Dutton's Nautical Navigation

FIFTEENTH EDITION

Thomas J. Cutler

with the U.S. Naval Institute
Navigation Board

Naval Institute Press
Annapolis, Maryland

Naval Institute Press
291 Wood Road
Annapolis, MD 21402

Library of Congress Cataloging-in-Publication Data
Dutton, Benjamin, 1883–1937.
  Dutton's nautical navigation.—15th ed. / Thomas J. Cutler.
      p. cm.
Rev. ed. of: Dutton's navigation & piloting. 14th ed. 1985.
Includes index.
  ISBN 1-55750-248-X (hardcover : alk. paper)
  1. Navigation. 2. Nautical astronomy. 3. Pilots and pilotage. I.
Cutler, Thomas J., 1947– II. Dutton, Benjamin, 1883–1937. Dut-
ton's navigation & piloting. III. Title.
  VK555.D9597 2003
  623.89—dc21
                                        2003011183

Printed in the United States of America on acid-free paper ∞
11 10 09 08 07 06 05 04   9 8 7 6 5 4 3 2
First printing

Contents

Preface

When Commander Benjamin Dutton, U.S. Navy, wrote his first edition of *Navigation and Nautical Astronomy*, it probably did not occur to him that his book would become one of the greats of navigation, continuing on for more than three-quarters of a century and enjoying a reputation exceeded only by that of the two-hundred-year-old *American Practical Navigator* by Nathaniel Bowditch. Originally written for midshipmen at the U.S. Naval Academy, Dutton's first edition was published in 1926 by the U.S. Naval Institute and has continued through fifteen editions, including this one. Enjoying the fresh insight of new authors while retaining many of the qualities of the original work, the book is still used extensively by Navy navigators, but its popularity has expanded to include many other nautical navigators of maritime industry and recreational boating.

Since celestial navigation was the primary means of establishing position on the open ocean in 1926, the original work reflected the technology of the day by including "nautical astronomy" in the title. In 1957, however, the title of the twelfth edition was changed to *Dutton's Navigation and Piloting*, incorporating the deceased author's name into the title and reflecting the changing technology of navigation. This fifteenth edition is again being retitled to more accurately reflect the nature of the subject while appropriately preserving the Dutton name.

Many technological advances of the twentieth and twenty-first centuries are reflected in this newest edition of an old icon. Early versions of *Dutton's* included chapters on aerial navigation, but these were eventually omitted when that subject became too extensive and unique to remain compatible in a single textbook. While aerial navigation may no longer be included and celestial navigation may not enjoy the primacy it once did, the "heavens" are still very much a vital part of nautical navigation. Today's navigators still peer into the skies through sextant telescopes, but they have the tremendous advantage of also being able to "observe" new constellations of manmade satellites through the wonders of electronics. Magnetic compasses are now enhanced by "digital flux gate" technology, chronometers have been joined by atomic clocks, and even paper charts are being replaced by "raster" and "vector" images on computer screens.

Much has changed, to be sure, but Benjamin Dutton would still recognize many of the basic concepts he first put down on paper many years ago. Updating his work has been a major undertaking, but the task would be a hundred times more difficult without the firm and lasting foundation he built. Even though this book is for all nautical navigators, Commander Dutton's emphasis on the Navy as his primary audience has been maintained by this Navy veteran, not for parochial reasons but in recognition of the Navy as a good navigational model. While merchant mariners are often more expert in navigation and recreational boaters usually less so, Navy navigators represent a useful median. They are generally cautious and professional—good attributes for any nautical navigator—yet most of them are also neophytes, coming to this wondrous but somewhat daunting science from the farmlands of Iowa or the streets of Detroit. Most naval personnel, whether they are the officer designated as "navigator" for a few years of a diverse career or those invaluable quartermasters who make it their primary occupation, come to the job with no prior experience. It is for them that this book is primarily written—and in so doing, it becomes a useful tool for others as well. While *Dutton's* is often used to good effect as a reference work, its primary purpose is as a teaching tool. For that reason, I have deliberately adopted a conversational tone—teacher to student—and have included many examples as a means to enhance this teaching process. Mnemonics and step-by-step explanations are designed to aid in the learning and retention of this complicated subject. My approach has been to empower the reader in the use of such things as geodesy, spherical trigonometry, and hydrodynamics without becoming overly immersed in them. My primary goal is to embrace both the *art* and the *science* of nautical navigation in such a way as to give both neophyte and veteran navigators the tools they need to navigate safely and to encourage in them an appreciation for this subject that has fascinated me for most of my adult life.

Non-naval readers will find the naval slant only slightly distracting. Those portions that apply solely to the Navy are apparent and easily ignored. Many of the examples assume a naval navigator who, as such, will "receive orders," "recommend," or "report," and so on, where a recreational navigator or fisherman would more likely just *do* the things explained.

Because it is assumed that not all readers will read the entire book cover to cover, some redundancy (various terms and concepts explained more than once in different chapters) and a great deal of cross-referencing has been included. To facilitate the latter, article numbers have been assigned. All illustrations have been identified with a number corresponding to the article number in which the illustration is first mentioned.

As explained in the text, I have addressed the role of computers in modern navigation, but the "manual" methods are retained because not every navigator will have a computer or the right software available and because understanding what lies behind the computer algorithms will separate true navigators from mere "users" of technology.

Some mention is made of various commercial products, not as an endorsement for them but because they are well known in the navigational world or have come to my attention during my research.

I am honored to be the new "Dutton" but can only take a portion of that honor because of the great deal of help I received in this project from individuals who made up the U.S. Naval Institute Navigation Board, which I was fortunate enough to be able to assemble for this project. A book as important as *Dutton's* should not be entrusted to one individual.

My confidence in the value of this project is greatly enhanced because of the help of such highly qualified individuals. This NAVBOARD (as we came to call ourselves) consists of a number of people with several important characteristics. Most important is their extensive knowledge of nautical navigation. Several of them, in a more perfect world, might have been the principal author of this revision, rather than me. Of nearly equal importance was their willingness to devote their time and energy to this project with little reward other than my eternal gratitude and the satisfaction of contributing to the safe navigation of vessels on the great waters of the world. I also appreciate the encouragement, patience, and humor that many of them provided during the many months that I worked on this project.

In addition to those members of the NAVBOARD, I am indebted to Lieutenant Commander John Shassberger, whose early review of the fourteenth edition and many valuable suggestions got me started on this project. Admiral Richard D. West (Navigator of the Navy) and several members of his staff (Captain Dan Soper, Captain C. R. Gunderson, Paul Witmer, and Commander Paul Heim, among others) were helpful in numerous important ways. Captain "Red" Smith and Warren Mazenac of the Naval Academy's Seamanship and Navigation Department and Chris Andreasen of the National Imagery and Mapping Agency provided much needed advice and assistance. John Watkins generously provided me with one of his highly regarded Celesticomp calculators for several months. Glenn Lawless and Hank Luniewski of Litton Marine Systems were very helpful in helping me understand new technologies, and Jim Bamberger, George Burkley, and Glen Paine very kindly opened the doors at the Maritime Institute and Graduate Technology Studies training facility in Linthicum Maryland.

As always, I am especially indebted to my wife, Debby, without whom this project could never have been completed. Not only did she put up with all the idiosyncratic behavior that authors frequently exhibit, but she used her extensive and impressive computer skills to transform the entire previous edition into an electronic version that made my revising considerably easier.

And finally, for posterity's sake (and because I obviously owe them a personal debt), I would like to acknowledge the many authors and contributors who have kept *Dutton's* current and valuable over the years. Many of their names were never recorded or were lost in group sobriquets such as "officer instructors in navigation," but among the names mentioned over the years, it is clear that several were the primary revisers, and they are here acknowledged (with the year in which they first began the honor of becoming principal authors of this navigation icon):

Commander H. F. Floyd and Lieutenant Commander L. H. McDonald—1942

Lieutenant Commander Alton B. Moody—1948
Commander Edwin A. Beito—1951
Commander John C. Hill II, Lieutenant Commander Thomas F. Utegaard, and Gerard Riordan—1957
G. D. Dunlap and Captain H. H. Schufeldt—1969
Elbert S. Maloney—1978

U.S. Naval Institute Navigation Board

These individuals voluntarily served as technical advisers, contributors, editors, and moral support for this fifteenth edition of *Dutton's Nautical Navigation*. This project would have been far more difficult and the final product considerably less effective had it not been for the generous sharing of their vast knowledge and expertise.

Captain John R. Bennett USNR (MMR)—Third Mate, Steam and Motor Vessels of any gross tons upon Oceans; First Class Pilot of unlimited tonnage between St. Regis, New York, and Port Weller, Ontario; Master of Great Lakes Steam and Motor Vessels up to 1,600 GRT; Commanding Officer, Military Sealift Command Atlantic 106; Acting Director, Great Lakes Pilotage (G-MW-1) U.S. Coast Guard.

Commander Giuseppe Berutti Bergotto, Italian Navy—Commanding Officer, 5th Class and Officer Candidate Courses, Italian Naval Academy; Navigation Course Coordinator, U.S. Naval Academy.

Michael B. Brown—Technical staff, Marine Chart Division, Office of Coast Survey, National Oceanographic and Atmospheric Administration; member, International Hydrographic Organization (IHO) Transfer Standard Maintenance and Application Development Working Group (S-57); member, International Organization for Standardization (ISO), Electronic Chart Systems Database Standard Working Group.

Captain William E. Clifford—New York Harbor Pilot; owner of vessels in passenger and cargo service; President of the Pilot's Association; Assistant Professor at the Global Marine and Transportation School (GMATS) at the U.S. Merchant Marine Academy; helped open the Port of Salem, New Jersey, to navigation after a one-hundred-year hiatus.

Lieutenant Commander Brian D. Connon USN—Certified as a Category A Hydrographer as defined by the International Hydrographic Organization (IHO); as a Hydrographer of the Naval Oceanographic Office Fleet Survey Team participated in operational survey/charting missions and the restructuring of the Navy with respect to electronic navigation; master of science degree in applied hydrographic science from the University of Southern Mississippi.

Commander Anthony Cowden USNR—Navigator, USS *Moosbrugger* (DD 980); two-time winner of the Jim Piner Cooper River Piloting Award for Navigation Excellence; Executive Officer, Naval Reserve Afloat Training Group Unit 101, responsible for conducting navigation, seamanship, and damage control training onboard cutters in Coast Guard District One.

Senior Chief Boatswain's Mate Dennis Dever USCG—Officer in Charge of Aids to Navigation Team Cape May, New Jersey, maintaining more than seven hundred navigational aids in 375 miles of waterways covering two states and the approaches to New York City, Philadelphia, and Wilmington, Delaware; one of the last genuine lighthouse keepers, Boston Light 1988–90; working with the University of Delaware laboratory at Fourteen Foot Bank Lighthouse, conducting sound transmissivity tests with the U.S. Navy; working with

Dutton's
Nautical
Navigation

Chapter 1

Introduction to Navigation

Science tells us that our origins are in the sea, and our earliest literature and historical records tell us that we have never strayed very far from it. We have been traveling on the great waters of the world for thousands of years, and from the very beginning we have been concerned with knowing where we are and where we are going on those vast waters. This, of course, is the essence of nautical navigation.

From its earliest days, navigation has been both an art and a science. Much of the navigator's work must be done with precise instruments, exact mathematics, and available technology, yet when the observations have been taken and the calculations made, the seasoned navigator must apply judgment based upon experience to interpret what the science is telling him or her.

TYPES OF NAVIGATION

101   Different schools of thought exist on how to categorize the various forms of nautical navigation. In actuality, these categorizations are not very important but merely serve as a means of helping the neophyte navigator organize the many aspects of a complex subject for learning purposes. The learner will do well to accept from the very beginning that there will be overlap among categories no matter how they are organized.

At one time a fairly simple way to organize the various forms of nautical navigation was to begin with three basic categories: terrestrial, celestial, and electronic. Within the terrestrial (or earthly) forms of navigation are the ancient but still valid methods of piloting and dead reckoning. Celestial (or heavenly) navigation takes advantage of the regularity of the Sun, Moon, stars, and planets to determine posi-

tion on the surface of the Earth. And electronic navigation began with the invention of radio, which quickly led to radio direction finding, then hyperbolic systems, and eventually satellite and inertial navigation. The problem with this categorization is that there are navigational methods that are not an obvious fit into one of these three categories but are not unique enough to justify their own. Radar navigation, for example, is clearly dependent upon electronics, yet the information it provides yields a form of piloting. Bathymetric navigation is similar. And some have argued that satellite navigation is a form of artificial celestial navigation, while others contend that inertial systems are a form of electronic dead reckoning.

Such confusion need not exist. The modern navigator should simply recognize that there are a great many navigational tools available, know their various capabilities and limitations, and use any or all of them when the appropriate situation arises. With that in mind, categorization will not be attempted, but the various types of navigation are here introduced and explained in greater detail in subsequent chapters.

Piloting

102   Early navigators often stayed close to shore and used familiar sights along the coast as a means of determining where they were. This is piloting in its simplest form. As time and technology advanced, this simple concept of "seeing where you are going" was extrapolated and refined, but the concept remained the same.

Piloting can be thought of as the main form of navigation used when a vessel is in coastal and inland waters. Proximity to land and the shallower depths associated with these waters offer certain advantages that a navigator does not have on the open sea.

Recognizable objects on a nearby shore can be used as a frame of reference to help determine a vessel's position. Early navigators were able to refine this technique by using instruments such as compasses and telescopes to determine their position relative to visible landmarks. Advancing technology improved these instruments and techniques, adding such things as radar to greatly enhance the mariners' ability to measure direction and distance to known objects and thereby fix their position. Some textbooks refer to radar navigation as a separate form of navigation, but because it is used to enhance the navigator's ability to "see" and is used only in inland waters for navigational purposes, it is really an electronically enhanced form of piloting.

In high traffic areas, recognizable objects (such as lighthouses) were added along the shore to serve specifically as navigational references. And because these waters were often shallow enough, markers (such as buoys) were placed in the water at key points (fixed to the bottom to prevent them from drifting away) to serve as virtual "road signs" for the mariner. These became and still are an important element in piloting.

The bottom beneath shallow waters can also be "mapped," providing navigators an additional clue to their position. Depth of water has always been an obvious concern for the navigator because of the fear of running aground, and early navigators dropped weighted lines over the sides of their vessels to determine how much water was beneath them. They eventually realized that there were patterns in the depths, and frequent measurements gave them a "picture" of what the sea bottom looked like. This led to their using bottom contours as another reference for piloting their vessels and is sometimes referred to as "bathymetric navigation." Modern technology has replaced the weighted line with very capable electronic sound transponders that provide a detailed "look" at the bottom, but the technique is essentially the same.

The advantages inherent to inland waters are attended by disadvantages as well. The proximity to land and the shallow waters that aid the navigator also present hazards that are not encountered on the open ocean. Because of the ever-present danger of running aground, there are highly specialized professional navigators in many ports of the world who are intimately familiar with local waters and are paid well to assist visiting ships in safely arriving and departing. Not surprisingly, these expert navigators are known as "pilots."

Dead Reckoning

103   As mariners became bolder in their ventures on the seas, they traveled beyond the range of visual references and into waters too deep to measure with their weighted lines. They then developed procedures to help estimate their position based upon deductive reasoning; in the terminology of the day, this was called "deduced reckoning," which was often abbreviated "ded. reckoning" and thus evolved into *dead reckoning* (DR), the term we still use today.

In its simplest form, dead reckoning can be thought of as simply keeping track of one's movements. If you proceed from a known location, traveling in a known direction for a known period of time at a known speed, it should be apparent that you will have a much better idea of where you are than if you do not keep track of these things. Of course, the "known" part of this supposition is the potential weak element. Starting from a known location is usually a given, but early navigators had only primitive means of determining direction, time, and distance.

Dead reckoning has another important purpose besides merely keeping track of your movements. DR is used to *predict* where you think you will be. This is a practice that takes place even in inland waters where there are visual reference points. As a navigator, one of your most important tasks is to prepare for your voyage by laying out your intended trip in advance on a *chart* (the nautical equivalent of a map). To accomplish this, you begin with your starting point, which is a known position, and then determine a safe and efficient path to follow to get to your destination. The path that you have chosen is marked by intended courses (directions) and speeds as well as predicted times of arrival at designated points (such as time intervals or points at which you intend to change course or speed). This is DR navigation and will be explained in more detail in chapter 9.

It is important to note a generally accepted distinction among navigators. DR navigation is based only upon assumptions relating to course, speed, and time, without taking into account the effects of winds, currents, steering errors, and other forces that might affect the actual travel of a vessel. Correcting a DR position for these additional factors redefines it as an *estimated position* (EP).

Celestial Navigation

104   Recognizing the deficiencies of dead reckoning when carried on for days without being certain of the effects of wind and current, navigators

looked for other means to find their way across the vast sameness of the sea. By carefully studying and recording the visual patterns and regular motions in the heavens above them, mariners long ago learned that they could use these celestial road maps to determine their position at sea.

Celestial navigation is the determination of position by observing the celestial bodies—the Sun, Moon, planets, and stars. In its simplest form, the angle of elevation above the horizon is measured for an identified heavenly body, and a series of mathematical calculations are then performed to compare this information to one's assumed position. Several of these observations and calculations can be used to arrive at a reasonably accurate position. Because the necessary mathematics is complex, navigators have relied for generations on precomputed tables to streamline the process. Today, electronic calculators and computers have almost completely automated the process.

Radio Navigation

105   Radio navigation is the determination of position—and to a lesser extent, direction-using information gained from radio waves received and processed on board a vessel or aircraft. This is accomplished by either radio direction finding or by the use of specially designed hyperbolic navigation systems.

Radio direction finding (RDF) is the oldest form of navigation making use of electronic technology. A vessel equipped with a specially designed directional antenna and receiver can determine with some accuracy the direction from which a radio signal is being broadcast. The navigator can then use this information to help determine the vessel's position.

A *hyperbolic navigation system* is more complicated but also more accurate. Specially designed radio transmitting stations broadcast signals that appropriately equipped vessels can receive and use to determine their position by comparing the time differences in the received signals. These time differences can be plotted as hyperbolas on charts. There have been a number of different systems created using this principle, but today only a system called "Loran-C" continues in active use in the United States (see chapter 16).

Satellite Navigation

106   As the name implies, satellite navigation involves the use of manmade satellites placed in orbit to aid navigators. While this is the most modern form of navigation, it has been around long enough to have had entire systems created, used, and abandoned in favor of improved methods. Today, the most widely used—and in many ways revolutionary—satellite system is the *Global Positioning System* (GPS), which has many applications besides nautical navigation. See chapter 17 for a detailed discussion of this and other satellite systems.

THE PROBLEMS OF NAVIGATION

107   Regardless of the specific methods of navigation used by a navigator, the procedures applied must provide a solution to the three basic problems of navigation. These problems are:
1. How to determine *position;*
2. How to determine the *direction* in which to proceed to get from one position to another; and
3. How to determine *distance,* and the related factors of *time* and *speed* as progress is made.

Position

108   The most basic problem facing the navigator is that of determining position. Unless you know where you are, you cannot direct the movements of your vessel with accuracy, safety, and efficiency. The term *position* refers to an identifiable location on the Earth or a point within a manmade system of artificial coordinates. The word position is frequently qualified by such adjectives as "known," "estimated," or "dead reckoning"; these will be further discussed in later chapters, but it is helpful to note at this point that there is a hierarchy of positions as follows: fix—running fix—estimated position—dead reckoning position. Your confidence in your position decreases as you move from left to right in this hierarchy. A *fix* is based upon very solid information which can be safely relied upon. If you are tied to a pier that shows on your chart, you have an excellent fix on your position. Under way in a narrow channel, as you pass beneath a bridge you again can fix your position on a chart with a great deal of certainty. While piloting, taking visual sightings (see article 109) on several objects can provide a reliable fix of your position. Nearly simultaneous observations of several celestial bodies can provide a fix that is accurate enough for open-ocean navigation, and electronic systems, such as Loran-C and GPS, are capable of providing accurate positioning information as well.

A *running fix* is similar to an ordinary fix, but because components of information are gathered at different times and artificially moved together, this type of fix is less reliable than a fix in which all the information is obtained simultaneously. Estimated and dead reckoning positions have been discussed above and will be further explained later in this book.

Another positioning term that is often used by modern navigators is *waypoint*. Defined in some publications as simply "sets of coordinates that describe a location of navigational interest," this term has come to be used primarily with electronic navigation systems and is probably more accurately understood in this context as a specific position that has been programmed into an electronic navigation system. Waypoints may be used to mark points along a planned track (see article 109) or as markers for some particular item of interest, such as a good fishing spot or the entrance to a channel. Modern electronic navigation systems, such as GPS (Global Positioning System) or Loran-C, have features that allow waypoints to be entered into the system and "remembered"; this has major advantages that will become obvious as you read further in this book.

Direction

109   Direction is the orientation of an imaginary line joining one point to another without regard to the distance between them. Direction is measured in angular units called *degrees*, measured relative to some reference—usually true north—from 0 to 360. A direction for navigational purposes is always presented as a three-digit number, with leading zeros as required; for example, a direction of 7° east of north would be written as 007°, and one of 36° east of north would be 036°. This convention applies whether you are writing or speaking; that is, 017° would be spoken "zero-one-seven degrees." Note that each digit is pronounced separately to avoid confusion. Therefore, north is 000 (said as "zero-zero-zero"), east is 090 ("zero-nine-zero" or, in military parlance, "zero-niner-zero"), south is 180 ("one-eight-zero"), and west is 270 ("two-seven-zero").

It is the knowledge of the spatial relationship between two positions—the direction from one to another—that makes it possible for you as a navigator to lay a course from where you are to where you want to go, and then to steer that course to proceed to that destination.

There are certain terms associated with direction that you will encounter many times as you read through this book. It will help to understand that, as already stated, all directions must have a reference. Most of the time, navigators will use either true or magnetic north (see chapter 7 for the difference), but other references are sometimes used. For example, lookouts on a naval vessel will use the bow of

their vessel as the reference and report sightings relative to that.

Course (C). As applied to marine navigation, the direction of travel through the water; the direction in which a vessel is being steered, or is going to be steered. Course may be designated as *true, magnetic, compass,* or (rarely) *grid* as determined by the reference being used. The course is measured from 000° clockwise from the reference direction to 360°. It should be apparent that if 000° is north, then east would be 090°, 180° due south, and 270° would be west.

Heading (Hdg. or SH). The direction in which a ship points or heads at any instant, expressed in angular units, 000° clockwise through 360°, from a reference point. The heading of a ship is also sometimes called "ship's head." Heading is a constantly changing value as a ship oscillates or yaws across the course due to effects of the sea and of steering error. In other words, "course" is your *intended* direction, while "heading" is the *actual* direction you are steering at any given instant.

Track (TR). The intended (anticipated, desired) direction of movement with respect to the Earth. A navigator plans a voyage by laying a track on a chart. Track is sometimes understood to include a planned speed as well as a planned direction.

Course over Ground (COG). The actual path of a vessel with respect to the Earth. This will not be a straight line if the vessel's heading varies as she yaws back and forth across the course.

Course Made Good (CMG). The single resultant direction from a given point of departure to a subsequent position (this *will* be a straight line); the direction of the net movement from one point to the other, disregarding any intermediate course changes en route. This may differ from the track by inaccuracies in steering, varying current effects, and so on (see fig. 109).

To summarize, as a navigator you plan a voyage by laying down a *track* on a chart. Once you have gotten under way, you will attempt to steer the chosen *course*, but because of wind, current, and/or

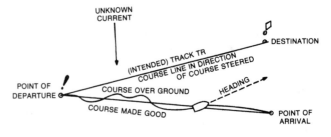

Figure 109. Course, track, course over ground (exaggerated), and course made good.

inattention, your vessel will rarely stay right on the exact course you want to steer, so for any given moment your actual *heading* may be right on the course you are trying to steer or something different. As you proceed, your actual movement will trace a somewhat wobbly path across the Earth's surface, and this is defined as your *course over ground*. Once you have traveled some distance, the "wobbles" can be averaged out to a straight line defined as your actual *course made good*. Ideally, the CMG will be very close to your intended TR.

Bearings and Azimuths. There is another element to direction besides that of steering courses. As already discussed, the navigator often relies upon points of reference, like objects on shore, or aids to navigation, or the heavenly bodies. To accomplish this, the navigator must be able to measure and express the direction of these things in relation to her or his own vessel. The terms associated with this aspect to navigation are *bearing* (B) and *azimuth* (Zn). These terms are sometimes used interchangeably, but bearing is more commonly used for terrestrial objects while azimuth is used more often to refer to the direction of a celestial body. In both cases, the direction is defined as a horizontal direction of an object expressed as the angular distance from a reference and, as with courses, that reference is often true or magnetic north and the angle is measured in degrees from 000 to 360. The same written and spoken conventions that apply to courses also apply to bearings—always three digits, spoken individually.

Distance

110 Distance is the spatial separation between two points without regard to direction. In navigation, it is measured by the length of a line on the surface of the Earth from one point to another; customary units are yards, miles, or kilometers. The "mile" commonly used by navigators is the *international nautical mile* (abbreviated n mi or, sometimes, nm) of 2,000 yards (approximately) or 6,076.1 feet or 1.852 kilometers. (For short distances, a nautical mile and 2,000 yards are often used interchangeably, the error being only 1.25 percent.) In practical terms the nautical mile is equivalent to one minute of latitude, or one minute of arc of any great circle (see article 202). The nautical mile is longer than the *statute mile* used on land, which is 5,280 feet or 1.609 kilometers. A close approximation of the ratio between the nautical mile and the statute mile is 38/33, but 8/7 is often used because of its simplicity. To convert nautical miles to statute miles, multiply the nautical miles by

1.15; to convert statute miles to nautical miles, multiply the statute miles by 0.87.

The statute mile is used in some inland U.S. waters such as the Great Lakes and the Intracoastal Waterways, but the nautical mile is used by most navigators most of the time. Therefore, unless otherwise qualified, the term "mile" (mi) when used in this book will mean the international nautical mile.

Two components of distance in navigation are time and speed. Indeed, distance is expressed mathematically as $D = vt$, where D is distance, v is speed (velocity), and t is time.

Time may be either the time of day of an event as indicated by a watch or clock or the interval between two successive events. Units used are hours, minutes, and seconds; decimal fractions of a second are rarely needed. In navigation, time is always stated or written as four digits in a 24-hour system, rather than the more conventional 12-hour system. This method removes the dangers of confusing "A.M." and "P.M." time; it is used by the U.S. Armed Forces and by hospitals, police forces, and other organizations who deal with life and death matters. To convert conventional 12-hour time to the more efficient 24-hour system, simply keep counting after noon (i.e., add twelve hours to all conventional times after noon) rather than starting over for a second (P.M.) twelve hours. Also, the 24-hour convention does not require a colon between hours and minutes but does require four digits for all times expressed (the first two digits represent the hours, from 00 to 24, and the latter two the minutes, from 00 to 59). This means that 9:32 A.M. would be written as 0932, and four minutes after midnight is 0004. One hour after noon in the 24-hour system is 1300 rather than 1:00 P.M., and 8:15 P.M. is 2015. When spoken, 1000 (10:00 A.M.) would be "ten hundred," not "one thousand," and 1637 would be "sixteen thirty-seven." The leading zero can be pronounced as "zero" (as in "zero-nine thirty-two") or as "oh" (as in "oh-nine thirty-two").

In other applications, such as celestial navigation, time measurement to seconds is critical. In this case time is normally expressed by writing hours, minutes, and seconds separated by dashes. Thus a conventional clock time of 10 hours, 57 minutes, and 17 seconds P.M. is written 22–57–17. If the number of hours, minutes, or seconds is less than 10, a zero is placed in front of each so that the hour, minutes, and seconds are each expressed by two digits; a time of 4 hours, 9 minutes, and 7 seconds A.M. is written as 04–09–07. Since the connotation of hours, minutes, and seconds is understood, no further labeling is required. Time zone descriptions may be applied if necessary (see chapter 23).

These conventions may seem arbitrary and confusing at first, but they are designed to avoid confusion and are a proven method of increasing safety and accuracy in nautical navigation.

Speed is defined as the rate of movement and in navigation is usually measured in *knots* (kn, or occasionally kt). Knots are defined as "nautical miles per hour." Note that the time element ("per hour") is included in the definition of "knot," so the use of "knots per hour" is obviously incorrect.

Later, as you become familiar with the various navigational techniques, you will find uses for two other terms relating to speed. *Speed of advance* (SOA) is defined as the speed *intended* to be made good when planning a voyage. It can also mean the *average* speed that must be maintained during a voyage to arrive at a destination at a specified time. *Speed over ground* (SOG) is the vessel's actual speed (in relation to Earth), determined by calculation (dividing the distance traveled by the elapsed time between successive fixes).

Speed made good (SMG) is similar to *course made good* in that it is the single resultant speed from a given point of departure to a subsequent position; the speed of the net movement from one point to the other.

Track Made Good (TMG). This term is similar to *course made good*, but is actually more useful because it incorporates the *speed made good* by the vessel as well. In other words, it is the actual (net) track (course and speed included) your vessel achieved despite other forces and factors. It averages out the effects of winds, currents, steering errors, and so on to come up with an overall course *and* speed made good. It can even be used to ignore large deviations such as maneuvering about to recover a man overboard or to retrieve a fishing net; in other words, once the maneuvers are completed and the vessel has resumed its original planned voyage, the track made good is a straight line drawn between two points on either side of the deviations that interfered with overall progress. You can use this to measure the course and the speed actually achieved in terms of voyage progress, ignoring the variations in between.

For example, in figure 110, a vessel has taken time out to run some man-overboard drills. The vessel's intended (planned) track is to make good the eight miles between points A and B in one hour, which translates to a planned track of course 105 at an SOA of 8 knots. The ship actually travels over a greater distance at higher speeds than planned because of the drill maneuvers, but those erratic movements are factored out in terms of voyage

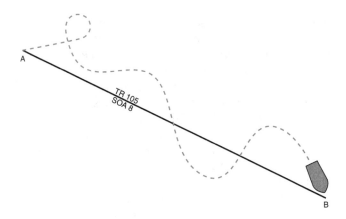

Figure 110. Track made good (TMG) vs. actual track.

progress by measuring the track made good. Those movements are important in terms of fuel consumption, training, and so on, but in navigational terms the TMG is what really matters because it is the real measure of progress in your overall voyage.

In this example, the TMG turned out the same as the original planned track and SOA, but that will not always be the case. The ship in the example could have taken more time than anticipated in doing the man-overboard drills, and the TMG could have ended up with the vessel behind the planned track and SOA, which would necessitate an increase of speed for a time to regain the original planned track. This, of course, is what navigation is all about: planning, executing, and adjusting courses and speeds to get from one place to another at a desired time.

NAVIGATIONAL ORGANIZATIONS

111   There are a number of organizations, both in the United States and abroad, that directly or indirectly support nautical navigation. Some of these organizations have a policy-making role, establishing conventions and standards for nautical navigators, while others provide goods and/or services needed by modern navigators.

International Maritime Organization (IMO)

112   The IMO is a specialized agency of the United Nations responsible for promoting maritime safety and efficient navigation. Serving as a vehicle for governments to cooperate with one another on such matters, it has established a number of conventions and standards that are recognized by most maritime nations of the world.

Among these conventions are several of particular importance to the nautical navigator. *The 1972 International Regulations for Preventing Collisions at Sea* (often referred to as the "COLREGS") are the basis for what are known as "the nautical rules of the road" and serve as "traffic regulations" for vessels.

One of the most far-reaching measures adopted by the IMO was the convention of *Safety of Life at Sea* (SOLAS), which you will read more about later in this book. Among the SOLAS regulations is V-20, which requires vessels to carry up-to-date charts and publications.

With the advent of electronic charts, IMO also developed minimum performance standards. These standards are known to the maritime world as ECDIS (Electronic Chart Display and Information System) and RCDS (Raster Chart Display System) (see chapter 4).

Another important contribution to nautical navigation was established by IMO in the form of a convention known as *Standards of Training, Certification, and Watchkeeping for Seafarers* (STCW). Among the provisions of STCW is the requirement for formal training on a number of important navigational methods and systems, such as Automatic Radar Plotting Aids (ARPA) and the Global Maritime Distress Safety System (GMDSS). Among its many provisions, this convention establishes minimum standards of rest for watchstanders with navigational responsibilities and specifies bridge teamwork procedures. Specific information about the impact and importance of STCW to American mariners can be found at a special Coast Guard web site, www.uscg.mil/stcw.

More information about IMO and its many activities is available at www.imo.org.

International Hydrographic Organization (IHO)

113 Formed in 1921, the IHO consists of representatives of many of the maritime nations of the world who work together in the coordination of hydrographic efforts. This cooperative effort has led to a great deal of uniformity in the format and content of charts and publications produced by the member nations.

The IHO web site is www.iho.shom.fr.

International Association of Lighthouse Authorities (IALA)

114 Member nations of the IALA work together to ensure uniformity of visual aids to navigation in the world, such as buoys and lighthouses. Since 1973, the organization has been working to reduce the number of buoyage systems in the world. When the IALA began this project, there were more than 30 different buoyage systems; today there are only two major ones remaining (see chapter 6).

IALA's web site is www.beta.ialahq.org.

National Oceanographic and Atmospheric Administration (NOAA)

115 The *Marine Chart Division* (MCD) of the *Office of Coast Survey* (which is a part of the *National Ocean Service*, a subdivision of NOAA) produces nautical charts and related publications for navigation in the coastal areas of the United States and the Great Lakes. MCD's paper and electronic charts cover more than 11 million square kilometers and serve many of the commercial and recreational needs of the nation.

To learn more about MCD and the other divisions of NOAA, go to www.noaa.gov.

National Imagery and Mapping Agency (NIMA)

116 When first organized in 1830, the purpose of the "Depot of Charts and Instruments" was to serve the U.S. Navy's navigational needs, storing and issuing to naval vessels the charts, sailing directions, and navigational instruments necessary to carry out their operations. Evolving through the years, merging with other government agencies, and undergoing several name changes (among them, "U.S. Hydrographic Office" and "Defense Mapping Agency"), today NIMA serves not only the Navy but the entire Department of Defense and the U.S. Intelligence Community. Charts needed for naval operations are created, collected, housed, and disseminated by the Marine Navigation Department of NIMA. This department also produces a number of important navigational publications, such as the *World Port Index, Sight Reduction Tables for Marine Navigation*, and the ultimate navigation reference book, *The American Practical Navigator* (originally by Nathaniel Bowditch in 1802 and often referred to simply as *Bowditch*).

Go to www.nima.mil for more information about NIMA.

To avoid some potential confusion, it is worthwhile to note that because NIMA has undergone a number of name changes over the years, you may still encounter references to the old names. For example, some publications that have not been updated since the last name change still bear the name "Defense Mapping Agency Hydrographic/Topographic Center" (or the abbreviation DMAHTC) rather than the new name.

United States Coast Guard

117 The U.S. Coast Guard maintains and operates more than forty thousand aids to navigation (buoys, lighthouses, foghorns, daybeacons, etc.) as well as the Loran-C and Differential GPS systems.

The modern nautical navigator will do well to periodically check the *U.S. Coast Guard's Naviga-*

tion Safety Center (NAVCEN) at www.navcen.uscg
.gov for important navigational information.

United States Navy

118 For obvious reasons, the U.S. Navy has long
been at the forefront of navigational development.
The *U.S. Naval Observatory* (USNO) has been the
nation's timekeeper for more than a century and a
half as well as the publisher (jointly with the British
Stationery Office) of *The Nautical Almanac* (see
chapter 24). In more recent times, USNO has developed and distributed the *System to Estimate Latitude and Longitude Astronomically* (STELLA), a software program that streamlines the process of sight
reduction in celestial navigation (see chapters
20–27).

Recognizing the growing importance and rapidly
changing nature of navigation, in January 2001 the
Chief of Naval Operations created the post of "Navigator of the Navy" to oversee the navigational needs
of the Navy.

Go to www.usno.navy.mil for the U.S. Naval
Observatory and www.navigator.navy.mil for the
Navigator of the Navy's web site.

U.S. Naval Institute (USNI)

119 In its role as an open forum for the
exchange of ideas to further the aims and well-being
of the sea services, the U.S. Naval Institute has
played a significant role in many areas of navigation
in its more than 130 years of existence. Its *Proceed-
ings* magazine has often provided a medium for
debate and a conduit of information relevant to navigational issues, and Naval Institute Press has produced a number of navigational text and reference
books over the years.

The Naval Institute's web site can be found at
www.navalinstitute.org or at www.usni.org. Several
navigational tables are available at this web site for
readers of this book (see articles 2501 and 3502).

METRIC SYSTEM OF MEASUREMENT

120 The "metric system of measurements," more
correctly known as the *International System of Units*,
abbreviated *SI* (from the name in French), has been
adopted in nearly all countries of the world. It is a
logical, systematic series of interrelated units with
larger and smaller units based on multiples of ten.

The Metric Conversion Act of 1975 declared that
the policy of the United States was to increase the
use of metric units on a voluntary basis with the
goal of a "nation predominately, although not exclu-
sively, metric." Progress toward this goal has slowed
in recent years, but the global use of metric units
makes this system of vital interest to navigators.
Accordingly, this book will often note metric units
where appropriate as approximate equivalents to
the customary (English) units.

The nautical mile is expected to remain the basic
unit of distance at sea. Depths and heights, however, are increasingly being shown in meters and
decimeters (tenths of meters). Conversion factors
are as follows:

> 1 nautical mile = 1.852 kilometer
> 1 fathom = 1.829 mile
> 1 foot = 0.3048 mile

To convert kilometers to nautical miles, multiply
the kilometers by 0.54 (or 0.5399). To convert nautical miles to kilometers, multiply the nautical miles
by 1.86 (or 1.85219).

help of a straightedge, such a line may be drawn on an engineering plan and the *distance* measured at the scale of the drawing. Similarly, the *direction* from one point to another may be measured by using an ordinary protractor to determine the angle that the line makes with the rectangular reference lines of the drawing. Because nautical navigation takes place on the surface of a sphere rather than a flat plane, some additional considerations come into play.

Great Circles

208   The shortest distance (abbreviated as Dist., symbol D) between any two points on the surface of the Earth is always along the great circle between them. The more closely the plane of a small circle approaches the center of the Earth, the more closely will distance measured along it approach the shortest distance. The converse is also true, of course.

Since a great circle is the shortest distance between two points on the surface of a sphere, it might be supposed that it would always be the route selected unless there were intervening dangers, such as reefs or shoals. The practical objection to following a great-circle route is that the direction of that great circle is constantly changing; it makes a different angle with each meridian it crosses from the starting point to the destination. This means the ship's course on a great-circle route would be subject to continuous alterations, which is not very practical.

Rhumb Lines

209   Since constant course changes are scarcely practical, it is customary to follow a *rhumb line,* or a series of rhumb lines, rather than to follow a great circle. For practical purposes, a rhumb line (also known as a *loxodrome* or loxodromic spiral) can be defined as a line that crosses every meridian of the terrestrial sphere at the same angle. In other words, a ship may maintain a true heading without change from starting point to destination (if one disregards factors such as currents, wind, etc.). Figure 209a shows what happens to a rhumb line if it is extended for a great distance; it takes the path of a continuous spiral from the equator to the North Pole.

Figure 209b shows a great circle and a rhumb line, both from a point on the equator to a point about 135° of longitude eastward and at a latitude near 52° north. In this view of the Earth (a spherical object on a flat page) it is not possible to show angular relationships correctly, but reference to a globe will show that the great circle leaves the equator at

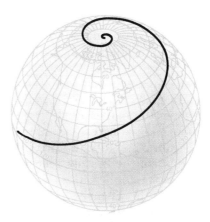

Fig. 209a. A rhumb line or loxodrome.

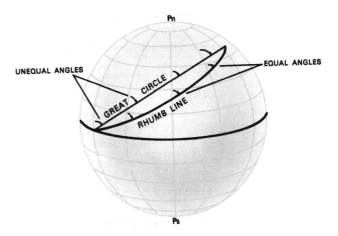

Fig. 209b. Comparison of great circle and rhumb line.

an angle of a little less than 30° with the meridian there; near the middle of the route, the angle with the meridian has increased to about 50° and, near the end of the route, to more than 100°. The rhumb line crosses each successive meridian at a constant angle of about 65°.

Comparison of Distances

210   A navigator is concerned with both great-circle distances and rhumb-line distances. Except for a few special cases where they are the same, great-circle distances are always shorter than rhumb-line distances, the amount of difference depending upon various combinations of latitude and longitude. The difference increases (1) as the latitude increases, (2) as the difference in latitude at the two points decreases, and (3) as the difference of longitude increases.

In article 203 it was seen that the equator is a great circle. But the equator is also a rhumb line, with a constant direction of 090° or 270°. Along the equator, then, great-circle and rhumb-line distances are identical; there is no difference at all.

As a vessel moves farther from the equator toward either pole, the saving in distance by way of a great circle becomes greater, and is always greatest for east-west courses (090° or 270°).

All meridians, too, are great circles by definition; they are also rhumb lines of constant direction, 000° or 180°. It thus can be quickly seen that along a meridian (as along the equator) great-circle distances and rhumb-line distances are identical; there is no difference. The difference begins to increase as the great-circle direction moves away from a north-south direction, reaching a maximum when east-west.

Near the equator, then, the saving in distance by use of a great-circle track is negligible, and it increases only slowly with increasing latitude. For an east-west distance of 1,000 miles, the saving is only 2.5 miles at latitude 40° (north or south), increasing to 10.6 miles at latitude 60°. For the route from New York City to London (mid-latitude about 40°), the great-circle distance is 3,016 nautical miles, and the rhumb-line distance is 3,139 miles—a difference of 123 miles.

Great-circle distances are often calculated rather than measured on a chart. When so computed, they are measured in degrees and minutes of arc. As is true for any great circle, one degree of arc is equal, for all practical navigational purposes, to 60 nautical miles, and one minute essentially equals 1 mile. The total number of minutes can thus be taken as the distance in nautical miles.

DIRECTIONS IN NAVIGATION

211 In navigation, *true direction* is the direction from one point on Earth's surface to another, without regard to the distance between them; it is expressed as an angle in degrees from 000° to 360°, referenced to true north. True north may be considered as either 000° or 360°, according to the problem at hand.

In figure 211, the true direction from A to B is 060°. The true direction from B to A is 240°; this is called the *reciprocal* direction and is 180° greater, or less, than the original direction. It is axiomatic that every line has two directions; hence the direction intended should be clearly indicated on a chart by arrow heads or some system of labeling. Direction can be shown as clearly by the *order of letters* used: thus AB is the direction from A to B; the reciprocal direction is BA.

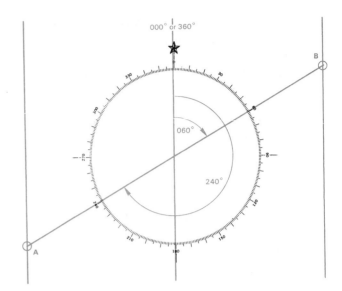

Fig. 211. Measurement of direction (course, track) in navigation.

All directions are *true directions* when measured from the true geographic meridian printed on the chart; *magnetic directions* when measured from magnetic north; and *compass directions* when measured with respect to compass north as indicated by the vessel's compass. *Relative directions* are those measured from the ship's head (the direction in which the ship is pointed).

GEODESY AND DATUMS

212 Geodesy in simplest terms is the science of measuring the Earth. More specifically, it is the use of observations and mathematical calculations to determine exact points and areas on the surface of the Earth, the actual size and shape of the Earth, and the significance of terrestrial gravity. While the nautical navigator does not need to be directly involved in the science and engineering of geodesy, the precision of modern navigational techniques makes a working knowledge of the purpose and outputs of this complex study necessary. How the Earth is measured—or more important, what assumptions and compromises are made in measuring the Earth—has a direct impact on the charts and systems the navigator must use to navigate.

It does not take much imagination to figure out that measuring something as vast and as irregular as the Earth is no small challenge. From space, Earth appears to be a perfectly spherical blue marble that should lend itself to a rather simple mathematical formula for measurement. For some purposes this is true. But when one first acknowledges a fact discovered long ago—that Earth is not a perfect sphere—the problem of measurement has already begun to get more complicated. Viewed from its surface, the planet obviously has many irregularities that quickly take the problem from very simple to impossibly complex. On a macro scale, continents and seas (differing in distribution by rotational and tidal forces) introduce a wide array of variables (some involving differences in gravitational force itself). Even closer scrutiny reveals the presence of mountains, plains, valleys, irregular bodies of water, and so on that make it abundantly clear that measuring and calculating the details of this planet are not simple tasks.

But a navigator without accurate charts is not much of a navigator at all. And the cartography that creates charts is based upon geodesy. Today, with the advent of satellites and other sophisticated navigational methods, the nautical navigator does not have to be a geodesist, but she or he must realize the importance of such things as which datum was used to create the chart in use.

Principles

213 In order to deal mathematically with this irregularly shaped planet, it is imperative to make certain assumptions that will simplify calculations, while having the least deleterious impact on the results. When a cartographer is dealing with a relatively small part of the Earth's surface—such as a city—it is acceptable to assume that the Earth is flat, even though we know otherwise. But as the area to be covered grows larger, the curvature of the Earth's surface must be taken into account.

While we know that the Earth is not a perfect sphere, we also know it is a close cousin to it. In the science of geodesy, several terms are used to describe the Earth: *spheroid*, *ellipsoid*, and *geoid*, depending on what the geodesist is trying to accomplish. These terms are all theoretical shapes and are listed in the order of their degree of accuracy, the geoid being a much closer approximation of Earth's shape than the spheroid and the ellipsoid a compromise between the two.

The ellipsoid can be thought of as a basketball with a small child sitting upon it. The child's weight will flatten the basketball somewhat, causing it to bulge at the middle, so that it is no longer a sphere. It should be apparent that this flattening will cause the diameter of the basketball to be slightly larger at the middle than at the top. In mathematical terms, the ellipsoid can be defined by the terms major axis (on Earth, this is the equatorial diameter), minor axis (polar axis), and eccentricity (flattening).

Actual measurements of the Earth reveal that the flattening results in a difference between the equatorial and polar diameters of the Earth that is only about 23 nautical miles. Against an equatorial diameter of nearly 7,000 nautical miles, it is apparent that the degree of flattening is very small, so the analogy of a *small* child is appropriate.

Taking this eccentricity into account, the geodesist has a working model—an ellipsoid—that can be used in calculations yielding small enough errors to be acceptable for most nautical cartographic purposes. The problem is that this theoretical ellipsoid changes somewhat, depending upon what part of Earth is being measured or charted. In other words, the ellipsoid that works well in the Atlantic Ocean does not necessarily fit well in the Indian Ocean. This means that different ellipsoids based upon different measurements must be used for different parts of the Earth.

In earlier times, navigators used charts for a local area based on measurements taken in that area, and because they navigated by taking bearings on local objects, different mathematical models did not matter. When transferring visual bearings to a chart, the exact longitude and latitude of a fix is not significant; that is, one does not care where one is in the absolute sense but only relative to the features on the chart being used. But the modern navigator using satellite fixes does not geometrically construct them using intersecting bearings; instead he or she accepts the satellite's fix and plots it on the chart. The potential problem not faced in earlier times is that today's navigator may be using a chart based upon a local ellipsoid while simultaneously receiving information from satellites that are using a different set of assumptions. This is a difficult concept for many people to grasp, since for most of their lives they were justified (and perfectly safe) in assuming that "a map is a map," never giving a thought as to the geodesy used by cartographers to create it. But the reality is that the great advantages realized by the advent of modern technology also bring with them an attendant peril, and ships have gone aground in more recent times because of this assumption. As has always been the seafarer's responsibility, the modern navigator must be aware of the pitfalls of the navigational techniques he or she is using, and take these into account. Today's nautical navigator must add a new and very important word to the ever-expanding glossary of navigational terms: the "datum."

Datums

214 One might argue that the plural of datum is data, and for syntactical purposes that would be

correct. But in the modern world of geodesy and navigation, the word datum takes on new meaning and therefore defies conventional English syntax.

When discussing datums in the geodetic or cartographic sense, confusion may arise because navigators have long referred to the reference level of tides on charts as datums. If one looks up "datum" in the index of older books on navigation, the referred pages will be in the section on tides only. But the geodetic datum that has taken on new significance for modern navigators is something very different and it must be taken into account to prevent potential disaster. More than one vessel has been lost because this new definition of datum was ignored or not understood.

If one traces the history of surveying in the United States before the advent of satellite technology, all of the measurements that have been taken by surveyors to establish known points, lines, and areas were taken relative to some other point. Obviously, there has to be an original (or first) point. In the United States, that point was established in 1879 in Maryland and was named, appropriately enough, *Principio*.

Once a point has been defined using very sophisticated measurements and calculations, other points may be defined relative to the original, using techniques such as triangulation, trilateration, and traverse surveying. Combining many of these known points into a network forms what is known technically as a Horizontal Geodetic Reference System. For geodetic purposes the datum is actually the starting or reference point for the network, but in common practice the whole network is often referred to as a datum. For navigational purposes one can think of a datum as a system consisting of a base (or reference) point combined with an appropriate ellipsoid such that consistent measurements can be made.

In geodesy, datums can be horizontal or vertical (the latter pertaining to altitude and/or depth), but for nautical navigation it is *horizontal* geodetic datums that are of primary concern. There are, in fact, many datums in use by cartographers. Many nations have developed datums which differ from those of neighboring nations (which has some interesting and potentially dangerous implications for national borders). The Tokyo Datum has its origin in Tokyo, and the European Datum originates in Potsdam, Germany. In the United States, the preferred datum for about fifty years was the North American Datum, 1927 (NAD 27) until replaced in 1989 by a new datum designated as NAD 83. The latter is currently the standard used by the National Ocean Service in the production of its charts.

Modern measuring techniques have significantly improved the geodesist's ability to measure the Earth and the result is a more accurate entity called the World Geodetic System (WGS). Based upon many points that have been fixed with precision using satellite technology and modern statistical methods, the WGS is actually based upon a geoid model that can be used for worldwide applications. The first WGS was completed in 1960 and is known as WGS 60. Several subsequent improved iterations are known as WGS 66, WGS 72, and WGS 84. The latter is currently the standard being used by the National Imagery and Mapping Agency in the production of its charts and the one used by the NAVSTAR GPS system. An important consideration for nautical navigators is that for all intents and purposes, WGS 84 and NAD 83 may be considered as equivalent. This means, among other things, that NOS and NIMA charts are compatible.

Datum Shift

215   As a nautical navigator, what is important to remember about datums is that they can be different, and this difference results in what is called *datum shift*, something that is ignored at the navigator's peril.

From the discussion above, it should be apparent that a problem develops when a navigation system (such as GPS) provides a fix based on a datum different from that which was used to create the nautical chart in use. The resulting plotted position may be different from the actual location on the chart. This difference varies greatly depending upon the datums in use. For example, if a GPS position (referenced to WGS 84) in New York Harbor were plotted on a chart that was created using the old NAD 27 datum, the datum shift would be about 11 meters, but a GPS position in the Sea of Japan plotted on a chart using the Tokyo Datum would have a datum shift of more than 700 meters.

A similar problem can result if the navigator shifts from one chart to another and the two charts were created using different datums. Simply transferring a position using longitude and latitude will result in the new position having a different location relative to the charted features. If one of those features happens to be a shoal, the datum shift can be rather significant!

Identifying the Datum

216   Most charts produced by NIMA and NOS include a *datum note*. Usually located in the title block or in the upper left margin of the chart, the note will say something like "North American Datum

of 1983 (World Geodetic System 1984)," or "World Geodetic System 1972 (WGS-72)," or "World Geodetic System 1984 (WGS 1984)," or sometimes just "World Geodetic System (WGS)." The latter note is sufficient because differences between the four WGS datums (60, 66, 72, and 84) are not significant enough to concern the nautical navigator—they can be treated as virtually identical.

Accompanying the note may be an additional notation indicating that positions obtained from satellite navigation systems may be plotted directly on the chart without corrections. If the chart is a NIMA reproduction of a foreign chart that is based upon a different (non-WGS) datum, it will have an additional note, such as "Positions obtained from satellite navigation systems referred to the WGS 84 datum must be moved 7.36 minutes northward and 3.65 minutes eastward to agree with this chart." Or there may be other notations, giving corrections to other datums.

A few charts are based on such early surveys that a conversion factor cannot be accurately determined. These charts will have a note saying "Adjustments to WGS cannot be determined for this chart" or "From various sources to (year)" with no reference to WGS.

Minimizing Datum Shift Errors

217 If the chart you are using is based upon a WGS datum or the NAD 83 datum, no corrections will be necessary. But if a chart is based upon any other datum, you will have to be aware of, and deal with, datum shift.

If you keep in mind that datum shift affects the latitude and longitude grid (graticule) of a chart but does not affect the relative position of features shown, then the most effective way to correct for datum shift is to compare an accurate fix taken by local means (visual or radar) to a satellite fix taken at the same time to determine a correction factor for the satellite information being used on that chart.

The difference between these two fixes can then be applied to all satellite fixes subsequently taken and plotted on that chart. Of course, the prudent navigator will repeat this process periodically to confirm or adjust the correction factor, especially as the vessel moves to other parts of the chart.

Another area of caution in dealing with datum shift problems is in applying chart corrections. Make certain that chart corrections are plotted only on the specific charts and editions for which they are intended. Mixing datums when applying chart corrections can introduce unwanted errors.

Keep in mind that some chart features, such as drill rigs, are temporary. Since they are usually positioned using satellites, WGS is the appropriate datum. If position information on such a feature is plotted on a chart of a different datum, a correction for datum shift will probably be necessary.

If you have any doubt as to the reference datum for plotted information, be wary and allow a margin of error that will compensate for any possible datum shifts that may be introduced.

SUMMARY

218 Latitude and longitude have long been the accepted means of defining position on Earth's surface. While other coordinate systems have been developed, none is as universally used as this tried and true system. An understanding of latitude and longitude is essential to the successful nautical navigator.

As already noted, you do not have to be a geodesist or cartographer in order to be a good navigator. You do not even have to fully understand such things as geoids, ellipsoids, and datums, but you *must* be aware of the importance of datums in terms of compatibility. In the U.S. Navy, "Check chart datum" has been added to every navigational checklist. This awareness, coupled with the corrections that may be required as a result, is absolutely imperative until the day arrives when all nautical charts and all navigational systems in the world are referenced to the same datum.

Chapter 3

Nautical Charts

A nautical chart is a representation of a portion of the Earth's spherical surface on a two-dimensional surface that has been specially designed for convenient use in navigation and therefore has to do primarily with areas of navigable water. A modern chart is intended to be worked upon, not merely looked at, and should readily permit the graphic solution of navigational problems, such as distance and direction, or the determination of position in terms of latitude and longitude. Although they are similar to maps in many ways and it is arguable that a nautical chart is a form of map, experienced mariners never refer to their charts as maps.

For many centuries mariners have used some form of graphic representation of shorelines and ports, hazards and safe waters, landmarks, and other features to assist them in safely guiding their vessels. In earlier times, charts were not published for general use but were often kept secret for the personal advantage of the captain or navigator who had prepared or purchased them.

In the second century A.D., the great astronomer and mathematician Ptolemy constructed a famous chart of the then-known world that listed several thousand places by latitude and longitude. Unfortunately, he based the chart on the faulty calculations of an earlier Greek philosopher who had estimated the Earth's circumference to be considerably less than its actual size. Ptolemy was rightfully held in high esteem, and his work—including this erroneous chart—remained a standard for many centuries, eventually leading Columbus to believe that he had reached the East Indies in 1492 when he had actually not gone nearly far enough.

The earliest charts of the Middle Ages still in existence are the Portolan charts prepared in Spain in the fourteenth century. They are remarkably accurate in their portrayal of the Mediterranean. In 1515, Leonardo da Vinci drew what has become a famous map of the world. Gerardus Mercator is considered the father of modern cartography because he used a scientific method to produce a world chart that is in use today and has been the basis for much of the chart making that has followed.

Today, charts are produced in many different ways for different purposes by official government agencies that ensure standardization and accuracy. They are constantly being revised to ensure that the most accurate and current data are represented.

A number of special-purpose charts have been created, such as pilot charts that provide weather and other information, tidal current charts, star charts, and so on. In the remainder of this chapter, primary consideration will be given to the more common nautical charts, to the projections upon which they are constructed, and to a navigator's use of them. Electronic charts, which are rapidly supplanting paper, will be covered in the next chapter.

CHART PROJECTIONS

301 Simple experimentation will show that no significant portion of a hollow rubber ball can be spread out flat without some stretching or tearing. Conversely, a sheet of tissue paper cannot be wrapped smoothly around a sphere; there will be numerous wrinkles and overlaps. Because Earth is also virtually round (a spheroid, ellipsoid, or geoid—see chapter 2; we will refer to it simply as a sphere for the purposes of this chapter), it should be apparent that, just like the rubber ball, it cannot be repre-

sented on a flat piece of paper without introducing some degree of distortion. The smaller the portion of the globe to be mapped, the less distortion present—conversely, the greater the area, the greater the distortion.

The process of transforming the spherical surface of the Earth to a flat surface is called projection, a term that comes from the earliest cartographic methods that involved physically projecting the features and accompanying coordinate system from one surface to the other. The truth is that many so-called projections are now derived from analytical and mathematical processes rather than the physical process of projecting, but the term has been used for so long it is now used to describe all cartographic procedures that result in maps or charts.

There are several hundred types of projections, each with some particular property that may make it desirable for some specific purpose. Of these, only a few are commonly used for nautical navigation.

Which projections will be used is determined by the desired properties of the chart. The properties that are most desirable in nautical charts are:
1. True shape of physical features such as bodies of land or water;
2. Equal area, that is, areas (such as land masses or bodies of water) are represented in correct relative proportions;
3. Correct angular relationships (known as *conformal*);
4. Distances are constant everywhere on the chart;
5. Great circles as straight lines;
6. Rhumb lines as straight lines.

A chart of a very small area may closely achieve most or all of these properties with almost any method of projection. As the area grows larger, however, there is a corresponding decline in the number and quality of the properties that can be achieved. For example, in a large-area chart either great circles or rhumb lines can be straight lines, but not both. *All* of the described properties can be obtained only on a *spherical* surface, so any projection to a flat surface will be a compromise based on the properties deemed most important.

Some of the projections commonly used for navigational purposes fall within three categories that are defined by the geometry used to create the resultant charts: *cylindrical, conic,* or *plane.* As indicated in figure 301, a cone and cylinder can be cut from top to bottom and rolled out flat without distortion. A limited portion of Earth's surface can also be shown ("projected") directly upon a plane surface while keeping distortion within acceptable limits.

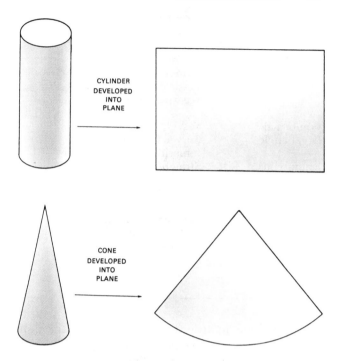

Fig. 301. Development of a cylinder and a cone.

The most-used projection for nautical charts is a *cylindrical* one known as the "Mercator." The best known *conic* projection that is sometimes used in nautical navigation, primarily in high latitudes, is the "Lambert conformal" projection. The *plane* projections best known to navigators are the various forms of "gnomonic" projections, also commonly known as "great-circle charts." The terms "stereographic," "azimuthal," and "zenithal" are also used for specific types of projections that are sometimes used for navigational charts.

The table on the next page compares some of the features of three of the more commonly used projections:

THE MERCATOR PROJECTION

302   Most of the charts used for marine navigation are based on the Mercator projection. For this reason, it is useful for a navigator to have a thorough understanding of these charts.

A Mercator projection can be visualized as the placement of a cylinder around the Earth touching it at a great circle, usually the equator. For this reason, it is generally classified as a cylindrical projection. Strictly speaking, however, the modern Mercator chart is derived from complex mathematical equations that introduce exactly the right amount of distortion to show every rhumb line as a straight line (see fig. 302a), an important consideration for navigational purposes (see article 209). When this

	Mercator	*Lambert Conformal*	*Gnomonic*
Parallels	Horizontal straight lines	Arcs of concentric circles	Curved (conic sections), except equator
Meridians	Vertical straight lines perpendicular to parallels	Straight-line radii of parallels, converging at the pole	Straight lines
Conformal	Yes	Yes	No
Great circle	Curved line (except meridians and equator)	Approximates straight line	Straight line
Rhumb line	Straight line; course angle measured with *any* meridian	Curved line; course angle measured at intersection of straight line and mid-meridian	Curved line
Distance scale	Varies; scale at mid-latitude of a particular course to be used	Nearly constant	No constant scale; can be measured by rules printed on most charts
Increase of scale	Increases with distance from equator	Increases with distance from central parallel of projection	Increases with distance from center of projection (point of tangency)

has been done, in order to keep all parts of the chart in their correct relative positions, great circles have been distorted into curved lines, always bending away from the equator, toward the nearest pole. Figure 302b is a portion of a Mercator chart showing both the great-circle route and the rhumb line between Norfolk, Virginia (Chesapeake Bay Entrance), and Brest, France. The great-circle route *appears* to be appreciably longer, but the distance is actually less. If you remember that the Earth's surface is actually curved, it will help you understand why this is so. Remember, a nautical chart must always make compromises in order to portray the properties desired.

Plotting Positions on Mercator Charts

303   A major advantage of the Mercator projection is that latitude and longitude appear as a rectangular graticule, simplifying the plotting of positions, the drawing of courses, and so on. A position of known latitude and longitude can be easily plotted on a Mercator projection, using a plotter or straightedge and a pair of dividers (see chapter 8). For example, a navigator's position at 1635 (Lat. 41° 09′ N, Long. 70° 44′ W) may be plotted as follows: first find the given latitude, 41° 09′ N, on the latitude scale along the right or left edge of the chart. Place a straightedge through this point parallel to any convenient parallel of latitude, aligning it in an east-west direction. Then set one point of the dividers at 71° 00′ W on the longitude scale along the top or bottom of the chart and the other point at 70° 44′ W, a spread of 16.0 minutes of longitude (the difference between 71° 00′ and 70° 44′). Without changing the setting of the dividers, lay off this dis-

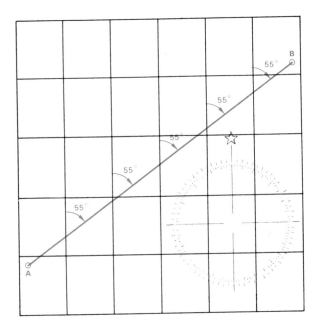

Fig. 302a. Measuring direction on a Mercator chart.

tance along the straightedge from the 71st meridian eastward, in the direction of the position. Circle this point and label with the appropriate time (1635).

The reverse problem—determining the latitude and longitude of a position that has been plotted on the chart—is also easily accomplished (see fig. 303). Place one point of a pair of dividers on the 1635 position and swing the other point in an arc, while adjusting its radius, until it becomes tangent to a parallel of latitude. The spread of the dividers then equals the difference of latitude from this reference parallel. Transfer the dividers to the latitude scale

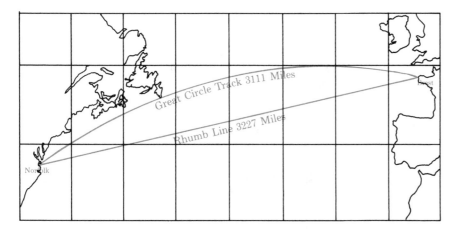

Fig. 302b. Great circle and rhumb line on a Mercator chart.

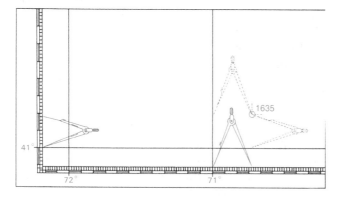

Fig. 303. Locating a position on a Mercator chart.

along the right or left edge of the chart, and placing one point at the reference parallel, read the latitude of the position at the other point. A similar procedure, measuring from the position to a meridian of longitude, will provide the longitude of the point. Be careful in each case to lay off the difference of latitude and longitude in the proper direction from the reference parallel or meridian.

Measuring and Plotting Distance on Mercator Charts

304   Another great convenience in using Mercator charts is that distances are easily obtainable by using latitude demarcations. For practical purposes, 1° of latitude everywhere on the Earth's surface may be considered to be 60 nautical miles in length. This means that *every minute of latitude is equal to one nautical mile*. Knowing this, you may quickly determine the distance between two points on your Mercator chart by setting the dividers to cover the space between the two locations on the chart (one divider point on each point to be measured on the chart) and then, without changing the spread of the dividers, move them to the nearest side of the chart

where you may then read the distance by measuring the number of minutes of latitude. The difference of latitude in minutes on the latitude scale, is the distance in nautical miles.

It is essential to note that this does *not* apply to longitude, because the length of 1° of longitude varies with the latitude, from 60 miles at the equator to zero at the poles (refer to fig. 205 in chapter 2). Therefore, it is always the *latitude scale* that must be used for measuring distance—*never the longitude scale*.

Also keep in mind that the latitude scale of a Mercator chart expands increasingly with distance from the equator, and this means that the scale of miles increases accordingly. That is, in the northerly part of a Mercator chart in the Northern Hemisphere, the length of each mile on the chart has been stretched, and there are fewer miles in an inch than in the southerly part. To avoid errors, therefore, you must always measure distances along the latitude scale in the same vicinity (i.e., approximately the same latitude) as the distance being measured. Do not, for example, measure the distance between two points at the lower part of your chart by moving the dividers to the latitude scale near the upper part of your chart. Simply make it a habit to always move your dividers laterally across the chart to the nearer edge, without moving north or south.

In the event that you are measuring a distance between two points with considerable north-south separation, use that part of the latitude scale which is at the mean latitude of the distance to be measured (see fig. 304a).

When the distance is great enough that the dividers cannot reach all the way from A to B in one step, one point of the dividers might be placed at A, the other point at a position about halfway between A and B. The length of this portion of the route could then be measured from the latitude scale with

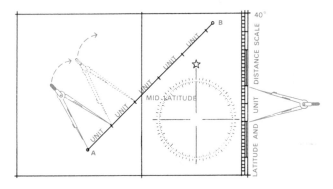

Fig. 304a. Measuring distance on a Mercator chart.

the dividers centered at about the mid-latitude of that part. Similarly, the length of the remainder could be read with the dividers centered at about mid-latitude of the other part. The two distances then would be added to obtain the total distance.

When the distance is too great for one or two settings of the dividers, some convenient unit—10 miles, in figure 304a—can be taken from the latitude scale at the mid-latitude and stepped off along the route, as shown. In the figure, it was stepped off five times: 5 × 10 = 50 miles, with a little left over. The small amount left over is then set on the dividers and laid off along the latitude scale, where it is found to measure 2 miles: 50 + 2 = 52 miles, the total distance from A to B.

Charts which cover a limited area (and therefore will have little change in latitude scale) often have a simple graphic *bar scale* for measuring distance, usually printed near the title of the chart. This may be simply a line, or a double line, divided into miles, or some other appropriate unit such as yards or kilometers; fractions of one major unit are conventionally marked to the *left* of the zero point. Frequently, such a chart will carry two or three such

graphic scales, each with different units (see fig. 304b).

To use a bar scale, set the dividers to cover the space between the two locations on the chart. Then move the dividers to the bar scale, placing the right-hand point on a mark for a whole unit so that the left-hand point is to the left of the 0 mark on the subdivided unit. For example: assume that the distance to be measured is between 2 and 3 miles; one point of the dividers is set on the bar scale graduation for 2 miles, and the other falls on the mark for 0.4 miles to the *left* of the 0 mark. The total distance is thus determined to be 2.4 miles.

For charts covering a wide band of latitude, a "scale diagram" (see fig. 304c) is sometimes used. This is, in effect, simply a series of bar scales, in parallel lines, with zero of each scale in the same vertical line. Smooth curves are then drawn through the corresponding graduations of each scale, keyed to latitude. Each scale in the diagram is correct for the latitude indicated, and distances should be measured with the scale for the average latitude of the distance required. Obviously, the correct scale for any latitude intermediate between two adjacent lines is also available. For example, if the average latitude between A and B is determined to be about 27° 30′ the dividers can be set on the diagram about halfway between the scales for 25° and 30°.

Disadvantages of Mercator Charts

305   As already discussed, any chart must compromise some of its properties, so there are disadvantages to Mercator charts as well. Great-circle distances and directions are not readily determinable without first plotting the great circle on a different (usually gnomonic) chart and transferring points along the line to the Mercator. Areas in high latitudes are greatly exaggerated. The example most

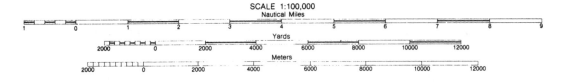

Fig. 304b. Various chart graphic (bar) scales.

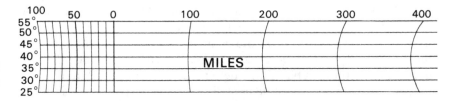

Fig. 304c. Scale diagram for a Lambert conformal chart of the United States, scale 1:5,000,000.

often cited is that of Greenland, which when shown complete on the Mercator appears to be larger than South America, although it actually is only one-ninth as large as that continent. Figure 305, which simulates the process used in creating a Mercator chart, will aid in understanding this weakness of the projection. In the figure, at A, one "gore" or section of an ordinary globe has been peeled off and stands vertically. Two true circles of the same size have been drawn on the gore, to serve as "test patterns." At B the sides of the gore have been stretched horizontally so that the two outer meridians are parallel to the central meridian of the gore. In the stretching, the two circles have become ellipses (represented by the shaded areas), the northerly one having been stretched much more than the southern one. To compensate for this horizontal stretching, the horizontally stretched gore must now be stretched vertically until the ellipses again become (approximately) circles, the diameter in each case approximating the major axis of the ellipse. Comparing the circles as they appear in figure 305 at A and C, and remembering that they are in reality the same size, you can see the problem created by Mercator projections in high latitudes.

In order for parallels and meridians to be rectangular on a Mercator chart (thus preserving the very desirable property of allowing rhumb lines to be drawn as straight lines), meridians cannot be extended all the way to the pole(s) on the chart. The poles have been projected to infinity, so most Mercator projections extend no farther from the equator than about 70°, and rarely beyond 80°. This is of no great disadvantage unless you are navigating in high northern or southern latitudes. For this purpose, a different kind of chart must be used.

Transverse and Oblique Mercator Projections

306   When one speaks of a "Mercator chart" it is commonly understood that the reference is to the Mercator *conformal* projection. There are, however, other forms of this cylindrical projection.

For the *transverse Mercator projection* the cylinder has been turned through 90° and is tangent along a selected meridian (see fig. 306a). For the polar regions it has the same desirable properties that the original Mercator possesses near the equator. For this reason, charts used in polar navigation (see chapter 34) sometimes are constructed using the transverse Mercator projection. As with the original Mercator projection, there has to be expansion of the parallel as one moves away from the line of tangency in order to maintain the relative shape of areas. Now, however, the areas of size distortion are those *distant from the pole*. A major disadvantage is the curvature of the meridians, making them less suitable for direction measurements. Within the limits of a single chart, however, this distortion is usually negligible.

The cylinder of the Mercator projection could have been turned through some angle other than 90°—any angle, and at any latitude between the equator and either pole. This is known as an *oblique Mercator* projection and is used for some special purpose charts. Figure 306b shows a portion of a cylinder tangent to the great circle joining Miami and Lisbon. On the resulting oblique Mercator projection, whether it is visible or not, this great circle becomes, in effect, the "equator" of the projection.

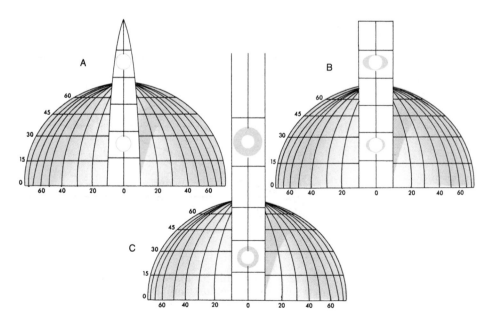

Fig. 305. Relationship between areas on a globe and their representation on a Mercator projection.

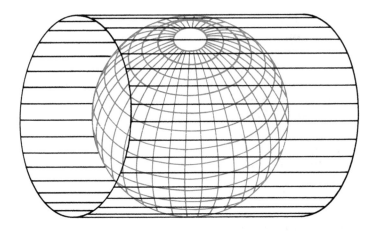

Fig. 306a. Transverse Mercator projection.

Meridians will be curves, the direction of curvature reversing as the meridian crosses the fictitious "equator," but the curvature is scarcely noticeable for areas within 700 to 800 miles on either side of this central line. Parallels are also curved lines.

GNOMONIC PROJECTION

307   Figure 307a illustrates the geometry of several kinds of cartographic projections. The most relevant one to nautical navigation is the gnomonic projection, in which the reference lines of the sphere are projected from the center of the Earth onto a tangent plane. The point of tangency may be on the equator (*equatorial*), at either pole (*polar*), or at any other latitude (*oblique*).

The Mercator projection was developed for the purpose of showing every rhumb line as a straight line. The gnomonic projection has been adapted to a number of special uses, but in navigation it is chiefly used because it shows *every great circle as a straight line*. In figure 307b the same great circle and rhumb line that appeared in figure 302b are again shown, but this time they are drawn on a gnomonic chart instead of a Mercator. On the gnomonic chart, the rhumb line is now curved instead of straight, and it bends *toward* the equator, away from the nearest pole.

In actual practice, a navigator planning this voyage from Norfolk to Brest would first plot the great-circle route on a gnomonic chart to determine the most direct route, and then transfer the route, one segment at a time, to a Mercator chart. Because great-circle courses yield the shortest distances, but

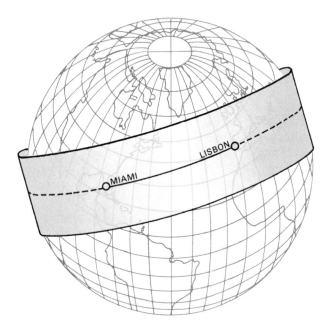

Fig. 306b. Oblique Mercator projection in which a selected great circle (Miami to Lisbon) serves as the "equator" of the projection.

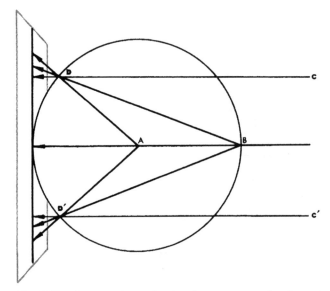

Fig. 307a. Gnomonic projection from center of sphere A; stereographic projection from B; orthographic projection from C and C′ (parallel rays).

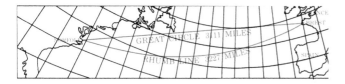

Fig. 307b. Rhumb line and great circle on a gnomonic chart.

rhumb-line courses are easier to steer (because of the unvarying heading), this compromise makes sense. Since great-circle routes yield a path of constantly changing direction, this method allows the course to be changed in steps at convenient intervals. When transferring from the gnomonic to the Mercator, a convenient and consistent method is to use points where the route crosses meridians or parallels at regular intervals to define the segments. These points are defined on the gnomonic chart, then transferred to the Mercator, where they are then connected by straight lines. The end result is a series of steerable rhumb lines closely approximating the great-circle route. For voyages that are long enough to justify the savings in distance, this combination of great-circle and rhumb-line navigation makes sense.

Limitations of Gnomonic Charts

308   Distance and direction cannot be measured directly on a gnomonic chart, so it is not usable as a working chart for normal plotting of navigational data. There are usually instructions printed on the chart for determining great-circle distances and the initial direction of a great circle, but these are not very practical for most navigational purposes.

Distortion of shape and scale increases as distance from the center of the projection (the point of tangency) increases. Within about 1,000 miles of the point of tangency, this distortion is not objectionable; beyond that, it increases rapidly and becomes a significant problem.

LAMBERT CONFORMAL PROJECTION

309   Derived from a conic projection, Lambert conformal charts first came into use during World War I as military maps. Since then, they have been used widely for aeronautical charts and as nautical charts for navigation in higher latitudes. Figure 309a illustrates a Lambert projection being developed for the United States. The cone intersects the Earth along two standard parallels of true scale. Between the standard parallels the scale is some-

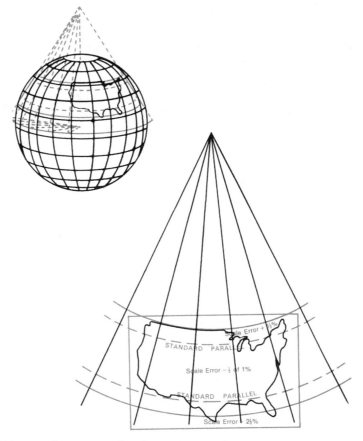

Fig. 309a. Development and scale properties of Lambert conformal projection.

what compressed, the maximum error being about $^1/_2$ of 1 percent; outside them, the scale is slightly expanded, reaching a maximum of nearly 2.25 percent at the tip of Florida.

It can be seen that the meridians are represented by straight lines that meet in a common point outside the limits of the chart (the tip of the developed cone) and that the parallels are represented by concentric arcs originating from this same point. Meridians and parallels intersect at right angles, and angles on the Earth are correctly represented on the chart. Stated another way, the *total* change in scale within the United States is about 3 percent. That is, from a point in the central United States to the tip of Florida, each 100-mile section would measure about 103 miles in figure 309a. By way of comparison, the total change of scale for a Mercator chart of the United States would be approximately 40 percent.

On a Lambert conformal chart, a great circle is very nearly a straight line, close enough for purposes of practical navigation (see fig. 309b). Points along such a line can be transferred to a Mercator chart for a series of rhumb lines in the same manner as for a gnomonic chart.

STEREOGRAPHIC AND ORTHOGRAPHIC PROJECTIONS

310   The polar stereographic projection is used for aeronautical (and some nautical) charts of the polar regions, from about 75° latitude poleward. Figure 310 shows a polar stereographic map of the Northern Hemisphere. Note that in this case the parallels are concentric circles and all meridians are straight-line radials.

Figure 307a showed the method of projection for stereographic charts. Instead of being projected from the center of the sphere, points are projected upon the tangent plane from the opposite end of the diameter from the point of tangency (from B in the figure). The case shown in the figure yields an equatorial stereographic. A polar stereographic or an oblique stereographic is as readily obtained. In each case, the point of projection is always the opposite end of the diameter from the point of tangency.

Another type of projection illustrated by figure 307a is the *orthographic*. Here the projection "rays" are from infinity, shown as C and C´, and thus are all parallel. The plane of the projection is usually tangent at the equator to depict half of the Earth, such as the Western Hemisphere, although conformality and equal area are sacrificed.

AZIMUTHAL CHARTS

311   Most polar projections are azimuthal (or zenithal). By this it is meant that all directions (azimuths) from the center of the projection are true. The polar stereographic projection mentioned above is azimuthal as well as conformal. All gnomonic projections are azimuthal, affording true directions from the point of tangency, regardless of the position of the point on the sphere.

In any family of projections, it is possible to obtain different properties simply by varying the spacing of the parallels. The polar stereographic projection is conformal, and scale along the meridians varies. The *polar equidistant* yields true scale along each meridian. A *polar equal area* projection is

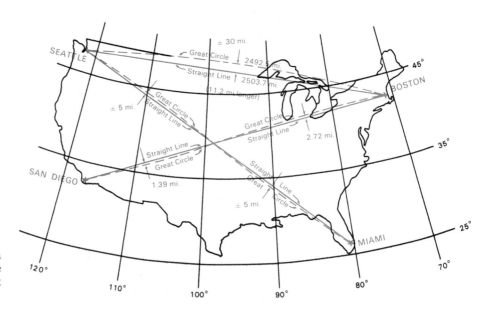

Fig. 309b. Straight lines on a Lambert conformal chart are close approximations of great circles.

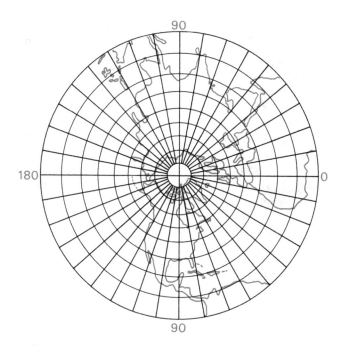

Fig. 310. Polar stereographic projection.

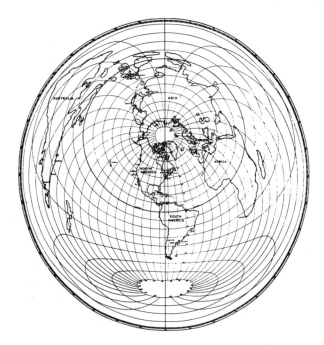

Fig. 311. An azimuthal equidistant chart centered on Washington, D.C.

also obtainable by another variation in the spacing of the parallels. All three are azimuthal.

In the same way, a cylindrical projection may be conformal (as with the ordinary Mercator) or equal area, by varying the spacing of the parallels. Conic projections, too, may be either conformal (as with the Lambert conformal) or equal area.

A specialized type of chart is the *azimuthal equidistant,* which is actually mathematically derived rather than being "projected." It is always centered on some place of particular significance, such as a nation's capital city or a major communications center. On this projection, it is possible to show the entire surface of the Earth in one flat chart, though with *great* distortion. For example, the *point* at the opposite end of Earth's diameter from the central point of the projection is stretched into a *line* throughout the entire 360° of the limiting circle, as in figure 311.

From the chosen central point of the projection all distances are true, and the distance to any place on Earth may be measured as accurately as the scale of the chart permits. From the same central point all directions are true, and the direction (azimuth) of any place on Earth may also be measured directly. A 360° scale is usually printed around the edge of the chart for this purpose.

Charts using the azimuthal equidistant method are particularly useful in communications as the great-circle paths followed by radio waves appear as radial lines, and the proper orientation for a direc-

tional antenna is easily obtained. For aviation interests, direction great-circle routes are easily plotted, and the various areas to be overflown are readily apparent. A number of these charts, centered on points of typical interest, are published by the National Imagery and Mapping Agency (NIMA).

PLOTTING SHEETS

312   At sea, where no large-scale charts are available, navigators use plotting sheets. These are basically Mercator charts showing only the grid of meridians and parallels with a compass rose, without any other chart data. There are two types available: Position Plotting Sheets, which are printed for a given band of latitude, and Universal Plotting Sheets, which can be used at any latitude.

Position Plotting Sheets

313   NIMA publishes several series of position plotting sheets at different scales; the value of the latitude is printed on the parallels of latitude, while the meridians are left blank. The navigator selects the plotting sheet with the appropriate latitude and then inserts the appropriate longitude. When labeling the meridians, it must be remembered that in west longitude the longitude becomes numerically greater toward the west (to the left) on the sheet. In east longitude it increases numerically to the east (to the right) on the sheet.

As on nearly all charts, north is at the top. When plotting sheets are used in north latitudes, the value of the latitude becomes numerically larger toward the north or top of the sheet. In south latitudes the reverse is true. The latitude markings will read appropriately for northern latitudes when the sheet is turned upright (with the words "Position Plotting Sheet" at the top and "Logarithmic Time, Speed, and Distance Scale" at the bottom) (see fig. 313). The sheet is turned upside down for southern latitudes, and the latitude markings will then read correspondingly. The compass rose is also designed for different hemispheric use: directions appropriate to north latitudes are marked on the inside of the circle, and those appropriate to south latitudes are marked on the outside. When the sheet is upright or inverted for the latitudes in use, the appropriate compass rose will become more readable.

Universal Plotting Sheets

314 These specialized sheets have a specialized compass rose, unnumbered parallels of latitude, and a single meridian in the center of the sheet. They are unusual in that they can be used for any latitude and longitude, exclusive of the polar areas where a Mercator chart is not practical. The navigator must draw in the appropriate meridians, making sure they are properly spaced for the mid-latitude of the area to be covered. This is accomplished by first labeling the existing lines as appropriate. For example, if you are operating off the east coast of the United States in the vicinity of 35° N 76° W, you would label the center latitude line on your universal plotting sheet as 35° N and the only meridian as 76° W (see fig. 314). You would then label the other parallels as appropriate (34° below and 36° above). Next, construct the other meridians by drawing a line parallel to the right of the central meridian so that it passes through the appropriate marking on the outer ring of the special compass rose (in this case, 35°). Note that the outer ring is not labeled with standard compass directions but with points representing angles from the horizontal instead. The resulting line would be the next whole-degree meridian (in this case, 75° W). The 74° line can then be constructed similarly or by simply marking off the same distance between the 75° and 76° meridians and then constructing a parallel line on the opposite side. Standard universal plotting sheets actually cover an area larger than the one shown in figure 314, so it will be necessary to construct the remaining whole-degree meridians using the latter method described (parallel lines at the same dis-

tance). Usually only two or three meridians will fit on either side of the central meridian (depending upon the latitude).

Universal Plotting Sheets are published with the designation VP-OS. They are 13 × 14 inches and are scaled at 20 miles per inch. Note that the central meridian has minutes of latitude marked off which can be used as a distance scale (1 minute = 1 nautical mile). There is also a longitude scale provided in the lower right-hand corner of the sheet (not shown in fig. 314) which can be used by measuring along the appropriate mid-latitude line.

IDENTIFICATION AND CLASSIFICATION OF NAUTICAL CHARTS

315 Because there are many, many nautical charts in existence, some means of identifying them is vital if the navigator is going to keep track of them. Charts can be classified in a number of different ways: by who produces them, by scale, by the area they cover, and so on.

U.S. Chart Agencies

316 The governmental agency for charting the coastal waters of the United States and its possessions for commercial and civil use is the *National Ocean Service* (NOS), a division of the National Oceanic and Atmospheric Administration (NOAA) within the Department of Commerce. NOS conducts hydrographic, topographic, and geodetic surveys from which charts are produced for coastal waters, most rivers, and the Great Lakes. The Army Corps of Engineers prepares navigational charts and maps for the Mississippi River and its tributaries and some larger inland lakes.

Nautical charts for use by the Defense Department are the responsibility of the *National Imagery and Mapping Agency* (NIMA). This activity produces charts from many sources, including its own field work, using U.S. Navy survey ships, and by reproducing charts of other nations. Both NOS and NIMA conduct continuing surveys, and their highly accurate charts are generally available to the mariners of all nations (although some NIMA charts are restricted to official governmental use only.)

The charts these two agencies produce come in a wide range of types and sizes. The most common are large sheets of high-quality paper, usually printed on one side only, and intended for flat or rolled storage. Recognizing that small craft will have difficulty both in using and storing a large flat chart, the National Ocean Service prints some in a special folding format.

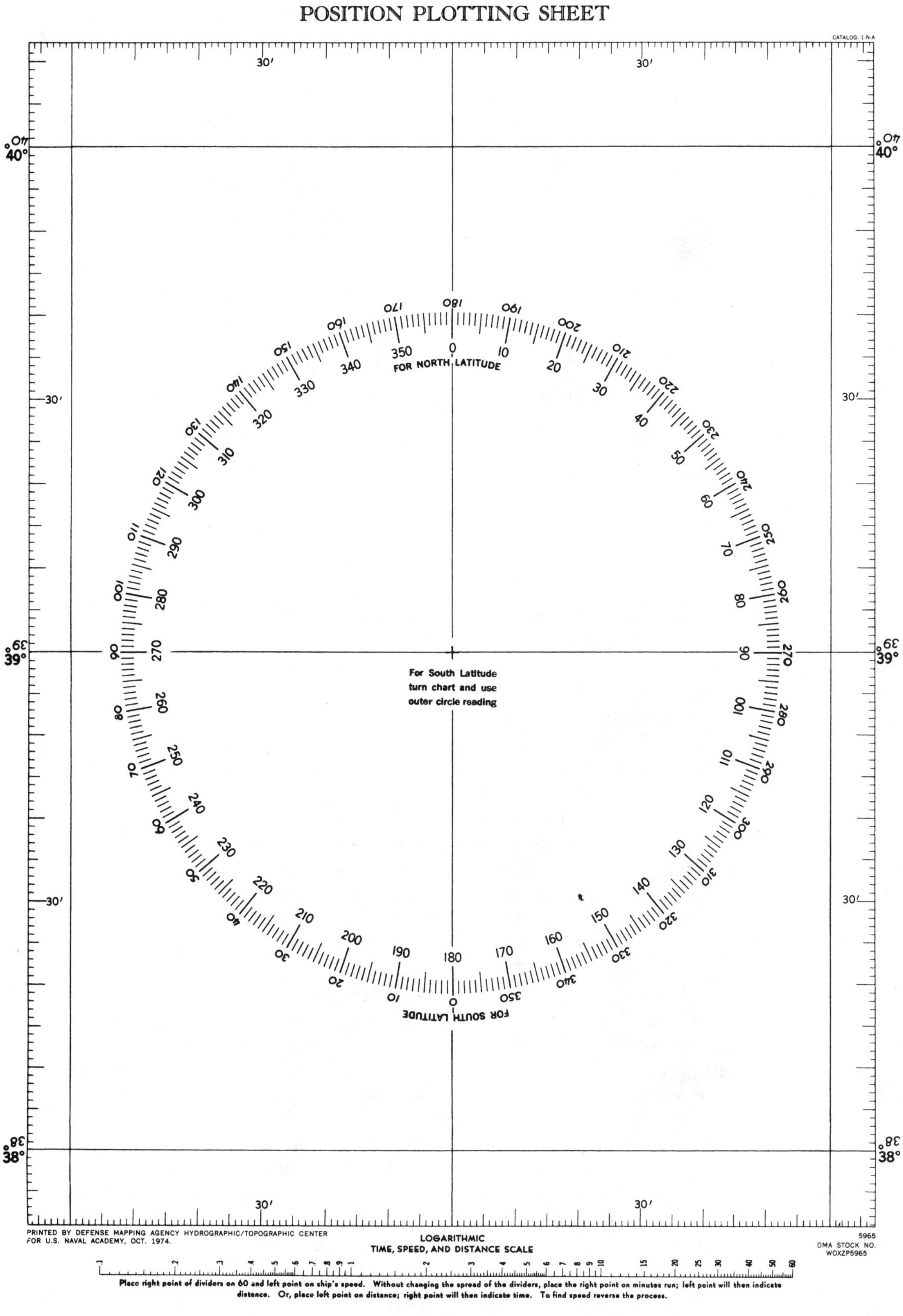

POSITION PLOTTING SHEET

For South Latitude
turn chart and use
outer circle reading

FOR NORTH LATITUDE

FOR SOUTH LATITUDE

PRINTED BY DEFENSE MAPPING AGENCY HYDROGRAPHIC/TOPOGRAPHIC CENTER
FOR U.S. NAVAL ACADEMY, OCT. 1974.

LOGARITHMIC
TIME, SPEED, AND DISTANCE SCALE

5965
DMA STOCK NO.
WOXZP5965

Place right point of dividers on 60 and left point on ship's speed. Without changing the spread of the dividers, place the right point on minutes run; left point will then indicate distance. Or, place left point on distance; right point will then indicate time. To find speed reverse the process.

Fig. 313. A typical position plotting sheet. Note that the sheet can be turned upside-down for use with southern latitudes.

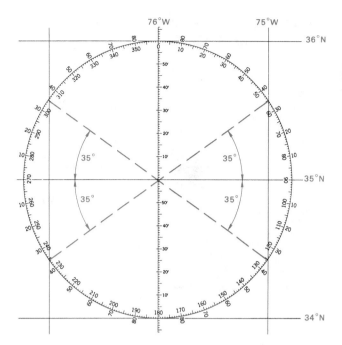

Fig. 314. Part of a universal plotting sheet.

Chart No. 1

317   Although NIMA and NOS publish their own charts, they use the same symbols and terms so that navigators having access to both will not have difficulty switching from one to the other. NIMA and NOS jointly publish an important booklet entitled *United States of America Nautical Symbols Abbreviations and Terms* that is more widely known by its numerical designation, *Chart No. 1* (even though it is a booklet and not a chart in the traditional sense). It explains all the various ways that information is represented on charts produced by the two agencies. It also incorporates the symbols contained in the international version, known as International Hydrographic Organization (IHO) Chart No. 1, sometimes abbreviated "INT 1."

NOS also produces a more detailed *Nautical Chart User's Manual* that "explains what is presented on the nautical chart, highlights the utility of this information, describes the charting conventions used to depict features and items of interest, and provides some practical pointers on how this information is used. Go to the National Oceanographic and Atmospheric Administration's web site, www.noaa.gov, for more information. The *Nautical Chart User's Manual* can be viewed at this web site and actually printed (warning: it is many pages long).

Editions and Revisions

318   Charts are published with an edition number and date so that the navigator will know how current is the information it contains. Revisions are periodically issued as explained below. When a significant number of revisions have been made to the information on a chart, a new edition is published; the interval between editions can vary from a year or less to more than twelve years. A chart is sometimes issued with a "Revised" date when the stock level requires another printing, and only a few changes have been incorporated; in this case, a new edition number is not warranted.

All charts in regular use onboard ships and boats should be corrected according to the latest information from all official sources such as "Notices to Mariners" (published by NIMA with the cooperation of NOS and the U.S. Coast Guard), "Local Notices to Mariners" (published by the Coast Guard), and urgent changes disseminated by radio in the appropriate series of warning notices (see articles 508 and 510). Also, procedures should be established whereby charts that are not used regularly can be quickly brought up to date when needed; one method used in the Navy is to keep a file of *Chart/Publication Record* cards (NIMA No. 8860/9). The growing use of electronic charts (see chapter 4) will modify or obviate some of the procedures required for revising paper charts.

For safety in navigation, every chart used must be the latest printing and fully corrected for changes that have occurred since the edition date. An old edition of a chart, or an uncorrected chart, is not safe to use and can lead to disaster.

Chart Scales

319   The scale of a chart is the ratio of a distance unit on the chart to the actual distance on the surface of the Earth; as this is a ratio, it does not matter what size the unit is, or in what system it is measured. For example, a scale of 1:80,000 means that one unit (inch, foot, meter, etc.) on the chart represents 80,000 such units on the Earth.

All charts have their scale shown in fractional form, but, as discussed earlier, charts representing relatively small areas will generally also carry graphic (bar) scales of distance, usually in more than one set of units. The bar scale shown in figure 304b, for example, is marked off in nautical miles, yards, and meters. Bar scales will only appear on charts of such scale and projection that the scale varies a negligible amount over the whole chart (usually scales of 1:75,000 or larger). Remember that because one minute of latitude equals one nautical mile, you can always use a nearby latitude scale in the absence of a bar scale (or even when it is present) to measure distance.

The terms *large scale* and *small scale* are often confusing to persons who are not accustomed to using charts. To begin with, they are relative terms—no clear dividing line exists to determine which scales are large and which are small. The other potential confusion comes from the seemingly opposite nature of the numbers involved. For example, if a chart is printed at a scale of 1:5,000,000, the very "bigness" of the second number makes it seem like a larger scale than one at 1:150,000. But remember that these scales can also be written as fractions—1/5,000,000 or 1/150,000—and the larger the denominator of a fraction, the smaller is the quantity. At a scale of 1:5,000,000, 1 mile is only 0.015 inch in length; at 1:150,000, it is 0.486 inch, roughly thirty-three times as long.

It follows, then, that a small scale chart covers a larger area than a large scale chart and that a small scale chart will include less detail than will a large scale chart. One way to help you remember this is to use the memory aid "LASS":

Large Area = Small Scale
For example,
1:1,000,000 = Small Scale = Large Area = Less Detail
and conversely,
1:10,000 = Large Scale = Small Area = More Detail

From all of this, it should be apparent that the nautical navigator may want to use a small scale for *planning* purposes, such as laying out a great-circle route across the Atlantic on a gnomonic chart, but he or she will almost always want to use the largest scale chart available for actual navigation, or *plotting* purposes, in order to take advantage of the greater detail available.

Chart Numbering System

320   To provide an orderly system for the numbering of U.S. charts, a worldwide scheme is used that generally identifies a chart by means of a scale range and geographic location. NOS and NIMA charts have numbers consisting of one to five digits as follows:

One digit	No scale involved
Two digits	1:9,000,001 and smaller
Three digits	1:2,000,001 to 1:9,000,000
Four digits	Special purpose
Five digits	1:2,000,000 and larger

Even though they are listed as charts, the one-digit category of publications actually contains symbol and abbreviation charts for the United States and some other nations, such as *Chart No. 1*, already discussed.

The two- and three-digit categories contain charts of very large areas such as entire oceans or major portions thereof. For these numbers, the world's waters have been divided into nine *ocean basins* numbered as shown in figure 320a. The first digit of a two- or three-digit chart number (with limited exceptions) indicates the ocean basin concerned. (There are no two-digit chart numbers used for Ocean Basins 3 and 4, as the limited areas of the Mediterranean and Caribbean seas make such very small scale charts inappropriate; thus two-digit chart numbers beginning with 3 or 4 do not fit into the overall numbering scheme.)

The four-digit category consists of a series of *non-navigational, special-purpose* charts, which are numbered arbitrarily.

The five-digit charts are those most often used by navigators. Except for bathymetric charts, the first of the five digits indicates one of the nine *coastal regions* of the world in which the chart is located (see fig. 320b). (Note that this "coastal region" number is *not* the same as the "ocean basin" number used in the two- and three-digit number series.) The first and second digits taken together identify a subregion (again, see fig. 320b). The final three digits associate the chart with a specific location; they are assigned in rough counterclockwise fashion around the subregion.

Many gaps are left in the assignment of numbers so that any future charts may be smoothly fitted into the system. Although the numbering system covers the world, it has as yet been applied only to U.S.–produced charts and foreign charts reissued by NIMA.

Chart Catalogs

321   The National Ocean Service and NIMA publish chart catalogs consisting of various pages or panels showing the area covered by each chart. Similar catalogs are also issued by the hydrographic survey authorities of other countries.

NOS has five marine chart catalogs: Nautical Chart Catalog 1, the Atlantic and Gulf Coasts, including Puerto Rico and the Virgin Islands; Nautical Chart Catalog 2, the Pacific Coast, including Hawaii, Guam, and Samoa Islands; Nautical Chart Catalog 3, Alaska, including the Aleutian Islands; Nautical Chart Catalog 4, the U.S. Great Lakes and Adjacent Waterways; Map and Chart Catalog 5, Bathymetric Charts and Special Purpose Charts.

These useful, free publications list all the charts available for the designated areas with their names,

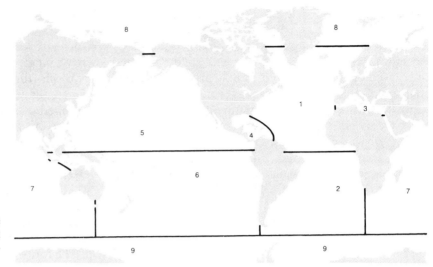

Fig. 320a. The "ocean basins" of the NIMA chart numbering system; the first digit of a two- or three-digit chart number.

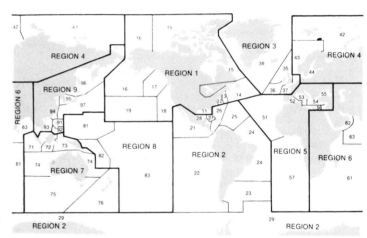

Fig. 320b. The "coastal regions" of the NIMA chart numbering system; the first digit of a five-digit chart number. The two-digit numbers are designations of subregions.

identifying numbers, and scales. A list of all authorized sales agents for NOS charts is included, and the catalogs also contain information on other NOS publications and where they may be obtained.

Charts and other publications prepared by NIMA are listed in the *NIMA Catalog of Maps, Charts, and Related Products, Part 2—Hydrographic Products* (part 1 lists aerospace products). This is divided into nine regional volumes (corresponding to the ocean basins discussed above) plus two others: Volume I, United States and Canada; Volume II, Central and South America; Volume III, Western Europe, Iceland, Greenland, and the Arctic; Volume IV, Scandanavia, Baltic, and Russia; Volume V, Western Africa and the Mediterranean; Volume VI, Indian Ocean; Volume VII, Australia, Indonesia, and New Zealand; Volume VIII, Oceania; Volume IX, East Asia; Volume X, Miscellaneous Charts and Publications; Volume XI, Classified (for security reasons) Charts and Publications. These volumes are issued to naval units, and Volumes I through X can be pur-

chased by civilian navigators from local sales agents for NIMA products.

Portfolios

322 The chart portfolio system provides a simple method for navigators of Navy, Coast Guard, and other federal vessels to order all the charts of a subregion rather than having to order them individually. The chart-numbering system based on regions and subregions provides an organized method of keeping track of charts issued by many various agencies, such as NIMA, NOS, the Canadian Hydrographic Service, British Admiralty, and others. For U.S. naval vessels, the required charts for each of the fifty-two subregions are grouped into a portfolio designated with the number of that subregion. This is further subdivided into "A" and "B" sections; for example, the charts of Subregion 26 are placed in Portfolios 26A and 26B. For each subregion, the A portfolio contains all the general charts and the principal approach and harbor charts; the B portfo-

lio contains more specialized charts that supplement the A coverage of the nautical charts within the subregion.

There are also three portfolios of general and international charts, Atlantic, Pacific, and the World; stock numbers of which charts begin with WOA, WOP, or WOB respectively (or WOX for charts of this type not in a portfolio). There are four other portfolios, each containing Bottom-Contour charts of a major area. The distribution of these charts is limited to naval activities.

Chart Series

323   The scales of nautical charts range from about 1:2,500 to about 1:5,000,000. Charts published by the National Ocean Service are classified into the following "series" according to their scale:

Sailing charts. Scales 1:600,001 and smaller. Used for offshore travel between distant coastal ports and for approaching the coast from the open ocean. (Note: Use of the term "sailing" is meant in the generic sense and does *not* apply only to sailing vessels.)

General charts. Scale 1:150,001 to 1:600,000. Used when a vessel is operating well offshore, but when her position can be fixed by landmarks, lights, buoys, and characteristic soundings (i.e., using piloting techniques).

Coast charts. Scale 1:50,001 to 1:150,000. Used for coastwise navigation inside the offshore reefs and shoals, when entering bays and harbors of considerable width, and for navigating certain large inland waterways.

Harbor charts. Scales larger than 1:50,000. Used in harbors, anchorage areas, and the smaller waterways.

Small craft charts. Scale of 1:80,000 and larger, designed for use primarily by small craft operators.

Intracoastal Waterway (Inside Route) charts. Scale of 1:40,000. These are special charts of the Intracoastal Waterways for use by recreational boaters.

Charts published by NIMA are classed as *world* (overlapping regions), *general* (scales smaller than 1:150,000), *operating area* (pertaining to naval "OPAREAs"), *harbor and approach,* and *coastal.*

Other Chart Numbers

324   For DOD procurement and inventory purposes, each chart is identified by a *NIMA reference number* (sometimes called a "NIMA Stock Number"). For example, the NIMA reference number for the chart covering Guantanamo Bay, Cuba is

26AHA26230

where the first two digits (26) refer to the coastal region and the subregion (see fig. 320b); the first "A" refers to the portfolio; the "HA" designates this as a "harbor and approach" chart; and the remaining five digits (26230) represent the individual chart number. Other abbreviations that might appear instead of *HA* are *CO* (Coastal), *OA* (Operating Area), *GN* (General), and *WO* (World). This reference number often appears in the lower left corner of NIMA charts and in the lower right corner of NOS charts.

U.S. charts also have a *National Stock Number* (NSN) used for federal inventory and procurement purposes. This number is usually accompanied by a bar code. Just to the right of the NSN, the *edition number* of the chart usually appears (with a corresponding bar code).

NAUTICAL CHART INFORMATION

325   Nautical charts provide navigators with vast amounts of information including the depth of the water and objects under and on the surface; features of the land, primarily those of specific interest to those traveling the waters; manmade features and shore facilities, again with emphasis on those that assist in navigation; information on tides and currents; laws and regulations; and more. All this is conveyed through the use of symbols, colors, abbreviations, and written statements. Even the style of lettering used can convey information useful to the mariner.

Title Block

326   Each chart has a title block, sometimes called a "legend," placed where it does not interfere with the presentation of essential navigational information (see fig. 326). Besides the title of the chart (which describes the area covered) and who produced it (usually NIMA or NOA), this block discloses the projection, scale, tidal information, and geodetic datum (such as WGS-84). (Note: The word "datum" is used for two different references in nautical navigation. The geodetic datum pertains to the reference used in measuring the Earth (such as WGS-84) and has important implications when navigating with satellite-based systems. The reference used in determining depths and heights on a nautical chart is called the *sounding datum,* the *tidal datum,* or the *vertical datum.* It is always based upon a chosen tidal average (such as "mean low water" or "mean high water"), but the terms "sounding datum" and "tidal datum" are more often used when referring to water depths, while "vertical

datum" is more frequently applied when referring to heights above water (such as bridges or power lines). You should be aware that the word "datum" is sometimes used without clarification, and it can be important for you to distinguish between the two. If the chart is based on foreign sources, as many NIMA charts are, the original authority and date of surveys will appear here in the title block.

Also in the title block are statements regarding the units of measurement used for depths and heights. If you have a vessel that draws five feet of water and has a mast twenty feet high, it is obviously quite important to know whether the track you have laid down will take you through waters of three feet, three fathoms, or three meters depth and whether the bridge you intend to pass beneath is ten feet or ten meters off the water.

Because water depth can change significantly with the tides, the plane of reference (datum) used for soundings shown on the chart must be explained; that is, at what point in the tidal range were the indicated depths measured. This is included in the title block of the chart and is generally some form of average low water so that at most states of the tide the mariner can count on at least the charted depth beneath the keel. Among the various levels used are "mean low water," "mean lower low water," and "mean low water springs" (see chapter 10 for a detailed explanation of these terms). It is important to remember that while it is a rare occurrence, it *is* possible for tidal conditions to occur that are *below* the mean level used on the chart, so that the depths encountered can be less than those shown on the chart. An extra margin of safety is therefore prudent.

Because tidal differences also affect the relative height of bridges, the plane of reference (datum) for the measurements of heights is usually chosen so that the mariner will have, at least at most times, the charted vertical clearance under bridges and other overhead obstructions, such as power transmission lines. "Mean high water" is commonly used and is assumed to be the reference plane on U.S. charts unless information to the contrary is shown. As with mean lows, some observed or predicted high-tide levels can be *above* mean high water, so caution must be exercised.

Chart Notes

327 Much valuable information is printed on charts in the form of notes and as boxes of data. Notes will relate to such topics as regulatory restrictions, cautions and warnings, unusual magnetic conditions, and so on. The boxes may show depths in major dredged channels, means and extremes of tidal stages at selected points on the chart (charts with scales of 1:75,000 and larger), anchorage information, and so on (see fig. 327). Notes and boxes may be printed in the margins or on the face of the chart at locations where they will not obscure navigational information.

Distance

328 While the unit of distance on most marine charts is the nautical mile, some will use statute miles or kilometers. On charts using nautical miles, the latitude scale can be used for measuring distances, or a graphic scale may be used when provided on larger scale charts. On charts using kilometers or statute miles, the latitude scale obviously will not yield distances in those units, so a graphic scale is essential.

Latitude and Longitude

329 As noted under the section on chart projections, each chart will have lines marking parallels and meridians—these are used to measure the geographic location of any point in terms of latitude and longitude. The intervals between these lines may be 2N, 5N, 10N or more as determined by the scale of the chart. Latitude scales will appear at the sides of conventional charts, with longitude scales at the top and bottom. Small-craft charts may be oriented so as to make the best use of rectangular sheets of pape; that is, north may *not* be "up," toward the top of the sheet.

Latitude and longitude scales will be marked with degrees and minutes. NOS charts with a scale larger than 1:49,000 will have minutes divided into seconds or multiples of seconds. Charts of a smaller scale will have subdivisions of tenths of minutes, while still smaller-scale charts will use fifths or halves of minutes or no subdivision at all.

Direction

330 Charts have *compass roses* distributed around the chart at various convenient locations (see fig. 330). The outer circle on the rose is aligned with true north; true directions may be measured here rather than using parallels and meridians. Graduations around this circle may be at intervals of 1°, 2°, or more as determined by the scale and use of the chart; note carefully the intervals between adjacent marks. An inner circle is offset from true north by the amount of variation (see chapter 7) and can be used for the direct measurement of magnetic directions without arithmetical calculations; the subdivisions on this inner scale

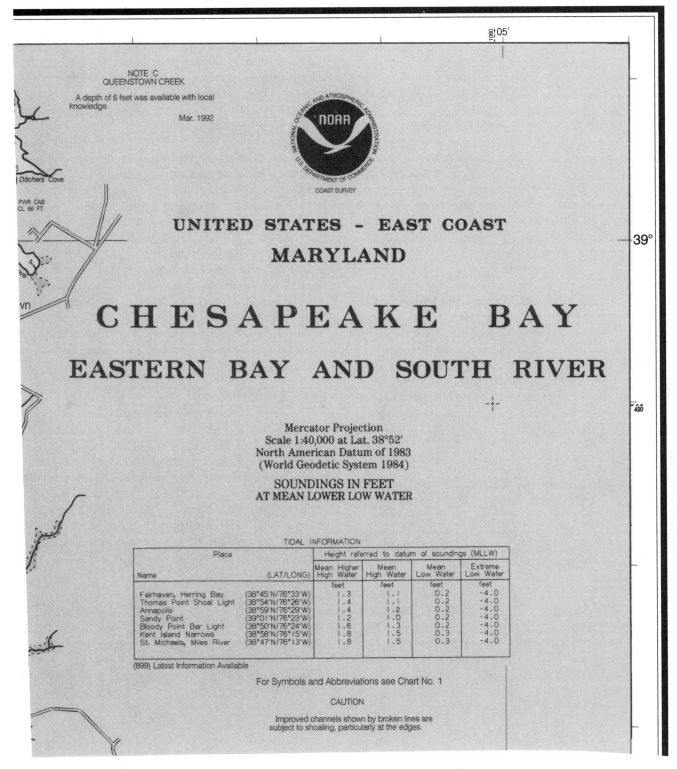

106°05'

NOTE C
QUEENSTOWN CREEK

A depth of 6 feet was available with local knowledge.

Mar. 1992

NOAA
NATIONAL OCEANIC AND ATMOSPHERIC ADMINISTRATION
U.S. DEPARTMENT OF COMMERCE

COAST SURVEY

39°

UNITED STATES – EAST COAST

MARYLAND

CHESAPEAKE BAY

EASTERN BAY AND SOUTH RIVER

420

Mercator Projection
Scale 1:40,000 at Lat. 38°52'
North American Datum of 1983
(World Geodetic System 1984)

SOUNDINGS IN FEET
AT MEAN LOWER LOW WATER

TIDAL INFORMATION

Place		Height referred to datum of soundings (MLLW)			
Name	(LAT/LONG)	Mean Higher High Water	Mean High Water	Mean Low Water	Extreme Low Water
		feet	feet	feet	feet
Fairhaven, Herring Bay	(38°45'N/76°33'W)	1.3	1.1	0.2	-4.0
Thomas Point Shoal Light	(38°54'N/76°26'W)	1.4	1.1	0.2	-4.0
Annapolis	(38°59'N/76°29'W)	1.4	1.2	0.2	-4.0
Sandy Point	(39°01'N/76°23'W)	1.2	1.0	0.2	-4.0
Bloody Point Bar Light	(38°50'N/76°24'W)	1.6	1.3	0.2	-4.0
Kent Island Narrows	(38°58'N/76°15'W)	1.8	1.5	0.3	-4.0
St. Michaels, Miles River	(38°47'N/76°13'W)	1.8	1.5	0.3	-4.0

(899) Latest Information Available

For Symbols and Abbreviations see Chart No. 1

CAUTION

Improved channels shown by broken lines are
subject to shoaling, particularly at the edges.

Ditchers Cove

PWR CAB
CL 66 FT

Fig. 326. Chart legend showing title, projection, scale, geodetic datum, and tidal information.

NOTE B
SPECIAL ANCHORAGES – anchor lights not required on vessels less than sixty-five feet long.

NOTE A
Navigation regulations are published in Chapter 2, Coast Pilot 2, or subsequent yearly supplements and weekly Notices to Mariners. Copies of the regulations may be obtained at the office of the District Engineer, Corps of Engineers in New York.
Refer to section numbers shown with area designation.

NOTE C
All vessels traversing the area shall pass directly through without unnecessary delay. No vessels having a height of more than 35 feet with reference to the plane of mean high water shall enter or pass through the area whenever visibility is less then one mile.

Fig. 327. Chart notes are used to provide information that cannot be shown by symbols or abbreviations.

may be different from those on the outer circle, typically 2° rather than 1°; carefully check each compass rose used. It is important to note that on smaller scale charts covering wider areas, the variation may be different at different locations—so always use the compass rose *nearest* the line whose direction is being measured.

Use of Color

331   Nearly all charts employ color to distinguish various categories of information such as deep water, shoal water, and land areas; "screening" is used to produce variations of the basic colors of black, blue, green, gray, magenta, gold, and white.

Deep-water areas are white (uncolored). All white may also be used on areas such as harbors that are not shown in detail on a chart but *are* shown on other, larger scale charts.

Shoal areas are colored blue; there may be two shades, and the dividing depth between white and blue will vary with the scale and use of the chart. Areas that cover and uncover with tidal changes are colored green. If a chart includes an area that has had a wire-drag survey to ensure the absence of all obstructions—wrecks, rocks, coral heads, and so on—this may be indicated in a screened-green tint with the depth of the drag indicated by words or symbols. Soundings (water depths) appear as black numbers.

On NOS charts, land areas are shown in a screened gold tint that appears as yellow. On charts published by NIMA, land areas are represented in a screened black tint that appears as gray. On larger scale charts, built-up areas of cities may be indicated by a darker land tint. Red is not used on nautical charts because navigators and watchstanders often use red lights to preserve their night vision while illuminating charts at night—red markings on charts would be invisible in these conditions. Dark magenta does, however, show up under red nighttime illumination, so it is used for printed information, compass roses, and some symbols for aids to navigation.

Lettering Styles

332   The style of lettering on a chart can provide information. For example, features that are dry at high water are identified in roman type, while submerged and floating hydrographic features (except the sounding figures that indicate depths) are identified in *italics* (see fig. 332). Often on small-scale charts it may be difficult to distinguish a small reef from a small islet, but the type of lettering will indicate the difference. To avoid confusion, periods are not used with abbreviations. Dots are used, how-

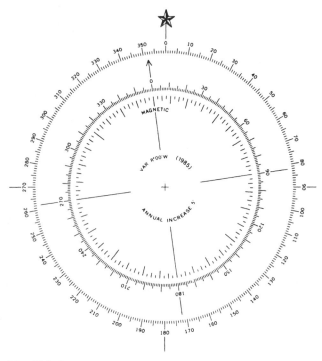

Fig. 330. A compass rose.

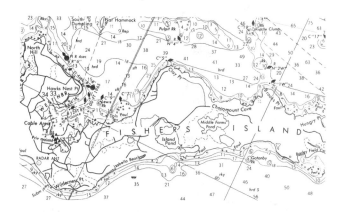

Fig. 332. Roman lettering is used for features that are dry at high water; italics are used for submerged and floating features.

ever, above each lower-case "i" and "j," and periods are used normally in chart notes and general statements.

Symbols and Abbreviations

333 Many symbols and abbreviations are used on charts. These constitute a shorthand that tells the navigator the physical characteristics of the charted area and details of the available aids to navigation. The symbols used are standardized, but are subject to some variation depending on the scale of the particular chart or chart series. It is not possible on a small-scale chart to show all the details that can be shown on a large-scale chart.

Many pages of text would be needed to describe all the symbols and abbreviations used to present the detailed information available on a modern chart. Only the more important will be described here. The full set of symbols and abbreviations is included in *Chart No. 1*, issued jointly by NOS and NIMA. New editions of *Chart No. 1* are published at irregular intervals as required by changes.

Features of Water Areas

334 In water areas, *soundings* (depths) are the items of greatest concern to navigators. These are shown as many small numbers in roman type. The unit of measurement and the sounding datum from which they measured are stated in the title block. As already discussed, actual depths will, of course, vary in tidal waters. Most charts will have lines connecting points of equal depth called *depth contours, depth curves,* or *fathom curves.* The number of such lines and the depth for which they are drawn will depend upon the type and scale of the chart. One of them will serve as the boundary between deeper areas in white and shallower water tinted blue; typically this is the 6-foot curve on harbor charts and the 12-, 18-, or 30-foot line on coastal charts, as determined by the rate of slope in these inshore waters.

Many charts will also have a *depth conversion scale* somewhere on the chart that permits quick conversion among feet, meters, and fathoms.

Artificial Channels

335 Dredged channels, deeper than the surrounding waters, are shown by a pair of parallel dashed lines. Information is normally printed within the lines or just outside for the depth and width of the channel and the date on which the last depth survey was taken. For major channels, this data may be presented in tabular form in a box elsewhere on the chart.

Character of the Bottom

336 Information on the composition of the bottom—mud, sand, rocks, coral, and so on—is of interest to mariners primarily when anchoring. This is shown on charts by abbreviations; many of these are self-evident and they may or may not be explained on the chart itself, but all are in *Chart No. 1.*

Features of the Shoreline

337 A chart will include information regarding the nature of the shoreline, defined as the mean high-water mark (see chapter 10) on most charts. Symbology is often used to indicate the nature of the shore (see fig. 337) and marshy areas or vegetation extending out into the water. A surveyed low-water line is marked by a series of dots. A natural shoreline is indicated by a slightly heavier line than the ones used to indicate a manmade shoreline such as a seawall. Unsurveyed stretches of any type are indicated by broken lines.

Aids to Navigation

338 Information on aids to navigation, being of prime importance to a navigator, is as complete as possible. Both symbols and abbreviations are used to this end. A mariner must be fully knowledgeable of these and should be able to read charts without reference to other sources. When in doubt, however, *referring* (to *Chart No. 1* or some other reference) is always preferable to *assuming.*

On NOS charts, channel marking buoys and other common types are indicated by a diamond shape above a very small circle (see fig. 338). The circle shows the position of the buoy and the diamond shape may be at any angle as required to avoid interference with other charted detail. The diamond may be filled in with the actual color of the buoy—green, or magenta (for red buoys). Other colors,

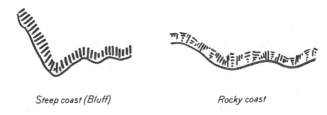

Steep coast (Bluff)   Rocky coast

Fig. 337. Charts can show the nature of the coastline.

Fig. 338. Chart symbols for aids to navigation (typical).

such as yellow, are sometimes shown with an "open"—uncolored—diamond. To facilitate color identification, a letter abbreviation—G, R, Y—is printed near the buoy symbol; two letters are used where necessary, such as "RG" for red and green.

A horizontally banded buoy will have a line across the *shorter* axis of the diamond shape, and the two halves will be colored magenta and green with the half away from the position circle matching the topmost band on the buoy; abbreviation "RG" or "GR" will be used as appropriate. A vertical striped buoy will have an open diamond symbol with a line along the *longer axis* and the letter abbreviations (such as RW) to identify the colors.

Lighted buoys have a small magenta disc or flare printed over the position circle (or dot) of the symbol. The color and rhythm of the light are identified by readily understood abbreviations placed close to the symbol. (No letter abbreviation is used for a white light.)

On NIMA charts, somewhat different symbols are used—a cone or can shape, for example. Because it is a joint publication of NOS and NIMA, *Chart No. 1* includes the symbology for both.

On both NOS and NIMA charts, a mooring buoy is represented by a downward tapering solid black trapezoid with a position circle on the lower side. A "superbuoy" has an open trapezoid with the shorter side upward; a large navigational buoy or an offshore data buoy has a "mast" pointing upward in addition to the position circle and a magenta "flare" if lighted.

Daybeacons have a small triangular symbol if the daymarks are triangular; this is colored magenta if the daymark is solid red; it is open with "RG" if it is red over green. All other daymarks, regardless of shape, are represented by small square symbols (see fig. 338). A square green daymark shows as a square green symbol; all other colors and shapes are shown as open squares with letter abbreviations for the colors.

Lights of all sizes, from minor lights to primary seacoast lights, are shown by a small black dot and magenta "flare"—the combination is much like an exclamation mark (see fig. 338). The size of the symbol normally has no significance, except that on some NIMA charts a larger symbol is used for lights with greater distances of visibility. The color (other than white) and rhythm of the light are shown by abbreviations as for lighted buoys. Additional abbreviations may be included for the height of the light (*not* the top of the structure) and its nominal range of visibility.

Articulated lights—a cross between a minor light and a lighted buoy—are shown by a unique symbol.

This combines a very small position circle, smaller than that used for buoys, with the magenta flare used for lights. The letters "Art" are placed nearby to further indicate this type of aid; light color, rhythm, and other identification data are shown in normal fashion. An explanatory note is placed on all charts with articulated lights.

Sound (fog) signals on buoys and at lights or elsewhere are labeled with the type of signal—BELL, GONG, HORN, or WHIS (for whistle).

The number and/or letter identification of a buoy, daybeacon, or light is printed near the symbol and is enclosed in quotation marks to prevent confusion with depth figures. Lights that have names may have this printed near the symbol in full or shortened form; quotation marks are not used.

Range markers are shown by a pair of symbols for the front and rear markers. A solid line is printed for the length on the chart that the range is intended for navigational use. Where the line crosses unnavigable water (such as close to shore), the line is shown as broken (dashed). The line between the two markers is also shown as broken.

The symbol for a radiobeacon is a magenta circle around a position dot if it is independently located, or around the symbol for the other navigational aid if it is co-located with another (atop a daybeacon, for example). The frequency, identifying signal (in dots and dashes and in letters), and operating periods (if not continuous) are shown near the abbreviation "RBn." Aeronautical radiobeacons are further identified by "AERO."

Other Buoyage Systems

339   The foregoing paragraphs on symbols for aids to navigation are based on the IALA-B system of buoyage, the implementation of which began in U.S. waters in 1982 (replacing the older "lateral" system). Differences will be encountered in the symbols on charts of foreign waters, but these will in general conform to one of the variations permitted in *Chart No. 1*. NOS metric charts of the Great Lakes, coproduced with the Canadian Hydrographic Service, will have specialized pictorial symbols for buoys, both lighted and unlighted.

Hazards to Navigation

340   Many types of symbols are used to show the location of dangers to navigation (such as shipwrecks). These can indicate whether the particular hazard is above water at all times, is submerged at all times (with the clearance over it), or covers and uncovers with tidal changes. Some symbols reveal the nature of the hazard; others are more general-

ized, some with a word or words, or abbreviations nearby. These are shown in detail and explained in *Chart No. 1*.

Land Features

341   Information shown on nautical charts that relates to land features is generally limited to items that will assist a navigator in establishing position and directing his or her vessel's movements safely.

The general form of the land may be shown by the use of *contours*, lines connecting points of equal elevation. The height above vertical datum, measured in feet or meters, is given by figures placed at intervals along the lines; the interval between contours will be uniform, but may vary from chart to chart based on the nature of the terrain and the scale of the chart. The height of conspicuous hills may be given within the closed lines of the highest contour. Contours are often omitted, however, if the land is relatively flat and featureless. Where contours would be useful, but exact surveys have not been made, generalized *form lines*, or *sketch contours* may be used. These are broken lines, and no height figures are placed on them.

Cliffs and steep slopes are shown by *hachures*, short lines at right angles to the rise of land. The length of such lines may indicate the height or steepness of the slope.

The nature of the shore may be shown by symbols—fine dots for sand, small circles of varying diameters for rocks or boulders—or by words such as "sand," "gravel," or "rocks." The presence of breakers in the surf is likewise indicated to warn mariners of this hazard.

Vegetation

342   Various forms of vegetation may be shown on a chart by symbols and/or abbreviations. This is not uniformly done, generally being omitted unless the information will assist the navigator. Specific types of trees (and especially single or small groups of isolated trees), and types of cultivation such as rice paddies or trees in rows (orchards) are shown where they can help establish a position offshore.

Manmade Features

343   Manmade features will be shown for both water and land areas. In water areas these include both aids and hazards to navigation. Bridges, piers, platforms, and overhead power cables are typical items above the water's surface; cable areas and pipelines are the most frequent below-surface manmade features.

On land, manmade features include landmarks—towers, stacks, tanks, and so on; buildings such as customs houses, post offices, and health offices; and structures of interest to mariners—breakwaters and jetties, wharves, and drydocks. Depending upon the scale of the chart, streets and roads may be shown in some detail; railroads are almost always indicated by a symbol and are often identified by lettering.

USING A CHART

344   Charts must be used intelligently, not blindly. Carefully read all notes appearing on the chart. Do not merely look at it is though it were a picture. Check the scale, note the date of the survey on which it is based, and determine whether or not the chart is corrected and up-to-date. Check whether soundings are in feet, fathoms, or meters. Check that the coverage is complete, and if not, note the areas where a paucity of information may indicate danger. Note the system of projection used, so that you can be sure how to measure direction and distance. Check both the geodetic datum and the tidal datum in use. Remember that a chart is a basic tool in the art of navigation. Learn to use it skillfully.

Keep in mind that a chart is no more accurate than the survey on which it is based. In order to judge the accuracy and completeness of a survey, note its source and date (which may be given in the title). Besides the changes that may have taken place since the date of the survey, earlier surveys often were made under circumstances that precluded great accuracy and completeness of detail. Until a chart based on such a survey is tested, it should be regarded with caution. Except in well-frequented waters, few surveys have been so thorough as to make certain that *all* dangers have been found. Noting the abundance or scantiness of the soundings is usually a dependable method of estimating the completeness of the survey, but it must also be remembered that the chart seldom shows all sounds that were obtained. If the soundings are sparse or unevenly distributed, it should be assumed, as a precautionary measure, that the survey was not in great detail. Large or irregular blank spaces among soundings can mean that no soundings were obtained in those particular areas. Where the nearby soundings are deep, it may be logically assumed that in the blank areas the water is also deep, but beware of such areas if they are remote or unfamiliar; it is always possible that a pinnacle or some other danger may be there. When the surrounding sounded water is shallow, or if it can be seen from the rest of the chart that reefs or banks are present in the vicinity, such blanks should be regarded with increased suspicion, avoided if possible, and entered only with great caution. This is particularly true in coral regions and off rocky coasts. These areas should be given a wide berth if at all possible.

Compromise is sometimes necessary in chart production, as scale, congestion, and various other factors may preclude the presentation of all data that have been collected for a given area. Such compromises are not to be made in such a manner as to compromise safety, but you should be aware that you may encounter some things that do not appear on your chart.

The National Ocean Service publishes nearly one thousand charts covering shorelines in excess of 86,000 miles. NIMA is responsible for an even greater number of charts. It is obvious that changes can and do occur in considerable quantities and may be detected by official survey parties only years later, if ever. Thus it is clear that charts must be used with all due caution—they are a navigational *aid*, not a guarantee of safety. It should be equally clear that it is the *duty* of every mariner to observe and report to the appropriate agency, promptly and in as full detail as possible, all inaccuracies noted on charts.

Chapter 4

Electronic Charts

Like the invention of the compass and the chronometer, the creation of Electronic Charts represents a revolution in nautical navigation. Like most revolutions, it has caused some consternation and met with some resistance while opening up new vistas of thought and creating significant improvements in capability and effectiveness. As with virtually all technological changes, the new paradigms and procedures accompanying the revolution have sparked healthy (if sometimes heated) debate. When looking back on the era when forward-looking sailors in the U.S. Navy urged the acceptance of the vast improvements of steam propulsion, there is a tendency to scorn those more conservative thinkers who insisted that masts and sails be retained as a form of redundant propulsion. Yet there is a measure of prudence in that kind of thinking, even if it may have remained a bit longer than necessary.

Today, mariners are faced with a whole new world of capability in the form of electronic charting, where charts are no longer large pieces of paper as they have been for centuries, but are presented on computer monitors or specially designed electronic plotters. Visionaries see piles of cumbersome paper replaced by a handful of compact discs, real-time (where *am* I?) navigation taking the place of time-late (where *was* I?) methods, and the time-consuming and tedious process of paper chart correcting exchanged for an instantaneous process initiated by a few keystrokes at a keyboard. Conservative thinkers see a system that is power dependent, methods that relinquish control, and the inherent dangers of complacency. Both are, of course, correct. As in any revolution, the major challenge faced is in finding the right balance between seizing the moment and not getting carried away. Modern mariners will do well to keep in mind the examples set by those who predicted "a CB radio in every car" and those who swore that "man will never fly."

Once the nautical navigator takes the plunge into the world of electronic charting, he or she is immediately confronted with a whole new lexicon and immersed in a sea of alphabet soup. The modern navigator must know what is meant by "raster" and "vector," be able to comprehend the meanings of ENCs, DNCs, and RNCs, and understand the differences between ECDIS and ECS. Other terms, such as VPF and S-57, are significant as well.

RASTER VS. VECTOR

401   While it is not the nautical navigator's job to produce Electronic Charts, a basic understanding of how they are made is essential. There are two basic ways that Electronic Charts are produced—raster and vector—and which method is used defines the capabilities of the chart.

Probably the simplest way to understand the difference between these two terms is to think of a raster chart as a kind of photograph (or xerographic copy) of a paper chart. With a vector chart, on the other hand, a database of chart features are used to create layers of digital data that, when combined, create an image of a chart on an electronic screen. Both methods present an image that looks like a nautical chart. Each has advantages and disadvantages that must be considered when determining which should be used.

Raster charts are essentially electronic reproductions of pictures, created by converting a paper chart into rows and columns of pixels (picture elements or colored dots) that accurately reproduce the image of the paper chart on a computer screen. Vector charts are built by breaking down individual components of charts into points, lines, polygons (areas), and text that are then merged into a new digital creation (a relational database) that not only allows navigational software to present a recognizable chartlike image but allows individual or collective manipulation of the various elements of data. Those familiar with computer technology will see that a raster chart is much like a facsimile (FAX) image, while vector charts are like word processor files. Just as a FAX image cannot be easily manipulated while a text file can, so raster charts cannot be easily manipulated while vector charts can.

The main advantage of raster is cost. Because vector charts require more sophisticated software and are much more complex, they are significantly more expensive to produce. Vector charts have appealing advantages over raster, however. Users are permitted a great deal more control because the component data can be individually manipulated. Symbology can be altered in a vector chart to meet particular needs. Vector charts can be "de-cluttered"; for example, if operating in deep water with a shallow-draft vessel, the navigator can temporarily remove some or all of the soundings from the display so that more important features are more readily discernible. Vector charts can be queried; for example, a buoy can be selected and a window will open up, giving the navigator a lot more information about that buoy than could normally be fit on a paper (or raster) chart. Vector charts are "smart"; they can be set up so that a warning is given when the vessel is approaching shallow water or some other danger. Depending upon pixel size, zooming in on a raster chart does not enhance the picture much, if at all, but a vector chart allows virtually unconstrained zooming (limited only by data density). And because vector charts can be broken down into data elements, they take up less computer disk space and can be efficiently transmitted through electronic communications circuitry, while raster charts can have a significant "clogging" effect.

ECDIS

402 The explosion of computer technology in modern times made electronic charting inevitable. The only real question to be answered is not *if* but *how* to merge the cyber-world with the nautical. In 1995, the International Maritime Organization (IMO) faced this question head-on by passing a res-

olution titled Electronic Chart Display and Information System. As with most modern technological advancements, the resolution and its implications quickly became defined by its acronym. ECDIS has become a navigational term in its own right, and while it does not define a specific system (as the *S* implies), it does define a concept that has become a standard. The concept includes a combination of hardware, software, data, and display standards for electronic charting that are recognized by IMO as meeting the requirements specified by the 1974 United Nations Safety-of-Life-at-Sea (SOLAS) Convention for carrying an up-to-date chart on board. In other words, for an Electronic Chart and its associated software to be equivalent to (or better than) a paper chart as defined by international standards, it must meet the requirements as spelled out by the resolution defining ECDIS.

The American view is spelled out in the Federal Radionavigation Plan (FRP), which defines ECDIS as "a real-time geographic information system (GIS) that combines both spatial and textual data into a readily useful operational tool. As an automated decision aid that is capable of continuously determining a vessel's position in relation to land, charted objects, aids to navigation, and unseen hazards, ECDIS represents an entirely new approach to maritime navigation and piloting." The FRP goes on to predict that "it is expected that ECDIS will eventually replace the need to carry paper charts."

The requirements as defined by the IMO resolution are generally grouped into three phases of the navigation problem: route planning before the voyage, route monitoring and adjustment during the voyage, and a means of recording the actual voyage made. The latter requirement serves as a great aid to training and for investigation and assessment in the event of a mishap.

Among the ECDIS requirements is the need for a continuous positioning system with a degree of accuracy consistent with the requirements of safe navigation. At present, this requirement is best fulfilled by the NAVSTAR Global Positioning System (GPS) (see chapter 17). A second, independent positioning method, such as an inertial navigation system (INS) (see chapter 18) or Loran-C (see chapter 16) is also required. ECDIS must be capable of detecting discrepancies between these primary and secondary positioning systems and alarms must be included that will alert the navigator when one or both positioning systems are lost or are malfunctioning. Other inputs may be incorporated as well, such as radar or bathymetric information, to further enhance the utility and flexibility of the system.

Inputs are displayed on an Electronic Chart in such a way as to simulate the kind of plotting that navigators routinely draw on a paper chart.

The Electronic Charts used by ECDIS must meet technical standards defined by the International Hydrographic Organization (IHO) in a special publication known as "S-57." IMO-recognized S-57 charts are vector charts, produced in a specific format that have come to be known as "S-57 format charts" or, more correctly, Electronic Navigational Charts (ENCs).

Not every vessel is bound by IMO or SOLAS requirements (U.S. naval vessels are a notable exception), but it makes sense for prudent mariners to consider these standards when attempting to embrace this "brave new world" of electronic charting. Accordingly, the U.S. Navy has adopted ECDIS as a baseline for its own system of standards that, not too surprisingly, has its own acronym of ECDIS-N (the *N* appropriately enough being defined as "Navy"). Guidance from the Chief of Naval Operations states that "ECDIS-N should comply to the greatest extent possible with international standards governing navigation."

Just as ECDIS is a defined set of standards and not a specific system, so is ECDIS-N. Consequently, there is more than one version. Navy guidance permits the use of commercially developed systems as long as they meet the specified requirements. In order to be considered a true ECDIS-N system, it must be certified by the Navy. In a certified ECDIS-N system, the navigator will have the following minimum capabilities:

ROUTE PLANNING

1. Route planning in both straight and curved segments is possible.
2. Designated waypoints (see article 108) in a planned route may be added/deleted/changed.
3. Alternate routes may be planned.
4. System feedback is provided when an operator plans a route across a designated safety contour (such as a depth less than the vessel's draft) or across a boundary of a prohibited area or a geographic area in which special conditions exist.
5. Navigation objects that may be used for obtaining visual bearings or radar bearings can be highlighted.

ROUTE MONITORING

1. Operators are able to enter visual bearings and radar ranges and to resolve this information into a fix or running fix.
2. Data from fathometers, anemometers, compasses, speed logs (see chapter 8) are automatically accepted and incorporated into the system.

Other information may be manually input (such as celestial observations or leadline soundings).

3. The system identifies discrepancies among automatic inputs and permits the operator to select the source he or she chooses to use.
4. Comparisons are possible between the ship's position as derived from a continuous positioning system (such as GPS) and estimated positions (EPs) that have been derived from manual inputs (fixes from visual bearings and radar ranges modified by set and drift calculations).
5. The system calculates and displays set and drift information (see chapter 13) at intervals designated by the operator.
6. Gyrocompass error may be entered, and a magnetic heading mode of operation is provided (see chapter 7). In the latter, automatic corrections for variation and deviation may be incorporated.
7. Other navigational information (such as a scaled overlay of radar information) may be included, but it must not degrade the other displayed information. It must also be possible for an operator to easily and quickly remove such added information from the Electronic Chart whenever she or he feels it necessary.
8. Alarms sound if the position-fixing system is lost, when a critical point (as predetermined by the operator) is coming up, and when a ship is approaching a safety contour or about to pass into a prohibited area.

VOYAGE RECORDING

1. Time, position, heading, and speed are recorded at one minute intervals for the previous 12 hours.
2. A means of preserving a twelve-hour record to a storage media is included.
3. Information on the chart(s) used is recorded.
4. Review of recorded data is possible.
5. Manipulation of recorded data is not possible.

There are many other requirements specified for a certifiable ECDIS-N system. Among them are alarms for various system malfunctions and an emergency source of electrical power. A backup system that operates on a separate power supply is required, and it must be capable of being implemented within 3 minutes.

There are requirements for display as well. Different modes of display to meet different lighting conditions are essential. The adding or removing of certain data elements (such as sounding information) can improve the display depending upon variable conditions. Pop-up windows that enhance information are a valuable advantage to an electronic system, but for obvious reasons, they must be moveable to a less important part of the display. Displays must always be capable of a traditional north orientation but others are possible (as long as it is clear what they are). Traditional chart symbology can be used or a new set of simplified symbols (specified by an IHO standard designated "S-52" and included in a NIMA product called Geosym) can be substituted.

Alternatives to ECDIS

403 Although ECDIS is the recognized world standard, not all forms of electronic charting live up to those standards. As previously mentioned, ECDIS is not required for a significant number of vessels (including pleasure craft) and costs a great deal more than less-capable systems. Consequently, commercial versions of Electronic Charts and the software needed to use them are available.

ECS

404 By definition, non-ECDIS systems are known as *electronic charting systems* (ECS). Despite their lack of IMO sanction, such systems may be very useful to nautical navigators with limited needs. ECS can also be useful as a supplement to another primary means of navigation, adding what is frequently referred to as *enhanced situational awareness*. ECS can be produced at considerably less cost and are therefore popular. While the prudent mariner will not likely rely solely upon a non-ECDIS system for navigation, an ECS is a welcome supplement to more traditional methods. Not being constrained by ECDIS regulations, ECS can use a variety of chart data types including ENCs, raster charts, and a range of commercially produced vector and raster charts. ECS can also be tailored to meet the specific requirements of certain applications such as river navigation, commercial fishing, and so on.

RCDS

405 The ENCs needed for ECDIS navigation (vector charts meeting the specific S-57 requirements) are being produced by national hydrographic offices worldwide, but it will take some time to attain world coverage. Meanwhile, because raster charts are considerably easier and less expensive to create, they have been developed by a number of commercial and governmental sources and coverage is virtually worldwide. For a number of years, professional mariners have been using these raster charts and reporting excellent results. As a result, in July of 1998, the IMO Sub-committee on Safety of Navigation (often referred to as "NAV 44") approved an amendment to the existing ECDIS performance standards that allows navigators to use raster charts in areas where vector charts have not yet been developed. The specifics of their use were clearly defined, using existing ECDIS standards as a model. The result is encapsulated in an added set of performance standards known as *Raster Chart Display System* (RCDS).

As with ECDIS and ECDIS-N, RCDS is not a specific system but a list of requirements that a system must meet in order to be considered RCDS. A significant difference, however, is that RCDS is not "stand-alone" but is an added component or mode of ECDIS. Systems capable of operating in vector and raster mode (i.e., ECDIS systems with RCDS mode capability) are known as *dual fuel* systems. Such a system is capable of taking advantage of the very latest in Electronic Chart technology, using ENCs in normal ECDIS mode where these charts are available, and using raster charts in RCDS mode when vector charts are not yet available.

It is important to note that current IMO policy is for RCDS to serve only as an interim measure to be used until full ENC coverage is available. Once that has been achieved, ECDIS (without RCDS) will be the standard. One of the reasons given for RCDS adoption is that by allowing mariners to use available raster charts in a "near-ECDIS" system, it will serve as a means of leading mariners into the eventual use of the more capable ECDIS technology.

TYPES OF ELECTRONIC CHARTS

406 The use of acronyms in modern technology has grown to astounding proportions and, while few would deny that the use of "CD-ROM" (or merely "CD") is preferable to the alternative ("compact disc–read only memory"), the proliferation of these terms can be confusing. The world of electronic charting is no exception.

The term *Electronic Chart* (EC) is a generic one that means any digitized form of nautical chart, but RNC, ENC, and DNC are all specific kinds of Electronic Charts that have some things in common while varying considerably in the ways they are made and somewhat in the ways in which they are used.

As already explained, an *ENC* (Electronic Navigational Chart) is a vector chart based on the IHO S-57 standard that are suitable for use with ECDIS. Because these are vector charts, they are complex and relatively expensive to produce. As already mentioned, only limited coverage is currently available and worldwide coverage is not likely for quite some time. The National Oceanographic and Atmospheric Administration (NOAA) has begun this process in the United States by first producing ENCs for the nation's forty major port areas and will continue the process until complete coverage of U.S. waters is achieved. When completed, it is anticipated that about 660 ENCs will be needed for complete coverage of U.S. waters. NOAA ENCs are being compiled by combining features from the largest scale paper charts with large scale, highly accurate information from sources such as U.S. Army Corps of Engineers channel blueprints and U.S. Coast Guard aid to navigation positions. This will improve the accuracy of critical features in the ENCs so that they will be more suitable for use with high accuracy positioning systems such as DGPS (see article 1712). Changes to these charts are issued through the Notice to Mariners system that has long served paper chart users well. Other nations are in the process of producing ENCs for their charting needs as well. NOAA has released ENCs for free download on the Internet for system development, testing, training, and user familiarization.

Digital Nautical Charts (DNC) are also vector charts but are produced by the U.S. National Imagery and Mapping Agency (NIMA), primarily for Department of Defense (DOD) use. Unlike ENCs, these Electronic Charts are not produced in the S-57 format but in something called *Vector Product Format* (VPF), which is essentially equivalent to S-57 and, by being based upon the Digital Geographic Information Exchange Standard (DIGEST), is also compatible with NATO requirements. There are significant differences in how ENCs and DNCs are produced. Technically, ENCs rely upon an exchange file that charting software converts into a database, while DNCs are based upon a relational data base that breaks chart features down into twelve thematic layers (aids to navigation, cultural landmarks, Earth cover, environment, hydrography, inland waterways, land cover, limits, obstructions, port facilities, relief, and data quality) that are more or less stand-alone elements. These differences are not readily apparent to users. Both technologies are capable of producing a chartlike display that can be manipulated in multiple ways to enhance navigational safety and awareness.

NIMA has produced a folio of approximately five thousand nautical charts of U.S. and foreign waters that is virtually worldwide in coverage. These Electronic Charts were arranged by geographic area into zones and stored on a series of twenty-nine CDs, each containing about 170 charts (see fig. 406). Even though the capability to distribute this data over the Internet and other electronic media exists, the original arrangement onto CD media was one of the factors that determined their grouping. Consequently, the zones are based upon the amount of data that can be stored on one CD as well the development of logical navigational scenarios. Within each of these zones the charts are grouped in four different "library" categories that are equivalent to NIMA's groupings of paper chart scales: General (1:500,000 and smaller scales) used for mission planning and open ocean navigation; Coastal (usually in the 1:75,000 to 1:500,000 range); Approach (ranging from 1:25,000 to 1:100,000) covering inshore areas; and Harbor (1:50,000 and larger). The system for updating DNCs is known as *VPF Database Update* (VDU) and is run by NIMA.

DNCs will ultimately be the primary (perhaps *only*) charts used by vessels of the U.S. Navy. Paper charts will continue to be produced by NIMA as long as there is a need, but eventually DNCs will meet all DOD needs. DOD policy on the release of DNCs for public use is under consideration.

A companion series called *Tactical Ocean Data* (TOD) charts has been developed by NIMA to support submerged navigation and for other military purposes. Because these charts contain classified data or information useful only for military purposes, TOD charts are not available for public use.

Raster Nautical Charts (RNC) are those raster charts that have been officially sanctioned by a national hydrographic office and are suitable for use with Raster Chart Display Systems (RCDS) as well as with ECS. In the United States they are produced by the Office of Coast Survey (a division of NOAA) by scanning at high resolution the original color separates that are used to print official OCS paper charts. Through an innovative public/private partnership between NOAA and a company known originally as BSB Electronic Charts and today as MapTech, Inc., the full inventory of NOAA charts was made available as RNCs for private and commercial use in May 1996. In Britain, the United Kingdom Hydrographic Office (UKHO) produces their own version of RNC, which they call ARCS (Admiralty Raster Chart Service) charts. Other nations, such as Australia, Canada, Iceland, and Brazil, are also producing RNCs.

The RNCs produced under the NOAA/MapTech agreement are available on CD-ROM packages that include approximately fifty-five raster charts as well as the appropriate Coast Pilot, Light List, Tide Tables, and Tidal Current Tables information. Another collaborative feature offered by NOAA and MapTech is a new update service for Electronic Charts that is delivered to subscribers by e-mail on a weekly basis. These updates include notices from

Fig. 406. One of the Digital Nautical Chart CDs produced by NIMA.

the U.S. Coast Guard, NIMA, NOAA's Critical Correction Database, and the Canadian Hydrographic Service.

NAVIGATING WITH ELECTRONIC CHARTS

407   The accuracy and reliability of modern Electronic Chart technology opens new doors and mandates change. Having GPS and other electronic systems input information directly to the Electronic Chart is a great time-saver, giving navigators more time to concentrate on other things; no small consideration in a crowded channel or aboard a military vessel charged with multiple missions. The great advantage of knowing where one *is* rather than where one has been is so obvious that it bears no discussion.

Yet there are tradeoffs that cannot be ignored. Power dependency is the obvious gremlin that haunts nearly all modern technological advances, but proponents argue that it is far more feasible to create power backup systems than it is to provide a backup to the human navigator who is subject to fatigue, far more likely to make a calculation error than is a computer, and statistically more responsible for accidents at sea than is any electronic navigation system. When using a paper chart, even a very capable and careful navigator may incorrectly plot the highly accurate fix information from the readout of a GPS receiver, whereas an Electronic Chart system essentially "cuts out the middle man" by inputting the fix information to an Electronic Chart.

A counterargument can be made that using Electronic Charts with automatic inputs such as GPS causes a fix to "magically" appear on the Electronic Chart, that by "cutting out the middle man," the navigator no longer has the advantage of seeing the fix constructed and therefore has less opportunity to realize a problem. For example, when navigators had to physically plot three visual LOPs to get a good fix (see article 1208), they might see a large triangle formed, which served as a warning that something was amiss. The automatic features afforded by Electronic Chart systems have removed that capability.

But with the more capable Electronic Chart systems like ECDIS, the modern navigator is not prevented from supplementing the information provided by electronic systems. Visual bearings and radar ranges can be entered and used to verify (or question) the information provided and plotted by electronics.

As with any sweeping change, no matter how advantageous, there is a natural human tendency to resist. But the hindrance of stubborn conservative thinking can be seen by considering that a pencil mark is about 1 mm in width when drawn on a paper chart. Working at a scale of 1:50,000, this translates to a line 50 meters in width. GPS positions are frequently accurate to less than half of that figure, so the mere act of replotting electronic positioning information onto paper charts can result in a significant loss of accuracy. Electronic Charts eliminate that factor.

The careful navigator knows that, despite all attempts to create completely accurate charts, errors still occur. The modern navigator who embraces Electronic Chart technology must also be aware that those same errors can be carried over into the new charts. The computer adage "Garbage in, garbage out" applies.

There is one very significant potential problem with electronic systems that is more psychological than real. The impressive accuracy, reliability, and ease of use of electronic systems brings with it a real danger of complacency. Lulled into a sense of well-being by the very things that make electronic navigation such an asset, mariners may be tempted to be more daring and pass hazards more closely than they would have when using more traditional navigational methods. Besides the obvious and unnecessary risks incurred by such thinking, it is important to keep in mind that the positions of hazards on charts may well have been determined using methods far less accurate than the method being used to navigate (such as GPS). Short of a life-and-death situation or a mission of high military importance that warrants extra risk, the nautical navigator should never cancel out the advantages gained through technology by being reckless.

Chapter 5

Navigational Publications

In addition to nautical charts, there are a number of publications that can enhance the mariner's ability to navigate. Most of these are prepared by various governmental agencies, although some originate from commercial sources. Some of these governmental agencies, such as the National Ocean Service (NOS) and the National Imagery and Mapping Agency (NIMA) have been discussed in some detail in previous chapters, but other agencies, such as the U.S. Naval Observatory and the U.S. Coast Guard, produce a number of publications that are essential to safe and efficient navigation.

LIGHT LISTS AND *LISTS OF LIGHTS*

501 Charts show as much information as possible regarding the many aids to navigation, but practical limitations of space necessitate a less-than-complete description. To supplement what is shown on the chart, and to provide the full amount of data to assist a navigator in locating, identifying, and using aids to navigation, there are two other series of publications; these are the *Light Lists* prepared by the U.S. Coast Guard and the *Lists of Lights* published by NIMA.

The Coast Guard *Light Lists* are published in seven volumes covering the U.S. coasts (including island possessions), the Great Lakes, and the Mississippi River system. These are complete listings of all lights, buoys, daybeacons, ranges, fog signals, radiobeacons, and radar beacons (RACONs). Detailed information is given on each aid, including its position, shape, color, and characteristics (see fig. 501). The fact that an emergency light of reduced intensity is provided when the main light is extinguished is an example of the kind of informa-

tion that you might find in a *Light List* that is too detailed to fit on a chart.

Each *Light List* volume contains introductory pages with additional information on aids to navigation and their use, contact information for the various Coast Guard district headquarters and glossaries of terms and abbreviations. Seacoast aids are listed first in the applicable volumes, followed by harbor and river aids, and then Intracoastal Waterways aids, if applicable. Each volume of the *Light Lists* is republished annually, but during the year should be kept continuously corrected from *Notices to Mariners* and *Local Notices to Mariners* (see articles 508 and 510).

Lists of Lights are published in seven volumes by NIMA (Pub. No. 110 through 116) and cover foreign coasts of the world (and limited portions of U.S. coasts). They include descriptive information similar to *Light Lists*, but because of their greater coverage areas, they list only lighted aids to navigation and fog signals; lighted buoys within harbors are also omitted. Each *List of Lights* is published in a new edition at intervals of approximately twelve months; changes and corrections are included as they are required in *Notices to Mariners*.

COAST PILOTS AND *SAILING DIRECTIONS*

502 Charts are limited in what can be shown by symbols and abbreviations regarding channels, hazards, winds and currents, restricted areas, port facilities, pilotage service, and many other types of information needed by a navigator for safe and efficient navigation. These deficiencies are remedied by the *Coast Pilots* published by NOS and the *Sailing Directions* published by NIMA.

(1) No.	(2) Name Characteristic	(3) Location Lat. N. Long. W.	(4) Nominal Range	(5) Ht. above water	(6) Structure Ht. above ground Daymark	(7) Remarks Year
	(Chart 13260) (For Gulf of Maine, see No. 199)					
1 227 J048	**MOUNT DESERT LIGHT** ...., Fl. W., 15s	On Mount Desert Rock, 20 miles south of Mount Desert Island. 43 58.1 68 07.7	24	75	Conical gray granite tower ... 58	HORN: 2 blasts ev 30s (2s bl-2s si-2s bl-24s si). Emergency light of reduced intensity when main light is extinguished. 1830
2 239 J116	**MATINICUS ROCK LIGHT** ..... Gp. Fl. W., (1 + 2), 15s 0.2s fl., 5.8s ec. 0.2s fl., 2.8s ec. 0.2s fl., 5.8s ec. (3 flashes.)	On south part of rock. 43 47.0 68 51.3	23	90	Cylindrical gray granite tower and dwelling. 48	RBN: 314 kHz MR(■ ■ ● ■ ●). Antenna on light tower. HORN: 1 blast ev 15s (2s bl). 1827—1857
3 282 J128	**MONHEGAN ISLAND LIGHT** ... Fl. W., 30s (2.8s fl)	Near center of island. 43 45.9 69 19.0	21	178	Gray conical tower covered way to dwelling. 47	Within 3 miles of island the light is obscured between west and southwest. 1824—1850
283 J130	Manana Island Fog Signal Station.	On west side of island, close to Monhegan Island. 43 45.8 69 19.7	....	....	Brown brick house	RBN: 286 kHz MI(■ ● ●)VI. Antenna 2,880 feet 259° from Monhegan Island light tower. HORN: 2 blasts ev 60s (3s bl-3s si-3s bl-51s si). 1855—1870
5 297 J146	**SEGUIN LIGHT** .... F. W.	On island, 2 miles south of mouth of Kennebec River. 43 42.5 69 45.5	18	180	White cylindrical granite tower connected to dwelling. 53	HORN: 2 blasts ev 20s (2s bl-2s si-2s bl-14s si). 1795—1857
6 320 J176	**HALFWAY ROCK LIGHT** ...... Fl. R., 5s	On rock, midway between Cape Small Point and Cape Elizabeth. 43 39.4 70 02.2	19	77	White granite tower attached to dwelling. 76	Emergency light of reduced intensity when main light is extinguished. RBN: 291 kHz HR(● ● ● ● ■ ●). Antenna on light tower. HORN: 2 blasts ev 30s (2s bl-2s si-2s bl-24s si). 1871
	(Chart 13286)					
7.10 334.10 J211	**Portland Lighted Horn Buoy** P (LNB). Fl. W., 2s F. W.	In 160 feet 43 31.6 70 05.5	14 8	42	Red	Equipped with passing light. RBN: 301 kHz PH(● ■ ■ ● ● ● ● ●). HORN: 1 blast ev 30s (3s bl). RACON: M(■ ■).
7.60 334.60	*Disposal Area Dumping Ground.* Lighted Buoy DG. Fl. W., 2.5s	In 181 feet 43 34.3 70 01.9	5	....	Orange and white horizontal bands.	Ra ref. Private aid.
7.70 334.70	*Portland Disposal Area* Lighted Buoy. Fl. Y., 4s	In 220 feet 43 34.1 70 01.9	....	....	Orange and white horizontal bands.	Ra ref. Private aid.
	(For Portland Harbor, see No. 334.10)					
8 338 J208	**CAPE ELIZABETH LIGHT** ...... Gp. Fl. W., 30s 0.2s fl., 2.3s ec. 0.2s fl., 2.3s ec. 0.2s fl., 2.3s ec. 0.2s fl., 2.3s ec. 0.2s fl., 2.3s ec. 0.2s fl., 17.3s ec. (6 flashes)	South of entrance to Portland Harbor. 43 34.0 70 12.0	27	129	White conical tower 67	HORN: 2 blasts ev 60s (3s bl-3s si-3s bl-51s si). Located 266 yards 146° from light tower. 1829—1874
	Taylor Reef Buoy 1TR	In 75 feet, off southeast side of reef.	....	....	Black can	Ra ref. Green reflector.
	Alden Rock Buoy 2AR	In 28 feet, 0.3 mile southwest of rock.	....	....	Red nun	Ra ref. Red reflector.

Fig. 501. *Light List* (extract).

U.S. Coast Pilots are published in nine numbered volumes to cover the waters of the United States and its possessions. These volumes contain a wealth of beneficial information, including such things as the operating schedules for drawbridges, radio frequencies for vessel traffic services, iceberg patterns, time zone changes, the presence of whales, berthing facilities and availabilities, weather patterns, and much, much more. They are of great value to a navigator when used in conjunction with charts of an area, particularly during the planning stage of a voyage. The contents of *Coast Pilots* have been stored in a computerized data bank, and volumes are reprinted annually with all intervening changes included (except CP8 and CP9, which cover Alaskan waters and are only revised every two years). Interim changes are published in *Notices to Mariners* and *Local Notices to Mariners* (see articles 508 and 510).

The NIMA-produced *Sailing Directions* provide information comparable to the *Coast Pilots*, but for foreign coasts and coastal waters. The appropriate volume of *Sailing Directions*, used with charts of a suitable scale, should enable a navigator to approach strange waters with adequate information for his vessel's safety. There are forty-three publications that make up the entire library of *Sailing Directions*: eight *Planning Guides* for ocean basin transits and thirty-five *Enroute Directions* for coastal waters and ports.

The *Sailing Directions* are based on a division of the world's waters into eight "ocean basins," but these are *not* the same as those used for two- and three-digit chart numbers. The *Sailing Directions* are given three-digit NIMA Pub. Nos. starting with a "1"; the second digit is a number according to the ocean basin concerned; the third digit is "0" for the *Planning Guide*, and "1" through "9" for the various *Enroute* directions. (Exceptions are ocean basin 5, the North Pacific—here the *Planning Guide* is Pub. No. 152, because the number "150" was already assigned to the *World Port Index* [see article 504] and "151" was given to the publication entitled *Distances Between Ports* [see article 505]—and ocean basin 2, the South Atlantic Ocean, where the *Planning Guide* is Pub. No. 121.)

The two components of the *Sailing Directions* contain information as follows.

Planning Guide. Each covers an ocean basin containing chapters of useful information about countries adjacent to that particular ocean basin; information relative to the physical environment and local coastal phenomena; references to publications and periodicals listing danger areas; recommended ship routes; details of electronic navigation systems;

and information relating to the buoyage systems pertaining to that ocean basin.

Enroute. Each includes detailed coastal and port approach information, supplementing the largest scale chart available from NIMA. It is intended for use in conjunction with the *Planning Guide* for the ocean basin concerned. Each *Enroute* volume is divided into a number of sectors, and for each sector, information is provided on available charts (with limits shown on an overall diagram as in U.S. chart catalogs); winds, tides, and currents (shown on an outline chart); off-lying dangers; coastal features; anchorages; and major ports (an annotated chartlet with line drawings of aids to navigation and prominent landmarks). Figure 502 shows the limits for the various enroute guides of the North Atlantic Ocean basin.

Changes for each *Planning Guide* and *Enroute* volume are prepared and published on an as-required basis as determined by the number of accumulated revisions.

The port facilities data, formerly scattered throughout the old *Sailing Directions*, has been computerized and tabulated in an expanded edition of Pub. No. 150, *World Port Index*, designed as a companion volume to be used in conjunction with the new *Sailing Directions*.

FLEET GUIDES

503 NIMA also publishes special *Fleet Guides* for U.S. Navy use only. These are Pub. No. 940, Atlantic Area, and Pub. No. 941, Pacific Area. These guides contain a number of chapters, each of which covers a port of major interest to naval vessels. They are prepared to provide important command, navigational, repair, and logistic information. This information is much like that contained in *Coast Pilots* and *Sailing Directions*, but is oriented toward naval interests and requirements; they are not needed by, nor are they available to, non-naval vessels.

Data in *Fleet Guides* are corrected and updated through the publication of changes and/or new editions when required; interim corrections are published in *Notices to Mariners* if the urgency so warrants. A CD-ROM version is included with each publication that can be used with a PC or can be downloaded to a handheld computer.

WORLD PORT INDEX

504 Published by NIMA as Pub. No. 150, the *World Port Index* lists important information about virtually every port in the world. By using the index, you can locate a port by name (such as Annapolis, Mary-

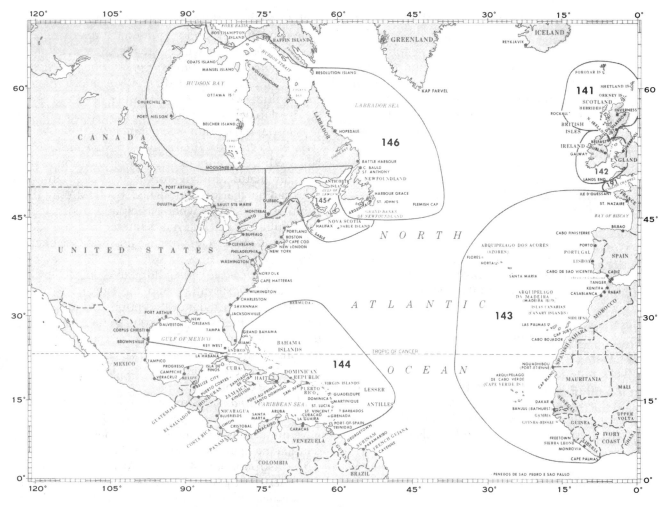

Fig. 502. Limits for *Enroute* volumes of *Sailing Directions* in the North Atlantic Ocean.

land) and find its index number (8225). Turning to the appropriate page to locate the index number (they are arranged sequentially), you may then read across the columns to obtain the information provided. Included are such things as the latitude and longitude of the port, the appropriate chart (by number) to use, applicable *Sailing Directions* (or the equivalent), the size and type of the harbor, and general information relating to anchorages, tides, repair facilities, communications, pilotage, and so on.

DISTANCES BETWEEN PORTS

505 Published by NIMA as Pub. No. 151, *Distances Between Ports* is useful in voyage planning for obvious reasons. Because it would be impractical to list the distances between every possible combination of ports, a system of *junction points* is used. For

example, if you wanted to know the distance between Norfolk, Virginia, and Bandar Abbas, Iran (located on the Gulf of Oman, near the Persian Gulf), you would first look at the junction point chartlets in the front of the book to identify all the junction points between Norfolk and Bandar Abbas. Since the shortest route would be across the Atlantic, through the Mediterranean and Red Seas (via the Suez Canal), you would be able to see from the applicable chartlets that there are two junction points between your departure point (Norfolk) and your destination (Bandar Abbas): the Strait of Gibraltar and Port Said. If you looked up Norfolk in the distance table (all ports are listed alphabetically in the book), you would see that there is a list of junction points and another list of ports after the entry for Norfolk. Scanning the list of ports (again alphabetical) you would see that Bandar Abbas is not included, so you would next find the listing for your first junction point (Strait of Gibraltar) and see that the distance is 3,335 nautical miles. In a similar manner, you would then locate the entry for Strait of Gibraltar in the distance table and find the distance to the Port Said junction point (1,943 nautical miles). Finally, you could then go to the listing for Port Said and find Bandar Abbas in the list of ports following that entry, or go to the entry for Bandar Abbas and find the distance back to the junction point at Port Said. In either case the distance would be listed as 2,842 nautical miles. Adding these three figures together (3,335 + 1,943 + 2,842) would give you the total distance between Norfolk and Bandar Abbas: 8,120 nautical miles. This procedure can be replicated for virtually any two ports in the world.

Also included in the back of Pub. No. 151 is a table for estimating time of transit (Norfolk to Bandar Abbas at 15 knots would take just over twenty-two days) and a conversion table for nautical and statute miles.

Pub. No. 151 does not include distances on the Great Lakes. These can be found in *U.S. Coast Pilot*, volume 6.

NOS also publishes a similar volume, called *Tables of Distances Between United States Ports*, which tabulates approximately 10,000 distances along the shortest routes marked by aids to navigation.

OTHER NAVIGATIONAL PUBLICATIONS

506   There are a number of other navigational publications that are covered in more detail in other parts of this book but are briefly described here.

Tide Tables: Annual prediction tables compiled by the National Ocean Service and published for DOD use in four volumes: *East Coast of North and South America, Including Greenland; West Coast of North and South America, Including the Hawaiian Islands; Europe and the West Coast of Africa, Including the Mediterranean Sea;* and *Central and Western Pacific Ocean and the Indian Ocean.* Each volume includes data on the height and time of high and low water at thousands of locations; also included are data on times of sunrise and sunset, moonrise and moonset, and other astronomical phenomena (see chapter 10).

Tidal Current Tables: Annual prediction tables compiled by NOS and published for DOD use in two volumes: *Atlantic Coast of North America* and *Pacific Coast of North America and Asia.* Each volume includes data on the times and strengths of flood and ebb currents and the time of slack water for thousands of locations. Also included are diagrams for certain heavily traveled bodies of water that facilitate the determination of optimum transit times and speeds, and astronomical data similar to that in *Tide Tables* (see chapter 11).

Sight Reduction Tables for Marine Navigation (Pub. No. 229): Published by NIMA in six volumes, each volume covers 16° of latitude, North or South (1° overlap between volumes). These tables are used in celestial navigation (see chapter 25).

Sight Reduction Tables for Air Navigation (Pub. No. 249): Despite its name, this publication is used by many nautical navigators as well as aviators for celestial navigation. Published by NIMA in three volumes, it is somewhat easier and faster to use than Pub. No. 229 but has a limited range of declination and yields a less precise position (see chapter 25).

The Nautical Almanac: Prepared jointly by the U.S. Naval Observatory and the Royal Greenwich Observatory in England, it is published annually to provide ephemeristic data useful to nautical navigators in celestial navigation and for routine determinations of such things as sunrise and sunset. There is also a cyber-version called the *Almanac for Computers* (see chapter 24).

The Air Almanac: Similar to the nautical version, but published twice a year and tailored more to air navigation, this publication is sometimes used by nautical navigators as well (see chapter 24).

The Astronomical Almanac: At one time entitled the *American Ephemeris and Nautical Almanac,* this book is also published by the Naval Observatory and contains the information in *The Nautical Almanac* plus a considerable amount of data of interest primarily to astronomers.

The American Practical Navigator: Published by NIMA as Pub. No. 9, this book is a comprehensive treatment of nearly every aspect of nautical navigation and is best known as *Bowditch,* after the name of its original author. When Nathaniel Bowditch's first edition of this book appeared in 1802, it was actually a revision of an even older British navigational text, *The Practical Navigator,* by John Hamilton Moore, by then in its thirteenth edition. Today it is primarily a reference book that no serious navigator will be without.

Handbook of Magnetic Compass Adjustment and Compensation: Designated Pub. No. 226, as of this writing this publication is in its fourth edition and still bears NIMA's previous name, *Defense Mapping Agency and Hydrographic/Topographic Center.* See chapter 7 and Appendix C for more information about magnetic compasses and their adjustment.

Radar Navigation Manual: Published as Pub. No. 1310 by NIMA (also bearing the old name, *Defense*

Mapping Agency and Hydrographic/Topographic Center as of this writing), this manual contains information regarding the fundamentals of shipboard radar, collision avoidance, navigation by radar, and a description of vessel traffic systems in U.S. waters.

Maneuvering Board Manual: While primarily a book about shiphandling and naval maneuvering, this publication includes a number of techniques applicable to navigation. Published as Pub. No. 217 by NIMA, as of this writing this, too, still bears the old name *Defense Mapping Agency and Hydrographic/Topographic Center.* (Note: NIMA has also combined *The Maneuvering Board Manual* and *Radar Navigation Manual* on a single CD that is available to authorized users.)

Radio Navigational Aids: NIMA Pub. No. 117 contains information on the various forms of radio navigational aids, including general descriptions, frequencies, regulations, and so on.

Loran-C User Handbook: Published by the U.S. Coast Guard as COMDTPUB P16562.6, the original (1980) edition of this book was commonly known as The Green Book (referring to the color of its cover). Today it is no longer green and has changed in other ways as well. Much of the material is user-friendly, but some parts are quite technical for those who have need of such information (most navigators will not). See chapter 16 for more information concerning Loran navigation.

Pilot Charts: Published by NIMA for the various ocean basins, these charts present available data in graphic form that will assist the mariner in selecting the safest and fastest routes. Pilot charts graphically depict magnetic variations, currents, prevailing winds and calms, percentages of gales, tracks of tropical cyclones, average wave heights, surface air and water temperatures, percentages of fog, surface barometric pressures, ice and iceberg limits, and recommended routes for different kinds of vessels. Additional information is included in brief paragraphs at the sides of each chart. Pilot charts are published quarterly and are furnished without charge to contributing observers and automatically to naval vessels after an initial request; they may also be purchased by others interested in their contents.

Guide to Marine Observing and Reporting: Pub. No. 606 is a collaborative effort of several U.S. governmental agencies to provide detailed guidance for submitting hydrographic and oceanographic reports. Check lists of key questions are included, where appropriate, as a means of ensuring that no essential facts will be inadvertently omitted from a report.

CORRECTIVE INFORMATION

507 As a sufficient number of changes and corrections accumulate to charts and other publications, they are reprinted as a revision with the same edition number or as a new edition. But in the interim, when changes occur to publications and charts and a new version has not yet been issued, some means of updating them is required to ensure safe navigation. This is where the Notice to Mariners systems come in.

Notice to Mariners

508 When the importance of the corrected or updated information is such that it cannot be delayed until the next revised or new edition, that information is included in the weekly *Notice to Mariners*, published by NIMA with the cooperation of NOS and the Coast Guard. This printed pamphlet includes corrections for charts, listed in numerical order, with a separate entry for each chart affected. To ensure that corrections will not be overlooked, each entry also indicates the number of the *Notice* carrying the last previous correction. Corrections for publications other than charts are also included, such as *Coast Pilots, Sailing Directions, Light Lists* and *Lists of Lights, Radio Navigational Aids, World Port Index, Fleet Guides*, tide and current tables, almanacs, and sight reduction tables. Small chartlets are often included, printed to the exact scale of the charts they are supposed to correct, so that they can be pasted directly onto the chart. Quarterly, a special issue of *Notice to Mariners* will contain a summary, listing by number the charts affected by changes during that period, with references to the numbers of the applicable *Notices*.

Summary of Corrections

509 Semiannually, NIMA publishes a *Summary of Corrections* in six volumes. Volume 1 covers the east coast of North and South America; volume 2 covers the eastern Atlantic and Arctic Oceans and the Mediterranean Sea; volume 3, the west coast of North and South America, including Antarctica; volume 4, the Western Pacific and Indian Oceans; volume 5 covers world and ocean basin charts, as well as *Coast Pilots, Sailing Directions, Fleet Guides*, and miscellaneous publications; and volume 6 is for classified charts and publications, with distribution limited to government activities on a need-to-know basis. The various volumes are published on a staggered basis; the schedule of publication for the volumes is listed in *Volume X* of the *NIMA Chart Catalog, Part 2.* Each issue of the *Summary of*

Corrections contains the full text of all applicable corrections; when any volume gets too large for convenient use, NIMA begins a new series. If a new edition of a chart is issued in the six-month period between issues, corrections for the old edition are omitted. Changes listed in a previous *Summary* are not repeated.

The *Summary of Corrections,* with the full text of all changes, is easier to use than the quarterly listings in *Notices to Mariners,* which give only the numbers of the charts affected without providing the information necessary to make the change. The *Summary* is particularly valuable in bringing charts fully up-to-date when they have been obtained some time after their publication date, such as the initial set of charts for a newly commissioned vessel, or when charts have not been used and kept corrected for some time. A given chart can be brought up to date by working from the proper volume of the *Summary* and all subsequent *Notices to Mariners.*

Local Notices to Mariners

510   Since the publications just described are worldwide in scope, changes are not included that are of local interest only, or are of no concern to oceangoing ships. Such information *is* published in *Local Notices to Mariners,* which are issued separately by each U.S. Coast Guard District at weekly intervals or as required. Items from the worldwide *Notices* are repeated in *Local Notices* if they are of interest to small vessels and craft of the waters covered.

Computerized Correction Data

511   Correction data is available from NIMA through the Maritime Safety Information Division web site, http://pollux.nss.nima.mil. Access is free, but the user must pay any applicable telephone charges. Users must register and obtain a password by calling 301-227-3296 or by writing NIMA, 4600 Sangamore Road, Bethesda, Maryland 20816.

The U.S. Coast and Geodetic Survey also operates a similar free computerized marine information bulletin board containing a list of wrecks and obstructions, a nautical chart locator, a list of marine sediment samples, a datum conversion program for NAD 27 to NAD 83 conversions (see chapter 2), and a list of aerial photographs available from NOAA. The telephone voice line is 301-713-2653, or write U.S. Coast and Geodetic Survey, 1315 East-West Highway, Silver Spring, Maryland 20910.

Corrections to electronic charts are discussed in chapter 4.

THE IMPORTANCE OF ACCURATE, UP-TO-DATE INFORMATION

512   There are many sources of valuable information available to the modern navigator. You should study all applicable publications and charts before getting under way and continually review them as you proceed through your voyage. Obviously, a time of danger or emergency is *not* the time to be hastily thumbing through an unfamiliar publication.

Failure to have on board and use the *latest* charts and other publications, *and to keep them corrected,* may adversely affect your legal position should you have the misfortune of a grounding, collision, or other mishap. Ignorance is no excuse in these matters.

Chapter 6

Aids to Navigation

While nautical navigators will make good use of natural and manmade features—such as mountain peaks and water tanks—to fix their position and find their way, they will rarely operate in coastal or inland waters without making use of some manmade aids to navigation, such as buoys, lights, and fog signals.

Aids to navigation (sometimes referred to as *navaids*) are vitally important to navigators in making a landfall when approaching from seaward, when navigating along a coast, and when piloting on inland waters. Their importance was first recognized by the ancient Mediterranean mariners, and a lighthouse was built at Sigeum, near Troy, before 600 B.C. The first lighthouse in the United States was built at Boston in 1716, and logs and kegs appeared as buoys in the Delaware River in 1767.

The *U.S. Coast Guard* has responsibility for the operation and maintenance of all lights and other aids to navigation along 40,000 miles of coastline in the United States and its possessions, plus additional thousands of miles along the shores of the Great Lakes and on most inland rivers. There are more than 12,000 lights, 24,000 lighted and unlighted buoys, and 10,000 daybeacons. There are also some "private aids" maintained by individuals, and local governments or federal agencies other than the Coast Guard maintain a number of additional aids, but these are relatively few in number, except in the Gulf of Mexico, where thousands of oil rigs are marked with private aids (yellow lights that flash "U" in Morse code).

Aids to navigation take a wide variety of forms. Some are very simple objects, others are more complex and costly, but all serve the same important purpose: the safety of vessels and those on board. In the discussion below, navaids have been grouped into categories—buoys, beacons, lights, ranges, and fog signals—but you will note as you read that there is considerable overlap in these categories. Many buoys have lights attached to them, some fog signals are mounted on beacons, and so on. Floating buoys and fixed beacons share many of the same purposes and characteristics, but are treated separately for discussion purposes.

CONVENTIONAL DIRECTION

601 An important concept that is used often in the description of many aids to navigation is that of conventional direction (often referred to in *Light Lists* and other official publications as "conventional direction of buoyage," even though the convention applies to some other aids besides buoys). Because mariners travel in both directions on waterways, what is the left (or port) side of a waterway when going in one direction becomes the right (or starboard) side of that same waterway when going in the opposite direction. In order to provide some means of reference when describing buoys and other navigational aids, certain conventions have been adopted.

For the majority of situations the conventional direction used is that of "entering from seaward" (sometimes expressed as "*returning* from seaward"). If you establish that you are entering from seaward (i.e., you have your back to the sea), you can then refer to a side of the channel as port (left) or starboard (right) and everyone can agree as to which side you are referring. This is an important concept that works in the majority of navigational situations. It means that no matter which way your vessel is heading, you may refer to one side of the channel as the starboard or port side. This is useful, for example, when transmitting or receiving information by radio. By means of the conventional direction concept, references can be made to the "port side of the channel," and everyone listening will know it is the left side of the channel for those vessels entering from seaward and the right side of the channel for those going in the opposite direction, heading toward the sea.

Obviously, when a vessel is entering the Hampton Roads channel from the Atlantic Ocean, it is "entering from seaward." It does not take too much deductive reasoning to further understand that you are still entering from seaward as you proceed northward through the Chesapeake Bay, and only a little more to realize that you are still doing so as you enter Baltimore Harbor.

But buoys are sometimes placed where this convention does not work, such as along sea coasts, in the Intracoastal Waterways, and on the Great Lakes. To cover these situations, some additional conventions have been adopted. The conventional direction of buoyage for a vessel traveling along the coasts of the United States is westerly and southerly along the coast of Maine; in a southerly direction along the remainder of the Atlantic Coast; westerly along the Gulf Coast; northerly on the Pacific Coast; and westerly on the Great Lakes (except southerly in Lake Michigan) (see fig. 601). Conventional directions for the Intracoastal Waterway, the Western Rivers system, and the Uniform State Waterway Marking System are discussed in articles 624, 625, and 626, respectively.

The importance of conventional direction will become clearer as you read on.

BUOYS

602 Used in a variety of shapes and sizes, buoys are the most numerous aids to navigation. These are floating objects, heavily anchored to the bottom so

Fig. 601. Direction of increasing numbers for coastal buoys—as if "returning from sea."

that they will remain in place. They are intended to convey information to a navigator by their shape and color, by the characteristics of a visible or audible signal, or a combination of two or more such features. Modern buoys have bands of reflective material to enhance their detection at night; these reflect brightly in the beam of a vessel's searchlight (or even a hand-held flashlight on smaller craft.) Some buoys are illuminated at night and are therefore in the category of "lights" as well. Many buoys also have special reflectors to make them more "visible" on radar.

Because buoys have been around for a long time, different nations (and different regions within nations) have developed their own systems of buoyage. Attempts have been made to standardize buoyage throughout the world, but these have been only partially successful. As a navigator, you must be familiar with the various systems of buoyage that you might encounter in your travels. Within the United States alone, you may encounter several different systems, depending upon the waters in which you are navigating. Those waterways used frequently by international traffic use IALA System B buoyage, while the Intracoastal Waterway and the Western Rivers (Mississippi and its tributaries) have systems of their own. These various systems will be explained below.

Lateral vs. Cardinal

603 One important classification of buoys is based upon how they are used. Buoys can be used in either a *lateral* system or a *cardinal* system, or a combination of both.

In a lateral system, aids are placed to indicate the sides of a navigable channel. They also mark junctions and bifurcations in channels, indicate the safe side on which to pass a hazard, and mark the general safe centerline of wide bodies of water. The majority of buoys in United States waters are based on the lateral system.

In a cardinal system, buoys are generally used to convey a geographic relationship with a hazard in terms of 90-degree quadrants, using the cardinal directions of north, east, south, and west (see Appendix D). Buoys are consequently named and clearly marked as north, south, east, or west. Mariners need only pass north of a north mark, south of a south mark, east of an east mark, and west of a west mark in order to remain in safe water. Identification of these buoys is enhanced by a specific color scheme and a system of topmarks as described below. Cardinal systems are not used in U.S. waters but are prevalent in Canadian and European waters.

IALA Systems

604 As mentioned above, more than thirty different buoyage systems have been used at one time or another by the world's maritime nations. Some features had exactly opposite meanings in different countries. Efforts toward standardization were made but achieved little success until the mid-1970s, when an organization then known as the International Association of Lighthouse Authorities (IALA) developed and secured nearly worldwide acceptance of two systems. Of course, one system would have been preferable, but in an international situation—where many nations were very used to doing things their own way—two is a lot better than thirty. The two systems adopted by most of the nations of the world have been designated System A and System B. Both systems use combinations of cardinal marks and lateral marks plus some unique marks for isolated dangers, safe-water areas, and special purposes. The cardinal and unique marks are the same in both systems; but the lateral marks have exactly *opposite* meanings in the two systems. To convey the desired information to the navigator, the IALA systems use buoy shape, color, topmarks, and, if lighted, the rhythm of the flashes.

IALA system A is used in Europe, Africa, and most of Asia, including Australia and New Zealand. It makes much use of cardinal marks and places red buoys to port and green buoys to starboard when entering from seaward.

The IALA-B system is used in the United States and the rest of the Western Hemisphere, plus Japan, South Korea, and the Philippines (see fig. 604). Although cardinal marks are permitted, less frequent use of them is made, and lateral buoys are colored the exact opposite of those in system A.

Except where otherwise indicated, references to buoys in this book are assumed to be adhering to IALA System B (see Appendix D). (Note: The IALA has changed its name to the "International Association of Marine Aids to Navigation and Lighthouse Authorities, but still uses the "IALA" acronym.)

Buoy Colors

605 *Green buoys* mark the port (left) sides of channels when heading in the conventional direction—that is, entering from seaward. Green buoys marking wrecks or obstructions should also be kept on your port side when returning from sea in order to remain in safe water. (Note: As previously mentioned, IALA System A is the exact opposite, so when entering European waters, these buoys would mark the starboard [right] side of the channel when entering from seaward.)

Red buoys mark the starboard (right) sides of channels when heading in the conventional direction—that is, entering from seaward. Red buoys marking wrecks or obstructions should also be kept on your starboard side when returning from sea in order to remain in safe water. The memory aid "red-right-returning" (sometimes called "the 3 'R's of navigation") refers to this convention: *red* buoys are kept on the *right* when *returning* from sea. (Note: In IALA System A, red buoys mark the port [left] side of the channel when entering from seaward.)

Buoys with horizontal red and green bands mark junctions (where two channels come together) or bifurcations (where two channels split off of one). If the topmost band is green, keeping the buoy on the port hand will follow the preferred channel, as if the whole buoy were green. If the topmost band is red, keeping the buoy to starboard ("red-right-returning"

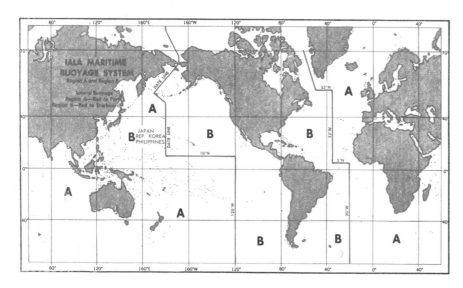

Fig. 604. The IALA Buoyage System differs in Regions A and B.

applies) will keep you in the preferred channel. (Note: In IALA System A, the opposite is true.)

Buoys with horizontal red and black bands mark isolated dangers, such as shoals or shipwrecks. (Note: This is the same in IALA System A.)

Buoys with red and white vertical stripes are "safe-water marks" used to indicate a fairway (midchannel) or a landfall. Such buoys are also used at the beginning of some vessel traffic separation schemes leading into busy ports, or in narrow passages congested with heavy traffic. Safe water marks are also at the termination of traffic separation schemes that direct traffic into a channel. (Note: This is the same in IALA System A.)

Solid yellow buoys are special-purpose buoys, typically marking anchorages, fishnet areas, and dredging sites. They may also mark the termination of traffic separation schemes, and they are used to mark the beginning of a traffic separation scheme when it is designed to coordinate traffic through an area, but not necessarily into a marked channel. (Note: These are used in the same manner in IALA System A.)

Cardinal buoys are colored as follows: north buoys are half black and half yellow, with the black half on top; south buoys are the exact opposite, yellow over black; east buoys are banded from top to bottom, black-yellow-black; and west buoys are banded from top to bottom, yellow-black-yellow (see Appendix D).

Buoy Types

606   A complete system of buoyage includes several different types of buoys, each type designed to meet the requirements of specific conditions. All buoys serve as guides during daylight and their shapes can be used to convey information as well as their colors; those having lights are also available for navigation at night; those having sound signals are more readily located in times of fog or other conditions of reduced visibility.

Can buoy. These buoys are shaped like a tin can, flat on top when seen from a distance. When used, can buoys are placed on the port side of the channel when entering from seaward and are therefore green in color (*red in IALA system A*). Junction buoys can also be can-shaped if the preferred channel is to starboard (i.e., the buoy should be left on the vessel's port hand to select the preferred channel). In this case, the top band of the buoy will be green.

Nun buoy. Sometimes called a "conical buoy," the above-water part of this buoy terminates in a cone, usually with a rounded tip. When used, nun buoys are either red (to mark the starboard side of the channel) or have red and green bands (with red on top) to mark a junction (preferred channel to port). (Note: In IALA System A, nun channel markers will be green, and junction buoys will have the green stripe on top.)

Spherical buoy. A buoy shaped like a sphere or globe. These buoys are only used to mark safe water and will always have red and white vertical stripes.

Spar buoy. A narrow buoy with an elongated cylindrical shape, resembling a pole. These buoys can be used for virtually any purpose (channel markers, junction buoys, safe water marks, etc.) but will be appropriately colored.

Cylindrical buoy. In some inland systems, small can buoys are referred to as "cylindrical."

Pillar buoy. Sometimes just referred to as a "lighted buoy" or a "whistle buoy," depending upon how they are equipped. These are buoys with a short tower (often skeletal in construction) mounted on a visible float in which a light, gong, or some other accessory is often housed (see fig. 606).

Lighted buoy. A pillar buoy equipped with a light to make it visible at night. A set of electric batteries (or other source of power such as a solar receptor) that operates the light is included.

Bell buoy. A bell with several clappers—usually four—hung externally so that they will strike the bell as it rocks with the motion of the sea.

Fig. 606. A pillar buoy.

Gong buoy. Generally similar in construction to a bell buoy except that it has several, usually four, gongs mounted in a vertical stack, each of which sounds a different note.

Whistle buoy. A buoy generally similar in construction to a bell or gong buoy, but which has a low-pitched whistle signal that is activated by the rise and fall of the buoy in a seaway.

Horn buoy. Similar to a whistle buoy except that its sound signal is electrically powered by batteries within the lower part of the buoy.

Combination buoy. A buoy having some combination of the light and sound accessories described above (for example, a lighted bell buoy, a lighted whistle buoy, etc.).

Topmarks

607   To enhance identification during daylight, pillar and spar buoys may have topmarks—distinctive shapes mounted at the very top of the buoy to facilitate its identification in the daytime from a distance, or under poor light conditions when the color might not be easily ascertained (see fig. 607 and Appendix D). Buoys will have topmarks as indicated:

1. Port hand channel markers—a can shape.
2. Starboard hand channel markers—a cone shape.
3. Junction buoys—a can shape to indicate preferred channel to starboard, or a cone shape to indicate the preferred channel to port.
4. Safe water marks—one spherical shape.
5. Isolated danger marks—two spherical shapes mounted one above the other.
6. Special purpose buoys—any shape that cannot be confused with other navigational marks.
7. North cardinal buoys—two triangles pointing up.
8. South cardinal buoys—two triangles pointing down.
9. East cardinal buoys—two triangles placed base-to-base (roughly a diamond).
10. West cardinal buoys—two triangles placed point-to-point (roughly an hourglass).

Note: There are a few simple memory aids that may help with cardinal topmarks. Note that the two triangles pointing up seem to be pointing northward (since most charts are oriented with north at the top); the opposite is true for south; and the two triangles oriented point-to-point for west can be remembered if one thinks of the resulting shape as resembling a wineglass and uses the first letters of "*w*est is *w*ineglass." The colors of cardinal system buoys can also be remembered by noting that the triangular topmarks always point toward the black color. For example, the northerly cardinal buoy is

Fig. 607. Topmarks may be added to lighted buoys to aid in daytime identification. Here a spherical topmark has been added, corresponding to an unlighted spherical buoy.

black over yellow and the triangles point up; for the westerly buoy the triangles point together, and the black band is sandwiched between the two yellow ones; and so on (see Appendix D).

Buoy Numbers and Letters

608   Most buoys are given numbers, letters, or combinations of numbers and letters that are painted conspicuously on them, or are applied in special reflective material. These markings facilitate identification and location of the buoys on the charts.

All solid-colored red and green buoys are given numbers or combinations of numbers and letters. Other colored buoys may be given letters. Numbers increase sequentially from seaward. Odd numbers are used *only* on solid green buoys. Even numbers are used *only* on solid red buoys. Numbers followed by letters are used on solid-colored red or green buoys when a letter is required so as not to disturb the sequence of numbers, such as when an additional buoy is placed after the numbering system has been established. Letters may also be used on certain important buoys, particularly those marking isolated offshore dangers. An example of the latter case would be a buoy marked "6 WQS." In this instance the number has the usual significance, while the letters "WQS" indicate the place as Winter Quarter Shoal. Letters without numbers are applied in some cases to red-and-white vertically striped buoys, red-and-green horizontally banded buoys, and solid yellow buoys.

Buoy Sound Signals

609   The IALA systems make no mention of sound signals—bells, gongs, whistles, horns—on buoys, but they are used frequently in U.S. waters to aid in identification during periods of restricted visibility.

In some areas, if both bell and gong buoys are used to mark a channel, the gongs are placed to port and the bells to starboard when entering from seaward. In other areas, different local arrangements are used to aid a navigator traversing a channel in fog or other reduced visibility situation. By studying the chart for an area, you will be able to discern any useful patterns.

Station Buoys

610   While buoys are carefully placed by the Coast Guard and are moored as securely as possible, worsening weather and current conditions can cause them to shift position. A smaller nun or can buoy, called a *station buoy* (also called a "watch-buoy"), is sometimes placed in close proximity to an important larger buoy to mark the station in case the regular aid is accidentally shifted from its designated location. Station buoys are colored and numbered in the same manner as the larger buoy.

Caution When Using Buoys

611   Despite their usefulness, buoys must be used with caution. The buoy symbol on a chart is used to indicate the *approximate* position of the buoy. This position must be considered "approximate" because of the practical limitations in positioning and maintaining buoys in precise geographic locations. These limitations include, but are not limited to, imprecise position-fixing methods (although modern methods are making this less likely), prevailing wind and sea conditions, and the slope and the makeup of the seabed. Keep in mind that buoy positions are not under continuous surveillance, but are normally checked only during periodic maintenance visits that may occur a year or more apart. It must also be remembered that buoys are moored to an anchor with varying lengths of chain to allow for changing tidal depths and to provide adequate stability (a scope of three times the depth of the water is typical, but it may be more), and a buoy can be expected to swing in a circle under the varying influences of current, wind, and waves. Buoys are subject to being carried away, shifted, capsized, or sunk; lighted buoys may become extinguished, and sound signals may malfunction.

Buoys marking wrecks will normally *not* be directly over the hazard, because of the potential danger to the vessel that places the buoy in position. Such buoys are usually put on the seaward or channelward side of the wreck; if two buoys are used, the wreck may lie between them. Wrecks may shift position due either to normal currents or storm conditions. Extra care must always be exercised in the vicinity of buoys marking wrecks.

As useful as buoys are, a smart navigator will not rely completely on the position or operation of floating aids to navigation, but will, whenever possible, give preference to bearings on fixed aids to navigation or natural landmarks.

One exception to the above cautions occurs in areas that have specially designated Vessel Traffic Schemes (VTS). The buoys in these carefully maintained channels are subject to constant radar monitoring. If they are moved by weather or collision, an alert pops up automatically and ships are warned by VTS controllers accordingly.

BEACONS

612   Beacons are those aids that are fixed in placed rather than floating and tethered. Beacons may or may not be lighted. Lighthouses (also known as "primary seacoast lights") are the largest form of beacon, but many smaller ones are merely a shape or a light mounted atop a single pile (large post) that has been driven into the ground along a shore or into the bottom in relatively shallow water. Beacons follow many of the conventions (colors, shapes, etc.) used by buoys.

Daybeacons are those that are not lighted and simply have a *daymark* that conveys information through its color, shape, and lettering or numbers. Like buoys, daymarks often have reflective material as part of their design so that they will show up at night.

Racons (the word is derived from the words *ra*dar and bea*con*) use radar to provide additional information to navigators. Racons are triggered by a vessel's search radar and respond with a distinctive Morse code signal that appears on the display of the querying radar, matching the letter on the chart. Racons are often co-located with other aids to navigation and may be on shore or in water areas on lights and buoys. They are sometimes used on bridges to mark the best point of passage.

Daymark Colors and Shapes

613   The daymark portion of a daybeacon is colored and shaped in a scheme that is similar to the one used for buoys. For example, the starboard side of a channel, when marked with buoys, will have red ones whose shape is either a spar, pillar, or (uniquely) nun or conical. Correspondingly, the daymarks for the starboard side of a channel are colored red and are triangularly shaped (similar to a cone or approximating the shape of the top of a nun buoy). Daymarks on the port side of a channel are green and square-shaped (similar to a can in profile).

When daymarks are used to mark a junction, they will be marked with the preferred channel color on top (green for starboard and red for port), and they will also be shaped accordingly (square if the preferred channel is to starboard, and triangular if the preferred channel is to port).

Midchannel daymarks are vertically divided into red and white and are octagonal (roughly corresponding to the spherical shape of buoys used for the same purpose).

Special daymarks are yellow and diamond shaped (a square rotated through 45 degrees).

Daybeacons will be numbered (and/or lettered) with reflective material in the same manner as buoys.

Some channels may be marked with a combination of buoys, daybeacons, and lights.

LIGHTS

614 While lights are often used in combination with other aids to navigation, such as buoys and beacons, they appear in many forms and have characteristics that are important to the navigator. Lights are classified in a number of confusing ways—major, minor, primary, secondary, and so on—that, for the most part, do not concern the navigator. What does matter is where they are and what characteristics they have that will aid the navigator in fixing his or her position. One classification that has significance to the navigator is whether a light is fixed or is attached to a floating buoy. When they are fixed in position, lights are useful sources of accurate bearing information, while those mounted on buoys serve as general demarcations of channels and obstructions but, because they are floating, must be treated as less reliable for fixing information.

Fixed lights on shore can be powered by continuous electrical sources, while buoys must rely upon either batteries or a combination of solar cells and batteries. To conserve electricity, lights are often equipped with a photoelectric cell that turns it off during the day. An automatic bulb-changing mechanism is included in most navigational lights to increase their dependability; if a bulb burns out, an internal device switches to a spare bulb. Some lights will have radio transmitters that will send out a signal if the light fails, so that Coast Guard personnel are alerted to make the necessary repairs.

Note: In this chapter, there will be frequent references to *Light Lists*. As discussed in chapter 5, we know that there are both *Light Lists* (published by the U.S. Coast Guard for U.S. waters) and *Lists of Lights* (published by NIMA for foreign waters). For simplicity, references to these publications will be abbreviated to simply "*Light Lists*" rather than repeating "*Light Lists* and *Lists of Lights*" each time.

Types of Lights

615 The most common lights are those that are combined with other navaids, such as buoys and beacons, but there are some specially designed lights that serve important navigational purposes as well.

Primary seacoast lights are those that serve as early indications of landfall for mariners returning from the open sea. The most familiar of these is the *lighthouse* (see fig. 615). Placed where they will be of most use, on prominent headlands, at entrances, on isolated dangers, or at other points where it is necessary that mariners be guided or warned, their principal purpose is to support a light at a considerable height above the water to maximize its range of visibility. They may also house a fog signal and/or radiobeacon equipment and may vary markedly in their outward appearance. Besides their different construction characteristics, lighthouses are deliberately painted with easily identifiable and discernible colors and patterns.

Until more modern times, *lightships* served the same purpose as lighthouses. These specially constructed vessels were anchored at key locations to warn mariners of dangers and to guide them safely along coasts and into harbors. But because they were very expensive to maintain (ships require

Fig. 615. The lighthouse at Cape Hatteras is an example of a primary seacoast light.

crews and manpower is expensive), lightships have been replaced by other aids to navigation.

Range lights are included as part of a range (see article 622). Like the daymarks that are mounted on them, these lights can be used at night or in periods of low visibility to stay in a designated channel or to accurately determine a turning point.

Sector lights use colored glass lenses that have been carefully aligned so that they show one color from most directions and a different color or colors over definite arcs of the horizon. These can be used to mark shoals or to warn mariners away from nearby land. The exact sectors covered by each color are listed in the appropriate *Light List* and clearly marked on the relevant chart(s). When viewed from the surface of the water, the light will appear to be one color when the vessel is in safe waters and will appear as a different color (usually red) when the vessel has strayed into dangerous waters. Sectors may be but a few degrees in width, marking an isolated rock or shoal, or of such width as to extend from deep water to the shore. Bearings referring to sectors are expressed in degrees as observed *from a vessel toward the light*. Charts normally show sector limits by a line of short dashes and include an arc labeled with the color of the light in that sector.

Directional lights use the same principle as sector lights but are used to aid mariners in staying within the limits of a channel in a manner similar to range lights (see article 622). Different-colored glass is carefully arranged so that the navigator will see a relatively narrow beam of white light when the vessel is in the center of a channel, but will see the light change to green when the vessel moves over to the side of the channel that is or would be marked with green buoys, and will see red when the vessel moves to the other side of the channel. Obviously, the safest passage is made when the directional light remains white.

Navigation lights on bridges are used to help mariners pass safely under or through these structures. Green lights may be used on drawbridges to indicate that the draw is open and a vessel may safely pass through. For bridges that are high enough for vessels to pass safely under, red lights are used to mark piers and supports, while green lights mark the centerline of the navigable channel passing beneath the bridge. If there is more than one channel through the bridge, the preferred route is marked by three white lights placed vertically.

Light Characteristics

616 The four standard *light colors* for lighted navaids are red, green, white, and yellow. Red lights only are used on red buoys, or red-and-green horizontally banded buoys with the topmost band red; green lights are used only on green buoys, or red-and-green horizontally banded buoys with the topmost band green. White lights are used only on safewater marks (red-and-white vertically striped buoys or beacons) and on isolated danger buoys (red and black horizontally striped buoys and beacons). Yellow is used on special-purpose buoys.

Lights used as navaids also have distinct characteristics (on/off patterns) to assist in their identification. The *period* of a light is the time it takes for it to complete one full cycle of on-and-off changes. By varying the lengths of the periods and the elements of a cycle, a considerable variety of light rhythms can be obtained. Advantage is taken of this to provide the necessary distinction between aids in the same area. These are illustrated with their commonly used abbreviations in figure 616.

Lights are described as *fixed* when they are continuously on; these are rarely used because of the attendant power consumption. A light is *flashing* when the time on is less than the time off ("eclipsed"). Conversely, lights are termed *occulting* when they are on more than they are off (sometimes called "flashing black"). If the times on and off are equal, the light is designated as *equal interval* or *isophase*. Group flashing and group occulting are those lights that flash or occult in regularly occurring patterns separated by periods of continuous light or darkness. *Composite group flashing lights* have more than one group making up their pattern. Lights can also flash in *Morse code* patterns to make them readily identifiable.

Lights can be further characterized by the *frequency* of their flashing. For example, those that flash at a rate of not more than 30 flashes per minute are called *flashing lights* and are often used to mark the sides of a channel (and can therefore be red or green). Those lights that flash at frequencies not less than 50 but not more than 80 flashes per minute (usually 50 or 60) are called *quick-flashing lights* and are often used to mark points in a channel where special caution is necessary—for example, at sharp turns, where a channel narrows, or to mark wrecks or other obstructions. *Very quick flashing lights* flash at a rate of more than 80 flashes per minute (usually 100 or 120) and are used primarily on cardinal buoys.

Identification of Lights

617 One of the most frequent causes of groundings is the failure to identify lights correctly. When expecting to make a landfall, you should consult the charts and appropriate *Light List* to learn the exact characteristics of the lights you expect to see first.

Illustration and phase description	Lights which do not change color	Lights which show color variations
A continuous steady light.	F. = Fixed	Alt. = Alternating.
A fixed light varied at regular intervals by a flash of greater brilliance.	F.Fl. = Fixed and flashing.	Alt.F.Fl. = Alternating fixed and flashing.
A fixed light varied at regular intervals by groups of 2 or more flashes of greater brilliance.	F.Gp.Fl. = Fixed and group flashing.	Alt.F.Gp.Fl. = Alternating fixed and group flashing.
Showing a single flash at regular intervals, the duration of light always being less than the duration of darkness; not more than 30 flashes per minute.	Fl. = Flashing	Alt.Fl. = Alternating flashing.
Showing at regular intervals groups of 2 or more flashes.	Gp.Fl. = Group flashing.	Alt.Gp.Fl. = Alternating group flashing.
Light flashes are combined in alternate groups of different numbers.	Gp.Fl. (1 + 2) = Composite group flashing.	
Light in which flashes of different duration are grouped in such a manner as to produce a Morse character or characters every 8 seconds.	Mo.(A) = Morse Code.	
Shows not less than 60 flashes per minute.	Qk.Fl. = Quick flashing.	
Shows a series of 6 quick flashes repeated at intervals of 10 seconds.	I.Qk.Fl. = Interrupted quick flashing.	
Light with all durations of light and darkness equal.	E.Int. = Equal interval. (Isophase)	
A light totally eclipsed at regular intervals, the duration of light always greater than the duration of darkness.	Occ. = Occulting.	Alt.Occ. = Alternating occulting.
A light with a group of 2 or more eclipses at regular intervals.	Gp.Occ. = Group occulting.	

Fig. 616. Light phase characteristics.

When a light is sighted, you should note its characteristics (color, period, etc.) and then correlate what you see with what is on your chart. Consult the chart and *Light List* to see if any other light in the general locality might be seen and mistaken for the desired light. If there is any doubt, a careful timing of the length of all flashes and dark intervals (using a stopwatch), and comparison with the *Light List* is usually conclusive. This process should be continued as you continue farther inland; that is, always be looking for the next light in your voyage, knowing in advance what characteristics to expect, so that sightings can be either confirmed or serve as warnings that something may be amiss.

In approaching a light with a complex characteristic of different colors and intensities, allowance must be made for the lesser range of the portion with inferior brightness. For example, a *fixed-and-flashing* light will have flashes much brighter than the fixed light. When initially seen from a distance, it is most likely that only the flashes will be bright enough to be seen, and the full characteristic will not develop until the observer has come closer to the light. Another example of a potential misunderstanding would be a light with a characteristic of alternating flashing using both white and red colors. It is a matter of physics that the red flashes will be less bright, and such a light, when first seen from a distance, will probably seem to have a simple flashing white characteristic; the intervening red flashes will be seen only after the observer comes closer. At short distances and in clear weather, some flashing lights may show a continuous faint light; this is because there are lights that do burn continuously, with the "flashes" being created by a revolving lens.

It is important to note that in *Light Lists* all bearings are stated in degrees true, reading clockwise from 000° at north; bearings relating to visibility of lights are given as *observed from a vessel*, not the light; distances are in nautical miles unless otherwise stated; and heights are referred to mean high water in the tidal range.

Determining Visibility

618 It is very useful for a navigator to know at what specific distance a given light will come into view. For example, when returning from sea, you can reassure yourself as to your navigational accuracy by sighting a light on shore at the moment you have predicted. Conversely, failure to sight a light when predicted can warn you that you may not be where you think you are.

If all things were constant, the *Light Lists* could include the range of visibility of lights and navigators could simply start looking for a given light when they believed they were within that range. But such things as atmospheric conditions and the height of the light and of the observer make these predictions more complicated.

To begin with, it is important to understand the concept of *meteorological visibility*. The amount of particulate matter and water vapor in the atmosphere has a considerable effect upon the visibility of a light. A scale has been set up called the "International Visibility Code" which classifies varying degrees of visibility that mariners may use to define existing conditions affecting optical ranges (see fig. 618a). This scale is also included in the front matter of the *Light Lists*. A mariner may use this scale to estimate conditions of visibility but is better off using other methods if they are available. For example, visibility conditions are included with marine

METEOROLOGICAL OPTICAL RANGE					
Code	Weather	Yards	Code	Weather	Nautical Miles
0	Dense fog	Less than 50	5	Haze	1 to 2
1	Thick fog	50 to 200	6	Light haze	2 to 5½
2	Moderate fog	200 to 500	7	Clear	5½ to 11
			8	Very clear	11.0 to 27.0
3	Light fog	500 to 1000	9	Exception-	
4	Thin fog	½ to 1		ally clear	Over 27.0

Fig. 618a. International Visibility Code.

weather broadcasts (broadcasting stations are listed in Pub. No. 117, *Radio Navigation Aids*). Another method is to take a radar range on visible landmarks or other vessels when they first become visible or disappear from sight.

To determine the predicted visibility of a light (sometimes referred to as the "computed visibility"), you must determine the *luminous range* and the *geographic range* of the light, and then compare the two. The lesser of the two is the range at which you should first sight the light.

There are two steps to finding the luminous range of a given light. The first step is to look the light up in the *Light List* to determine its *nominal range* (see fig. 501 in chapter 5), which is defined as the maximum range at which the light could be seen if the meteorological visibility were 10 miles. The nominal range (rounded to nearest whole mile) is also sometimes provided on the chart; this is called the "charted range" or the "charted visibility."

The next step in finding the luminous range of the light is to use a *Luminous Range Diagram* (see fig.

618b), which can be found in the front of the *Light List*. By entering the diagram with the nominal range (obtained from the *Light List*) and the meteorological visibility (obtained as described above), you identify the point where the visibility curve intersects the nominal range, then read across to the scale on the side of the column to obtain the luminous range. For example, if you are expecting to encounter a light that is listed as having a nominal range of 16 miles and you know your meteorological visibility is approximately 2 miles (obtained by noting the radar range of a passing vessel when it first became visible), you can then enter the Luminous Range Diagram and find the luminous range of the light to be 5 miles.

Once you have come up with the luminous range of the light, you must next determine the *geographic range*. This is defined as the visible range of a light based upon the heights of the light and the observer (without considering the meteorological conditions). Because the Earth's surface is curved, the height of a light becomes a factor in how far it can be seen. The taller an object is, the farther away it can be seen. This becomes fairly obvious when you realize that the masts and sails of a vessel become visible on an approaching vessel before you can see the hull. The same is true with the height of the observer (often called "height of eye"); you can see a great deal farther from the top of a building than you can from the ground. Therefore, both the height of the light and the height of eye of the observer must be considered when determining

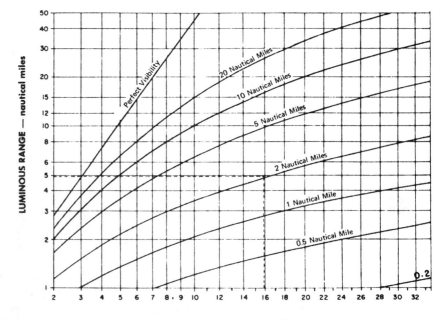

Fig. 618b. Luminous Range Diagram.

NOMINAL RANGE — nautical miles

geographic range. To do this, you must rely upon a table or use a mathematical formula to determine what is often called the *horizon distance* for each, then add them together to get the geographic range.

Tables used to determine horizon distance are available in the front matter of the *Light Lists* and in *Bowditch*. An example is provided in figure 618c. As an alternative you may calculate the horizon distance by multiplying the square root of the height in feet (of the light or of the observer—remember, you must do *both* and add the results in order to find the geographic range) by 1.17. This will yield a horizon distance in nautical miles. You may use the height in meters instead of feet but must use 2.12 as your multiplier (instead of 1.17). Once you have obtained the horizon distances for the light and for the observer, you must add them together to get the geographic range.

Height Feet	Nautical Miles	Height Feet	Nautical Miles	Height Feet	Nautical Miles
1	1.2	33	6.7	125	13.1
2	1.7	34	6.8	130	13.3
3	2.0	35	6.9	135	13.6
4	2.3	36	7.0	140	13.8
5	2.6	37	7.1	145	14.1
6	2.9	38	7.2	150	14.3
7	3.1	39	7.3	160	14.8
8	3.3	40	7.4	170	15.3
9	3.5	41	7.5	180	15.7
10	3.7	42	7.6	190	16.1
11	3.9	43	7.7	200	16.5
12	4.1	44	7.8	210	17.0
13	4.2	45	7.8	220	17.4
14	4.4	46	7.9	230	17.7
15	4.5	47	8.0	240	18.1
16	4.7	48	8.1	250	18.5
17	4.8	49	8.2	260	18.9
18	5.0	50	8.3	270	19.2
19	5.1	55	8.7	280	19.6
20	5.2	60	9.1	290	19.9
21	5.4	65	9.4	300	20.3
22	5.5	70	9.8	310	20.6
23	5.6	75	10.1	320	20.9
24	5.7	80	10.5	330	21.3
25	5.9	85	10.8	340	21.6
26	6.0	90	11.1	350	21.9
27	6.1	95	11.4	360	22.2
28	6.2	100	11.7	370	22.5
29	6.3	105	12.0	380	22.8
30	6.4	110	12.3	390	23.1
31	6.5	115	12.5	400	23.4
32	6.6	120	12.8	450	24.8

Fig. 618c. Table of distances to the horizon for various heights of eye.

Having determined both the luminous range and the geographic range, you must then compare them and select the lesser of the two as your *computed visibility*. This is the range that you would expect to first see the light in question.

Example: Determine the computed visibility of Mount Desert Light. Meteorological visibility is about 20 nautical miles and the observer is standing on the bridge of his ship and knows that gives him a height of eye of 70 feet above the water.

Solution: From the *Light List* (see fig. 501 in chapter 5) find the nominal range of Mount Desert Light (24 nm) and then determine the luminous range by entering the Luminous Range Diagram (see fig. 618b) at the 24-mile point and finding where that line intersects with the 20-nautical-mile visibility curve, then read the luminous range of 40 nm on the left side of the diagram. Next consult the *Light List* again to determine the height of Mount Desert Light (75 feet). Using the appropriate table (see fig. 618c) or multiplying the square root of 75 (8.66) by 1.17, find the horizon distance for the light to be 10.1 nautical miles. Doing the same for the observer's height of eye (70 feet), you find the observer's horizon distance to be 9.8 nm. Adding the two horizon distances (10.1 + 9.8), you determine the geographic range to be 19.9 nautical miles. Comparing the two, you find the geographic range (19.9) to be less than the luminous range (40 nm).

Answer: Computed visibility for Mount Desert Light in these circumstances is 19.9 nautical miles.

Bobbing a Light

619 If your computed visibility turns out to be the geographic range of the light rather than its luminous range, it is helpful to know when the light has first appeared at the horizon. An age-old technique of determining this is to "bob the light." This entails simply lowering your height of eye (by stooping or flexing your knees) while keeping your eye on the light. If the light disappears right away, you can be certain that you are at the extreme limit of the geographic range (because the relatively small reduction in your height of eye when you "bobbed" caused the light to fall below the horizon). The corollary is that if you have to stoop a great deal (or even go to a lower deck) to make the light disappear, you then know that you are closer than the geographic range of the light.

By shooting a bearing to this light at this moment, you then have a relatively accurate range and bearing you can plot on your chart. This method is not reliable enough to yield a fix but *can* be used as an estimated position.

Predicting Time and Bearing for Sighting a Light

620   Once the computed visibility of a light has been determined, an arc representing this visibility can be drawn on the chart. This arc is centered at the charted position of the light, and its radius is the computed visibility (see fig. 620). The arc is labeled with the name of the light above the arc, and the visibility below it. The point at which this circle intersects your intended track indicates the position at which the light should become visible. The time of arrival at this point is determined by dead reckoning (see chapter 9); the bearing on which the light should be sighted is its direction from this point. The true bearing obtained from the chart can be converted to a relative bearing to assist lookouts in locating the light.

Variables

621   Keep in mind that there are other factors that can affect the visibility of a light. In clear weather, the loom of a powerful light may appear before the light itself comes into sight. In a dense fog, you might not be able to see your own bow, but a very strong light may defy the luminous range curves and "burn through" the fog at a significant distance. Background lights (like the neon lights of a string of shore hotels) can be so bright as to make it very difficult for you to spot the navigation light you are looking for.

RANGES

622   One of the most useful aids to navigation is something called a "range." In the Royal Navy the potential confusion of using the same term that is

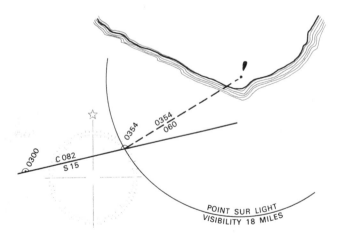

Fig. 620. Predicting the time and bearing for sighting a light.

used to describe a measured distance is avoided by calling it a "transit." Ranges can occur naturally or are deliberately created for navigational purposes. The latter are pairs of fixed markers (often, but not always, lighted) that are carefully positioned some distance apart in line with a channel, the rear one higher than the front one. When the navigator of an approaching vessel sees the front and rear daymarks or lights aligned, it can safely be assumed that the vessel is in the prescribed channel (see fig. 622). You can see how this works by placing two objects (like a pair of bottles) centered at the back of a room, one behind and slightly higher than the other. From the other end of the room, walk slowly toward the two bottles. As long as you keep the two lined up (the lower one in front of the higher one), you will be on the straight path defined by their positions (simulating a channel). If you move to the left of that straight path, the closest object will appear to move to the right of the one farther away. The opposite occurs when you move to the right.

Ranges can also be used to mark turning points in channels or to establish specific directions for compass adjustment. They are especially useful in places where tidal currents set across or at an angle to a dredged channel that has shoal water on either side.

Range lights may be red, green, white, or yellow, and may be fixed, flashing, or occulting. They are carefully designed to ensure that they stand out distinctly among their surroundings. Some have very bright lights that can be seen in daytime.

Often the range markers are located on shore or in shallow water, so it is important to examine the chart carefully to determine how far the range line can be safely followed. If you look at figure 622, you can see that the range shown has been useful in keeping the vessel in the channel, but it will soon be time for the vessel to cease relying on the range and turn in order to stay in the channel. You cannot determine this information from the *Light Lists*, so it is important to consult the chart so that a wonderful navigation aid does not turn into a device for disaster.

You should also be aware that *side ranges* also exist (particularly on Western Rivers). These are used to mark the sides of channels rather than the middle; seeing *them* lined up indicates that you are standing into danger.

As mentioned earlier, ranges can also occur naturally. The nautical navigator will do well to be watching for natural ranges when planning the voyage and while actually under way. Prior to getting under way, by studying the charts you will be using,

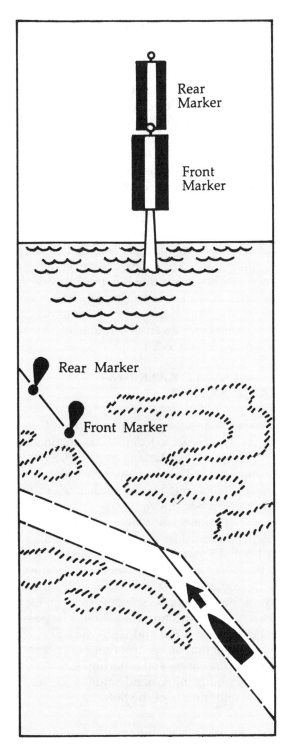

Fig. 622. A range is formed by two objects or aids to navigation in line, with the rear one higher than the front one.

you may see certain features that line up when you are on your planned track or that may serve as good turning markers. *Coast Pilots* and *Sailing Directions* often note these relationships as well. While actually under way, you might notice that when you are on track, a certain flag pole and steeple are lined up. Noting this for future transits of that same channel will prove very useful.

FOG SIGNALS

623   Fog signals are audible signals used to indicate the location of an aid to navigation when it cannot be seen because of conditions of reduced visibility. They serve to warn the mariner of a danger or to indicate a general direction to steer. They may be on shore, on a fixed structure in the water, or on a buoy, and they are often co-located with another form of aid such as a light. Some signals on buoys are operated by the motion of the sea, so they will not produce sounds in a calm sea without swells. Others are battery powered so that they will operate in such conditions, and these are placed on a regular cycle of operation, permitting different types of signals and characteristics to be assigned various locations in the same general area for identification purposes.

To be effective as an aid to navigation, a mariner must be able to identify the signal and know from what location it originates. The different types most frequently used are horns, whistles, bells, and gongs. Some, called diaphones or "two-tone," produce separate tones of different pitch to help in identification.

The navigator must always bear in mind that sound signals in fog can be very deceptive. At times, they may be completely inaudible even when near at hand. They may also be somewhat refracted, so that the sound may seem to be coming from a direction other than the actual bearing of the signal source. It goes without saying that extra caution is mandatory when operating in reduced visibility, and that navigators should use all means available (reduced speed, radar, extra lookouts, soundings, etc.) in addition to relying on fog signals.

AIDS TO NAVIGATION ON THE INTRACOASTAL WATERWAY

624   The Intracoastal Waterway (ICW) is a largely sheltered waterway, suitable for year-round use, extending some 2,400 miles along the Atlantic and Gulf Coasts of the United States, from Manasquan, New Jersey, to Brownsville, Texas. For vessels using the ICW, the conventional direction is southerly along the Atlantic Coast and westerly along the Gulf Coast. This means that the starboard side of the channel will be the western bank along the Atlantic

portions of the waterway and the northern bank along the Gulf Coast parts.

Along the ICW, the usual daymark and buoy painting schemes are used, but an additional *yellow* stripe is added. In many areas, this yellow stripe has been replaced by yellow squares and triangles as appropriate. As mentioned earlier, the colors used for ICW aids are governed by the following rules:

The *port side* of the channel, when traveling toward the south and west, is marked with *green aids* (and a yellow stripe) with *odd numbers*.

The *starboard side* of the channel, when traveling toward the south and west, is marked with *red aids* (and a yellow stripe) with *even numbers*.

All *green* daymarks on daybeacons are *square*, while the *red* daymarks are *triangular* in shape. All have a yellow stripe.

In certain areas, the ICW coincides with other waterways that are buoyed in accordance with the standard practice—that is, green buoys on the left hand when proceeding from seaward, and red buoys on the right. In such joint waterways the standard system of coloring for entering from seaward prevails, and the ICW numbers and yellow markings are omitted, but yellow triangles or squares are added to the regular markings to alert the mariner that these aids have significance in the ICW as well as in the shared waterway. This can cause some serious confusion if the navigator is not alert, because the color of aids may be reversed under such conditions. A vessel proceeding south down the ICW will have red aids on her starboard hand until the channel becomes a joint waterway; at this point the red aids may suddenly be on her port hand. However, the yellow shapes painted on the buoys (squares for the port side of the ICW channel and triangles for the starboard side of the ICW channel) should alert the navigator and be useful in maintaining a consistent orientation. The yellow squares on the red buoys will serve as a reminder that this is a joint waterway and explain the sudden reversal.

AIDS TO NAVIGATION ON THE WESTERN RIVERS

625   The Mississippi River and its tributaries, as well as a number of other rivers that flow into the Gulf of Mexico, use a somewhat different scheme from other U.S. waters. The color system conforms to the U.S. lateral system (of red-right-returning from sea), but mariners *refer* to "right side" and "left side" of the channels (the conventional direction) as proceeding downstream *toward* the sea. Buoys are not numbered. Lights and daybeacons *are* numbered, but *not* in the even-odd style of the lateral system; numbers relate to the distance upstream in *statute* miles from some designated point of origin. Lights and lighted buoys on the starboard side proceeding downriver show a single green or white flash; those on the port side show a *double* red or white flash. Special diamond-shape "crossing" daymarks are used at bends where the deeper channel crosses from one side of the river to the other (see Appendix D).

UNIFORM STATE WATERWAY MARKING SYSTEM

626   To provide for consistent marking of U.S. internal waters not subject to federal jurisdiction, the Uniform State Waterway Marking System (USWMS) has been established. This consists of regulatory buoys and signs, plus buoys in either the lateral system or a cardinal system (see Appendix D).

The conventional direction in the USWMS is upstream or toward the head of navigation.

The USWMS uses black buoys instead of green to mark the port sides of channels; white buoys with red tops indicate an obstruction that should be passed to the south or west; white buoys with black tops mark an obstruction that should be passed to the north or east; a red and white vertically striped buoy indicates that an obstruction exists between it and the nearest shore; and mooring buoys are white with a horizontal blue band midway between the water line and the top of the buoy.

Chapter 7   Compasses

THE MAGNETIC COMPASS

701   The origins of the magnetic compass are not precisely recorded by history; it is one of the oldest, if not the oldest, of the navigator's instruments. It was almost certainly developed independently in several different seagoing cultures. The Vikings were apparently familiar with it in the eleventh century and the Chinese possibly even earlier, as seamen in those areas were familiar with the natural magnetic properties of lodestone, a type of iron ore. Although historical records are lacking, the first compasses most likely consisted of a piece of lodestone placed on a chip of wood floating in a bowl of water. Soon this developed into an iron needle thrust through a straw and floated on the surface of a container of water; a lodestone had to be applied to the needle to magnetize it each time this "compass" was to be used.

Initially, compasses were used only to indicate north, but subsequently the concept of marking other directions around the rim of the bowl was introduced. The directions were given the names of the various winds, now known as North, East, South, and West; these are the *cardinal* directions. For more accuracy, *intercardinal* directions were introduced: NE, SE, SW, and NW. Still finer subdivisions are the *combination directions:* NNE (spoken "north-north-east"), ENE, ESE, and so on; and the *bypoints:* N by E (spoken "north-by-east"), NE by E (spoken "north-east-by-east"), and so on. This system results in a complete circle divided into 32 points (1 point = 11^1/$_4$°), and there are half-points and quarter-points (see fig. 701). The point system was widely used until relatively modern times but is now obsolete except for some minor use on sailing

craft and generalized use in indicating the direction of wind. Modern compasses use the standard 360-degree system instead of the archaic 32-point system that served mariners for centuries.

Because of the difficulty at sea in using a needle floating freely in an open bowl of water, the next development was that of using a needle attached to a pivot at the center of a dry bowl. Not for some centuries was the liquid put back in, this time in an enclosed chamber, as now is the case with the modern magnetic compass.

The magnetic compass still retains its importance despite the invention of the gyrocompass. While the latter is an extremely accurate instrument, it is relatively expensive, highly complex, dependent on an electrical power supply, and subject to mechanical damage. The magnetic compass, on the other hand, is less expensive, entirely self-contained, fairly simple, and not easily damaged.

One problem with the magnetic compass is that set-up and maintenance can be somewhat intimidating to the inexperienced mariner. There are professional compass adjustors whose services are available to those unwilling to take on the relative complexity of setting up or periodically adjusting magnetic compasses. Compass adjustment is explained in Appendix C.

Standard and Steering Compasses

702   Some vessels carry two magnetic compasses called the "standard compass" and the "steering compass." The standard compass, whenever possible, is located on the ship's centerline at a point where it will be least affected by unfavorable magnetic influences. Headings read from this compass are termed *per standard compass* (psc). The steering

	Points	Angular measure (° ′ ″)		Points	Angular measure (° ′ ″)
NORTH TO EAST			**SOUTH TO WEST**		
North	0	0 00 00	South	16	180 00 00
N¼E	¼	2 48 45	S¼W	16¼	182 48 45
N½E	½	5 37 30	S½W	16½	185 37 30
N¾E	¾	8 26 15	S¾W	16¾	188 26 15
N by E	1	11 15 00	S by W	17	191 15 00
N by E¼E	1¼	14 03 45	S by W¼W	17¼	194 03 45
N by E½E	1½	16 52 30	S by W½W	17½	196 52 30
N by E¾E	1¾	19 41 15	S by W¾W	17¾	199 41 15
NNE	2	22 30 00	SSW	18	202 30 00
NNE¼E	2¼	25 18 45	SSW¼W	18¼	205 18 45
NNE½E	2½	28 07 30	SSW½W	18½	208 07 30
NNE¾E	2¾	30 56 15	SSW¾W	18¾	210 56 15
NE by N	3	33 45 00	SW by S	19	213 45 00
NE¾N	3¼	36 33 45	SW¾S	19¼	216 33 45
NE½N	3½	39 22 30	SW½S	19½	219 22 30
NE¼N	3¾	42 11 15	SW¼S	19¾	222 11 15
NE	4	45 00 00	SW	20	225 00 00
NE¼E	4¼	47 48 45	SW¼W	20¼	227 48 45
NE½E	4½	50 37 30	SW½W	20½	230 37 30
NE¾E	4¾	53 26 15	SW¾W	20¾	233 26 15
NE by E	5	56 15 00	SW by W	21	236 15 00
NE by E¼E	5¼	59 03 45	SW by W¼W	21¼	239 03 45
NE by E½E	5½	61 52 30	SW by W½W	21½	241 52 30
NE by E¾E	5¾	64 41 15	SW by W¾W	21¾	244 41 15
ENE	6	67 30 00	WSW	22	247 30 00
ENE¼E	6¼	70 18 45	WSW¼W	22¼	250 18 45
ENE½E	6½	73 07 30	WSW½W	22½	253 07 30
ENE¾E	6¾	75 56 15	WSW¾W	22¾	255 56 15
E by N	7	78 45 00	W by S	23	258 45 00
E¾N	7¼	81 33 45	W¾S	23¼	261 33 45
E½N	7½	84 22 30	W½S	23½	264 22 30
E¼N	7¾	87 11 15	W¼S	23¾	267 11 15
EAST TO SOUTH			**WEST TO NORTH**		
East	8	90 00 00	West	24	270 00 00
E¼S	8¼	92 48 45	W¼N	24¼	272 48 45
E½S	8½	95 37 30	W½N	24½	275 37 30
E¾S	8¾	98 26 15	W¾N	24¾	278 26 15
E by S	9	101 15 00	W by N	25	281 15 00
ESE¾E	9¼	104 03 45	WNW¾W	25¼	284 03 45
ESE½E	9½	106 52 30	WNW½W	25½	286 52 30
ESE¼E	9¾	109 41 15	WNW¼W	25¾	289 41 15
ESE	10	112 30 00	WNW	26	292 30 00
SE by E¾E	10¼	115 18 45	NW by W¾W	26¼	295 18 45
SE by E½E	10½	118 07 30	NW by W½W	26½	298 07 30
SE by E¼E	10¾	120 56 15	NW by W¼W	26¾	300 56 15
SE by E	11	123 45 00	NW by W	27	303 45 00
SE¾E	11¼	126 33 45	NW¾W	27¼	306 33 45
SE½E	11½	129 22 30	NW½W	27½	309 22 30
SE¼E	11¾	132 11 15	NW¼W	27¾	312 11 15
SE	12	135 00 00	NW	28	315 00 00
SE¼S	12¼	137 48 45	NW¼N	28¼	317 48 45
SE½S	12½	140 37 30	NW½N	28½	320 37 30
SE¾S	12¾	143 26 15	NW¾N	28¾	323 26 15
SE by S	13	146 15 00	NW by N	29	326 15 00
SSE¾E	13¼	149 03 45	NNW¾W	29¼	329 03 45
SSE½E	13½	151 52 30	NNW½W	29½	331 52 30
SSE¼E	13¾	154 41 15	NNW¼W	29¾	334 41 15
SSE	14	157 30 00	NNW	30	337 30 00
S by E¾E	14¼	160 18 45	N by W¾W	30¼	340 18 45
S by E½E	14½	163 07 30	N by W½W	30½	343 07 30
S by E¼E	14¾	165 56 15	N by W¼W	30¾	345 56 15
S by E	15	168 45 00	N by W	31	348 45 00
S¾E	15¼	171 33 45	N¾W	31¼	351 33 45
S½E	15½	174 22 30	N½W	31½	354 22 30
S¼E	15¾	177 11 15	N¼W	31¾	357 11 15
South	16	180 00 00	North	32	360 00 00

Fig. 701. Conversion table, points to degrees.

compass in most ships is also located near the centerline, just forward of the ship's helm, where it can be seen easily by the helmsman. Its headings are termed *per steering compass* (p stg c).

Many small craft will have only a single magnetic compass to serve both functions described above for larger vessels. In some instances it will not be possible to mount it on the centerline, but it still must be properly aligned parallel to the vessel's keel. Another useful form of magnetic compass usually found on small craft is a *hand-bearing compass*. This is a small, portable unit that is used for taking bearings all around the horizon from many locations on the craft (see fig. 702).

The information that follows takes note of the continuing importance of the magnetic compass, despite the great advances made in the field of the

Fig. 702. A hand-bearing compass.

gyrocompass. It deals only briefly with the theory of magnetism, and is not intended as a treatise for the professional compass adjustor. Compasses require some rather intricate adjustments to assure maximum efficiency and the theory of compass adjustment is covered in detail in Bowditch's *American Practical Navigator* (NIMA Pub. No. 9).

Magnetic Principles

703   Magnetism is a fundamental physical phenomenon that occurs both naturally, as in a lodestone mentioned above, and artificially by the electrical process of induction. It is the property of certain metals to attract or repel items of like material or certain other metals. An object that exhibits the property of magnetism is called a magnet. It can be elongated, as in a bar magnet, shaped like a horseshoe, or take other forms. The space around each magnet in which its influence can be detected is called its *field;* this can be pictured as being composed of many lines of force that represent its field. The ends of a magnet are called *poles,* and they exhibit different properties of repulsion and attraction, called *polarity.* Each magnet will have a *north pole* and a *south pole* and they will be exactly opposite in polarity. A basic law of magnetism is that poles of the *same polarity repel* each other and those of *opposite polarity attract.* Thus the north pole of one magnet attracts the south pole of another magnet but repels another north pole.

The Earth as a Magnet

704   The Earth may be visualized as having a bar magnet within it, radiating lines of force that may be detected on the surface. Like a simple bar magnet, the Earth has a north magnetic pole and a south magnetic pole (see fig. 704). This "internal magnet" is not exactly aligned with the Earth's axis but is nearly so. The consequence of this divergence is that the magnetic poles are *not* at the same locations as the geographic poles; furthermore, the locations of the magnetic poles vary with time. These two factors complicate the use of a magnetic compass. The Earth's north magnetic pole is currently in the vicinity of latitude 78.9° N, longitude 103.8° W, and the south magnetic pole is near 65.4° S, 139.5° E; these positions are somewhat indefinite and change irregularly over the years. Some studies have shown that the poles appear to move in daily cycles over an elliptical path having a major axis of about 50 miles; this movement is too slight to affect practical navigation except in nonpolar latitudes.

The Earth's magnetic field is not constant in either direction or intensity. The changes in direc-

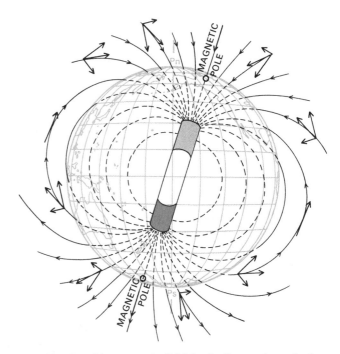

Fig. 704. Earth's magnetic field is similar to that of a bar magnet.

tion are significant in navigation, but the changes in intensity are not of immediate importance to a navigator. Though not well understood, it is known that there have been twelve reversals of the Earth's magnetic polarity over the past nine million years and that we are overdue for another. The Earth's field intensity has decreased 50 percent in the last 4,000 years, and one study predicts that in 1,200 years or so magnetic compasses will become useless—there will be no field to direct them and they will point in any direction. Although all decreases do not result in reversal, when the field returns a few centuries later, its polarity is more likely than not to have reversed.

Variation

705   The lines of force running between the magnetic poles can be defined as *magnetic meridians.* As has already been pointed out, the Earth's magnetic poles are not in the same positions as those poles defined by the Earth's axis of rotation (geographic poles). If they were, and if the Earth were made up of a uniformly magnetic material, the magnetic meridians would line up exactly with the geographic ones. Instead, we find that the magnetic meridians do not coincide and are somewhat irregular (primarily caused by the non-uniform distribution of magnetic material within the Earth). The difference at any location between the directions of the magnetic and true meridians is called *variation.* It

can also be described as the difference between true north and the direction that a compass would point if free of all local influences. Variation is labeled *easterly* and marked *E* if the compass needle, aligned with the magnetic meridian, points eastward or to the *right* of true north; and *westerly* (marked *W*), if it points to the *left*.

Variation is important to the navigator because a magnetic compass, responding to the Earth's magnetic field, is in error in measuring true geographic direction by the amount of the variation (Var. or V). Since variation is caused by the Earth's magnetic field, its value changes with the geographic location of a vessel, but is the same for all headings of that vessel at any specific position and for all vessels at or near that position.

To further complicate things, variation is not constant. It changes over time and some of those changes must be taken into account by the navigator. There are diurnal (daily) changes, but they are too small to be significant (except in polar regions, where diurnal changes of as much as 7° have been observed). But those changes occurring over a longer period of time, called *secular changes,* must be taken into account to prevent serious errors. Although secular change to the Earth's magnetic field has been under observation for more than three hundred years, the length of its period has not been fully established. The change generally consists of a reasonably steady increase or decrease, which may continue for many years, sometimes reaching large values. It can then remain nearly unvarying for a few years and ultimately reverse its trend.

Fortunately for the navigator, future values of secular change to variation can be predicted with reasonable accuracy, and this information is printed on modern charts within special diagrams known as *compass roses* (see fig. 705). True (geographic) directions are printed around the outside of the rose and magnetic directions are indicated on an inner ring, offset by the amount of variation for that part of the world when the chart was made. The amount of the variation for that year and the amount of predicted annual change in variation are indicated in the center of the rings as shown. To get the new variation for the current year the navigator need only multiply the annual change indicated by the number of years that have transpired since the chart was made, and add or subtract that amount as appropriate from the initial variation indicated. It is important to realize that the predictions of change in the variation are intended for short-term use—a period of only a few years. With time, those predic-

tions become less reliable and predictions on an older chart may be in error, so the latest chart editions available should always be used.

Compass Construction

706 The basic mechanism of modern magnetic compasses is the same as that of the very earliest ones used—a magnet freely suspended so that it is able to align itself with the magnetic field of the Earth. Refinements have been added for greater accuracy, steadiness of indication, and ease of reading, but the fundamental mechanism remains unchanged.

The modern marine magnetic compass is contained in a glass-topped bowl made of nonmagnetic material. One example of a venerable old compass that has served the U.S. Navy for many decades is the Navy standard No. 1 seven-and-one-half-inch compass, shown in figure 706a. A sectional view (see fig. 706b) illustrates the construction of the compass and some of the components. In the photograph, one can see the *lubber's line* (at about 355°), which is permanently mounted so that it is aligned with the ship's centerline and indicates the direction of the vessel's head. The card is marked around its outer edge with graduations at 10-degree intervals from 000° clockwise through 360°. Cardinal and intercardinal directions are also shown.

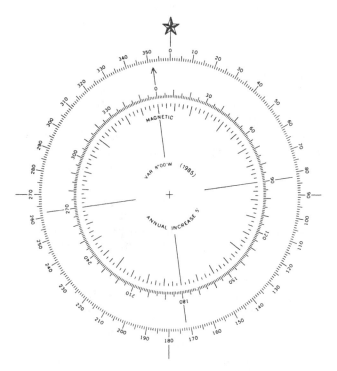

Fig. 705. Compass rose, showing variation and annual rate of change.

Fig. 706a. U.S. Navy standard compass.

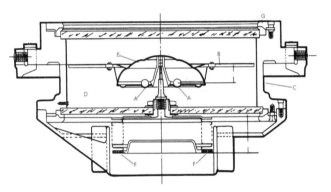

Fig. 706b. Sectional view of a magnetic compass.

Fig. 706c. A compass binnacle.

In the sectional view, the letter *C* indicates the bowl with its cover secured by the bezel ring (*G*). At the center of the bottom of the bowl is a vertical pin, the pivot, upon which the compass card (*B*), rests. Attached to the bottom of this card are two or more magnets (*A*) aligned with the north-south axis of the compass card. In order to reduce friction on the pivot and to dampen vibration, the compass bowl is filled with a clear fluid (*D*) that is resistant to freezing. The card has a *float* or air chamber (*E*), designed so that it will support all but a very small percentage of the weight of the card with its attached magnets. Lastly, the bowl is fitted with an *expansion bellows* (*F*), which permits the bowl to remain filled as the liquid expands and contracts with temperature changes.

The bowl is supported in *gimbals*, or double rings, hinged on both the fore and aft and the athwartships axes. These gimbals permit the compass bowl to remain horizontal, or nearly so, regardless of the vessel's rolling or pitching. The gimbaled compass is mounted in a *binnacle*, or stand, made of nonmagnetic material. One type of binnacle is shown in figure 706c.

Much research has gone into the development of the magnetic compass to bring it to its present high state of accuracy and reliability. Metallic alloys have been intensively studied in order that magnets of increased strength and retentivity might be produced. Alloys of nickel, cobalt, and other metals have proven far superior to the iron formerly used in both these respects. In addition, many advances have been made in protecting the needle from mechanical disturbances, in reducing its oscillations (called *hunting*) and in the presentation of the directional readout.

On some modern compasses a circular or ring magnet is used, replacing the bar magnets attached to the compass card. Because of its circular shape, the ring magnet causes less friction with the fluid in the compass bowl as the ship turns, producing an exceptionally steady card.

There are other components that are used to offset various forces that can affect the accuracy of the compass. The most obvious on some magnetic compasses are the large metal balls called *quadrantal spheres* mounted on adjustable rails on either side of the compass. They are used to compensate for induced magnetism in vessels constructed of steel. Others, such as a *Flinders bar* are less obvious but no less important. These components are explained in more detail in Appendix C.

A *spherical compass* is illustrated in figure 706d. This type of compass is popular among yachtsmen, as well as with some commercial operators, because it offers several advantages over the conventional flat-topped compass. These compasses are internally gimbaled, and the compass card is pivoted at the center of the sphere, assuring maximum stability of the card in all conditions of pitch, roll, and heave. In addition, the transparent spherical dome of the compass acts as a powerful magnifying glass, and greatly increases the apparent size of the compass card in the area of the lubber's line. A "dished" card, slightly concave, together with spherical dome, permits such a compass to be read accurately from a distance of 10 feet (3 m) or more. When fitted with shock-absorbing mounts, a spherical compass functions very well in high-speed boats, despite vibration and shock in heavy seas.

Operation of a Magnetic Compass

707 Assuming for the moment that there are no local influences (objects of magnetic material or electrical currents), when a compass is mounted on a vessel, its magnets align themselves with Earth's magnetic field. The compass card will maintain this alignment regardless of the vessel's heading and the 000° mark on the card always points in the direction of *compass north.*

The vessel's *compass heading* is indicated by the lubber's line. When a compass is first installed, great care is taken to align the lubber's line exactly parallel to the centerline of the ship. The compass bowl and lubber's line will then turn with the vessel, and the direction of the lubber's line from the center of the compass will always represent the direction of the ship's head. Since the 000° mark on the card is always toward the magnetic north, the direction indicated on the compass card by the lubber's line is the ship's heading. As the ship turns, the lubber's line turns with it, while the compass card remains

Fig. 706d. A spherical compass.

aligned with compass north, virtually suspended in space, so that the heading at any moment is indicated at the lubber's line. *Remember—it is the lubber's line, and not the compass card, that turns.*

Deviation

708 As stated above, a compass needle free to turn horizontally tends to align itself with Earth's magnetic lines of force. But because ships and boats have marked magnetic properties of their own, a compass needle can be significantly deflected from the Earth's magnetic meridian. This divergence between the north-south axis of the compass card and the magnetic meridian is called *deviation* (Dev. or D). It is particularly present in a steel-hulled vessel, but even in a vessel made of wood or fiberglass there is enough magnetic material on board—engines, fuel and water tanks, rigging, and so on—to cause some deviation.

Direct currents flowing in straight wires also create magnetic fields that can cause deviation. Care must be taken that wiring in the vicinity of a compass is properly installed to eliminate or reduce effects on the compass; checks must be made for deviation with the circuits turned on and off.

If no deviation is present, the compass card lies with its axis in the magnetic meridian, and its north point indicates the direction of magnetic north. If deviation is present and the north point of the compass points eastward of magnetic north, the deviation is considered *easterly* and marked *E.* If it points westward of magnetic north, the deviation is *westerly* and marked *W.*

While variation is caused by Earth's natural magnetism and deviation is the result of local influences, the two are similar in their effects and in the way they must be treated by the navigator. The navigator finds the correct variation by referring to the chart of his area. Deviation, however, is not so simple to ascertain. It varies not only on different ships, but it also varies with changes in the ship's heading.

Compass Error

709 The algebraic sum of variation and deviation is termed *compass error.* The navigator must understand thoroughly how to apply variation, deviation, and compass error, as he or she is frequently required to use them in converting one kind of direction to another.

From the foregoing it should be apparent that there are three ways in which a direction can be expressed:

As *true,* when referred to the *true (geographic) meridian* as the origin of measurement.

As *magnetic,* when referred to the *magnetic meridian* as the origin of measurement.

As *compass,* when referred to the axis of the *compass card* as the origin of measurement.

Any given direction may be expressed in all three of these ways, if it is understood that:

True differs from *magnetic* by *variation.*
Magnetic differs from *compass* by *deviation.*
Compass differs from *true* by *compass error* (variation *and* deviation).

Figure 709a shows a compass card surrounded by a compass rose similar to the type you would find on a chart, with the outline of a vessel superimposed in blue. The outer circle of the compass rose indicates true directions, while the inner ring shows magnetic directions. From this diagram, it can be seen that the ship's compass heading (read off the compass card) is 301°, that the ship's magnetic heading (read off the magnetic compass rose) is 309°, and that the ship's true heading (read off the true compass rose is 321°. From the discussion above, it should be apparent that the deviation in this case is 8° E (the alignment of the compass card is 8° eastward of the magnetic meridian), and that the variation is 12° E (the magnetic meridian is 12° eastward of the true meridian).

Viewed another way, consider the observer to be at the blue "O" in the figure. The ship's head is marked by the line labeled LL (for lubber's line). The blue line OC shows the direction of the compass needle. OM is the direction of the magnetic meridian, and OT the true meridian. It can be seen that OM is 12° eastward (right) of OT; therefore, the variation at that position is 12° E. OC is 8° eastward (right) of OM; therefore, the deviation is 8° E.

Since compass error is the algebraic sum of the variation and deviation, in this case CE = 20° E. It is added to the compass direction of C (0° on compass card) to obtain the true direction of C (020° on the true rose).

The bearing of object A from the ship is shown as 020° compass, 028° magnetic, and 040° true. (Remember that bearings are always expressed in three-numeral groups.)

As already noted, easterly deviation is added to compass and easterly variation is added to magnetic when converting to true. Conversely, they are subtracted when converting in the reverse order.

Figures 709b and 709c show different directional combinations of variation and deviation.

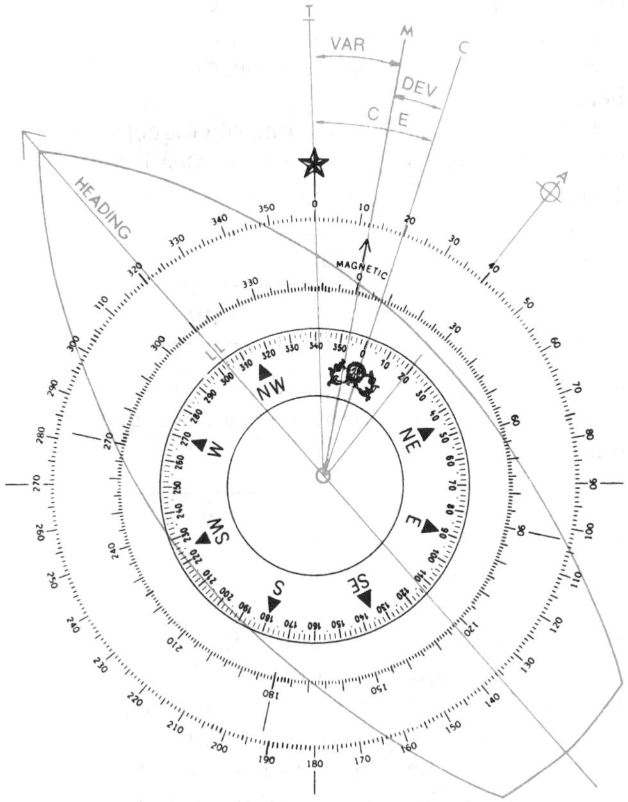

Fig. 709a. Compass error.

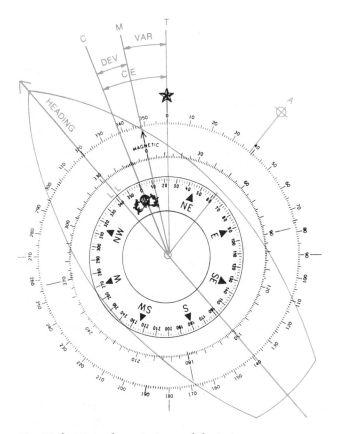

Fig. 709b. Westerly variation and deviation.

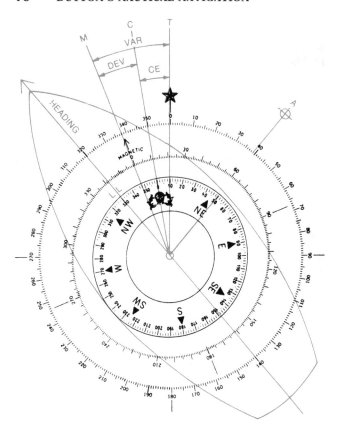

Fig. 709c. Westerly variation, but easterly deviation.

Rules for Applying Compass Errors

710 It is convenient to have a rule of thumb to serve as a memory aid in applying the above principles. The following has served mariners for a long time: *When correcting, easterly errors are added,* or simply, *correcting add east.* When applying this rule, it is necessary to consider a compass direction as the "least correct" expression of direction, as it contains two "errors," variation and deviation. Magnetic direction is thus "more correct" than compass as it contains only one error, variation. This is the case even when the axis of the compass card is closer to the true meridian than is the magnetic meridian (because the errors are offsetting). Magnetic direction is, however, "less correct" than true direction, which contains *no errors.* Hence the process of converting a compass direction to a magnetic or true direction, or of converting a magnetic direction to a true direction, is one of "correcting," or removing errors. If easterly errors are added, it is obvious that westerly errors are subtracted, and no separate rule is needed.

Navigators must also be able to convert a true direction to a magnetic one, or a magnetic direction to a compass direction, by applying the known errors of variation and deviation, and this process is

logically called *uncorrecting.* If easterly errors are added and westerly errors subtracted when correcting, then the *reverse is true when uncorrecting.* Hence, the one rule, *correcting add east,* is sufficient to cover all four possible situations:

Correcting—add east, subtract west.
Uncorrecting—add west, subtract east.

Another method for remembering the rules of correcting and uncorrecting that works for many people involves using the first letters of the appropriate words: Compass, Deviation, Magnetic, Variation, and True and letting these be the initial letters of words that form a nonsensical but easy-to-remember sentence: *Can Dead Men Vote Twice?* The addition of "*At Elections*" to the sentence will assist in remembering that in the direction C-D-M-V-T the procedure is to *Add East.* Using this memory aid, write down just the initial letters of the sentence and use them to guide you through the calculations. (Do not feel foolish for resorting to these methods. Mariners have been doing so for centuries.) By placing the given information in the appropriate places, the unknown values can easily be computed following the rule of add east (*At Elections*).

Example: A ship is heading 127° per standard compass. For this heading the deviation is 16° E, and the variation is 4° W in the area.

Required: (1) The magnetic heading. (2) The true heading.

Solution: The problem is one of correcting (going from compass to true), so Can Dead Men Vote Twice applies. Filling in the known quantities:

C	D	M	V	T
127	16E		4W	

and then applying the "add east" rule ("at elections"), the other quantities can be determined mathematically:

C	D	M	V	T
127	16E	143	4W	139

The deviation is easterly, so it must be added. Hence, the magnetic heading is 127° + 16° = 143°. To find the true direction we are again correcting, and since the variation is westerly, it is subtracted. Hence, the true heading is 143° - 4° = 139°.

Answers: (1) Magnetic heading is 143°. (2) True heading is 139°.

Another memory aid that has been around long before the advent of so-called political correctness may not meet everyone's standards of sensitivity but has proven useful in remembering the opposite process. Again using the first letters, but going in the opposite direction, the memory aid becomes *True Virgins Make Dull Companions*. Since some may feel this memory aid is "politically uncorrect," it is that much more appropriate because it describes the process of "uncorrecting." "*At Weddings*" can be added to the saying to remember to *Add West* in this situation. For those who prefer a less controversial memory aid, the Navy has sanctioned the use of *Timely Vessels Make Distance Count At War* in its Quartermaster rate training manual, and the U.S. Naval Academy teaches *Truly Valiant Marines Don't Cry At Weddings*.

Example: From a chart the true course between two places is found to be 221°. The variation is 9° E and the deviation is 2° W.

Required: (1) The magnetic course. (2) The compass course.

Solution: Since we are going from true to magnetic and then to compass, it is necessary to uncorrect. Using the uncorrecting memory aid, fill in the known information:

T	V	M	D	C
221	9E		2W	

and then applying the "add west" rule ("at weddings"), the other quantities can be determined mathematically:

T	V	M	D	C
221	9E	212	2W	214

The easterly variation is subtracted and the westerly deviation is added. The magnetic course is 221° – 9° = 212°. The compass course is 212° + 2° = 214°.

Answers: (1) Magnetic Course is 212°. (2) Compass Course is 214°.

Naming Variation, Deviation, or Compass Error

711 Another problem that can arise is that of assigning a "name"—east or west—to variation, deviation, or compass error when the numerical value has been found by calculating the differences between two directions. Here, we can use the simple rhyming phrase:

Compass least, error east;
Compass best, error west.

"Least" means lesser numerically, and "best" means greater numerically. For variation from true directions, "magnetic" can be substituted for "compass" in the rhyme.

Example: From a nautical chart we know that two aids to navigation are so placed that when seen in line from seaward they mark the direction of a channel as 161° T. Seen in line from your ship heading up the channel, they bear 157.5° by your magnetic compass. The chart shows the variation for the locality to be 2.5° E.

Required: (1) The compass error. (2) The deviation.

Solution: The numerical difference is 161° – 157.5° = 3.5°. Since "compass is least," the "error is east." Because the compass error is the algebraic sum of the variation and deviation, the deviation can be determined by subtracting the variation from the compass error (3.5° – 2.5° = 1.0°).

Answers: (1) Compass error is 3.5° E. (2) Deviation is 1.0° E.

Deviation Table

712 As stated above, deviation changes with a change in the vessel's heading. The deviation is determined by comparing a direction shown on the compass with the known magnetic direction. Several methods of accomplishing this are explained in Appendix C.

In the Navy, the deviation on various headings is tabulated on a form called a deviation table (or magnetic compass table) and posted near the compass. A copy of the table should also be kept posted in the charthouse and at any other navigation station that is likely to make use of magnetic directions.

Figures 712a and 712b illustrate the standard U.S. Navy form, used for tabulating deviation, compass history, and performance data. Non-naval craft will have deviation tables that are similar to the Navy one.

The Navy form provides blanks for filling in certain information regarding the compass. Note that there are two columns marked "DGOFF" and "DGON." "DG" refers to a ship's degaussing coils, which are installed in many naval vessels and are used to change the ship's magnetic "signature" in order to counter magnetic influence mines. Since the deviation may be different when the degaussing coils are energized, it is necessary to determine the deviation under both conditions. A deviation table for a vessel without degaussing coils obviously would be simpler.

The deviations shown in this illustration are somewhat larger than would be acceptable under

MAGNETIC COMPASS TABLE   NAVSHIPS PP1 3539
NAVSHIPS 3120/4 (REV. 6-72) (FRONT) (Formerly NAVSHIPS 1792)

U.S.S. **S. P. Lee**   NO. **AG 192** (BB, CL, DD, etc.)

[X] PILOT HOUSE   [ ] SECONDARY CONNING STATION   [ ] OTHER

BINNACLE TYPE   [ ] NAVY ST'D   [ ] OTHER

COMPASS **7½"** MAKE **Lionel** SERIAL NO. **12792**

TYPE CC COILS **K**   DATE **15 Sept 1984**

READ INSTRUCTIONS ON BACK BEFORE STARTING ADJUSTMENT

SHIPS HEAD MAGNETIC	DEVIATIONS DG OFF	DG ON	SHIPS HEAD MAGNETIC	DEVIATIONS DG OFF	DG ON
0	4.0 W	4.5 W	180	4.0 E	3.5 E
15	4.0 W	4.0 W	195	5.5 E	5.0 E
30	3.5 W	4.0 W	210	6.5 E	6.0 E
45	3.0 W	3.5 W	225	6.5 E	6.0 E
60	2.5 W	3.0 W	240	6.0 E	5.5 E
75	2.5 W	2.5 W	255	4.5 E	4.0 E
90	2.0 W	2.5 W	270	3.0 E	2.5 E
105	2.0 W	2.0 W	285	0.5 E	0.5 E
120	2.0 W	2.0 W	300	1.0 W	1.0 W
135	1.5 W	1.5 W	315	2.5 W	3.0 W
150	0.5 W	0.5 W	330	3.5 W	3.5 W
165	1.5 E	1.5 E	345	4.0 W	4.0 W

DEVIATIONS DETERMINED BY [ ] SUN'S AZIMUTH [X] GYRO [ ] SHORE BEARINGS

B **4** MAGNETS RED [ ] FORE [ ] AFT AT **13**° FROM COMPASS CARD

C **6** MAGNETS RED [ ] PORT [ ] STBD AT **15**° FROM COMPASS CARD

D **2-7"** [X] SPHERES AT **12**° [X] ATHWARTSHIP [ ] CLOCKWISE [ ] CYLS [ ] SLEWED [ ] CTR. CLOCKWISE

HEELING MAGNET: [X] RED UP [ ] BLUE UP **18**° FROM COMPASS CARD   FLINDERS BAR [X] FORE [ ] AFT **15**°

[ ] LAT **0.190**   [ ] LONG **+0.530**   [X] H   [ ] Z

SIGNED (Navigator)   APPROVED (Commanding)

Fig. 712a. Navy deviation table (front).

VERTICAL INDUCTION DATA
(Fill out completely before adjusting)

RECORD DEVIATION ON AT LEAST TWO ADJACENT CARDINAL HEADINGS

BEFORE STATING ADJUSTMENT: N **5.5W** E **4.0W** S **5.5E** W **6.0E**

RECORD BELOW INFORMATION FROM LAST NAVSHIPS 3120/4 DEVIATION TABLE

DATE **1 Mar 1984** [X] LAT **41° 22' N** [X] LONG **71° 18'W** [ ] H [ ] Z

15 FLINDERS BAR [X] FORWARD [ ] AFT   DEVIATIONS N **4.5W** E **2.0W** S **4.5E** W **3.0E**

RECORD HERE DATA ON RECENT OVERHAULS, GUNFIRE, STRUCTURAL CHANGES, FLASHING, DEPERMING WITH DATES AND EFFECT ON MAGNETIC COMPASSES

Annual shipyard overhaul:
3 June - 7 Sept 1984
Depermed Norfolk NSY: 12 Sept 1984
Abnormal deviation observed

PERFORMANCE DATA

COMPASS AT SEA   [ ] UNSTEADY   [ ] STEADY
COMPASS ACTION   [ ] SLOW   [X] SATISFACTORY
NORMAL DEVIATIONS   [X] CHANGE   [ ] REMAIN RELIABLE
DEGAUSSED DEVIATIONS [X] VARY   [ ] DO NOT VARY

REMARKS   None

INSTRUCTIONS

1. This form shall be filled out by the Navigator for each magnetic compass as set forth in Chapter 9240 of NAVAL SHIPS TECHNICAL MANUAL.

2. When a swing for deviations is made, the deviations should be recorded both with degaussing coils off and with degaussing coils energized at the proper currents for heading and magnetic zone.

3. Each time this form is filled out after a swing for deviations, a copy shall be submitted to: Naval Ship Engineering Center, Hyattsville, Maryland 20782. A letter of transmittal is not required.

4. When choice of box is given, check applicable box.

5. Before adjusting, fill in section on "Vertical Induction Data" above.

NAVSHIPS 3120/4 (REV. 6-72) (REVERSE)

Fig. 712b. Navy deviation table (reverse).

normal conditions for a properly adjusted compass. These larger values are used here to provide practice in calculation and interpolation, the procedure for determining an intermediate value between two tabular listings.

To find the compass course when a magnetic heading deviation table is available, proceed in the manner discussed in the following examples.

Example 1: A ship is to steer course 201° true. The variation is 9° W. DG is off.

Required: The compass course to be steered.

Solution: Applying the variation, the magnetic course is 201° + 9° = 210°.

Enter the deviation table (figure 712a) with the 210° magnetic heading and find that the deviation is 6.5° E. Using the rules explained above, the deviation should be *subtracted* (210° − 6.5° = 203.5°).

Answer: The compass course to be steered is 203.5°.

Example 2: The ship's head is 270° magnetic. A lighthouse bears 136° by compass. The variation is 4° E. DG is off.

Required: The true bearing of the lighthouse.

Solution: Because the deviation depends on the ship's head, *not* the bearing of the lighthouse, we enter the table with 270° and find that the deviation is 3° E. Applying this to the observed bearing of the lighthouse, we add the 3° deviation to get the magnetic bearing of the lighthouse 136° + 3° = 139°, then add the 4° of easterly variation to get the true bearing of the lighthouse (139° + 4 = 143).

Answer: The lighthouse bears 143° T.

Example 3: Using the deviation table of figure 712a, determine the compass courses corresponding to the following true courses in an area where the variation is 12° W and the degaussing is on: 093°, 168°, 228°.

Solution: Add the westerly variation and then either add (if westerly) or subtract (if easterly) the deviations found in the table.

Answers: The compass courses are 107°, 176.5°, and 234.5°.

Example 4: Obviously, headings and bearings will not always come out exactly on the whole figures represented in the deviation table as has been the case in the examples above. But a simple mathematical interpolation will remedy that problem and render an accurate answer. For example, if we wanted to find the compass course corresponding to a true course of 238° in an area where the variation is 12° W, an interpolation would be necessary.

Solution: Add the westerly variation (238° + 12° = 250°) and enter the deviation table with the result. Since there is no entry in the table for 250°, interpolation using the straddling entries (240° and 255°) is necessary and yields 5° E.

Answer: The compass course is 245°.

The degree of precision to which calculations are carried out should be determined by the application of the final figures. In this book, interpolation and other calculations of direction will be carried out to the nearest half-degree. In the practice of navigation at sea, it is not likely that any greater degree of precision in the steering of a vessel could be obtained, and in smaller craft it is probable that the nearest whole would be used.

Critical Values Table

713 A simplified form of deviation table that is easier to use, eliminates interpolation, and is frequently employed on small craft, is the critical values table. It is considerably quicker and easier to use, requiring no interpolation for any whole degree heading. See figure 713 for an example of a partial critical values table.

Digital Flux Gate Magnetic Compass

714 Modern technology improved on an ancient device with the development of the digital flux gate magnetic compass (DFGMC). Intended as a replacement for the Navy standard magnetic compass, this new compass has several advantages.

As should be apparent from the preceding discussions, deviation represents a major inconvenience for mariners. The DFGMC effectively eliminates this error by placing a flux gate sensor atop a mast away from the ship's magnetic fields. An additional benefit is that, unlike a conventional magnetic compass, the DFGMC can provide remote repeaters wherever they are needed without regard to the ship's magnetic field. Each of these repeaters is controlled by the central sensor on the mast so no individual adjustments are necessary.

Ships Heading Compass	Deviation DG Off
000–034	4W
035–077	3W
078–133	2 W
134–150	1 W
151–159	0 W
. . . .	. . .
286–293	0 W
294–303	1 W
304–314	2 W
315–330	3 W
331–360	4 W

Fig. 713. Deviation shown by a table of critical values (extract).

The DFGMC offers several functions not found on conventional compasses. One feature allows the operator to set a reference heading in memory by pressing a "set course" button. A "display damping" feature allows the operator to select how often the digital display is updated ("FAST" = every three seconds; "MED" = every nine seconds; and "SLOW" = every seventeen seconds). FAST is selected for restricted waters and MED or SLOW is used in rough seas or when running at high speeds.

Local variation may be preset in the compass to automatically convert magnetic heading to true. Some caution must be employed with this function since variation changes with location and therefore must be periodically adjusted.

One of the best features of the DFGMC is the capability of the compass to perform an automatic adjustment (known as *auto-compensation*). When selected, this feature allows the compass to automatically correct for even very small changes in the ship's magnetic signature each time the ship completes a 360° turn. An *intentional auto-compensation* can be completed when conditions warrant by deliberately turning the ship through 360° twice at a turn rate that does not exceed 3° per second so that each turn takes more than two minutes to complete. The prudent navigator will ensure that an intentional auto-compensation is among the preparations for entering port or for conducting some other potentially hazardous operation, such as an underway replenishment.

As with most innovations, the many advantages are offset somewhat by fewer disadvantages. The most obvious disadvantage is that the DFGMC is power-dependent. A backup power supply is therefore mandatory, or a conventional magnetic compass must be maintained in addition to the DFGMC to be used in the event of a power failure.

Turning a ship's degaussing system on and off can degrade the accuracy of the DFGMC. This can be corrected by conducting an intentional auto-compensation after a change in degaussing has occurred, but that is not always feasible (particularly when entering or leaving port). One precaution that can be taken, if conditions warrant, is to leave the degaussing system turned on or off (i.e., do not change its status) when operating in restricted waters, waiting until it is feasible to perform an intentional auto-compensation before changing the status of the degaussing system.

GYROCOMPASSES

715 For many centuries, the magnetic compass was the only instrument available at sea for the determination of direction. Early in the twentieth century, an American, Elmer Sperry, and a German, Anshutz Kampfe, independently developed their own versions of an electrical instrument that was capable of indicating true north rather than magnetic north. Because it was based upon a device invented by the French physicist Leon Foucault that he called a *gyroscope*, this new navigational tool became known as a *gyrocompass*.

This important breakthrough was based upon the principle that if a heavy disc or flywheel is mounted to a spindle so that it can spin rapidly and is placed in supporting rings so that it is free to move about its spinning axis as well as its horizontal and vertical axes, it will maintain its original direction in space as long as it is kept spinning. If it is aligned with the true meridian, it will remain that way, virtually unaffected by movements or by terrestrial magnetism. Because it is aligned with the meridian, it will, therefore, remain aligned with true north.

The spinning disc is called a *rotor* and the supporting rings are called *gimbals*. Figure 715a illustrates a simple gyroscope and shows the three degrees of freedom that keep the rotor fixed in space. One degree of freedom for the mass of the wheel or rotor is provided by the spin axis (1) itself. The remaining two degrees of freedom, which allow the spin axis to be pointed in any direction, are provided by the axes of the supporting gimbals, designated as the *torque axis* (2) and the *precession axis* (3). Note that all the axes are mutually perpendicular through the center of gravity of the rotor, thus providing the necessary degrees of freedom.

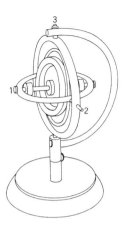

Fig. 715a. A simple gyroscope with three axes of freedom.

The intuitive thinker will have discerned by this time that there is a practical problem inherent in the theoretical concept. If the gyrocompass remains fixed in space, it will lose its orientation to true north as the Earth rotates. For purposes of illustration, if the spin axis were directed toward a star, the axis would continue to point toward the star during its apparent motion across the sky. To an observer on Earth the spin axis would appear to change direction as the Earth rotated eastward. This is illustrated in figure 715b, in which it can be seen that with one rotation of the Earth the direction of the spin axis relative to the Earth would have moved through a complete 360°; it therefore becomes apparent that the gyroscope in this form is not suitable as a compass as it is not north-seeking. To make the gyroscope useful as a direction-indicating instrument with respect to the Earth rather than space, a force (called torque) must be applied that causes it to move (precess) an amount exactly opposite to the apparent movement caused by the rotation of the Earth. If this is accurately accomplished, the gyrocompass will remain oriented to true north.

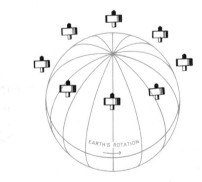

Fig. 715b. A gyroscope with its spin axis horizontal at any point away from the equator, observed from a point in space above the gyroscope.

To take the gyrocompass from the theoretical to the practical, other correctives must be employed. Latitude, for example, affects the operation of the compass in ways that require compensation, and environmental factors cause other problems that must be considered and corrected. But all of these problems are surmountable, and the modern gyrocompass has become an extremely valuable navigational asset for those who can afford them. The high cost of these devices make them impractical for many smaller craft, but they are standard equipment on many commercial and virtually all naval ships.

Basic Gyrocompasses

716 A gyrocompass fundamentally consists of one or more north-seeking gyroscopes with suitable housing, power supply, and so on. To each gyroscope there must be added control elements to apply torques of the correct phase and magnitude to ensure that it will precess in such a manner that the spin axis is brought parallel to the geographic meridian within a reasonable time (a few hours) after the wheel is set spinning, that it will remain so, and that it can quickly return to the meridian if it becomes displaced. A modern gyrocompass system consists of a master unit (or two on larger vessels) with remote readout units called *repeaters* located at various locations in the ship as necessary for navigation and weapons control.

Gyro repeaters are accurate electronic servo-mechanisms, connected to the master unit(s) by cabling, that reproduce the indications of the master gyrocompass at remote locations. There is no practical limit to the number of repeaters that can operate from a single master gyrocompass. Most repeaters are self-synchronous, so that if they become out of step with the master gyro during a temporary power failure, they will automatically line up with the transmitter when power is restored. Like the master gyro, repeaters are generally provided with a damping device to prevent undesirable oscillation when the heading is changed rapidly. Adjustable, self-contained lighting is provided in each repeater so they can be used at night and in low-light conditions.

The gyrocompass is normally kept in continuous operation at sea. Most compasses are equipped with a standby power supply and failure alarms to indicate any malfunction of the compass or loss of the power supply. A standby power supply can be used to automatically operate the compass for a period of time until ship's power can be restored. When in port in safe conditions for a considerable period of time, the gyro can be switched off. A navigator must be aware of the fact that when the gyro is restarted, several hours will be required for the rotor to attain operating speed and for the compass to settle on the meridian. Instruction manuals contain methods to externally precess the compass to speed up this settling period. If a vessel is apt to be ordered to get under way on short notice, her gyrocompass should be kept running. Modern merchant vessels, particularly container ships, are often in port for cargo handling for relatively short periods only, and gyrocompasses are normally not secured.

Advantages and Limitations of Gyrocompasses

717 The advantages of the gyrocompass over the magnetic compass are many. The most obvious is that the gyrocompass seeks the true meridian instead of the magnetic meridian, thereby eliminating the need for variation corrections. For this reason, it can be used near the Earth's magnetic poles, where the magnetic compass is useless. Because it is not affected by surrounding magnetic material, no deviation corrections are necessary either. If an error does exist, it is the same on all headings, and correction is a simple process. Gyrocompass information can be fed electronically into automatic steering equipment, course (DR) recorders, and inertial navigation systems. On warships, data can be injected into weapons control systems.

In spite of the many advantages of a modern gyrocompass, there are certain limitations inherent in its design. Foremost is its need for a constant source of power. Maintenance and repair are more complex than with a magnetic compass, and the gyro's accuracy decreases in latitudes above 75 degrees. If operation is interrupted long enough for it to become disoriented, as much as four hours may be required for it to settle back into reliable operation.

Gyrocompass Errors and Corrections

718 Although the error of a modern, properly adjusted gyrocompass seldom exceeds 1°, and is usually such a small fraction of this that for practical purposes it can be considered zero, this does not mean that it must not be checked frequently. A small error carried for a long time will take a vessel far to one side of the desired objective. Large errors introduced by temporary mechanical failure, when undetected, have caused disasters.

When a gyrocompass is mounted on land, it is affected only by gravity and the Earth's motion. When it is mounted in a ship at sea, consideration must be given to additional factors due to motions of the ship—such as roll, pitch, turning, speed over the ground, and course being steered—and the latitude. The effect of these factors differs in compasses of different basic design. Reference should be made to the appropriate instruction books for a detailed exposition of the theory of a particular compass design, including a description of the automatic and manual corrective features incorporated in the design.

At both the gyrocompass itself and its repeaters, a compass card is attached and is graduated in degrees from 0° to 360°. Just as with a magnetic compass, the direction of the ship's head is indicated by the lubber's line, and as the ship turns, the lubber's line turns with it so that the changing heading is properly indicated on the card (as with the magnetic compass, it is the lubber's line and not the compass card that actually turns). The 0° point on the card always points true north if there is no gyrocompass error. If there is compass error, the 0° point on the compass card will not indicate true north, but a direction either to the left or to the right of the meridian. If the 0° point is to the left, the card has been rotated counterclockwise and all readings of course and bearing made with this error will be too high—this is a westerly error and must be subtracted. And, of course, the opposite is true: if the gyro error results in the compass card being rotated clockwise, its readings will be right (or east) of the true bearings, causing them to be too low and therefore requiring the error to be added in order to obtain true directions. Two memory aids that may help are:

Compass least, error east; compass best, error west.
"GET" can be used to remember *Gyro* + *East* = *True*.

The first memory aid is the same one introduced in the above discussion regarding magnetic compasses and is applicable in this case also to help in remembering how to identify the error (as east or west). The second tells what must be done with the error once it is identified. For example, if you determine that your compass bearing is reading less than a known true bearing, you know that the error is easterly ("compass least, error east") and that the error must be added to any direction determined by your gyrocompass in order to know the true direction. Conversely, a compass reading determined to be more than a true direction means it is westerly and must, therefore, be subtracted. The memory aid described earlier for magnetic compasses applies here too: correcting add east (C-A-E).

When a ship is at sea, the navigator should determine the gyrocompass error at least once each day;

this is required for naval vessels and is desirable on any ship. Over and above this bare minimum, the prudent navigator will take advantage of every opportunity to check the accuracy of his gyro. The importance of so doing is emphasized by a grounding case on record where the failure of a ship's gyro went undetected for a period of over twelve hours, with the result that, at the time of grounding the vessel was more than 110° off course and more than 200 miles out of position.

In order to know whether your compass has an error, you must have some means of determining an actual true bearing. There are several methods of accomplishing this, several of which are summarized and briefly discussed as follows:

1. By comparing the observed gyro bearing of an artificial or natural range with the charted true bearing of the range. When two fixed objects are perfectly aligned, their true bearing can be determined from a chart. Observing them in line with your gyrocompass will give you a bearing, and combining the two will permit you to determine the gyro error.

2. By comparing the gyro bearing of a celestial body, usually the Sun, with the computed true bearing (azimuth) of the same body. At sea, the azimuth method is the only one available, and any time a sight of a celestial body is taken for a line of position, the bearing of the body observed may be taken at the same instant. Azimuths of the Sun at sunrise and sunset, and when its altitude is low in the early morning and late afternoon, are particularly useful for this purpose. The azimuth obtained by computation, when compared with the gyro azimuth, gives a check on the accuracy of the compass. Polaris ("the north star") can be used to check the azimuth at night in low northern latitudes.

3. By "trial and error" adjustment of the observed bearings of three or more lines of position obtained on charted objects equally spaced around the ship until a point fix is obtained. A set of bearings is taken with the repeater on three objects that will yield suitable angles of intersection; these are plotted on the chart. If they meet in a point, the repeater is "on" and there is no gyro error. If the three lines form a triangle, the lines can be adjusted to meet in a point by trial and error; that is, 1° is added to or subtracted from each bearing, and they are again plotted. If the size of the triangle is reduced, the proper estimate of the direction of the error has been made, and after a proper correction is applied, the lines should meet in a point. When they do meet, the

total amount of correction applied to any one bearing is the error of the compass.

4. By comparison with a compass of known error, as for example, a standby gyro compared with a master gyro. If a compass of unknown error is compared with one whose errors are known, the difference in their readings on various headings will provide information from which the errors of the former can be determined. This comparison is generally only possible in ships having two gyrocompasses installed aboard.

Some examples of determining gyro error follow.

Example 1: Two fixed aids to navigation in line are sighted with a gyrocompass repeater, and found to be bearing 136.5° per gyrocompass. According to the chart, the bearing of these aids when in line is 138° true.

Required: The gyro error (GE).

Solution: Numerically, the gyro error is the difference between gyro and true bearings of the objects in range, or 138° – 136.5° = 1.5°. Since this 1.5° would have to be added to the gyro bearing to obtain true bearing, the direction of the error is easterly.

Answer: GE 1.5° E. This means that all bearings shot or courses steered using your gyrocompass must have 1.5° added in order to be true. For example, after determining this error, you look at your chart and decide that to get to the main channel you need to steer a course of 073° T, you should actually steer 074.5° by your compass in order to make good the true course determined. As mentioned above, this error remains the same no matter what the heading (unlike a magnetic compass for which the deviation differs according to the vessel's heading).

Example 2: A round of gyro bearings is taken on three terrestrial objects with the following results:

Tower: 058.0°
Light: 183.0°
Beacon: 310.0°

The three lines of position, when plotted, formed a small triangle. By trial and error, it was found that when 2.0° was subtracted from each bearing, a point fix resulted.

Required: The gyro error (GE).

Solution: Since 2.0° had to be subtracted from each bearing to obtain a perfect fix, and since westerly errors are subtracted, the gyro error is 2.0° W.

Answer: GE 2.0° W. This would mean that 2° would have to be subtracted from all gyro readings in order to get the true bearing or course.

Ring Laser Gyrocompasses

719 A relatively recent technological improvement on the gyrocompass is the ring laser gyro (RLG). Using carefully aligned mirrors, two laser beams travel around a closed circuit (or "ring") in opposite directions until they meet at a special detector. If the vessel in which the gyro is mounted is stationary, the two beams will arrive at the sensor simultaneously and with no difference in the laser frequency. But if the vessel is turning, there will be a shift in frequency caused by the resultant differences in travel time around the ring. Using the Doppler principle, the frequency shift can be measured and translated into compensating information, thereby replicating the functions of a conventional gyroscope without relying upon cumbersome mechanical devices such as rotors, gimbals, and motors. This reliance on electronic rather than mechanical technology allows RLGs to be smaller and less sensitive to shock and vibration. They require less power to run, less maintenance to keep them running, and less cooling to keep them from overheating. Gravity and magnetic fields have no effect upon them, and they require much less start-up time (ten minutes dockside; thirty minutes at sea) than do mechanical gyrocompasses. With these advantages, RLGs are steadily replacing their mechanical forerunners.

Chapter 8

Navigational Equipment

As noted in chapter 1, navigation is both an art and a science, and the scientific aspect is reflected in the "tools of the trade." Some navigational equipment has been discussed in detail in earlier chapters (compasses and charts, for example), so they will be only briefly mentioned here. Equipment used primarily with celestial navigation (such as sextants and chronometers) and electronic equipment (such as GPS and Loran receivers) will be covered in detail in later chapters. This chapter will concentrate on general navigational equipment that does not fit into those more specific categories.

Navigational instruments can be classified in various ways, any of which will result in some overlap. Here they will be considered in groups according to their primary purpose—for measuring direction, speed, depth, and so on.

DIRECTION

801 Whether it is to steer a specific course or to fix one's position by means of bearings, one of the key components of navigation is being able to determine direction. While compasses are the primary instruments for determining direction, there are a number of associated devices used by navigators in conjunction with them.

Azimuth and Bearing Circles

802 As discussed in chapter 1, the term *azimuth* is most often used for stating the direction of a celestial body, while *bearing* is mostly used for the direction of terrestrial objects. This division, however, is not rigid, and at times the terms are used interchangeably. Terrestrial bearings and azimuths are expressed in degrees, using three digits, from 000° at north clockwise through 360°. *True* azimuth or bearing refers to direction with respect to true north, *magnetic* bearing with respect to magnetic north, and *compass* bearing with respect to north as indicated by the compass being used. A *relative* bearing is measured from the ship's head, measuring clockwise with 000° being dead ahead.

Technically, an *azimuth circle* can be used for determining both azimuths of celestial bodies and bearings of terrestrial objects, while a *bearing circle* is equipped only for the latter (having no prism-mirror to assist in celestial observations), but in practice, mariners will often refer to both devices by either name. Both the azimuth circle and bearing circle have a nonmagnetic ring formed to fit snugly over the top of a compass bowl (or onto the top of a gyrocompass repeater), about which it can be turned to any desired direction (see fig. 802). Mounted on the ring is a pair of sighting vanes, consisting of a peep vane (A) and a vertical wire mounted in a suitable frame opposite (B). To observe the bearing of a terrestrial object, the observer looks through the peep vane in the direction of the object, and by means of the finger lugs (C, C´) provided on the circle, she or he rotates the circle until the observed object appears on the vertical wire of the opposite vane. At the base of the opposite vane is a mirror (D) marked with a centerline agreeing with the vertical wire of the vane. This mirror reflects the compass card into the observer's field of view so that the observed object and its bearing can be read simultaneously.

On the azimuth circle, there is also a reflector of dark glass (E) attached to the far vane (called *far* vane because it is *farther* from the eye than is the peep vane when observing). This reflector is mov-

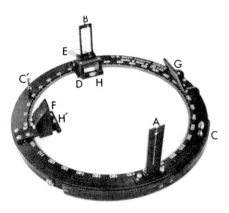

Fig. 802. An azimuth circle.

able about a horizontal axis, enabling the observer to adjust it so that the reflected image of a celestial body can be brought to the eye, and a compass azimuth obtained as has been described for a terrestrial object.

At right angles to the line of sight of the pair of vanes just described, there is a second set of observing devices, designed especially for obtaining a compass azimuth of the Sun. At one extremity of the diameter on which these appliances are mounted is a 45° reflecting prism encased in a metal housing (F). This housing is provided with a narrow slit in which light may be received from a concave mirror diametrically opposite (G), the slit being at the focus of the concave mirror. Light so received is reflected downward by the prism and appears on the graduations of the compass card as a bright narrow band. To observe the compass bearing of the Sun with this arrangement, the observer turns the azimuth circle until the Sun's rays are reflected by the mirror across the card to the prism, and the bearing can then be read on the compass card by means of the narrow band of light.

Two leveling bubbles (H, H′) are provided, one under each far sight vane. The appropriate bubble is used to level the instrument when taking a bearing to eliminate a possible source of inaccuracy.

Telescopic Alidade

803 A telescopic alidade is similar to a bearing circle except that the alidade circle mounts a telescope instead of the sighting vanes. The telescope contains a reticle that can be aligned with the object being observed for greater precision in determining the bearing. The image is magnified, making distant objects appear larger to the observer. A prism arrangement reflects the compass card into the field of vision, enabling the observer to sight the object and its bearing simultaneously.

A more modern version ties in directly to sophisticated electronic navigation systems by permitting the operator to line up the alidade on the object being sighted, then press a button, which automatically transmits the bearing from the compass repeater to the electronic chart (see chapter 4) in use.

Pelorus

804 Though not often used anymore, the pelorus is an adequate (though not desirable) substitute for a compass in places on a vessel where it is not practical to place an actual compass. It is sometimes called a "dumb compass" and is merely a compass card without any magnetic or gyroscopic input.

A pelorus consists essentially of a flat, nonmagnetic, metallic ring mounted in gimbals on a vertical stand, looking much like a compass. The inner edge of the ring is graduated in degrees from 000° at the ship's head clockwise through 360°. This ring encloses a compass card called a *pelorus card*. The card, flush with the ring and the top of the bowl, is rotatable, so that any chosen degree of its graduation may be set to the lubber's line. A small set screw is provided for temporarily securing the card to the ring. Upon the card is mounted a pair of sighting vanes similar to those of a bearing circle. They may be revolved about the center of the card, *independently of the card itself,* and held in any desired position by a central clamp screw. On some models an electric light inside the stand illuminates the card from underneath for night work.

True bearings are obtained by setting the pelorus to the ship's true course, and then turning the card until its true-course graduation coincides with the lubber's line. Secure the card. Line up the sighting vanes approximately on the object to be observed. Direct the steersman to say "Mark! Mark! Mark!" at the instant of the observation. If the steersman was on his course, the bearing was true. If not, it may be corrected by applying the number of degrees the steersman was off, being careful to apply the correction in the proper direction.

Magnetic or compass bearings are taken in exactly the same manner as true bearings, the pelorus card being set beforehand to the magnetic or compass course, respectively. By applying the variation or the compass error to the bearings obtained as appropriate, they can be converted to true bearings for plotting on a chart.

Relative bearings are the easiest to obtain when using the pelorus. Set the 0° graduation of the card to the lubber's line and observe the object. Relative bearings are converted to true bearings for plotting by adding the true heading of the ship to the bearings observed. (Note: In the Royal Navy, a pelorus is the centerline compass repeater on the bridge that is used by the navigator or officer of the watch to navigate.)

Hand-bearing Compass

805 As mentioned in chapter 7, on small craft, bearings are often taken with a hand-bearing compass. Its advantages stem from its ability to be carried to any place on deck from which a bearing can be taken on an object that might not be visible from the steering station due to the vessel's superstructure, sails, and so on. Deviation may or may not exist at locations from which a hand-bearing compass is used; caution is advised. In the event of a failure (unlikely, but possible) of a boat's steering compass, a hand-bearing compass can be used quite adequately if consideration is given to the probability of different values of deviation.

SPEED AND DISTANCE

806 The navigator must have speed and distance information in order to successfully maintain an accurate plot. In nautical navigation, a device used to determine a vessel's speed or distance traveled through the water is called a *log.*

Before modern technology found more efficient means, logs consisted of rather cumbersome and inaccurate devices that involved trailing a line along behind the vessel that had been knotted at specific intervals. By counting the number of knots paid out over a specific interval of time, the ship's speed could be estimated. This device survived for centuries and is the reason why nautical navigators today use the term *knot* to describe a vessel's speed.

It is important to note that there are two kinds of speed used in nautical navigation. *Speed over the ground* (SOG), also called *true speed,* is the vessel's speed relative to the surface of the Earth and is calculated empirically by measuring the time required for a vessel to travel a known distance. *Speed through the water* is measured by instruments that sense the vessel's motion through the water, using some mechanical or electromagnetic principle.

Speed over the ground can be obtained by several means, including a simple calculation of distance covered and time elapsed between fixes on a chart. GPS units (see chapter 17) provide speed readings of the SOG type because they are calculated relative to the Earth's surface and are measured without being affected by the water surrounding the vessel.

There are a number of different logs in use today to measure speed through the water. Some of these integrate values of speed to determine distance traveled as well as speed. Logs usually require the use of a device known as a *rodmeter* that projects through the bottom of the ship into the water and contains a sensing device of some kind that is used to determine speed. Because a rodmeter can be damaged by striking submerged objects, it may be necessary to retract the unit when entering shallow water. A sea valve usually provides a means for closing the hull opening when the rodmeter is withdrawn or housed. The signal received from the sensing device is converted into a readout of speed and distance traveled, which is then transmitted electronically or by synchronous motors to display units where needed on the vessel.

Because logs are subject to the motion of the water, a consequence that should be remembered is that they tend to overread somewhat when moving through a head sea, and to underread with a following sea.

The *pitot-static log,* sometimes called a *pitometer log* (*pit sword* or *pit log*), uses a pitot tube—a device that measures pressures—mounted in the rodmeter to detect differences in the static and dynamic pressures in the water. Static pressure is present when water is not in motion, and dynamic pressure is caused by the motion of the vessel through the water. The device consists of two tubes, one inside the other. One tube is open on the forward side and is subjected to dynamic pressure when the ship is in motion; the other is open on the sides and is exposed only to static pressure. The difference in the two pressures will vary with the speed of the ship.

The pitometer measures the difference in the two pressures and is calibrated to convert those differences into measurable speed.

An *impeller-type log* uses a propeller-like device to produce an electrical signal by which the speed and distance traveled are measured and indicated at one or more remote locations. Typically, the rodmeter head assembly contains an impeller-driven frequency generator. The impeller rotates as it moves through the water, and the frequency generated by the rotary motion is directly proportional to the ship's speed.

The *electromagnetic (EM) log* is generally calibrated for speeds from 0 to 40 knots. Any conductor will produce an electromagnetic field or voltage when it is moved across a magnetic field, or when a magnetic field is moved with respect to the conductor. It is this relative movement of the conductor and the magnetic field producing a measurable induced signal voltage that is used in the EM log. The rodmeter contains an induction device which produces a signal voltage that varies with the speed of the ship through the water. The magnetic field, produced by a coil in the sensing unit, is set up in the water in which the ship is floating. Two Monel buttons, one on each side of the rodmeter, pick up the induced voltage as the ship moves through the water. These logs do not function very efficiently when the vessel has sternway on because the churning water affects the surrounding magnetic field.

Engine revolution counters provide a convenient means of determining speed and distance and are widely used, especially on merchant ships. One of these instruments is in the engine room for each shaft and automatically counts the revolutions of the propellers. By means of a master counter connected to the individual counters, the average revolutions made by all propellers can be obtained. The output from these devices may be either a total number of revolutions or the rate in revolutions per minute (RPM), or both. The records of the acceptance trials of a ship furnish data as to the revolutions required for a mile, as well as the RPM for various speeds. Such data can be derived, or verified, from runs over a measured mile or any known distance. This information is used to construct a curve with RPM as ordinates and corresponding speed in knots as abscissas. From the curve, a *revolution table* is prepared for use on the bridge while under way. It gives the RPM required for each knot of speed. In making use of engine revolutions as speed indicators, the draft of the ship, the condition of its bottom as to cleanliness, and the state of the sea must be considered for additional accuracy.

A few small craft, chiefly ocean-cruising sailboats, still use the traditional *taffrail log,* which consists of a rotor streamed at the end of a braided log line sufficiently far astern to be clear of the wake effect. The log line is connected to an indicating device, usually reading nautical miles and tenths on two separate dials. In sailing ships, this indicator was frequently attached to the taffrail, the hand rail at the after end of the ship, hence the name. Good taffrail logs are quite reliable if kept clean of weeds and other floating debris.

Distances of objects can also be ascertained by using a sextant (see chapter 22) to determine the angle subtended by an object of known height. The angle so measured can be converted to distance by means of trigonometric calculations or by using Tables 15, 16, or 17 in *Bowditch.*

A *stadimeter* is an optical instrument, in some ways similar to a sextant, that is designed to allow the user to sight an object of known height and read the distance of the object directly off the instrument without the need to make additional calculations or to refer to tables. The two general types in use, the Fisk and the Brandon sextant type, are illustrated in figure 806. Both use a system of mirrored optics that permit the user to observe an object directly while simultaneously observing a reflected image of the same object. The stadimeter is constructed in such a way as to use the compared images to measure angles and mechanically compute trigonometric functions, allowing the user to read the distance on a micrometer drum etched with a graduated scale. By first setting in the height of the object being observed (for example, a lighthouse whose height is provided on a chart or in a *Light List*) and then sighting the object through the attached scope, the drum is then turned until the top of the reflected image is brought into coincidence with the bottom of the direct image. The range is then read off the micrometer drum.

One of the most useful means for determining distances is radar. Modern radar systems have great versatility and are very accurate and reliable. The downsides to radar are the expense, sophisticated maintenance requirements, and the need for a continuous power source.

DEPTH

807 Since the days of man's first ventures onto the waters, one of the mariner's major concerns has been the need to know the depth of the water so as to prevent grounding. Thousands of years ago, mariner's in shallow waters used a pole with measured markings to probe the water ahead. A weighted and measured line followed for use in deeper waters and has been part of the mariner's tool kit ever since. Because the weights used were often made of lead, this navigational tool became known as the *lead line.* An added feature was to have a concave base, so that the hollow could be "armed" with tallow or salt-water soap, which could then bring up a sample of bottom sediment to assist in determining position. From the *Historia* of the Greek historian, Herodotus, one learns that this technique was used in and around the mouth of the Nile in the fourth century B.C.: "When one gets 11 fathoms and ooze on the lead, he is one day's journey from Alexandria."

Of the various types of lead lines used for taking soundings, the two most common are the *hand lead,*

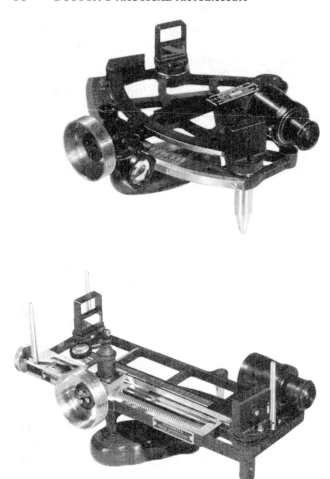

Fig. 806. Stadimeters: Brandon sextant type *(top)* and Fisk type *(bottom)*.

weighing from 7 to 14 pounds, with a line marked to about 25 fathoms; and the *deep-sea lead*, weighing from 30 to 100 pounds, the line being 100 fathoms or more in length. Fathoms that correspond with the marked depths are termed *marks* and intermediate fathoms are called *deeps*. The only fractions of a fathom used are a half and a quarter.

Small vessels often use a lead line with a weight of 2 to 5 pounds on a line of 20 to 30 feet. The line is normally marked with plastic tags giving the depth directly in feet or meters. Boatmen may find a sounding pole useful in some circumstances, particularly if it is marked with the craft's draft and at whole feet above that depth.

Soundings using the lead line can be obtained only in the vicinity of the continental shelf, and only at comparatively long intervals, due to the time consumed in recovering by hand a lead of fifty or more pounds and a hundred or more fathoms of line. A device was eventually invented, called a *sounding machine*, that used fine steel wire and mechanical

methods for retrieving the weight and devices at its end. Because currents and the forward motion of the ship often prevented the sounding wire from being vertical, "sounding bottles" were attached to the wire that measured pressure at the bottom, which could be translated to a measurement of depth. The sounding machine allowed accurate measurements of considerable depths, but even this improvement permitted only a very few measurements to be taken in an hour of continuous effort.

Once electronics came into being, a few simple physical principles could be incorporated to make more accurate and far more convenient depth sounders. A sound pulse generated in the water will echo from most bottoms and can be received by a hydrophone (an underwater microphone). Since the speed of sound in water is known fairly closely, the depth can be determined by measuring the time interval between the generation of the sound and the return of the echo, according to the equation: *depth = speed × ¹/₂ time interval between sound pulse and echo.*

The speed of sound waves in water does vary somewhat with the salinity of the water, its temperature, and the pressure (depth). The variation is not great, and most echo-sounding equipment of American manufacture is calibrated for a speed of 4,800 feet per second (1,463 m/s). Since this assumed speed is equivalent to 800 fathoms per minute, an elapsed time of one second indicates a depth of 400 fathoms (2,400 feet or 731.5 meters). At sea, the actual speed of travel of sound waves is nearly always slightly greater than this calibration speed, and any error introduced lies on the side of safety (except where the water is fresh or extremely cold).

Devices for measuring depth in this manner are variously known as *echo sounders* or *electronic depth sounders*. (The term "fathometer" is often used, but this is properly applied only to the equipment of one manufacturer whose trademark it is.) The essential components of an electronic depth sounder are a transmitter, a transducer, a receiver, and a display (indicator or recorder).

The transmitter generates a pulse of electrical energy at a sonic (audible) frequency in the range of 20 to 20,000 hertz or at an *ultrasonic* frequency, usually 150 to 200 kHz. The returning echo is picked up by the transducer, converted to electrical energy, and sent back to the receiver. The receiver amplifies the very weak returned echo and converts it to a form suitable for visual display.

The transmitted sound signal is actually shaped like a cone as it leaves the transducer. Because the area of the bottom covered by the sound cone is a function of depth, in deep water it can become quite large. Therefore, the trend in the development of newer echo-sounding equipment is toward narrower beams, obtained by using higher frequencies (generally around 200 kHz). Higher frequencies, however, have the disadvantage of greater attenuation and lesser depth range. For survey work, complex arrays of multiple transducers may be used. Transducers may be stabilized to counter the vessel's rolling and pitching motions that could result in erroneous data.

Depth sounders for smaller vessels commonly use either 50 or 200 kHz. Deeper depth penetration is achieved by the lower frequency pulses that employ transducers with sound cones of 40° to 60°. The higher frequency pulses are sent and received with transducers having sound cones of 8° to 12° that provide much sharper definition. Some more expensive models operate on multiple frequencies, using a specially designed transducer that has a different sound cone to match the frequency being used.

Electronic depth sounder displays vary greatly in detail, some providing a digital readout while others use a cathode-ray tube display to show bottom contours. Some provide a paper printout to serve as a record of the depths encountered. Others use multiple colors to indicate different intensities of echoes that can be used to differentiate between the actual bottom and those echoes reflected off schools of fish. Alarm buzzers are included in many units that will sound when depths decrease below a preset figure. Some models have the capability of operating on more than one scale or displaying depth measurements in a choice of units—feet, fathoms, or meters; *it is, of course, essential that the navigator be certain what range and unit of measurement is being used.*

PLOTTING EQUIPMENT

808   Some of the items used by navigators in plotting are as simple as pencils and erasers, while others are very specialized devices.

Dividers are frequently used by the navigator. While there are different designs, all are simply a means of measuring a distance by placing sharp points at two different places on a chart or plotting sheet and then moving that distance to a measurable scale (see fig. 808a). Learning to use the dividers with one hand will keep your other hand free for other purposes. Your dividers should be tight enough to remain as set, but not so tight that setting is difficult. They all have some means of adjustment (usually a simple set screw) that will permit you to make this adjustment. Some navigators prefer to

use "one-hand" dividers that are shaped so that a squeeze in one position closes the distance between the points, while a squeeze in another position opens the gap. Dividers with long legs will allow you to measure greater distances with one setting but are more likely to "slip," while shorter legged dividers are more stable. One kind of divider that is very stable but less easily used is the "bow" style in which the distance between the points is set and maintained by a cross arm with a setting screw (see fig. 808b). The choice is really up to you as which type you find most comfortable and efficient.

Fig. 808a. Dividers are a basic plotting tool for measuring distances and plotting positions.

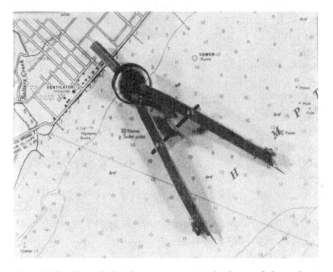

Fig. 808b. "Bow" dividers are particularly useful as their setting cannot be accidentally changed.

Fig. 808c. Parallel rulers.

Drafting *compasses* (not to be confused with magnetic compasses) are convenient for drawing circles and arcs. They are essentially the same as dividers except that there is a pencil lead in place of one of the points. They are used for drawing in the computed visibility circles of lights, constructing arcs as lines of position based upon radar ranges, and other purposes.

Although there are many different kinds of directional plotters, *parallel rulers* are among the simplest (see fig. 808c). While there are variations, the best known consists of two bars—the "rulers"—of the same length connected by a mechanical linkage in such a manner that when one ruler is held in place on the chart and the other moved, the orientation of the ruler that is moved will remain parallel to the stationary ruler. This allows you to move lines from one place on a chart to another (by "walking" the rulers across the chart) while maintaining the direction of the original line.

One example of how this is done would be if you laid a track on a chart down the middle of a channel and wanted to know what course to steer to follow that track (i.e., the direction of the line). You would begin by placing one of the rulers along the track line and hold it firmly in place while opening the other ruler away from the fixed ruler in the direction of the nearest *compass rose*. Then, holding that ruler firmly in place, close the original ruler up to the one you just moved. Holding that one in place, again open the one closest to the rose. Repeat the process as many times as necessary, essentially "walking" the rulers across the chart by alternating the two rulers as stationary and moving, until you have reached the center of the compass rose. You will then be able to read the direction of your track from the compass rose. The key to successful operation is to press the stationary ruler *firmly* against the chart while the other ruler is being moved—slippage at this time will destroy the accuracy of the measurement.

Parallel rulers are somewhat slow, and it is sometimes difficult to keep them from slipping when a direction is to be moved a considerable distance across the chart. Moreover, they are of little value for measuring direction when no compass rose is shown on the chart, as on those of Lambert conformal projections.

For these reasons and as a matter of personal preference, many navigators use one of the various other plotters that are available. Most of these consist of some form of protractor and a straightedge. The AN plotter is an example of this type (see fig. 808d). The 180° scale is used for measuring directions relative to any meridian with an auxiliary scale, rotated 90°, that permits measuring direction relative to any parallel of latitude (as shown it is measuring 186° from A to B). Some plotters have distance markings on the longer edges at typical chart scales.

The *parallel plotter* shown in figure 808e is a device that can be used as either a plotter or a roller-type parallel ruler. It is convenient for use on small craft and has been adopted by many ship navigators.

A pair of ordinary *draftsman's triangles* are also useful in plotting. They need not be of the same type or size. The two hypotenuse (longest) sides are placed together, and the pair is aligned so that the chart line or desired direction is along one of the other four sides (see fig. 808f). By holding one triangle firmly in place and sliding the other with respect to it, alternating between them if the distance is great, the original direction, or one at right angles to it, can be transferred across a chart. The use of two triangles provides a fairly easy and accurate means of drawing both a line and another line at right angles to the first one—something that is often done when plotting celestial sight reductions.

Chart plotting on most large ships is done with a universal drafting machine, also called a *parallel motion protractor*. Figure 808g shows such a device, but smaller and simplified models are sometimes used on recreational and commercial boats. A typical unit consists of a protractor carried on a parallel-

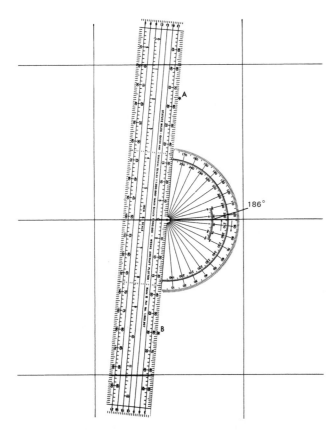

Fig. 808d. Aircraft-type "AN" plotter, often used in nautical navigation.

motion linkage system fastened to the upper left-hand corner of the chart table. The graduated protractor rim (similar to a compass rose) can be rotated and clamped in any position desired. Hence, by orienting it to the directions on a chart (using compass roses or latitude/longitude lines), the linkage permits the movement of the protractor to any part of the chart without change of orientation. Direction can then be instantly determined anywhere on the chart. Several graduated rulers of different length are usually provided. On some models any two of these can be mounted, one as shown and the other at right angles to the first, to facilitate plotting of lines of position from celestial observations. However, most navigators prefer to use a right triangle to obtain the perpendicular rather than deal with the more cumbersome two-ruler arrangement.

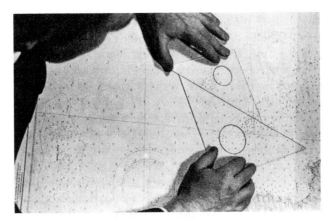

Fig. 808f. Two drafting triangles can be used to transfer a direction across a chart.

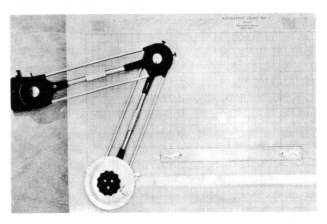

Fig. 808g. A universal drafting machine (also called a "parallel motion protractor") is excellent for navigational plotting.

Plotting Techniques

809   Neatness and accuracy in plotting are essential for safe navigation. Skill will come with experience and practice, but a few hints and suggestions may be of assistance toward both accuracy and speed in plotting.

Use No. 2 pencils for plotting, and keep a number of them handy and well sharpened. Hexagonal pencils are less likely to roll off a chart table than are round pencils. Because of the width of the pencil lead and the conical shape of the sharpened end, a line drawn on a chart with a straightedge will be a

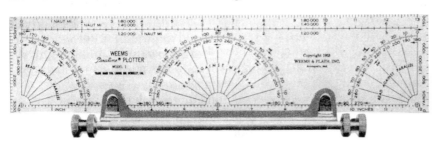

Fig. 808e. Parallel plotter.

slight distance from that edge. Allowing for this distance when placing the straightedge in position will avoid a needless error. Another important point to remember is that the pencil should make the same angle with respect to the straightedge throughout the length of the line.

Draw only light lines on the chart, so that they can be easily erased. Avoid drawing lines longer than necessary, and erase extra lengths. Label all lines and points as soon as drawn. An unlabeled line on a chart is a possible source of error. Avoid drawing lines through symbols for navigational aids, so that the symbols will not be made less distinct when the line is later erased. Be sure to test erasers on an unimportant portion of a chart to be sure they are the right kind that will clean your chart without damaging it.

Tape the chart to the table or desk used to maintain proper orientation. Because thumbtacks are apt to tear the chart and allow it to shift, tape is preferable. Masking tape should be used because it will not harm the surface of the chart when removed, provided it has not been left in place for an extended time and allowed to harden.

If the chart is too large to fit on the table used, determine the extent of the chart that must be used, then fold under the portions that will not be required. Be sure to leave one latitude scale and one longitude scale available for measurement.

CALCULATING EQUIPMENT

810   The *nautical slide rule* is a circular device that allows you to quickly solve time-speed-distance problems (see fig. 810a). Given any two of these factors, the third may be easily obtained. The yards scale is based on the assumption that 1 nautical mile equals 2,000 yards; this is an assumption frequently used in maritime surface navigation—the slight error, 1.25 percent, is ignored for the convenience gained. Therefore, if the distance scale is set at 3 miles, it will also read 6,000 yards. The figures on the distance scale may also be used in solving problems involving statute miles; however, in this case, the yard scale must *not* be used. In using the slide rule, when the distance is one of the known factors, the distance setting should be made *first*. When speed is a known factor, it should always be set last, as the speed scale is read through both dials.

Many nautical charts include a *Logarithmic Time, Speed, and Distance Scale* along with instructions for its use (see fig. 810b). Very simply, all you need do is place the right point of your divider on the right edge (marked "60") and the

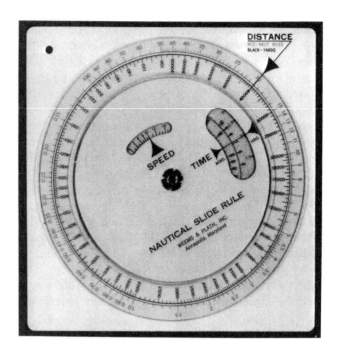

Fig. 810a. Nautical slide rule.

left point on the number representing the ship's speed; then, without changing the spread of the dividers, lift them and place the right point on the number representing the minutes of time that you are measuring, and the left point will come to rest on the distance traveled. Other ways to use this scale are explained in the accompanying instructions and will become obvious and second-nature to you with practice.

A regular electronic calculator is very useful for solving many navigational problems. Some specialized electronic navigational calculators are available as well, obviating the need for the mariner to know the requisite formulas. A programmable calculator can further enhance the navigator's capabilities, and specially designed software programs for computers have taken a lot of the guesswork out of navigation.

TIME MEASUREMENT

811   Knowledge of the time of day and of elapsed time is essential in many phases of navigation. A stop watch or a navigational timer, which can be started and stopped at will, is of particular value in timing the period of a navigational light to determine its characteristic for purposes of identification. When equipped with a luminous dial and sweep-second hand, the watch may be read without the use of artificial light, thereby maintaining night-adapted vision.

Fig. 810b. Logarithmic speed-time-distance scale.

Chronographs that accurately keep the time of day while allowing separate timing events to be measured are particularly useful (see fig. 811).

Chronometers are highly accurate mechanical timepieces that have been an essential part of the navigator's kit for hundreds of years. These sensitive instruments were essential for celestial navigation (and still are, in the absence of other electronic replacements).

Global Positioning Systems (GPS) (see chapter 17) keep time even more accurately than chronometers and can be safely relied upon as long as electrical power is available.

WEATHER INSTRUMENTS

812   While weather is not used as a factor in determining position and is, therefore, not an actual component of the science of navigation, mariners make few navigational decisions without considering the weather. There are various instruments that are essential in monitoring and predicting weather conditions.

A *barometer* is an instrument for determining the atmospheric pressure, a meteorological element of considerable interest to a mariner, because its fluctuations provide an index useful in predicting weather, an important factor in navigation. Because bad weather is usually associated with regions of low atmospheric pressure and good weather with areas of high pressure, a rapidly falling barometer usually indicates the approach of a storm.

Two general types of barometers are used. The *mercurial barometer* consists essentially of a column of mercury in a tube, the upper end of which is closed and the lower end open to the atmosphere. The height of the column of mercury supported by the atmosphere is read by a suitable scale. Readings are in inches of mercury. The standard atmospheric pressure used for reference is 29.92 inches.

An *aneroid barometer* consists essentially of a short metal cylinder from which the air has been partly exhausted. The ends of the cylinder, being of thin metal, expand or contract as the external atmospheric pressure changes. This motion is transferred by a suitable mechanical linkage to a registering device that may be graduated in either inches of mercury or millibars (equivalent to 1,000 dynes per square centimeter—a standard atmospheric pressure is 1,013.25 millibars), or both. A reading of one scale can be converted to one of the other by table or arithmetically if both scales are not shown.

A *barograph* is a recording instrument that provides a permanent record of atmospheric pressure over a period of time. It is a relatively sensitive instrument and must be protected from shock and vibration; it is not normally affected by motions of the vessel, including rough weather.

For measuring temperature on board vessels *thermometers* are usually graduated to the Fahrenheit scale (water freezes at 32° and boils at 212° at standard atmospheric pressure), but use of the metric scale of Celsius (formerly centigrade) degrees (0° is freezing, 100° is boiling) is increasing, particularly in international applications. The reading of one scale can be easily converted to that of the other by means of table 29 in *Bowditch,* or mathematically, using the formulas:

$$°F = {}^9\!/_5\,(C° + 32°)$$
$$°C = {}^5\!/_9\,(F° - 32°)$$

in which °F = degrees Fahrenheit, and °C = degrees Celsius.

There are some electronic means of measuring humidity, but one simple method often used is to mount two thermometers together in an instrument shelter, a wooden box with louvered sides to protect the instruments from direct rays of the Sun and

Fig. 811. A stopwatch (*left*) and a chronograph with split-second capability.

other conditions that would render their readings inaccurate. The instrument shelter is installed at some exposed position aboard the vessel. One of the thermometers has its bulb covered with a wet fabric, and the other is exposed to the air. The rate of evaporation of the water is dependent upon the relative humidity of the air, or the relative amount of water vapor in the air. The evaporating water cools the bulb of the thermometer, resulting in a lower temperature. Knowing the air temperature (reading of the dry bulb thermometer) and the difference between this and the reading of the wet bulb thermometer, the relative humidity and *dew point* (the temperature to which the air must be cooled for condensation to take place) can be easily determined using tables available in *Bowditch*. Calculations of relative humidity and dew point are of special interest to the mariner in connection with the formation of fog. A instrument combining wet and dry thermometers is known as a *psychrometer*.

An *anemometer* is an instrument for measuring wind force or speed, usually in knots. It is important to remember that wind speed measured on a moving vessel is not the true wind because the vessel's motion affects it. The anemometer reading is actually the relative wind (or apparent wind). The true wind can be determined by a graphic solution using a maneuvering board worksheet (see the Maneuvering Board Manual, NIMA Pub. No. 217) or by using the "Direction and Speed of True Wind in Units of Ship's Speed" table in *Bowditch*. There are also navigational calculators and computer software programs that can be used for this purpose.

MISCELLANEOUS EQUIPMENT

813   *Binoculars* are an essential item of navigational equipment, useful for locating aids to navigation, especially small ones like buoys, and in reading their identifying markings. (Note: The term "set [or pair] of binoculars" is commonly used for a single unit, but this is not strictly correct; the proper term is the single form "binocular"—as in "bicycle." However, the plural form is more common, so it has been used here.) When binoculars are being used, the strap should be placed around the user's neck to prevent dropping them or losing them overboard—an expensive and potentially dangerous mistake all too common at sea. Those binoculars deemed most useful for marine work are 7 × 50. The first number tells you that the object being observed will appear seven times larger or closer. The second number tells you that the objective lenses (the ones closest to the object rather than the ones closest to your eye) are 50 mm in diameter. The larger the lens, the more light it takes in, the brighter (and therefore sharper) the image. The tradeoffs are that the larger the lens, the greater the size and weight of the binoculars, factors which can make them cumbersome to use and harder to hold steady. Also the field of view is affected by the ratio of these factors. Other types, such as 10 × 50 or 6 × 30, are preferred by some mariners, but most U.S. Navy binoculars are 7 × 50. This ratio of magnification to lens size is a satisfying compromise between the need for magnification and the reduction of field of view that results as the magnification is increased. Objective lenses of 50-mm diameter have excellent light-gathering characteristics, making them particularly suitable for night use.

At least one good *flashlight* should be kept handy for an accurate reading of watches and sextants during twilight observations if the latter are not equipped with their own light, and for timing light characteristics, and so on, during the hours of darkness. To protect dark-adapted vision, your flashlight should be equipped with a *red bulb* or a *red lens* (night vision is not affected by red light as it is with white). Lacking these, a red plastic or cellophane filter should be fitted.

Chapter 9   Dead Reckoning

As discussed in chapter 1, within the category of terrestrial navigation are two methods known as piloting and dead reckoning (DR). Some of the tools of piloting (charts, aids to navigation, etc.) have been discussed in earlier chapters, and in some ways the piloting phase of navigation precedes the DR phase, but dead reckoning has two different purposes and one of them requires discussion before going into the details of piloting.

Under ordinary conditions, when a mariner first gets under way, it is from a known position (such as a marina or naval base), and there will usually be a number of familiar surroundings to aid the navigator in piloting his or her way down the channel(s) and out to sea. Such things as buoys, familiar objects on shore that lend themselves to visual sightings for lines of position, known bottom contours, and so on will allow the navigator to immediately begin fixing her or his position using piloting as the preferred method of navigation. Once the navigator reaches the open sea, however, those elements are no longer present and, in the absence of other sources of navigational information (such as electronic or celestial), the only method left to employ is dead reckoning in its simplest form; that is, keeping track of one's movements to make a best estimate of position. Traveling in a known direction for a known period of time at a known speed gives you a much better idea of where you are than if you do not keep track of these things. Before the invention of the chronometer and the advent of electronics, this was the only means available to navigators for "knowing" their position on the vast expanses of the ocean. Even today, unusual circumstances may require the navigator to rely on this method alone.

Dead reckoning is also used to *predict* where you think you will be in a given period of time. A navigator must know his position, or approximate position, to determine when to make changes in course and/or speed, to predict the time of sighting lights or other aids to navigation, and to identify landmarks. Maintaining a DR plot accomplishes this and serves as a baseline or reference which is then further refined as more reliable information becomes available. In other words, the navigator lays down a DR track based upon his or her intended direction and speed and then adjusts this track as lines of position and fixes are obtained that show reality rather than prediction. In this manner, DR is employed when a navigator first plans a voyage, but it is also an ongoing process that is employed even while the navigator is using other forms of navigation—a "fill-in" for those periods of time between fixes, while sightings, calculations, and plotting of information are taking place. Therefore, DR is actually basic to all phases of navigation.

DR VS. EP

901   If a ship made good the exact course and speed ordered, and there were no wind or current, dead reckoning would at all times provide an accurate indication of position and no other means of navigation would be necessary. Such conditions rarely exist, however, and a DR position is therefore only an approximation of the true position, a "best guess."

The navigator will sometimes have additional information that improves the navigational picture but is not enough to define a fix with confidence. Knowing the prevailing wind speed, estimating the current, taking a series of soundings, or obtaining a line of position of questionable accuracy are examples of some of these circumstances. When this occurs, the navigator may choose to use this information to plot an estimated position (EP). This is a judgment call and cannot be defined empirically—an example of where navigation becomes *art* as well *science*.

An EP can be defined as a DR position that has been corrected using additional information, most often for the effects of wind, current, heavy seas, steering error, instrument inaccuracies, and so on. Measuring or quantifying these factors is not easy, but you can measure their cumulative effect by comparing simultaneous fix and DR positions.

THE DR PLOT

902   Maintaining a graphical representation on the nautical chart of the intended courses and speeds constitutes a DR plot. If no additional information is available to modify it, the DR plot becomes a record of the ship's track until additional information becomes available.

As already stated, the DR plot originates at a known position and is suitably labeled with courses, speeds, and times. If a new fix, running fix, or even a single line of position (LOP) is plotted, a new DR plot is begun at that point, running it out from that point. This can happen within minutes if fix information is readily available. If no fix information is available, the DR plot is maintained with all changes in course and speed represented and with periodic intervals labeled. In other words, you should update the DR plot:

After every fix
After every running fix
After plotting a single LOP
After every change of course
After every change of speed
At least every hour on the hour

It is of the utmost importance that all points and lines plotted on a chart be properly labeled as indicated in figure 902. The use of standardized methods and symbology will avoid confusion and ensure that the plot will mean the same thing to others as it did to the navigator who made it. Immediately after drawing any line or plotting any point, it should be labeled as follows:

1. The symbol for a fix obtained by electronic means (radar, GPS, etc.) is a triangle with the time (always four-digit, 24-hour time; no colons or dashes or any other symbols) written *horizontally* (east-west on a chart oriented to true north).
2. The symbol for a fix derived from visual bearings is a circle, also labeled horizontally with the time.
3. If a fix is obtained using a combination of visual and electronic means (one radar range and two visual bearings, for example), a triangle is used.
4. The symbol for a running fix is also a circle, but the letters "R FIX" are added to the time to distinguish it from a fix.
5. The symbol for an estimated position is a small square with time written *horizontally.*
6. The symbol for a DR position is a semicircle around a dot on a straight segment of a course line. When plotting a change of direction, the semicircle surrounds the point of change (and may therefore appear as slightly more or slightly less than a semicircle). The time of the DR position is also labeled with the time (as always, four-digit, 24-hour) but is written *diagonally* to distinguish it from horizontal fix times.

Labels indicating direction and speed should be written along the course line with the course above the line and the speed below. The course should be preceded by the letter *C* and always written in three digits with no degree symbol. If the course is something other than *true,* it should be appropriately labeled after the numerals (with an *M* for magnetic, for example). Speed is preceded with the letter *S.*

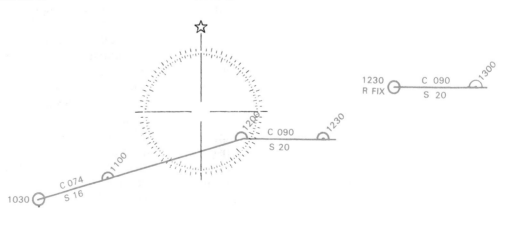

Fig. 902. Labeling a DR plot.

Example of a DR Plot

903 The following example illustrates a typical dead reckoning plot (see fig. 903).

A partial extract from a ship's deck log reads as follows:

1045 With Tide Rip Light bearing 315°, distant 6 miles, took departure for operating area V-22 on course 090°, speed 15 knots.

 1120   Changed speed to 10 knots.

 1130   Changed course to 145° and increased speed to 20 knots.

 1145   Changed course to 075°.

 1210   Made radar contact on Buoy 1A bearing 010°, distant 8 miles. Depth sounding on Garrett pinnacle.

 1215   Changed course to 090° and changed speed to 18 knots to arrive at the rendezvous point at 1230.

The plot for these events would appear as indicated in figure 903. Note the applicability of the rules for dead reckoning as they pertain to this example. Commencing at the initial known position (the 1045 fix), the navigator plotted the course line in a direction of 090° with the course indicated above the line and the speed of 15 knots indicated below it. According to the rules of DR, the next required plot is the DR position *on the hour* (1100). Computing the distance traveled in fifteen minutes (from the 1045 fix to the 1100 DR position) the navigator then plotted the 1100 DR in the appropriate position and labeled it.

At 1120 the speed was changed, so the navigator plotted the 1120 position (based upon the distance traveled in the twenty minutes of elapsed time) and labeled it appropriately.

At 1130, both the course and speed were changed, while at 1145, only the course was changed. Each of these occurrences requires a separate DR position on the plot, while segments of the course lines are labeled to indicate what the course and speed were at that time.

The 1200 DR was plotted on the whole hour as prescribed ("every hour on the hour"). At 1210 the navigator determined that there was enough information for a reliable fix. That new position was then plotted and appropriately labeled. Note that both the old DR position at 1210 and the new fix are plotted in their appropriate positions and labeled. The new fix at 1210 required a new position to be plotted and a new DR course and speed line to be drawn from that point. The ship then continued on briefly on the old course and speed while a revised course and speed were being determined—in this example, for five minutes—before a new course of 090 at 18 knots was ordered to arrive at the operating area at 1230 as scheduled. The ship continued on this course until reaching the rendezvous point at 1230.

DR IN VOYAGE PLANNING

904 Another form of DR is used before the ship ever gets under way and is an important component of voyage planning. The entire process of voyage planning (also called "navigational planning") involves using as much information as is available (from charts, publications, etc.) to prepare for a voyage in advance. The DR component consists of laying down a predicted track based on the best information available at the time. It is similar to a flight plan used by aviators and is one of the most important parts of the process of voyage planning because it gives the navigator a plan that can be executed or (more often) that serves as a model that will be modified as the actual voyage takes place and unpredictable variables take effect. It is important to understand this, to realize that the DR track that is laid down is more for reference than for actual execution. An inexperienced navigator may be reluctant to deviate from this plan and may encounter unnecessary trouble as a result. Deviation from the planned track will nearly always become necessary when those things that cannot be predicted occur (vessel traffic, unexpected currents

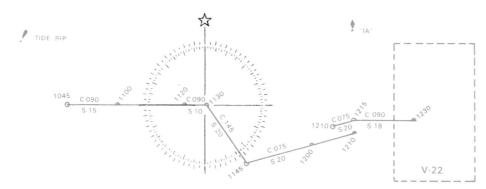

Fig. 903. A typical navigator's DR plot.

or winds, engine trouble, etc.). For example, you may encounter a large tanker heading down the center of the same channel you are using, and you may have to alter course to get around her or slow down to stay behind her if there is not enough deep water available to allow safe passing. Once this occurs, your DR track is no longer valid as planned and you must either make adjustments to get back on the planned DR track (by altering course or speeding up once the tanker is no longer in your way) or modify the rest of your voyage plan if complete recovery is not possible (as when you have been forced to slow down for so long that "catching up" to your DR track is not feasible). What is important to note is that the original DR track is there as a *reference*, something to regain or to modify, but in either case much better than simply "winging it."

The DR component of voyage planning, in its simplest form is first deciding where you want to go and what time you want to get there, and then laying out a track line that will determine the course or courses to steer and the speed or speeds you will need to get to your destination on time. The following description of a short voyage will serve to illustrate this process.

Referring to figure 904, assume that your ship is located at point A, and you receive orders to depart at 0800 for point B, 90 miles distant, and that you must be there at 1300 to rendezvous with another ship. Upon receipt of this information, you would locate points A and B on the appropriate chart of the area. By measuring the direction of B from A, you would determine the course to get there would be 070°, and you would note it on the DR plot as "C 070." Dividing the distance between A and B by the five hours (between 0800 and 1300), you determine the required speed to be 18 knots and label it accordingly. Next, starting at the known position, or fix, at 0800, step off and mark the successive hourly positions that your ship is expected to pass through.

The plot is now complete and barring any unforeseen circumstances, represents the track that the ship will follow from the point of departure to her destination. As already stated, in actual practice the odds are that there will indeed be unforeseen circumstances and that, once under way, you will have to deviate from this planned track.

Departures from Plan

905   An example of what might happen in actual practice follows. The ship gets under way as scheduled in figure 904 and sets course 070° true and speed 18 knots to arrive at B at 1300. Once under way, your responsibility as navigator is to use whatever means are available to establish the ship's actual position from time to time, in order to be sure that the ship is following the intended track. If it is not, you must recommend changes in course or speed, or both, that will bring the ship safely back to the intended track at some selected point on it.

In our example, the weather is poor and you are unable to establish your position until about noon, at which time you obtain a 1200 fix. When the fix is plotted, you find that the ship is actually about 10 miles south and a bit east of your 1200 DR position (see fig. 905). You further note that if your ship maintains the same course from the 1200 fix as it had from point A, she will be in danger of grounding on the indicated shoal.

Since the ship will not reach the desired destination on a course of 070° and a speed of 18 knots, you must determine a new course and speed to arrive at point B by 1300, based upon the relationship between point B and the latest fix at 1200.

Because time was required to record the fix, evaluate it, and decide upon a new course and speed, this change cannot be effected from the 1200 fix, but rather from a DR position some time later. Making a rough estimate of how long it will take you to determine a new course and speed and get approval, you

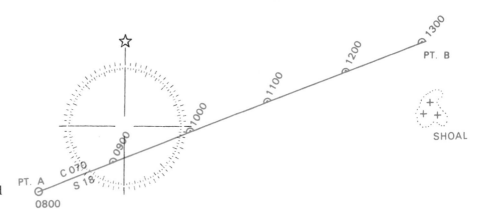

Fig. 904. Intended DR, plotted and labeled in advance.

Fig. 905. The practice of dead reckoning.

plot a 1215 DR position based on the old, and still maintained, course and speed. From here you calculate a new course and a new speed to reach your rendezvous point on time. In this case, you determine that a course of 028° and a speed of 24 knots at 1215 will get you to point B at 1300. Note: Although it is apparent that something (like the wind or a current) caused you to stray from your intended track, it was not considered in this simplified example. The techniques of computing and allowing for current are explained later in chapter 13.

In the absence of other information, your best option was to believe that the ship was following the intended track. Once you obtained and plotted your 1200 fix, it became apparent that adjustment was necessary. This illustrates the fundamental weakness of relying solely on dead reckoning, and demonstrates why dead reckoning should *not* be relied upon if it is possible to obtain information to determine the position by other means. The many volumes of records on maritime disasters are filled with reports of vessels having been lost because of a navigator's adherence to a course that was laid in safe waters, while the actual movement was an unknown path leading to danger.

Alternative Procedures

906   An alternative labeling procedure for the DR track used in voyage planning is shown in figure 906. Here *distances to go* are given at each change of

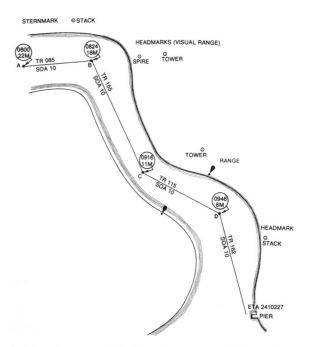

Fig. 906. Alternative labeling of a proposed DR track.

course, and the line is labeled with "TR" for track and SOA for speed of advance. This method has several obvious advantages and is more easily distinguished from the running DR that will likely be added once the ship gets under way.

Sometimes, when laying out a DR track in advance, the times of departure and arrival may not be known yet. In that case, speeds are not plotted but distances are. This is done with the letter *D* followed by the distance in nautical miles (statute miles in some areas), usually to the nearest tenth of a mile, and is placed below the course line where the speed would be plotted if known. Once the times are known, the terms ETD and ETA may be used for "estimated time of departure" and "estimated time of arrival," respectively.

Chapter 10   Tides

When approaching a harbor, or pilot waters in general, one of the most important preparatory actions to be taken by a vessel's navigator is consideration of the available depths of water at the expected time of arrival. The natural phenomenon known as *tide* will cause such depths to vary from time to time in most areas of the world. The nautical navigator must have a thorough knowledge of tidal action and how the height of tide, which in turn determines the depth of water, can be predicted and calculated. Having enough water under your keel at one time does not necessarily mean you will have enough at *all* times. Tides can also have an effect on mooring lines. As the depth of water alongside a pier changes with the tide, it can cause your mooring lines to become excessively slack or taut, causing serious problems when the tidal range is large. Adjusting your mooring lines to take into account the range of tide can prevent them from parting or suffering excessive wear and can keep your vessel from "wandering" at its mooring.

In addition to concern over adequate depths of water in channels, across bars, alongside piers and wharves, and so on, in some locations there may be concern as to sufficient vertical clearance beneath a fixed bridge. Here, too, tides play a major role, for as depths increase for improved clearance under the hull, available vertical clearances for masts and superstructures decrease by the same amount.

BASIC DEFINITIONS

1001   The vertical rise and fall of the ocean level due to gravitational and centrifugal forces between the Earth and the Moon, and, to a lesser extent, the Sun, is called *tide*. Local conditions cause considerable variations in tidal phenomena from place to place, but most places on the Earth's oceans and connecting waters experience two high tides and two low tides each lunar day. *High tide*, or *high water*, is the highest level reached by an ascending tide. When the tide is rising (i.e., water is getting deeper) it is often referred to as a *flood tide*. From high tide the level of the water decreases until it reaches a minimum level called *low tide*, or *low water*. When the water is falling it is called an *ebb tide*. At high water and at low water there is a brief period when no change in the water level can be detected. This period is called *stand*. The total rise or fall from a consecutive low water to high water, or vice versa, is called the *range of tide*. *Mean sea level* is the average height of the surface of the sea for all stages of tide (calculated over an approximately nineteen-year period), differing slightly from *half-tide level*, which is the plane midway between mean high water and mean low water.

CAUSES OF TIDE

1002   In any consideration of tidal theory, it is convenient to begin by assuming a theoretically spherical Earth uniformly covered with water. It is also convenient to consider the effects of the Moon and Sun separately, following this with a consideration of the combined effects of both bodies. Because the Moon exerts the larger influence, its effects will be studied first. Before A.D. 100, the Roman naturalist Pliny observed and wrote of the influence of the Moon on tides, but a better understanding had to wait for Newton's scientific description of gravity in 1687.

Lunar Effects

1003 The oceans are affected by the gravitational attraction between the Earth and the Moon, and by the centrifugal forces resulting from the movement of these bodies. While it appears that the Moon revolves around the Earth, both the Earth and Moon are revolving together around their common center of mass, which is a point located *within* the Earth about 810 miles (1,500 km) beneath the surface called the barycenter. The gravitational and centrifugal forces are in balance, and so the Earth and Moon neither collide nor fly away from each other. The centrifugal force is the same everywhere on Earth's surface, since all points describe the same motion around the center of mass; these forces are all parallel to each other and to a line joining the centers of the Earth and Moon. On the other hand, the gravitational force is *not* everywhere the same—particles at points nearer the Moon feel a greater attractional force than those on the far side of the Earth—so these forces are *not* parallel, each being in the direction from that point toward the center of the Moon. A diagram of these forces, much exaggerated for emphasis, is shown in figure 1003. Note that there are a series of resultant forces that will cause the surface water to flow toward the points on the Earth's surface that are then nearest and farthest from the Moon. This flow causes higher than normal levels of water at these points, and lower than normal levels at the areas from which the flow comes. Although at the nearest and farthest points there is an indicated outward force, this is very slight and not nearly enough to cause an appreciable tide; the true tide results from the near-horizontal forces causing the flow described above.

If the Moon's orbit coincided with the Earth's equator, the tides would occur evenly each day. But because the Earth's axis of rotation is tilted with respect to the Moon's orbit, the line of direction toward the Moon changes as the Earth rotates each day. This results in the daily occurrence of two high tides and two low tides that are not normally of equal levels.

Because the Moon's orbit around the Earth is elliptical, it's distance from the Earth will vary. Tidal effects will be somewhat more (15–20 percent) when the Moon is at its closest point (perigee) to the Earth and somewhat less when it is at its farthest point (apogee). Appropriately enough these tides are known *perigean* and *apogean tides.*

Solar Effects

1004 This somewhat simplified explanation must now be complicated by the presence of the Sun, a body of immensely greater mass than the Moon, but relatively so much more distant that its effect is less (only about 46 percent as great). The tides that occur on Earth are the result of both lunar and solar influences. When these two bodies are in line with the Earth—as at both new and full Moon—the two influences act together, and the result is higher than average high tides and lower than normal low tides; these are called *spring tides* (the word "spring" here has nothing to do with the season of the year of the same name). This is true whether the Moon is between the Earth and the Sun or is on the opposite side. Figure 1004a illustrates these situations.

When the directions of the Sun and Moon are 90° apart, as at both first- and third-quarter Moons, the effect of the Sun is to partially counteract the Moon's influence (see fig. 1004b). At these times, the high tides are lower and the lower tides are higher than normal; these are called *neap* tides.

Other factors involving the relative positions of the Earth, Sun, and Moon such as the equinoxes in September and March and the solstices in June and December (see article 1909) can have significant effects upon the tides.

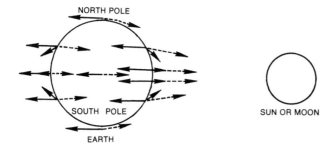

Fig. 1003. Gravitational forces (dashed lines) and centrifugal forces (solid lines). (Not to scale.)

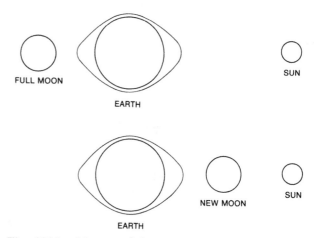

Fig. 1004a. Moon and Sun acting together to produce spring tides.

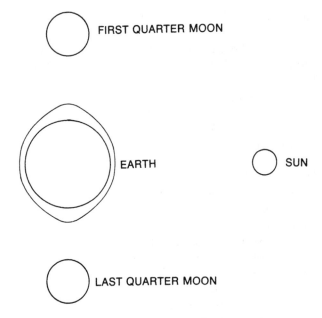

Fig. 1004b. Moon and Sun in quadrature acting to produce neap tides.

As the Moon revolves about the Earth once each lunar month of roughly twenty-nine and a half days, its transit of any meridian on Earth occurs approximately every twenty-four hours and fifty minutes. This is the period for two high waters and two low waters and is called a *tidal day;* the period of one high and one low is referred to as a *tidal cycle.* In actuality, the daily rotation of the Earth on its axis has a frictional effect on the tides, so that high tides normally lag the time of the Moon's transit across the meridian of any location. Additional irregularities are introduced into the heights and times of tide by the Moon's varying angle and distance from the Earth. The many effects result in a pattern of tides that repeats only at intervals of roughly nineteen years.

Other Influences

1005 The assumption of a spherical Earth uniformly covered with water is, of course, purely hypothetical. Tides in the open oceans are only about 1 to 2 feet high (0.3–0.6 m). Actual coastal tides are often much greater, in some places as much as 40 or 50 feet (12 to 15 m) or more. This is the result of large land masses restricting the flow of water, of ocean bottom and shoreline variations, the internal friction (viscosity) of the flowing water, and other factors. These combine with the basic tidal influences to establish complicated but predictable periods of oscillation for seas, gulfs, large bays, and estuaries.

Our Restless Tides

1006 A more detailed explanation of the causes of tides is available from the National Oceanic and Atmospheric Administration (NOAA) in booklet form (for a small fee) called *Our Restless Tides.* The entire text is also available at their web site, www.co-ops.nos.noaa.gov/restles1.html.

TIDAL CYCLES

1007 Because of the influences described above, a body of water has a natural period of oscillation that is dependent upon its dimensions. No ocean appears to be a single oscillating body; instead, each one is made up of a number of individually oscillating basins. As these basins are acted upon by the tide-producing forces, some respond more readily to daily (diurnal) forces, others to semidiurnal (twice per day) forces, and still others respond almost equally to both. Hence, tides at a given place are classified as semidiurnal, diurnal, or mixed- according to the characteristics of the tidal pattern occurring at that place.

Semidiurnal. In this type of tide, there are two high and two low waters each tidal day with relatively small inequality in the consecutive high and low water heights (see fig. 1007a). Tides on the Atlantic Coast of the United States are representative of the semidiurnal type.

Diurnal. In this tide, only a single high and a single low water occur each tidal day. Tides of the diurnal type occur along the northern shore of the Gulf of Mexico, in the Java Sea, in the Gulf of Tonkin (off the Vietnamese-Chinese coast), and in a few other localities. The tide curve for Pakhoi, China, illustrated in figure 1007b is an example of the diurnal type.

Mixed. Here the diurnal and semidiurnal oscillations are both important factors, and the tide is characterized by a large inequality in the high-water heights, low-water heights, or in both. There are

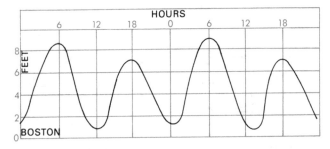

Fig. 1007a. Semidiurnal tides.

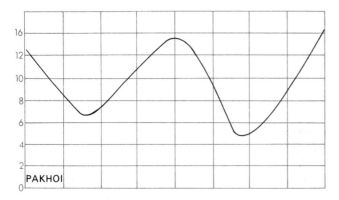

Fig. 1007b. Diurnal tides.

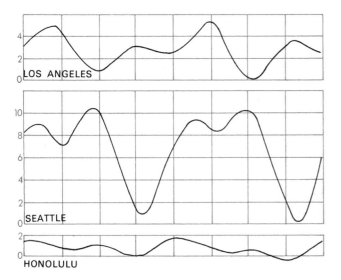

Fig. 1007c. Mixed tides.

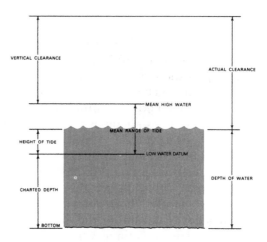

Fig. 1008. Relationship of terms used in measurement of depths and heights.

usually two high and two low waters each day, but occasionally the tide may become diurnal. Mixed tides are prevalent along the Pacific Coast of the United States and in many other parts of the world. Examples of mixed types of tides are shown in figure 1007c. At Los Angeles, it is typical that the inequalities in the high and low waters are about the same. At Seattle the greater inequalities are typically in the low waters, while at Honolulu the high waters have the greater inequalities.

REFERENCE PLANES FOR TIDAL DATA

1008 You will recall that depths are shown on charts by numbers (also called soundings) representing meters, feet, or fathoms on charts. But if we know that tides are continually raising and lowering the water level, what do those numbers actually represent? Known as the *charted depth,* these numbers refer to the depth as measured from the bottom to a chosen reference plane.

Chart makers could use mean sea level as the reference plane for determining the depths and heights on charts, but because lower waters are a potential detriment to a vessel's staying afloat and higher waters can reduce the amount of clearance available for a vessel to pass beneath a bridge or some other overhead obstruction, using two different reference planes—one for depths and one for heights—makes more sense. The depths of water on a chart are in relation to a reference plane based upon an average of the low tides that are present in the area. Heights on the same chart are in relation to a different reference plane that is based upon an average of the *high* tides in the area (see fig. 1008). This means that if you rely on the readings you find on your chart, you will be using something akin to a "worse case scenario," which should give you an extra margin of safety.

As discussed below, there are a number of different reference planes that can be (and are) used, but the most frequently used on U.S. charts are *mean high water* for heights and *mean lower low water* for depths. On your chart, somewhere close to the title, the reference plane used will be indicated and what units of measurement (meters, feet, or fathoms) are being used (see fig. 326 in chapter 3).

One other plane of reference used on charts is the *shoreline plane of reference.* Since it is obvious that the actual shoreline is subject to change because of tides, some reference must be chosen in order to draw the line where land ends and sea begins. *Mean high water* (explained below) is normally used for this plane of reference.

Depths

1009   The reference plane used in determining the depth of water may differ from chart to chart, depending upon the locality and the country making the survey on which the chart is based. This reference plane is often known as simply the *tidal reference plane* but is also sometimes referred to as the *tidal datum* or *chart datum*. This latter term can cause some confusion since, as discussed in chapter 2, there is another datum used in navigation which is a geodetic one used in the creation of charts. The latter is known as the "horizontal datum" or the "horizontal geodetic datum" or the "horizontal control datum" and is something very different from the tidal datums discussed here.

The chosen reference plane for charted depths can be any of several described below:

Mean low water (MLW). The average of all low tides.

Mean lower low water (MLLW). The average of only the lower of the two daily low tides. Remember that in each day there may be two low tides (semidiurnal); this reference plane considers only the lower of the two. It is the most commonly used reference plane for low-water predictions on U.S. charts.

Mean low-water springs (MLWS). The average of the low waters at spring tides.

Mean lower low-water springs (MLLWS). The average of the lower of the two daily low tides on the days of spring tides.

Lowest astronomical tides (LAT). The lowest level that can be predicted to occur under average meteorological conditions and under any combination of astronomical conditions over a period of one lunar nodal cycle epoch (18.6 years). This reference plane is gaining favor in the international community and is now standard for charts produced in the United Kingdom.

(Note: It should be apparent that these low-water planes of reference are listed in order, such that you are less likely to go aground relying on the charted depths on a chart that uses MLLWS as its tidal datum than if you are using one based upon MLW. That is not to say that a chart using MLW is not safe, but one using MLLWS has an extra margin of safety built in. As a navigator, you should exercise more caution [i.e., assume the water could be less deep] when using charts that use tidal reference planes that are closer to the top of the above list than when using one farther down the list.)

Heights

1010   A second reference plane based on a selected *high-water* average is used as a basis for the measurement of *charted heights* of objects above the water and *vertical clearances* under structures such as bridges and power lines. Note that elevations (heights of geographic features such as hills and mountains) are generally referenced to mean sea level, while charted heights (of lighthouses and the like) and vertical clearances (under bridges, etc.) are generally based upon mean high water as discussed below:

Mean high water (MHW). The average height of all high tides. This is the most commonly used high-water reference plane on U.S. charts.

Mean higher high water (MHHW). The average of only the higher of the two daily high tides. This is the reference plane used on United Kingdom charts when there is a diurnal inequality of heights.

Mean high water springs (MHWS). The average of the high waters at spring tides. This is the reference plane used on United Kingdom charts when tides are semidiurnal.

Mean higher high-water springs (MHHWS). The average of the higher of the two daily high tides on the days of spring tides.

(Note: It should be apparent that these high-water planes of reference are listed in order such that passing beneath a bridge is safer when using a chart based upon MHHWS than when using a chart based upon MHW.)

Cautions

1011   It is important to determine which planes of reference are in use for the chart(s) you are using. Each chart normally carries a statement of the planes of reference used. However, these may be in doubt on charts compiled from old or questionable data. If there is any doubt, assume the worst case (i.e., that it is mean low water for soundings and mean high water for heights) for the greatest margin of safety.

Also be aware that even though the depth of the water will seldom be lower than the charted depth if lowest astronomical tides (LAT) is used as a tidal reference plane and seldom higher when mean higher high-water springs (MHHWS) is the height reference, aberrations *can* occur, even at these extremes. Always allow an extra margin of safety.

Keep in mind that the terms *height of tide, charted depth,* and *depth of water* mean very different things but are interrelated (see fig. 1008). *Height of tide* refers to the vertical distance from the surface of the water to the selected reference plane discussed above. *Depth of water* refers to the vertical distance from the surface of the water to the bottom at any given moment, depending upon the height of tide at that time. And *charted depth* is the depth shown on the chart based upon the reference plane but not accounting for the height of tide at any specific time. Reliance upon your chart alone is therefore working with an incomplete picture. To increase your situational awareness (and your safety) incorporate the information available in the *Tide Tables*.

TIDE TABLES

1012   As already stated, despite the many variables involved in the determination of tides, they are predictable. Predictions of tidal heights have been calculated and compiled annually by the National Ocean Service (and its predecessor agencies, the Coast & Geodetic Survey and National Ocean Survey) since 1853. Because the tides vary from year to year, this data must be recomputed each year. For many years NOS published this data as annual tide tables in book format, but since 1997 it no longer does so. NOS continues to provide the data—it is available on the Internet and via CD-ROM—but leaves the book publishing to commercial publishers for civilian use and to NIMA, who continues to publish these tables in book format for DOD use. Other commercial companies produce navigational software packages that include tide prediction capabilities.

To keep the volumes of *Tide Tables* a reasonable size when printed, the data provided by NOS are presented in tables of *reference stations* and *subordinate stations* that can be cross-referenced to find the tides for specific areas. This method significantly streamlines the data by eliminating a great deal of repetition. By using this method, tidal information is available for literally thousands of locations but, when printed, can be presented in reasonably sized volumes.

Commercial Tide Table Publications

1013   Several private printers use the NOS data to publish tide tables in book form. NOS provides the needed data to these companies with the stipulation that they are free to provide additional information before or after the data, but they must not alter the tables themselves. Three publishers who produce tide tables are:

International Marine Division
McGraw Hill
P.O. Box 545
Columbus, OH 42318
800-722-4726

Prostar Publications
8643 Hayden Place

Culver City, CA 90232
and
3 Church Circle, Suite 109
Annapolis, MD 21401
800-481-6277

Reed's Nautical Almanacs
Thomas Reed Publications, Inc.
293 S. Main St.
Providence, RI 02903
800-995-4995

The telephone and address information provided above was current as of this writing. For a current list of companies who publish tide tables based on NOS data, write or call:

National Ocean Service
User Services Branch, N/CS44
1305 East-West Highway
Silver Spring, MD 20910
301-713-2815

Additionally, various other organizations produce their own versions of tide tables (nearly always based on NOS data) for local use. The United New York Sandy Hook Pilots Benevolent Association and Moran Towing & Transportation Company are examples.

Software Tide Tables

1014   There are a number of navigational software programs that include tide prediction capabilities. Among them are Nautical Software Tides & Currents, Xtides, Cap'n, and UKHO TotalTides. As of this writing, the U.S. Navy is in the process of evaluating software packages with an eye toward possible fleet adoption. However, preliminary findings of some of those evaluations have indicated that some commercial products are based on out-of-date harmonic constituents that could predict incorrect tidal heights and result in groundings. Prudent navigators will avoid using publications and products that have not been government approved.

Tide Information from the Internet

1015   NOS tide information is available on the Internet for the current year at www.tidesonline.nos.noaa.gov. The data is listed by geographic area and is available in two formats.

The *International Format* is an electronic ASCII file that provides time and height of tide information for a single location in a columnar format suitable for importing into databases or other computer programs. The data is provided in 24-hour clock format for the local time zone, but can be modified to show A.M./P.M. time and/or Daylight Savings Time.

NOS calls their other electronic offering *Standard Format,* and is in what they refer to as "page readable format." Making it a bit more readable are high (H) and low (L) indications, days of the week, and other useful notations.

As mentioned above, tidal information for subordinate stations is also available in the form of "differences" from a specified reference station. Figures given are preceded by a positive sign (+), negative sign (–), or asterisk (*). These figures are added, subtracted, or multiplied to those figures provided for the indicated reference station.

For tidal data outside the United States, there are links to those foreign hydrographic offices that maintain their own web sites. Foreign information is also available from NOS by contacting them by telephone at 301-713-2815 (between 0700 and 1500 Eastern Time) or by e-mailing a request to TidePredictions @noaa.gov. There may be a fee involved, depending upon the amount of data you are seeking.

Tide Tables for DOD Use

1016 As already mentioned, NIMA produces *Tide Tables* in book form for DOD use. They are compiled in four volumes as follows:
1. Europe and West Coast of Africa (including the Mediterranean Sea)
2. East Coast of North and South America (including Greenland)
3. West Coast of North and South America (including the Hawaiian Islands)
4. Central and Western Pacific Ocean and Indian Ocean.

Included in these volumes is a series of tables. The most useful ones for tide predictions are the first three:

Table 1: Times and heights of high and low tides for selected reference stations.

Table 2: Differences in times and heights for specific secondary stations.

Table 3: Used for determining tidal heights at specific times (between highs and lows).

Reference Stations

1017 To keep the volumes of *Tide Tables* a reasonable size when printed, the data provided by NOS is maintained just as it is found on the NOS web site: in tables of reference stations and subordinate stations that can be cross-referenced to find the tides for specific areas.

Table 1 is a many-page listing of the reference stations used. The times and heights of the high and low tides are listed in chronological order for each day of the year for these stations. Figure 1017 is an extract from Table 1 of the *Tide Tables for the East Coast of North and South America (including Greenland)* for the months of January, February, and March (of a certain year) at the reference station, Portland, Maine.

In studying this table you will see that each day of the month is listed along with an indication (M, Tu, W, Th, or F) as to the day of the week. Beside each day is a listing of the times (in hours and minutes) for each of the high and low tides occurring that day. As always in navigation, times are listed using the 24-hour clock. Next to the time is the height of the tide in both feet and centimeters. Some of the days have circular symbols representing the phases of the Moon; the white portion of the circle depicted indicates how much of the Moon would be illuminated (visible) on that particular day. For example, on 28 January, the Moon will be new (completely dark) as indicated by the completely black circle; it will be in first quarter on 3 February, full on 11 February, and so on.

It is important to realize that what you are seeing in this table are *corrections* to charted depth. In other words, at the times indicated, the depth of water you will encounter at that location (Portland, Maine) will differ from what your chart is telling you by the amount indicated. Because the predicted depth of water is equal to the algebraic sum of the charted depth and the height of tide, it should be obvious that when the corrections in Table 1 are preceded by a minus sign, the water level will actually be *below the charted depth.* In other words, the numerical value of the height of tide is subtracted from the charted depth to find the depth of water when the height of tide is a negative number, giving you an actual depth of water that is less than that which is indicated on the chart. (Note that for the month of January in figure 1017, 28 of the listed tidal corrections are negative and will, therefore, be less than the charted depths at the times indicated.)

Two notes at the bottom of the page provide additional important information about the times and heights used. The note explaining the time meridian in use for that page tells you that the times are local standard times (see chapter 23). Keep in mind that if you are in a region using daylight saving time, an adjustment will have to be made.

The other note explains what tidal datum is being used. As indicated, this is the same datum that is used on charts for the area.

Because the lunar or tidal day is a little more than twenty-four hours in length (an average of about

January | February | March

January

Day	Time	ft (Height)	cm	Day	Time	ft (Height)	cm
1 Th	0026	9.5	290	**16** F	0117	9.0	274
	0621	-0.1	-3		0713	0.6	18
	1234	10.8	329		1324	9.6	293
	1857	-1.2	-37		1943	0.0	0
2 F	0113	9.7	296	**17** Sa	0157	8.8	268
	0711	-0.2	-6		0756	0.8	24
	1324	10.6	323		1406	9.2	280
	1946	-1.1	-34		2023	0.4	12
3 Sa	0204	9.8	299	**18** Su	0238	8.7	265
	0805	-0.1	-3		0840	1.1	34
	1418	10.4	317		1450	8.8	268
	2038	-0.9	-27		2104	0.7	21
4 Su	0258	9.8	299	**19** M	0322	8.5	259
	0903	0.0	0		0928	1.3	40
	1516	10.0	305		1537	8.4	256
	2134	-0.6	-18		2148	1.0	30
5 M ◐	0356	9.8	299	**20** Tu ◐	0408	8.4	256
	1007	0.0	0		1019	1.4	43
	1619	9.6	293		1629	8.0	244
	2234	-0.3	-9		2236	1.3	40
6 Tu	0457	9.9	302	**21** W	0457	8.4	256
	1114	0.0	0		1114	1.5	46
	1726	9.3	283		1724	7.8	238
	2336	-0.1	-3		2327	1.5	46
7 W	0600	10.0	305	**22** Th	0548	8.5	259
	1222	-0.1	-3		1211	1.4	43
	1835	9.1	277		1822	7.7	235
8 Th	0040	0.1	3	**23** F	0020	1.5	46
	0703	10.1	308		0641	8.7	265
	1328	-0.3	-9		1307	1.1	34
	1941	9.1	277		1919	7.8	238
9 F	0141	0.1	3	**24** Sa	0113	1.4	43
	0803	10.3	314		0733	9.0	274
	1428	-0.6	-18		1400	0.7	21
	2042	9.2	280		2012	8.1	247
10 Sa	0239	0.1	3	**25** Su	0205	1.1	34
	0858	10.5	320		0823	9.5	290
	1523	-0.8	-24		1449	0.2	6
	2137	9.3	283		2101	8.5	259
11 Su	0332	0.0	0	**26** M	0254	0.6	18
	0949	10.6	323		0910	10.0	305
	1614	-1.0	-30		1535	-0.4	-12
	2227	9.4	287		2148	8.9	271
12 M ○	0421	0.0	0	**27** Tu	0341	0.2	6
	1036	10.6	323		0956	10.5	320
	1700	-1.0	-30		1620	-0.9	-27
	2313	9.4	287		2233	9.4	287
13 Tu	0506	0.1	3	**28** W ●	0428	-0.3	-9
	1120	10.5	320		1043	10.9	332
	1743	-0.8	-24		1705	-1.3	-40
	2356	9.3	283		2318	9.8	299
14 W	0550	0.2	6	**29** Th	0516	-0.7	-21
	1202	10.2	311		1130	11.1	338
	1824	-0.6	-18		1750	-1.6	-49
15 Th	0037	9.1	277	**30** F	0005	10.2	311
	0631	0.4	12		0605	-0.9	-27
	1243	9.9	302		1219	11.2	341
	1904	-0.3	-9		1838	-1.7	-52
				31 Sa	0053	10.4	317
					0656	-1.0	-30
					1310	11.0	335
					1927	-1.5	-46

February

Day	Time	ft (Height)	cm	Day	Time	ft (Height)	cm
1 Su	0143	10.4	317	**16** M	0156	8.9	271
	0750	-0.9	-27		0802	0.7	21
	1404	10.6	323		1413	8.8	268
	2018	-1.2	-37		2021	0.7	21
2 M	0237	10.4	317	**17** Tu	0235	8.8	268
	0848	-0.7	-21		0844	0.9	27
	1502	10.1	308		1456	8.5	259
	2114	-0.7	-21		2101	1.0	30
3 Tu ◐	0334	10.2	311	**18** W	0316	8.7	265
	0950	-0.4	-12		0930	1.1	34
	1604	9.5	290		1542	8.1	247
	2213	-0.2	-6		2145	1.3	40
4 W	0435	10.0	305	**19** Th ○	0403	8.6	262
	1057	-0.2	-6		1021	1.2	37
	1712	9.0	274		1634	7.8	238
	2317	0.2	6		2235	1.5	46
5 Th	0540	9.9	302	**20** F	0454	8.6	262
	1206	0.0	0		1118	1.2	37
	1822	8.7	265		1732	7.7	235
					2331	1.5	46
6 F	0023	0.5	15	**21** Sa	0551	8.7	265
	0647	9.8	299		1218	1.1	34
	1314	-0.1	-3		1833	7.8	238
	1930	8.7	265				
7 Sa	0128	0.5	15	**22** Su	0029	1.4	43
	0750	9.9	302		0649	9.0	274
	1416	-0.2	-6		1317	0.7	21
	2032	8.8	268		1932	8.1	247
8 Su	0228	0.5	15	**23** M	0128	1.0	30
	0847	10.0	305		0746	9.5	290
	1512	-0.4	-12		1413	0.1	3
	2126	8.9	271		2027	8.6	262
9 M	0321	0.4	12	**24** Tu	0224	0.5	15
	0938	10.1	308		0841	10.0	305
	1601	-0.5	-15		1505	-0.5	-15
	2214	9.1	277		2118	9.2	280
10 Tu	0409	0.2	6	**25** W	0317	-0.1	-3
	1024	10.1	308		0932	10.6	323
	1644	-0.5	-15		1553	-1.1	-34
	2257	9.2	280		2207	9.9	302
11 W ●	0452	0.2	6	**26** Th ●	0407	-0.8	-24
	1105	10.1	308		1023	11.1	338
	1724	-0.5	-15		1641	-1.5	-46
	2335	9.2	280		2254	10.5	320
12 Th	0532	0.2	6	**27** F	0458	-1.3	-40
	1144	10.0	305		1113	11.4	347
	1800	-0.3	-9		1728	-1.8	-55
					2342	10.9	332
13 F	0011	9.2	280	**28** Sa	0548	-1.6	-49
	0609	0.2	6		1203	11.4	347
	1220	9.8	299		1816	-1.8	-55
	1835	-0.1	-3				
14 Sa	0046	9.1	277				
	0646	0.4	12				
	1257	9.5	290				
	1909	0.1	3				
15 Su	0121	9.0	274				
	0723	0.5	15				
	1334	9.2	280				
	1944	0.4	12				

March

Day	Time	ft (Height)	cm	Day	Time	ft (Height)	cm
1 Su	0031	11.1	338	**16** M	0046	9.3	283
	0640	-1.7	-52		0654	0.3	9
	1255	11.2	341		1306	9.2	280
	1906	-1.6	-49		1909	0.6	18
2 M	0121	11.1	338	**17** Tu	0119	9.3	283
	0734	-1.5	-46		0730	0.4	12
	1349	10.7	326		1343	8.9	271
	1958	-1.2	-37		1944	0.8	24
3 Tu	0214	10.9	332	**18** W	0155	9.2	280
	0831	-1.2	-37		0809	0.6	18
	1447	10.1	308		1422	8.6	262
	2053	-0.6	-18		2022	1.1	34
4 W	0311	10.5	320	**19** Th	0235	9.0	274
	0932	-0.7	-21		0852	0.8	24
	1549	9.5	290		1506	8.3	253
	2153	0.0	0		2106	1.3	40
5 Th ◐	0413	10.1	308	**20** F	0320	8.9	271
	1038	-0.2	-6		0940	0.9	27
	1656	9.0	274		1556	8.1	247
	2258	0.5	15		2155	1.5	46
6 F	0519	9.7	296	**21** Sa ◐	0411	8.8	268
	1148	0.1	3		1035	1.0	30
	1806	8.6	262		1652	8.0	244
					2251	1.5	46
7 Sa	0006	0.8	24	**22** Su	0508	8.9	271
	0628	9.5	290		1136	0.9	27
	1256	0.2	6		1753	8.1	247
	1914	8.6	262		2353	1.4	43
8 Su	0113	0.9	27	**23** M	0611	9.1	277
	0733	9.5	290		1238	0.6	18
	1359	0.2	6		1856	8.5	259
	2015	8.7	265				
9 M	0214	0.8	24	**24** Tu	0057	0.9	27
	0832	9.5	290		0713	9.6	293
	1454	0.1	3		1338	0.1	3
	2108	8.9	271		1955	9.0	274
10 Tu	0307	0.6	18	**25** W	0157	0.3	9
	0923	9.7	296		0813	10.1	308
	1541	0.0	0		1434	-0.5	-15
	2154	9.1	277		2049	9.7	296
11 W	0353	0.4	12	**26** Th	0254	-0.4	-12
	1007	9.8	299		0909	10.7	326
	1623	-0.1	-3		1526	-1.0	-30
	2234	9.2	280		2140	10.5	320
12 Th ○	0434	0.3	9	**27** F ●	0348	-1.1	-34
	1047	9.8	299		1003	11.1	338
	1659	-0.1	-3		1616	-1.5	-46
	2310	9.3	283		2230	11.1	338
13 F	0511	0.2	6	**28** Sa	0440	-1.7	-52
	1123	9.7	296		1055	11.4	347
	1733	0.0	0		1705	-1.7	-52
	2343	9.4	287		2319	11.5	351
14 Sa	0546	0.1	3	**29** Su	0532	-2.0	-61
	1157	9.6	293		1147	11.4	347
	1805	0.2	6		1754	-1.6	-49
15 Su	0014	9.4	287	**30** M	0008	11.6	354
	0620	0.2	6		0624	-2.0	-61
	1231	9.4	287		1239	11.1	338
	1836	0.3	9		1844	-1.4	-43
				31 Tu	0059	11.5	351
					0717	-1.8	-55
					1334	10.7	326
					1937	-0.9	-27

Time meridian 75° W. 0000 is midnight. 1200 is noon.
Heights are referred to mean lower low water which is the chart datum of soundings.

Fig. 1017. Extract from Table 1 of the *Tide Tables*.

24^{h}50^m), the time between successive high or low tides is a little more than twelve hours. When a high (or low) tide occurs just before midnight, the next high (or low) tide occurs about noon of the following day, and the next one occurs just after midnight. Under these conditions, three consecutive high (or low) tides may occur on three different dates, although the total interval may be no more than the average period of a lunar day, 24^{h}50^m. This means that on the middle of the three days, there is but one high (or low) water. An example of this is seen in figure 1017; only one low tide occurs at Portland on 7 January.

Subordinate Stations

1018   The information described above is very useful if you are at Portland, Maine. But if you are going somewhere that is not listed as a reference station in the *Tide Tables*, you will need to dig deeper to get the information you need. Let us assume that your dock landing ship, USS *Tortuga*, has been ordered to go to Berth 6A at Seavey Island in Portsmouth Naval Shipyard, arriving on 28 January at 1300. Checking the Fleet Guide, you determine that the depth at the berth is 25 feet. Since your vessel draws 20 feet, you should have enough water under your keel when moored. However, if Portsmouth is one of those areas of the world where the tidal range is substantial, you could have a problem.

By checking the index of the *Tide Tables for the East Coast of North and South America*, you would find a listing for Seavey Island with the number 893 after it. Because the listing does *not* have an asterisk and a page number following it, you know that it is a secondary or *subordinate station* and is therefore listed in Table 2, which lists several thousand additional locations in geographical order.

Turning to Table 2 (see fig. 1018), you would find Seavey by going to the number 893; listings are in sequential order. There you can see the latitude-longitude location of Seavey Island along with differences in time and height of high and low water, ranges of mean and spring tides and the mean tide level. Note that the difference figures are used in relation to the reference station listed above in bold type—in this case, Portland—along with the page number (32) where the data for this reference station can be found.

Determining Height of High or Low Tide at Subordinate Stations

1019   By reading across the columns in Table 2 (fig. 1018), you can see that the height differences for high and low water are tabulated. These will

appear in Table 2 in two forms. Sometimes they will be listed as a simple positive or negative number; this number is the difference in tidal height from that of the reference station. You would algebraically sum the two figures (i.e., add or subtract the substation differences from the reference station's high and low tides as appropriate) to determine the heights of tides for the substation.

More frequently you will encounter a number with an asterisk before it—this is the case for Seavey Island in figure 1018 (*0.89 for both high waters and low waters). The number is a ratio and is used by *multiplying* the heights at the reference station (Portland) to get the heights for the subordinate station (Seavey Island).

Referring again to Table 1 (fig. 1017), you can see that the high tides for Portland on 28 January are 10.9 feet (332 centimeters) and 9.8 feet (299 cm). You can tell the high tides from the low by comparing the heights—in this case, the two low tides are negative numbers and the highs are positive.

By multiplying these high tides by the high water ratio figure of 0.89 listed in Table 2, you know the high tides at Seavey Island will be 9.7 feet (0.89 × 10.9 = 9.701) or 295 cm (0.89 × 332 = 295.48) and 8.7 feet (0.89 × 9.8 = 8.722) or 266 cm (0.89 × 299 = 266.11).

Similarly, you can use the 0.89 ratio for low waters to find that the first low tide at Seavey Island on 28 January will be negligible (0.89 × 3 = .267) and that the second low tide will be a little more than a foot (0.89 × 1.3 = 1.157 ft). When applied to the charted depth of 25 feet at your mooring at Berth 6A, you can see that these low tides are of little concern. Your vessel will have adequate water at low tides and ample water at high tides.

Determining Time of High and Low Tides at Subordinate Stations

1020   Even though you now know that you will have enough water beneath your keel at Berth 6A at all times, it would be helpful to know when the different tides would occur. For example, knowing the range of tide can help you use the right amount of mooring line to keep your vessel properly secured to the pier. Or you might want to schedule a stores load when the tide is low rather than high because the brow would be at a more convenient angle at that time, making the job easier for the sailors who have to carry the stores aboard. By again reading across the columns in Table 2 (fig. 1018), you can see that there are time differences for high and low water tabulated. These time differences must be applied to the respective high and low waters at the

TABLE 2 – TIDAL DIFFERENCES AND OTHER CONSTANTS

No.	PLACE	POSITION		DIFFERENCES				RANGES		Mean Tide Level
				Time		Height				
		Latitude	Longitude	High Water	Low Water	High Water	Low Water	Mean	Spring	
		North	West	h m	h m	ft	ft	ft	ft	ft
	MAINE, Casco Bay–cont. Time meridian, 75° W			on Portland, p.32						
833	Little Flying Point, Maquoit Bay	43° 50'	70° 03'	−0 01	−0 01	*0.99	*0.99	9.0	10.3	4.8
835	South Freeport	43° 49'	70° 06'	+0 12	+0 10	*0.99	*0.99	9.0	10.3	4.8
837	Chebeague Point, Great Chebeague Island.	43° 46'	70° 06'	−0 04	−0 09	*0.99	*0.99	9.0	10.4	4.8
839	Prince Point	43° 46'	70° 10'	0 00	0 00	*1.01	*1.00	9.2	10.6	4.9
841	Doyle Point	43° 45'	70° 08'	−0 02	−0 03	*1.00	*0.88	9.2	10.5	4.9
843	Falmouth Foreside	43° 44'	70° 12'	+0 01	0 00	*1.00	*1.03	9.1	10.5	4.9
845	Great Chebeague Island	43° 43'	70° 08'	+0 03	+0 03	*1.00	*1.00	9.1	10.5	4.9
847	Cliff Island, Luckse Sound	43° 42'	70° 07'	−0 02	−0 02	*1.00	*1.00	9.1	10.4	4.9
849	Vaill Island	43° 41'	70° 09'	+0 05	+0 01	*0.98	*1.03	9.0	10.3	4.8
851	Long Island	43° 41'	70° 10'	−0 01	0 00	*1.00	*1.00	9.1	10.4	4.9
853	Cow Island	43° 41'	70° 11'	−0 01	0 00	*1.00	*1.00	9.1	10.5	4.9
855	Presumpscot River Bridge	43° 41'	70° 15'	+0 01	+0 04	*1.01	*1.06	9.2	10.6	5.0
857	Back Cove	43° 41'	70° 15'	+0 02	+0 06	*0.97	*0.97	9.1	10.5	4.9
859	Great Diamond Island	43° 40'	70° 12'	−0 01	0 00	*0.99	*1.00	9.0	10.4	4.9
861	Peaks Island	43° 39'	70° 12'	−0 04	−0 08	*0.99	*0.99	9.0	10.4	4.8
863	Cushing Island	43° 39'	70° 12'	+0 01	0 00	*0.99	*1.00	9.0	10.4	4.9
865	PORTLAND	43° 40'	70° 15'	Daily predictions				9.1	10.4	4.9
867	Fore River	43° 38'	70° 17'	+0 02	+0 02	*1.00	*1.00	9.1	10.5	4.9
869	Portland Head Light	43° 37'	70° 12'	−0 02	−0 02	*0.97	*0.97	8.9	10.2	4.8
	MAINE, outer coast–cont.									
871	Richmond Island	43° 33'	70° 14'	−0 03	−0 03	*0.98	*0.98	8.9	10.1	4.8
873	Old Orchard Beach	43° 31'	70° 22'	0 00	−0 06	*0.97	*0.97	8.8	10.1	4.7
875	Wood Island Harbor	43° 27'	70° 21'	+0 02	−0 04	*0.96	*0.96	8.7	9.9	4.7
877	Cape Porpoise	43° 22'	70° 26'	+0 12	+0 14	*0.95	*0.95	8.7	9.9	4.7
879	Kennebunkport	43° 21'	70° 28'	+0 16	+0 16	*0.94	*0.94	8.6	9.9	4.6
881	York Harbor	43° 08'	70° 38'	+0 03	+0 13	*0.95	*0.95	8.6	9.9	4.6
883	Seapoint, Cutts Island	43° 05'	70° 40'	+0 01	−0 04	*0.96	*0.96	8.8	10.1	4.7
	MAINE and NEW HAMPSHIRE									
	Portsmouth Harbor									
885	Jaffrey Point	43° 03'	70° 43'	−0 03	−0 05	*0.95	*0.95	8.7	10.0	4.7
887	Gerrish Island	43° 04'	70° 42'	−0 02	−0 03	*0.95	*0.95	8.7	10.0	4.7
889	Fort Point	43° 04'	70° 43'	+0 03	+0 07	*0.94	*0.94	8.6	9.9	4.6
891	Kittery Point	43° 05'	70° 42'	−0 07	+0 01	*0.96	*0.96	8.7	10.0	4.7
893	Seavey Island	43° 05'	70° 45'	+0 20	+0 18	*0.89	*0.89	8.1	9.4	4.4
895	Portsmouth	43° 05'	70° 45'	+0 22	+0 17	*0.86	*0.86	7.8	9.0	4.2
	Piscataqua River									
897	Atlantic Heights	43° 05'	70° 46'	+0 37	+0 28	*0.82	*0.82	7.5	8.6	4.0
899	Dover Point	43° 07'	70° 50'	+1 33	+1 27	*0.70	*0.70	6.4	7.4	3.4
901	Salmon Falls River entrance	43° 11'	70° 50'	+1 35	+1 42	*0.75	*0.75	6.8	7.8	3.6
903	Squamscott River RR. Bridge	43° 03'	70° 55'	+2 19	+2 41	*0.75	*0.75	6.8	7.8	3.6
905	Gosport Harbor, Isles of Shoals	42° 59'	70° 37'	+0 02	−0 02	*0.93	*0.93	8.5	9.8	4.5
907	Hampton Harbor	42° 54'	70° 49'	+0 14	+0 32	*0.91	*0.91	8.3	9.5	4.5
	MASSACHUSETTS, outer coast									
909	Merrimack River entrance	42° 49'	70° 49'	+0 20	+0 24	*0.91	*0.91	8.3	9.5	4.4
911	Newburyport, Merrimack River	42° 49'	70° 52'	+0 31	+1 11	*0.86	*0.86	7.8	9.0	4.2
913	Plum Island Sound (south end)	42° 43'	70° 47'	+0 12	+0 37	*0.94	*0.94	8.6	9.9	4.6
915	Annisquam	42° 39'	70° 41'	0 00	−0 07	*0.96	*0.96	8.7	10.1	4.7
917	Rockport	42° 40'	70° 37'	+0 04	+0 02	*0.94	*0.94	8.6	10.0	4.6
				on Boston, p.36						
919	Gloucester Harbor	42° 36'	70° 40'	−0 01	−0 04	*0.91	*0.91	8.7	10.1	4.6
921	Manchester Harbor	42° 34'	70° 47'	0 00	−0 04	*0.92	*0.92	8.8	10.2	4.7
923	Beverly	42° 32'	70° 53'	+0 02	−0 03	*0.94	*0.94	9.0	10.4	4.8
925	Salem	42° 31'	70° 53'	+0 04	+0 03	*0.92	*0.92	8.8	10.2	4.7
927	Marblehead	42° 30'	70° 51'	0 00	−0 04	*0.95	*0.95	9.1	10.6	4.8
	Broad Sound									
929	Nahant	42° 25'	70° 55'	+0 01	0 00	*0.94	*0.94	9.0	10.4	4.8
931	Lynn Harbor	42° 27'	70° 58'	+0 10	+0 06	*0.96	*0.96	9.2	10.7	4.9
	Boston Harbor									
933	Boston Light	42° 20'	70° 53'	+0 02	+0 03	*0.94	*0.94	9.0	10.4	4.8
935	Lovell Island, The Narrows	42° 20'	70° 56'	+0 04	+0 03	*0.95	*0.95	9.1	10.6	4.8
937	Deer Island (south end)	42° 21'	70° 58'	+0 01	0 00	*0.97	*0.97	9.3	10.8	4.9
939	Belle Isle Inlet entrance	42° 23'	71° 00'	+0 20	+0 17	*1.00	*1.00	9.5	11.0	5.0
941	Castle Island	42° 20'	71° 01'	0 00	+0 02	*0.99	*0.99	9.4	10.9	5.0
943	BOSTON	42° 21'	71° 03'	Daily predictions				9.5	11.0	5.1
945	Dover St. Bridge, Fort Point Channel	42° 21'	71° 04'	+0 06	+0 08	*1.01	*1.01	9.6	11.0	5.1
	Charles River									
947	Charlestown Bridge	42° 22'	71° 04'	+0 04	+0 04	*1.00	*1.00	9.5	11.0	5.0
949	Charles River Dam	42° 22'	71° 04'	+0 07	+0 06	*1.00	*1.00	9.5	11.0	5.0
951	Charlestown	42° 22'	71° 03'	0 00	+0 01	*1.00	*1.00	9.5	11.0	5.0
953	Chelsea St. Bridge, Chelsea River	42° 23'	71° 01'	+0 01	+0 06	*1.01	*1.01	9.6	11.1	5.1
955	Neponset, Neponset River	42° 17'	71° 02'	−0 02	+0 03	*1.00	*1.00	9.5	11.0	5.0
957	Moon Head	42° 19'	70° 59'	+0 01	+0 04	*0.99	*0.99	9.4	10.9	5.0
959	Rainsford Island, Nantasket Roads	42° 19'	70° 57'	0 00	+0 02	*0.95	*0.95	9.1	10.6	4.8

Endnotes can be found at the end of table 2.

Fig. 1018. Extract from Table 2 of the *Tide Tables.*

reference station in order to know the times at the subordinate station. In the case of Seavey Island, you can see that high tides will occur twenty minutes later ($+0^h20^m$) than at Portland and low tides will occur eighteen minutes later ($+0^h18^m$). If the tides at Seavey Island occurred earlier than those at the Portland reference station, the times would be preceded by a minus (–) sign instead of the plus sign you see here.

Referring back to Table 1 (fig. 1017), you see that for 28 January, the two high tides occur at 1043 and 2318, and the two low tides are at 0428 and 1705. By applying the time differences from Table 2 to these figures, we can determine the times of the high and low tides for Seavey Island.

Since the difference for high tides at Seavey Island was determined from Table 2 to be $+0^h20^m,$ the high tides there will occur at 1103 ($10^h43^m + 0^h20^m = 11^h03^m$) and 2338 ($23^h18^m + 0^h20^m = 23^h38^m$). By this same means, you can determine that the low tides at your berth will occur at 0446 ($04^h28^m + 0^h18^m$) and 1723 ($17^h05^m + 0^h18^m$).

Keep in mind that the figures listed for subordinate stations in Table 2 are corrections to the figures found in Table 1 for the indicated reference station. Do not make the mistake of applying the differences found in Table 2 to the depths found on your chart. These figures must be applied to those in Table 1 and the results must then be applied to the charted depths in order to get an accurate depth of water.

Determining Height of Tide for a Specific Time

1021   Once you have determined the times of high and low tides for a specific location such as Seavey Island, it is then possible to determine the height of tide (and, therefore, the depth of water) for a specific time by using Table 3 in the *Tide Tables* (see fig. 1021).

In our example, *Tortuga* is scheduled to arrive at 1300 on 28 January. If you wanted to know the height of tide at your berth upon your arrival, you could enter Table 3 with several pieces of information to get your answer. You know from using Tables 1 and 2 that 1300 falls between the 1103 high tide of 9.7 feet and the 1723 low tide of –1.2 feet. By simple calculation you know that the elapsed time between the two extremes is six hours and twenty minutes ($17^h23^m – 11^h03^m = 6^h20^m$) and that the elapsed time from the nearest tide to your arrival time is one hour and fifty-seven minutes (1300–1103). You also know that from the high tide to the low tide the range is from +9.7 to –1.2, a total of 10.9 feet. These pieces of information are used to enter Table 3 as follows:

1. Enter the top portion of the table with the elapsed time between the two tides straddling your arrival time of 1300; this is called the "Duration of rise or fall" in the table. Use the figure in the table closest to your calculated difference in time; in this example, "6 20" is an exact match.
2. Move across the table until you reach the closest "Time from the nearest high water or low water"; in this case "1 54" in the table would be closest to the one hour and fifty-seven minutes between the 1103 high tide and the 1300 arrival time.
3. Move down the column from 1 54 to the lower part of the table and find the line that intersects with the figure on the left that most closely matches the range of tide (10.9 feet in this example). "11.0" is the closest match, so you then read the figure at the intersection of these two lines; in this case, the intersection occurs at "2.3" and that would be the "correction to height."

By this process, you have determined that the correction to the height of tide would be 2.3 feet, and since the tide was falling between the 1103 high tide and the 1723 low tide, you would *subtract* the 2.3 from the 1103 height of water to obtain the height of tide for 1300 (9.7 – 2.3 = 7.4). Using Table 3 in conjunction with the data you derived from Tables 1 and 2, you have determined that the height of tide when you arrive at Berth 6A will be 7.4 feet above the charted depth of 25 feet.

Note that additional interpolation is not used when using Table 3. The predictions of times and heights of tide are influenced by local conditions to the extent that they are not exact enough to make meaningful any further interpolation for more precise values.

Graphing Tidal Data

1022   Because you can never be certain that you will arrive at a particular place at an exact time, it can be very useful to prepare a graphic representation of the tidal information available that straddles your ETA or ETD by an appropriate margin. In the Navy, navigators will graph the entire day (or days) that their ship is expected to be in restricted waters and make copies for all concerned (the conning officer, officer of the deck, etc.). This graph provides a quick (though somewhat approximate) reference for finding the tide for whatever time is desired without having to go into Table 3 each time a specific time is required. The procedures for graphing the tidal data obtained from the tables are explained in the notes accompanying Table 3.

Some of the commercially available software programs also permit a graphing function.

TABLE 3. —HEIGHT OF TIDE AT ANY TIME

Duration of rise or fall, see footnote

Time from the nearest high water or low water

h. m.	h. m.	h. m.	h. m.	h. m.	h. m.	h. m.	h. m.	h. m.	h. m.	h. m.	h. m.	h. m.	h. m.	h. m.	h. m.
4 10	0 08	0 16	0 24	0 32	0 40	0 48	0 56	1 04	1 12	1 20	1 28	1 36	1 44	1 52	2 00
4 20	0 09	0 17	0 26	0 35	0 43	0 52	1 01	1 09	1 18	1 27	1 35	1 44	1 53	2 01	2 10
4 40	0 09	0 19	0 28	0 37	0 47	0 56	1 05	1 15	1 24	1 33	1 43	1 52	2 01	2 11	2 20
5 00	0 10	0 20	0 30	0 40	0 50	1 00	1 10	1 20	1 30	1 40	1 50	2 00	2 10	2 20	2 30
5 20	0 11	0 21	0 32	0 43	0 53	1 04	1 15	1 25	1 36	1 47	1 57	2 08	2 19	2 29	2 40
5 40	0 11	0 23	0 34	0 45	0 57	1 08	1 19	1 31	1 42	1 53	2 05	2 16	2 27	2 39	2 50
6 00	0 12	0 24	0 36	0 48	1 00	1 12	1 24	1 36	1 48	2 00	2 12	2 24	2 36	2 48	3 00
6 20	0 13	0 25	0 38	0 51	1 03	1 16	1 29	1 41	1 54	2 07	2 19	2 32	2 45	2 57	3 10
6 40	0 13	0 27	0 40	0 53	1 07	1 20	1 33	1 47	2 00	2 13	2 27	2 40	2 53	3 07	3 20
7 00	0 14	0 28	0 42	0 56	1 10	1 24	1 38	1 52	2 06	2 20	2 34	2 48	3 02	3 16	3 30
7 20	0 15	0 29	0 44	0 59	1 13	1 28	1 43	1 57	2 12	2 27	2 41	2 56	3 11	3 25	3 40
7 40	0 15	0 31	0 46	1 01	1 17	1 32	1 47	2 03	2 18	2 33	2 49	3 04	3 19	3 35	3 50
8 00	0 16	0 32	0 48	1 04	1 20	1 36	1 52	2 08	2 24	2 40	2 56	3 12	3 28	3 44	4 00
8 20	0 17	0 33	0 50	1 07	1 23	1 40	1 57	2 13	2 30	2 47	3 03	3 20	3 37	3 53	4 10
8 40	0 17	0 35	0 52	1 09	1 27	1 44	2 01	2 19	2 36	2 53	3 11	3 28	3 45	4 03	4 20
9 00	0 18	0 36	0 54	1 12	1 30	1 48	2 06	2 24	2 42	3 00	3 18	3 36	3 54	4 12	4 30
9 20	0 19	0 37	0 56	1 15	1 33	1 52	2 11	2 29	2 48	3 07	3 25	3 44	4 03	4 21	4 40
9 40	0 19	0 39	0 58	1 17	1 37	1 56	2 15	2 35	2 54	3 13	3 33	3 52	4 11	4 31	4 50
10 00	0 20	0 40	1 00	1 20	1 40	2 00	2 20	2 40	3 00	3 20	3 40	4 00	4 20	4 40	5 00
10 20	0 21	0 41	1 02	1 23	1 43	2 04	2 25	2 45	3 06	3 27	3 47	4 08	4 29	4 49	5 10
10 40	0 21	0 43	1 04	1 25	1 47	2 08	2 29	2 51	3 12	3 33	3 55	4 16	4 37	4 59	5 20

Range of tide, see footnote

Correction to height

Ft.	Ft.	Ft.	Ft.	Ft.	Ft.	Ft.	Ft.	Ft.	Ft.	Ft.	Ft.	Ft.	Ft.	Ft.	Ft.
0.5	0.0	0.0	0.0	0.0	0.0	0.0	0.1	0.1	0.1	0.1	0.1	0.2	0.2	0.2	0.2
1.0	0.0	0.0	0.0	0.0	0.1	0.1	0.1	0.2	0.2	0.2	0.3	0.3	0.4	0.4	0.5
1.5	0.0	0.0	0.0	0.1	0.1	0.1	0.2	0.2	0.3	0.4	0.4	0.5	0.6	0.7	0.8
2.0	0.0	0.0	0.0	0.1	0.1	0.2	0.3	0.3	0.4	0.5	0.6	0.7	0.8	0.9	1.0
2.5	0.0	0.0	0.1	0.1	0.2	0.2	0.3	0.4	0.5	0.6	0.7	0.9	1.0	1.1	1.2
3.0	0.0	0.0	0.1	0.1	0.2	0.3	0.4	0.5	0.6	0.8	0.9	1.0	1.2	1.3	1.5
3.5	0.0	0.0	0.1	0.2	0.2	0.3	0.4	0.6	0.7	0.9	1.0	1.2	1.4	1.6	1.8
4.0	0.0	0.0	0.1	0.2	0.3	0.4	0.5	0.7	0.8	1.0	1.2	1.4	1.6	1.8	2.0
4.5	0.0	0.0	0.1	0.2	0.3	0.4	0.6	0.7	0.9	1.1	1.3	1.6	1.8	2.0	2.2
5.0	0.0	0.1	0.1	0.2	0.3	0.5	0.6	0.8	1.0	1.2	1.5	1.7	2.0	2.2	2.5
5.5	0.0	0.1	0.1	0.2	0.4	0.5	0.7	0.9	1.1	1.4	1.6	1.9	2.2	2.5	2.8
6.0	0.0	0.1	0.1	0.3	0.4	0.6	0.8	1.0	1.2	1.5	1.8	2.1	2.4	2.7	3.0
6.5	0.0	0.1	0.2	0.3	0.4	0.6	0.8	1.1	1.3	1.6	1.9	2.2	2.6	2.9	3.2
7.0	0.0	0.1	0.2	0.3	0.5	0.7	0.9	1.2	1.4	1.8	2.1	2.4	2.8	3.1	3.5
7.5	0.0	0.1	0.2	0.3	0.5	0.7	1.0	1.2	1.5	1.9	2.2	2.6	3.0	3.4	3.8
8.0	0.0	0.1	0.2	0.3	0.5	0.8	1.0	1.3	1.6	2.0	2.4	2.8	3.2	3.6	4.0
8.5	0.0	0.1	0.2	0.4	0.6	0.8	1.1	1.4	1.8	2.1	2.5	2.9	3.4	3.8	4.2
9.0	0.0	0.1	0.2	0.4	0.6	0.9	1.2	1.5	1.9	2.2	2.7	3.1	3.6	4.0	4.5
9.5	0.0	0.1	0.2	0.4	0.6	0.9	1.2	1.6	2.0	2.4	2.8	3.3	3.8	4.3	4.8
10.0	0.0	0.1	0.2	0.4	0.7	1.0	1.3	1.7	2.1	2.5	3.0	3.5	4.0	4.5	5.0
10.5	0.0	0.1	0.3	0.5	0.7	1.0	1.3	1.7	2.2	2.6	3.1	3.6	4.2	4.7	5.2
11.0	0.0	0.1	0.3	0.5	0.7	1.1	1.4	1.7	2.3	2.8	3.3	3.8	4.4	4.9	5.5
11.5	0.0	0.1	0.3	0.5	0.8	1.1	1.5	1.8	2.3	2.9	3.4	4.0	4.6	5.1	5.8
12.0	0.0	0.1	0.3	0.5	0.8	1.1	1.5	1.9	2.5	3.0	3.6	4.1	4.8	5.4	6.0
12.5	0.0	0.1	0.3	0.5	0.8	1.2	2.6	1.9	2.6	3.1	3.7	4.3	5.0	5.6	6.2
13.0	0.0	0.1	0.3	0.6	0.9	1.2	1.7	2.2	2.7	3.2	3.9	4.5	5.1	5.8	6.5
13.5	0.0	0.1	0.3	0.6	0.9	1.3	1.7	2.2	2.8	3.4	4.0	4.7	5.3	6.0	6.8
14.0	0.0	0.2	0.3	0.6	0.9	1.3	1.8	2.3	2.9	3.5	4.2	4.8	5.5	6.3	7.0
14.5	0.0	0.2	0.4	0.6	1.0	1.4	1.9	2.4	3.0	3.6	4.3	5.0	5.7	6.5	7.2
15.0	0.0	0.2	0.4	0.6	1.0	1.4	1.9	2.5	3.1	3.8	4.4	5.2	5.9	6.7	7.5
15.5	0.0	0.2	0.4	0.7	1.0	1.5	2.0	2.6	3.2	3.9	4.6	5.4	6.1	6.9	7.8
16.0	0.0	0.2	0.4	0.7	1.1	1.5	2.1	2.6	3.3	4.0	4.7	5.5	6.3	7.2	8.0
16.5	0.0	0.2	0.4	0.7	1.1	1.6	2.1	2.7	3.4	4.1	4.9	5.7	6.5	7.4	8.2
17.0	0.0	0.2	0.4	0.7	1.1	1.6	2.2	2.8	3.5	4.2	5.0	5.9	6.7	7.6	8.5
17.5	0.0	0.2	0.4	0.8	1.2	1.7	2.2	2.9	3.6	4.4	5.2	6.0	6.9	7.8	8.8
18.0	0.0	0.2	0.4	0.8	1.2	1.7	2.3	3.0	3.7	4.5	5.3	6.2	7.1	8.1	9.0
18.5	0.1	0.2	0.5	0.8	1.2	1.8	2.4	3.1	3.8	4.6	5.5	6.4	7.3	8.3	9.2
19.0	0.1	0.2	0.5	0.9	1.3	1.8	2.4	3.1	3.9	4.8	5.6	6.6	7.5	8.5	9.5
19.5	0.1	0.2	0.5	0.8	1.3	1.9	2.5	3.2	4.0	4.9	5.8	6.7	7.7	8.7	9.8
20.0	0.1	0.2	0.5	0.9	1.3	1.9	2.6	3.3	4.1	5.0	5.9	6.9	7.9	9.0	10.0

Obtain from the predictions the high water and low water, one of which is before and the other after the time for which the height is required. The difference between the times of occurrence of these tides is the duration of rise or fall, and the difference between their heights is the range of tide for the above table. Find the difference between the nearest high or low water and the time for which the height is required.

Enter the table with the duration of rise or fall, printed in heavy-faced type, which most nearly agrees with the actual value, and on that horizontal line find the time from the nearest high or low water which agrees most nearly with the corresponding actual difference. The correction sought is in the column directly below, on the line with the range of tide.

When the nearest tide is high water, subtract the correction.

When the nearest tide is low, add the correction.

Fig. 1021. Extract from Table 3 of the *Tide Tables*.

Summary of Procedures

1023   To sum up the procedures for determining tidal information from the *Tide Tables* for a given location:

1. Look up your desired location in the index. If it is a reference station (identified by an asterisk and a page number in parentheses), simply go to the page number (skipping steps 2, 3, and 4) and use the data provided there.
2. If your location is a subordinate station, use the sequential number provided to find it in Table 2.
3. Record the subordinate station's difference information.
4. Identify the reference station (indicated in bold somewhere above the information for your subordinate station).
5. Go to the reference station in Table 1 and record the time and height information for the appropriate day(s).
6. If Daylight Savings Time is in effect locally, add one hour to the times provided.
7. Construct time and height information for your location by applying the differences in Table 2 to the information obtained in Table 1.
8. If desired, determine specific times required by using Table 3.
9. Graph your tidal data for quick reference.

Other Tables

1024   The *Tide Tables* also contain additional information that can be useful. Table 4 provides a handy reference for determining the Local Mean Time of sunrise and sunset. Table 5 can be used to reduce Local Mean Time to standard time (see chapter 23), and Table 6 provides moonrise and moonset data. Table 7 is used to convert feet to centimeters, should you have the need to do so. Table 8 provides some additional explanatory information regarding the accuracy of tide predictions, and a glossary in the back of the book can be most helpful in understanding the terminology used in the book.

Uses of Tidal Information

1025   As you can see from the above examples, using the *Tide Tables* can reassure you that you will have enough water beneath your keel to stay afloat (or warn you that you will not). You can also determine in advance how long your brow must be in order to reach from the pier to your deck at a reasonable angle (too short a brow can result in too steep an angle in regions where the tidal range is great). Tidal range can have an effect on the scope of your anchor chain, and it can be extremely important if you need to pass beneath any bridges as you make your way to your destination.

The Shoal Problem

1026   One practical application for using tidal data is to figure a window of time that it will be safe for your vessel to pass over a shoal (or through some other shallow water area where the right tidal conditions can provide sufficient water for a safe passage). Using your prepared graph, bracket the time that the tide is above the required level by identifying the two points where the water becomes deep enough and where it ceases to be. Read the times corresponding to these points and you have your "window."

The Bridge Problem

1027   When planning to pass beneath a bridge keep in mind that overhead clearance is usually based upon mean high water (MHW) and depths of water are based upon mean lower low water (MLLW). The difference between the two is the "Mean Tide Level" plus one half the "Mean Range." Both of these figures are included in Table 2 for all stations (both subordinate and reference). By adding the mean tide level and half the mean range to the published clearance at MHW, you now have a figure that you can compare to your masthead height to determine the height of tide required for your vessel to pass safely beneath the bridge. Using your tidal graph, you can then compute the times when it is safe to pass beneath the bridge.

It is advisable to factor a margin of safety for both the bridge and shoal problems.

Cautions

1028   While *Tide Tables* enhance your navigational abilities significantly, you should keep in mind that the information provided is not absolute and at times will be superseded by local conditions. In many coastal areas, the actual height of tide at any time may be considerably influenced by winds from a particular direction, especially if the winds are strong and persist for several days. At such times, the predicted tide variations may be completely masked by the temporary conditions and you may find considerably higher water on a shore that has had sustained and strong onshore winds virtually piling water up on it (and considerably *lower* water where a strong *offshore* wind has been blowing). This can be further exacerbated by sustained periods of heavy rains. Periods of abnormally low barometric pressure also may result in higher water levels for both high and low tides.

Generally, predictions for stations along the outer coasts are more accurate than those for stations farther inland. Stations in relatively shallow water, or those with a small tidal range are also more susceptible to meteorological effects.

As always, because of these uncertainties, an extra measure of caution is appropriate when incorporating tidal information into your navigational plan. As has been shown, there is a wealth of useful information available that can enhance navigational safety, but overreliance on this information without factoring in possible (and unexpected) variables can cause serious problems.

Keep in mind that the charted depths may be worsened by normal tidal changes and that tidal data may be further worsened by abnormal conditions.

Do not forget that the times listed in your tide table may need to be adjusted for Daylight Savings Time.

When applying corrections be careful to apply the differences appropriately; positives, negatives, and whether the water is rising or falling must be taken into account to avoid errors.

Remember that high tides may mean more water beneath your keel when crossing a bar but also means less clearance for your mast when passing beneath a bridge (and vice versa).

Chapter 11   Currents

In addition to the vertical changes in water levels caused by tides, as discussed in the preceding chapter, the nautical navigator must be concerned with currents, those *horizontal* movements of the body of water in which a vessel floats and moves. Currents can be the result of several causes: the daily changes in tidal levels, the normal flow of rivers from higher elevations to the sea, the steady blowing of wind from approximately the same direction for several days or more, or long-term climatic and weather conditions. Often two or more of these causes combine in temporary local conditions, such as when tidal action is superimposed on a river's natural flow, or when a number of days of steady winds alter a normal ocean current. The effect of current on a vessel, whatever its cause, is to set it off course, change its speed with respect to the Earth, or, more likely, both of these actions combined. The direction of a current is referred to as its *set,* and the speed of a current is known as its *drift,* usually expressed in knots.

The first part of this chapter will deal with the various *ocean current systems,* their location, and where data concerning them may be found. In considering these current systems, it must be borne in mind that strong winds, blowing contrary to the prevailing wind pattern for prolonged periods, can have a marked effect on the drift (speed) of an ocean current, and, to a lesser degree, on its set (direction) in the affected area. Drift for ocean currents is often described in terms of nautical miles per *day,* rather than knots (nautical miles per hour). When the weather returns to normal, the ocean current system will also return to its usual flow, which can often be predicted with considerable precision and accuracy.

The remainder of the chapter will deal with tidal currents. The rise and fall of water as described in the previous chapter results in a flow of water in and out of bays, rivers, and so on. As with the tides that cause them, tidal currents are predictable, and mariners take advantage of that predictability in their planning.

OCEAN CURRENT SYSTEMS

1101   A number of well-defined, permanent current systems exist in the open oceans, as charted in figure 1101. The chief cause of these currents is wind. Blowing almost continuously with considerable force and in the same general direction over large areas of the globe, these consistent winds have long been an important consideration to mariners making long voyages and are known by various appropriate names, such as "westerlies," "trade winds," and so on. The direction, steadiness, and force of a prevailing wind determines to a large extent the set, drift, depth, and permanence of the current it generates.

Currents with a generally northerly or southerly drift are also considerably affected by the *Coriolis force.* Caused by the rotation of the Earth, this force causes currents to be deflected to the right in a clockwise direction in the Northern Hemisphere, and counterclockwise in the Southern Hemisphere. Its effect increases with latitude; north-south currents are "bent" more as they head toward the poles. The Coriolis force is largely responsible for the circular pattern of the flow of currents in the North and South Atlantic, the North and South Pacific, and in the Indian Ocean. Because of seasonal variations in the wind systems and other seasonal changes, the characteristics of most ocean currents change considerably, but quite predictably, at certain times of the year.

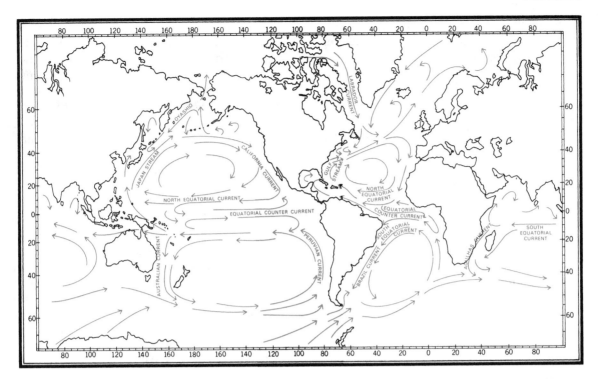

Fig. 1101. The principal ocean currents.

Currents are often described as warm or cold. These terms are relative, and are based on the latitudes in which they originate, and on the effect they have on climate. For example, the northeast drift current off the northern coast of Norway is a "warm" current, although it may be lower in temperature than the southern extremity of the "cold" Labrador Current off the New England coast.

Currents as well as winds were of great importance in the days of sail. Clipper ships in the nineteenth century, bound from England for Australia, would go out via the Cape of Good Hope, but return via Cape Horn, thus taking advantage of the strong prevailing westerly ocean currents (see fig. 1101). Similarly, the sixteenth-century Spanish "treasure galleons" sailed from Acapulco, Mexico, for Manila via the North Equatorial Current, but returned via the Japan Stream and the California Current.

Much useful information about these currents may be obtained from the *Pilot Charts* and *Pilot Chart Atlases* published by NIMA. These publications, covering the principal ocean areas of the world, in most instances show the mean direction and force of the surface currents in specific quadrangles of latitude and longitude for each month, as well as the frequency of direction and average drifts.

While there is some disagreement as to the names of ocean currents, certain conventions prevail. Some of the more significant ocean currents are discussed below.

Atlantic Ocean Currents

1102   The effect of the trade winds is to form two currents flowing westward across the Atlantic at the rate of about two thirds of a knot known as the *North and South Equatorial Currents*. Between them flows the somewhat weaker *Equatorial Counter Current*.

At the western edge of the Atlantic, the South Equatorial Current divides at the eastern tip of South America, part of it flowing southward and part continuing on into the Caribbean or northwestward along the West Indies. This current is joined by the North Equatorial Current, which has flowed westward from an area to the north of the Cape Verde Islands. Water flows up the Caribbean, through the Yucatan Strait, across the Gulf of Mexico, and back into the Atlantic through the Straits of Florida. Here it meets with the flow that flows east of the West Indies to form the famous *Gulf Stream*, which flows northerly along the east coast of the United States, picking up even more flow from currents eastward of the Bahamas. The indigo blue water of this sharply defined current of warm water roughly follows the coastline as far as Cape Hatteras, where it curves eastward, widens, and gradually loses some of its velocity. In an area south of North Carolina, there is a phenomenon associated with the Gulf Stream known as the "North Wall" where the warm water meeting with colder waters can cause very rough conditions.

Off the Grand Banks, the Gulf Stream loses its identity as such, but continues on eastward as a general circulatory flow or drift. It meets the cold water of the *Labrador Current* in this area, part of which accompanies it toward the east. However, the water mass remains comparatively warm, and has a very marked effect on the climate of northwestern Europe. On the eastern side of the Atlantic it divides to form the *northeast, easterly,* and *southeast drift currents.*

The circulation of the South Atlantic is generally similar. That part of the South Equatorial Current curving southward eventually forms the *Brazil Current,* which roughly follows the coast of South America. Off the coast of Uruguay the current divides, part of it continuing on to the south and part curving eastward back across the South Atlantic. This part, known as the *Southern Current,* is joined in the eastern Atlantic by water flowing northward from the Antarctic, and continues along the western coast of Africa to connect with the South Equatorial Current and complete the circulation, much as does the southeast drift current in the North Atlantic.

Pacific Ocean Currents

1103 The circulation in the Pacific is similar to that in the Atlantic. Here, as in the Atlantic, the *North* and *South Equatorial Currents* set westward, with the *Equatorial Counter Current* between them setting to the east.

In the western Pacific the North Equatorial Current curves northward forming the *Japan Stream,* which is similar to the Gulf Stream in the Atlantic. Roughly following the coastline of the Japanese islands, the Japanese name for this current is *Kuroshio* or "Black Stream," named for the noticeably dark color of the water. The main stream passes east of Japan and flows northward and eastward, widening as it does so and losing velocity while one part continues northerly and easterly to the region of the Aleutian Islands, and another part continues on east where it joins the weak north and northeast drift currents in this area.

Similar to the Labrador Current, the cold *Oyashio* flows out of the Bering Sea to the south and west close to the shores of the Kuril Islands and Japan. Like the Labrador Current, the Oyashio often brings ice from the Arctic Ocean.

Along the Pacific coast of the United States the cold *California Current* flows southward, generally following the coastline. This current is 200 to 300 miles wide and is not as strong as narrower currents, having an average velocity of only about 0.8 knots.

In the western Pacific the South Equatorial Current becomes the *Australia Current* as it flows southward past the east coast of Australia.

A current of cold water emerges from the Antarctic, southwest of South America, and then divides at the southern tip of Patagonia. Part of it, the *Cape Horn Current,* crosses into the southern Atlantic and part of it continues up the west coast of South America, as the *Peruvian Current.* Near Cape Blanco it curves to the western part of the Galapagos Islands and finally joins the South Equatorial Current.

INDIAN OCEAN CURRENTS

1104 The South Equatorial Current is the largest system in the Indian Ocean, circulating in a counterclockwise direction such that it flows northward off the western coast of Australia and southward off the eastern coast of southern Africa. The North Equatorial Current flows in a generally westward direction along the south coast of Asia, and the Equatorial Countercurrent is sandwiched between the other two, flowing in an opposite manner.

TEMPORARY WIND-DRIVEN CURRENTS

1105 Temporary, local wind-driven currents sometimes develop outside the well-defined ocean current systems. The drift of such a current depends largely on the force of the wind and its duration. If a wind has been blowing fairly steadily for some time at sea, a reasonable assumption would be that the drift of the current roughly equals 2 percent of the sustained average wind speed.

In the open ocean the set of a temporary wind current will *not* be in the direction the wind is blowing because it will be deflected by the Coriolis force. As discussed earlier, this deflection is to the right in the Northern Hemisphere. In the open sea, the deflection is about 40°; near a coastline it is considerably less, probably nearer 20°. Deflection of a wind-driven current is affected by the land structure and varies with depth, being more deflected at greater depths. The *Tidal Current Tables* (explained below) give information on offshore conditions that may be expected in certain areas.

TIDAL CURRENTS

1106 The previous chapter discussed the causes of tides and noted that the waters in the oceans and connecting waterways rise and fall periodically. It is obvious that as the amount of water changes, thus varying its level, there must be a flow back and forth between different areas; these flows are *tidal currents.* Such water movements are little noticed on the high seas, but they become significant, and sometimes critically important, along coasts and in bays, estuaries, and the lower reaches of rivers. The effect of tidal current is at times more important than the height of tide; in any body of water subject to tidal action, both must be considered.

Rotary Tidal Currents

1107   Offshore and in some of the wider indentations on the coast, where the direction of flow under tidal influence is not restricted by land, the Coriolis force influences the tidal flow just as it does with the wind driven current systems discussed earlier. Tidal current becomes *rotary*, flowing continuously, with the direction changing through all points of the compass during the tidal period. The change is clockwise in the Northern Hemisphere, and counterclockwise in the Southern Hemisphere. The speed usually varies throughout the tidal cycle, passing through two maximums in approximately opposite directions, and two minimums about halfway between the maximums in time and direction. Rotary currents are depicted as in figure 1107 by a series of vector arrows representing the direction and speed of the current at each hour. This depiction is sometimes called a *current rose.*

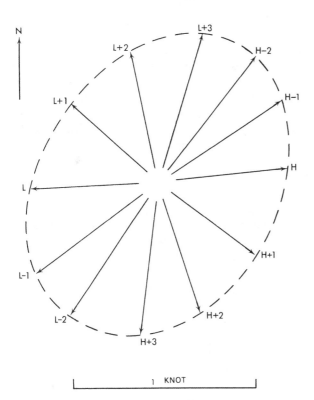

Fig. 1107. Rotary tidal currents. Times are hours before and after high and low tides at a specified reference station (former location of Nantucket Lightship). The bearing and length of each arrow represent the direction and strength of the current at the labeled time.

A distinguishing feature of a rotary current is that it has no time of slack water (see below). Although the current varies in strength, the variation is from a maximum to a minimum and back to the next maximum without any occurrence of slack.

Reversing Tidal Currents

1108   In rivers, bays, and straits, where the direction of flow is restricted to certain channels, the tidal current is called a *reversing current;* that is, it flows alternately in approximately opposite directions. The horizontal movement of water away from the sea (*upriver,* in the case of rivers) is called *flood current,* and the horizontal movement away from the land is called *ebb current.* Between these two, when the current changes direction, there is a brief period when no horizontal motion can be detected; this is *slack water.* During the flow in each direction, the speed varies from zero at the time of slack water to the *maximum flood* or *ebb* about midway between the slacks.

The symmetry of reversing currents can be significantly affected by the configuration of surrounding land. For example, the effect of tidal current will be magnified in a rapidly narrowing bay or hindered by a jutting peninsula. A swift current, called a *hydraulic current,* often occurs in a narrow passage connecting two large bodies of water, and is characterized by the current's strength being reached much more quickly, after a very brief period of slack water, and remaining strong for a greater part of the cycle than with normal reversing tidal currents.

As tidal currents supplement or oppose the natural flow of a river, its speed will increase during ebbs and slow down during flood tides. Rivers with a weaker natural flow can actually be reversed by the stronger influence of the tidal currents. The swiftest current in straight portions of tidal rivers is usually in the middle of the river, but in curved portions the most rapid current is toward the outer edge of the curve.

In areas where a rapid current moves along an irregular bottom, erratic movements of the water can form and are called *rips* or tide rips. A relatively small, somewhat circular movement of water can form where currents pass close to obstructions (natural or manmade); this is called an *eddy* (sometimes a whirlpool) and can have a significant effect on a small craft caught in its influence.

Reversing currents can be represented graphically by arrows or curves that indicate the strength of the current at each hour, as in figure 1108.

Tidal Current Predictions

1109   Just as with *Tide Tables* (see chapter 10), the National Ocean Service compiles and makes available the data needed for predictions. These

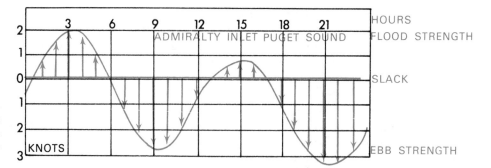

Fig. 1108. Reversing tidal currents; note asymmetrical nature of flood and ebb currents. (Some such graphs may show only the curve without the arrows.)

data are available on the Internet at the NOS web site, in commercially produced publications and software, and (for DOD use only) in book form from the National Imagery and Mapping Agency.

The availability of tidal current predictions and observed data is limited compared to the availability of tide data, but there is a significant amount available and it should be used whenever possible.

At the NOS web site, tidal current predictions are available in *international format* and *standard format* just as they are for tide predictions. Many of the same commercially produced navigational software programs and publications that include tide data also include tidal current predictions.

NIMA publishes the NOS data in book form in two volumes for DOD use: *Tidal Current Tables for the Atlantic Coast of North America*, and *Tidal Current Tables for the Pacific Coast of North America and Asia*. These publications are organized in a format generally similar to the *Tide Tables* discussed in chapter 10 and are used in much the same manner.

Table 1

1110   Just as the *Tide Tables* were arranged using separate tables of reference stations and subordinate stations to reduce the overall size of the volumes of data, the same method is used for the *Tidal Current Tables*. Table 1 provides essential data for a number of selected *reference stations*. Listed for each station in chronological order are the times of slack water and the times and speeds of maximum current flow. The latter are marked with an "E" or and "F" to identify them as ebbing or flooding. As with the *Tide Tables*, all times are 24-hour and are *not* adjusted for Daylight Savings Time. Also included, at the top of each page, are the general directions of flow of the currents.

For example, in figure 1110 you can see a sample page from the *Tidal Current Tables* for the Atlantic Coast of North America. If you were planning on entering Baltimore Harbor on the afternoon of 8 December, you can see from the table that at noon

you would have no current to contend with as you passed Sandy Point because there is a slack water listed for 1200. Looking across at the next entry you can see that it is an ebbing current reaching its maximum of 0.6 knots at 1442. Looking at the top of the table, you see that the general direction of ebb currents in this area is 190° True. Since the channel leading to Baltimore tends northward from Sandy Point, it is apparent that as you continue on, you will be sailing in the opposite direction of the 0.6-knot current and will therefore be impeded by it. You can also see in the table that the next slack water will be at 1722, and that will be followed by a flood current of 0.9 knots at 2046 that evening (in the direction 025° True).

Just as with the *Tide Tables*, the table also indicates the central meridian for time at the bottom of the page and provides some phase of the Moon information as indicated by the circular symbols on the appropriate days. You can see that the time meridian for Baltimore is 75° West and that the Moon will be somewhere between full and first quarter on 8 December.

Table 2

1111   A list of secondary or *subordinate stations* are arranged in geographical order in Table 2. To obtain the data for your location, look it up in the index and find its corresponding sequential number. Note that if there is an asterisk after the name of the location, it is a *reference station* and you need only go to the page indicated to find the data you need in *Table 1*. The vast majority of locations are subordinate stations and the number following the name is listed sequentially in Table 2. If, for example, you wanted to find the tidal current data for Greenbury Point, you would look it up in the index and find the number 6021. Turning to Table 2, you would then find the listing for Greenbury Point matched to that number (see fig. 1111). Given for each station in the table is its position in latitude and longitude to the nearest minute, the difference

Baltimore Harbor Approach (off Sandy Pt.), Maryland

F–Flood, Dir. 025° True   E–Ebb, Dir. 190° True

October

Day	Slack h m	Maximum h m	knots
1 Th		0052	0.8F
	0413	0730	0.8E
	1058	1343	0.5F
	1635	1933	0.6E
	2222		
2 F		0147	0.8F
	0503	0816	0.8E
	1136	1429	0.7F
	1727	2028	0.7E
	2324		
3 Sa		0240	0.8F
	0550	0900	0.9E
	1211	1512	0.8F
	1816	2120	0.8E
4 Su	0022	0330	0.9F
	0635	0941	0.9E
	1246	1555	0.9F
	1903	2209	0.9E
5 M ○	0119	0418	0.9F
	0718	1022	0.9E
	1322	1637	1.1F
	1950	2258	1.0E
6 Tu	0213	0506	0.8F
	0802	1104	0.9E
	1400	1721	1.2F
	2037	2347	1.1E
7 W	0308	0554	0.8F
	0846	1147	0.9E
	1440	1806	1.2F
	2126		
8 Th		0037	1.1E
	0402	0644	0.7F
	0932	1233	0.9E
	1523	1853	1.2F
	2216		
9 F		0129	1.1E
	0458	0736	0.7F
	1022	1322	0.8E
	1611	1943	1.2F
	2309		
10 Sa		0223	1.1E
	0556	0832	0.6F
	1117	1416	0.7E
	1703	2037	1.1F
11 Su	0004	0320	1.0E
	0655	0932	0.6F
	1219	1515	0.7E
	1801	2136	1.0F
12 M ◐	0101	0419	1.0E
	0754	1035	0.6F
	1327	1621	0.6E
	1907	2239	0.9F
13 Tu	0201	0520	0.9E
	0852	1139	0.6F
	1437	1731	0.6E
	2019	2345	0.9F
14 W	0301	0620	0.9E
	0946	1241	0.7F
	1545	1840	0.6E
	2132		
15 Th		0050	0.8F
	0359	0716	0.8E
	1036	1337	0.8F
	1646	1943	0.7E
	2241		
16 F		0150	0.8F
	0454	0808	0.9E
	1120	1428	0.8F
	1740	2040	0.8E
	2344		
17 Sa		0245	0.8F
	0545	0855	0.8E
	1202	1514	0.9F
	1828	2131	0.8E
18 Su	0040	0336	0.7F
	0632	0938	0.8E
	1240	1556	1.0F
	1912	2218	0.9E
19 M	0132	0422	0.7F
	0715	1019	0.8E
	1315	1635	1.0F
	1953	2301	0.9E
20 Tu ●	0220	0506	0.7F
	0757	1057	0.7E
	1349	1713	1.0F
	2032	2342	0.9E
21 W	0307	0548	0.6F
	0837	1134	0.7E
	1422	1750	1.0F
	2110		
22 Th		0023	0.9E
	0353	0630	0.6F
	0917	1212	0.6E
	1456	1827	1.0F
	2149		
23 F		0105	0.9E
	0439	0713	0.5F
	0959	1250	0.6E
	1530	1906	1.0F
	2230		
24 Sa		0148	0.9E
	0527	0759	0.5F
	1043	1331	0.5E
	1607	1947	0.9F
	2312		
25 Su		0233	0.9E
	0617	0847	0.4F
	1131	1416	0.4E
	1649	2032	0.9F
	2358		
26 M		0321	0.8E
	0707	0938	0.4F
	1225	1507	0.4E
	1739	2122	0.8F
27 Tu	0046	0411	0.8E
	0756	1032	0.4F
	1323	1605	0.4E
	1838	2217	0.7F
28 W ◐	0138	0503	0.8E
	0842	1126	0.5F
	1424	1708	0.4E
	1946	2316	0.7F
29 Th	0231	0554	0.8E
	0924	1218	0.6F
	1523	1812	0.5E
	2059		
30 F		0017	0.7F
	0324	0644	0.8E
	1003	1307	0.7F
	1617	1913	0.6E
	2210		
31 Sa		0116	0.7F
	0416	0731	0.8E
	1040	1353	0.8F
	1708	2010	0.7E
	2317		

November

Day	Slack h m	Maximum h m	knots
1 Su		0213	0.7F
	0506	0817	0.8E
	1118	1438	1.0F
	1756	2103	0.9E
2 M	0019	0306	0.7F
	0555	0901	0.8E
	1157	1523	1.1F
	1844	2154	1.0E
3 Tu	0117	0358	0.7F
	0643	0946	0.8E
	1237	1608	1.2F
	1931	2243	1.1E
4 W ○	0212	0448	0.7F
	0731	1032	0.8E
	1319	1653	1.3F
	2018	2332	1.2E
5 Th	0305	0538	0.7F
	0820	1119	0.8E
	1404	1740	1.3F
	2106		
6 F		0022	1.2E
	0357	0630	0.7F
	0912	1208	0.8E
	1451	1828	1.3F
	2154		
7 Sa		0112	1.2E
	0449	0723	0.7F
	1007	1300	0.7E
	1542	1919	1.2F
	2244		
8 Su		0203	1.2E
	0541	0818	0.7F
	1107	1357	0.7E
	1638	2013	1.1F
	2336		
9 M		0257	1.1E
	0634	0916	0.7F
	1212	1459	0.6E
	1740	2111	1.0F
10 Tu ◑	0029	0352	1.0E
	0726	1016	0.7F
	1321	1606	0.6E
	1848	2212	0.8F
11 W	0124	0448	0.9E
	0817	1116	0.7F
	1429	1715	0.6E
	2003	2317	0.7F
12 Th	0220	0543	0.9E
	0906	1214	0.8F
	1532	1823	0.6E
	2119		
13 F		0021	0.7F
	0316	0637	0.8E
	0952	1307	0.8F
	1630	1925	0.7E
	2230		
14 Sa		0122	0.6F
	0411	0728	0.8E
	1035	1357	0.9F
	1720	2021	0.8E
	2334		
15 Su		0219	0.6F
	0503	0815	0.8E
	1115	1442	1.0F
	1806	2112	0.8E
16 M	0032	0311	0.6F
	0553	0900	0.7E
	1153	1523	1.0F
	1848	2157	0.9E
17 Tu	0124	0359	0.6F
	0639	0941	0.7E
	1230	1603	1.1F
	1928	2241	1.0E
18 W ●	0213	0444	0.5F
	0724	1021	0.7E
	1304	1641	1.1F
	2006	2322	1.0E
19 Th	0259	0528	0.5F
	0808	1100	0.6E
	1339	1718	1.1F
	2044		
20 F		0003	1.0E
	0344	0611	0.5F
	0851	1139	0.6E
	1414	1756	1.1F
	2122		
21 Sa		0043	1.0E
	0428	0655	0.5F
	0936	1220	0.5E
	1450	1835	1.0F
	2201		
22 Su		0125	1.0E
	0512	0739	0.5F
	1022	1303	0.5E
	1530	1916	1.0F
	2242		
23 M		0207	1.0E
	0555	0825	0.5F
	1113	1350	0.4E
	1616	2001	0.9F
	2324		
24 Tu		0251	0.9E
	0637	0913	0.5F
	1207	1442	0.4E
	1710	2049	0.8F
25 W	0008	0336	0.9E
	0717	1002	0.5F
	1305	1541	0.4E
	1813	2143	0.7F
26 Th ◐	0055	0422	0.8E
	0755	1052	0.6F
	1404	1645	0.5E
	1926	2242	0.6F
27 F	0144	0510	0.8E
	0833	1142	0.7F
	1501	1750	0.5E
	2044	2344	0.6F
28 Sa	0236	0559	0.8E
	0912	1231	0.8F
	1556	1853	0.7E
	2200		
29 Su		0046	0.5F
	0329	0648	0.8E
	0951	1320	1.0F
	1648	1951	0.8E
	2311		
30 M		0146	0.5F
	0422	0737	0.8E
	1033	1408	1.1F
	1738	2046	0.9E

December

Day	Slack h m	Maximum h m	knots
1 Tu	0015	0244	0.5F
	0516	0826	0.8E
	1116	1455	1.2F
	1826	2138	1.1E
2 W	0113	0338	0.6F
	0610	0915	0.8E
	1201	1543	1.3F
	1914	2228	1.2E
3 Th ○	0207	0431	0.6F
	0704	1005	0.8E
	1249	1631	1.4F
	2001	2317	1.2E
4 F	0257	0523	0.6F
	0759	1056	0.8E
	1338	1719	1.4F
	2048		
5 Sa		0006	1.2E
	0346	0615	0.6F
	0856	1149	0.7E
	1429	1809	1.3F
	2135		
6 Su		0054	1.2E
	0433	0708	0.7F
	0955	1244	0.7E
	1522	1859	1.2F
	2222		
7 M		0143	1.2E
	0520	0801	0.7F
	1056	1341	0.6E
	1620	1951	1.1F
	2309		
8 Tu		0232	1.1E
	0607	0855	0.7F
	1200	1442	0.6E
	1722	2046	0.9F
	2357		
9 W		0322	1.0E
	0653	0950	0.8F
	1305	1546	0.6E
	1830	2144	0.8F
10 Th ◑	0047	0413	1.0E
	0739	1046	0.8F
	1408	1652	0.6E
	1943	2245	0.7F
11 F	0138	0504	0.9E
	0824	1140	0.9F
	1509	1757	0.6E
	2058	2347	0.5F
12 Sa	0231	0556	0.8E
	0907	1232	0.9F
	1604	1859	0.6E
	2211		
13 Su		0048	0.5F
	0324	0646	0.7E
	0950	1321	1.0F
	1654	1955	0.7E
	2317		
14 M		0147	0.4F
	0418	0734	0.7E
	1031	1407	1.0F
	1739	2047	0.8E
15 Tu	0017	0242	0.4F
	0511	0820	0.7E
	1110	1450	1.1F
	1822	2134	0.9E
16 W	0110	0333	0.4F
	0602	0905	0.6E
	1148	1531	1.1F
	1902	2218	1.0E
17 Th	0159	0420	0.5F
	0651	0948	0.6E
	1226	1611	1.1F
	1941	2300	1.0E
18 F ●	0245	0506	0.5F
	0738	1029	0.6E
	1304	1650	1.1F
	2019	2340	1.1E
19 Sa	0327	0550	0.5F
	0825	1111	0.5E
	1343	1730	1.1F
	2058		
20 Su		0020	1.1E
	0408	0632	0.5F
	0911	1154	0.5E
	1424	1810	1.1F
	2136		
21 M		0100	1.1E
	0446	0715	0.5F
	0959	1239	0.5E
	1508	1852	1.0F
	2215		
22 Tu		0139	1.0E
	0523	0758	0.5F
	1049	1328	0.5E
	1558	1936	0.9F
	2255		
23 W		0219	1.0E
	0558	0842	0.6F
	1142	1421	0.5E
	1654	2023	0.8F
	2336		
24 Th		0301	0.9E
	0633	0927	0.7F
	1238	1518	0.5E
	1759	2115	0.7F
25 F ◐	0019	0344	0.9E
	0709	1015	0.7F
	1336	1621	0.5E
	1912	2213	0.6F
26 Sa ◐	0104	0430	0.8E
	0746	1105	0.8F
	1434	1726	0.6E
	2030	2314	0.5F
27 Su	0154	0519	0.8E
	0827	1157	1.0F
	1531	1830	0.7E
	2149		
28 M		0019	0.4F
	0247	0610	0.8E
	0911	1249	1.1F
	1626	1931	0.8E
	2302		
29 Tu		0122	0.4F
	0345	0704	0.7E
	0958	1341	1.2F
	1718	2029	0.9E
30 W	0007	0224	0.4F
	0445	0758	0.7E
	1047	1433	1.3F
	1809	2122	1.1E
31 Th	0103	0321	0.5F
	0546	0853	0.7E
	1138	1524	1.3F
	1857	2213	1.1E

Time meridian 75° W. 0000 is midnight. 1200 is noon.

Fig. 1110. Extract from Table 1 of the *Tidal Current Tables.*

TABLE 2 – CURRENT DIFFERENCES AND OTHER CONSTANTS

No.	PLACE	Meter Depth (ft)	Position Lat. North	Position Long. West	Time Diff. Min. before Flood (h m)	Time Diff. Flood (h m)	Time Diff. Min. before Ebb (h m)	Time Diff. Ebb (h m)	Speed Ratio Flood	Speed Ratio Ebb	Min. before Flood (knots)	Min. before Flood (Dir.)	Maximum Flood (knots)	Maximum Flood (Dir.)	Min. before Ebb (knots)	Min. before Ebb (Dir.)	Maximum Ebb (knots)	Maximum Ebb (Dir.)
	PATUXENT RIVER—cont. Time meridian, 75° W				on Baltimore Harbor Approach, p.48													
5861	Point Patience, 0.1 mile southwest of	15	38° 19.70'	76° 29.20'	−5 07	−6 12	−6 46	−6 01	0.6	1.0	0.0	---	0.5	315°	0.0	---	0.8	145°
5866	Broomes Island, 0.4 mile south of		38° 23.70'	76° 33.25'	−5 01	−5 16	−5 02	−5 02	0.5	0.6	0.0	---	0.4	290°	0.0	---	0.5	110°
5871	Sheridan Point, 0.1 mile southwest of		38° 27.97'	76° 38.88'	−4 33	−4 54	−4 38	−4 16	0.8	0.8	0.0	---	0.6	320°	0.0	---	0.6	135°
5876	Benedict, highway bridge		38° 30.70'	76° 40.33'	−4 45	−4 38	−4 09	−4 35	1.0	0.6	0.0	---	0.8	025°	0.0	---	0.5	190°
5881	Lyons Creek Wharf		38° 44.8'	76° 41.1'	−3 14	−3 24	−3 52	−3 29	1.4	1.1	0.0	---	1.1	315°	0.0	---	0.9	140°
	LITTLE CHOPTANK RIVER																	
5886	Hills Point, 1.0 mile south of		38° 33.0'	76° 18.7'	Current weak and variable													
5891	Ragged Point, 1.5 miles east of		38° 31.80'	76° 14.65'	−4 53	−5 15	−4 29	−4 57	0.5	0.2	0.0	---	0.4	045°	0.0	---	0.2	235°
	CHOPTANK RIVER																	
5896	Cook Point, 1.4 n.mi. NNW of	15d	38° 38.83'	76° 18.40'	−3 52	−4 06	−4 06	−4 24	0.8	0.7	0.0	---	0.6	049°	0.0	---	0.5	241°
	do.	45d	38° 38.83'	76° 18.40'	−4 09	−4 05	−4 03	−4 12	0.6	0.6	0.0	---	0.5	068°	0.0	---	0.5	232°
5901	Holland Point, 2.0 n.mi. SSW of	17d	38° 40.43'	76° 15.45'	−3 54	−4 21	−3 26	−4 00	0.3	0.2	0.1	145°	0.2	089°	0.0	---	0.2	262°
5906	Chlora Point, 0.5 n.mi. SSW of	24d	38° 37.70'	76° 09.10'	−3 45	−3 32	−3 22	−3 58	0.4	0.4	0.0	---	0.5	139°	0.0	---	0.4	332°
	do.	18d	38° 37.70'	76° 09.10'	−3 48	−3 33	−3 13	−3 42	0.4	0.5	0.0	---	0.4	143°	0.0	---	0.3	323°
5911	Martin Point, 0.6 n.mi. west of	7d	38° 37.63'	76° 08.15'	−3 18	−3 42	−3 22	−3 34	0.3	0.2	0.0	---	0.2	155°	0.0	---	0.2	341°
5916	Howell Point, 0.5 n.mi. south of	18d	38° 36.23'	76° 06.87'	−3 17	−4 04	−3 52	−3 42	0.4	0.5	0.0	---	0.3	122°	0.0	---	0.4	274°
5921	Cambridge hwy. bridge, W. of Swing Span		38° 34.78'	76° 03.67'	−2 48	−3 05	−1 07	−2 13	0.6	0.8	0.0	---	0.4	132°	0.0	---	0.4	316°
5926	Off Jamaica Point		38° 36.58'	75° 58.97'	−2 13	−2 32	−2 44	−2 26	0.6	0.3	0.0	---	0.5	000°	0.0	---	0.6	205°
5931	Poplar Point, south of		38° 40.52'	75° 57.98'	−1 52	−2 05	−1 56	−2 15	1.0	1.0	0.0	---	0.8	305°	0.0	---	0.8	100°
5936	Dover Bridge		38° 45.40'	75° 59.92'	−1 19	−1 50	−1 25	−1 47	1.1	1.0	0.0	---	0.9	050°	0.0	---	0.8	235°
5941	Oxford, Tred Avon River		38° 41.72'	76° 10.67'	---	−4 05	---	−4 03	0.4	0.2	0.0	---	0.3	040°	0.0	---	0.2	225°
5946	Easton Pt., 0.5 mi. below, Tred Avon River		38° 45.8'	76° 06.2'	Current weak and variable													
5951	Mulberry Pt., 0.6 mi. S of, Broad Creek		38° 44.33'	76° 14.95'	---	−4 10	---	−4 18	0.4	0.2	0.0	---	0.3	350°	0.0	---	0.2	170°
5956	Bald Eagle Pt., east of, Harris Creek		38° 43.75'	76° 18.30'	−4 07	−4 27	−4 07	−4 14	0.5	0.5	0.0	---	0.4	010°	0.0	---	0.4	175°
	EASTERN BAY																	
5961	Poplar Island, east of south end	15d	38° 44.9'	76° 21.2'	−2 20	−2 20	−2 20	−2 20	1.2	0.8	0.0	---	1.0	000°	0.0	---	0.6	170°
5966	Kent Point, 1.4 n.mi. east of		38° 50.33'	76° 20.25'	−3 04	−3 18	−3 49	−3 12	0.5	0.4	0.0	---	0.4	043°	0.0	---	0.3	233°
5971	Long Point, 1 mile southeast of		38° 50.6'	76° 19.6'	−3 40	−3 40	−3 40	−3 40	0.6	0.5	0.0	---	0.5	040°	0.0	---	0.4	235°
5976	Turkey Point, 1.3 miles WSW of		38° 53.68'	76° 19.55'	Current weak and variable													
5981	Parson Island, 1.4 miles west of		38° 54.83'	76° 16.77'	Current weak and variable													
5986	Parson Island, 0.7 mile NNE of		38° 55.48'	76° 14.33'	---	−2 45	−2 33	−2 50	0.2	0.2	0.0	---	0.2	305°	0.0	---	0.2	150°
5991	Tilghman Point, 1 mile north of	9	38° 52.78'	76° 15.18'	−2 33	−3 15	−3 17	−3 55	0.4	0.4	0.0	---	0.3	060°	0.0	---	0.3	265°
5996	Wye River, west of Bruffs Island		38° 51.28'	76° 11.88'	−3 48	−3 18	−3 43	−3 00	0.8	0.9	0.0	---	0.6	030°	0.0	---	0.7	190°
6001	Deepwater Point, Miles River		38° 48.33'	76° 12.55'	---	−3 52	---	−4 14	0.6	0.6	0.0	---	0.5	215°	0.0	---	0.5	025°
6006	Long Point, 0.8 mi. east of, Miles River		38° 46.43'	76° 09.32'	---	−3 24	---	−3 45	0.4	0.2	0.0	---	0.3	055°	0.0	---	0.2	245°
	WEST and SOUTH RIVERS																	
6011	Cheston Point, south of, West River		38° 51.33'	76° 31.43'	Current weak and variable													
6016	South River entrance		38° 54.77'	76° 29.43'	Current weak and variable													
	SEVERN and MAGOTHY RIVERS																	
6021	Greenbury Point, 1.8 miles east of	8	38° 58.40'	76° 25.00'	−0 57	−1 05	−0 51	−0 47	0.8	0.8	0.0	---	0.6	070°	0.0	---	0.6	245°
6026	Annapolis		38° 58.95'	76° 28.50'	---	−3 35	---	−2 26	0.5	0.4	0.0	---	0.4	320°	0.0	---	0.3	110°
6031	Brewer Point, Severn River		39° 01.83'	76° 31.73'	---	−1 22	---	−1 50	0.4	0.4	0.0	---	0.3	275°	0.0	---	0.3	155°
6036	Mountain Point, Magothy River entrance		39° 03.47'	76° 26.23'	−2 20	−2 00	−1 29	−2 04	0.8	0.4	0.0	---	0.6	315°	0.0	---	0.3	125°

Endnotes can be found at the end of table 2.

Fig. 1111. Extract from Table 2 of the *Tidal Current Tables*.

in times of minimum (slack) and maximum (flood and ebb) currents in hours and minutes with respect to the reference station, the maximum flood and maximum ebb velocity *ratios* with respect to similar current at the reference station, and the direction and average velocity of the maximum flood and ebb currents. Separate time differences may also be given for minimum current before flood begins and before ebb begins. Note that the term used is "minimum current" rather than "slack;" this is because at many locations the current may not diminish to a true slack water or zero speed stage.

Looking at the Greenbury Point subordinate station in figure 1111, you can see that the reference station is Baltimore (in bold letters with the page number near the top of the page). By studying the table entries, you can see that Greenbury Point reaches minimum before flood (or slack) fifty-seven minutes earlier than does Baltimore (indicated by the "–0 57" entry under the "Min. before Flood" column). You can also see that tidal current will reach its maximum flood stage one hour and five minutes earlier (–1 05) than will Baltimore, and that the minimum before ebb is fifty-one minutes earlier and maximum ebb occurs forty-seven minutes before Baltimore.

The entries under the "Speed Ratios" column tell you that both the flood and ebb currents at Greenbury Point will be 0.8 times that experienced at Baltimore. To obtain the speed of those currents, you would multiply the flood and ebb currents at Baltimore by the ratios provided, 0.5 and 0.4 respectively.

Because the entries under "Minimum before Flood" and "Minimum before Ebb" columns (under the general heading "Average Speed and Directions") are "0.0" knots with no direction indicated, you know that Greenbury Point's "minimum before flood" and "minimum before ebb" entries are true slack waters. From the remaining entries you know that the *average* floods flow at 0.6 knots in the direction of 070° and that the average ebbs flow at the same speed at 245°.

Combining the information for the subordinate station at Greenbury Point with the reference station at Baltimore for 18 December, you would learn that the first slack water on that date will be at 0148 (because the first slack time of 0245 at Baltimore precedes a flood current occurring at 0506, you would subtract the Greenbury Point "Min. before Flood" time of fifty-seven minutes from the Baltimore "Slack" time of 0245). The next slack water at Greenbury Point would occur at 0647 (subtract the

Greenbury Point "Min. before *Ebb*" time of fifty-one minutes from the next Baltimore "Slack" time of 0738). In like manner, two more slack waters would occur at Greenbury Point at 1207 ($13^h04^m - 0^h57^m$), and 1928 ($20^h19^m - 0^h51^m$).

Caution must be used when subtracting times. Remember that there are sixty minutes, not one hundred, in an hour; this seemingly obvious fact is often overlooked. It is convenient when subtracting a larger number of minutes from a smaller number to restate the time as one hour less but sixty minutes more; for example:

$$1304 = 12^h64^m \qquad 1500 = 14^h60^m$$
$$\underline{-0^h57^m} \qquad \qquad \underline{-13^h24^m}$$
$$12^h07^m \text{ (or 1207)} \qquad 1^h36^m \text{ (or 0136)}$$

To figure the times of maximum flood and ebb currents, you would proceed in a similar manner. From Table 2 you know that the flood currents occur at Greenbury Point one hour and five minutes before (-1 05) those at Baltimore, so you would simply subtract that time from the flood times provided in Table 1 for that date. This would tell you that flood tides would occur at 0401 ($05^h06^m - 1^h05^m$) and at 1545 ($16^h50^m - 1^h05^m$) on 18 December. The speed of these flood tides would be 0.4 knots and 0.9 knots (because the 0.5 and 1.1 speeds at Baltimore must be multiplied by the 0.8 ratio found in Table 2 for Greenbury Point).

Likewise the ebb currents would occur at 0942 ($10^h29^m - 0^h47^m$) and 2253 ($23^h40^m - 0^h47^m$), and their respective speeds would be 0.5 knots (0.6×0.8) and 0.9 knots (1.1×0.8).

Note that if this were a time of year when Daylight Savings Time was in effect, all times from Table 1 would have to be adjusted. Also be aware that in the examples used above, all the time differences at Greenbury Point were preceded by a minus sign and were therefore earlier than the times for Baltimore in Table 1. If any of these time differences had been preceded by a *plus* sign, they would have indicated occurrences that were *later* than those in Table 1.

An inspection of Table 2 reveals an additional column labeled "Meter Depth" preceding the ones listing the latitude and longitude positions of the subordinate stations. While this is of no great import to most navigators, a brief explanation may be useful in understanding the finer points of Table 2. In order to obtain the data for this table, a flow meter was placed in the water to measure the various currents. This data column tells you at what depth the meter was placed in the water. Note that for "Cook Point" (subordinate station number 5896), meters were placed at two separate depths (15 and 45 feet) and that there are consequently two sets of data listed. (Keep in mind that "meter" here refers to the instrument used and not a unit of measurement—the measurements are actually in *feet* as indicated at the head of the column.) The "d" following the depths indicates that the meters were anchored on the bottom (as opposed to being suspended from survey vessels) and that the depths indicated are referenced to chart datum (as opposed to being measured from the surface, as is the case for those measurements taken from survey vessels).

One last observation is that the "Minimum before Flood" reading for the second depth at Cook Point is 0.1 knots in the direction of 145°. This means that a true slack water is never reached at this station at this depth; unlike all the other subordinate stations on this page. As mentioned earlier, it is because of readings like this that the column is labeled "Minimum before Flood" instead of "Slack Water."

Table 3

1112 Just as Table 3 in the Tide Tables was used to determine *exact* times and heights of tides, so Table 3 of the *Tidal Current Tables* can be used to determine the speed of a current at any specific time (see fig. 1112). Here the entering arguments are the time intervals between the slack and maximum currents surrounding the exact time desired and between the preceding slack and the desired time. Where these intersect you will find a factor that is used to multiply the maximum velocity in order to obtain the approximate current velocity at the time desired. Note that the figure obtained at the intersection of values is a *factor*, abbreviated "ft"; this should not be confused with *feet*, which makes no sense here.

Note that there are two tables provided, one labeled "Table A" and the other "Table B." Checking the notes provided beneath these tables, you would find that Table B is to be used only for the stations (both reference and subordinate) associated with Cape Cod, Hell Gate, and the Chesapeake and Delaware Canal. For all other stations, you should use Table A.

If, for example, you wanted to know the current velocity in Baltimore Harbor at 2000 on 31 December, you would enter Table 3 with the intervals between slack and desired time and slack and maximum current. Inspecting Table 1 for 31 December (see fig. 1110), you would see that the slack and maximum current times straddling 2000 would be 1857 (slack) and 2213 (maximum current—a 1.1 knot ebb). Simple calculation would tell you that the interval between slack water and the desired time would be one hour and three minutes ($20^h00^m - 18^h57^m$) and that the interval between the slack and maximum current times would be three hours and sixteen minutes ($22^h13^m - 18^h57^m$). Entering Table A of Table 3 at the appropriate places (the intervals closest to those obtained), you would find that 0.5 is the factor at their intersection. Multiplying that factor by the maximum current for that period (0.5×1.1) gives you the approximate current of 0.6 knots that you would expect to encounter in Baltimore at 2000. Because it is an ebbing current, you would know (from the information provided at the top of the Table 1 page) that this current would be flowing in the general direction of 190° True.

Other Tables and Information

1113 *Table 4* (see fig. 1113a) is used to find the *duration of slack*. Although slack water, or the time of zero velocity, lasts but an instant, there is a period on each side of slack during which the current is so weak that for practical purposes it can be considered negligible. Table 4 tabulates the periods (half on each side of slack) during which the current does not exceed velocities of 0.1 to 0.5 knot. The velocities are tabulated for various maximum currents. Like Table 3, this table also has "A" and "B" components, the latter provided for specified stations and Table A for all others.

Table 5 (see fig. 1113b) is included in the Atlantic tables only. As explained earlier, certain areas have *rotary tidal currents*, or currents that change their direction continually and never come to a slack, so that in a tidal cycle of about twelve and a half hours they set in all directions successively. Such currents occur offshore and in some wide indentations of the coast, a situation that occurs in only a relatively few locations.

Following Table 5 is some information about the Gulf Stream, a discussion of wind-driven currents (including an unnumbered table that can be used to refine predictions), and some information about the combination of currents.

Also included are some useful diagrams of average current direction and strength for certain bodies of water (Martha's Vineyard and Nantucket Sounds, New York Harbor via Ambrose Channel, the East River of New York, Delaware Bay and River, and Chesapeake Bay). These diagrams are very useful in determining a time of departure and the appropriate speed to use to make maximum use of favorable ("fair") currents or minimize adverse

TABLE 3.—SPEED OF CURRENT AT ANY TIME

TABLE A

Interval between slack and maximum current

Interval between slack and desired time	1 20	1 40	2 00	2 20	2 40	3 00	3 20	3 40	4 00	4 20	4 40	5 00	5 20	5 40
	ft.	ft.	ft.	ft.	ft.	ft.	ft.	ft.	ft.	ft.	ft.	ft.	ft.	ft.
0 20	0.4	0.3	0.3	0.2	0.2	0.2	0.2	0.1	0.1	0.1	0.1	0.1	0.1	0.1
0 40	0.7	0.6	0.5	0.4	0.4	0.3	0.3	0.3	0.3	0.2	0.2	0.2	0.2	0.2
1 00	0.9	0.8	0.7	0.6	0.6	0.5	0.5	0.4	0.4	0.4	0.3	0.3	0.3	0.3
1 20	1.0	1.0	0.9	0.8	0.7	0.6	0.6	0.5	0.5	0.5	0.4	0.4	0.4	0.4
1 40	- - - -	1.0	1.0	0.9	0.8	0.8	0.7	0.7	0.6	0.6	0.5	0.5	0.5	0.4
2 00	- - - -	- - - -	1.0	1.0	0.9	0.9	0.8	0.8	0.7	0.7	0.6	0.6	0.6	0.5
2 20	- - - -	- - - -	- - - -	1.0	1.0	0.9	0.9	0.8	0.8	0.7	0.7	0.7	0.6	0.6
2 40	- - - -	- - - -	- - - -	- - - -	1.0	1.0	1.0	0.9	0.9	0.8	0.8	0.7	0.7	0.7
3 00	- - - -	- - - -	- - - -	- - - -	- - - -	1.0	1.0	1.0	0.9	0.9	0.8	0.8	0.8	0.7
3 20	- - - -	- - - -	- - - -	- - - -	- - - -	- - - -	1.0	1.0	1.0	0.9	0.9	0.9	0.8	0.8
3 40	- - - -	- - - -	- - - -	- - - -	- - - -	- - - -	- - - -	1.0	1.0	1.0	0.9	0.9	0.9	0.9
4 00	- - - -	- - - -	- - - -	- - - -	- - - -	- - - -	- - - -	- - - -	1.0	1.0	1.0	1.0	0.9	0.9
4 20	- - - -	- - - -	- - - -	- - - -	- - - -	- - - -	- - - -	- - - -	- - - -	1.0	1.0	1.0	1.0	0.9
4 40	- - - -	- - - -	- - - -	- - - -	- - - -	- - - -	- - - -	- - - -	- - - -	- - - -	1.0	1.0	1.0	1.0
5 00	- - - -	- - - -	- - - -	- - - -	- - - -	- - - -	- - - -	- - - -	- - - -	- - - -	- - - -	1.0	1.0	1.0
5 20	- - - -	- - - -	- - - -	- - - -	- - - -	- - - -	- - - -	- - - -	- - - -	- - - -	- - - -	- - - -	1.0	1.0
5 40	- - - -	- - - -	- - - -	- - - -	- - - -	- - - -	- - - -	- - - -	- - - -	- - - -	- - - -	- - - -	- - - -	1.0

TABLE B

Interval between slack and maximum current

Interval between slack and desired time	1 20	1 40	2 00	2 20	2 40	3 00	3 20	3 40	4 00	4 20	4 40	5 00	5 20	5 40
	ft.	ft.	ft.	ft.	ft.	ft.	ft.	ft.	ft.	ft.	ft.	ft.	ft.	ft.
0 20	0.5	0.4	0.4	0.3	0.3	0.3	0.3	0.3	0.2	0.2	0.2	0.2	0.2	0.2
0 40	0.8	0.7	0.6	0.5	0.5	0.5	0.4	0.4	0.4	0.4	0.3	0.3	0.3	0.3
1 00	0.9	0.8	0.8	0.7	0.7	0.6	0.6	0.5	0.5	0.5	0.4	0.4	0.4	0.4
1 20	1.0	1.0	0.9	0.8	0.8	0.7	0.7	0.6	0.6	0.6	0.5	0.5	0.5	0.5
1 40	- - - -	1.0	1.0	0.9	0.9	0.8	0.8	0.7	0.7	0.7	0.6	0.6	0.6	0.6
2 00	- - - -	- - - -	1.0	1.0	0.9	0.9	0.9	0.8	0.8	0.7	0.7	0.7	0.7	0.6
2 20	- - - -	- - - -	- - - -	1.0	1.0	1.0	0.9	0.9	0.8	0.8	0.8	0.7	0.7	0.7
2 40	- - - -	- - - -	- - - -	- - - -	1.0	1.0	1.0	0.9	0.9	0.9	0.8	0.8	0.8	0.7
3 00	- - - -	- - - -	- - - -	- - - -	- - - -	1.0	1.0	1.0	0.9	0.9	0.9	0.9	0.8	0.8
3 20	- - - -	- - - -	- - - -	- - - -	- - - -	- - - -	1.0	1.0	1.0	1.0	0.9	0.9	0.9	0.9
3 40	- - - -	- - - -	- - - -	- - - -	- - - -	- - - -	- - - -	1.0	1.0	1.0	1.0	0.9	0.9	0.9
4 00	- - - -	- - - -	- - - -	- - - -	- - - -	- - - -	- - - -	- - - -	1.0	1.0	1.0	1.0	0.9	0.9
4 20	- - - -	- - - -	- - - -	- - - -	- - - -	- - - -	- - - -	- - - -	- - - -	1.0	1.0	1.0	1.0	0.9
4 40	- - - -	- - - -	- - - -	- - - -	- - - -	- - - -	- - - -	- - - -	- - - -	- - - -	1.0	1.0	1.0	1.0
5 00	- - - -	- - - -	- - - -	- - - -	- - - -	- - - -	- - - -	- - - -	- - - -	- - - -	- - - -	1.0	1.0	1.0
5 20	- - - -	- - - -	- - - -	- - - -	- - - -	- - - -	- - - -	- - - -	- - - -	- - - -	- - - -	- - - -	1.0	1.0
5 40	- - - -	- - - -	- - - -	- - - -	- - - -	- - - -	- - - -	- - - -	- - - -	- - - -	- - - -	- - - -	- - - -	1.0

Use table A for all places except those listed below for table B.
Use table B for Cape Code Canal, Hell Gate, Chesapeake and Delaware Canal, and all stations in table 2 which are referred to them.

1. From predictions find the time of slack water and the time and velocity of maximum current (flood or ebb), one of which is immediately before and the other after the time for which the velocity is desired.
2. Find the interval of time between the above slack and maximum current, and enter the top of table A or B with the interval which most nearly agrees with this value.
3. Find the interval of time between the above slack and the time desired, and enter the side of table A or B with the interval which most nearly agrees with this value.
4. Find, in the table, the factor corresponding to the above two intervals, and multiply the maximum velocity by this factor. The result will be the approximate velocity at the time desired.

Fig. 1112. Extract from Table 3 of the *Tidal Current Tables*.

TABLE 4.—DURATION OF SLACK

The predicted times of slack water given in this publication indicate the instant of zero speed, which is only momentary. There is a period on each side of the slack water, however, during which the current is so weak that for practical purposes it may be considered negligible.

The following tables give, for various maximum currents, the approximate period of time during which weak currents not exceeding 0.1 to 0.5 knot will be encountered. This duration includes the last of the flood or ebb and the beginning of the following ebb or flood, that is, half of the duration will be before and half after the time of slack water.

Table A should be used for all places except those listed below for table B.

Table B should be used for Cape Cod Canal, Hell Gate, Chesapeake and Delaware Canal, and all stations in Table 2 which are referred to them.

Duration of weak current near time of slack water

TABLE A

Maximum current	Period with a speed not more than -				
	0.1 knot	0.2 knot	0.3 knot	0.4 knot	0.5 knot
Knots	Minutes	Minutes	Minutes	Minutes	Minutes
1.0	23	46	70	94	120
1.5	15	31	46	62	78
2.0	11	23	35	46	58
3.0	8	15	23	31	38
4.0	6	11	17	23	29
5.0	5	9	14	18	23
6.0	4	8	11	15	19
7.0	3	7	10	13	16
8.0	3	6	9	11	14
9.0	3	5	8	10	13
10.0	2	5	7	9	11

TABLE B

Maximum current	Period with a speed not more than -				
	0.1 knot	0.2 knot	0.3 knot	0.4 knot	0.5 knot
Knots	Minutes	Minutes	Minutes	Minutes	Minutes
1.0	13	28	46	66	89
1.5	8	18	28	39	52
2.0	6	13	20	28	36
3.0	4	8	13	18	22
4.0	3	6	9	13	17
5.0	3	5	8	10	13

When there is a difference between the speeds of the maximum flood and ebb preceding and following the slack for which the duration is desired, it will be sufficiently accurate for practical purposes to find a separate duration for each maximum speed and take the average of the two as the duration of the weak current.

Fig. 1113a. Extract from Table 4 of the *Tidal Current Tables*.

TABLE 5.—ROTARY TIDAL CURRENTS

Great Round Shoal Channel, 4 miles NE. of Great Pt., Nantucket Sound. Lat. 41°26' N., long. 69°59' W.			Cuttyhunk I., 3¼ miles SW. of Lat. 41°23' N., long. 71°00' W.			Gooseberry Neck, 2 miles SSE. of Buzzards Bay entrance. Lat. 41°27' N., long. 71°01' W.		
Time	Direction (true)	Velocity	Time	Direction (true)	Velocity	Time	Direction (true)	Velocity
Hours after maximum flood at Pollock Rip Channel, see page 28	Degrees	Knots	Hours after maximum flood at Pollock Rip Channel, see page 28	Degrees	Knots	Hours after maximum flood at Pollock Rip Channel, see page 28	Degrees	Knots
0	80	0.8	0	356	0.4	0	52	0.6
1	88	1.1	1	15	0.3	1	65	0.4
2	96	1.3	2	80	0.2	2	108	0.2
3	104	1.0	3	123	0.3	3	168	0.3
4	129	0.5	4	146	0.5	4	210	0.4
5	213	0.5	5	158	0.5	5	223	0.5
6	267	1.1	6	173	0.4	6	232	0.5
7	275	1.4	7	208	0.3	7	249	0.3
8	280	1.2	8	267	0.2	8	274	0.2
9	284	0.7	9	306	0.3	9	321	0.2
10	328	0.2	10	322	0.3	10	16	0.3
11	42	0.4	11	335	0.4	11	38	0.5

Browns Ledge, Massachusetts. Lat. 41°20' N., long. 71°06' W.			Point Judith, Harbor of Refuge, Block Island Sound (west entrance). Lat. 41°22' N., long. 71°31' W.			Point Judith, 4.5 miles SW. of, Block Island Sound. Lat. 41°18' N., long. 71°33' W.		
Time	Direction (true)	Velocity	Time	Direction (true)	Velocity	Time	Direction (true)	Velocity
Hours after maximum flood at Pollock Rip Channel, see page 28	Degrees	Knots	Hours after maximum flood at The Race, see page 34	Degrees	Knots	Hours after maximum flood at The Race, see page 31	Degrees	Knots
0	330	0.3	0	197	0.2	0	264	0.6
1	12	0.3	1	160	0.2	1	270	0.6
2	28	0.3	2	151	0.4	2	270	0.5
3	104	0.4	3	159	0.5	3	280	0.2
4	118	0.4	4	146	0.5	4	62	0.2
5	123	0.4	5	124	0.5	5	70	0.6
6	168	0.3	6	109	0.4	6	78	0.7
7	205	0.2	7	104	0.2	7	95	0.5
8	201	0.3	8	90	0.1	8	105	0.3
9	270	0.3	9	30	0.1	9	120	0.1
10	282	0.4	10	336	0.1	10	286	0.1
11	318	0.5	11	209	0.1	11	277	0.3

Fig. 1113b. Extract from Table 5 of the *Tidal Current Tables*.

("foul") currents. Using the diagrams and the accompanying instructions, vessel speeds can be selected which, with a properly selected starting time, will permit the vessel to "ride the tide" (have a favorable current) when traversing the waters covered.

At the back of the *Tidal Current Tables* volumes, just before the index, there is a useful glossary included, and the lunar and solar astronomical data on the inside back cover is the same as that given in the *Tide Tables*.

Tidal Prediction Forms

1114   Just as with predicting tides, using a form can assist you in the process of predicting tidal currents by walking you through the procedure and making sure you do not forget needed components or steps. Figure 1114 is an example of a form that has been filled out to predict the tidal current at 1600 local time in Jacksonville, Florida. Note that the navigator has identified the location as "Washington Street" because there are two subordinate stations at Jacksonville (the other at "F.E.C. RR Bridge") and has also written in the reference number (7701) that

locates the station in the *Tidal Current Tables*. Because the date is in August, Daylight Savings Time is in effect, so the time has been converted from Eastern Daylight Time to Eastern Standard Time. Using the tables, the navigator has plugged in the acquired data and performed the necessary calculations to determine that the tidal current at the desired time (1600 EDT) will be flooding in a direction of 281° True at a speed of 1.1 knots.

IMPORTANCE OF CURRENTS

1115   Currents can help or hinder the passage of a vessel on the high seas or in pilot waters; they can set her off course and into hazardous waters. Every serious navigator must know where to get information on the various currents that may be encountered and must be able to make all the necessary calculations.

General information on ocean currents can be found in books such as this or *Bowditch*. More specific information may be obtained from *Pilot Charts, Pilot Chart Atlases, Sailing Directions,* and *Coast Pilots,* as well as the *Tidal Current Tables*.

VEL OF CURRENT	
Date	12 August
Location	Jacksonville, Wash. St. 7701
Time	1600 EDT (1500 EST)
Ref Sta	St. Johns River Entrance
Time Diff Minimum before Ebb	+ 2:39
Time Diff Max Flood	+ 2:31
Vel Ratio Max Flood	0.9
Vel Ratio Max Ebb	0.8
Flood Dir	281°
Ebb Dir	118°
Ref Sta Slack Water Time	1324
Time Diff	2:39
Local Sta Slack Water Time	1603
Ref Sta Max Current Time	1030 flooding
Time Diff	+ 2:31
Local Sta Max Current Time	1301
Ref Sta Max Current Vel	2.5
Vel Ratio	0.9
Local Sta Max Current Vel	2.2
Int Between Slack and Desired Time	1:03
Int Between Slack and Max Current	3:02
Max Current	
Factor Table 3	0.5
Velocity	1.1
Direction	Flooding, 281°

Fig. 1114. Calculation of the predicted velocity of current at a given time at a subordinate station.

Chapter 12   Piloting

In the first chapter of this book, we determined that navigation in its simplest terms is the art and science of knowing where we are and where we are going. Chapter 9 explained the navigational technique known as dead reckoning in which a "best guess" plot is maintained, based only upon course, speed, and time without considering any of the factors that can cause a vessel to deviate from her intended track. But we know that a wandering helmsman, barnacles on the hull, strong winds and currents, or any number of other conditions can (and often will) render a dead reckoning position inaccurate. Thus it is necessary to find the means to do better, to *fix* your position, rather than merely estimate it.

While there are a number of ways to do this—celestial, electronic, and so on—determining the position and directing the movements of a vessel by visual reference to landmarks, by measurements of depth, or by radar is called *piloting*. Those areas in which piloting is the normal method of navigation, usually coastal or inland regions, are known as *pilot waters*.

While piloting primarily relies on the proximity of land and therefore has certain advantages, it can be the most unforgiving form of navigation. Mistakes in navigation on the open sea can generally be discovered and corrected before the next danger looms ahead. In pilot waters there is often little or no opportunity to correct errors before danger is upon you.

LINES OF POSITION (LOP)

1201   Probably the most important and elemental concept in navigation is that of the *line of position* (LOP). Whereas an exact position (or fix) is a *point* on a chart, telling you exactly where you are, an LOP (as indicated by its name) is a *line*, along which the navigator knows he or she is located. A single LOP can be very useful by providing a significant piece to the navigational puzzle, but cannot fix your position by itself. A minimum of two LOPs is needed for a fix, and three or more LOPs yield a more reliable fix. A line of position *can* provide useful *negative* information, telling the observer that his or her vessel is *not* somewhere else, such as in shoal water. A single LOP of good quality, therefore, while not establishing a position, takes one giant step toward fixing your position and can at least rule out some worries if it has no hazards along its length or nearby.

As will be seen in forthcoming chapters, LOPs can be obtained in many ways—as the result of a celestial observation, for example, or as a readout on a Loran-C radio navigation set—but in piloting, the two primary means are the visual bearing and the radar range. Bearings can also be obtained under ideal circumstances by radar, and ranges can be obtained by visual means, but these methods are employed infrequently compared to the visual bearing and the radar range. You will remember from chapter 6 that it is also possible to obtain a very accurate visual bearing using either a manmade or a natural *range* (do not confuse this "range" with the one connoting distance) where two objects line up in such a way as to give a reliable bearing that can be used to stay in a channel or as a turn bearing.

Technically, because of the curvature of the Earth, a visual LOP is a segment of a great circle, but in piloting the segment is so short that it may be plotted as a straight, or rhumb, line on a Mercator chart (see chapter 2).

It is important to bear in mind that there is a significant difference between the DR track and lines of position. Dead reckoning is a statement of *intention,* a graphic representation of ordered courses and speeds, a *calculated* position or a kind of "best guess" in the absence of other information. Accurately obtained lines of position are statements of *fact,* since the vessel is somewhere on the LOP, regardless of any courses steered and speeds used.

Bearings as LOPs

1202 Visual bearings are used extensively in piloting. The observer sights across a pelorus, hand-bearing compass, bearing circle, or gyro repeater toward a fixed, known object and thus determines the direction of the line of sight to that object. The bearing is then plotted on the chart by replicating the direction of the bearing using a parallel motion protractor or some other appropriate plotting device (see chapter 8) and moving it to the same object on the chart. A segment of the bearing line is drawn in the approximate area on the chart where you believe you are located (based upon your last fix and DR plot). The line is then labeled with the time (mandatory) and the direction (optional). Note that the line you are drawing is actually the *reciprocal* of the bearing you took on the object, since you are drawing it *from* the observed object rather than *to* it. In figure 1202, for example, you can see that the bearing taken at noon on the spire was approximately 045° T, but the line drawn is actually in the direction of 225° T, the reciprocal (045 + 180) of the bearing.

Visual bearings are nearly always preferable to radar bearings. Although modern radar systems yield reasonably accurate bearings, they are significantly more accurate in assessing ranges (distances) than bearings (directions). You are also less likely to make an error if you can *see* the object rather than trusting that the electronic image you are using is the same one that you think it is.

You must exercise some judgment and forethought in choosing the objects you will use for your bearings. Most important, the objects must appear on the chart; it does no good to shoot a bearing to a flagpole on the near shore if it does not appear on the chart you are using. Another important consideration is to choose objects that will yield bearings that are widely separated (see article 1206).

Using Relative Bearings

1203 The *relative bearing* of an object is its direction from the ship, relative to the ship's head. It is the angle between the fore-and-aft line of the vessel and the bearing line of the object, measured clockwise from 000° at the ship's head through 360°. In figure 1203 the relative bearings of objects *A, B, C,* and *D* are 135°, 180°, 270°, and 340°, respectively. As explained in chapter 8, a pelorus can be used for taking relative bearings by setting the 000° graduation of the pelorus card to the lubber's line, then observing the object and reading the card. An

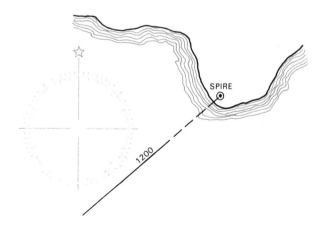

Fig. 1202. A line of position (LOP) from a bearing.

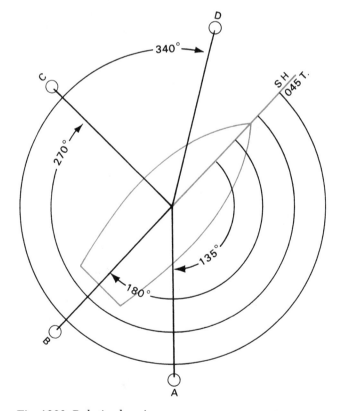

Fig. 1203. Relative bearings.

azimuth circle or a bearing circle are more frequently used, however.

Relative bearings are converted to true bearings before they are plotted on the chart. This is accomplished simply by adding their value to the vessel's true heading when the relative bearings were taken (and subtracting 360° if the sum equals or exceeds that amount). Thus, assuming the vessel is steady on 045° T during observations, the corresponding true bearings of *A, B, C,* and *D* are 180°, 225°, 315°, and 025°. Conversely, true bearings can be converted to relative bearings by subtracting the vessel's true heading from the true bearings (first adding 360° if necessary).

TB = RB + SH(–360°)   TB is true bearing
RB = TB(+360°) – SH   RB is relative bearing
    SH is ship's head (true)

Using Distances to Obtain LOPs

1204   Because the word "range" can have two meanings in navigation—two objects lining up visually to provide a bearing is one form of "range," and the other is simply a distance—this section is entitled "Using *Distances* to Obtain LOPs" to prevent any initial confusion. In practice however, mariners will often use the word "range" when talking about a measured distance, so that term will be used here. A discussion of visual ranges as LOPs follows in the next section.

Attach a piece of line of known length (6 feet—one fathom—for example) to an object, say a flagstaff. Walk away from the flagstaff in any direction until the line is taut. You now know that you are 6 feet from the flagstaff. If you walk around the flagstaff, keeping the line taut, you will define an arc that will become a circle if you continue all the way around. From this simple illustration, you can see that knowing the distance (or *range*) to an object from your vessel means that your vessel lies somewhere on a circle centered on that object. If you use a scale on your chart to set a drafting compass (dividers with a point and a pencil on their tips; see chapter 8) to that range, you can then place the point on the object on your chart and inscribe an arc using the pencil point of the drafting compass. You know your vessel is somewhere on that arc. In theory, you really only know that you are somewhere on the entire circle (known as a *circle of position*) that your pencil point can inscribe, but in practice this will almost never be the case. In figure 1204, the range was taken on an object surrounded by water, but this will not happen very often. Most objects that are suitable for measuring range in pilot waters will be located somewhere along a

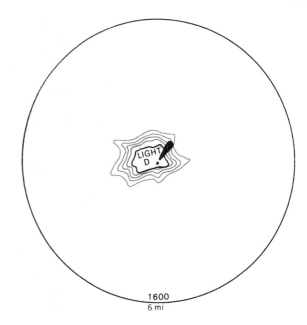

Fig. 1204. A circular line of position (LOP) results from a distance measurement.

shoreline, which means a large segment of your circle of position will fall across land. Obviously you can discount any land areas that your circle falls upon—assuming you are afloat. And just as was the case with a visual bearing, your DR plot will give you an approximate idea of where you are, so you need only inscribe that part of the arc that makes sense—that which is in the reasonable vicinity of your assumed location. Depending upon conditions then, your arc may be relatively small or large. It should be apparent that this arc, like the straight line derived from taking a visual bearing, is an LOP.

Range is most efficiently obtained by radar. Just as when taking visual bearings, the objects you choose for taking ranges must be on your chart if you are going to use them to plot LOPs. Matching an object chosen from your chart with the image that appears on your radar scope is the most difficult part of using radar for obtaining range LOPs, but it will become second nature with practice.

If the height of a charted object is known, its range may be determined using a stadimeter or sextant, both of which can be used to measure angles. The angle measured by sighting on the top of the object can be used as an entering argument in a table found in *Bowditch* that has the rather long but very descriptive title of "Distance by Vertical Angle Measured between Waterline at Object and Top of Object" (Table 16 in the 1995 edition of *Bowditch*, but it may have a different number in future editions).

The distance to an object of known height can also be calculated by using the equation $D = H \div \tan A$, where D is the distance to the object, H is its height, and A is the vertical angle measured. D will be in the same units as H (usually feet) and should be converted to the unit of measurement you are using on your chart (usually yards) before plotting.

When measuring objects of known height, care must be taken to make certain that you measure appropriately with your stadimeter or sextant. For example, if the object you are observing is a lighthouse, the known height you obtained from the chart or publication will be qualified as either "height above water," "height of structure," or "height of light." The first must obviously be measured using the surface of the water as the base of measurement, while the "height of structure" must be measured from its base (which may be perched on a high rock above the water, therefore yielding a very different angle). If the "height of light" is provided, you must be careful not to use the actual top of the lighthouse for your upper measurement but use the glass from which the light emits (which can be some distance below the top of the lighthouse structure).

Visual Ranges as LOPs

1205   In earlier discussions we saw the value of a visual range in providing a bearing that can be used to stay in a channel or as a turn bearing. Visual ranges can also be used as a reliable method of obtaining an LOP. If you see two objects line up and can locate these same two objects on a chart, you may place a straight-edge so that it connects the two objects and then extend the connecting line to the vicinity of your DR plot. You know you are somewhere along that line and have, therefore, obtained an LOP (see fig. 1205). Using a visual range to obtain an LOP does not even require a compass.

In following a narrow channel, particularly one that is not well marked, the value of ranges, either artificial or natural, as guides in navigation cannot be overemphasized. Excellent fixes to check the progress of a ship can be obtained by following a range and noting the instant that other pairs of objects near the beam are in range. A study of the chart in advance will often reveal several good natural ranges to use as checkpoints along a channel. One near a turn is especially valuable.

THE FIX

1206   Taking advantage of the visual range's ability to provide an LOP without the need for a compass, try a simple experiment in a room. Place two objects (a pair of drinking glasses or candlesticks, for example) so that one is closer to a wall in the room, represented by the two Xs in figure 1206a. Then place two other objects similarly in a line near one of the adjoining walls, represented by the Os in the figure. Stand in the room so that the two pairs of objects are each in line ("F" in the figure). By moving around the room, you can see that both pairs of objects can never be in a line simultaneously unless you are standing at that one point ("F"). From this experiment you can see that the intersection of these two "LOPs" results in a single unique position. Instead of knowing that you are somewhere along either line, you know that you are at a point defined by the intersection of the two lines. In navigational terms, this is called a "fixed position" or more simply a *fix*.

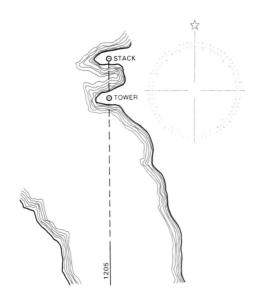

Fig. 1205. Plotting a visual range.

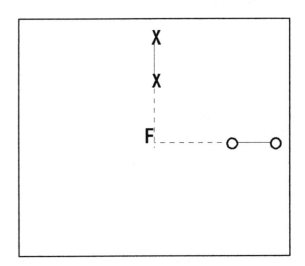

Fig. 1206a. Geometry of the fix.

In the real world you will almost never be able to line up two visual ranges simultaneously as we did in the experiment. But by relying on LOPs derived from compass bearings or radar ranges of objects you have located on a chart, you will have many opportunities to acquire LOPs. Where two or more of these LOPs intersect, you will have a fix. Keep in mind that if you are moving, these LOPs have to be taken *simultaneously* to yield an accurate fix. That is one of the reasons why a navigational *team* is so much more valuable than a single individual when piloting. If simultaneous bearings are not possible, an alternative is to employ the "running fix" (see article 1207).

Any combination of bearings and ranges (two or more bearings, two or more ranges, and one or more of each) will yield a fix. In figure 1206b the navigator has obtained a fix by obtaining a range and bearing of the same object ("Double Point Light"). In figure 1206c a fix was obtained by simultaneously shooting a bearing on Tower ("Tr") A and reading the radar range to Sandy Point Light (note the straight-line bearing and curved-line range).

The more LOPs you can obtain, the more accurate your fix will be. Multiple LOPs will also make an error very obvious—the bad LOP will fall outside the intersection by a noticeable amount.

An important consideration in planning is to remember that using objects that are too close in bearing will be much less likely to yield a good fix. Ideally, two bearings should be 90 degrees apart (for example, 235 and 325) and three bearings should be 120 degrees apart (041, 161, and 281, for example). Use bearings that are less than 30 degrees apart only if no others are available; and consider positions

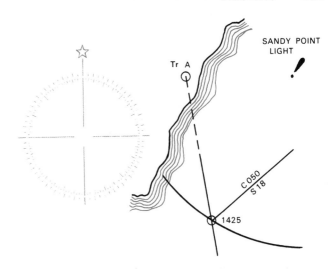

Fig. 1206c. A fix by a bearing on one object and distance from another.

that are obtained with such close bearings as unreliable (better than nothing, but far from ideal). Of course, objects will rarely be available in exactly the right positions for these ideals, so you must compromise with the situation at hand. But keeping these ideals in mind will guide you toward the best navigation possible under the circumstances, particularly in the planning stages.

THE RUNNING FIX

1207   Since it is not always possible to obtain two simultaneous observations, the navigator may have to use two lines of position that are obtained by observations at *different times*. A fix obtained in this manner is called a *running fix* and, while it is less reliable than a normal fix derived from simultaneous observations, it is much better than *no* fix or a simple DR position. In order to plot a running fix, you must make allowance for the time elapsed between the first observation and the second. This is done by *advancing* (moving) the earlier line of position to the time of the second observation. (It is also possible to obtain a running fix by *retiring* the second LOP to the time of the first observation, but this is seldom desirable in actual navigation, as the first method gives a more recent position.) The navigator assumes that, for the limited period of time between the two observations, the vessel makes good over the ground a definite distance in a definite direction. He moves the earlier LOP, *parallel to itself*, to this advanced position (see fig. 1207a). If this advanced LOP intersects with one derived from a new observation, it will provide a running fix. If you think about it, a running fix is a *blend of fix and DR.*

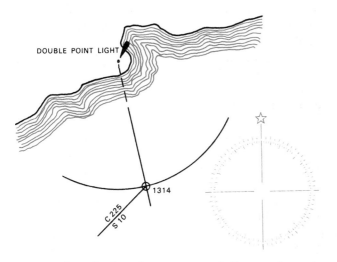

Fig. 1206b. A fix by a bearing on and distance from the same object.

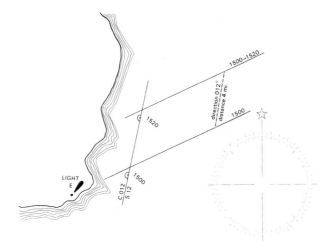

Fig. 1207a. Advancing a line of position.

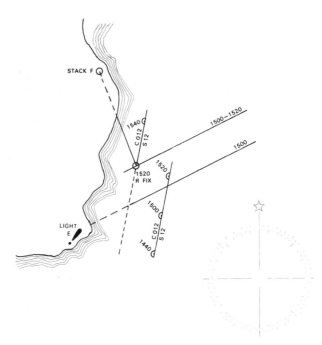

Fig. 1207b. A running fix.

Example: A ship is on course 012° T at 12 knots while running parallel to a coast. At 1500, a light is sighted bearing 245° T, but because it is foggy, no other charted objects are visible at that time. Twenty minutes later, the light has been swallowed by the fog, but a tall smokestack looms into view and the navigator is able to shoot a bearing to it (340° T).

Required: Plot a running fix based upon the two sightings.

Solution: Referring to figure 1207b, you can see from the DR plot that the ship is on course 012° T at 12 knots when light *E* is sighted on bearing 245° T. The LOP is plotted as the reciprocal of 245 (065° T) and labeled with the time (1500). At 1520 stack *F* is observed at bearing 340° T, and the appropriate LOP is drawn on the chart. Using parallel rulers, the first LOP is then advanced by moving it the appropriate distance that the ship would be expected to travel in the elapsed time between sightings, so that it is in the appropriate DR position; in other words, the first LOP is moved ahead by 4 miles because, at 12 knots, the vessel would travel that distance in twenty minutes (20/60 × 12). (Note: this distance of advance can be quickly derived using a nautical slide rule; see chapter 8.) This advanced LOP is labeled with the two times ("1500–1520") to make it clear that this is an advanced LOP. Where the new LOP (from the observation on the stack) and the advanced LOP (from the light twenty minutes earlier) intersect, you have a running fix (labeled "R FIX" with the time on the chart). From your new fixed position, you would then start a new DR using the appropriate course and speed (012° T at 12 knots, since no changes were made).

The length of time between observations for a running fix should be kept as short as possible, consistent

with other considerations. There is no rule as to how far a line of position can be advanced and still give a well-determined position. This is a matter of judgment and depends upon individual circumstances, but a good general rule in piloting is to avoid advancing a line of position more than 30 minutes.

A running fix may also be obtained by taking successive bearings on the *same* object.

Example: A ship is on course 018° T at 12 knots. At 1430, Light *G* bears 042° T and at 1452, it is observed at 083° T.

Required: Plot and label the 1452 running fix.

Solution: Referring to figure 1207c, plot the 1430 DR position on the course line that corresponds with the time of the first observation and plot the 1430 line of position on a bearing of 042° to the light, labeling the plot as indicated. In a like manner, plot the 1452 DR (using a nautical slide rule or other appropriate method to determine where it should be). Then plot the corresponding line of position as a reciprocal of the bearing 083° from the light. Using the distance measured between the two DR positions (1430 and 1452) advance the earlier line of position in the direction of the course 018°. Construct a line parallel to the original 1430 line of position. (It may be desirable to label direction on the initial LOP so that this information can be used for drawing the advanced LOP.) The intersection of the 1452 LOP with the 1430 LOP advanced to 1452 determines the 1452 running fix. A new course line is started from the 1452 running fix as indicated.

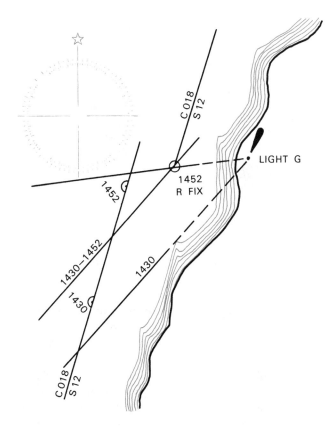

Fig. 1207c. A running fix from two bearings on the same object at different times.

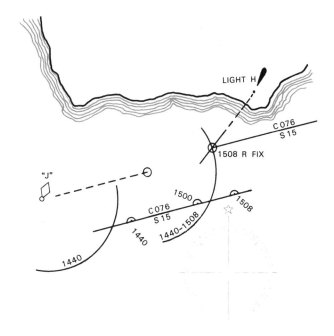

Fig. 1207d. Advancing a circle of position.

If the earlier LOP was a *circle of position* (obtained by radar or some other method of ranging), the resulting arc is advanced by moving the *center of the circle* (the object used to obtain the range) by the appropriate amount.

Example: A ship is on course 076°, speed 15 knots. The 1440 DR position has been plotted as shown in figure 1207d. At 1440, the distance to Buoy *J*, obscured by fog, is found by radar to be 4.7 miles. At 1508, Light *H* is sighted bearing 040°, and the radar has become inoperable.

Required: Plot and label the 1508 running fix using the information available.

Solution: Note that the center of the circle (the buoy) is advanced in the direction 076° for a distance traveled in the 28 minutes between LOPs (28/60 × 15 knots = 7 miles). From this point, the distance circle of position is constructed again with a radius of 4.7 miles (the original range obtained by radar) and labeled as indicated. The 1508 line of position to Light *H* is plotted as the reciprocal of bearing 040°. The intersection of this LOP with the advanced distance circle of position determines the 1508 running fix, from which a new DR plot is started.

Note that if you extended the bearing line farther than is shown in the figure, there are two possible intersections of the bearing line of position with the advanced distance circle of position. In ordinary circumstances, the intersection closest to the DR position is used as the running fix. In cases of doubt and in the absence of additional information that will confirm either one as the correct running fix, you would be wise to commence DR plots from both positions, and then assume the ship to be on the course that is potentially more dangerous (taking appropriate actions) until you have more reliable position information.

Running Fixes with Changes in Course or Speed

1208   A line can be advanced to determine a running fix even though the vessel's course or speed is changed in the period between the two observations, as illustrated in the following examples.

Example: A ship is on course 063°, speed 18 knots. The 2100 DR position is plotted as shown in figure 1208a. At 2105 Light *P* bears 340° and disappears shortly thereafter. The 2105 DR position is plotted. At 2120 the ship's course is changed to 138° and the 2120 DR position is plotted. AT 2132 Light *Q* is sighted bearing 047°.

Required: Plot and label the 2132 running fix.

Solution: Plot the 2105 DR and 2132 DR positions. The 2105 line of position is advanced by using the course and distance made good through the water between the DR position corresponding to the line of each visual observation. This is shown by a

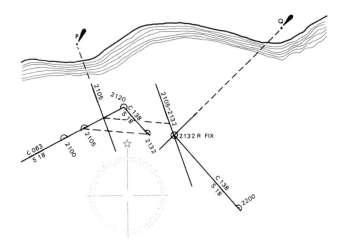

Fig. 1208a. A running fix with a change of course between times of bearings.

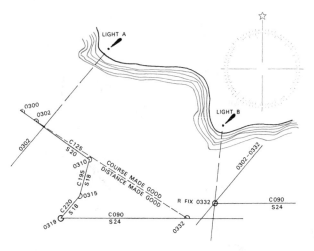

Fig. 1208b. A running fix with multiple changes of course and speed.

dashed line, usually not drawn in practice, but used here for clarity, connecting the 2105 DR and the 2132 DR. Advance the 2105 line of position parallel to itself in the direction of the *course made good* (essentially a blending of the two courses steered in the interim into a theoretical most direct course between the points) by a distance equal to the *distance made good* (again, a theoretical direct distance ignoring the course changes) between the 2105 and the 2132 DR positions. The 2105 line of position advanced becomes the 2105–2132 line of position. In this example, the point of origin for the measurement of this advance was at the intersection of the 2105 LOP with the DR course line as shown. Similar advance of any other point on the 2105 LOP would have produced the identical result.

Plot the 2132 line of position to Light Q on a bearing of 047°. The intersection of this line of position with the 2105–2132 LOP determines the 2132 running fix, from which a new DR is started. The plot is labeled as indicated.

Running fixes may be derived even when *multiple* course and/or speed changes are made between LOPs.

Example: At 0300, a ship is on course 125°, speed 20 knots. At 0302, Light A is observed on a bearing of 040° and is soon lost sight of in the haze. At 0310 course is changed to 195°, and speed is reduced to 18 knots. At 0315, course is changed to 220°. At 0319, course is changed to 090°, and speed is increased to 24 knots. At 0332, Light B is sighted on a bearing of 006° T.

Required: Plot and label the 0332 running fix (as shown in figure 1208b).

Solution: Use the same technique described in the foregoing example to construct the 0332 running

fix. The accuracy of measurement will depend, of course, upon the accuracy with which the DR plot was maintained between 0302 and 0332. *This is true for any running fix obtained by construction.*

The 0302 line of position is advanced parallel to itself in the direction of the course made good a distance equal to the distance made good between the 0302 and 0332 DR position. This advanced line now defines the 0302–0332 LOP. The intersection of this line of position with the 0332 line of position on a bearing of 006° to Light *B* establishes the 0332 running fix, from which a new DR plot is started. The plot is labeled as indicated.

PASSING CLOSE ABOARD AN AID TO NAVIGATION

1209 A vessel's position can also be determined approximately by passing close aboard a navigational aid, such as a buoy or offshore light tower, the position of which is indicated on the chart. The accuracy of a position obtained in this manner depends upon two factors: (1) the accuracy of the measurement of the relationship between the ship and the observed aid (in other words how close are you to it and in what direction), and (2) the amount of displacement between the actual and plotted positions of the aid (in the case of a buoy). If the aid is a fixed structure, such as a beacon or light platform, only the determination of your direction and distance off the object will affect the accuracy of your position. In a case where you are passing close aboard such a structure, you are probably safe in considering your determined position a fix. If a moored aid (buoy) is involved, the possibility for error increases markedly. In some cases (such as at low tide in an area where the tether must be long enough to accommodate a large range of tide), a buoy can be a significant distance from its charted position. Relying on this as a means of fixing your position should be used only if more accurate means are not available; in this case it may be prudent to consider the position determined as an *estimated position* rather than as a fix.

LABELING LOPS AND FIXES

1210 LOPs and their resulting fixes should be labeled as shown in the preceding examples and in figure 1210. A single LOP, whether a bearing or a range, should always be labeled on the upper side of the line with the time of observation expressed in four digits. When plotting a bearing, the actual numeric value of direction is of little value because the line is drawn on the chart and can be seen and easily remeasured if necessary, so it is often omitted. If it *is* labeled on the chart to avoid any possible confusion, it is shown as a three-digit number directly *beneath* the time label; true direction is assumed unless "M" is suffixed, indicating magnetic direction.

As already discussed in chapter 9, *fixes* obtained by visual bearings are circled and labeled with the time horizontally. Fixes obtained by electronic means are marked by a triangle instead of a circle. The LOPs used to form a simultaneous fix need not be labeled with the time, since the fix itself is so labeled.

Running fixes are also circled and labeled with the time (of the subsequent observation), but the term "R FIX" is included to distinguish it from a simultaneous (and more reliable) fix. The single line of position that was advanced to form the running

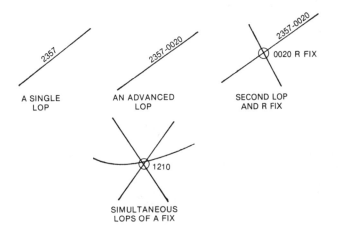

Fig. 1210. Labels for lines of positions (LOPs) and fixes.

fix, however, is labeled with the original time of observation and the time to which it has been advanced, with a hyphen between the two, to make the advance clear. The *second* line of position in a running fix need not be labeled, since it takes its time from that of the running fix itself.

Use sufficient labels to make it clear to you and others what is transpiring, but try not to unnecessarily clutter your chart. Subject to the rules above, *every line must be labeled as soon as it is plotted;* an unlabeled line can be a source of confusion and possible error, especially after a change of watch. Care must be taken not to confuse a course line with a line of position. Draw light lines on the chart and make them no longer than necessary. Particularly avoid drawing them through chart symbols for aids to navigation and other objects that might be made indistinct by erasures. In the illustrations for this chapter, broken lines have been extended from the symbols on the chart to illustrate principles; in reality, the solid segment of the line of position that appears in the illustrations is all that is normally plotted on the chart.

SPECIAL CASES

1211 The methods of fixing your position in pilot waters that are described below are infrequently used, but can be useful in special circumstances.

Sextant and Three-Arm Protractor

1212 A fix can be determined by the measurement of the two horizontal angles between the lines of sight to three identifiable objects. A compass is not used in this method and the actual *directions* of these lines of sight are therefore *not* measured; but the two angles must be measured simultaneously, usually when the vessel has no way on. The angles are normally measured by a sextant held horizontally.

The two angles so measured are usually plotted with a *three-arm protractor*. This instrument, made of brass or plastic, consists of a circular scale that can be read to fractions of a degree or minutes of arc, and to which the three arms are attached (see fig. 1212). The center or index arm is fixed, and the zero graduation of the protractor coincides with the straightedge of this arm. The other two arms are rotatable, and can be set and locked at any angle relative to the fixed arm.

To obtain a fix, three fixed objects that can be identified on the chart must be visible. The angles between the right and central objects, and the left and central objects, are measured with the sextant. The two movable arms are set to these angles and

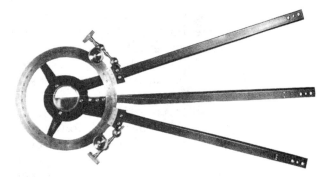

Fig. 1212. A three-arm protractor.

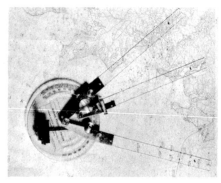

Fig. 1213b. Using a position finder on a chart.

locked, and the protractor is placed on the chart, with the index arm passing through the center object. The instrument is now moved slowly on the chart until all three arms are aligned with the three objects. The vessel's position may now be marked on the chart with the point of a pencil through the hole at the center of the protractor.

Care must be used in selecting the three objects to be observed; if they and the vessel all lie on the circumference of a circle, no fix can be obtained. To avoid this possibility, the objects should be selected to ensure that the center one is closer to the estimated position than the right and left objects.

The three-arm protractor gives chart positions of great accuracy; these positions are not affected by any compass error (since a compass is not used). If a three-arm protractor is not available, a variation on the protractor method can be used by drawing straight lines at the appropriate angles on clear plastic or transparent paper, which is then placed on the chart and moved about until the lines pass over all three objects; the position is beneath the intersection point of the lines.

Position Finder

1213   In lieu of a sextant, a special instrument called a *position finder* can be substituted, which is,

in effect, a three-arm protractor with mirrors attached that permit using this same instrument for observing and plotting. It is necessary to read the value of the angles measured, as the plotting arms are properly positioned when making the observations. Figure 1213a illustrates the optics of the position finder, and figure 1213b shows it positioned on the chart for plotting.

Geometric Solutions

1214   *Doubling the angle on the bow* uses basic geometrical principles to arrive at a practical relationship as can be seen in figure 1214a:

$$b = 180° - 2a$$

$$a + b + c = 180°$$

$$a + (180° - 2a) + c = 180°$$

$$a - 2a + c = 0°$$

$$\text{and } a = c$$

Therefore, *ABC* is an isosceles triangle, and *AB = BC*.

Hence, when the angular distance of the object on the bow is doubled, the run between bearings equals the object's distance at the second bearing.

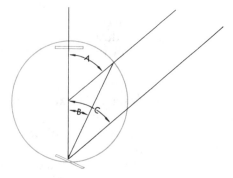

Fig. 1213a. Optical principle of a position finder; B = A, C = A.

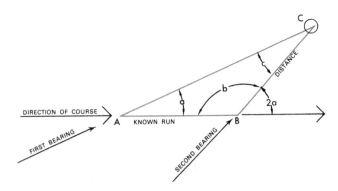

Fig. 1214a. Doubling the angle on the bow.

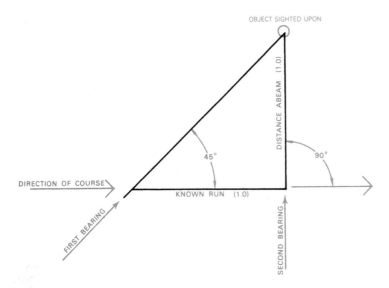

Fig. 1214b. Bow and beam bearings.

Thus, if you use 30° and 60° as your two angles (thereby doubling the angle on the bow), the distance run will equal the object's distance at the second bearing just as it did in the bow and beam bearing method. Similarly, 22½° and 45° may be used as angles on the bow, and other combinations as well. Keep in mind that "angle on the bow" is not the same thing as relative bearing. The former is measured from the bow in either direction as an angle, whereas relative bearings are measured clockwise from the bow through 360°.

The *bow and beam bearing method* uses the relationship described above in its most extreme case and is more consistent with normal shiphandling practices in that it uses *relative bearings* to arrive at a quick visual solution. If you consider the extreme case of *doubling the angle on the bow* described above—45° and 90°—and convert to relative bearings, you can see that when an object is observed on either bow (045° or 315° relative), and then subsequently when the same object is on your beam (090°R or 270°R), the distance traveled between the two observations (noted by dead reckoning), will tell you that you are that same distance from the object you have been observing. You will therefore have fixed your position because you know the range and bearing to the object. You can see this relationship in figure 1214b.

ADDITIONAL PILOTING TECHNIQUES

1215 Along a straight coast where the various depth curves roughly parallel the shore, the echo sounder or lead can be constantly used and any tendency of the ship to be set in toward the beach will soon be apparent. Such a method, of course, must be used intelligently. If a given fathom curve is blindly followed, it may lead into trouble. It is necessary to look ahead and anticipate the results. If the given fathom curve on the chart makes a sharp turn, for instance, a ship following a steady course might find itself in rapidly shoaling water before it could make the turn. The given fathom line, while affording plenty of water under the keel, might pass close to isolated dangers, such as wrecks, shoals, or rocks. Use this procedure *only with due caution.*

If a visual range is not available, using a constant bearing on a distant object ahead can function in a similar manner. This is less reliable and more difficult to achieve but worth employing if the situation warrants.

Knowing when to turn is essential when following a narrow channel. Bends in a channel are usually (but not always) marked by turn buoys. A vessel can usually be taken safely on a change of course around a point of land that has a prominent, identifiable landmark by gradually altering course as the landmark draws abeam, making sure you keep the landmark abeam (or nearly so) but *never forward of the beam;* frequent small changes of course are made to maintain this condition. Be aware, however, that this technique can be dangerous if there is appreciable current.

DANGER BEARINGS

1216 A *danger bearing* is used by the navigator to keep clear of an area of danger close to which the vessel must pass. This is particularly useful in an area where the danger is plotted on the chart but no visible warning of its presence is available. Examples of such dangers are submerged rocks, reefs, wrecks, and shoals. A danger bearing is established between two fixed objects, one of which is the danger area. The other object must be selected to satisfy certain important conditions: it should be clearly visible; it should appear on the chart; the true bearing to it should be in the *same general direction* as the course of the ship as it proceeds through the area.

As shown in figure 1216, a ship is standing up a coast on course 000°, speed 15 knots. The 0430 DR is at Point *A*. A charted area of shoal water and sunken rocks off the coast must be avoided. On the chart draw line "GO" from light "O" (the visible object), tangent to the danger area (the invisible object). The measured direction of this line from G to O, 015°, is the danger bearing. It is usually hachured on the dangerous side, and is labeled with "NLT 015" (meaning *not less than* 015°) on the side opposite the hachures; any bearing less than 015° to Light O could indicate a hazardous situation.

As the ship proceeds up the coast, frequent visual bearings of Light O are taken. If each bearing is numerically *greater* than the charted bearing GO (the danger bearing), such as EO or FO, the ship must be in safe water. If, however, a bearing is observed to be less than GO, such as HO, the ship may be standing into danger as illustrated. In this case, if the position of the ship cannot be determined by a fix, the ship should change course *radically* to the left until the danger bearing is exceeded, after which it is safe to resume the original course.

Similarly, if the hazard were to the left of the course, a danger bearing could be plotted with hachures on the other side and a label reading "NMT" meaning *not more than*. In some waters, it is useful to use a pair of danger bearings, one NLT and one NMT, to keep the vessel on a safe course between hazards to either side.

Even if there are other objects visible by which to plot accurate fixes, it is a simple matter to note, by an occasional check of this bearing, between fixes, that the vessel is making good a safe course. The value of this method decreases, however, as the angle between the course and the danger bearing increases. Unless the visible object is *nearly dead ahead*, the danger bearing is of little value in keeping the vessel in safe water. If there is a large angle between the course and the danger bearing, the object might better be used to obtain running fixes as the vessel proceeds.

RADAR PILOTING

1217   Radar (*r*adio *d*etection *a*nd *r*anging) operates on the principle of reflected energy. In its simplest form, a beam of microwave radio energy is emitted in a sharply defined beam, reflects off an object, and returns. Because radio waves travel at a fixed speed (the same as light waves), distance (range) can be determined by measuring the time between the transmission of the signal and the return of the "echo." The bearing of an echo returned by a "target" is determined from the orientation of a directional antenna.

Radars come in many different varieties. Some are relatively simple and inexpensive, while others offer many sophisticated features and can cost a great deal. Modern radars can even have color displays that can show land and water in contrasting colors and can help the operator differentiate between different types of targets. Coverage of all the different types and of the many features available is beyond the scope of this book. Hands-on practice and reading the accompanying documentation for the radar(s) available on your vessel will ensure that you make full use of this important nav-

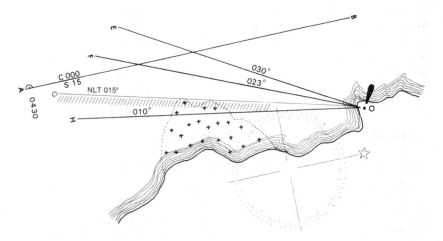

Fig. 1216. A danger bearing.

igational technology. NIMA publication number 1310—the *Radar Navigation Manual*—also contains a great deal of additional information concerning the theory and practical applications of navigational radar.

Radar Fixes

1218 Radar can be used in several ways to obtain position. As with visual piloting, well-determined positions are labeled as *fixes* and less reliable ones as *EPs,* depending upon the judgment of the navigator. Radar or radar-assisted position fixes are listed below in descending order of reliability:
1. Radar ranges and visual bearings of prominent isolated objects.
2. Radar ranges of several radar-conspicuous objects plotted as position circles.
3. Radar range and radar bearing of a single charted feature.
4. Radar bearings of two or more charted features.

Advantages of Radar

1219 Radar has several advantages over other navigational aids for piloting:
1. It can be used at night and during periods of low visibility, when most other methods are limited, or are not available at all.
2. Fixes may be available at greater distances from land than in most other methods of piloting.
3. A fix or EP can be obtained from a single object, since both range and bearing are provided.
4. LOPs and fixes can be obtained rapidly.

Disadvantages of Radar

1220 As a navigational aid, radar is subject to certain limitations and disadvantages:
1. It is subject to mechanical and electrical failure.
2. There are both minimum and maximum range limitations.
3. Interpretation of the information presented on the scope is not always easy, even after considerable training.
4. Charts do not always give adequate information for the identification of radar echoes.
5. Buoys or other small objects may not be detected, especially if a high sea is running, or if they are near shore or other objects.
6. Radar requires active transmission of signals from the vessel, which can be a limiting factor in naval operations (can be detected by an enemy).
7. Radar requires a substantial amount of electrical power (a limiting consideration on small craft with limited power sources).

Racons

1221 As discussed in chapter 6, racons (the word is derived from the words *ra*dar and bea*con*) use radar to provide additional information to navigators. Racons are triggered by a vessel's search radar and respond with a distinctive Morse Code signal that appears on the display of the querying radar, matching the letter on the chart. They can also be coded for positive identification and range measurement to the beacon.

ESTIMATED POSITIONS

1222 At times, the information available to a navigator is insufficient to fix the position of the vessel accurately. However, under these conditions it is often possible to improve on the DR by using the data at hand. A position determined under these conditions is called an *estimated position* (EP). An EP is indicated on the chart by a small square with the corresponding time, written horizontally.

One method of obtaining an estimated position from limited information involves the ship's DR position. The DR position at the time of observation represents the best position available before a line of position is plotted. Once plotted, a line of position represents the locus of all the possible points the ship could have occupied at the time of the observation. The most probable position of the ship is that point on the line of position that is *closest* to the DR position.

Example: The 0600 DR of a ship is as indicated in figure 1222. Course is 025°, speed 10 knots. At 0627, Light *A* was observed through a rift in the fog, bearing 260°.

Required: Plot and label the 0627 EP.

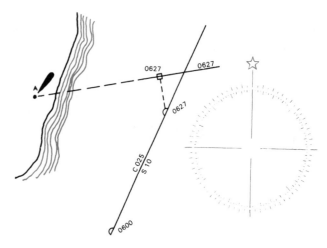

Fig. 1222. Estimated position.

Solution: Plot the 0627 LOP and the corresponding 0627 DR. From the 0627 DR, draw a perpendicular to the LOP. The intersection of the LOP and the perpendicular locates the 0627 EP, labeled as shown. This is the most probable position of the ship on the 0627 LOP, as it is not only on the observed line of position, but it also represents the nearest point thereon to the 0627 DR. It should be obvious that this is a best guess only, and while not as accurate as a fix is more reliable than a simple DR position.

An EP can also be obtained using depth information. Charts often show a number of precise depth soundings and, on many charts, depth contours (lines of equal depths) are shown as light blue lines. If the bottom has a general slope, or there are areas of pronounced features, such as a sharp "valley" or ridge, a sounding can be combined with other positioning information to establish at least an estimated position. This will not be possible on a flat, featureless bottom.

One of the best ways to establish an estimated position from depth information is to use a *line of soundings.* The manner of employing this method is largely determined by the chart covering the area.

Either of the two procedures requires a piece of tracing paper or plastic, on which is drawn a straight line representing the ship's course. If bottom contour lines are printed on the chart, the depth values of the contour lines should be noted; assume, for example, that these are given for every 20 fathoms. When a sounding of a multiple of 20 fathoms true depth is obtained from your echo sounder, a mark is made at one end of the course line on the tracing paper, with the depth and time noted opposite the mark. When the depth changes by 20 fathoms, note the time, and using the latitude scale of the chart, calculate the vessel's run for the time interval; make another mark on the tracing paper at the appropriate distance from the first, and write the depth and time next to the mark. After this process has been repeated several times, place the tracing paper on the chart in the vicinity of the vessel's DR position, with the marks oriented in the same direction as the vessel's course. You can now move it around on the chart until the depth marks on the paper agree with the contour lines on the

chart. Your vessel's position may now be determined with reasonable accuracy.

Note that if the echo sounder reads depth under the keel, the soundings must be adjusted to represent depth below the surface. For example, if the vessel draws 24 feet (4 fathoms), use echo-sounder readings of 16, 36, 56 (and so on) fathoms to get the 20 fathom marks you want. Also, remember that if the vessel is in tidal waters, all charted depths must be adjusted for the height of the tide at the time that this method is used. Do not forget the possibility of a current setting the vessel to one side of its intended track or affecting the speed made good.

When contour lines are not shown on the chart, use the individual soundings in a similar manner by marking off the course line in equal distances on a piece of tracing paper, each mark representing the vessel's advance for a convenient length of time or distance, such as six or ten minutes or 1 mile. (On small-scale charts, these intervals will be greater than when using a large-scale chart.) When a number of soundings have been recorded, orient the tracing paper strip to the course line and move it about the chart in the same manner as described until it matches the charted soundings (or very nearly so) above to determine an estimated position.

It is a good idea to use depth contours for position determination and for planning courses *in advance,* particularly where characteristic bottom features are available. These may be combined with other information such as radio bearings, visual bearings, or lines of position from celestial bodies.

The negative value of depth information should never be overlooked—if the depths being measured at a location vary markedly from those shown on the chart, you are *not* at the position indicated by whatever other method is being used. Depth soundings may not be able to conclusively confirm a fix, but they can warn you of a problem.

Since an EP is not a well-determined position, it is not customary to run a new DR plot from such a position. However, a light line representing the estimated course and speed being made good should be run from an EP to indicate any possibility of the ship standing into danger, allowing the navigator to take appropriate avoiding action before a dangerous situation develops.

Chapter 13

Current Sailing

In chapter 9 ("Dead Reckoning") we considered the movement of a vessel through the water without regard to current. Then, in chapter 11 ("Currents") we considered the movement of the water itself. Chapter 12 ("Piloting") presented methods by which the actual—rather than the DR—position of the vessel could be fixed, thereby verifying the DR plot or making clear the need for correction(s). This chapter carries the process further by showing how the net effect of current can be determined from the difference between DR positions and actual fixes, and also how allowances can be made in advance for the anticipated effect of currents. This is called "current sailing" in navigational parlance.

TERMS DEFINED

1301 Actually, the term *current* used in this chapter should be stated as "current"—in quotation marks—for more must be considered than the horizontal movement of the waters. In navigation, especially in current sailing, the total of *all* the factors that may cause a ship to depart from its intended course and DR are lumped together and termed *current*. Among the factors included in the term are:

Ocean current
Tidal current
Wind-driven current
The effect of wind on the ship itself
Heavy seas
Inaccurate steering by the helmsman
Undetermined compass error
Inaccurate determination of speed
Error in engine calibration
Error in speed log calibration

Excessively fouled bottom
Unusual conditions of trim

It can be seen from the foregoing that *current*, unfortunately, has two meanings as commonly used in marine navigation. First, as discussed in chapter 11, it refers to the horizontal movement of water due to ocean currents, tidal currents, or wind currents. Second, in common usage it *refers to the combined effect of all the factors listed above* (inaccurate steering, wind, etc.). This second composite meaning of the word is used because, in most cases, this movement of water is the one factor that will have the greatest effect on the ship's course, but you should keep in mind that these other factors contribute as well. In the rest of this chapter, the *composite* meaning will apply when the word "current" is used, rather than the simpler "movement of water" meaning.

Current sailing is the art of selecting courses and speeds through the water, making due allowance for the effect of a predicted or estimated current, so that upon completion of travel, the intended track and the actual track will coincide, and you will have arrived at your desired destination. Primarily, current sailing is the application of the best available current information to the intended track in order to determine what course and speed to use to get where you want to go. In other words, it is the application of *compensating* actions to offset the effects of current.

In actual practice, there can be two separate but related procedures used when current sailing. One is the determination of *actual current,* and the other is the compensation for *predicted current* (sometimes called "estimated current") in order to make good the course and speed desired. Actual current is determined by measuring the distance and direction between a fix and the DR position of a vessel for that same time; it can be determined only when an accurate fix can be obtained. Predicted current is the compensation for actual current as described above. Examples of both are provided below.

A *current triangle* is a vector diagram, in which one side represents the set and drift of the current, one side represents the ship's ordered course and speed, and the third side represents the actual track (course and speed) made good. If any two sides are known, the third can be determined by measurement or calculation. Keep in mind that a vector is a line that has both magnitude and direction—it represents a particular speed (by its length) and a particular direction (by the way it is pointing).

Reviewing some of the definitions introduced in earlier chapters:

Track (TR). The intended (anticipated, desired) horizontal direction of travel with respect to the Earth. A navigator plans a voyage by laying a track on a chart. Track is sometimes understood to include a planned speed as well as a planned direction.

Speed of Advance (SOA). Defined as the speed *intended* to be made good when planning a voyage. It can also mean the *average* speed that must be maintained during a voyage to arrive at a destination at a specified time.

Set. The direction *toward* which a current is flowing; if the broader definition of "current" is used, set can be more accurately defined as the resultant direction of all offsetting influences. Note that the description of the set of a current is directly *opposite* to the naming of a wind—a westerly *current* sets *toward* the west, a westerly *wind* blows *from* the west.

Drift. The speed of a current (or the speed of the resultant of all offsetting influences), usually stated in knots. As already noted in chapter 11 (Currents) some publications, notably pilot charts and atlases, express drift in terms of nautical miles per *day*.

Course Made Good (CMG). The resultant direction from a given point of departure to a subsequent position; the direction of the net movement from one point to another, disregarding any intermediate course changes en route. This may differ from the planned track by inaccuracies in steering, wind effects, and so on.

Speed Made Good (SMG). The net speed based on distance and time of passage directly from one point to another, disregarding any intermediate speed changes; speed along the course actually made good.

Track Made Good (TMG). A term sometimes used that, in essence, is a combination of CMG and SMG.

All of these terms and the actual practice of current sailing can be better explained through examples.

DETERMINATION OF ACTUAL CURRENT

1302 Assume your intention is to get from one place to another in a specified time, and a major portion of your planned track and speed of advance requires you to make good a course of 090° T at 15 knots in order to arrive at your destination on time. Let us assume that you departed from a known position at 0800 and, as planned, you steered 090 at 15 knots for two hours, at which time you obtained a good fix. As you can see in figure 1302a, the fix shows your actual position to be southeast of your DR position (where you expected to be at 1000). Drawing and measuring a line from your 0800 known position to your 1000 known (fix) position tells you that you have actually made good a course and speed different from the one you expected to make (Course Made Good is 106° T and Speed Made Good is 19 knots).

Drawing another line connecting the 1000 DR position to your 1000 fix position completes a current triangle (see fig. 1302b), and by measurement you can determine the amount of current that was acting upon your vessel to cause it to wind up at the 1000 fix position instead of the 1000 DR you

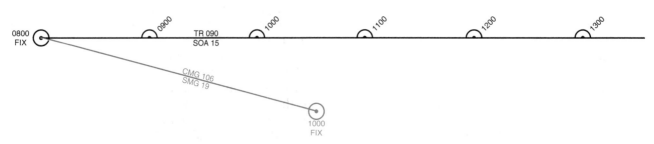

Fig. 1302a. *Course* and *speed made good* derived from a fix.

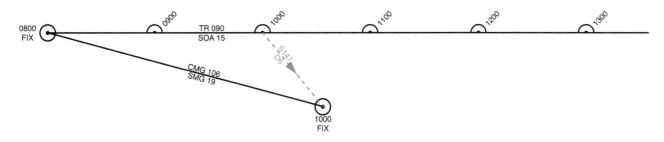

Fig. 1302b. Determining the current.

intended. By measuring this line against a compass rose on your chart, you determine that its direction is 147° T. This is the *set* of the current. By measuring the distance between the fix and DR positions, you determine that it is 12 nautical miles. Knowing that this distance is the result of two hours travel time (0800 to 1000 between fixes), a simple calculation (Speed = Distance ÷ Time) tells you that the speed (drift) of the current is 6 knots.

You have just solved a vector diagram in which the three vectors involved are the *ordered course and speed* (090° at 15 knots), the *course and speed made good* (106° T at 19 knots), and the *set and drift of the current* (147° T at 6 knots). This diagram could have been solved on a maneuvering board sheet as well as directly on the chart; some mariners prefer this method. Computer solutions are available in some systems as well, but it is worthwhile to understand the basis for the computer algorithm.

PREDICTING CURRENT

1303   Once you have determined what the current (combined effects of wind, ocean or tidal current, steering error, etc.) has done to your planned track, it is obvious that continuing to steer 090° T at 15 knots will not get you where you want to go. Assuming the actual current remains the same (and that would be your most reasonable assumption unless you obtained other information), you will have to compensate for it.

The best way to accomplish this is to first regain your original track, and then to figure out what adjustments to your original plan will effectively compensate for the actual current and keep you on that planned track. Regaining your original track will minimize the amount of adjustments you will need to make, and it will simplify your calculations by ensuring that you are in the proper position to take advantage of the preparations you have made for the voyage (turn bearings, rendezvous points, etc.). Making the appropriate adjustments once you have regained track will minimize future adjustments to your track. Failing to make these two compensations (regaining your planned track and adjusting course and speed to make it good) makes much of your advance planning useless and increases the chances of your standing into danger.

The first step toward regaining the original track is accomplished by picking a point on that track that you will aim for—which point you choose is up to you and will be determined by the circumstances. For example, if you were in restricted waters, where there were a number of hazards in relatively close proximity, you would want to regain your planned track quickly and would therefore make a radical course change to get yourself back on track quickly. In more open waters, where there is no immediate danger, you might want to take less radical action in order to save fuel. In our example, the latter is the case, so you decide that aiming for the 1200 DR position will get you back on track in a reasonable

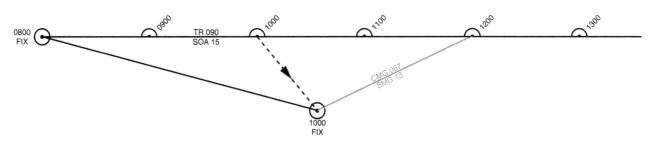

Fig. 1303a. *Course* and *speed made good* to regain track.

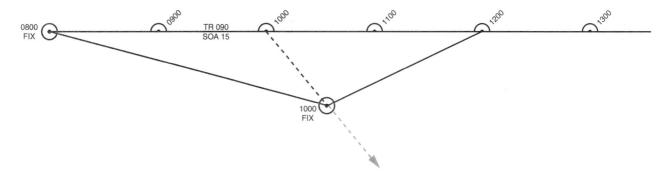

Fig. 1303b. Applying the actual current vector.

time (two hours) without sacrificing any important components of your plan and requiring a less radical deviation than if you headed for the 1100 DR position, for example.

Having decided upon the 1200 DR position as your target, you would draw a line to it from the 1000 fix. This line represents the course and speed you need to make good in order to regain your track at the desired (1200 DR) position (see fig. 1303a), and it is also one leg of a new vector diagram you will use to determine what your ordered course and speed should be to regain track. By measurement, you can see that the course and speed you wish to make good is 067° T at 13 knots.

Because you have determined that a current exists, it is apparent that you cannot merely steer 067° at 13 knots to get back to your track. So you must next apply the actual current. From your calculation above, you know that the actual current has been 147° T at 6 knots for the last two hours. Draw a current vector from the 1000 fix in the direction of the set you determined (147° T) and use the appropriate drift (6 knots) to determine how long this vector should be; in this case, it should be 12 miles long because the drift of 6 knots will be affecting your passage for a total of two hours (between the 1000 fix and the 1200 DR) (see fig. 1303b). If we

had chosen the 1100 DR, this vector would be only 6 miles long, and if we had chosen the 1130 DR, it would be 9 miles long. Always be sure to match this vector with the appropriate time so that you can determine the appropriate length of the current vector. Remember that the length of this vector is determined by the drift (speed) multiplied by the elapsed time ($D = S \times T$).

Next, simply connect the end of the new set-and-drift vector with the 1200 DR (see fig. 1303c). This determines the final vector in the predicted current triangle, and it tells you what course and speed to order. Measuring this vector reveals that you need to steer 034° T at 17 knots in order to return to your track at the 1200 point. By ordering this course and speed at 1000, you should regain your track at the 1200 DR position.

Once you have arrived at the 1200 DR, it should be apparent that if you remained on 034° T at 17 knots your vessel would continue on beyond the 1200 DR and place you north of your intended track. It should also be apparent that coming back to the originally planned track course and speed of 090° T at 15 knots would (assuming the current is the same) carry you off your intended track to the southeast, just as it did between the 0800 and 1000 fixes.

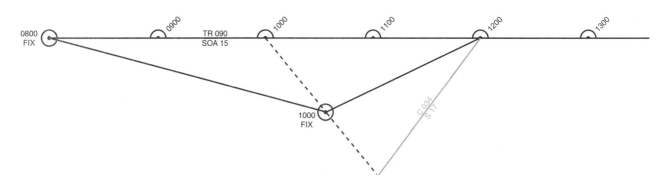

Fig. 1303c. Course and speed to order to regain track.

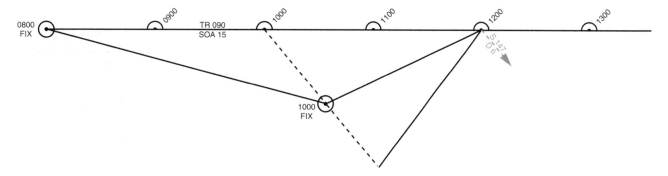

Fig. 1303d. In order to remain on track, first construct a set and drift vector.

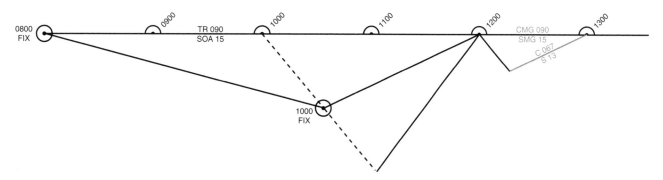

Fig. 1303e. Connect end of vector to future DR position to determine course and speed required to make good your intended track.

To remain on your planned track, therefore, you need to solve another current vector diagram. This time, you draw a current vector from the 1200 position, using the appropriate direction (set) and speed (drift). In this case, a vector drawn as 147° T and 6 miles long will represent the current over a one-hour period (see fig. 1303d). Connect the end of that vector to the 1300 DR (one hour later) and the new vector created tells you what course and speed you should order in order to compensate for the existing (actual) current in order to make good your planned track (see fig. 1303e). In this example, you should order 067° T at 13 knots in order to make good your planned track of 090° T at 15 knots. If the actual current does not change, you will be able to remain on your planned track for as long as you want by continuing to steer 063° T at 13 knots.

ADDITIONAL CONSIDERATIONS FOR CURRENT SAILING

1304 The examples above make it clear that the navigator cannot afford to ignore the effects of current. An inexperienced navigator, however, may be tempted to blindly assume that a current is continuing without change. The assessment of current should be considered an ongoing process and should not be limited to those times when definitive fix information is available. The wise mariner will gather what information he or she can and use it to think in terms of estimated positions in the absence of more reliable information.

Judgment born of experience is the best guide, but there are some considerations that even a beginner can apply. The estimates of current given in official tables, pilot charts, and so on are usually quite accurate under normal conditions and should not be ignored; but neither should they be accepted as absolute. When there is a strong, steady wind, it can increase or decrease the predicted current, or it can cause a temporary wind-driven current. The effect of wind on a vessel differs with the type of vessel, her draft, and the relative direction of the wind. The current acting on a vessel can change with the tidal cycle, changes in sustained wind, changes in geographical position, and so on. "Current" normally changes with a change of helmsman. Hence, it is generally unwise to blindly assume that the current that has acted since the last fix will continue. All the factors mentioned above should go into an estimate of the present current and to one or more estimated positions. Whether or not you believe in the inevitability of "Murphy's

Law," for safety's sake, always assume the most unfavorable conditions when trying to predict the effects of current.

Another consideration of current sailing is that since a running fix is obtained from two bearings not taken simultaneously, the running fix will be in error if current is present. Unless the actual movement of the vessel between the observations is correctly estimated, the effect of current will degrade the quality of the running fix because it will affect the LOP brought forward. This is one of the main reasons why running fixes are considered less reliable than fixes.

As was stated in the very first chapter of this book, nautical navigation is a combination of art and science. The use of vectors and mathematical calculations is the science part; the art comes in because of the many variables that are not always easy to quantify—judgment replaces calculation in these cases. Current sailing is an excellent example of this. Modern sensors and computers coupled with satellite technology have tipped the balance in favor of science, but the best nautical navigators will still prove to be the ones who understand what is happening even when computer algorithms are doing the work.

Chapter 14

Ship Characteristics in Piloting

Up to this point it has been conveniently assumed that at the instant of an ordered course change the vessel came immediately to the new course, and that when a new speed was ordered, the ship attained that speed instantly. Such, of course, is not the case in "real life." To increase or decrease speed by 10 knots may require twenty minutes or more before the new speed is attained, depending on the size of the vessel, her initial speed, and the flexibility of the engineering plant. A course change of 90° may require half a mile or more of sea room to complete, depending on the type of ship, the rudder angle used, the wind and sea conditions, and various other factors. Each ship reacts in a different way to a given rudder or speed order and reacts differently under different conditions of wind and sea. A navigator must be able to take these factors into consideration in order to know what order must be given to achieve a desired result.

The term *handling characteristics* refers to the ways a vessel responds to engine and rudder orders. For naval vessels, these are called the *tactical characteristics* of the ship. Tables of tactical characteristics are maintained on the bridge of all U.S. naval vessels. Coast Guard regulations require that U.S. merchant ships post data on handling characteristics where they can easily be seen by bridge watchstanders. On smaller craft the data will not normally be formalized, but they do exist, even if only in the mind of the skipper.

When a ship is traveling singly in the open sea, her navigator may ignore the time and travel required to effect course and speed changes, for the scale of the plot is too small to be affected by the resulting errors. In restricted waters however, the situation is entirely different. Here, the navigator frequently needs to know the vessel's position within a few yards, and the effect of the ship's travel in the time required to complete a change of course or speed is comparatively large enough that it must be taken into account. The term *precise piloting* is sometimes applied when taking into consideration these small, but very important, factors.

TURNING CHARACTERISTICS

1401 When approaching an anchorage, turning onto a range, piloting in a restricted channel, maintaining an intended track, or at any time when precise piloting is necessary, the navigator must allow for the turning characteristics of the ship. These characteristics are usually determined during the builder's trials of a new vessel (or for the first of a class of naval ships), but these values can vary somewhat as a ship ages or is modified, so they should be verified or updated when circumstances permit. Instructions for obtaining tactical data for U.S. Navy ships are contained in NWP 50-A, *Shipboard Procedures*.

The standard method of finding a ship's turning characteristics is to run tests in which the vessel is turned in various complete and partial circles under varying conditions and the results recorded for each. The minimum variables used are right and left rudder of specified angles, steady speeds of different value, and notable differences in draft and trim. When turning data is taken, the effects of differing wind and sea conditions should be evaluated as much as practicable. When actually navigating, course changes are not usually as much as 360°, but by studying the complete turning circle of your vessel, the ship's behavior for turns of any extent can be determined.

In considering the track actually followed by a ship during a turn, an understanding of certain definitions used by the U.S. Navy is helpful. Understanding these terms will help you to know how your vessel will respond under various conditions and help you to make appropriate allowance for these responses while navigating—both in the planning and execution stages. Once you have considered these things, it will be apparent why they cannot be ignored in restricted waters.

The *pivot point* of a vessel is the point about which the vessel turns when her rudder is put over. It is a point—a kind of "axis" about which a vessel rotates when it is turning—and is typically located about one-third of the way aft from the bow when a vessel is under way. On a typical destroyer, for example, the pivot point would be somewhere close to the center of the bridge when the ship is under way. It typically moves aft when a vessel slows down and will be about two-thirds of the way aft when a vessel is backing. The pivot point will also vary from one vessel to another and may vary for a given vessel under different conditions of a longitudinal trim. The bow of a vessel moves inside the track followed by the pivot point and the stern "skids" along outside it, something like a car oversteering on a slippery road.

Turning circle is the path inscribed by the vessel's longitudinal center of gravity in making a turn of 360° or more at a constant rudder angle and speed. Although not technically correct, when a vessel is moving forward you may assume this path to be inscribed by the vessel's *pivot point*, since that is easier to identify (or estimate) than is the longitudinal center of gravity. The diameter of a turning circle for a given ship will vary with both her rudder angle and her speed through the water.

Advance is the distance gained in the original direction until the vessel steadies on her new course; it is measured from the point at which the rudder is put over. The advance will be maximum when the ship has turned through 90° (see fig. 1401a).

Transfer is the distance gained at right angles to the original course, measured from the line representing the original direction of travel to the point of completion of the turn. Transfer is maximized at 180°.

Tactical diameter is the distance gained to the right or left of the original course when a turn of 180° has been completed.

Final diameter is the distance perpendicular to the original course between tangents drawn at the points where 180° and 360° of the turn have been

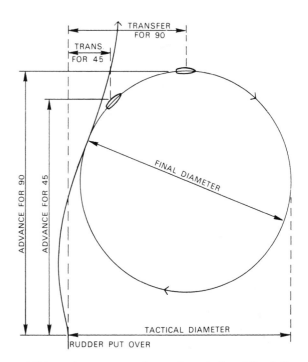

Fig. 1401a. Advance, transfer, and tactical and final diameters.

completed. Should the ship continue turning indefinitely with the same speed and rudder angle, she will keep on turning in a circle of this diameter. It will nearly always be less than the tactical diameter.

Standard tactical diameter is a specific distance chosen to be uniform for naval vessels of a particular type. Using this will ensure that naval vessels will maintain their relative positions when turning together.

Standard rudder is the amount of rudder angle necessary to cause the ship to turn in the standard tactical diameter at standard speed.

Angle of turn is the arc, measured in degrees, through which the ship turns from the original course to the final course (see fig. 1401b).

The speed at which a ship makes a turn may affect the turning diameter markedly, particularly if the *speed-length ratio* (ratio of speed to the square root of the length) is high enough. Thus a 300-foot ship at 30 knots has a considerably larger turning circle than at 15 knots. A short vessel will have a smaller turning circle than a longer one with the same general tonnage.

Sample Turning Data

1402   Figure 1402 is a partial set of typical data on the turning characteristics of a naval ship using standard rudder at standard speed. Other values would be applicable for different speeds and rudder

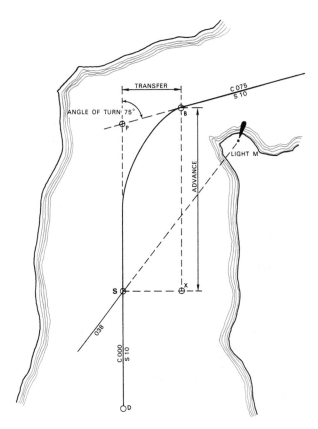

Fig. 1401b. Angle of turn, advance, and transfer.

angles. These figures are representative of one particular ship and are for use only with problems in this book. Note that the table has been prepared for every 15° of turn. Data required for increments between these 15-degree points may be obtained by interpolation.

USING A TURN BEARING

1403 From the preceding discussion it can be seen that during conditions when precise piloting is required a navigator must know at what point the rudder must be put over, so that when allowance has been made for the advance and transfer of the ship, she will steady on the desired heading at the time the new desired track is reached. Having determined this point on your plot, your next task is to establish a means by which you will know when you have arrived at that point so that you will know it is time to put your rudder over to begin your turn. This is accomplished by selecting a prominent mark, such as an aid to navigation or a landmark ashore, and predetermining the bearing to that mark from the point at which the turn is to begin; this is the *turn bearing*. Many navigators prefer using an object upon which the turn bearing is taken that is abeam at the time of starting the turn; this gives the greatest rate of change of bearing and hence an easily and precisely determined point for turning. If the vessel is known to be on track when approaching the turn point, a beam point works well, but if the vessel is off track before the turn, it will still be off track after the turn. Choosing an object that is nearly parallel to the new course actually works better in these circumstances. If practicable, you should choose an object on the side of the channel *toward* which the turn is to be made (the inside of the turn), since the conning officer will be giving that side the greater part of her or his attention. In figure 1401b, the navigator has selected Light M for this purpose, which is a compromise between parallel and beam. The ship is standing up the channel on course 000° T and, after rounding the point of land marked by Light M, will come to new course 075° T to continue up the river.

To allow for the turning characteristics of the vessel, the navigator would draw the desired course line up the next reach of the river, then draw a line parallel to the vessel's present track at a distance out to the side equal to the transfer for a 75° turn (513 yards from the table in fig. 1402). The intersection of this line with the final course, 075° T, will be the point B at which the turn will be completed. From this point, the navigator would measure back along the line drawn parallel to the present track a distance equal to the advance (1,007 yards from fig. 1402) locating point X. From point X, drawing a perpendicular to the original course line will locate

Angle of Turn	Advance	Transfer	Angle of Turn	Advance	Transfer
15°	500	38	105°	993	853
30°	680	100	120°	933	1013°
45°	827	207	135°	827	1140
60°	940	347	150°	687	1247
75°	1007	513	165°	533	1413
90°	1020	687	180°	367	1500

Standard Tactical Diameter, 1500 Yards—Standard Rudder 15°

Fig. 1402. Typical amounts of advance and transfer for various angles of turn for a specific vessel.

the point at which the rudder must be put over to complete the turn at the required point. The bearing from that point to Light M is the turn bearing—038° T in this case.

When actually moving up the channel, the navigator will make continuous observations on Light M. It should be apparent that the bearings will initially be less than 038 but will gradually get closer to it as the vessel continues northward. When Light M bears 038 (at point S in fig. 1401b) the order "Right Standard Rudder" would be given. When the turn is complete, the ship will be heading on the final course of 075 at point B. The solid line SB represents the actual track of the ship through the turn.

Some mariners use a method known as the *slide bar* technique to assist the navigator in quickly revising a turn bearing if the vessel is off track just prior to a turn. Draw the slide bar parallel to the new course through the turning point on the original course (see fig. 1403). You may then determine a new turn bearing by dead reckoning ahead from your last fix. From the point where the DR intersects the slide bar, determine the bearing from that intersection to the navigational aid being used for your turn bearing. Because charts often get cluttered around turn points, it helps to draw the slide bar using a different color from the one used to lay down your track; this will distinguish the two and avoid confusion.

Yet another related technique is the use of a radar range on an identifiable (stationary) target ahead or astern. By knowing the range at which the object should be when the turn is to commence, you may use that figure as the determinant for commencing your turn when that actual range is reached.

ANCHORING IN A SPECIFIC SPOT

1404   Charts showing specific anchorage berths are published by NOS, NIMA, and/or local maritime authorities for a port. They are simply harbor charts with anchorage berths overprinted in colored circles of various diameters corresponding to the swinging area required by vessels of various types and sizes. The center of the circles marks the center of the berth, and each berth is designated by a number or letter printed inside the circle.

In harbors for which no standard anchorage chart is available, berths are assigned by giving the bearing and distance of the berth from a landmark or aid to navigation, together with its diameter. It is the duty of the navigator to cause the ship to be maneuvered in such a manner that the anchor may be let go in the center of the ship's assigned berth. This should be accomplished with a maximum permissible error of 10–50 yards (9–46 m), depending upon the type of ship.

There are a number of terms associated with the anchoring process.

Approach track is defined as the track that a vessel must make good in order to arrive at the center of her assigned berth.

While taking bearings, the navigator is not normally standing at the same spot on the vessel where

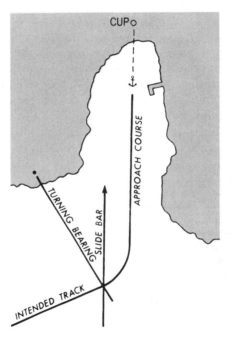

Fig. 1403. The slide bar technique.

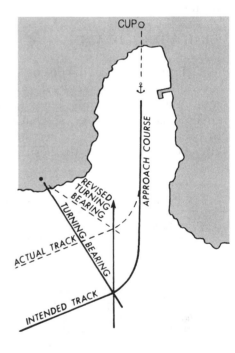

the anchor will be let go. To compensate for this separation, the navigator should draw a *letting-go circle* around the center of the berth while preparing for anchoring. The radius of that circle is equal to the horizontal distance from the point on the vessel where the anchor will be let go (the "hawsepipe" on a naval vessel) to the point where the instrument that will be used in taking bearings is located (a gyro repeater on the port bridge wing, for example). Obviously, the distance between the two locations can be very large on an aircraft carrier and virtually insignificant on a small craft.

The *letting-go bearing* is a bearing to any convenient landmark from the point of intersection of the letting-go circle and the final approach track. As with a turn bearing, the selected object should, if possible, be near the beam to maximize effectiveness.

The *letting-go point* is the intersection of the approach track and the letting-go circle.

Range circles are distance circles of varying radii *plotted* from the center of the berth with distances

measured from the letting-go circle. In other words, you will measure the distance between the letting-go point and the center of the berth and add that amount to each of your measurements for range circles; then place one point of your dividers on the center of the berth while inscribing the arcs of the range circles. The letting-go circle is then labeled 0 yards, while the other range circles are labeled with their distance from the letting-go point (even though they were inscribed using the center of the anchorage). This may seem confusing at first, but if you think about it for a moment, it makes sense. Range circles are used as references to let the navigation team know where the vessel is in relation to the drop point for the anchorage.

Preparations

1405   When the ship has been ordered to anchor in a specific berth (see fig. 1405), the navigator consults the chart and prepares for the approach to the anchorage.

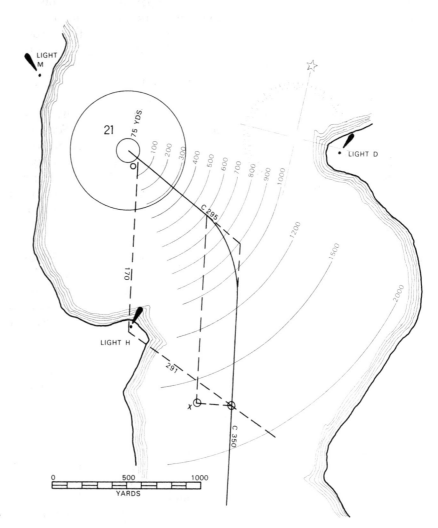

Fig. 1405. Anchoring in an assigned berth.

The letting-go circle is plotted as described above. Next comes the approach track, selecting an appropriate course that will make best use of available landmarks and navigational aids for fixing the ship's position en route, and for locating turn bearing marks at predetermined points where turns are necessary. The approach track must be long enough for the final turn to have been completed and any last-minute adjustments of track accomplished before reaching the center of the berth. The final approach should, if possible, be made with the vessel heading into the current (or into the *wind* if it is expected to have more of an effect than the current). It is also desirable for the approach track to be headed directly toward an identifiable aid to navigation or landmark during the final leg; as the approach is made, the constant bearing (termed a *head bearing*) of the aid or landmark can then be maintained. If no such aid is available, or if the aid previously selected becomes obscured, the positions of consecutive fixes with respect to the approach track (to the right of it or to the left of it) will permit the navigator to recommend a change of course to conn the ship back on the approach course.

Range circles of varying radii are also plotted. In most cases it is necessary to draw in only the arcs of the range circle adjacent to the approach track rather than the full circles. In practice it is customary to draw arcs every 100 yards out to 1,000 yards, then at 1,200 yards, 1,500 yards, and 2,000 yards.

When planning to bring a ship to anchor, the navigator should determine the depth of the water and the characteristics of the bottom as they may be shown on the chart, as well as the nature of and distance to any nearby areas of shoal water or other hazards.

Using the planned drop point as a center, a radius equal to the ship's length plus the horizontal component of the length of anchor cable to be used is plotted; called a *swing circle* this construction allows the chart to be closely examined to be sure that no hazards exist within this circle, nor does it infringe on any other charted anchorage.

The navigator also plots a *drag circle*, using the actual anchor position as a center and the horizontal component of the anchor cable length plus the letting-go circle distance as the radius. Therefore, once anchored, any check bearing, taken to determine if the anchor is holding, must fall within this circle, which is of smaller diameter than the swing circle. If a bearing places you outside this circle, it is an indication that your anchor is not holding you securely in position and is probably dragging.

All of this information should then be passed to the captain and other officers directly concerned with the anchoring. In naval vessels, a formal navigational brief is required to be held to ensure that all concerned are aware of the plan. This not only ensures that everyone involved knows in advance what their responsibilities are going to be, but also brings the plan under more scrutiny and thus improves the chances that potential problems or errors will be identified.

A good practice is to prepare a template for the anticipated anchoring. This template is constructed of clear plastic and replicates the planned approach —range rings, letting-go circle, and so on—in the same scale as the chart in use. By having this template at hand, if you find the planned anchorage unusable for some reason (another vessel is already anchored there, for example) you can quickly shift the template to a new location and use it to accomplish a safe anchoring.

Execution

1406 *Example:* A ship is assigned Berth 21 for anchoring (see fig. 1405). The initial approach into the harbor is on a course of 350° T. A final approach track directly toward Light M is possible and is selected. Distance from the hawsepipe to the gyro repeater used for taking bearings is 75 yards.

Required: (1) Approach track to the berth. (2) Turn bearing. (3) Letting-go bearing.

Solution: The selected approach track is plotted back from Light M through the center of the berth; its direction is measured as 295°. The letting-go circle with a radius of 75 yards is plotted around the center of the berth. The intersection of this circle and the approach track is the letting-go point and is labeled 0 yards.

The initial approach track into the harbor is plotted. By use of the table of the ship's characteristics, the navigator can determine the advance and transfer of the final turn at the speed to be used. With this data, he or she determines the point at which the turn is to be completed and the point at which the rudder is to be put over. The navigator then plots this and determines the turn bearing as 291° using Light H (selected because it best meets the criteria described above).

Range circles are plotted from the center of the berth, measuring the distances from the letting-go point as described above. Thus, the radius used to plot the "100-yard" range circle is actually 100 + 75 = 175 yards; similarly, all other range circles are plotted with a radius 75 yards greater than the labeled distance to allow for the difference between the center of the berth (where you ideally want your hawsepipe to be when the anchor is let go) and the point from which you are taking your measurements (usually from the bridge, which can be some distance away—on an aircraft carrier, it can be more than a quarter of a mile).

As the ship enters the harbor and proceeds along the track, frequent bearings are taken and fixes plotted to ensure that the desired track is maintained. As the range circles are crossed, the navigator advises the captain of the distance to the letting-go point so that the speed may be adjusted to bring the ship nearly dead in the water when the letting-go point is reached.

When Light H bears 291° the rudder is put over and the turn commences. Upon completion of the turn Light M should bear 295° dead ahead. As the ship approaches the anchorage, the heading of the ship is adjusted so that a constant bearing of 295° is maintained on Light M. Bearings on Lights H and M are plotted continuously, and the captain is advised of the distance to go. When Light H bears 170° and Light M 295°, the vessel is at the letting-go point and the anchor is let go. At that instant, bearings are taken on all navigational aids visible so that the

exact location of the anchor can be accurately determined. The ship's exact heading at the time of the final fix are also observed and noted. A distance of 75 yards is then plotted from the fix, in the direction of the observed heading to determine the exact position of the anchor.

Answers: (1) Approach track is 350° initially, then (using light M) 295° for the final leg. (2) Turn bearing is 291° on Light H. (3) The letting-go bearing is 170 on Light H.

Procedures After Anchoring

1407   Immediately after the anchor is down and holding, and the intended length of anchor cable has been let out, the navigator should plot the actual position of the anchor from the bearings taken at the moment it was dropped. Using this as a center, the actual swing circle and drag circle should be plotted. Frequent fixes should then be taken using all available resources (visual, radar, etc.) to ensure that the vessel is remaining within the anchorage and not dragging anchor. As a backup, many GPS units have an alarm function that can provide a warning that the vessel is dragging anchor.

Chapter 15

Basic Radio Navigation

The use of radio waves in navigation is a relatively new phenomenon when compared to techniques such as piloting and celestial navigation, yet various forms have been in existence for more than a century. The radio time signal was the first navigational aid to take advantage of the properties of radio waves. It made precise time available to the navigator for use in connection with celestial navigation. The next major development was the use of radio transmissions to obtain bearings—radio LOPs—by means of radio direction finding equipment. An advancement of this technique used shore-based direction-finding stations that were a significant distance apart but were linked together by telegraph lines into a net so that a fix could be determined from several radio bearings and transmitted by radio to the ship.

Eventually, the advance of technology led electronic engineers to the use of hyperbolic techniques for more refined radio navigation. A number of these systems were eventually developed and some continue in use today. Radio is an important part of satellite navigation as well.

This chapter provides an introduction to radio fundamentals and discusses radio direction finding. Hyperbolic and satellite radio-navigation systems will be discussed in the next chapter.

FUNDAMENTALS OF RADIO NAVIGATION

1501 While a detailed discussion of radio-navigation fundamentals is beyond the scope of this text, a review of some of the basics is provided with an emphasis upon those aspects which are most useful in navigation.

Generation of Radio Waves

1502 In the simplest of terms, electrical current can be considered as the flow of electrons along a conductor (wire). That flow can be continuous in the same direction—known as *direct current*—or it can flow back and forth, first in one direction and then in the opposite direction—known as *alternating current*.

One of the resulting phenomena caused by this flow of electrons is the creation of an electromagnetic field around the conductor. If the current is stopped, this field will—after a brief but finite amount of time—collapse back into the conductor. In the case of alternating current, the current increases to a maximum (while generating a corresponding electromagnetic field) and then decreases until it reaches zero, which causes the electromagnetic field to collapse as expected. However, because the conductor is again filling with current (this time flowing in the opposite direction) the collapsing field is prevented from returning to the conductor and is instead detached and is thrown outward into the surrounding space. This is repeated time and again as long as the current is alternating through the conductor. This is the basic principle of a radio broadcast—these electromagnetic fields that are cast off into space from the conductor (antenna) are radio waves, and they can be configured (modulated) to carry intelligence or to perform specific tasks.

The reason these castaway fields are called "waves" is related to the method of their generation and to the "picture" that results when one represents them graphically. In its simplest form, alternating current is created (generated) by rotating a specially shaped conductor (called a rotor) through a magnetic field. The amount (magnitude) and direction (polarity) of current flowing through the rotor varies according to the position of the rotor relative to the magnetic field. When the rotor has completed one quarter turn through the magnetic field, it will be at its maximum amount and will begin to decline as the rotor continues to turn. Halfway through one complete turn, the rotor will be oriented relative to the magnetic field in such a way that no current flows. As the rotor continues to turn, it will be oriented differently from its original half turn and the current will begin to flow in the opposite direction, continuing until it reaches another maximum one quarter turn more, before starting to decline to zero again. One complete turn (cycle) of the rotor then will result in two moments of zero flow and two maximums (in opposite directions). Plotted on a graph (see fig. 1502), this action looks similar to the undulating waves flowing into a beach and has been given the name *sine wave*.

An understanding of some radio wave terminology will be useful when discussing radio navigation. The completion of an entire sine wave is called a *cycle*. The amount of time used to complete one cycle is called the *period* of the wave. The maximum points are called peaks and are distinguished by the qualifiers crest and trough. The height of a wave (above zero) defines its *amplitude*. The distance covered by one complete wave is called, appropriately enough, *wavelength*.

How often complete sine waves are formed in a given amount of time is called *frequency* and is most often expressed in terms of *hertz*, which is another name for "cycles per second." (Note: For many years, frequency was expressed simply as cycles per second, but was eventually changed to honor Heinrich Hertz, one of the "founding fathers" in the field of electronics.) When dealing with greater frequencies (as you often will), metric prefixes (kilo, mega, and giga) are used as a form of shorthand:

1 kilohertz (kHz)	= 1,000 hertz (Hz)
1 megahertz (MHz)	= 1,000,000 Hz or 1,000 kHz
1 gigahertz (GHz)	= 1,000,000,000 Hz
	or 1,000,000 kHz
	or 1,000 MHz

Sometimes one wave is compared to another wave and the term *phase* becomes important. Phase is usually expressed in terms of circular measure (with a complete cycle represented as 360°) so that two waves whose crests are ¼ cycle apart are said to be 90° *out of phase*. If the crest of one wave occurs at the trough of another, the two waves are 180° out of phase.

The Electromagnetic Spectrum

1503   Among the radio terms discussed above, frequency is a particularly important one. If you tune in a radio station in your car, the number you select is the frequency. There is a wide range of frequencies (known conventionally as the electromagnetic spectrum), and radio frequencies are only a small part (10 kHz to 300,000 mHz) of that entire spectrum. As you can see in figure 1503, other wave forms are also included in this vast spectrum, including infrared, visible light, ultraviolet, and x-rays above the radio spectrum and audible sounds below.

Another important characteristic of radio waves is their wavelength. This characteristic figures in the design of antennas, among other things. It is important to note that *the higher the frequency, the shorter the wavelength* and, conversely, the lower the frequency, the longer the wavelength. This relationship plays a major role in the design of radio equipment and in the use of radio waves for various pur-

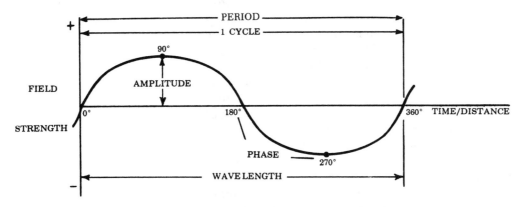

Fig. 1502. Components of an electromagnetic (sine) wave.

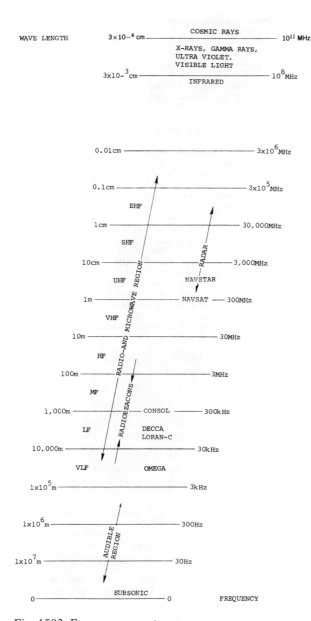

Fig. 1503. Frequency spectrum.

Band	Abbrevia-tion	Frequency	Wavelength
Very low frequency	VLF	10–30 kHz	30,000–10,000 meters
Low frequency	LF	30–300 kHz	10,000–1,000 meters
Medium frequency	MF	300–3,000 kHz	1,000–100 meters
High frequency	HF	3–30 MHz	100–10 meters
Very high frequency	VHF	30–300 MHz	10–1 meters
Ultra high frequency	UHF	300–3,000 MHz	100–10 centimeters
Super high frequency	SHF	3–30 GHz	10–1 centimeters
Extremely high frequency	EHF	30–300 GHz	1–0.1 centimeters

These bands will be discussed in further detail relating to their practical uses later in the chapter.

It should be noted that potential confusion may arise because the military and some scientific circles also refer to frequencies above 1,000 MHz (1 GHz) by another system as follows:

L-band	1,000–2,000 MHz	(1–2 GHz)
S-band	2,000–4,000 MHz	(2–4 GHz)
C-band	4,000–8,000 MHz	(4–8 GHz)
X-band	8,000–12,500 MHz	(8–12.5 GHz)
K-band	12,500–40,000 MHz	(12.5–40 GHz)

And because severe absorption of radio waves occurs near the resonant frequency of water vapor (22.2 GHz), the K-band is subdivided into the lower K-band (12.5–18 GHz) and the upper K-band (26.5–40 GHz).

Reflection, Refraction, and Diffraction

1504 Radio waves and light waves are both forms of electromagnetic waves, differing only in frequency. Some of the laws learned in the science of optics are also applicable to radio waves.

In the simplest terms, *reflection* occurs when light or radio waves are "bounced off" surfaces; *refraction* occurs when light or radio waves are "bent" as a result of passing from one medium to another; and *diffraction* occurs when light or radio waves "bleed" into the shadow zones behind opaque objects.

Reflection. When light waves encounter a surface, the light is reflected (bounced off), absorbed, or scattered. If the surface is smooth and polished, the light is reflected in a *specular* fashion, as with a mirror. A rougher surface will reflect in a more *diffuse* fashion because of scattering and will result in dis-

poses, including navigation. The transmission characteristic of a given electronic system is often stated either as wavelength or frequency. The relationship between the two can be stated as a simple equation:

$$\lambda = 300/F$$

λ is the wavelength in meters, F is the frequency in megahertz, and the constant 300 is the velocity of light in meters per microsecond (a more precise figure is 299.793).

Recognizing these characteristics of frequency and wavelength, the radio portion of the electromagnetic spectrum has been divided into various bands for conventional reference as follows:

tortion of the image. Dark surfaces will absorb much of the incoming light and convert it to heat.

Like light, radio waves are also reflected, specularly from smooth surfaces and diffusely from rough surfaces. When a radio wave is reflected specularly, the character of the wave is unchanged. When it is reflected more diffusely, the character of the radio wave will be more distorted.

In terms of radio waves, an important characteristic to remember is that the higher the frequency, the more likely it is to be reflected.

Refraction. In free space, an electromagnetic wave travels in a straight line; however, when traveling through an area containing matter or material particles, the wave may be bent or refracted. Similarly, bending in the direction of travel of a wave occurs when the wave passes from one medium to another of different density. Thus, when a wave front enters a medium of different density at an oblique angle, the change in velocity affects the first portion of the wave front, entering the new medium before the remainder of the wave is affected, and the alignment of the wave front is changed. The direction of travel, as previously stated, is perpendicular to the wave front; therefore, the direction of travel changes toward the direction of reduced velocity. The practical effect of this is that radio waves can, under the right conditions, follow the curvature of the Earth, an important consideration in some circumstances.

Diffraction. When an electromagnetic wave, either radio or light, is partially obstructed by an object of opaque material, the area behind the object is shadowed as the unobstructed portion of the wave front continues in its original direction. But some of the light enters the shadow zone (by means of a rather complex process beyond the scope of this book). This is why you do not find yourself in complete darkness when you are standing in the shadow of an object even though the source of light is being blocked by the object (see fig. 1504). This is also the reason why a radio signal can reach some distance beyond the horizon.

Trapping. Sometimes called "ducting," this is actually a form of extreme reflection that occurs when radio waves are trapped between the Earth's surface and an atmospheric layer (or between layers of the atmosphere) in such a way that they continue to reflect in a kind of tunnel effect. The result is that the waves are transmitted over much longer distances than would otherwise be possible. This is the reason why sometimes you are able to hear radio stations from very distant cities that you would not normally expect to hear. This is an aberrant condition that occurs only under certain specific atmospheric conditions. You should not *expect* to encounter it, but you should be able to recognize it when it occurs.

Ground Waves and Sky Waves

1505 In order to maximize the use of radio waves, it is important to know that once radio waves are transmitted from an antenna, they travel in two basic ways: as ground waves that hug the sur-

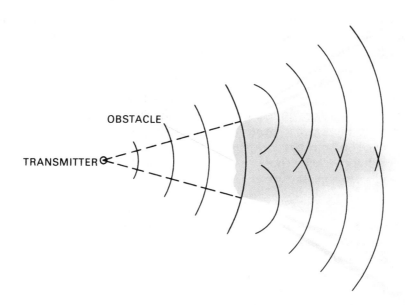

Fig. 1504. Diffraction of a wavefront.

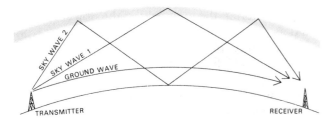

Fig. 1505. Radio ground-wave and sky-wave propagation paths. (Vertical distances in this sketch have been exaggerated for clarity; the distance between the transmitter and receiver is normally hundreds of miles, while the ionosphere is only 30 to 215 miles above Earth.)

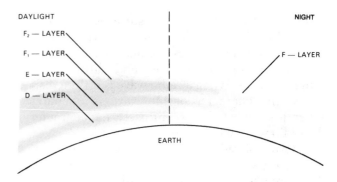

Fig. 1506a. Layers of ionization: during daytime (*left*) and at night (*right*).

face of the Earth or as sky waves that can, in some circumstances, bounce off the upper layers of the atmosphere and return to Earth.

Ground waves occur with all radio transmissions, but they are most significant when low frequency signals are used because they are able to remain in contact with the Earth's surface for great distances. This characteristic allows them to follow the curvature of the Earth. Because the Earth's surface absorbs some of the signal as it travels along, these ground waves require high power to make sure they have enough energy to go the long distances desired. The amount of absorption of the ocean's surface is rather constant, allowing more accurate predictions than when transmitting over land surfaces. The variability of the characteristics of land areas complicates the prediction of its effects on ground-wave transmission.

Electromagnetic energy, as transmitted from the antenna, radiates outward in all directions. As discussed above, a portion of this energy proceeds out parallel to the Earth's surface, while the remainder travels upward as well as outward. Some of this upward and outward energy continues on a straight line, penetrating the Earth's atmosphere and continuing on into outer space. Other parts of this signal strike one or more layers of ionized gases in the Earth's upper atmosphere and, through reflection and refraction, are returned to the Earth's surface. This normally occurs only once but may be repeated as shown by "sky wave 2" in figure 1505. (These are referred to as "one-hop" and "two-hop" sky waves.)

Ionospheric Layers

1506   That part of Earth's atmosphere that causes sky waves to return to Earth is known as the *ionosphere*. Electrons and ions are not uniformly distributed in the ionosphere, but rather tend to form layers. These layers change, disappear, combine, and separate as they are affected by the local time of day, season of the year, and the level of sunspot activity;

the layers are also, at times, affected by apparent random changes from moment to moment.

Four ionized layers are involved in the phenomenon of radio-wave propagation (see fig. 1506a). The most intense ionization occurs near the center of each layer. The greater the intensity of ionization in any layer the greater is the bending back (refraction) toward Earth of the radio waves; lower frequencies are more easily reflected than are higher frequencies, which have a greater tendency to penetrate the ionosphere and "escape" into space.

The ionized layer nearest Earth's surface is called the *D layer*. This layer, which occurs at heights of 30 to 50 nautical miles (55 to 90 km) above the Earth, exists only during daylight hours and disappears completely at night. It has more of an absorbing than reflecting effect.

Located at a height of about 65 nm (120 km), the *E layer* is densest in the region directly beneath the Sun and virtually disappears at night.

The ionization layer designated as *F* occurs in two separate zones during the day, and the two collapse into one much denser layer at night. The F_1 *layer* is usually between 95 and 135 nm (175 to 250 km) and the F_2 *layer* is found at altitudes of 160 to 215 nm (300 to 400 km) during the day.

As the Sun sets, the ionosphere undergoes a significant change, both physically and electrically. The D and F layers disappear, and the F_1 and F_2 combine to form a much denser single layer. The bottom level of the ionosphere is raised to about 100 nautical miles (185 km) above the Earth's surface. This newly formed layer causes radio waves to return to the Earth much more readily than during daylight hours. This results in better reception and clarity as well as improved range of transmission for mariners using radio in the appropriate frequencies.

The practical effects of all this are that during daylight, radio transmissions are essentially limited to ground waves; during twilight, while the layers

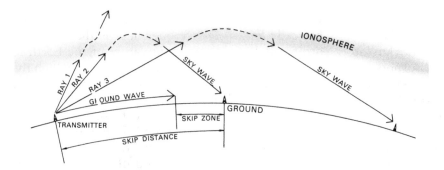

are transforming, significant interference occurs so that radio reception may be lost entirely; and during the hours of darkness, reception range can be significantly improved by the addition of reflected sky waves.

In figure 1506b you can see the effects of these phenomena. A vessel which is beyond the effective range of the ground wave but is not far enough out to receive the sky wave is in the skip zone and will not receive any signal.

Another problem can occur when a vessel receives both a ground wave and a sky wave. Because the latter has farther to travel, the two signals will be out of phase when received and can interfere with one another. Appropriately designed equipment is able to sort out these signals and take advantage of the presence of both.

Radio Frequency Bands

1507   The radio frequency bands introduced earlier in the chapter have general characteristics that translate into various practical applications as described below. Because radio waves are used in radar and communications equipment as well as in some equipment designed specifically for navigational purposes, an understanding of these spectrum definitions is useful to the nautical navigator.

Very Low Frequency (VLF)

1508   The VLF band includes those frequencies between 10 and 30 kHz. Because of the low frequency, these radio waves have a long wavelength, which makes them very stable over long distances, but they also require very high power in order to overcome the effects of absorption.

VLF sky waves are reflected by the ionosphere with comparatively little loss of energy because of the short distance they travel within the ionized layer. However, the ensuring reflection from the Earth's surface undergoes significant loss by absorption, especially over land areas.

Despite these limitations, high-powered VLF signals travel efficiently between the Earth's surface and the ionosphere. VLF waves may be propagated for distances as great as 8,000 nautical miles (15,000 km).

Diffraction is greater in the VLF band than in the higher frequencies which allows the signals to efficiently penetrate shadow zones. VLF waves will also penetrate the surface of the Earth (land or water) and hence are used for transmissions to submerged submarines. In the lower part of the VLF band, signals may be received with good readability at depths of 40 to 50 feet (12 to 15 m).

It is much more difficult and expensive to build efficient antennas at these frequencies than at higher ones. Also, radiation of high power, which is required if good reliability over long distances is to be realized, becomes very costly.

The now-defunct Omega hyperbolic navigation system operated in the VLF band before it was superceded by more modern systems. With stations strategically located around the world, this U.S. Navy system used the favorable characteristics of VLF radiation to provide nearly worldwide coverage.

Low Frequency (LF)

1509   The LF band (30 to 300 kHz) is not reflected as efficiently by the ionosphere as are VLF signals. Ground losses increase as the frequency is increased and diffraction decreases. However, antennas for use in the LF band are generally more efficient than those in the VLF band. Good ground-wave propagation is still possible over moderate distances. LF signals are usable, to a limited degree, for transmissions to submerged submarines; at 100 kHz, usable signals are available for a short distance beneath the surface.

The primary navigational use of the LF band is Loran-C (see chapter 16). Decca, a navigational system still in use in certain parts of the world, also makes use of LF signals.

Medium Frequency (MF)

1510   The MF band extends from 300 to 3,000 kHz. Frequencies in this band provide reliable ground-wave propagation over distances ranging from approximately 400 nautical miles (740 km) at the lower end of the band to about 15 nm (28 km) at the upper end. Daytime ionospheric absorption is high and limits sky-wave propagation. Long-distance sky-wave transmission is possible at night. Antenna requirements are not as stringent as they are in the VLF and LF bands.

Loran-A, a forerunner to Loran-C, operated in the MF band, and commercial radio stations (sometimes used by nautical navigators for radio direction finding) are also in this band.

High Frequency (HF)

1511 The HF band (3 to 30 MHz) is heavily employed for long-distance communications, often relying upon the ionized layers in the ionosphere. At these frequencies, antenna efficiency is much more easily obtained than at the lower frequencies. Communications over long distances are possible with moderate transmitter power. Frequencies must be selected, however, with respect to the conditions prevailing at the moment. Under some conditions the higher frequencies travel great distances in the ionosphere before being refracted sufficiently to reflect the wave back to Earth. Signals entering the ionosphere at an angle of incidence that prevents their being refracted back toward the Earth penetrate the ionized layers and are lost in space. In daylight, energy propagated at the lower frequencies of this band has high absorption losses and fades out a short distance from the source. Higher frequencies, during hours of darkness, if reflected at all, return to Earth at great distances from the transmitting antenna, so that they skip over distances of several hundred or more miles.

An example of the need to select proper frequencies is apparent in the case of receiving a National Bureau of Standards time signal from station WWV (see article 2326). This signal can be readily received by day on a standard radio set at 15 MHz at a location 1,300 miles (2,400 km) from its transmission site in Colorado, but at night the 5 MHz signal must be used.

Frequencies in the HF band do not propagate with suitable characteristics for obtaining bearings or distance measurements; thus they are not used for radio-navigation systems. But mariners make extensive use of the HF band for long-distance ship-to-ship and ship-to-shore communications.

Very High Frequency (VHF) and Ultra High Frequency (UHF)

1512 Frequencies in the VHF band (30 to 300 MHz) and the UHF band (300 to 3,000 MHz) are widely used for marine communications. They are basically *line-of-sight* frequencies, as their range is ordinarily limited by the curvature of the Earth to distances approximately equal to those at which the top of one antenna could be seen from the top of the other under ideal weather conditions. VHF and UHF frequencies are also used to some extent for communications over several hundred miles in what is termed a "scatter mode" of operation. Under the right conditions, a portion of very high power electromagnetic waves in the 30 to 60 MHz frequency range are scattered by particles in the ionosphere and returned to Earth, permitting signal reception at ranges of 600 to 1,200 miles (1,100–2,200 km).

A similar scatter effect can be obtained in the *troposphere* by emissions in the 400 to 4,000 MHz range. The troposphere, situated below the stratosphere, is much nearer the Earth than the ionosphere. By means of tropospheric scatter, ranges of about 600 miles (1,100 km) have been obtained. For navigational purposes, VHF and UHF frequencies provide good line-of-sight propagation at moderate transmitter power. VHF is used for navigational purposes but almost entirely in *air* navigation (such as the TACAN system used by military aircraft). Some radars use frequencies in the upper regions of the UHF band.

The most significant electronic navigational system in use today is the NAVSTAR Global Positioning System (GPS) (see chapter 17), which uses UHF signals transmitted from satellites to provide precise positioning information.

Commercial television broadcasts also use these bands.

Super High Frequency (SHF) and Extremely High Frequency (EHF)

1513 The SHF (3 to 30 GHz) and EHF (30 to 300 GHz) bands are useful only as direct line-of-sight signals. Signals reaching the ionosphere are not reflected or refracted but simply pass through into outer space (although *some* scattering may occur when particles of the right dimensions are encountered). Highly directional antennas are able to make good use of these "microwave" signals (so called because of their extremely short wavelengths); networks of these antennas are used to pass signals over land areas, thereby obviating the need for a great deal of transmission wire. These short wavelengths are also ideally suited for precise range measurements, providing better definition than UHF radars, which makes them a better choice for navigational purposes.

RADIO DIRECTION FINDING (RDF)

1514 The simplest of radio-navigation systems is that of radio direction finding (RDF). Equipment for RDF is used on some recreational craft, on fishing vessels of all sizes, and on oceangoing merchant ships. The extent that RDF is used varies with the availability of more sophisticated equipment, but it remains a basic radio-navigation system.

In the early days of RDF, the actual direction finder was located on shore, taking bearings on radio transmissions from a ship and then radioing bearing information to the navigator. Coastal networks were established so that several simultaneous measurements could yield a fix. Such a network existed along the U.S. coasts during the 1920s and 1930s; shore-based direction finder service is still available in a few foreign locations.

With modern RDF systems for marine navigation, the radio bearing is determined aboard the vessel rather than ashore. Specially designed marine radiobeacons were once the best signal source for RDF navigation, but they are no longer considered cost-effective, and their use has been discontinued. Commercial broadcasting stations (standard AM band), some aeronautical radiobeacons, and a number of other miscellaneous sources can still be used.

A bearing obtained by RDF can be used in the same manner as any other line of position. The exact location of the transmitting antenna must be known; nautical charts will often show the position of aeronautical radiobeacons and some commercial broadcasting stations.

In its simplest form, a radio direction finder makes use of the directional properties of a *loop antenna*. If the plane of such an antenna is *parallel* to the direction of travel of the radio waves, the signal received will be at maximum strength. If the plane of the loop is *perpendicular* to the direction of travel, the signal will be at minimum strength or entirely missing. When a dial is attached to a loop antenna that can be rotated, the orientation of the antenna, and therefore the direction of the signal, can be determined. The pointer indicates the direction of the transmitter from the receiver when the loop is perpendicular to this direction, indicating the minimum signal. The minimum, generally called the "null," rather than the maximum, is used because a sharper reading is then obtained. Some RDFs use *two fixed* loops at right angles to each other and "rotation" is accomplished by electronic circuitry.

Because there are two possible nulls (and two possible maximums) 180° apart with this basic design, modern RDF systems often have built-in circuitry that can differentiate between the actual bearing and its reciprocal. It should be obvious which is the correct bearing (based upon your DR position), but a squadron of destroyers ran up on the rocks of Southern California in 1923 (with the loss of six ships) because of this confusion.

Since radio waves travel a great-circle path, a correction must be applied for plotting long bearings on a Mercator chart (see article 1517); some other chart projections may permit direct plotting of radio bearings.

RDF Equipment

1515 Radio direction finder equipment can be either manual (RDF) or automatic (ADF). In the former case, the antenna is rotated by hand until a direction is obtained. The antenna can be mounted on top of the receiver or separately.

Automatic direction finders rotate a loop either mechanically or electronically. A direct-reading visual display continuously indicates the bearing of the transmitter being received, corrected for 180° ambiguity as discussed above. The operator of an ADF set needs only to tune it to the correct frequency and confirm the identification of the station.

Radio Direction Finder Stations

1516 In some foreign countries radio direction finder equipment is installed at points ashore, and these *radio direction finder stations* will take radio bearings on ships when requested, passing that information by radio. Such stations are also called *radio compass stations*, and can be located by reference to NIMA Pub. No. 117 (*Radio Navigational Aids*), or by the letters "RDF" placed near a radio station symbol on a chart.

Bearings taken by radio direction finder stations, and reported to the ships, are corrected for all determinable errors except the difference between a great circle and a rhumb line, and are normally accurate within 2° for distances under 50 nautical miles.

In some instances, several shore-based radio direction finding stations operate together in a net, and a vessel may be advised of its *position* rather than being given bearings. There may be a charge for this service.

Plotting Radio Bearings

1517 Radio bearings are plotted and labeled in the same manner as visual bearings. RDF bearings are, however, usually much less precise and accurate; a position found with one or more radio bearings must be identified as an "RDF fix," or as an estimated position (EP). A series of estimated positions obtained from RDF bearings and supplemented by a line of soundings can often provide a vessel's position with acceptable accuracy.

In addition to the usual possible errors of plotting, there are two additional sources of error that must be avoided when working with radio bearings. First, be careful to plot from the correct position. If the bearing is observed aboard ship, it must be plotted from the position of the transmitting antenna; if observed at a radio compass station, it must be plotted from the position of the *receiving* antenna. Second, radio waves travel great circles and if they are to be plotted on a Mercator chart at a great enough distance (more than 50 nautical miles), a correction will have to be applied to convert the great circle to the corresponding rhumb line between the broadcasting and receiving antennas. If needed, the correction can be found in the "Radio Bearing Conversion Table" in NIMA Pub. No. 117 (*Radio Navigational Aids*) (see fig. 1517a). As can be seen in the table, the amount of the correction depends on the latitude and the difference of longitude. A bearing from a transmitter 200 miles away that is near the equator or in a nearly north-south direction from the receiver may require a smaller correction than one that is 100 miles away in an east-west direction in high latitudes. The only way to be sure is to enter a correction table and determine the magnitude of the correction.

Having found the correction, it is necessary to determine its sign before applying it to the observed bearing. This is easy to determine if it is remembered that the *great-circle direction is always nearer the pole than the Mercator direction.* Drawing a diagram, mentally or otherwise, for each problem can help you determine the sign as indicated in figure 1517b will

help you visualize how the sign should be applied. The important thing to remember is that the sign depends on the relative position of the receiver and the transmitter, regardless of which is on your ship.

Accuracy of Radio Bearings

1518   The accuracy of RDF bearings depends on the following factors:

Strength of signals. The best bearings can be taken on transmitters whose signals are steady, clear, and strong. Weak signals and those receiving interference may give inaccurate bearings at best.

Radio deviation. Direction finders are subject to radio deviation, which affects the accuracy of their readings in much the same manner as magnetic compass deviation, although for different reasons. Incoming waves are picked up by metallic objects, particularly items of rigging, and re-radiated in such a way as to cause incorrect nulls on the vessel's RDF. Calibration for these errors can be accomplished by observing simultaneous radio and visual bearings on various headings and preparing an RDF deviation table. Deviation errors should be checked periodically, particularly after the ship's structure has been altered or major changes have been made in electrical wiring. Bearings should be taken only when other antennas and movable equipment such as davits, cranes, and so on, are in the same position as during calibration if at all possible.

Reciprocal bearings. With some equipment it is not apparent from which of two directions differing by 180° the bearing is coming. It is usually possible to tell which bearing to use by the dead-reckoning position of the ship, but if there is any doubt, take several bearings and note the direction of change. The station should draw aft if you are using the correct bearing rather than the reciprocal.

RADIO NAVIGATIONAL AIDS

RADIO DIRECTION—FINDER AND RADAR STATIONS

200F.   Radio Bearing Conversion Table

Correction to be applied to radio bearing to convert to Mercator bearing

Difference of longitude

Mid. lat.	0.5°	1°	1.5°	2°	2.5°	3°	3.5°	4°	4.5°	5°	5.5°	6°	6.5°	7°	7.5°	Mid. lat.
°	°	°	°	°	°	°	°	°	°	°	°	°	°	°	°	°
4	...	...	...	...	0.1	0.1	0.1	0.1	0.2	0.2	0.2	0.2	0.2	0.2	0.3	4
5	...	0.1	0.1	.1	.1	.1	.2	.2	.2	.2	.2	.3	.3	.3	.3	5
6	...	.1	.1	.1	.1	.2	.2	.2	.2	.3	.3	.3	.3	.4	.4	6
7	...	.1	.1	.1	.2	.2	.2	.3	.3	.3	.3	.4	.4	.4	.5	7
8	...	.1	.1	.1	.2	.2	.2	.3	.3	.4	.4	.4	.5	.5	.5	8
9	...	.1	.1	.1	.2	.2	.2	.3	.3	.4	.4	.5	.5	.6	.6	9
10	...	.1	.1	.1	.2	.2	.3	.4	.4	.4	.5	.5	.6	.6	.6	10
11	...	.1	.1	.2	.2	.3	.3	.4	.4	.5	.5	.6	.6	.7	.7	11
12	.1	.1	.1	.2	.3	.3	.4	.4	.5	.5	.6	.6	.7	.7	.8	12

Fig. 1517a. Radio Bearing Conversion Table (extract from Pub. No. 117).

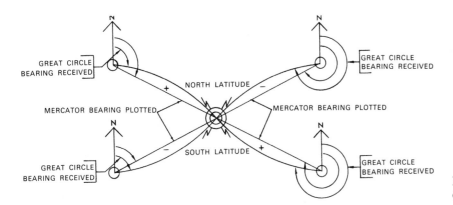

Fig. 1517b. Diagram for determination of the sign of a conversion angle.

Night effect. Within half an hour of sunrise and sunset, and to a lesser extent throughout the night, radio bearings may be less accurate than at other times, due largely to what is called the "polarization effect." This is manifested by a broadening and shifting of the minimum signal.

Land effect. When a radio signal crosses a shore line at an oblique angle, or if it passes over an island or peninsula of high land, the direction of travel may be bent a slight amount in a manner similar to the refraction of light. When a bearing is taken under these conditions, it should be considered of doubtful accuracy.

Personal error. The skill of the operator is perhaps the most important factor in obtaining accurate readings. Frequent practice is essential if this source of error is to be reduced to a minimum.

VHF Direction Finding

1519 Direction finding using VHF-FM signals is not as common as on the lower bands; it can, however, be useful in certain situations. The continuous weather broadcasts in U.S. waters by NOAA on frequencies between 162 and 163 MHz can be used if the antenna locations are plotted on the charts being used. Transmissions from Coast Guard stations and Marine Operators should be used with caution, because these activities often have more than one transmitting antenna and it cannot be known which one is in use at any given time. VHF direction finding is often useful in a "homing" mode for search-and-rescue operations or when two vessels desire to rendezvous at sea.

Bearings are typically read to a precision of only 5°, but this is usually adequate. A special antenna is required on the vessel and each installation must be carefully checked for radio deviation.

RADIO COMMUNICATIONS

1520 An indirect use of radio for navigation is for communications. Time signals and weather information are available to the mariner through radio communications. Information on changes to aids to navigation are transmitted regularly, including announcements of scheduled interruptions in service for various stations or radio-navigation systems. Ships at sea or in remote ports can request and receive current information from *Notices to Mariners.*

Much information of interest and value to a navigator will be found in NIMA Publication No. 117, *Radio Navigational Aids,* and information on weather broadcasts will be found in the publication *Worldwide Weather Broadcasts* of the National Oceanic and Atmospheric Administration. Systems in U.S. waters will be covered by the various volumes of the *Light Lists.*

Chapter 16

Hyperbolic Navigation

The theory behind hyperbolic navigation was known prior to World War II, but it was not until that great conflict that scientists were effectively motivated and funded to make it a reality. By early 1942, the British Royal Air Force was using such a system, called Gee, that operated in the VHF range to guide bombers to and from their targets in Europe. The U.S. Coast Guard began operating a chain of transmitters the following year that was dubbed Loran-A (LORAN is an acronym meaning *long ra*nge *n*avigation). (Note: Like radar and sonar, the term "LORAN" has been around so long that it has ceased to be treated as an acronym and is now simply written as "Loran" or "loran.") A follow-on system called Loran-B was developed but never used as a functioning navigational system, but its successor Loran-C has been in service for decades and is still in use today.

Other hyperbolic systems have come and gone, with a few still in use in certain parts of the world. Decca was one of the more successful hyperbolic systems, and Omega was used extensively by the U.S. Navy until the advent of GPS (see chapter 17).

Today, the GPS satellite system is more capable and accurate than any hyperbolic system, but the U.S. government keeps Loran-C in operation for several reasons. Countless mariners still depend upon Loran-C because of its familiarity and because of their reluctance to take on the expense of replacing their Loran-C receivers with GPS equipment. Also, the age-old principle of navigation that urges redundancy in methods for fixing position keeps Loran-C alive as both collaborator and backup.

PRINCIPLES OF OPERATION

1601   In simplest terms, hyperbolic navigation is based upon the simple formula $D = S \times T$ (Distance = Speed × Time). Accepting that the speed of a radio transmission is predictable, it becomes a constant in the formula, and using time as the variable between two signals broadcast from two different locations, a discerning receiver can determine a distance.

Imagine that your ship is located between two stations (M and S) that are broadcasting radio signals at the exact same instant. If you drew a line between the two stations (assume for simplicity that it is an exact east-west line as indicated in figure 1601a), and if your vessel was on that line exactly halfway between the two stations as indicated by V, you would receive both signals at the exact same instant. If you move along that line closer to one of the stations than to the other (point V_1), you will receive one station's signal before the other. By calculation, you could convert this time difference to a distance (i.e., determine how much closer you are to one than to the other).

It should be apparent that you need not be exactly on the line drawn between the two stations M and S to be equidistant to them. You could, for example, move due north (point V_2) and remain at exactly the same distance to each station. Vessels at points V_3 or V_4 are also equidistant from the two transmitting stations. Connecting these various points yields a straight line running due north and south in our example. As long as a vessel is located somewhere on that line, it will receive both signals simultaneously.

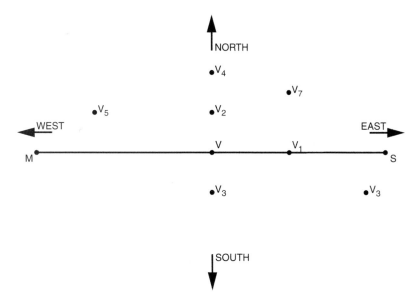

Fig. 1601a. Basic principle of hyperbolic navigation.

But if your vessel is anywhere else (i.e., *not* equidistant from the two stations—at positions V_5, V_6, or V_7, for example), then you will receive one signal before the other; there will be a *time difference* between the two signals. And mathematically, this time difference can also be converted to a distance.

By connecting the positions where there was no time difference, we constructed a straight line. But this is the only situation in which a *straight* line will emerge when connecting points of the same time difference. Connecting other points, where there *is* a time difference but that difference is the same, yields a uniquely shaped line instead of a straight line. This special line is a *hyperbola*. In figure 1601b, a vessel located at point B would receive the two signals from stations M and S with the same time difference of a vessel located at point B′ and are on the same hyperbola. The same would be true for vessels at C and C′, D and D′, and so on.

Two stations transmitting simultaneous signals will yield an infinite number of hyperbolas based upon time differences. With an electronic receiver that is capable of identifying these special signals and accurately measuring the time differences between them, the navigator can discern which of these hyperbolas she or he is on. The hyperbola so defined is, therefore, an LOP. As with any LOP, the navigator will not know specifically where along that hyperbola he or she is; but if there are more pairs of stations transmitting identifiable signals, the navigator may then obtain two or more of these hyperbolas to use as LOPs, and where they intersect is a reliable *fix* of the vessel's position (see fig. 1601c).

In actual hyperbolic navigation systems, stations may be grouped in configurations of more than two and are called "chains"; one of the stations in a chain will be designated a *master station* and the others as *secondary* (the terms "slave" and "subordinate" have also been used, but "secondary" is the most common usage now). For more efficient operation, transmissions for the secondary stations are usually delayed rather than being simultaneous with the master, but the principle of operation remains the same. In a basic configuration, the straight line between the master and secondary stations is called the *baseline* (see fig. 1601b), and the continuation of that line beyond the two stations is called the *baseline extension*.

This hyperbolic concept has been used to make remarkable systems that can provide reliable fixes under conditions that would prevent piloting or celestial navigation techniques from being effective (out of sight of land, in darkness or bad weather, etc.). Such systems do, however, require very sophisticated equipment (able to discern minute time differences) and special charts (overlaid with appropriate hyperbolas) or tables.

LORAN-C

1602   As already mentioned, Loran-C is the main hyperbolic navigation system still in use today. (Note:

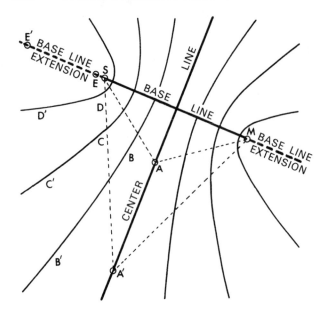

Fig. 1601b. A hyperbolic system.

For simplicity, the word "Loran" as used here will refer to the *Loran-C* system unless otherwise noted.)

The technical principle that distinguishes the various versions of Loran from most other hyperbolic navigation systems is the use of *pulse emissions*. This technology permits the nonambiguous measurement of time differences of signals from different stations and further provides the means of discrimination at the receiving location between ground waves and sky waves. The ability to select and use a particular transmission provides maximum accuracy consistent with the system's inherent geometric configuration.

Loran operates on a single frequency centered on 100 kHz. Because of the use of this low frequency, the baseline distance between stations can be 1,000 miles or more, and position information can be provided to approximately 1,200 miles by means of ground waves, and to more than 3,000 miles with sky waves. The power of a Loran-C transmitter varies with the specific station and is normally between 165 kW and 1.8 MW.

The time interval between transmissions of signals from a pair of Loran stations is very closely controlled, operating with multiple atomic time standards of extremely high accuracy and stability.

Loran-C Stations

1603   The master and secondary stations of a Loran-C chain are located so that signals from the master and at least two secondary stations may be received through the desired coverage area. (In some instances, a common site is used for a secondary station of two different chains, or for the master

of one chain and a secondary of another chain.) For convenience, the master station is designated by the letter *M* and the secondary stations are designated *W, X, Y,* and/or *Z*.

Stations may be grouped in different configurations, depending upon the number of stations and the available geography. Four stations will be ideally placed in a "Y" configuration (see fig. 1603a), and five would be set up in a cross-shaped configuration (sometimes called a "Star" configuration) with the master at the center and the secondaries (W, X, Y, and Z) at the ends of the crossing arms. In some instances, the master for one chain can also serve as a secondary for another chain (see fig. 1603b).

Each Loran station uses pulse groups and extremely precise timing to make possible the sharing of the same frequency by all stations in the system. Provision has been made in the Loran-C system for as many as seventy-eight different pulse *group repetition intervals*, abbreviated as GRI, to make it possible to distinguish among stations. Each station transmits one pulse group, nine pulses for the master station and eight for each secondary station, in each group repetition interval spaced 1,000 microseconds apart. The master station's extra pulse aids in identification. Multiple pulses are used so that more signal energy is available at the receiver, improving the signal-to-noise ratio without having to increase the peak power capability of the transmitters. In addition, Loran-C employs *cycle-matching* technique for greater precision. A rough measurement is made of the difference in arrival time of the pulsed signals, and this is refined by a comparison of the phase of the signal within each pulse. This phase comparison is made automatically in the receiver and does not involve a separate operation by the navigator.

Chain Operation

1604   All transmitting stations are equipped with cesium time and frequency standards. The extremely high accuracy and stability of these standards permit each station to establish its own time of transmission without reference to another station. (In the older Loran-A system, subordinate stations were "slaved" to the master station, transmitting only after receipt of the master pulse; this is not so in Loran-C.)

The objective for control of a Loran-C chain is to keep the observed time difference (TD) of each master-secondary pair constant at any location throughout the coverage area. Frequency offsets in the cesium standards and changes in propagation conditions can cause the observed TD to vary. Therefore, one or more system area monitoring (SAM) sta-

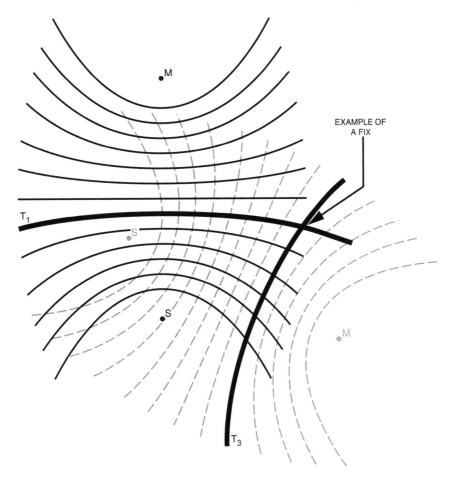

Fig. 1601c. Intersecting hyperbolic systems. Receiving time differences define a unique hyperbolic line in each system; where they intersect is the receiving vessel's position (fix).

tions are established with precise receiving equipment to monitor continuously the TDs of the master-secondary pairs. In some instances, a transmitting station is suitably located and can perform the monitoring function. A control TD is established during system calibration. When the observed TD varies from the control TD by more than one-half the prescribed tolerance, the SAM directs a change in the timing of the secondary station to remove the error. If the observed TD becomes different from the control TD by more than the established tolerance, then a *blink* is ordered to alert all users that the time difference is not usable.

The master station transmitter's ninth pulse in each group is used for this "blink" function as well as for identification. Blinking is used to warn users that there is an error in the transmission of a particular station or stations; it is accomplished by turning the ninth pulse off and on in a specified code as shown in figure 1604. The secondary station of the unusable pair also blinks by turning off and on the first two pulses of its pulse group. Most modern receivers automatically detect secondary station blink only, because this is enough to trigger alarm indicators.

Loran-C Equipment

1605 Loran receivers normally provide both automatic signal acquisition and cycle matching once the set is turned on.

Because a master station is common to two or more pairs, the receiver will automatically give two time differences for two lines of position and automatically track these signals once they have been acquired; some receivers will track more than two station pairs, displaying time differences for those of adequate signal quality. The receiver will give a direct readout of the time differences; if two pairs are being tracked, a single digital display will alternately show each time difference, or there may be a

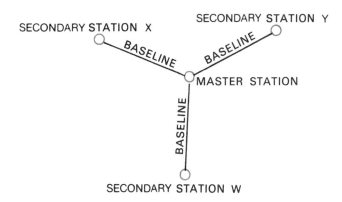

Fig. 1603a. Loran-C "Y" configuration of one master and three secondary stations.

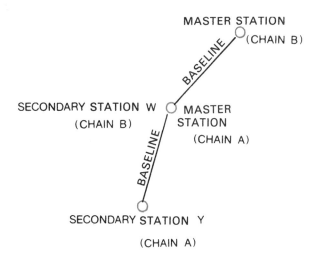

Fig. 1603b. Loran-C configuration where one station (*center*) serves as the master station of one chain and a secondary station of another chain.

dual display to give both readings simultaneously. Some Loran-C receivers provide a direct readout in latitude and longitude, and many Loran-C receivers have a "coordinate conversion" capability; an internal microprocessor automatically changes the measured time differences to a display of position directly in latitude and longitude. Many sets can also provide a flow of digital data to a position plotter that will automatically and continuously plot the vessel's position in N-S and E-W coordinates to any selected chart scale within wide limits.

Most Loran-C receivers will compute a great-circle track to a destination described in terms of time differences or latitude and longitude. A number of waypoints may be entered and tracks for successive legs computed. These sets can display information such as course and speed being made good

(computed from changes in the Loran-derived positions), directions and distance to a previously entered destination or waypoint, cross-track error (distance off course to right or left of direct track), a direct-reading steering indicator, and distance and time to go to the next waypoint or destination plus a warning signal just before that point is reached. Some sets will even talk to you—using synthesized speech to give you selected items from the above list at intervals of six seconds to one hour as desired.

Position information in terms of time-difference readings can be transferred between receivers with excellent results. If, however, latitude/longitude data are used, the results may be less accurate because different receivers may have different coordinate conversion programs.

Many models of Loran-C receivers can be connected, through an interface unit, to a vessel's automatic steering mechanism (commonly called an "autopilot"). Thus the vessel may be steered, without human action, so as to continuously be on the great-circle track previously computed in the receiver.

Once started with accurate time, several receivers can function as a chronometer with an error no greater than about two seconds per month. A Loran-C set often contains highly sophisticated self-testing and signal-status circuitry to give a navigator confidence in its output data.

Remote readout units are available for some Loran-C receivers. These may show position in time differences or latitude/longitude, or may be a steering indicator only. There are also portable receivers powered by an attached battery pack.

A Loran receiver must be properly installed if it is to operate satisfactorily; this is a task for a qualified technician. The antenna should be mounted as high as possible, but it is even more necessary that it be well away from other antennas, stays, and metallic objects. No other equipment should be connected to the Loran antenna. Equally important is the proper grounding of the antenna coupler and the receiver.

Like all radionavigation systems, Loran can be adversely affected by interference. This can make it difficult to acquire the Loran signals and/or make the readings fluctuate more than usual. Most manufacturers provide tunable "notch" filters that can be used to minimize such interference. Once these filters are properly set by the manufacturer or his local representative, it will probably never be necessary to readjust these filters if you are always going to remain in the same general area (a radius of several hundred miles from a center point). If you are

LORAN-C BLINK CODE

MASTER STATION NINTH PULSE: ▬ = APPROXIMATELY 0.25 SECOND
▬▬ = APPROXIMATELY 0.75 SECOND

UNUSABLE TD (S)	ON-OFF PATTERN — 12 SECONDS
NONE	(continuous)
X	
Y	
Z	
W	
XY	
XZ	
XW	
YZ	
YW	
ZW	
XYZ	
XYW	
XZW	
YZW	
XYZW	

SECONDARY STATION FIRST TWO PULSES:
TURNED ON (BLINKED) FOR APPROXIMATELY 0.25 SECONDS
EVERY 4.0 SECONDS. ALL SECONDARIES USE SAME CODE,
AUTOMATICALLY RECOGNIZED BY MOST MODERN LORAN–C
RECEIVERS.

Fig. 1604. Loran-C blink codes.

going to travel great distances, you will need to learn how to readjust the filters.

To start the acquisition process of the receiver, the GRI of the Loran-C chain to be used is entered into the set. With the long baselines of this system, a single GRI is used over a wide area, such as the U.S. Atlantic and Gulf coasts, or the U.S. Pacific Coast. The speed at which the receiver will find the Loran signals depends upon the signal strength and how much noise is present. In some receivers, you can speed up the process by preselecting the approximate Loran readings he expects to read. Most modern receivers will be automatically tracking within five minutes of initial turn-on, and will continue to track until the receiver is turned off. If the vessel is at a known location (at a pier and ready for departure, for example) it will be obvious when the receiver is providing the correct information. In any event, most receivers display some type of an alarm that remains lighted until the receiver is tracking properly.

Initially acquiring Loran-C signals when arriving from far out at sea (several hundred miles or more) is a more difficult problem, so the receiver may take somewhat longer to acquire the signals. When first entering a Loran-C coverage area, the receiver should be checked frequently to ensure that all alarm lights are out. Sometimes, due to weak signals and high noise, the receiver alarms will go out even though the receiver is not tracking precisely. As the vessel continues to enter the stronger signal area, however, the receiver will automatically recognize that it has made an error and will provide an alarm light. This should occur well before entering coastal waters.

Other alarms that may be on a Loran-C receiver include one to indicate that a station is transmitting a "blink" warning, or one indicating that an incorrect cycle is being tracked on one or more signals so that the reading is off by a multiple of 10 microseconds. (This alarm may come on when the receiver is, in fact, tracking properly, but has not yet completed all internal tests to verify correct operation.)

Whenever an alarm light is on, use extreme caution. Do not use a time difference reading unless all alarm lights are out.

Loran Operation

1606   Loran is a complex system of radionavigation developed by skilled engineers and maintained by highly trained electronics technicians. However, the *use* of Loran-C for navigation does *not* require technical expertise; determining a vessel's position can be quite simple. A fix can be obtained by using either a chart or a set of tables. Use of a chart is simpler and quicker and yields results of satisfactory precision for ordinary navigation. Use of a tabular solution is more complex, but gives a more precise position; the use of tables also allows a position to be determined if a Loran-C chart does not exist for the area or is not onboard.

Charts of U.S. coastal waters published by the National Ocean Service at a scale of 1:80,000 or smaller will have Loran-C lines of position printed on them (using different colors for the various usable pairs of stations). Read one Loran-C time difference from the receiver and find the pair of lines for time-difference values that bracket the observed reading; interpolate by eye or measurement for an exact LOP. Follow the same procedure for a second Loran reading from the receiver; the fix is at the intersection of these lines to an accuracy determined by the range from the Loran transmitters and other factors. If a third time difference and LOP can be obtained, this will improve the accuracy of the fix, and the navigator's confidence in it.

Some Loran-C transmitters are located inland from the coasts—in a few instances, several hundred miles or more. The overland path of signals from these stations results in phase shifts that are difficult to predict accurately. When Loran-C lines were first applied to charts, they were drawn using theoretical values for propagation shifts of the signals. Actual conditions often turn out to be different, resulting from the fact that the pulses travel partly over land and partly over water. The sets of lines bear a correct relationship to each other, but the grid as a whole may be offset from true locations by ¼ to 2 miles. Field surveys—taking Loran readings at known geographic positions—have resulted in more accurate hyperbolic lattices on later editions of charts.

Loran-C charts will carry one of the following notes:

The Loran-C lines of position overprinted on this chart have been prepared for use with ground-wave signals and are presently compensated only for theoretical propagation delays, which have not yet been verified by observed data. Mariners are cautioned not to rely entirely on the lattices in inshore waters. Sky-wave corrections are not provided.

The Loran-C lines of position overprinted on this chart have been prepared for use with ground-wave signals and are compensated with propagation delays computed from observed data. Mariners are cautioned not to rely entirely on the lattices in inshore water. Sky-wave corrections are not provided.

There may be continual slight changes in the last digit of the readout of a Loran-C receiver; this is termed "jitter" or jumping. This may occur even though the vessel is not moving; it is caused by noise interfering with the Loran signal. For the most precise navigation, readings should be averaged over a brief period; note the smallest and largest values and average them mentally.

Many receivers have a "Memory" or "Hold" switch. This locks the display on the present reading while the receiver continues to track internally. The memory capability can be most helpful in situations such as a crewman overboard, or marking the location of a float. It must be recognized that the reading shown may be 0.1 or 0.2 microseconds different from the average reading if there is noise jitter present.

In some instances, one or both of the following conditions may cause difficulties for a navigator:
1. The lines of position are almost parallel, thus making it difficult to determine accurately the vessel's position.
2. A small change in the Loran-C reading will cause a large change in the position of the corresponding LOP (i.e., the lines are spaced farther apart than are other sets on the same chart).

If either or both of these conditions exist, the proper procedure is to relock one channel of the receiver on the signal of a different secondary station, using the set's instruction manual. To determine which signal to use, examine the chart and find a set of LOPs that result in a good crossing angle (greater than 30E) with the other Loran LOP and/or which shows a small change in position for small changes in time-difference readings.

Never use a master-secondary pair near their baseline extension; here the gradients become very large and there is also the possibility of introducing very large errors in position for lack of knowledge as to which side of the baseline the vessel is situated; baseline extensions are labeled on charts.

Loran-C lines are primarily shown for offshore waters; they are carried into larger inshore bodies, but not into harbors, rivers, and so on, because of the effects of close-by land masses and the consequent lack of the precision and accuracy required for piloting. For example: Loran-C lines are shown on charts of the coastal waters of Virginia and up the Chesapeake Bay, but not into Hampton Roads and Norfolk Harbor. But a navigator operating frequently in any given area can make his or her own "Loran chart" by recording time differences at a series of known positions, such as turns in channels or designated anchorage berths. The Coast Guard has published Loran-C time differences at selected "waypoints" along heavily traveled inland routes such as New York Harbor and Delaware Bay.

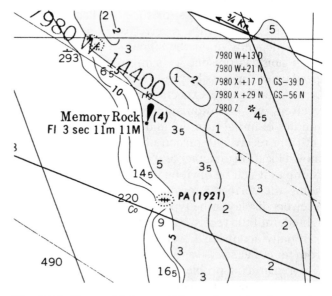

Fig. 1606. Chart with Loran-C lines of position (extract).

A further correction is required if sky-wave signals must be used. On many NIMA charts with Loran lines, small blocks of figures will be found at regular intervals of the intersections of meridians and parallels. The values given are microseconds to be added to or subtracted from the Loran-C receiver reading. Separate values may be shown for day and night reception, and some areas may have a symbol for one or more station pairs indicating, "Do not use sky waves in this area." The appropriate figure from the nearest block should be applied to the receiver reading before the LOP is drawn. For example, in figure 1606, the "7980 W" signifies that the sky-wave corrections are for the 7980 W lines of position. The "+13" means that 13 microseconds must be added to the receiver reading; "D" means that this correction is to be applied during daylight navigation only, and "N" has the corresponding meaning for night-time use. For the 7980 X readings, the "GS-39D" means that 39 microseconds must be subtracted before plotting the LOP if the receiver is tracking a ground-wave master signal and a sky-wave secondary signal during daylight hours. If the letters G and S are reversed, the correction factor applies when receiving a sky-wave master signal and a ground-wave secondary signal. The asterisk on the line for 7980 Z refers to a note elsewhere on the chart that states that sky-wave signals from this secondary station should not be used.

You must be able to know when your receiver is tracking a sky-wave signal. By using the receiver's digital readout and special functions, you can look for one or more of the following indicators of sky-wave tracking:

1. A signal strength or signal-to-noise ratio much larger than would be expected in the area for a ground-wave signal;
2. Signal strengths that vary more than normal;
3. Time differences that vary more than normal;
4. Large position errors.

When looking for these indications, be sure to determine which specific stations have abnormal signals, since these are the ones for which corrections must be used. Consult the operator manual for the receiver being used for additional information, and remember to use sky-waves with extreme caution, as they are less accurate and much more difficult to use than ground-wave signals.

Loran-C Position Accuracy

1607 Position accuracy degrades with increasing distance from the transmitting stations as a result of variation in propagation conditions, losses over the signal path, and internal receiver conditions. Accuracies cannot be stated absolutely, but using range as the distance to the master station of the pair, groundwave accuracies may be generally stated as follows:

> At 200 miles, 50–300 feet (15–90 m)
> 500 miles, 200–700 feet (60–210 m)
> 750 miles, 300–1,100 feet (90–340 m)
> 1,000 miles, 500–1,700 feet (150–520 m)

Accuracies are stated as a range of values rather than as fixed amounts, as the error will vary with the position of the receiver with respect to the master and secondary stations, variations from standard propagation conditions, and other factors.

Sky-wave reception of Loran-C signals gives greater range, but lesser accuracy. At 1,500 miles, position accuracy may be as poor as 10 miles (18 km); at 2,000 miles, it may degrade to as much as 17 miles (31 km)—these are "worst case" values, and sky-wave accuracies are often better.

One useful feature of the Loran-C system is that it provides excellent "repeatability," which means that a Loran-C fix taken many times at a known location will give positions normally varying less than 300 feet (91 m), and often less than 50 feet (15 m). Thus, the knowledge of previously obtained readings at a specific location can be extremely useful if a navigator wants to return to that same spot at a later date; these readings can be used instead of values of latitude and longitude. The repeatability of Loran-C time-difference readings has led to the use of such coordinates for search-and-rescue operations offshore; these are often *more* useful than geographic coordinates derived from Loran or other sources.

The repeatability capability of Loran-C makes it useful in inshore and harbor navigation where data have previously been taken and recorded. Used in this manner and in conjunction with other navigational aids and systems, Loran may be employed where its accuracy when used with overprinted charts is not adequate for safe navigation.

LORAN-D

1608 Some years ago, the need developed for a low-frequency, hyperbolic navigation system that would be mobile for military applications. Loran-D was developed to fill this need. It is designed to be readily transportable, so that lines of position can be furnished in a new area as the need develops, and to minimize downtime required to correct equipment failure.

Like Loran-C, Loran-D operates in the low-frequency band, in the range 90–110 kHz, and its signal characteristics are very similar to those of Loran-C. Three or four transmitting stations operate together on a time-shared basis to provide ground-wave signals of high accuracy out to a maximum range of about 500 miles. Its signals are equally dependable whether over land or water.

Primarily, Loran-D differs from Loran-C in its signal format; it uses repeated groups of sixteen pulses spaced 500 microseconds apart.

The system is highly resistant to electronic jamming. This characteristic, and its mobility—stations can be set up anywhere within twenty-four hours—make it exceptionally useful when areas of operations are changing rapidly. The system is equally satisfactory for use aboard naval vessels or high-speed aircraft.

Chapter 17

Global Positioning System

For centuries, mariners have looked to the skies, relying on the natural heavenly bodies for navigational guidance. Modern mariners also scan the heavens, but it is sightless circuit boards and odd-looking antennas, rather than the optics of a sextant, that are now their primary tools. The Sun, Moon, planets, and stars are supplemented by a new constellation of heavenly bodies sown by man himself.

As discussed in an earlier chapter, satellites have been a major part of the navigational arsenal since the early 1960s. This evolutionary development of space technology has led in recent times to the deployment of two global satellite navigational systems that are expected to continue well into the twenty-first century. In 1973, the U.S. Department of Defense inaugurated a new satellite navigation system called NAVSTAR GPS (Navigation Satellite Timing and Ranging Global Positioning System), and in 1982 the Russians (then Soviets) followed suit by launching the first satellites of their similar GLONASS (Global Navigation Satellite System). A joint European initiative known as Galileo has been under consideration for quite some time and will be another GPS system when and if it is implemented. NAVSTAR has been fully operational since 1993 and GLONASS less reliably since 1996.

NAVSTAR GPS

1701 While the Russian GLONASS has experienced reliability problems, the U.S. NAVSTAR GPS (more commonly referred to as simply "GPS") has rapidly become the premier navigation system in the world. Carefully positioned satellites continuously transmit information signals to receivers on the Earth, making it a completely passive system for users. Besides ensuring a degree of military security, this passivity means that receivers can be small and relatively inexpensive with low power requirements, making them suitable for many civil uses, including recreation. Aside from the cost to the American taxpayer and the necessary investment in a receiver, there is no cost to users.

Much less vulnerable to weather conditions than most traditional methods of navigation and available to an unlimited number of users, the GPS system provides a worldwide common grid reference system with marine applications ranging from open ocean to restricted waterways. But because GPS is a notable improvement on earlier navigation satellite systems, its utility goes beyond mere surface marine navigation. The Navy's NAVSAT (or Transit) system, by contrast, only provided positioning information in two dimensions, while GPS provides altitude and precise timing information that make it, in essence, a four-dimensional system suitable for aviation, land surveying, and many other civil and military uses. Augmentations to the system further enhance its accuracy and utility, but the basic GPS system consists of three segments: the space segment, the control segment, and the user segment.

Space Segment

1702 The space segment consists of 24 satellites in six different orbital planes angled at 55 degrees to the equator (see fig. 1702). Each satellite is 10,900 miles (20,200 km) above the Earth, traveling at about 7,000 miles per hour, and circling the Earth twice a sidereal day. They are solar powered with battery backup, weigh about 2,000 pounds each, and are approximately 17 feet across with their solar panels extended. Transmitter power is only 50 watts or less, yet this carefully arranged constellation of satellites ensures that users will have continuous access to the number of satellites necessary for a good fix under all but the most unusual conditions.

The first satellite was launched in 1978 and the full constellation of twenty-four was reached in 1996. Each satellite lasts about seven to ten years, requiring the periodic launch of replacement satellites. Several spares are kept in orbit for immediate activation in the event of the failure of an operational satellite. Small rocket engines attached to each satellite allow them to be moved about in space for repositioning or for fine-tuning their orbits.

Later generation satellites are designed to continue functioning for 180 days without control segment (see below) contact. Navigational accuracy will degrade during that period, however. Each of these later generation satellites has two cesium and two rubidium atomic clocks for accuracy in time keeping, but for peak efficiency they require periodic adjustments from the control segment.

Control Segment

1703   A Master Control Station (MCS) is located at Schriever Air Force Base (formerly Falcon AFB) near Colorado Springs, Colorado, and is supplemented by four other stations in Hawaii and Kwajalein in the Pacific, Diego Garcia in the Indian

Ocean, and Ascension Island in the Atlantic (see fig. 1703). This network monitors satellite telemetry, evaluating their "health" (power status, thermal condition, spatial attitude, etc.), and sends time and orbital corrections to the satellites as needed.

The control segment also includes a Prelaunch Compatibility Station (PCS) at Cape Canaveral, Florida, which handles the launching and setup of satellites and also is available as a back-up MCS should there be problems with the Colorado station.

Primary responsibility for the NAVSTAR system lies with the U.S. Air Force's 1st and 2d Space Operations Squadrons (SOPS). Launching of the satellites and initial orbital operations are the responsibility of 1st SOPS, while day-to-day operations of the system are controlled by 2d SOPS.

User Segment

1704   Thousands of users across a wide spectrum of utility make up this segment, from backpackers hiking in the wilderness to aircraft carriers threading their way through islands in the Java Sea. Besides the obvious navigational uses of GPS, scientists make use of the system's precision timing attributes for such things as astronomical observations and laboratory standards.

The keys to the user segment are receivers and their antennas. Without these components and the people to take advantage of them, NAVSTAR GPS is just a lot of expensive space clutter. Equipment can range in size from portable handheld units with built-in antennas to much larger permanent installations inside buildings, ships, or other vehicles linked to external antennas. The range of capabilities is equally diverse, the primary determinant being cost. Some very expensive surveying GPS equipment can provide measurements down to a millimeter, while other less capable units can be purchased by nearly anyone with a need or desire to know where they are.

Because the geometry of GPS is capable of yielding a fix in three dimensions instead of two (as was the case with the old Transit or NAVSAT system), the NAVSTAR system can be used for altitude measurements as well as surface positions.

Theory of Operation

1705   GPS technology, while very sophisticated and in some ways complicated, is based upon a very simple physical principle, the same one that children use when they count the seconds between lightning flashes and the following thunder to tell how far away a storm is. $D = vt$ (or distance equals velocity multiplied by time) is the governing for-

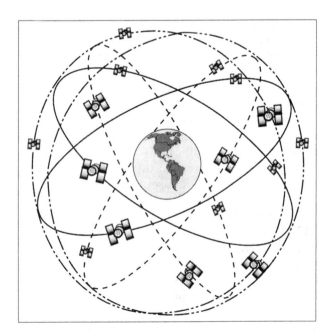

Fig. 1702. The GPS constellation.

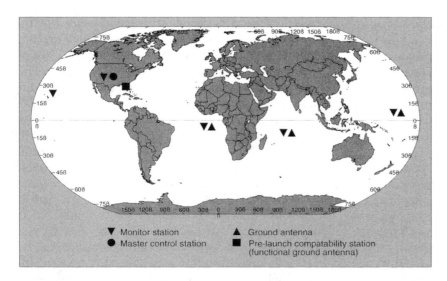

▼ Monitor station   ▲ Ground antenna
● Master control station   ■ Pre-launch compatability station
                             (functional ground antenna)

Fig. 1703. The GPS control segment.

mula behind GPS technology. Each satellite in the NAVSTAR constellation emits an identifiable unique signal that allows your GPS receiver to determine its distance by measuring the amount of time that it takes for that radio signal to travel from the satellite to the receiver. The velocity part of the formula is constant since radio waves travel at the speed of light (approximately 186,000 land miles or 162,000 nautical miles per second or 3×10^8 meters per second). If you think about a radio signal traveling outward from a satellite in every direction simultaneously, you can envision an ever-expanding sphere, much like a balloon filling with air. One part of that sphere will reach your receiver at a measurable time, allowing your receiver to calculate the distance between it and the satellite. This does not yet tell your position because your receiver only knows that you are somewhere on that sphere but cannot tell exactly where. But when additional satellites are brought into the picture, your receiver obtains enough information to determine your position.

It helps to pause and think about the geometry of the situation at this point. In visual piloting, you shoot bearings to objects of known (from a chart) location and the result is straight lines of positions. Where these straight lines intersect is your position (fix). In radar piloting, you measure ranges to known objects (measured using the same D = vt formula that is the basis of GPS) which are drawn as arcs on your chart that intersect to yield a fix. In radar piloting both you and the objects you are ranging are on the surface of the Earth, so you are working, for all intents and purposes, in only two dimensions. With satellites in space, the geometry becomes three dimensional, which means we are working with spheres instead of mere arcs.

Two satellites yield two spheres, and as they merge into one another, the points at which they intersect define a circle in space. This effectively eliminates one of the three dimensions so that the receiver now knows that it is somewhere on that circle rather than on a sphere of possible locations. Introduce a third satellite and the geometry is reduced to only two possible points in space where the defined circles intersect (see fig. 1705). In most cases, only one of those points is reasonable, since the other will be somewhere in outer space. It may help to visualize the Earth itself as a fourth sphere thereby eliminating the other position which is not on or near the Earth's surface.

In actuality, your receiver needs a fourth satellite to precisely fix your position because of the need for precision timing. If GPS receivers had their own rubidium or cesium atomic clocks (capable of measuring time in nanoseconds—billionths of a sec-

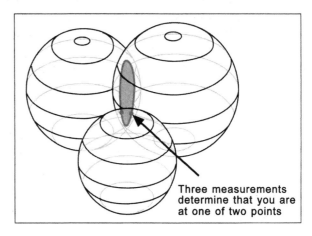

Three measurements
determine that you are
at one of two points

Fig. 1705. The positional spheres of three satellites provide two possible positions in space, only one of which will be on the Earth's surface.

ond), you would not need a fourth satellite to accurately fix your position. But because the addition of an atomic clock to your receiver would increase its size and weight significantly and its cost astronomically, it makes more sense to house the atomic clocks in the satellites instead. Using its much less capable (nonatomic) built-in clock and incorporating a process of measured trial and error your receiver is able to use four satellites to precisely determine your position. The receiver accomplishes this by adding a few nanoseconds to its internal clock time to see if that improves the calculated fix (brings it closer to a precise pinpoint) or makes it worse. Then it subtracts a few and continues the process until it arrives at the most precise fix (least amount of dispersion). This may sound lengthy, but the entire process is completed in microseconds. In fact, the more times the receiver does this, the more accurate the fix (and the more expensive the receiver).

Specifics of Operation

1706 Each satellite broadcasts two different L-band signals (L1 at 1575.42 MHz and L2 at 1227.6 MHz). Using ultra high frequency (UHF) signals has a number of advantages, including minimizing ionospheric interference and only requiring small antennas. The signals are pseudo-random noise, sequence-modulated radio signals (sometimes referred to more simply as "pseudorandom codes" or simply "PRN codes"), which is a complicated way of saying that the signals have been carefully engineered to allow the receiver to differentiate the signals from other radio noise in the Earth's atmosphere while keeping power requirements low.

Each satellite is assigned one of 31 coarse acquisition (C/A) codes that repeats once every millisecond and helps the receiver quickly acquire and identify the satellite. It is carried only on the L1 frequency.

A navigation data message is superimposed on both the C/A code and the P(Y) codes (explained below). This message contains data unique to the individual satellite and data common to all the satellites. Included is almanac and ephemeris data (explained below), atmospheric propagation data, and satellite clock corrections.

There are two types of GPS service available: *Standard Positioning Service* (SPS) and *Precise Positioning Service* (PPS). SPS is available to users worldwide, civilian and military, and is carried on the L1 frequency. As the name implies, PPS is more accurate than SPS and is available only to authorized users (military and certain U.S. allies and civilian contractors).

For a time, SPS was deliberately degraded by the U.S. government as a security measure by introducing an error called *Selective Availability* (SA), which reduced the accuracy to about 100 meters. This deliberate degradation of the signal was intended to prevent unfriendly entities from taking advantage of GPS accuracy for targeting or positioning purposes. However, during the Gulf War, SA was actually turned off because so many friendly military units were using commercial GPS receivers to navigate about the deserts, and the Iraqis had no weapons systems that relied upon GPS technology. Subsequent discussions on the matter eventually led to the conclusion that since SA could be turned on at any time it was deemed necessary, and because SA can be targeted (i.e., used in specific areas of the world while not in others), it was not necessary to leave it on at all times. On 1 May 2000, SA was set to zero, thereby increasing the accuracy of SPS to about 10 meters or better for all users. This is expected to remain the normal mode of operation.

The more accurate PPS signal, called the *Precise Code* (P-code), is carried on both the L1 and L2 frequencies and can be protected from unauthorized users by encryption. This is accomplished by adding SA and/or another protection called *Anti-Spoofing* (A-S), which prevents the receiver from being fooled by an enemy-generated false signal. If the P-code has been encrypted, it is referred to as the *Y-code*, and only users with tightly controlled decryption capability can then take advantage of the greater accuracy of PPS. Because this code can be operated in either the unencrypted "P" or the encrypted "Y" mode, it is sometimes referred to as the P(Y) code. Since the removal of SA from SPS, this standard service is much more accurate, but maximum GPS accuracy is obtained by using the P(Y) code on both L1 and L2.

Because GPS signals are transmitted on low power (20–50 watts, compared to a typical 100,000 watts from your local radio station), the signal cannot be detected when shielded by solid objects such as mountains or buildings. Therefore, a receiver that is to be used inside the skin of a vessel must have an external antenna in place. Signals will pass through clouds and transparent substances such as glass or plastic but will not function underwater.

In order to fix their own position, GPS receivers must first know the location of the satellites it is using. To accomplish this, the receiver uses two types of information called *almanac and ephemeris data*, referring to constellation and individual satellite information respectively. Almanac data gives the receiver a rough configuration of the satellite constellation, telling it where the satellites are supposed to be. This information is stored in the receiver as a kind of reference map and helps the receiver determine which satellites to use for obtaining a fix. Because the individual satellites do drift slightly out of position, the receiver is provided frequent correction information, and this is referred to as ephemeris data. Armed with these data, the receiver knows the exact location of the satellites it is using to fix its position.

Ephemeris data is updated virtually continuously when a receiver is using an individual satellite. Because almanac data is less time-sensitive than ephemeris data, it does not need to be updated as often. However, a GPS receiver that has been turned off for a while may become "cold," meaning that the almanac data is too old to be usable. Typically, a receiver goes cold after four to six hours. When starting up a cold receiver, it will take some time (called "acquisition time" and varying with the type of receiver) for the receiver to reacquire the necessary almanac data.

GPS Errors

1707 As with all technological wonders, theory and actuality are not always a perfect match. Certain conditions can produce errors in GPS. While they are generally relatively small, they can be significant, particularly when using less-sophisticated equipment. Receivers approved for military use are very effective in eliminating errors, but civilian equipment varies widely in its ability to cope with sources of error.

Because GPS depends upon radio signals, radiation layers in the atmosphere can have a deleterious effect upon the system's ability to provide an accurate fix. This effect is more significant when the Sun is high and less so at night. GPS technology counters this error in two ways. Because PPS-capable military receivers have access to both the L1 and L2 signals, they can compare the different atmospheric effects on the two frequencies to determine the errors and make appropriate corrections. Civilian receivers, using only the L1 signal for SPS, do not have that advantage and must rely only on an approximated model instead of actual measurements and are, therefore, less accurate.

The configuration of satellite orbits is such that it is theoretically possible for all four satellites being used to be overhead at the same time. Just as in visual, radar, and celestial navigation, where objects or heavenly bodies cannot be clustered too closely together, so GPS satellites must not be too close together in azimuth when used for a fix (see fig.

1707). The ideal GPS fix would occur with one satellite directly overhead and three others spaced at 120-degree intervals around the horizon. Actual GPS fixes are obtained with satellites in configurations somewhere between the two extremes just described, and their accuracy is determined by their relative approximations to one or the other. The degree to which the satellites differ from the ideal is sometimes called *Geometrical Dilution of Position* (GDOP). The GPS constellation is maintained in such a way as to minimize this error, but it is impossible to eliminate it altogether.

Another source of error is called multipath reflection and comes into play when GPS receivers are used in close enough proximity to objects capable of causing the radio signal to reflect, such as concrete buildings. Reflected signals will reach the receiver later than straight line-of-sight signals and thereby impair the receiver's ability to correctly evaluate the incoming signals. This does not usually occur to any great degree with vessels unless they are in restricted waters near tall buildings or other reflective surfaces, although some reflection can occur off the surface of the water under certain conditions. When multipath reflection does exist, good receivers can detect and correct it by comparing the power level of signals received. Reflected signals will have a lower power level than those received directly (line-of-sight) because there will typically be some signal absorption by the reflecting surface. After comparing the line-of-sight and reflected signals, the receiver can filter out the weaker of the two to correct the potential error.

GPS Vulnerability

1708 While there are safeguards built in to the NAVSTAR system, and it would take an enemy with a high technological capability to physically assault the very high altitude satellites, the low power signals of the system make it vulnerable to simple noise jamming on a fairly low technological level. Studies are under way to combat this potential problem, but the most obvious remedy is redundancy—the user must have backup systems (such as Loran-C, which requires a higher output of jamming signal, or inertial systems, which are not vulnerable to jamming at all), particularly if the user's requirements are military or safety related.

One system under development involves a backup system in which high-powered, GPS-like transmitters would deploy on aircraft over combat zones. While such a system would have a vulnerability of its own (aircraft are more easily shot down than are satellites), the high-powered signals would be more

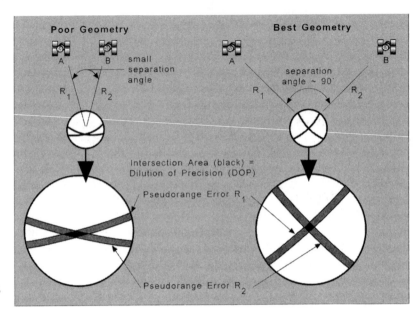

Fig. 1707. Accuracy improves when GPS satellites are not clustered too closely.

difficult to jam, and this redundancy in systems would complicate the enemy's problem of effectively neutralizing friendly navigational and targeting capabilities.

Navigating by GPS

1709   While it is indisputable that GPS is a marvelous technological achievement—capable of telling you where you are, where you are going, how fast you are going, how far you are from your destination, and how long it is going to take you to get there—it is, like all such technological wonders, still only as good as the user's ability to take advantage of it. Without meaningful inputs, much of its capability is useless. In the worst case scenario, it can significantly contribute to a dangerous situation.

For example, let us assume you are following the buoys out of Annapolis Harbor and, as you pass buoy 5 in the channel, you decide that you want to go to the middle span of the Chesapeake Bay Bridge where you have been told the fishing is good. Your GPS receiver can tell you where you are when you start, but without giving it more information, it will not know where it is you want to go. A simple solution would be to refer to a chart and read the latitude and longitude of the middle span of the bridge. By using your current position as the starting point and entering the latitude and longitude of your destination along with the time you wish to arrive, the receiver can now tell you what course to steer, what speed to use, and, as you progress, how far you have to go. But true navigators at this point are wary. This seems too simple—and it is. If the draft of your vessel is less than 2 feet, you *might* make it to your

destination by relying solely upon your GPS receiver. Only capable of processing the data you give it, this incredibly sophisticated, multibillion-dollar system has no idea that there is dangerous shoal water between the two points you have entered.

To counter this problem, you must use a series of waypoints that will keep you in safe water. By plotting a safe track on your chart and entering the points where you must change course (and/or speed) as waypoints, the receiver can now help you safely and efficiently get to your defined destination. Some of the many advantages that are available in GPS navigation are that you can store these waypoints for future use, tell the system to take you back the same way you came, and record and review your actual voyage after it is over. As you steer from waypoint to waypoint, your GPS receiver can tell you that you are left or right of the desired track (often called "cross track error") and recommend a new course and speed to arrive at the next waypoint. By including an estimated time of arrival (ETA) at your final destination, most receivers will constantly update the speed of advance (SOA) required to arrive on time, based upon the current speed over ground (SOG) as calculated by the receiver as it updates the position. Good GPS receivers will also tell you how much time is left until you reach the next waypoint.

Besides the obvious need for referring to a chart (either paper or electronic) in order to plan a safe route, there are other considerations to using GPS that must not be overlooked. Your receiver needs to know whether it is working with true or magnetic compass directions. While latitude and longitude are the most common grid references, GPS must be told what coordinate system to use. It must also know what datum the chart was based upon or serious errors can occur (see chapter 2). Vessels have gone aground while navigating by the dangerous combination of GPS and an incompatible chart.

There are psychological considerations as well. An uncertainty factor is introduced because GPS fixes are automatically constructed electronically by the receiver and transformed into a coordinate readout or plotted directly onto an electronic chart display. Before GPS, a navigator constructed fixes on a chart by physically plotting the LOPs. When something was amiss, such as three LOPs forming a large triangle instead of converging toward a single point, the navigator could see this discrepancy and be warned. This problem can be offset by checking the fix information provided by GPS with more conventional means; for example, by obtaining and plotting a visual bearing or radar range to ensure that it coincides with the position supplied by GPS.

Another psychological problem can arise because the accuracy, reliability, and ease of use of GPS can cause a navigator to become complacent or even reckless by allowing the vessel to come closer to dangers than he or she might have before the advent of GPS. This problem is exacerbated by GPS receivers that have readouts showing coordinate positions with minutes of arc out to three decimal places; this corresponds to a precision of about two yards, which is actually beyond the accuracy of the GPS system itself. The same kind of discipline that has always differentiated good navigators from bad ones will prevent this problem from occurring. The successful navigator will keep the safety of the vessel paramount among all considerations by treating GPS with the respect it is due but not by succumbing to overreliance.

GPS Equipment

1710 As already mentioned, GPS equipment varies a great deal in capability and consequent cost. The most inexpensive units are useful for recreational purposes and as backups for situational awareness in navigation, but serious navigators must be careful to ensure that they understand the capabilities and limitations of their equipment.

Early units worked on a single channel, requiring them to read each satellite signal in sequence. This of course slowed down the process and eliminated the possibility of incorporating some of the more sophisticated features found in better units. Multi-channel receivers allow the simultaneous processing of multiple signals. Not only does this speed up the process considerably, but it allows comparison of signals. Some of the better GPS receivers can track as many satellites as are "visible" (above the celestial horizon) and select the four that allow the least GDOP and therefore provide the best fix. Having an extra channel to separately handle almanac and ephemeris data is an obvious plus, as well.

The NAVSTAR GPS system is referenced to the World Geodetic System 1984 (WGS 84) datum. An added feature on many GPS units is a datum transformer that allows the user to use charts based on a different datum. As already mentioned, without this feature, navigational safety can be seriously compromised. The datum used by the equipment and by the chart must match or significant (and sometimes disastrous) errors will occur.

GPS displays vary with the type of equipment and manufacturer's design. Some provide a numerical display which may tell the user such things as current position (in latitude and longitude or some other grid system, such as the Military Grid Reference System), course and speed, cross-track error, and course to steer to the next waypoint. Terminology differs with manufacturer, so you may encounter varied terms like SOG (Speed Over Ground), SMG (Speed Made Good), of GS (Ground Speed) depicting your vessel's speed. Some initial familiarization of your equipment's idiosyncrasies in terminology will eliminate any confusion.

Some units will provide a graphic display of a map or a schematic representation of the trackline that has been entered into the unit.

One important display feature is the *cross track error*, commonly shown as "XTE" or "OT" (for "off track"). This helps you to stay on your planned track by telling you how much you have deviated from it. It can be shown as a numerical quantity, such as ".037 RIGHT" or "00.037NMR," or it can be shown graphically. A simple graphic version uses a sliding horizontal bar scale, while some will simply use an arrow or a dogleg symbol to tell you which way you must steer to return to your track. One popular display shows lanes (much like a road is shown in a video auto-racing game), showing your vessel's position relative to the track and providing the course/speed corrections needed to get to the next waypoint.

The display may also tell the user how many and/or which satellites are in use at the moment. Some units, such as the AN/WRN-6 receiver used aboard many U.S. naval vessels, include a display of the *figure of merit*, an indication of the degree of accuracy ranging from one (the most accurate) to nine (the least). This evaluation is based upon the degree to which GDOP, atmospheric interference, and other error factors have affected the fix.

One useful feature found on many GPS sets is the "quicksave" function (sometimes called "man overboard" or "waypoint dump" or some other name). When activated, it automatically marks the vessel's position at that instant and saves it into memory as a new waypoint. Very useful in a man overboard situation, this feature can also be used for marking any position you might want to return to, such as a good fishing spot or the site of a whale sighting.

Most GPS receivers will keep a *track log*, which records every movement your vessel makes. Among other things, this allows the user to employ the age-old navigational technique made famous by the fairy tale characters Hansel and Gretel, who left a trail of bread crumbs through the forest so that they could find their way back. But birds will not eat the electronic bread crumbs created by GPS, and the user can simply use this track log in reverse to return along the reciprocal track.

GPS information can be fed directly to an electronic chart system or into an autopilot. Such things as Loran-C, Differential GPS (explained below), inertial navigation, or even Russian GLONASS inputs can be integrated into a GPS receiver for comparison or augmentation. The degree of sophistication (and expense) determines whether this type of equipment operates in an either/or mode (using either GPS or Loran-C, for example) or an integrated mode (in which all inputs are evaluated simultaneously to arrive at the most accurate fix).

The smart navigator will keep in mind the relative abilities of her or his equipment. For example, because a GPS receiver's main capability is determining a real-time position, it must derive other information, such as course and speed, by comparing a series of positions. The accuracy of such added information depends upon the "smoothing" algorithm used by the receiver. The more times it compares positional data in a given period of time the more accurate will be the outputs provided. This means that the course information provided by a less-expensive receiver will fluctuate noticeably while a better receiver will provide a steady course to the next waypoint.

GPS AUGMENTATION

1711 Despite its amazing capabilities, GPS cannot meet every positioning need. For example, federal aviation requirements cannot be met by GPS alone, so some form of augmentation is necessary if aircraft are going to be able to take advantage of GPS.

There are a number of enhancements in operation or in various stages of development to increase the capabilities of the basic GPS system. Some are still being developed and others do not have marine applications and are beyond the scope of this book, but there are two systems currently in use that mariners should be aware of.

DGPS

1712 SPS is accurate enough for open ocean and coastal navigation, but it is not sufficient in harbors and restricted waterways. Even the increased accuracy of PPS, which is not available to all users, does not meet the requirements for "harbor and harbor approach" situations as defined in the Federal Radionavigation Plan. To overcome this shortcoming, the U.S. Coast Guard maintains an augmenting system known as *Maritime Differential GPS*, or, as it is most often called, simply *DGPS*.

The principle of operation of DGPS is fairly simple and quite logical. Placing a GPS receiver at a fixed *known* location, called a reference station, allows it to compare its known position to the position information coming from the GPS satellites (see fig. 1712a). The resulting difference (or "differential") accurately measures whatever error there might be in the GPS signal. The resulting correction can then be transmitted on a separate frequency that users can apply to their GPS signal for more accurate positioning. A simplified version of this system may be visualized as a triangle, the corners of which are a GPS satellite, a DGPS receiver/transmitter site, and the user. Both the user and the DGPS site receive the GPS signal from the satellite while the user also receives a correction signal from the DGPS site.

In practice, the Coast Guard has set up a network of DGPS components at key locations to provide extensive coverage in "harbor and harbor approach areas" and "critical waterways" (see fig. 1712b). Human centralized control is provided by two stations that are manned twenty-four hours a day: the East Coast Control Station in Alexandria, Virginia, and the West Coast Control Station in Petaluma, California. DGPS currently covers both U.S. coasts, most of the Great Lakes, the Hawaiian Islands, Puerto Rico, the Aleutians, the southern Alaskan coast, the entire west coast of Canada, the waters around Nova Scotia, and the entrance to the St. Lawrence Seaway. Additional areas (such as the western rivers and northern Alaskan waters) may be added as practical. Though planned for coverage

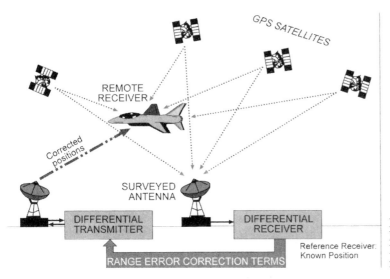

Fig. 1712a. Differential GPS uses signals from known reference stations on the surface of the Earth for comparison in order to improve accuracy.

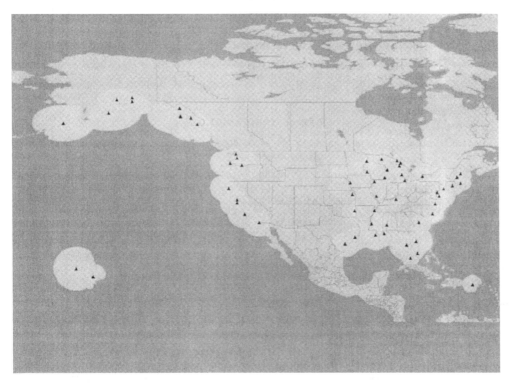

Fig. 1712b. U.S. maritime DGPS service coverage.

out to 150 miles offshore, mariners have reported getting good fixes as far out as 1,000 miles.

For the sake of efficiency and economy, the Coast Guard placed most of these DGPS receiver/transmitter sites (called *reference stations*) at existing radiobeacon locations. The transmitting range varies from station to station from 40 to 300 miles, and there is a great deal of overlapping coverage. The DGPS signal is transmitted on the low end of the medium-frequency band (285–325 kHz), superimposed upon the existing beacon signal using minimum shift keying (MSK) modulation which relies

upon a minimal shifting of the carrier frequency to transmit the data. This technology is both efficient and relatively inexpensive to implement. Each reference station monitors all satellites "in view" (technically, all those above an elevation angle of 7.5 degrees), and separate corrections are calculated for each one (up to nine at a time).

Mobile antennas also exist that can be set up and operated anywhere in the world. These units require proper setup and configuration to function properly but they provide an added capability that can be used effectively in remote locations if necessary.

DGPS users must have receivers and antennas that are capable of receiving both GPS and DGPS signals. These components may be integrated or add-on. One obvious limitation of DGPS is that users must be within range of one or more stations to make use of the signal, and the degree of accuracy diminishes with distance from the DGPS transmitter. Another limiting factor the navigator should be aware of is that the MF signal is subject to radiofrequency interference caused by ionospheric disturbances during sunrise and sunset and by thunderstorms. A correlating advantage is that the MF signals do not have the line-of-sight restrictions associated with the GPS UHF signals and can more effectively make use of diffraction to receive signals in the presence of objects that would block UHF transmissions.

WAAS

1713   To meet air navigation needs, the Federal Aviation Administration (FAA) and the Department of Transportation are developing an augmentation system for GPS called the *Wide Area Augmentation System* (WAAS). Although not yet certified for aviation use, the system is largely in place in North America and can be used by mariners with the right equipment.

WAAS is similar to the Coast Guard's DGPS system in that it uses a number of ground reference stations located at precisely surveyed spots to compare satellite positioning information to their own known fixed positions, and master stations then collect data from the ground reference stations to create a GPS correction message. But WAAS differs significantly from DGPS in its method of disseminating that information. Instead of broadcasting the correction directly to users, the master stations send the correction messages to one of two geostationary satellites in fixed orbits over the equator. These satellites then rebroadcast the corrections on the same frequency as the GPS L1 signal (1575.42 MHz) using the same modulation method as that used for GPS itself. Users with WAAS-capable receivers can then apply the correction to their GPS information for a more accurate fix than can be obtained without augmentation.

WAAS-related equipment is more compatible with GPS equipment than is DGPS, since the frequencies and modulation techniques are the same. This obviates the need for an MF antenna and related receiver circuitry. Because the correction signal is in the UHF range, it does not suffer the consequent noise sometimes experienced on the lower MF frequencies of the DGPS system. WAAS requires fewer stations than DGPS, even when counting the required ground reference stations. One potential problem with WAAS for mariners is that the equatorial location of the geostationary satellites means that they will decrease in altitude the farther north the user is. This increases the likelihood of encountering obstructions (mountains, tall buildings, etc.) to the line-of-sight UHF signal when operating in coastal or inland waters. As has already been mentioned, the Earth-hugging, wraparound nature of the MF signals used by DGPS are less likely to be degraded by obstructions.

The Coast Guard is working with the FAA to expand WAAS coverage through dual signal transmissions from established Loran-C antennas. This will provide unbroken nationwide coverage.

Overall, WAAS and DGPS are virtually the same in terms of capability and accuracy, but DGPS has a slight edge when the user is near a transmitting site. One important thing for the navigator to remember is that both systems are GPS dependent. Any malfunction or damage to the GPS system renders all three useless.

Other Augmentations

1714   The FAA is also developing a *Local Area Augmentation System* (LAAS), but this will function only in the immediate vicinity of airports and will have little or no maritime use. Other nations are developing similar satellite-based systems to augment GPS. In Europe, it is the *Euro Geostationary Navigation Overlay Service* (EGNOS), and the Japanese version is *Multi-Functional Satellite Augmentation System* (MSAS).

As an extrapolation of the Maritime DGPS system, seven U.S. federal agencies are cooperating on the development of a *Nationwide DGPS* (NDGPS) system to cover the surface areas in the continental United States and portions of Alaska and Hawaii not covered by the Maritime system. This will ensure that a differential GPS signal will be available to railroad systems, farmers, truckers, hikers, and all others who have GPS needs in the inland areas of the nation. This system should be fully operational by 2004.

GLONASS

1715   The Russian equivalent of NAVSTAR GPS is the GLONASS (Global Navigation Satellite Service). Run jointly since 1999 by the Defense Ministry and the Russian Space Agency, GLONASS is identical in theory and very similar in actual design to its American counterpart.

The space segment of GLONASS consists of a constellation of 24 satellites in roughly circular orbits 19,100 km (10,300 miles) above Earth in three orbital planes separated by 120 degrees. Each satellite transmits on two UHF frequencies designated L1 and L2, but unlike GPS, each Russian satellite transmits on a slightly different frequency beginning at 1602 MHz for L1 (and increasing by .5625 MHz for each succeeding satellite) and 1246 MHz for L2 (and increasing by .5833 MHz for each succeeding satellite). After the system was originally deployed it was noted that this proliferation of L-band frequencies overlapped a frequency important to radio-astronomy so, as a frequency spectrum conservation measure, the Russians reassigned half of their satellites to share frequencies, so that those in antipodal positions (i.e., on opposite sides of the Earth) in the same orbit now operate on the same frequency.

The ground segment is centered on a control station in Moscow with supporting tracking stations in various locations in what was the Soviet Union. The orbital configuration chosen by the Russians (three planes containing eight satellites each at a slightly lower altitude than the four-plane six-satellite configuration of GPS) is partially driven by the location of these ground stations and partially because this configuration provides better security and makes "spoofing" more difficult.

GLONASS has not enjoyed the same level of reliability as GPS. The Russian satellites are heftier (described by some scientists as "over-engineered") and have a shorter life (one to three years compared to GPS's seven to ten). There have been significant periods of system failure and the Russian govern- ment does not appear to have a firm timetable of satellite replenishment (in 1995, for example, nine satellites were launched, but no more were sent into orbit for the next three years). The following table compares the American NAVSTAR GPS and Russian GLONASS systems:

	NAVSTAR GPS	*GLONASS*
Satellites in constellation	24	24
Orbital planes	6	3
Orbital periods	11^{h}56^m	11^{h}15^m
Orbit altitudes (km)	20,200	19,100
Orbit altitudes (nm)	10,900	10,300
L1 frequencies	1575.42 MHz	Multiples from 1602 MHz
L2 frequencies	1227.6 MHz	Multiples from 1246 MHz
First launch	1978	1982
Fully operational	1993	(1996)
Launch vehicles	Atlas and Delta	Proton

Despite the differences, the Russian and American systems are very similar, prompting many discussions of systems integration to take advantage of the potentially increased reliability and accuracy of having a forty-eight-satellite constellation. Civil aviation needs alone make this a highly desirable outcome. Indeed, some commercial manufacturers have already produced receivers that are capable of using both systems. However, it should be fairly obvious that much has to be worked out before such an integration can be achieved. As a first step, GLONASS reliability must be improved and, for security reasons, it is doubtful that a total integration will ever be achieved.

Chapter 18   Inertial Navigation

Inertial navigation is the process of measuring accelerations in known spatial directions and employing the Newtonian laws of motion to detect and direct the motions of a vessel. A single integration of acceleration with respect to time yields velocity; a second integration provides distance data that can be used to give position fixes based on departure from a known starting location. The basic components used in an inertial navigation system are gyros, accelerometers, and digital computers.

As discussed in chapter 7, a simple gyrocompass tells mariners in what direction their vessel is heading. An inertial navigation system takes gyroscopic technology a step further by yielding *position* information in addition to directional information.

Nautical inertial navigation systems have been developed for naval use primarily. Some research vessels have employed inertial systems as supplements to their navigation package.

SHIP'S INERTIAL NAVIGATION SYSTEM (SINS)

1801 Developed as an accurate, all-weather, dead-reckoning system, the Ship's Inertial Navigation System (SINS) employs gyroscopes, accelerometers, and associated electronics to sense turning rates and accelerations associated with the rotation of the Earth, and with a vessel's movement relative to the surface of the Earth.

Since Newton's laws of motion remain valid throughout the entire range of speeds of any vessel, inertial navigation, which is based on these laws, can be of tremendous assistance to a navigator. Inertial systems can furnish a wide range of information in addition to position coordinates. They

provide a continuous readout of latitude, longitude, and ship's heading, as well as information on roll, pitch, and velocity, which is useful for the stabilization of other instruments. They are capable of extreme accuracy; their accuracy depends directly on how faithfully the component gyroscopes and accelerometers mechanize the laws of motion. SINS is of necessity extremely complex compared to other navigational methods; consequently, it has a high initial cost and requires expert maintenance and operating personnel.

Similar inertial systems are also available for civilian applications requiring very high accuracies, such as offshore geophysical surveys.

DEVELOPMENT OF SINS

1802 Inertial navigation systems were originally developed for military aircraft and missiles and eventually were adapted for use in spacecraft. The Ship's Inertial Navigation System was originally developed for the Polaris submarines, but its use was extended to include surface ships. Inertial navigation is used in long-distance commercial airline flights and in some merchant vessels.

PRINCIPLES OF OPERATION

1803 Inertial systems derive their basic name from the fact that gyroscopes and accelerometers have a sense of *inertia* in the classic Newtonian sense in that they have a tendency to maintain their orientation in space and are sensitive to forces that interfere with their initial equilibrium. A rough analogy may be drawn by closing your eyes when traveling in an automobile. When the car is moving down a straight highway, you have little sense of motion. But if the car turns, or accelerates, or slows down, you can sense it. Inertial navigation systems replicate that ability to sense changes using sophisticated electronic systems so that your vessel is "aware" of changes to its position in space. Deviations from an original orientation are sensed and measured by specially designed components. Accelerometers measure the individual components of horizontal and vertical accelerations, while the included gyroscopes stabilize the accelerometers in a desired orientation. A computer, which is also included in the system, determines position and velocity by integrating the acceleration components sensed in the vehicle and by calculating orientation corrections caused by motion over the Earth, rotation of the Earth, and other factors.

GYROSCOPES

1804   A *gyroscope* is, in effect, a miniaturized version of the Earth, used here to hold an inertial platform in alignment. When affected by disturbing torques, it cannot maintain direction in space as well as the Earth does, because of its much smaller mass, which is only partially offset by its much higher speed of rotation. For this reason it is necessary to use several motors and gear drives or direct-drive torquing mechanisms to drive the gimbals in response to the gyroscope's signals to maintain platform stabilization. A "package" consisting of several gyroscopes can control the alignment of a platform from which accelerometer measurements are made. The velocity meters (accelerometers) can be mounted on the gyro-stabilized platform. Velocity signals from these accelerometers are used to precess or torque the gyroscopes in their respective axes. This feedback from one instrument to the other produces an oscillation, which can best be visualized by considering a simple pendulum that has motion across the vertical when any force is applied to it, rather than simply moving to a new position and stopping.

Rate Gyroscopes

1805   A simplified schematic of a *rate gyroscope*, having a single degree of freedom, is shown in figure 1805. The precessional rotation around the output axis is restrained by a spring. The amount of precession around this axis is a function of the *rate* of rotational motion, as in the case of an integrating gyroscope. The rate of rotation around the input axis results in an output torque that is opposed by a restraining force illustrated by the spring device.

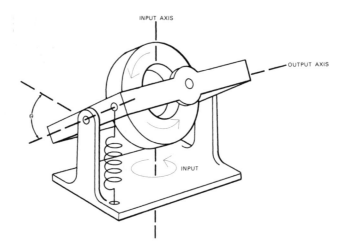

Fig. 1805. Schematic of a rate gyro.

The gyro will precess through angle 2 until precessional torque is balanced by the force exerted by the spring. It follows, then, that as long as the rate of input remains constant, the gyro will maintain its position. When the rate of input decreases, the gyro will feel the force of the spring applied as an input torque, and this torque will cause the rotor to return toward its normal position. The angle 2 is always proportional to the angular input rate.

Rate Integrating Gyroscopes

1806   Three rate gyros are normally used on the platform of a basic inertial system. The z axis of the platform is vertical, while axes x and y may be aligned north and east or in other azimuthal directions, depending upon the coordinates used in designing the system.

The basic sensing element of a modern inertial system is the *rate integrating gyroscope* (see fig. 1806a). The accuracy of the inertial data output depends largely upon the ability of such a gyro to maintain its orientation; this ability, while based to a great extent on the internal construction of the gyro, also depends upon the accuracy of calibration and alignment of the system, which are the responsibility of the shipboard operator. Motions and their effects are illustrated in figure 1806b when applied to a gyroscope having a single degree of freedom. For a given torque around the input axis (IA), a given angular rate of precession about the output axis (OA) is generated, assuming the angular momentum of the wheel stays constant. The rule for precession can be stated as follows: a spin axis (SA) precesses about the output axis (OA) toward the input axis (IA) about which the torque is applied. In other words, with the force exerted by a torque acting directly on the wheel, the

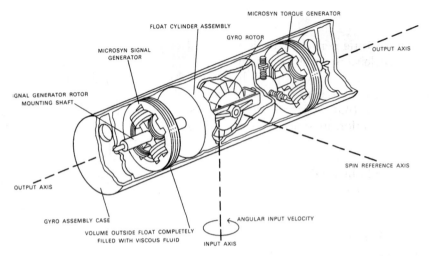

Fig. 1806a. Rate integrating gyro.

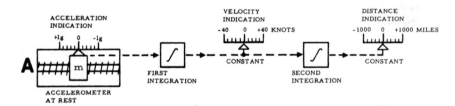

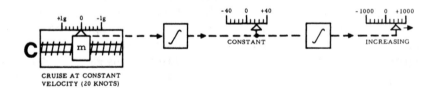

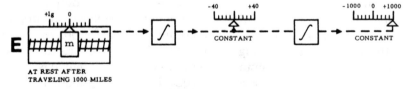

Fig. 1806b. Illustrations of accelerometer action and integration for velocity and distance.

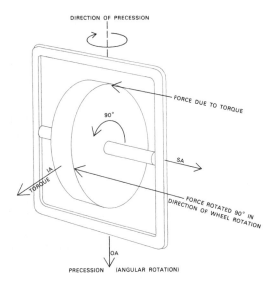

Fig. 1806c. The rule for precession.

precession of the wheel is in the direction of the force rotated around 90° in the direction of wheel rotation, as shown in figure 1806c.

ACCELEROMETERS

1807 Inertial navigation is based on the sensing of movement of the vehicle and integrating this movement or acceleration with respect to time to determine velocity and distance (position). The stable platform established by means of gyroscopes is used to establish the horizontal for the accelerometers. In actual practice, the accelerometers need not be physically mounted on the gyro platform; they can be installed on an accelerometer platform controlled by the gyros.

Acceleration-sensing instruments may be of three basic types:

1. An *accelerometer* in which the output is a measure of acceleration;
2. A *velocity meter*—a single-integrating device with an output signal proportional to velocity; and
3. A *distance meter*—a double-integrating device with an output signal proportional to distance traveled.

The term "accelerometer" is often used to denote any one of these instruments, however.

THE COMPLETE SYSTEM

1808 Two basic physical principles can be stated that summarize the use of gyroscopes and accelerometers in an inertial navigation system:

Linear momentum of a rotating mass remains constant unless an external force is applied.

Angular momentum of a rotating mass remains constant unless an angular torque is applied.

By practical application of the first principle, if acceleration is accurately measured, and is integrated twice with respect to time, then the distance traveled is determined. Applying the second principle, a gyroscope can be used to find the direction. Having determined both distance and direction, a form of dead-reckoning navigation system is created.

Figure 1808 shows the schematic of a gimbaled inertial design using separate gyroscopes and accelerometers for the three axes, *x*, *y*, and *z*.

INACCURACIES IN INERTIAL NAVIGATION

1809 Inertial systems are not subject to the various errors of dead-reckoning navigation we generally group together under the heading "current." In theory, an inertial system is limited in accuracy only by the degree of perfection of the instrumentation used.

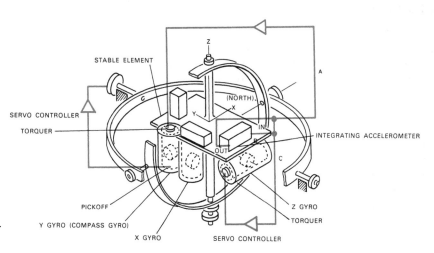

Fig. 1808. Components of an inertial guidance platform.

When the inertial system is used aboard ship over a considerable period of time, the dominant error sources are *gyro-loop uncompensated drift rates*. These drift rates are composed of many variables, depending on the mechanization and configuration of the system. They may be due to imperfections in manufacturing or to instabilities arising subsequent to the installation of the system, or they can be caused by erratic or complex vehicle movement. The ultimate result, however, is that they appear as gyro platform drift, causing erroneous presentation of the output data. The principal known causes of this apparent gyro drift are outlined below.

Because an accelerometer is sensitive only to acceleration along one axis, if two accelerometers are mounted with their sensitive axes at right angles to one another, they can be used to measure any arbitrary acceleration in the plane in which they are mounted. Assuming for the sake of simplicity that the system is so designed that one accelerometer is mounted with a north-south axis while the other is in the east-west axis, then in measuring accelerations along any course each will measure one component of the acceleration. These components can be integrated separately and interpreted as distances traveled north-south or east-west from the assumed starting point.

Errors in Alignment

1810   Obviously, an exact initial alignment of the platform is necessary. If there is a misalignment in azimuth of the system, and the vessel is traveling on a precise course of 000°, the east-west accelerometer will detect a very slight signal that will produce an erroneous indication that the vessel has moved slightly to the east or west, and the north distance readout will be slightly too low.

Earth Rate

1811   As the Earth completes one rotation about its axis in twenty-four hours, the accelerometer platform must be continuously adjusted to remain level with respect to the Earth during this entire period. If the platform is permitted to tilt, the accelerometer will sense a component of gravity. This adjustment for the computed *Earth rate* is automatically applied to the platform by the computer system. While the computed Earth rate may be equal in *magnitude* to the true Earth rate, if its *direction* is incorrect due to a misalignment of the platform in heading, there will be an error in the rate supplied to the platform. The resultant error in the accelerometer platform position is generally known as the "twenty-four-

hour error," as it is based upon erroneous sensing of the daily rotation of the Earth.

Aligning the Platform Using the Earth Rate

1812   The fact that the computed Earth rate must match the true rate is used in aligning the inertial platform. With the system at rest, the platform is leveled and aligned as closely as possible in azimuth. The accelerometer outputs are then monitored, and any indicated acceleration is considered to be the result of platform tilt caused by residual error in the azimuth alignment. Azimuth alignment is then corrected until no measurable platform tilt is detected. When this procedure is followed, the platform is aligned by using the Earth's rate of rotation as a reference.

The orientation of the inertial package when carried over the surface of the Earth must be adjusted for the curvature of the Earth in order that it will remain level. When the computer arrives at an incorrect value of the angular distance traveled by the vehicle, because of incorrect alignment or other errors in the system effectively causing an error in the direction of Earth rate, it will supply an incorrect signal to the drive motor used for leveling the accelerometer platform. This causes the accelerometer, which cannot distinguish between gravity and vehicle acceleration, to sense a gravity component, and an erroneous acceleration signal is fed back through the closed loop. The attempt of the system to correct itself produces an undamped oscillation, which in a properly designed system would have a period of twenty-four hours (see fig. 1812).

Gyro Drift

1813   Since a gyroscope cannot be constructed to be mechanically perfect, some *drift rate* will always be present. This drift of the platform tends to produce an acceleration error that increases linearly with time. Due to the closed feedback loop, however, the accelerometer platform oscillates about a zero mean error rather than building up a linear error. Constant components of gyro drift tend to cause offsets in the position and heading sinusoid, as well as a ramp in longitude. Thus, as indicated in figure 1812, there will be a consistent pattern of error propagation with respect to time resulting from unpredictable gyro drift, producing an error in the indicated position of the vehicle.

Miscellaneous Sources of Error

1814   The precise requirements of an inertial system make it necessary to take secondary effects into account; these are caused by the Coriolis effect

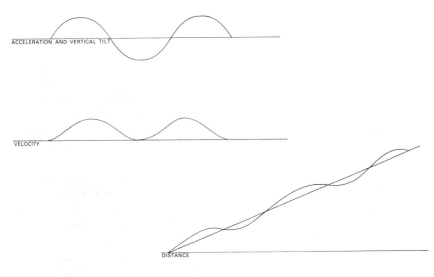

Fig. 1812. System errors plotted against time.

and the Earth's shape, which is not perfectly spherical. These error sources are automatically compensated for by the computer. For long periods of inertial navigation, dynamic coupling between various parts of the system produces a small rate error that must also be considered.

It must be realized that error sources can better be described statistically than as constants. Using this concept, the long-term buildup of errors can be determined and reduced more readily than by attempting to evaluate and use only constant error sources.

RESET PROCEDURES

1815   The early methods of resetting the system were based on the assumption that the drift rate remained constant during the sampling period. This did not prove entirely satisfactory because accurate drift rate measurements can be made only at intervals, and it was not always true that the drift rate was essentially constant, or that any random errors were accurately known. Accurate position information, external to the inertial system, is needed and is used to recalibrate or reset the system, regardless of the reset technique. These data are fed through the computer, which calculates and applies proper torquing to the stabilized platforms. All of the data that is fed to the computers needs to be smoothed out, as frequent resetting or use of data that may itself be inaccurate can cause errors in determining and correcting the drift rate of the system.

USE OF A MONITORING GYROSCOPE

1816   One method of determining the drift rate is by employing a monitoring gyro. Including a monitor (a rate gyro) in the system improves performance because it senses and supplies data to the computer on any uncompensated fixed or slowly varying components of drift in the x and y gyros; a significant reduction in the random error component is also obtained. The monitoring technique utilizes a redundant gyro mounted on a rotating platform. An integrating rate gyro, with high-gain feedback from pickoff to torquer, is used to effectively yield an accurate rate gyro. This platform, an integral part of the heading gimbal, rotates about an axis parallel to the heading gimbal axis, and does not compensate the z axis, or heading gyro. Reversal of the direction of the input axis of the monitor inertial component, with respect to the navigational component, represents the basic technique used. Case reversal is instrumented by successively positioning the monitor table to each of the four quadrant positions, under control of a computer program. The monitoring gyro provides an output at each quadrant that is equivalent to the relative drift between the controlling gyro and the monitoring gyro. The torque applied from the computer to the monitor gyro for Earth rate and vessel's velocity over the Earth is the same as the torque computed for the gyro for Earth rate, and vessel's velocity over the Earth is the same as the torque computed for the gyro being monitored. Since the system computes the vessel's position from accelerations resulting from the vessel's movement, it is important that gyro drift be known as accurately as practicable. The monitoring gyro improves overall performance of the system by detecting gyro drift that has not been compensated; it particularly helps to maintain heading accuracy.

SYSTEM UPDATING

1817 Because of the errors just discussed, inertial navigation systems must have the capability of being updated or reset through the computer. Continuous compensation can be made for a known gyro drift. Discrete position information obtained, for example, from GPS can also be used to correct the system by manual or automatic insertion of the position into the computer.

ADVANCEMENTS IN INERTIAL NAVIGATION

1818 As with nearly all technologies, there have been improvements in inertial navigation systems. One such refinement is the use of a device called an *electrostatic gyro* (ESG). This improvement makes use of a solid beryllium sphere spinning at very high velocity in a nearly perfect vacuum. Functioning as a rotor, it is supported by an electrostatic field, rather than a mechanical axle. The clearance between this rapidly spinning sphere and the case that encloses it is a mere few thousandths of an inch. This arrangement frees the device from the bearing friction present in more traditional gyroscopes and virtually eliminates many of the undesir-

able torques that are inherent to a mechanical support system. Systems employing this near-perfect gyro can function for an entire month without an external input to update its accuracy.

As discussed in article 719, a relatively recent technological improvement on the gyrocompass is the ring laser gyro (RLG). Using carefully aligned mirrors, two laser beams travel around a closed circuit (or "ring") in opposite directions until they meet at a special detector. If the vessel in which the gyro is mounted is stationary, the two beams will arrive at the sensor simultaneously and with no difference in the laser frequency. But if the vessel is turning, there will be a shift in frequency caused by the resultant differences in travel time around the ring. Using the Doppler principle, the frequency shift can be measured and translated into compensating information, thereby replicating the functions of a conventional gyroscope without relying upon cumbersome mechanical devices such as rotors, gimbals, and motors. This reliance on electronic rather than mechanical technology allows RLGs to be smaller and less sensitive to shock and vibration. They require less power to run, less maintenance to keep them running, and less cooling to keep them from overheating. Gravity and magnetic fields have no effect upon them, and they require much less start-up time (ten minutes dockside; thirty minutes at sea) than do mechanical gyrocompasses. With these advantages, RLGs are steadily replacing their mechanical forerunners.

Chapter 19

Navigational Astronomy

Astronomy is one of the oldest of the sciences to which humans have devoted their attention; it is a fascinating subject, so broad that it can be studied for a lifetime. Undoubtedly, primitive men gazed at the sky in awe and wonderment; folklore and legends reflect their interest in the heavens and their crude explanations for the phenomena they saw. Progress in the science of astronomy is closely linked with the history of the human race. The Egyptians, Babylonians, Chinese, Hindus, Mayas, and Aztecs all pursued the science of astronomy, which they associated with their religious beliefs. These studies were written down and have been well researched, and the science of astronomy has greatly advanced in more recent times by scientists using the wonders of modern technology.

The study of celestial navigation should properly start with a brief consideration of the basics of astronomy. A navigator certainly need not be an astronomer, but a degree of knowledge of the stars and other celestial bodies—their size, distance, location, and movement—can aid in understanding the necessary calculations and diagrams that make celestial navigation workable. Some of the descriptions and explanations used here should rightfully be considered simplistic, and students of pure astronomy may be inclined to say, "Yes . . . but." The word "gravity" alone can stimulate complicated discussions of space-time, the curvature of space, and so on. But these matters are beyond the scope of this book, and consideration of this vast subject area will be limited to a small amount of background and to the specialized study one might call *navigational astronomy*—those aspects of astronomy of interest and value to a navigator in fixing positions and directing the course and speeds of a vessel.

MEASUREMENTS

1901 In a universe where galaxies have been observed at distances greater than ten billion trillion (10^{22}) miles, special units of measurement are required. Among these are the astronomical unit (AU), the light-year, and the parsec. Because the brightness of individual stars is important in making navigational observations, a comparative system has been devised to rank them in terms of their relative luminosity.

Astronomical Distances

1902 The value of the *astronomical unit* is the mean distance between the Earth and the Sun, approximately 92.9 million statute miles, or 150 million kilometers. (Note: In this chapter, the use of the word "miles" will be understood to be in *statute* miles, as used in texts on astronomy, rather than in nautical miles as is the practice in the rest of this book.)

A *light-year* is the distance that light travels in one year, or roughly 5.88 trillion miles (9.46 trillion km). The speed of light is approximately 186,282 miles (299,792 km) per second, and one year is equivalent to approximately 31.6 million seconds.

One *parsec* (derived from the words *parallax* and *second*) is the distance at which a body as viewed from the Earth and from the center of the Sun, will differ in apparent position (parallax) by 1 second of arc. It is, therefore, the radius of an arc of 1 second whose chord is one astronomical unit. The length of this radius amounts to about 3.26 light-years.

The universe is made up of countless galaxies. An immense number of galaxies have been counted by astronomers. Each galaxy is an assemblage of perhaps 100 billion stars, dust clouds, and masses of

Fig. 1902. Photograph of a spiral galaxy.

thin gas, held in their orbits together by gravitational force in a lens-shaped arrangement as viewed in cross section. Most galaxies are spiral in shape (see fig. 1902).

Measuring Brightness

1903   The brightness of a celestial body is of obvious interest to a navigator and is expressed in terms of *magnitude*. One of the earliest known astronomers, Ptolemy of Egypt, devised a system of dividing the visible stars into six groups according to brightness, and the system used today is derived from his. The first group is considered to be 100 times brighter than the sixth group. Thus, the magnitude ratio is computed as the fifth root of 100 or 2.512. Thus, a zero magnitude body is 2.512 times brighter than a first magnitude body, which is 2.512 times brighter than a second magnitude body, and so on. Using this scale, the two brightest stars, Sirius and Canopus, have negative magnitudes of -1.6 and -0.9 respectively. Some are *variable stars* whose brightness varies slightly or considerably over regular or irregular intervals; for example, Betelgeuse varies in brightness by more than a factor of two over an irregular period.

THE MILKY WAY

1904   Our own galaxy, the Milky Way, derives its name from the milky appearance of the night sky to the unaided eye as an observer looks along its major axis. This milky appearance is caused by the con-centration of stars—uncounted and uncountable by the naked eye—in this area. The Milky Way is considered to be about average among galaxies in star population. The stars are not evenly distributed; they tend to be concentrated in two spiral arms extending outward from the center, with the whole galaxy in rotation. It is about 100,000 light-years in diameter, has a maximum thickness of some 10,000 light-years, and contains (perhaps!) 100 billion stars. Near the inner edge of one of the spiral arms and about halfway between the "top" and the "bottom" of the galaxy, there is a quite ordinary star, as stars go, but one of supreme importance to man— our *sun*.

The stars that make up the Milky Way galaxy vary greatly in size. Our Sun, an average-sized star, is approximately 864,400 miles in diameter, and the largest known star is Antares with a diameter about 428 times that of the Sun, giving it a diameter greater than that of the Earth's orbit. Even though we know that the Sun is a star, for navigational purposes, we will often refer to it as a separate (and different) entity.

The navigator is concerned only with stars within our galaxy, astronomically speaking, in our immediate neighborhood. The *Nautical Almanac* and the *Air Almanac* tabulate data on a total of 173 stars suitable for use in celestial navigation. Only 58 of these are normally used; they are the fifty-seven so-called selected stars, plus Polaris, which is a special (and very useful) case because it is conveniently located above the North Pole and can therefore (for reasons that will become more clear later) be used for the determination of latitude in the Northern Hemisphere. Because of its coincident location above the Earth's north pole, Polaris is sometimes referred as the *pole star*.

The *planets* of our solar system and the Earth's *moon* are also valuable to the navigator, and their data are also included in the almanacs. Because the stars are so much farther away than the Sun, Moon, and planets, there are some differences in the way they are used. For example, the stars can be considered as being at a virtually infinite distance, while the Sun, Moon, and planets are at finite distances. Because the Moon is only about 1¼ light-seconds distant from the Earth, and the Sun is less than 8½ light-minutes away, these relatively close distances necessitate a correction for *geocentric parallax*, that difference in apparent direction or position of a celestial body when observed from a point on the surface of the Earth (using a line of sight from the center of the Earth outward) (see fig. 1904a). But the great distances of stars allows us to ignore par-

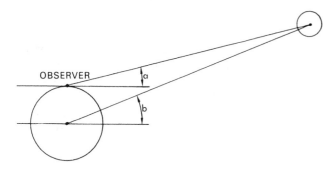

Fig. 1904a. Parallax occurs because the observer is not positioned at the center of the Earth.

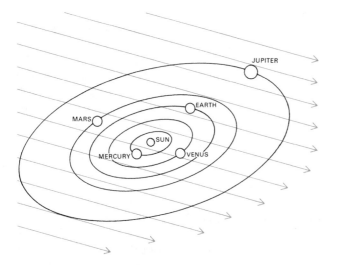

Fig. 1904b. Light rays from stars are essentially parallel all across the solar system.

allax in their case because, for example, Rigil Kentaurus—the nearest navigational star at more than four light-years distant—when observed from opposite points on the Earth's orbit around the Sun, differs in angle by only approximately 1.5 seconds of arc. A navigator is not equipped to measure angles to this precision, so light rays coming from the stars may be considered as parallel and parallax may therefore be disregarded (see fig. 1904b).

Despite their huge actual dimensions, stars may be considered, for navigational purposes, as point sources of light with no measurable diameter when viewed through a sextant telescope. However, because of their relative proximity, the Sun and Moon appear to us as sizable spheres rather than mere points of light. As you will see in a subsequent chapter, when observing these bodies with a sextant, it is more efficient to use the upper edge—

called the *upper limb*—or the lower edge (*lower limb*), rather than trying to sight the exact center of the body. Because there is an angular difference, a correction will be necessary to compensate. That correction is called *semidiameter*. With the Sun and the Moon, this correction is sizable enough to be necessary, but the semidiameter of planets is limited to not more than about 32 seconds of arc, and is seldom considered in marine navigation.

THE SOLAR SYSTEM

1905 Oriented around the Sun in elliptical orbits are the nine known planets and thousands of planetoids or asteroids. Of these major planets, only Venus, Mars, Jupiter, and Saturn are normally used in navigation; they are often referred to as the *navigational planets* for this reason. Mean distances of these four planets from the Sun range from 67 million miles (1.08×10^8 km) for Venus, to 886 million miles (1.43×10^9 km) for Saturn; the periods required by each to complete a revolution around the Sun vary from about 225 days for Venus, to 29½ years for Saturn. See figure 1905 for some comparative data on the planets.

While some of the planets have satellites orbiting them, only the Earth's natural satellite—the Moon—is of current interest to the nautical navigator.

Planets and other celestial bodies in our solar system *rotate* on internal *axes* and *revolve* around the Sun in paths called *orbits*. The Sun too is thought to revolve in a much longer orbit about the center of our galaxy, the Earth and the rest of our solar system going with it. All four navigational planets rotate in the same direction (west to east in the Earth's reference system), except for Venus, which has an opposite rotation.

Planet	Mean Distance from Sun		Mean Diameter (in miles)	Sidereal Period		Axial Rotation	Known Satellites
	Millions of Miles	Astronomical Units					
Mercury	36	0.4	3031	88	days	60^d	none
Venus	67	0.7	7521	224.7	days	243	none
Earth	93	1.0	7926	365.24	days	23^{h}56^m	1
Mars	142	1.5	4222	687	days	24^{h}37^m	2
Jupiter	484	5.2	88729	11.86	years	9^{h}50^m	16
Saturn	887	9.5	74565	29.46	years	10^{h}14^m	17
Uranus	1783	19.2	31566	84.02	years	17^{h}14^m	15
Neptune	2794	30.1	30199	164.8	years	15^{h}40^m	2
Pluto	3666	39.4	1423	248.4	years	6.4^d?	1

Fig. 1905. Distance, diameter, and other planetary data.

THE EARTH AND THE SUN

1906 The Earth's rotation on its axis and its revolution around the Sun have effects that are both important and measurable. For example, because the Earth's orbit around the Sun is elliptical rather than circular, the distance between the Earth and Sun varies. Among other effects, this variation in distance results in a noticeable difference in the apparent diameter of the Sun depending upon where the two are in relation to one another. At *perihelion*, the point of nearest approach, the apparent diameter of the Sun is approximately 32.6 minutes of arc. At *aphelion*, the point of greatest separation, the apparent diameter is about 31.5 minutes. Perihelion and aphelion are illustrated in figure 1906a.

The Earth rotates 360° about its axis once in 23 hours, 56 minutes, 4 seconds; this is termed the *sidereal day*, and differs from the solar day, which averages 24 full hours, because of the Earth's motion in its orbit. This difference between the sidereal and solar days is illustrated in figure 1906b. At position (1) the Sun is over the (celestial) meridian *M* (defined by the parallel light coming from the stars). Rotation is counterclockwise in this diagram and when the Earth has arrived at position (2) in its orbit, it has rotated 360° on its axis, but the Sun is still east of the meridian *M* and will not be on it

until the Earth has rotated for an additional period averaging some four minutes. This period varies slightly during the year, and depends on the Earth's position in its orbit. Compounding this effect and often accounting for most of it, is the apparent slope of the Sun's annual path against the background of stars. The *ecliptic* as that path is called, is tilted with respect to the plane of the Earth's equator, not coincident with it or parallel to it.

The daily rotation of the Earth on its axis has the effect of making the other heavenly bodies appear to move across the sky from east to west. We all are familiar with that *apparent motion* in the case of the Sun, but only the more observant among us have noticed this same effect in the case of the stars. The daily paths of the stars would appear as concentric full circles (called *diurnal circles*) if you were standing at one of the Earth's poles. Looking directly upward, you would see the circular tracks as parallel to the plane of the horizon and centered on a single point in the sky directly overhead. Moving away from the pole (say southward from the north pole) you would notice that the planes of the circles seem to tilt, so that some of the circles would be interrupted by the northern horizon, while short arcs of new paths of additional stars would begin to appear above the southern horizon. All the star paths, however, would remain concentric about the same axis. Continuing southward, you would eventually reach the equator and there find that the stars' diurnal circles would appear to be arcs of semicircles, the stars rising perpendicularly to the horizon in the eastern half of the sky and setting perpendicularly to it in the western half.

At the pole, stars near the horizon seemed to circle all around it, ever westward and neither rising nor setting. In intermediate latitudes, some stars stayed always above the horizon and seemed to circle around the same common center as they did when observed for the pole. In figure 1906c, the bright arc near the center of is most likely the path of the star Polaris. Notice that the arcs that are individually discernible are all of the same length as measured in degrees, each arc giving a common indication of the duration of time that the photographic film was exposed (assuming that the camera remained fixed in place with its shutter open throughout the exposure).

It is important to note that at all latitudes, the stars all appear to revolve together, circling the Earth's axis and maintaining constant positions relative to each other. This apparently constant, though rotating, field of stars forms a sort of "backdrop" that surrounds the entire Earth and, for navi-

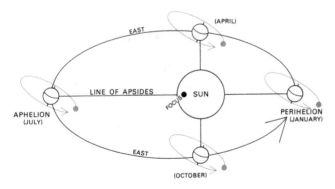

Fig. 1906a. Perihelion and aphelion resulting from the elliptical orbit of the Earth.

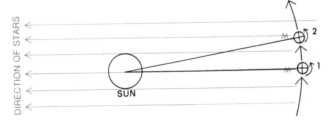

Fig. 1906b. Sidereal and solar days.

Fig. 1906c. Observatory photograph of circumpolar stars.

gational purposes, is known as the *celestial sphere.* Notice that (unlike the stars) the Sun, Moon, and planets keep moving relative to one another and so are always changing their positions as seen against the background of the celestial sphere.

To better understand these phenomena, some additional terminology will help. The terms *geographical position* and *declination* and their uses in celestial navigation will be explained in greater detail in succeeding chapters, but a brief explanation is useful here.

Geographical Position and Declination

1907 The point on the Earth directly below a celestial body is defined as the body's *geographical position* (GP). In other words, if you dropped a line straight down from a celestial body and connected it to the center of the Earth, where it touched the surface of the Earth would be that celestial body's GP (see fig. 1907a). The *declination* of a body is identical to the *latitude of the GP.* The apparent motion of the celestial bodies caused by the rotation of the Earth on its axis results in the GP of the body moving westward along a parallel of latitude equal in angular value to the declination of the body. Figure 1907b illustrates three stars with declinations of 0°, 30° S, and 60° N. As the Earth rotates, the GPs of the bodies will trace lines across the Earth following the equator, the 30° south parallel of latitude, and the 60° north parallel of latitude respectively.

In figure 1907c an observer is at 30° north latitude. The plane of the observer's horizon is shown as passing through the Earth's center; circle 1 represents the apparent daily path or diurnal circle of a body having a declination of approximately 80° north. In moving along its diurnal circle, it is therefore constantly above some point on the eightieth parallel of north latitude. Note that for the observer in latitude 30° north, this body never sets below the horizon. This, of course, will be equally true for all bodies having a declination of 60° or more North (90° minus observer's latitude of 30°). All such bodies will bear due north of the observer at the highest and lowest points on their diurnal circles, and since they do not set below the horizon they are referred to as *circumpolar* stars.

Although there actually are very small changes over many years (for reasons beyond the scope of this discussion), the declination of each star can be considered as fixed, and an observer in a given

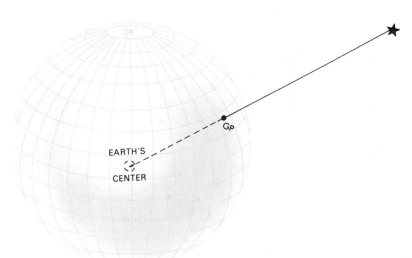

Fig. 1907a. Geographical position (GP) of a celestial body.

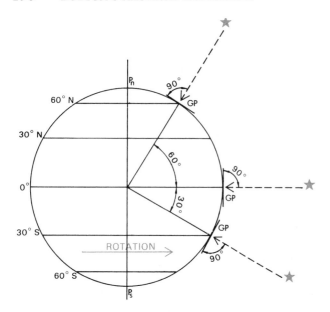

Fig. 1907b. The declination of a star equals the latitude of its GP.

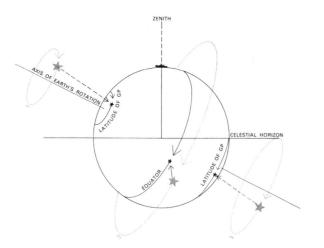

Fig. 1907c. Diurnal circles.

latitude will have essentially the same continuous view of the diurnal circle of that star night after night. On the other hand, the declination of each body *in the solar system* changes with comparative rapidity, and thus the apparent motion of these bodies changes at a similar high rate. For reasons relating to the revolution of the Earth and the tilt of its axis as well as other factors, the declination of the Sun, Moon, and navigational planets varies between roughly 25° N and 25° S, and at any time their diurnal circles will lie between these limits.

Effects of the Earth's Axis

1908   Because the Earth is essentially a sphere (a simplifying assumption, but a highly useful and

practical one), the half facing the Sun is illuminated by the Sun and the half facing away is essentially in darkness (receiving light only from the stars and planets and that which is reflected from the Moon). The Earth's rotation causes that half-and-half arrangement to be constantly changing, giving us the phenomenon of day and night. If the Earth's axis were perpendicular to the plane of its orbit, an observer on any point on the Earth (other than the poles) would be in daylight exactly half of each day and the other half would be spent in relative darkness. But the Earth's axis is *not* perpendicular to its orbit around the Sun, and is in fact inclined at an angle of about 23½° from the vertical. This means that the length of an observer's day will be determined by where she or he is on the Earth and where the Earth is its orbit around the Sun. These combined effects create other phenomena that are worthy of note.

Solstices and Equinoxes

1909   Because the Earth's axis is inclined at an angle of about 23½° from the vertical (see fig. 1909), this causes the North Pole to be inclined toward the Sun from the latter part of March to the latter part of September. Those parts of the Earth located in the Northern Hemisphere will therefore be warmer during those times because of the increased exposure to the Sun's radiation. During the balance of the year, the *South Pole* is inclined toward the Sun, reversing the effect. This is what causes the seasons and explains why it is winter in Australia when it is summer in the United States and vice-versa.

As illustrated in figure 1909, about 21 June each year the North Pole is at its maximum inclination toward the Sun. Understanding the definition of declination will tell you that the Sun's declination at this point is 23½° North. As the Earth moves on in

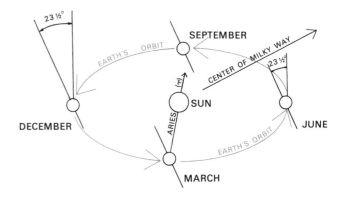

Fig. 1909. The annual revolution of the Earth around the Sun.

its orbit about the Sun, the northerly declination of the Sun decreases slowly (each day being slightly lower), until it reaches 0° (is directly over the equator) about 22 September. The Sun then continues southward until about 21 December, when it reaches 23½° South, its maximum southerly declination. The Sun's declination then begin moving northward, crossing the equator on 21 March and reaching maximum northern declination (23½° North) again on about 21 June. This entire cycle represents one revolution of the Sun around the Earth and takes one year to complete. (Note: It actually takes approximately 365¼ days to complete. This extra quarter-day longer than the calendar year is why we have a leap year, of 366 days versus 365, almost every four years. In the civil calendar now in common use, century years are not leap years, unless integrally divisible by 400. Thus, year 2000 was a leap year, but 1900 was not. Adding the extra day to the calendar ensures that the relative positions of the Sun and Earth will remain the same year after year, season by season. Without this correction, the seasons would gradually migrate so that we would eventually have snow falling in August in the city of New York.)

The continuing change in the Sun's declination throughout a yearly cycle explains the changing seasons experienced on Earth, which are caused by the angle at which the Sun's rays strike the Earth, and the comparative length of daylight and darkness. The points of maximum declination are called the *solstices;* the points of 0° declination are called the *equinoxes*. These words are derived from Latin, *solstice* meaning "sun standing still," and *equinox* meaning "equal night." The early thinkers who devised these reference systems named them after the seasons in which they occurred, and because these thinkers were all residents of the Northern Hemisphere, the points were named according to those seasons occurring at that time for that hemisphere. Therefore, the solstice occurring in June is known as the *summer solstice* (even though residents of the Southern Hemisphere are experiencing *winter* at that time), and the one in December is known as the *winter solstice*. The equinoxes are also named according to the seasons occurring simultaneously in the Northern Hemisphere: the one in September is the *autumnal equinox* and the one in March is the *vernal (spring) equinox*. Also contributing to seasonal effects is the varying distance from the Sun as the Earth proceeds in its elliptical yearly orbit. The Earth, in approaching closest to the Sun in January and departing farthest from it in July, thereby slightly intensifies seasonal extremes of weather in the Southern Hemisphere and attenuates them in the Northern.

That portion of the Earth's surface that at some time during the year has the Sun directly above it is known as the *torrid zone*. It should be apparent that this zone is defined as falling between latitudes 23½° North (called the *Tropic of Cancer*) and 23½° South (called the *Tropic of Capricorn*).

The revolution of the Earth about the Sun also affects the apparent positions of the stars, which surround the solar system on all sides. The ones that can be seen from the Earth on a given night are those in a direction generally opposite to that of the Sun. Because of this, the stars appear to make one complete revolution around the Earth each year independently of their nightly revolution, due to the Earth's rotation on its axis; each succeeding night at the same time at a given place, each star will be almost 1° farther west, and it requires an average of 365¼ days to complete the revolution of 360°.

The Ecliptic and Aries

1910 As already noted, the celestial bodies in our solar system noticeably move relative to the backdrop of stars known as the celestial sphere. In the case of the Sun, this relative movement traces a path across the field of stars and this path is called the *ecliptic*. The early astronomers grouped the stars into arbitrary constellations; the twelve constellations through which the Sun passes during the year (i.e., those located along the plane of the ecliptic) are collectively known as the *zodiac*.

An arbitrary but conventionally very important concept for nautical navigation is that of the *first point of Aries* (or simply *Aries*), and it is represented by the symbol ♈. It is used in the celestial system of coordinates in a manner similar to the Greenwich meridian in the terrestrial coordinate system. The first point of Aries is defined as that point in space where the vernal equinox occurs. When this point was first named, the vernal equinox coincided with the time when the Sun's path crossed into the constellation of Aries. That is no longer true (today it is in the constellation Pisces) because of precession (see below), but the nomenclature remains unchanged.

Effects of Precession

1911 The Earth is, in effect, a gigantic gyroscope, and is subject to the laws of gyroscopic motion. The Moon and Sun exert gravitational forces on the Earth, and the Earth's resistance to these forces causes it to react like a gyroscope and *precess* in a direction that is at right angles to the direction of the external force. This means that over time the Earth's orientation relative to the celestial sphere is changing.

Among other effects, this precession causes a slow rotation of the Earth's axis about an axis projected outward at right angles to the plane of its orbit, therefore slowly tracing a circle on the celestial sphere—a kind of "wobble" of the Earth's axis relative to the space around it. The period of this precession is about 25,800 years, so it would seem that it is not something a navigator would have to be concerned about. However, there is a long-term effect that has some navigational significance. Figure 1911 shows the path of the Earth's axis in space over the period of precession. Because of this "wobbling" of the Earth's axis, you can see that Polaris will not always be the convenient "polestar" that it is today. Over time, other stars will replace it in that role. At present, the Earth's axis is actually getting closer to Polaris and will be at its closest point of approach (about 28 minutes) in 2102. After that time, the Earth's axis will move farther away from Polaris and will eventually be replaced by Deneb in approximately eight thousand years.

Another effect is known as *precession of the equinoxes.* As noted before, the apparent location of the Sun among the stars when its declination is 0° is termed an equinox; this occurs each spring and fall. The gyroscopic action of the Earth causes the equinox to move at a rate of about 50 seconds of arc per year in a westerly direction, that is, clockwise as seen from the north. This is the *opposite* direction to both the Earth's rotation and its revolution. The rate of the Earth's precession is not uniform due to the varying positions of the Moon relative to the Earth's equator and some small effects of other bodies; this slight variation is termed *nutation.*

Minor Motions of the Earth

1912   In addition to the major motions described above, there are several motions of the Earth of minor importance. Two of the more significant in navigation are the *wandering of the terrestrial poles* and the *variations in speed of rotation* of the Earth.

The north and south terrestrial poles, or the points where the Earth's axis of rotation theoretically pierces the Earth's surface, are not stationary. Instead, they wander slightly in somewhat circular paths. The movement is believed to be caused by meteorological effects. Each pole wanders in an area smaller than a baseball diamond, and neither has been known to move more than 40 feet (12 m) from its average position. The phenomenon is also called *variation in latitude.*

The rotational speed of the Earth on its axis is steadily decreasing by a small amount, causing the length of the day to increase at the rate of about 0.001 second a century. There are also small irregular changes in the rotational period, the causes of which are uncertain. With the introduction of atomic time standards, which keep uniformly linear time, variations in the speed of rotation of the Earth, which affect its rotational position and hence astronomical observations, are of interest to the navigator; see chapter 23 for further discussion of the differences between "perfect" time and "correct" time for navigational use.

THE MOON

1913   The most obvious effect of the Moon's revolution about the Earth is the cycle of *phases* through which it passes. The Moon shines by the Sun's reflected light. Excluding occasional eclipses, the side facing the Sun is lit and the opposite side is dark; the Moon's appearance from the Earth depends on its orientation relative to the Earth and Sun.

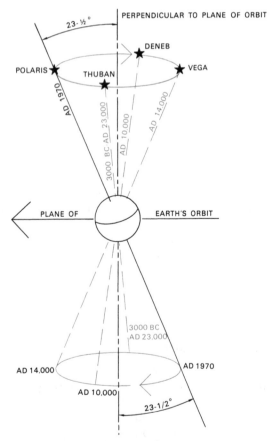

Fig. 1911. Precession of the Earth.

The Moon passes through its cycle of phases during a 29.5-day *synodic period*. The synodic period of a celestial body is its average period of revolution with respect to the Sun, as seen from the Earth. It differs from the 360° sidereal period because of the motions of the Earth and the Moon in their orbits. Figure 1913 illustrates the positions of the Moon relative to the Sun and Earth during its synodic period, and the resulting phases. When the Moon is between the Sun and the Earth, its sunlit half faces away from the Earth, and it cannot be seen; this is the *new Moon*. As it revolves in its orbit, (counterclockwise in fig. 1913), an observer on Earth first sees a part of the sunlit half as a thin *crescent*, which will then *wax* (grow) slowly until it reaches *first quarter*, when it appears as a semicircle. After passing through the first quarter, it enters the *gibbous* phase until it becomes full, and the entire sunlit half can be seen. From full it is said to *wane*, becoming gibbous again to the last quarter, and then crescent until the cycle is completed. The term "age of the Moon" refers to the number of days that have passed since the preceding new Moon, and is an indication of both the phase and the amount of light it sheds. On the average, the Moon rises about 50 minutes later each day, although that interval varies considerably. In high northern latitudes, the full or nearly full Moon that occurs near the start of the fall season may actually rise *earlier* from day to day.

Other effects of the Moon's revolution about the Earth are *eclipses* that occur when the Sun, the Earth, and the Moon are in line. The Earth and the Moon both cast shadows into space, in a direction away from the Sun. A *solar eclipse* occurs whenever the shadow of the Moon falls on a part of the surface of the Earth, blocking light from the Sun. As determined by the alignment of the three bodies and the position of the observer, one may witness a *total*

eclipse, or only a *partial eclipse*, if part of the disc of the Sun is visible. A solar eclipse is further defined as *annular* when the Moon's distance from the Earth is sufficiently great to permit a narrow ring of sunlight to appear around the Moon. A *lunar eclipse* occurs when the Moon passes through the shadow of the Earth, and it, too, may be partial or total. Owing to the light-focusing properties of the Earth's atmosphere, the whole side of the Moon toward the Earth remains visible throughout a total lunar eclipse, though at significantly reduced brilliance and usually appearing more reddish in color.

THE PLANETS

1914   The combination of the revolutions of the Earth and the planets about the Sun results in the comparatively rapid change of position of the planets on the celestial sphere. Mars, Jupiter, and Saturn are called *superior planets* because their orbits lie outside that of the Earth. (Note: The other superior planets—Uranus, Neptune, and Pluto—are all too far away to be used as navigational bodies.) They appear to move always westward with respect to the Sun, meaning that they rise earlier and cross the observer's meridian earlier on each succeeding day. With respect to the stars, the superior planets appear to move constantly eastward from night to night, except when they are nearest the Earth. At this time, their motion is *retrograde*, appearing to move backward (westward) among the stars. Figure 1914 illustrates the retrograde motion of a superior planet. When the Earth is at E_1, E_2, E_3, and so on, the superior planet is at P_1, P_2, P_3, and so on, and appears at positions 1, 2, 3, and so on at the left.

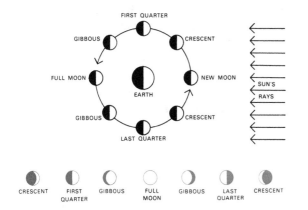

Fig. 1913. Phases of the Moon; conventional symbols are shown below.

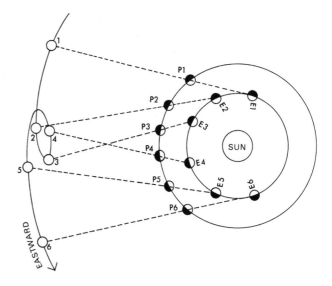

Fig. 1914. Retrograde movement of a superior planet.

Mercury and Venus are called *inferior planets* because their orbits lie *inside* that of the Earth. They appear to oscillate with respect to the Sun. Venus always appears comparatively near the Sun, alternating as a morning and evening planet, often popularly referred to as the "morning star" or "evening star," because it rises and sets within about three hours of sunrise and sunset. Mercury is a bright celestial body, but because of its closeness to the Sun it can be seen only rarely, and its coordinates are therefore not listed in the *Nautical Almanac*.

Like the Moon, the planets shine by the reflected light of the Sun; the inferior planets go through all the same phases as the Moon, being "full" when on the opposite side of the Sun from the Earth, and "new" when on the same side. The superior planets never pass between the Earth and Sun, and thus are never seen in the "new" phase; they vary only between "full" and "gibbous" when viewed through a telescope.

THE EARTH'S ATMOSPHERE

1915 The atmosphere of the Earth has some important effects on celestial navigation; it is a great blanket of air, consisting principally of 78 percent nitrogen and 21 percent oxygen, with very small amounts of other gases and contaminants. Half of the atmosphere is concentrated within about 3½ miles (5½ km) of the surface; the remainder thins out to an altitude of roughly 1,000 miles (1,600 km).

Atmospheric Diffusion

1916 Without the diffusing effect of the atmosphere, the stars and the Sun would be visible at the same time. However, the molecules that make up the atmosphere, aided by suspended dust, scatter the Sun's light in all directions and make it difficult to see the stars. The short-wavelength blue light from the Sun is particularly affected by this scattering, thus giving the sky its characteristic blue color. Astronauts report that at altitudes of over 100 miles (160 km) they are still unable to see most stars in daytime, but that from true "outer space" they can.

When a celestial body is near the horizon, its light must pass through a greater volume of air than

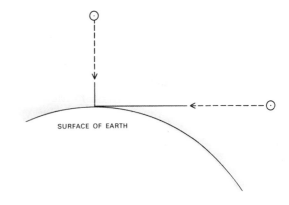

Fig. 1916. At low altitudes, the Sun's rays travel through greater distances in the Earth's atmosphere, resulting in the characteristic red color.

when it is overhead, as is shown in figure 1916. This longer air path causes additional scattering, and permits very little blue light to reach the observer, leaving only the long-wavelength red light. This filtering action causes the reddish-orange appearance of the Sun and Moon near the horizon.

Refraction of Light

1917 The atmosphere also causes light rays to be refracted, or bent, as they enter it from space. This refraction of the Sun's rays has the effect of prolonging the twilight. In addition, except when a celestial body is directly overhead, refraction affects its apparent altitude, causing it to appear higher than it actually is. At sunset, the entire disc of the Sun can still be visible after the upper limb has, in fact, passed geometrically below the horizon.

The atmosphere also reduces the apparent brightness of celestial bodies, again having its greatest effect when the body is on the horizon and its light rays are passing through the maximum distance and density of air. As its altitude decreases from 90° (straight overhead) to 5° (near the horizon), a star's brightness may be reduced by a full magnitude. Atmospheric turbulence often causes the light from a star to fluctuate; hence the popular notion that stars "twinkle." The light from planets is normally much steadier, because they are comparatively near the Earth and thus have appreciable size, rather than appearing as mere points of light.

Chapter 20

Introduction to Celestial Navigation

Celestial Navigation may be defined as the art and science of using observations of the Sun, Moon, certain planets, and the brighter stars for navigational purposes. In the process, principles of optics, geometry, spherical trigonometry, and, of course, astronomy all come into play. Fortunately for the modern navigator, one does not have to be a physicist or mathematician to employ the wonders of celestial navigation. Strenuous calculations have long given way to the simplicity of tables that require only simple addition and subtraction to use, and computer programs have simplified the process even further. But, just as any elementary school teacher would never consider teaching arithmetic solely by showing the students how to push the buttons of a calculator, neither should any navigator be satisfied with only punching numbers through a series of tables or a computer program. As a nautical navigator, you should certainly not hesitate to take advantage of the time-saving and improved accuracy that such things offer, but you should also have an understanding of the theory behind the practice of celestial navigation. This will not only stand you in good stead should a crisis arise that eliminates the availability of these conveniences or removes the electrical power needed to make them run, but it will make you a better navigator as well.

A frequently used term among navigators today is "situational awareness," an encompassing idea that, among other things, refers to the navigator's use of as many sources of information as possible to safely navigate. Directly using celestial navigation can certainly improve situational awareness by providing additional information that can be used to correlate or corroborate information from other sources; the importance of redundancy in naviga-

tion cannot be overemphasized. But there is also an *indirect* benefit for a navigator who has a good working knowledge of how the heavens work and how their behavior relates to nautical navigation. The navigator's situational awareness is improved by that knowledge, even if he or she is not actively taking Sun lines or star sights with a sextant. Without referring to a single piece of electronic equipment, a navigator can know that the vessel is significantly off course simply by looking up at the night sky. Just as a traveler on land is much more comfortable (and less apt to get lost) if she or he recognizes certain landmarks along the way, so the nautical navigator who knows the heavens and how they work will be more "in tune" with the surroundings, more *situationally aware*.

BASICS

2001   There is no question that celestial navigation is complicated. Unlike many other concepts in nautical navigation, such as shooting bearings to a visible object, the process used to fix a position using the heavenly bodies is not easily visualized. To understand the theory behind this practice requires a certain degree of imagination and the suspension of the conventional thinking we use in everyday life. At times you will be asked to imagine yourself in space looking down on the Earth with geometric figures inscribed above and below; at others you will be looking up from your tiny spot on the Earth and visualizing all sorts of lines running across the sky. All of this is not necessary in the actual practice of celestial navigation, but understanding the theory behind what you are doing will make the practice less mystifying and will lessen the likelihood of errors, and help you to detect them and determine their source when they do occur.

A brief explanation of the theory and of the practice of celestial navigation may help you to understand where we are going as the ensuing discussion progresses. Too often students begin learning the various coordinate systems and the components of sight forms without knowing where all of this is taking them. Obviously, the end result is to fix your position, but how that is accomplished by looking at a star through a sextant is not intuitively apparent. To help alleviate this potential problem we will begin with simplified explanations of the theory and the practice of celestial navigation. Later in the chapter, and in the chapters that follow, we will go into these matters in more detail.

The process described in the following summaries focuses primarily upon using a celestial body to obtain a line of position. This is obviously an important part of celestial navigation and serves as a useful example. However, there are other functions of celestial navigation (such as predicting times of sunrise and moonset, determining compass errors, and calculating the times of transit of celestial bodies) that you will learn about in subsequent chapters.

Celestial Navigation *Theory* Summarized

2002   As with most other forms of nautical navigation, the goal in celestial navigation is to obtain lines of position (LOPs). Each sighting of a heavenly body yields a single LOP. The rules for LOPs that apply in piloting apply to celestial LOPs as well. In fact, one might think of the celestial bodies as roughly equivalent to the visual landmarks used in piloting. We must use more than one body in order to get a fix. Using bodies that are too close together in the sky will not provide a good fix; to get the most reliable fix, you should use bodies with a wide separation of bearing (*azimuth* is the preferred term in celestial navigation). In the night sky, there will often be much to choose from—stars, planets, the Moon—but in daytime it is only the Sun (and sometimes the Moon, rarely a planet) that is available to the navigator. But just as was the case with visual LOPs, celestial LOPs may also be advanced or retarded to obtain a running fix.

Basically, obtaining a celestial LOP relies on a simple rule of mathematics. You may recall from your early studies of geometry that it is possible to deduce the values of all six parts (sides and angles) of a triangle if we know the values of, say, only two sides and one angle. To accomplish this feat in celestial navigation, we begin with what we know. Because of the regularity of the universe, and

because astronomers long ago began keeping track of the locations and relative motions of the celestial bodies, we are able to predict the location of any of the navigational bodies (Sun, Moon, planets, and stars, etc.) relative to the Earth at any given instant. This information (sometimes referred to as *ephemeral data*) is contained in an *astronomical almanac* (also called an *ephemeris*) such as the *Nautical Almanac* or the *Air Almanac*. By referring to one of these books (or a software program with ephemeral data incorporated) and using the concept of a celestial body's geographical position or GP (explained in the previous chapter), we can identify a specific point on Earth's surface. We also know the location of the north and south poles, so one of those can be used in our deduction. We now have two points and can connect them to create one side of a triangle.

To obtain another side of the triangle, we must rely upon what is actually not a *known* quantity but an *assumed* one. Although we do not know our exact location on the face of the Earth (if we did, we would have no need of celestial LOPs), we do know our *approximate* position. When all else fails in navigation, we have our dead reckoning (DR) position. This "best guess" can be used (somewhat refined as explained later) to define our point, which in celestial navigation is called an *assumed position* (AP).

Having identified three points on the surface of the Earth—a geographic position (GP) of a celestial body, one of the poles, and an assumed position (AP)—we have defined a triangle. The GP and AP can each be defined in terms of latitude and longitude, and the difference in the longitude of the two provides an angle (called the *meridian angle*). We now have a fully defined triangle, the sides being defined by connecting these three points and the angles determined by the resultant geometry.

By calculation, or by using specially prepared tables, or by the use of specialized software, all needed parts of the triangle can be obtained. We can then determine where in the sky the celestial body we are using *should be;* that is, what we would expect its azimuth and altitude above the horizon to be relative to our assumed position. By actually sighting that body using our sextant, we can then *compare* the *actual* altitude of the body (called the *observed altitude*) with the one we *predicted* (called the *computed altitude*). The difference between these two altitudes can then be used to refine our assumed position to something closer to the actual.

As noted earlier, this process only yields a single LOP, and it will be necessary to repeat the procedure with another celestial sight in order to obtain a celestial fix. This is a simplistic explanation of the process, and it will become much clearer as you proceed through this and the following chapters, exploring the theory of celestial navigation, methods of locating and identifying celestial bodies, the use of sextants, time, almanacs, tables, and plots.

Celestial Navigation *Practice* Summarized

2003   The actual practice of obtaining a celestial LOP takes place in six steps. (Note: The process described here assumes the navigator is using an almanac and sight reduction tables to obtain a solution. The process is somewhat different, but *essentially* the same, when using a software program or when calculating a solution directly by using mathematical formulas.) There are many components to these basic steps that will be subsequently explained, but it is useful to recall these six primary steps as you move ahead through the following chapters.

1. *Identify and locate the celestial body* or bodies you are going to use. If it is the Sun or Moon, this process is obviously a simple matter, but if it is a star or planet, you will need some assistance from special charts, almanacs, devices, or software.
2. Using a sextant and timepiece, *take your sighting* and record it.
3. *Determine the actual position of the celestial body* (or bodies) at the time of the sighting(s). This is accomplished by using an almanac or other source of ephemeral data. This information will give you the body's GP in terms of celestial coordinates that can be translated into those of a terrestrial position.
4. *Determine your assumed position.* As mentioned above, your AP is based upon your DR but will be refined for convenience when using sight reduction tables. The AP will give you an assumed latitude and longitude to work with.
5. *Enter the sight reduction tables* with the local hour angle, declination, and latitude (all deduced from the ephemeral and assumed position data) to obtain the computed altitude and azimuth.
6. Comparing the computed altitude with the observed altitude and using the azimuth, *plot an LOP.*

Sight Forms

2004   As mentioned above, there are many refinements to the six steps described (corrections for the many variables involved, adjustments for specific celestial bodies in use, etc.). As a result, the six-step process can have many substeps. Many mariners and the authors of most of the books on celestial navigation have resorted to guides called "sight forms" (one might refer to them less kindly as "cheat sheets") that ensure no steps (or substeps) are overlooked. Some mariners regard these forms as harmful because they take too much of the thinking out of the process. Others believe that a navigator is less likely to make an error with a sight form as a guide.

For many navigators, computer programs have replaced sight forms and tables as the preferred method of compiling the data used in celestial problem solving, but many continue to rely on them. In this book, while we will address the various methods in use, we will devote a fair amount of attention to sight forms as a means of stepping through the process. This is useful as a methodical way of dealing with the various components of the process and can help in understanding the algorithms used by computer programs and some of the mathematical calculations as well. Making the transition from sight form to software is a much simpler process than trying to go the other way. Using the more rigorous method of direct mathematical calculation is also enhanced by an understanding of the structured approach afforded by the sight form.

There are many different versions of sight forms available and trying to explain all of them would be impossible, but the differences in forms are not significant, and understanding the use of one easily leads to understanding others.

Computer Applications

2005   While there are a number of good computer programs available that are celestial capable, it is not practical to cover them all here. Probably the most capable (and accurate) of these programs is the STELLA program developed for Navy use by the U.S. Naval Observatory. The rather labored acronym STELLA stands for System to Estimate Latitude and Longitude Astronomically. The STELLA version in use as of this writing is Version 2.0, a Windows-compatible system that fits on one CD. This program has enjoyed wide acceptance within the Navy and serves as a good illustration of the advantages and limitations of computer technology in celestial navigation. Unfortunately, STELLA is listed as LIMDIS (limited distribution) by the Navy and is therefore not available to the general public, but because this book is used extensively by the U.S. Navy, we will focus on the STELLA program as an excellent example of how the celestial process can be made considerably simpler when using a good computer program.

Most navigators agree that the danger in using a computer program lies in the "masking" effect; that is, so much is done with internal algorithms that the user has little understanding of the *process* when relying on computers. In other words, users who "blindly" use programs such as STELLA will do fine as long as the power remains on and the computer is functioning properly, but in the event of a casualty such as a power loss, such users can no longer navigate.

The bottom line is that using STELLA and other similar programs as a form of convenience and efficiency is an intelligent thing to do and is recommended, but the true navigator, who has the ultimate safety of her or his vessel in mind, will take the time to learn the theory and the mechanics behind celestial navigation so that he or she is not merely a slave to technology.

EARTH AND THE CELESTIAL SPHERE

2006   In celestial navigation, the Earth is assumed to be a perfect sphere, located at the center of the universe. The rest of the universe is assumed to be a second sphere surrounding the Earth and concentric with it. This second sphere is called the *celestial sphere*, and all heavenly bodies are considered to be located on it. Despite the great actual differences in the distance of the various celestial bodies, it is useful and mathematically acceptable to assume the radius of the celestial sphere to be what we might call arbitrarily large. This is a bit more comforting than the definition you may sometimes encounter, which says that the radius of the celestial sphere is *infinite*. While the infinite definition assists in the understanding of some of the concepts used in celestial navigation, it introduces other mathematical and philosophical complications that are better left out of the discussion. The important thing to keep in mind is that for most celestial navigation purposes, there is no need to differentiate between the distances of objects that theoretically rest upon this celestial sphere. With a few exceptions, all of the bodies (Sun, Moon, stars, and planets) are considered to be the same (very great) distance from the Earth, resting upon this theoretical but very useful sphere.

The Earth's rotation from west to east causes the celestial sphere to appear to rotate in the opposite direction; bodies are seen to rise in the east and then set in the west. Remembering that the celestial sphere is "moving" in this manner is an important fact in celestial navigation and explains why time is such a crucial component when practicing celestial navigation. Keep in mind that the stars are all fixed on the celestial sphere and that they, therefore,

appear to move together, maintaining their same positions relative to one another. Meanwhile, the Sun, Moon, and planets are also considered to be located on the celestial sphere but are constantly changing their positions on that sphere relative to the fixed pattern of stars and relative to each other.

Once the Earth and its motions have been related to the heavens using the theoretical expedient of the celestial sphere, two systems of relational coordinates can be derived to establish the geometrical relationships that will eventually lead us to a celestial LOP and, ultimately, a fix. These coordinate systems are known as the *celestial equator* system of coordinates and the *horizon* system of coordinates, and each is similar to the terrestrial system of coordinates (latitude and longitude) in many ways, but each also has unique properties that make it useful to the theory of celestial navigation.

Celestial Equator System of Coordinates

2007   The Earth's axis is theoretically extended outward to form the north and south *celestial poles*. Similarly, the plane of Earth's equator is extended outward to form the *celestial equator* (also known as the *equinoctial*) on the sphere. Earth's meridians can also be projected out to form *celestial meridians*. The most frequently used celestial meridian is the one that passes through an observer's position when he or she is taking a sight, and often this meridian is referred to in celestial navigation as *the* celestial meridian, as though there were no others. Visualize yourself on the Earth at a specific point. Conceptualize a line of longitude passing through your position and then imagine that line projected upward onto the celestial sphere. That is your celestial meridian.

Another common use of a celestial meridian is the projection of the Greenwich (or *prime*) meridian onto the celestial sphere to become the *Greenwich celestial meridian*. This forms a useful reference meridian and its use will be explained later.

Keep in mind that these celestial meridians are constantly moving in relation to the celestial sphere, sweeping across it, as it were. Because of this motion, another form of reference used by celestial navigators is the *hour circle*. Defined as great circles on the celestial sphere that pass through both celestial poles, these circles (unlike celestial meridians) are fixed in position on the celestial sphere (but move in relation to the Earth). Each star, for example, has a specific hour circle that functions much as a line of longitude does on the surface of the Earth but locating its position on the celestial sphere instead.

On Earth, the location of any spot can be pinpointed by using the Earth's system of coordinates—latitude and longitude. A similar system of coordinates exists for the celestial sphere, by means of which a heavenly body can be located exactly on that sphere.

Both astronomers and navigators use *declination* (Dec. or d) as the virtual equivalent of latitude on the celestial sphere, measured as angular distance north or south of the equinoctial (celestial equator). Note that declination is defined on the hour circle of the celestial body and, just as is the case with latitude, a parallel of declination may be defined, and the body appears to move along that parallel as the Earth rotates.

For the longitude equivalent, astronomers and navigators differ. *Right ascension* (RA) is the coordinate of choice for astronomers and is measured eastward from the first point of Aries (see article 1910) in units of time. Occasionally, you will need to understand and use right ascension, but most of the time, navigators use *hour angle* instead, which is measured *westward* and expressed in units of *arc* rather than time. Depending upon the point of origin, the hour angle used will be called the Greenwich hour angle, local hour angle, or sidereal hour angle.

In many cases, we will want to use the *Greenwich hour angle* (GHA). As its name implies, the Greenwich celestial meridian is its point of origin (see fig. 2007a). The use of GHA relates the celestial sphere to the revolving Earth by referring all values of hour angle to the Earth's Greenwich meridian. The GHA of every celestial body is therefore constantly changing with time, as the Earth with its Greenwich meridian rotates on its axis.

Another frequently used hour angle is *local hour angle* (LHA). Measured from 0° to 360° in arc *westward* from the observer's meridian to the hour circle of a body, it is a vital part of the celestial solution as will become clear later. One way of determining the LHA of a body is to apply the observer's longitude to the value of the GHA by *adding* east longitude or *subtracting* west longitude.

Sometimes LHA is converted to *meridian angle* (t) for convenience. It is equivalent to LHA, but it is measured from 0° to 180° *east* or *west* from the observer's meridian to the hour circle of a body rather than westward through 360°. Meridian angle, like longitude, is labeled with the suffix E or W, depending on whether the direction of measurement is toward the east or west. Some navigational formulas and sight reduction tables use meridian angle instead of LHA, but the latter is most often used.

Yet another form of hour angle is the *sidereal hour angle* (SHA). Used to locate the fixed stars on the celestial sphere, it uses the hour circle of the First Point of Aries (K) as its point of origin and is measured *westward* from 0° through 360°. To tabulate the GHA of all the navigational stars in an almanac would require publishing extremely large volumes. The GHA of the first point of Aries is therefore tabulated for various increments of time, and the SHA and declination of the navigational stars are listed separately. The GHA of a star equals the GHA of Aries plus the SHA of the star (see fig. 2007b). GHAs

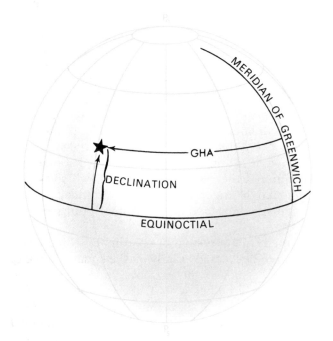

Fig. 2007a. Equinoctial coordinates.

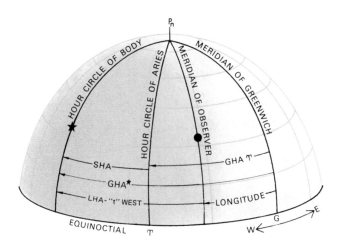

Fig. 2007b. The various hour angles.

of the Sun, Moon, and navigational planets are tabulated separately in almanacs because they constantly move through the fixed pattern of the stars on the celestial sphere and cannot be located with a simple reference to Aries as can the fixed stars.

Horizon System of Coordinates

2008   A second system of coordinates required in the practice of celestial navigation is known as the "horizon system of coordinates." It differs from the celestial system in that it is based on the position of the observer. Whereas the celestial system uses the poles and the celestial equator for its orientation, the horizon system is oriented about the observer's horizon and zenith. The observer's *celestial horizon* (see fig. 2008a) is defined as a plane passing through the center of the Earth that is perpendicular to a line drawn from the position of the observer to the Earth's center. This same line, when extended outward from the Earth's center through the observer's position, defines his or her *zenith* on the celestial sphere. The zenith is exactly 90° above the celestial horizon; it could also be defined as the point on the celestial sphere directly above the observer. Extended in the opposite direction through the Earth's center, this line marks the observer's *nadir* on the celestial sphere. The imaginary line from zenith to nadir forms the axis of the observer's celestial horizon system. The celestial horizon is parallel to the plane of the observer's visible horizon at sea. The *visible horizon* (also called the sea horizon and, sometimes, the natural horizon) is the line where, to an observer, sea and sky appear to meet. Because the radius of the Earth is effectively negligible relative to the infinity of the celestial sphere, the celestial horizon and the visible horizon may be considered coincident.

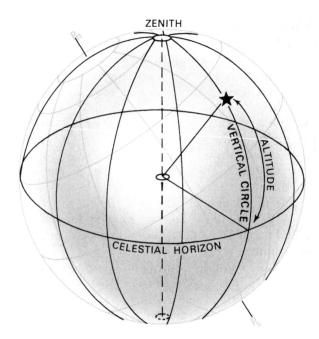

Fig. 2008b. Altitude measured above the celestial horizon.

Another useful term is *vertical circle*, which is defined as a great circle on the celestial sphere passing through the observer's zenith and nadir. When an observer measures the altitude of a body, the angle measured is along a vertical circle and is defined in reference to the celestial horizon (see fig. 2008b). A circle passing through the observer's zenith (and nadir) and the celestial poles is the *principal vertical circle* and is used as a reference as described later. Note that this circle is also the *observer's celestial meridian* in the celestial system of coordinates. Another reference you will sometimes encounter is the *prime vertical circle*, which is perpendicular to the principal vertical circle, passing through the east and west cardinal points on the horizon.

In the horizon system of coordinates (unless you happen to be located exactly on the equator), one of the celestial poles will be above your horizon and the other will be below it. These are referred to as the *elevated pole* and the *depressed pole*, respectively.

Just as a celestial body's position can be defined by coordinates on the celestial sphere (using declination and hour angle as the equivalents to latitude

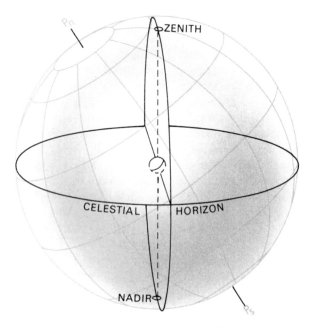

Fig. 2008a. Zenith, nadir, and celestial horizon.

and longitude) so may a body's position be defined using the horizon system. In this case, the equivalent of latitude is the body's altitude above the celestial horizon and the equivalent of longitude is the body's true azimuth. This is defined as the horizontal angle measured along the celestial horizon in a clockwise direction from the principal vertical circle to the vertical circle of the body. Because, as noted above, the principal vertical circle is also the observer's celestial meridian, this can also be thought of as simply the true bearing of a celestial body from the observer's position.

THE CELESTIAL AND NAVIGATIONAL TRIANGLES

2009   The celestial triangle (sometimes called "the astronomical triangle") is the basis for much of what we call celestial navigation. It is theoretically inscribed on the celestial sphere and its vertices are the elevated celestial pole, the observer's zenith, and the position of the celestial body. The sides of the triangle are defined by portions (arcs) of the observer's celestial meridian, the hour circle passing through the observed celestial body and the vertical circle passing through that body (see fig. 2009a). These sides are made up of what might be thought of as *complements*. The side consisting of a portion of the observer's celestial meridian can be defined as 90° minus the observer's latitude and is called *colatitude*. The side that is a portion of the hour circle of the observed body is 90° minus the declination of the body and can be thought of as *codeclination*. The side consisting of a portion of the vertical circle is 90° minus the altitude of the body and is called *coaltitude*. Note that codeclination is derived from the *celestial equator* coordinate system, coaltitude is derived from the *horizon* system of coordinates, and colatitude is actually derived from the *terrestrial* (latitude and longitude) system.

In practice, this celestial (or astronomical) triangle is modified somewhat to become what is sometimes called the *navigational triangle*. A bit of imagination is called for (though no more than when imagining a triangle etched onto the night sky) in creating this theoretical but very useful geometric form. Imagine lowering the celestial triangle down to the surface of the Earth. The celestial pole is now the actual (terrestrial) pole and is labeled either *Pn* or *Ps*, depending upon which pole (north or south) is being used. The observer's zenith becomes the observer's actual position on the Earth and is labeled *M*. And the third point of the triangle is no longer the celestial body but its geographic position

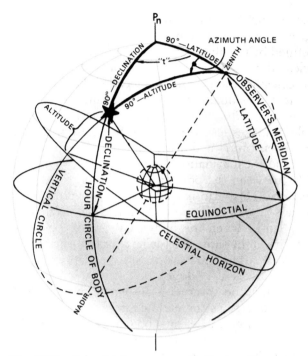

Fig. 2009a. Celestial (or astronomical) triangle.

or *GP* (as described in article 1907) and is so labeled (see fig. 2009b).

Sides of the Navigational Triangle

2010   The sides of this navigational triangle are the same as those of the celestial triangle with one

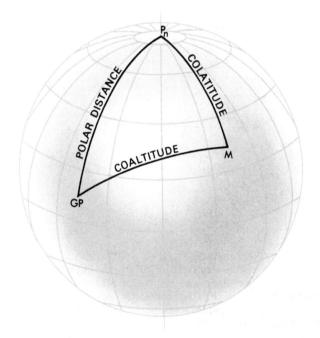

Fig. 2009b. Navigational triangle, with sides labeled.

exception. The side defined by the pole and the observer's position remains the colatitude. The side defined by the observer's position and the GP of the celestial body retains the name of its equivalent in the celestial triangle and is still called the coaltitude. (Note: Occasionally, you may see coaltitude referred to as the *zenith distance*. While this term is acceptable, it makes less sense when the celestial triangle has been brought down to the Earth's surface to become the navigational triangle.) The remaining side (between the pole and the GP) is called *polar distance*. This term is used instead of *codeclination* because the definition of 90° minus the declination only works when the body's GP and the elevated pole are in the same hemisphere (unless one considers declinations in the opposite hemisphere to be negative, as is often done).

Although the observer is always on the same side of the equator as the elevated pole, at times he or she may observe a celestial body having a GP with a latitude of *contrary name;* that is, a navigator in *north* latitude may observe a celestial body whose GP is in *south* latitude or vice versa. When this situation of opposite names occurs, the absolute value of the latitude of the GP must be *added* to 90°, rather than subtracted, to get the true value of this side of the triangle (polar distance) (see fig. 2010). The rule is very simple: when the latitudes of GP and M have the *same* name, the polar distance equals 90° *minus*

the latitude of the GP; when GP and M have *opposite* names, polar distance equals 90° *plus* the latitude of the GP (again, unless the opposite-named entity is considered negative, for subtraction of a negative quantity is numerically equivalent to adding its absolute value).

Angles of the Navigational Triangle

2011   The angle at the pole between the meridian of the observer and the meridian of the GP is called, appropriately enough, the *meridian angle*. Less appropriately, it is labeled *t*. The choice of "t" as the label comes from the meridian angle's relation to time. As discussed earlier, meridian angle is related to the local hour angle (LHA), but meridian angle is used in the creation of the navigational triangle in order to accommodate those situations when LHA is greater than 180°. As previously explained, t is measured either east or west of the observer's meridian and is so labeled.

The other important angle within the navigational triangle is the *azimuth angle*. Measured at the observer's position, this angle is derived from the observer's meridian and the vertical circle running through the position of the GP and that of the observer (see fig. 2009a). Azimuth angle is always measured from the observer's meridian toward the vertical circle joining the observer and the GP. It is labeled with the *prefix* "N" (north) or "S" (south) to agree with the name of the observer's elevated pole, and with the *suffix* "E" (east) or "W" (west) to indicate the direction of measurement. In the final plotting of position this angle is converted to *true azimuth*, which is measured clockwise from north through 360°.

Unfortunately, the abbreviations used for azimuth angle and true azimuth can be a bit confusing to the unwary navigator. There are two abbreviations in use for azimuth angle: *Az* and *Z*. The conventional abbreviation for true azimuth is *Zn*. To further confuse the issue, *Z* is also the commonly used abbreviation for zenith. In this book, *Z* for *azimuth angle* and *Zn* for *true azimuth* will be the abbreviations used. As you progress through this chapter it may help to realize that the azimuth angle and zenith are closely related and that azimuth is always measured from true north (which makes the "n" sensible). Figure 2011 illustrates the various possible relationships between azimuth angle (Z) and azimuth (Zn).

The third angle in the navigational triangle is called the *parallactic angle*. Although it is sometimes used in alternative navigational formulas, it is not used directly in the more common practices of

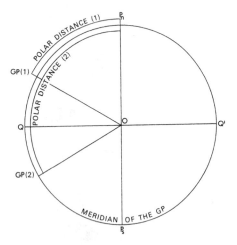

Fig. 2010. Polar distance of GP(1) = 90° *minus* its latitude. Polar distance of GP(2) = 90° *plus* its latitude, which is of opposite name. Point *O* is the center of the Earth; *QQ'* marks the Earth's equator; and *Pn* is the North Pole, which in this instance is the elevated pole for the observer, whose position though not shown is somewhere in the northern hemisphere and near enough to GP(2) for its coaltitude not to exceed 90°.

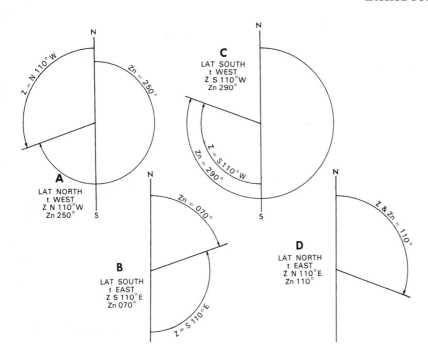

Fig. 2011. Azimuth angle (Z) and true azimuth (Zn).

celestial navigation, and need not be considered here.

Triangle Terminology

2012   It is helpful to be aware that different terms are used at different times to describe the various components of the celestial and navigational triangles. Fig. 2012 below illustrates those differences in terminology. Bear in mind that these different terms and/or their abbreviations are used in different combinations depending upon the circumstances and the reference being used; do not become too concerned about which to use when as long as you understand what part of the triangles they represent and what are their relationships to one another.

CIRCLES OF EQUAL ALTITUDE

2013   To make the transition from navigational triangle to fix, we need to consider the concept of the *circle of equal altitude*. Imagine a pole of known height erected vertically on level ground, and stayed with a number of guy wires of equal length attached to the top of the pole and stretched taut to points on the ground equidistant from the base as illustrated in figure 2013. Think of the top of the pole as a celestial body. The base of the pole can be thought of as its GP. The angle between the ground and the top of the pole is equivalent to the altitude of a celestial body as measured by a sextant.

It should be apparent that wherever these guy wires touch the ground, the angle to the top of the

Vertices		
Pole (Pn or Ps)	Observer (M)	Geographic position (GP)
Celestial pole	Zenith (Z)	Body (star, Sun, etc.)
Elevated pole	Assumed position (AP)	
Angles		
Meridian angle (t)	Azimuth angle (Zn or Az)	Parallactic angle
Sides		
Colatitude	Coaltitude	Codeclination
90°-latitude	90°-altitude	90°-declination
	Zenith distance (z)	Polar distance

Fig. 2012. The various names used for the components of the celestial/navigational triangles.

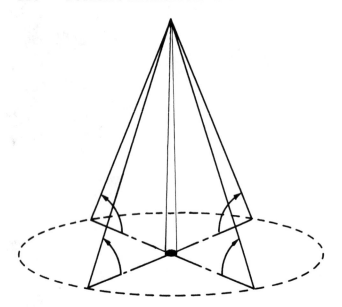

Fig. 2013. Circle of equal altitude around a pole.

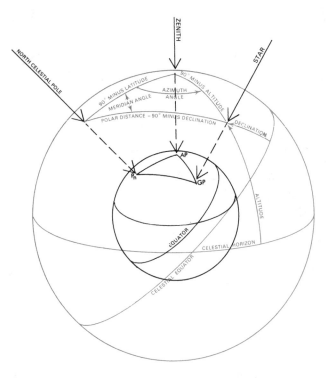

Fig. 2014a. The combined coordinate systems.

pole will be the same. Visualize a lot of these guy wires and it will be obvious that they would inscribe a circle on the ground with the base of the pole at its center.

This concept of the circle of equal altitude can be used on the surface of the Earth. By measuring the altitude of a celestial body, we know that we are somewhere on a circle of equal altitude that is inscribed on the surface of the Earth. In the case of the pole of known height, the distance from the base of the pole can be determined by plane trigonometry if the angle it subtends is known. This is *partially* analogous to determining a ship's distance from the GP of a star by observing the star's altitude. The analogy, however, is not completely valid, as the ship is on the curved surface of the Earth, rather than on a flat plane, so that *spherical* rather than *plane* trigonometry is used and there are some differences in the geometric model being used. For practical purposes, however, the analogy can be assumed and is useful in understanding how celestial navigation works.

RELATIONSHIPS AMONG COORDINATE SYSTEMS

2014   By studying figure 2009a and 2014a you can see the relationships between the celestial coordinate system and the horizon coordinate system. Note that figure 2009a is oriented with the celestial pole at the top and that you are viewing the navigational triangle from the coaltitude side (shown as 90°-latitude); figure 2014a is oriented with the observer's zenith at the top and your point of view is from the polar distance side (shown as 90°-declination).

Because the neophyte to celestial navigation is usually familiar with the earthly, or terrestrial, system of coordinates used in basic geography, the following table may be helpful by demonstrating the analogous relationships of the three coordinate systems used in nautical navigation:

Terrestrial	Celestial	Horizon
Equator	Celestial equator	Horizon
Poles	Celestial poles	Zenith; nadir
Meridians	Celestial meridians; hour circles	Vertical circles
Prime (Greenwich) Meridian	Greenwich celestial meridian; Hour Circle of Aries (Vernal Equinox)	Principal Vertical Circle
Latitude	Declination	Altitude
Longitude	Greenwich hour angle; local hour angle; sidereal hour angle; meridian angle, right ascension	Azimuth; azimuth angle

The polar distance side of the triangle is a portion of an hour circle and the colatitude side is a portion of a celestial meridian. You will remember that celestial meridians remain fixed in relation to the Earth and therefore move across the celestial sphere (as the Earth rotates), while hour circles remain fixed on the celestial sphere and therefore move in relation to the Earth. What this continuous relative movement means is that the navigational triangle is a very transient thing—that when we are referring to the parts of a navigational triangle, they are only relevant for an instant in time (the exact instant that you have taken your observation). A second later, the movement of the Earth in relation to the celestial sphere has redefined the navigational triangle.

The coaltitude side of the triangle is an arc of a vertical circle, and perhaps the most important key to understanding the relationship between the coordinate systems is to realize that when making a celestial observation, *the radius of the circle of equal altitude is equal to the coaltitude of the navigational triangle.* If you think about it for a moment, this will make sense. The altitude of a celestial body is measured from your position to the celestial body. The geographical distance between your position and the GP of the body is defined by the radius of the circle of equal altitude, as explained above. The coaltitude side of the navigational triangle is also defined as connecting the observer's position (M) with the GP of the body. This relationship is demonstrated in figures 2014b and 2014c.

This relationship can be taken a step further if you recall that coaltitude is also defined as 90°

minus the altitude. You will remember from an earlier chapter that there is a convenient relationship between measurements of arc and distance on the surface of the Earth, namely, that 1 minute of arc equals 1 nautical mile. Therefore, the coaltitude (90° minus the altitude) can be converted to nautical miles and that distance is the geographical length of the radius of the circle of equal altitude.

THE CELESTIAL LOP

2015   If you sighted a star directly overhead (at your zenith), its altitude would be 90°. Remembering that 1 minute of arc equals 1 nautical mile, if you moved in any direction 1 nautical mile, the altitude of the star would then be 89° 59′. If you continued to move out from under the star until the altitude measured 89° 00′, you would have traveled a distance of 60 nautical miles. By definition then, the radius of the circle of equal altitude would be 60 nautical miles and so would the length of the coaltitude side of the navigational triangle. Therefore, as the altitude of a celestial body decreases, the distance of the observer from the body's GP increases. This inverse relationship means that the length of the radius of the circle of equal altitude can get quite large (3,300 nautical miles for a body with an altitude of 35° for example). Because these circles are too large to fit on a chart of practical scale, the entire circle is seldom, if ever, drawn on the plotting chart. In practice, only a very short segment of its arc, in the vicinity of the DR position, is actually needed. Further, the usually large radius of

Fig. 2014b. Coaltitude = 90° minus altitude.

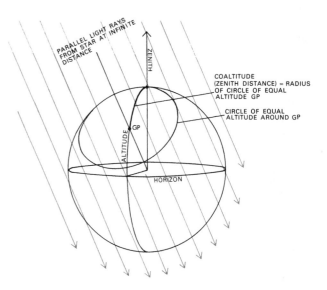

Fig. 2014c. Coaltitude equals the radius of the circle of equal altitude.

the circle means that this short curved arc can, for practical purposes, be represented as a straight line segment on your chart without causing significant distortion. This short curved arc of a circle of equal altitude is a celestial line of position (LOP).

From this description we can see that the LOP we are seeking is not a part of the navigational triangle, but it is defined by it. A celestial LOP is actually a line segment perpendicular to the coaltitude side of the navigational triangle and, therefore, also perpendicular to the azimuth of the celestial body. Its distance from the GP of the body being observed is defined by the length of the coaltitude.

Another way of thinking about the celestial LOP is that it is analogous to the LOP we get when we take a radar range to an object on shore during coastal piloting. A radar range is inscribed as a partial arc of a circle on your chart, using the object on shore as the center of the circle and the size of the circle being defined by the range as determined by the radar. We only draw part of the range circle in the vicinity of our DR and we know that our vessel lies somewhere on that arc. With the celestial LOP, the center of the circle is the GP of the celestial body being observed and the distance (radius of the circle of equal altitude) is defined by the coaltitude as calculated using the geometry of the navigational triangle. As already mentioned, the great distances involved usually mean that the celestial LOP is drawn as a straight line rather than as an arc.

Assumed Position

2016   It is tempting at this point to think we have derived all we need to know to determine a celestial fix, but remember that one important component of the celestial triangle is based not on fact but on *assumption*. One point defining the navigational triangle is the observer's position. As explained earlier, if we knew the exact location of that point, there would be no need to bother with celestial navigation. But by assuming our location to be at or near our DR position, we can accurately compute a navigational triangle for that position. Geometry being the unyielding discipline that it is, that computed navigational triangle demands a specific altitude (remember the relationship between the circle of equal altitude and the coaltitude side of the triangle) for the celestial body being used. Once we compare the computed altitude with the actual one we observed, unless we were very lucky and happened to be exactly at our assumed position, there will be a difference. Using techniques explained below, we can then use that difference to plot our LOP.

Computing the Triangle

2017   In order to have a computed altitude that we can use to compare to our actual, we must have some means of solving the navigational triangle. As discussed earlier, the navigational triangle can be easily solved by entering the right values into a specially designed computer software program. It can also be computed directly using mathematical formulas and either trigonometric tables or a calculator with those values built in. A compromise method is to solve the triangle by using the sight reduction tables. In all cases, the object is to solve the navigational triangle so that we know the coaltitude side and azimuth angle. The former tells us how far away the GP would be if our assumed position were correct and the latter can be used to tell us the direction of the GP from our position.

Determining Your Position

2018   Solving the navigational triangle as described above yields an altitude that is known as the *computed altitude* and is identified by the abbreviation *Hc*. We then compare that computed altitude with the one actually sighted through the sextant (after certain corrections have been applied as explained in chapter 22). This is called the *observed altitude* and is abbreviated as *Ho*. The difference between Hc and Ho is known as the *altitude intercept* (a) and represents the difference in length of the two coaltitudes (which are also the radii of the *computed* and *observed* circles of equal altitude).

As previously demonstrated, a lesser altitude angle places the circle of equal altitude, and therefore the resulting LOP, farther away from the GP of the body than does a larger altitude. Accordingly, if Hc (the computed altitude) for the assumed position is greater than Ho (the observed altitude), the actual position from which the observation was made would be farther from the GP of the body than is the assumed position. Similarly, if Ho is the greater, the actual position would be nearer the GP. The intercept should always be labeled accordingly, using the suffix "T" (toward) or "A" (away), to make it clear which direction it is to be measured.

Solving the navigational triangle also yields an azimuth angle (Z). By converting Z to a true azimuth measured from north (Zn), you can conveniently plot on your chart the direction of the GP from the AP. Using the AP as a reference point, this azimuth line is drawn through it indicating the direction of the GP (even though that point is, in most cases, off the area of the chart being used). Since (a) is the difference in miles between the

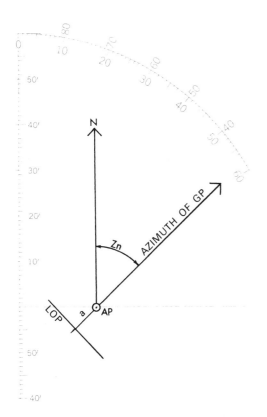

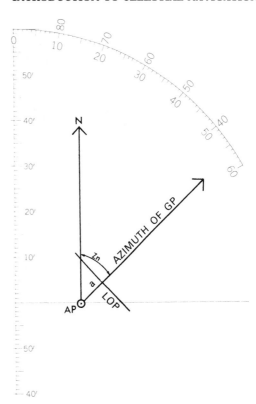

Fig. 2018. The line of position (LOP) plotted. Altitude intercept is "a." If Hc is *greater* than Ho, "a" is *away* from the GP (*left*). If Hc is *less* than Ho, "a" is *toward* the GP (*right*).

circles of equal altitude passing through the actual and assumed positions, the navigator can plot either *toward* or *away* for the value of (a) along this azimuth line as appropriate. From the description given in the preceding paragraph of how the intercept is determined to be toward or away, the phrase "Computed Greater Away" can be derived. A useful "memory aid" for this is "*Coast Guard Academy.*" Another frequently used memory aid is the acronym "HoMoTo" for "*Ho More Toward.*" The point on the azimuth line represented by marking off the intercept (a) is a point on the observer's circle of equal altitude. The celestial line of position (LOP) is then drawn through this point *perpendicular* to the azimuth line as shown in figure 2018 to represent an arc of the circle of equal altitude corresponding to the *observed* altitude. This is the LOP we have been seeking.

As with any LOP, a single celestial LOP does not produce an absolute position or fix but merely a line somewhere on which the observer is located (or nearly so). At least two LOPs are therefore required to obtain a fix. Three LOPs from different bodies will give a fix with a greater degree of confidence, and four or five are not too many. The position of the vessel is determined by the intersection of the LOPs. In actual practice, three or more LOPs will rarely intersect at a point, but will more often form a small polygon instead, often popularly referred to as a "cocked hat." It is normally assumed that the actual position of the ship is at this figure's center, which can, for practical purposes, be estimated by eye.

SUMMARY

2019 A bare-bones description of the elementary celestial navigation process can be briefly summarized as follows: Using almanac data along with some assumed data, construct and solve a theoretical spherical triangle in order to find one of its sides (coaltitude) and one of its angles (azimuth angle). By comparing one of the results (computed altitude) to an actual measured result (corrected sextant altitude), determine the altitude difference (intercept) and use it as a distance plotted from the assumed position along the azimuth line, toward or away from (as the case may be) the geographical position of the celestial body. At the point so located on the azimuth line, construct the celestial LOP as a short straight line segment at right angles to the azimuth.

Things helpful to remember are that the coaltitude and circle of equal altitude are equivalent, that Hc is based upon an assumption while Ho is an actual observation, that Z must be converted to Zn for convenient plotting, and that the resulting LOP is perpendicular to the coaltitude and must be plotted either toward or away from the observed body's GP.

In the chapters that follow, the steps and procedures introduced here will be explained in more detail. If you refer back to the section titled "Celestial Navigation *Practice* Summarized," you will see that the following chapters are presented in the same order as the six steps listed there. Chapter 21 explains how celestial bodies are identified and located. The next two chapters (22 and 23) describe the use of the sextant and give you a thorough understanding of time and how it relates to celestial navigation. Chapter 24 describes how to use almanacs and other sources of ephemeral data to locate the GPs of celestial bodies at the precise moment of observation. Chapter 25 then tells you how to use mathematical calculations, sight reduction tables, or computer software to complete the solutions to your navigational triangles, and chapter 26 describes the plotting procedures used in celestial navigation. Chapter 27 ties all of these elements together in completing the standard celestial solution. Chapters 28 and 29 address some of the specific applications of celestial navigation. Finally, chapter 30 discusses the actual practice of celestial navigation.

Chapter 21

Identification of Celestial Bodies

Before you can start a series of observations of celestial bodies, you must first predict which ones will be available, and which will yield the better lines of position. With this information, you must next be able to identify these bodies in the sky. The Sun and the Moon obviously present no problem, but distinguishing stars among the many in the night sky can be challenging. Planets—the name is derived from "wanderer"—change their position in the sky and can present difficulties of identification.

The usual procedure in identifying stars and planets is to select, in advance of twilight, a number of these bodies, so located that lines of position obtained from them will result in a good fix. Only occasionally is an unknown body observed and identified afterward. The approximate altitudes and azimuths of these bodies are predetermined so that they may be located in the night sky.

With experience, a navigator gains the ability to locate the most used navigational stars without the aid of mechanical or electronic devices. Many, but far from all, navigational stars can be quickly identified from the constellations of which they are a part, and apparent differences in brightness, and occasionally in color, can sometimes be used to pick out the desired body. But you will probably need help locating lesser-known stars. For the benefit of less-experienced navigators, this chapter will consider the use of such devices and the various "star charts" that are available from various sources such as the *Nautical Almanac* and the *Air Almanac*.

As you go through this chapter, you will encounter the names of many stars and constellations. For convenience, two useful tables from *Bowditch*'s *American Practical Navigator* are included as Appendix E. Refer to these for additional information, including pronunciations.

THE STAR FINDER AND IDENTIFIER 2102-D

2101 The star finder most used by navigators is generally referred to as "2102-D"; this was its "H.O." number when it was produced by the Navy Hydrographic Office. This Navy star finder is no longer available to nongovernment personnel, but identical units can be obtained from civilian sources and some of them use the same number for identification. The device is a development from the original Rude Starfinder created by Capt. G. T. Rude, USC&GS, and it is still referred to by many by its original name.

The 2102-D Star Finder and Identifier is designed to permit a user to determine the approximate altitude and azimuth of those of the fifty-seven "selected navigational stars" listed on the daily pages of the *Nautical* and *Air Almanac*s (see chapter 24) that are above the celestial horizon at a given place and time. With some minor additional effort, it can also be set up to indicate the positions of the navigational planets and other stars of interest (and even the Sun and/or Moon if desired, although this is rarely needed). The Star Finder can also be used in the reverse operation: identification of an unknown body whose altitude and azimuth have been measured.

The Star Finder consists of a circular *base* and ten circular *templates*, all contained in a flexible slipcase, together with a sheet of instructions. The base (see fig. 2101a) is a white opaque plastic disc, with a

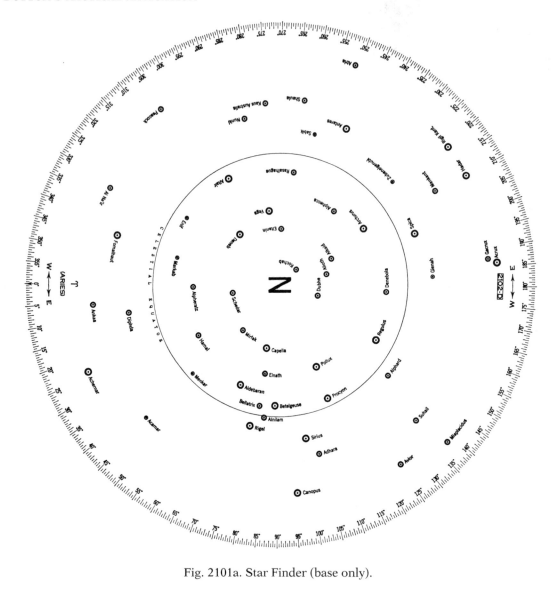

Fig. 2101a. Star Finder (base only).

small pin at its center. On one side, the north celestial pole is shown at the center; on the opposite side the south celestial pole is at the center. On both sides the circumference is graduated in half degrees of LHA ♈, and reverse-labeled toward the east, at 5° intervals. All fifty-seven stars are shown on each side of the base on a polar azimuthal equidistant projection extending toward the opposite pole. Each star is named, and the approximate magnitude is indicated by a symbol—a large, heavy-ringed dot for first magnitude; a smaller, heavy-ringed dot for second magnitude; and a yet smaller and thinner ring for third magnitude. The celestial equator is shown as a circle about half the diameter of the base. Because of the distortion caused by the projection, the relative positions of the stars shown on the base do *not* correspond to their apparent positions in the

sky, and the device *cannot* be compared directly with the heavens.

The ten circular templates are made of transparent plastic. Nine of these are printed with blue ink and are designed for apparent altitude and azimuth determinations, while the tenth, printed in *red* ink, is intended for the plotting of bodies other than the fifty-seven selected stars on the base plate.

There is one blue template for every 10° of latitude between 5° and 85°. One side of each template is for use in north latitudes and the other side for south latitudes. Each of these "latitude" templates is printed with a set of oval blue altitude curves at 5° intervals from 0° to 80°, with the outermost curve representing the observer's celestial horizon. Also included is a set of curved azimuth lines, also at 5° intervals, ranging from 0° to 360°. In figure

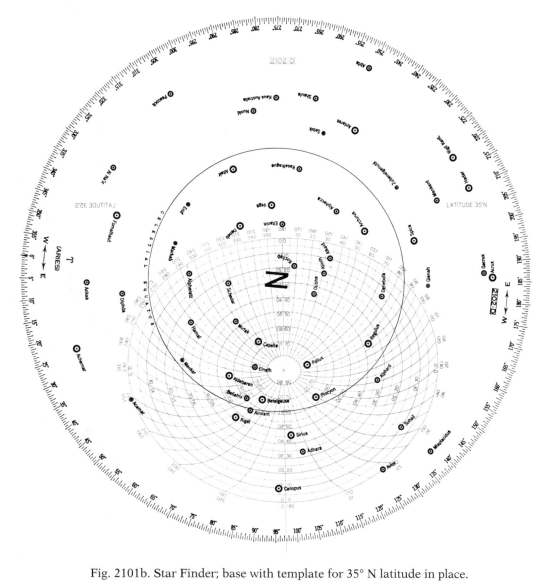

Fig. 2101b. Star Finder; base with template for 35° N latitude in place.

2101b the blue template for latitude 35° has been attached to the north side of the Star Finder base. Note that the blue "LATITUDE 35°N" can be read on the upper right and that "LATITUDE 35°S" reads *backward* on the upper left of the template. This labeling tells you that the template has been properly attached. If you were operating in the Southern Hemisphere, you would use the other sides of the template and baseplate (with a large "S" in the baseplate center instead of the "N" you see in figure 2101b).

The red template is provided for plotting the planets and other bodies not included among the fifty-seven stars printed on the base. It is noticeably different from the other templates, with concentric circles representing declination, and straight radial lines representing meridians (see fig. 2101c).

Using the Star Finder to Determine Altitude and Azimuth of a Star

2102 The Star Finder is most convenient for determining which of the fifty-seven selected stars will be favorably suited for observation at twilight and what will be their approximate altitudes and azimuths. First, the LHA of ♈ must be determined for the mid-time of the period during which observations are to be made. LHA ♈ equals GHA ♈ (obtained from an almanac) minus west longitude, or plus east longitude. For morning sights, the beginning of civil twilight (see chapter 24) or a time shortly thereafter is often used. For the evening, the time would be based on the ending of civil twilight. The most suitable time to select depends largely on the ability of the observer and the quality of the sextant to be used, and can best

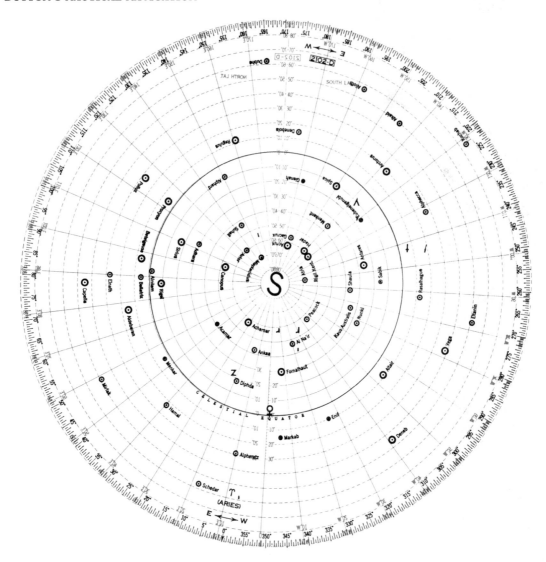

Fig. 2101c. Star Finder; base with red plotting template in place (shown here in blue).

be determined by experience. Arriving early for taking sights at morning twilight helps in identifying stars by their constellations.

The following examples illustrate the use of the Star Finder.

Example: Your DR position at the time of the ending of civil twilight will be Lat. 37° 14.8′ N, Long. 144° 25.6′ E. From the *Nautical Almanac*, you determine the GHA of Aries to be 312° 46.8′ at that time.

Required: The approximate altitudes and azimuths of all first-magnitude stars above the horizon at that time, using the Star Finder.

Solution: First, determine LHA by adding the longitude (since it is *east*); in this case, 312° 46.8′ + 144° 25.6′ = 457° 12.4′ – 360° = 97° 12.4′. Next, select the blue-ink template for the latitude closest to the DR latitude. Place this on the star base so that the labels

for both correspond to the name of the DR latitude. In this case, the template for latitude 35° N is selected and placed over the side of the star base that has the letter *N* at the center, as shown. Orient the template so that the arrow extending from the 0°–180° azimuth line points to the value on the base plate of LHA ♈ for the time desired; in this case, the arrow is aligned, as closely as possible by eye, with 97.2° (see fig. 2101b).

Finally, note the approximate altitudes and azimuths of the desired celestial bodies. The approximate altitudes and azimuths of the first-magnitude stars are tabulated below, in order of increasing azimuth.

In this instance, there are a considerable number of first-magnitude stars above the horizon, but they are not evenly distributed in azimuth. At sea, you

Body	Ha	Zn
Regulus	38°	098°
Pollux	76°	106°
Procyon	58°	149°
Sirius	39°	177°
Canopus	2°	181°
Betelgeuse	60°	201°
Rigel	42°	207°
Aldebaran	56°	241°
Capella	70°	305°

would include some tabulated stars of lesser magnitude to your north, such as Dubhe, Kochab, and so on. You would probably not observe Canopus, except from necessity, due to its low altitude. Pollux and Capella might be difficult to observe, both being very high in altitude; Regulus and Mirfak would be easier to observe and give equivalent coverage in azimuth.

It is always wise to list more stars than you actually expect to observe, as some may be obscured by clouds. The stars listed for observation should not be limited to those of the first magnitude; all the stars shown on the Star Finder are readily visible in clear weather. The stars should be selected not only for good distribution in azimuth, but also on the basis of altitude. The most convenient altitude band for observation lies roughly between 15° and 60°, but it is preferable to obtain observations considerably lower or higher than these approximate limits, rather than to have poor distribution in azimuth.

Using the Star Finder with Planets

2103   The Star Finder may be used in the same manner to predict the position in the heavens of the planets. To accomplish that, you must manually plot them on your star base. This plotting is necessary because the planets are constantly moving in relation to the stars and therefore cannot be fixed on the star base by the manufacturer as are the stars. You may want to plot the planets on your base even if you do not plan to take sightings on them for navigational purposes because you may confuse them with a star if you are not aware of their presence.

While the planets do move in position relative to the stars, they do not change their relative positions rapidly, so their plotted positions will be satisfactory for several days. Thus, for a vessel departing on a two-week passage, the positions of the planets could be plotted on the star base for a date approximately one week after departure.

To plot the position of a planet on the star base, you must first obtain its GHA and declination from an almanac. The Star Finder is designed such that you must convert the GHA to the angular equivalent of right ascension (RA). This conversion sounds more complicated than it is and is accomplished in one of two ways. First, by simply subtracting the GHA of the planet from the GHA of ♈ for the time of observation (adding 360° if necessary), you can ascertain the appropriate RA figure; both of the needed GHAs (Aries and the planet) can be found by turning to the appropriate page of either the *Nautical Almanac* or the *Air Almanac*. The alternative method is available when you have a *Nautical Almanac*. Unlike the *Air Almanac*, the *Nautical Almanac* also includes the SHA of each of the planets for a three day period that yields an average RA by subtracting it from 360.

For example, suppose you have been navigating in waters south of the equator for several days and you have noted that Venus has been visible. You decide to plot it on your Star Finder to confirm that what you are seeing is Venus and to ensure that you do not confuse it with any of the stars you are planning to sight. From the *Nautical Almanac*, for a time near the middle of the anticipated observation period, you obtain the following data:

GHA ♈	339° 07.9′
GHA Venus	346° 15.0′
Dec. of Venus	S2° 10.9′

Using that information, you would then subtract the GHA of Venus from that of Aries (adding 360 since the GHA of Venus is larger than GHA ♈) to obtain an SHA for Venus of 352° 52.9′ or about 352.9° that you would then use along with Venus's declination to properly place Venus on your Star Finder. (Alternatively, from the *Nautical Almanac*, you could have directly read the SHA of Venus tabulated at the bottom of the left-hand page as a usable average for a three-day period and subtracted this value from 360°; this procedure is accurate enough for Star Finder use.)

To do the actual plotting, the red plotting template is placed, south latitude side up, on the south (S) side of the star base as indicated in figure 2101c. On the template, a radial line is printed to represent every 10° of meridian angle, and a concentric circle is printed for every 10° of declination, with the median circle being the celestial equator. When in place on the base plate, this median circle should be concurrent with the celestial equator circle on the base plate. The solid circles within the celestial equator circle then represent declination of the same name (north or south) as the base plate, while the dashed circles outside the equator represent declinations of contrary name.

The index arrow is now aligned with 352.9°. The position of Venus is then plotted on the base by marking with a pencil through the cut-out slot at the proper point on the declination scale. In this case, south declination is on the side of the circle for the celestial equator toward the S pole at the center of the base; if the declination of the body had been of the *contrary* name to the name of the center of the base plate, it would have been plotted on the side of the equatorial circle *away* from the center. The proper symbol for Venus, ♀, is drawn in on the base after the template is removed. The date for this plot should be marked in some clear area of the base as a guide to indicate when the position will need to be recalculated and replotted.

Similar procedures can be followed to plot an unlisted star, the Moon, or the Sun. A star's plot will remain unchanged for a number of years, but any plot of the Moon or Sun must be corrected to a specific time of use.

Identifying Unknown Celestial Bodies

2104   At times, you may obtain an observation of an unknown body. In such a case, if both its altitude and azimuth are noted, as well as the time of the observation, it may be identified by means of the Star Finder.

If the star is one of those shown on the base plate of the Star Finder, the identification is quite simple. The index arrow of the blue template is aligned to the appropriate LHA ♈ for the time of the observation. The point of intersection of the altitude and azimuth curve of the body is then located on the blue template, and the body listed on the star base at or quite near this position can usually be assumed to be the one observed.

The observed body may be a planet rather than a star. If you had plotted the visible planets in advance as outlined above, it will be clear which planet you have sighted.

If no star or planet appears at or near that point, the red template can be used to determine the approximate Dec. and SHA of the star. These two arguments can then be used with the list of stars in the *Almanac* for proper identification.

To determine the SHA and Dec. of the "mystery" body, the red template is placed over the appropriate blue template on the base with all three properly aligned for the appropriate latitude. The index arrows of the two templates are then lined up with the value of LHA ♈ on the base, and you may then use the red template to read off the approximate declination and meridian angle of the location. Coupling the meridian angle with your longitude at the time of the observation, the approximate GHA of the body may be computed; using the computed GHA and the determined declination, you may then scan the appropriate page of the *Nautical Almanac* to see if any of the visible planets match these figures. If that yields nothing, you may then compute the SHA and search the list of additional stars near the back of the *Nautical Almanac* for a match. This process can be significantly streamlined by the use of a computer star finder program.

Improving Accuracy of the Star Finder

2105   If your latitude is notably different from that which is provided for by the various templates—say your latitude is close to 40°, which is not very close to either 35° or 45°—you can improve the accuracy of the Star Finder by removing the template from the pin and adjusting it appropriately.

Notice that the pin on the base fits the center hole of the blue template where the 0–180 line intersects the altitude oval that matches the value of the latitude for that template; for example, on the blue template for 35° latitude, the pin comes through the template at the 35° altitude line. By removing the template and realigning it so that the appropriate latitude is over the pin (a small adjustment to be sure), your readings will improve. In most cases, the difference is not great, but this technique does improve the accuracy of your readings if carefully done; do take care not to damage the template by denting or piercing it over the pin.

STAR IDENTIFICATION BY PUB. NO. 229

2106   Although no formal star identification tables are included in NIMA Pub. No. 229, *Sight Reduction Tables for Marine Navigation*, a simple approach to star identification is to scan the pages for the applicable latitude having a combination of arguments that give altitude and azimuth angle for an unidentified body. Thus the approximate declination and LHA of the body are determined directly. The star's SHA is found from SHA star = LHA star – LHA ♈. With declination and SHA roughly known, the *Air* or *Nautical Almanac* is consulted for identification and exact values. Each volume of Pub. No. 229 describes this method, and an alternative, in greater detail.

STAR CHARTS AND SKY DIAGRAMS

2107   In addition to the 2102-D Star Finder and Identifier, the identification of celestial bodies may be ascertained pictorially; remember that the Star Finder does *not* give a visualization of the heavens. *Star charts* come much closer to doing so. They are photograph-like representations of the night sky at certain times of the year. They are representations of the celestial sphere, or of a part of it, on a flat surface. On most star charts, north is at the top and south at the bottom, but east is at the *left,* and west at the *right;* this is the reverse of a terrestrial chart presentation. If the chart is held overhead, and the N-S axis is properly oriented, this presentation approximates the appearance of the heavens. Some star charts are polar projections; these show the star groups around the pole and are especially helpful in visualizing the movement and relationship of circumpolar stars. Star charts are more often used for *learning* the identification of stars than in the normal practice of actually taking navigational sightings at sea.

Sky diagrams are drawings of the heavens as they would be seen from certain locations at various times. Although intended for the same purpose, there are differences in design and use.

Nautical Almanac Star Charts

2108 The *Nautical Almanac* star charts consist of four charts; one polar projection for each hemisphere, covering declinations 10° through 90°, of the same name, and two rectangular projections covering Dec. 30° N to 30° S, around the celestial sphere (see fig. 2108).

A planetary diagram giving LMT of meridian passage of the planets is also provided in the *Nautical Almanac* shortly before the daily pages. By means of this diagram, the approximate positions of the planets relative to the Sun, and to each other, may be determined. The planet Mercury, usually not of much use in navigation, is included in this diagram, because being aware of its relatively rare appearances helps avoid mistaking Mercury for another body.

Air Almanac Star Charts

2109 A fold-in, white-on-black star chart is located in the back of the *Air Almanac*. It presents the entire celestial sphere on a rectangular projection, the top and bottom edges representing the north and south celestial poles, respectively. This projection causes great distortion in the relative positions of stars near the poles, but provides a means of determining the order of appearance of the stars and constellations as they move across the heavens.

Air Almanac Sky Diagrams

2110 The *Air Almanac* also contains a series of sky diagrams that show the appearance of the sky in various latitudes at different times of the day. Although their small scale limits their use, they are helpful in selecting the most useful stars and planets for navigation, and for identifying prominent bodies when sighted. For each month, there is a series of diagrams for different latitudes (at intervals from 70° N to 30° S) at two-hour intervals during the entire day. The diagrams for a given latitude are in a horizontal row and show the changes as the day progresses. The appearance of the sky for different latitudes and different times is shown on a pair of facing pages; thus, the appearance of the sky for an intermediate latitude and/or time is easily visualized. A separate set of diagrams is included for the north polar region.

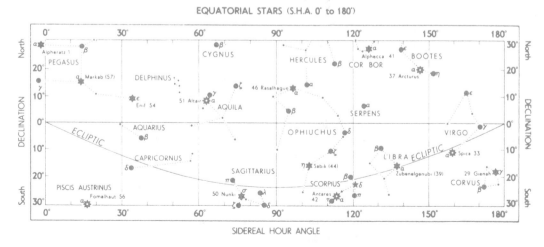

Fig. 2108. Star chart from the *Nautical Almanac.*

Because they are prepared for each month, the sky diagrams of the *Air Almanac* have an advantage over sky charts, making them usable without reference to tables or calculations. A diagram for a specific month also allows the inclusion of the planets and the Moon, in addition to the fifty-seven selected navigational stars and Polaris. The north and south celestial poles are also shown as NP and SP where appropriate. Stars are shown by a symbol indicating their magnitude and a number for identification; planets are identified by a single-letter abbreviation, and the Sun by its symbol. The position of the Moon is shown separately for each day by a small circle around figures representing the day of the month.

The positions of the stars and planets in each diagram are indicated for the fifteenth of the month and will usually serve for the entire month. If it is desired to allow for the motion of the stars during the month, it is necessary only to remember that a given configuration will occur at the beginning of each month one hour later than the time indicated, and at the end of the month one hour earlier. In those months during which Venus moves considerably with respect to the stars, the positions for the first and last of the month are shown; the position toward the west is for the first of the month.

It must be remembered that the sky diagrams of the *Air Almanac* are to be used flat on the chart table and that they show bearings as they appear on the navigator's chart, east to the right. The star chart and the planet location diagram, on the other hand, are both designed to be held over the head for comparison with the sky, and on them east is to the left.

A BRIEF GUIDE TO THE NIGHT SKY

2111   Six numbered star charts are included in this chapter. They show all the brighter stars, necessarily with some repetition; the various constellations are described in addition to navigational stars. There are two charts of the polar skies usable all year long, plus four lower-latitude charts, one for each season of the year. The two charts of the polar regions are azimuthal equidistant polar projections; the others are transverse Mercator projections.

To use a polar chart, face the elevated pole and hold the correct chart with the name of the month on top (not directly overhead but in the general direction of the pole). It will then be correctly oriented for that month for 2200 Local Mean Time (LMT) (see article 2307). For each hour that the LMT differs from 2200, rotate the chart one hour, as shown by the radial lines. These are labeled for LHA Υ in *time units*, in which case it is called *local sidereal time* (LST), and for sidereal hour angle (SHA) in degrees. The sidereal time indicates the direction of rotation, as earlier sidereal times occur at earlier solar times. The region about the *elevated* pole will be the only polar region visible.

To use one of the transverse Mercator star charts, hold it overhead with the top of the page toward north. The left edge will then be east, the right edge west, and the bottom south. The numbers along the central hour circle indicate declination and can be used to orient for latitude. The charts are made for LMT 2200 on the dates specified. For each half month later, subtract one hour to determine the time at which the heavens appear as depicted in the chart; for each half month earlier, add one hour to LMT 2200. The numbers below the celestial equator line indicate local sidereal time; those above indicate sidereal hour angle. If the LMT of observation is not 2200, these can be used to determine which hour circle coincides with the celestial meridian. The lighter broken lines connect stars of some of the more easily distinguishable constellations. The heavier broken lines are shown to aid in the identification of stars of different constellations that have an especially useful spatial relationship to each other.

It should be kept in mind that the apparent positions of the stars are constantly changing because of the motions of the Earth. If the observer changes his or her position on the Earth, a further change in the apparent positions of the stars will result. Remember, too, that the limits of the transverse Mercator charts represent the approximate limits of observation only at the equator. Observers elsewhere will see beyond their elevated pole to a portion of the opposing seasonal chart, and an equal amount of the opposite polar region shown on the chart in use will actually be hidden from view.

The approximate appearance of the heavens at any given time can be determined by obtaining LHA (from the observer's longitude and the GHA Υ, which is tabulated in the almanacs) and converting it to time units. The resulting local sidereal time (LST) is then found on the star charts. The celestial meridian on the transverse Mercator chart that is labeled with that time is the one that is approximately overhead. The same celestial meridian on the polar charts, labeled in the same way, is the one that is *up*. Thus, if LHA Υ is 225°, LST is 15^h. This appears on the transverse Mercator charts of both figures 2116 and 2120. The stars to the east of the celestial meridian at this time appear in figure 2120 (in the direction of increasing LST and increasing SHA). By orienting each polar chart so that the celestial meridian labeled 15^h is up, the stars toward and beyond each celestial pole can be seen. You can view only half of the celestial sphere at a given time, of course, and the stars actually visible depend upon your latitude.

THE NORTH POLAR SKY

2112 In the north polar sky (Star Chart 1, fig. 2112) nearly everyone is familiar with the *Big Dipper*, the popular name for the constellation *Ursa Major* (the big bear). This is composed of seven stars in the shape of a dipper, with the open part toward the north celestial pole. For observers in the United States, most of the dipper is circumpolar and is therefore visible the year around. Dubhe, Alioth, and Alkaid are the stars of this constellation most used by navigators. Dubhe and Merak, forming part of the bowl of the dipper, are called the pointers, for if the line connecting them is extended northward, it passes very near Polaris, less than one degree from the north celestial pole. If the line is extended across the pole, it leads very near to Caph in *Cassiopeia*, which is very near the hour circle for the vernal equinox (First Point of Aries). These stars point straight *down* to Polaris in the evening sky of mid-April. By the middle of July they are to the left

of Polaris. In mid-October they are directly below the pole, and three months later, in the middle of January, they are to the right.

Ursa Minor (Little Dipper)

2113 Polaris is part of the *Little Dipper*, as the constellation *Ursa Minor* (the little bear) is popularly known; this star is not conspicuous until the sky has become quite dark. Only Polaris at one end and Kochab at the other, both second-magnitude stars, are used by the navigator. The *Little Dipper* is roughly parallel to the *Big Dipper*, but upside down with respect to it. In the autumn, the *Big Dipper* is under the *Little Dipper*, and there is a folktale that liquid spilling out of the little one will be caught by the big one. The handles of the two dippers curve in opposite directions relative to their bowls.

Cassiopeia

2114 Across the pole from the handle of the *Big Dipper*, and approximately the same distance from Polaris, will be found the constellation *Cassiopeia* (the queen), also known as *Cassiopeia's Chair*. The principal stars of this constellation form a well-defined *W* or *M*, depending on their position with

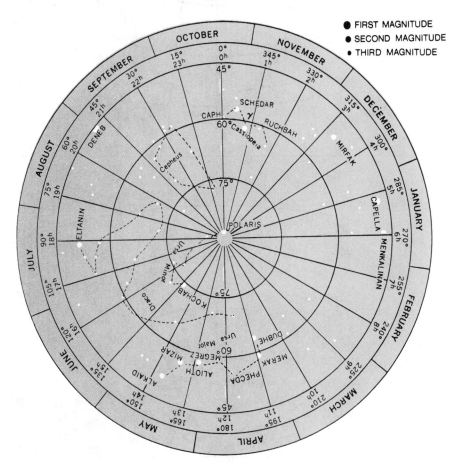

- ● FIRST MAGNITUDE
- ● SECOND MAGNITUDE
- • THIRD MAGNITUDE

Fig. 2112. Star Chart 1, the north polar region. Hold the chart toward the north at 2200 LMT with the name of the current month at the top.

respect to the pole. Schedar, the second star from the right when the figure appears as a *W,* is a second-magnitude star sometimes used by navigators. Second-magnitude Caph, the right-hand star when the figure appears as a *W,* is of interest because it is situated close to the hour circle of the vernal equinox.

Draco

2115   The constellation *Draco* (the dragon) is about halfway from *Cassiopeia* to the *Big Dipper* in a westerly direction, but its navigational star, Eltanin, probably is easier to identify by following the western arm of the *Northern Cross* as described in the *Scorpio* group.

THE SPRING SKY

2116   In the spring sky (Star Chart 2, fig. 2116) the *Big Dipper* is above the pole, high in the sky, and serves to point out several excellent navigational stars. Starting at the bowl, follow the curvature of the handle. If the curved arc is continued, it leads first to Arcturus, the only navigational star in *Boötes* (the herdsman) and then to Spica in *Virgo* (the virgin), both first-magnitude stars much used by the navigator.

Leo

2117   A line northward through the pointers of the *Big Dipper* leads to Polaris. If this line is fol-

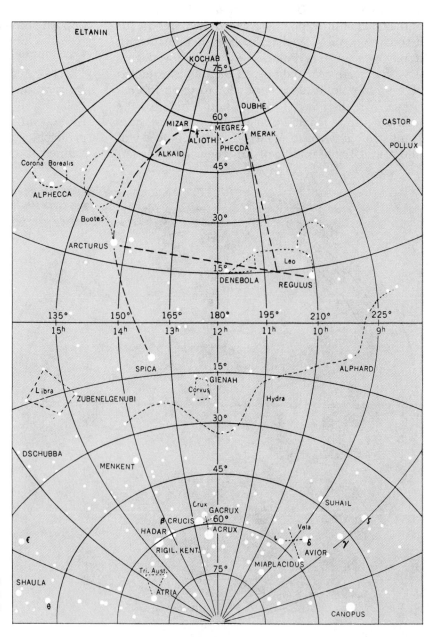

Fig. 2116. Star Chart 2. The spring sky as seen at 2200 LMT on 22 April. Hold the chart overhead with the top of the page toward the north.

lowed in the opposite direction, it leads in the general direction of Regulus, the end of the handle of the sickle in the constellation *Leo* (the lion). This much-used navigational star is of the first magnitude and the brightest star in its part of the sky. A line connecting Regulus and Arcturus passes close to second-magnitude Denebola (tail of the lion), sometimes used by navigators.

Corvus

2118   The constellation *Corvus* (the crow) more nearly resembles a quadrilateral sail. It is not difficult to find, and contains the third-magnitude navigational star Gienah. Due south of *Corvus* is the *Southern Cross*.

Hydra

2119   The only navigational star in *Hydra* (the serpent), a long, inconspicuous constellation near *Corvus*, is the second-magnitude Alphard. This star is more easily identified by its being close to the extension of a line from the pointer of the *Big Dipper* through Regulus and extending southward.

THE SUMMER SKY

2120   In the summer sky (Star Chart 3, fig. 2120), the curve from Antares, the main navigational star in *Scorpio* (the scorpion), to Shaula is particularly suggestive of a scorpion's tail. Immediately to the

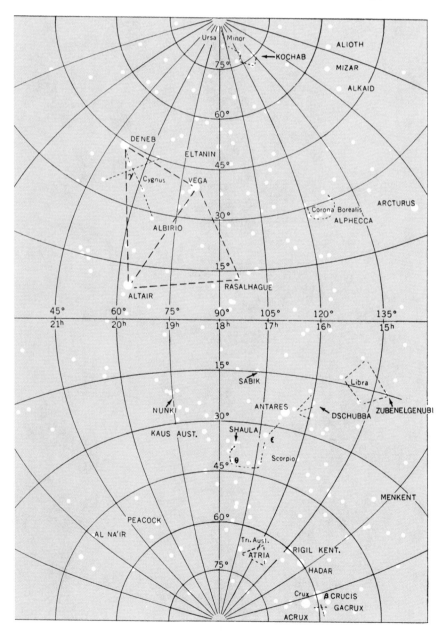

Fig. 2120. Star Chart 3. The summer sky as seen at 2200 LMT on 22 July. Hold the chart overhead with the top of the page toward the north.

east is a group forming the shape of a teapot with the star Nunki in the handle.

Cygnus

2121 To the north of the above-mentioned stars are the first-magnitude stars Vega, Deneb, and Altair. They form a distinct right triangle (right angle at Vega), which many people use as an identification feature. However, each one is in a different constellation, which should enable one to identify it without reference to either of the two other stars. Deneb is in the Northern Cross (*Cygnus*); the eastern arm of the cross points to Enif, the western arm to Eltanin (remember that east and west are reversed from normal charts), and the bisectors of the lower right angles point to Altair and Vega. Altair is readily identified by the small stars on either side of it, sometimes called the "guardians." It should be kept in mind, however, that the southern guardian is only a fourth-magnitude star and may not show very plainly on very hazy or bright moonlight nights.

Corona Borealis

2122 The Northern Crown (*Corona Borealis*) is a group of stars shaped like a bowl about two thirds of the distance from Vega toward Arcturus. This constellation forms a distinctive pattern and con-

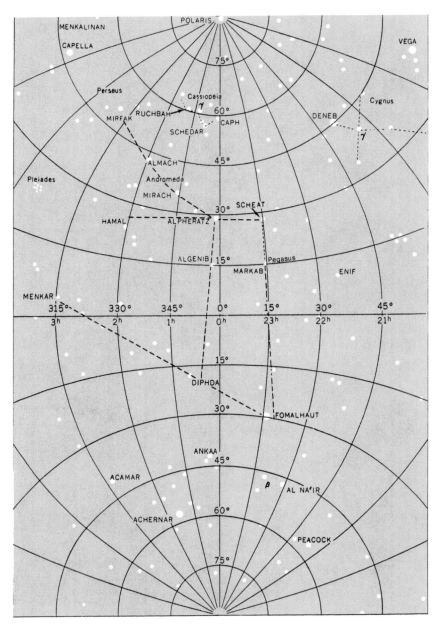

Fig. 2123. Star Chart 4. The autumn sky as seen at 2200 LMT on 21 October. Hold the chart overhead with the top of the page toward the north.

nects the dipper group to the Northern Cross to the east. Second-magnitude Alphecca in this group is sometimes used by navigators.

Rasalhague forms nearly an equilateral triangle with Vega and Altair. This second-magnitude star and third-magnitude Sabik, to the south, are occasionally used by navigators.

THE AUTUMN SKY

2123   The autumn sky (Star Chart 4, fig. 2123) is marked by a scarcity of first-magnitude stars. The *Northern Cross* has moved to a position low in the western sky, and *Cassiopeia* is nearly on the meridian to the north. A little south of the zenith for most observers in the United States, the great square of *Pegasus* (the winged horse) appears nearly on the meridian. The eastern side of this square, and Caph in *Cassiopeia*, nearly mark the hour circle of the vernal equinox (First Point of Aries). Alpheratz and Markab, second-magnitude stars at opposite corners of the square, are the principal navigational stars of this constellation. Second-magnitude Enif is occasionally used.

The square of *Pegasus* is useful in locating several navigational stars. The navigational stars associated with *Pegasus* are Alpheratz, Markab, Diphda, Fomalhaut, and Hamal.

The line joining the stars of the eastern side of the square, if continued southward, leads close to second-magnitude Diphda in *Cetus* (the sea monster). Similarly, a line joining the stars of the western side of the square, if continued southward, leads close to first-magnitude Fomalhaut. A line extending eastward from the north side of the square leads close to second-magnitude Hamal, in *Aries* (the ram). This was the location of the vernal equinox some 2,000 years ago, when it was designated the "first point of Aries."

A curved line from Alpheratz through *Andromeda* leads to *Perseus*. The only navigational star frequently used in *Perseus* is the second-magnitude Mirfak. The curved line from Mirfak to Alpheratz forms a handle to a huge dipper of which the square of *Pegasus* is the bowl.

A line from Fomalhaut through Diphda extended about forty degrees leads to Menkar, an inconspicuous third-magnitude star in *Cetus;* and Ankaa, a second-magnitude star in *Phoenix*, is found about twenty degrees southeasterly from Fomalhaut. Both stars are listed among the navigational stars.

Capella, rising in the east as *Pegasus* is overhead, connects this group to the *Orion* group while Enif acts as a link to the west.

THE WINTER SKY

2124   At no other time do the heavens contain so many bright stars as in the winter sky (Star Chart 5, fig. 2124). The principal constellation of this region is *Orion* (the hunter), probably the best-known constellation in the entire sky with the exception of the *Big Dipper*. This figure is well known to observers in both the Northern and Southern Hemispheres, as the belt of *Orion* lies almost exactly on the celestial equator.

Stars Relative to Orion

2125   Several good navigational stars may be found by the use of *Orion*. Brilliant Rigel and first-magnitude Betelgeuse are situated at approximately equal distances below and above the belt, respectively. If the line of the belt is continued to the westward, it leads near first-magnitude, reddish Aldebaran (the "follower," so named because it follows the "seven sisters" of *Pleiades*), in the V-shaped head of *Taurus* (the bull). If the line of the belt is followed in the opposite direction, it leads almost to Sirius, the brightest of all the stars; this is the principal star in the constellation of *Canis Major*, the hunter's large dog. Starting with Sirius, a rough circle can be drawn through Procyon in *Canis Minor* (the little dog), Pollux and Castor in *Gemini* (the twins), Capella in *Auriga* (the charioteer), Aldebaran, Rigel, and back to Sirius. All of these, except Castor, are first-magnitude stars.

Several second-magnitude stars in the general area of *Orion* are bright enough for navigational purposes, but are seldom used because there are so many first-magnitude stars nearby. Four of these second-magnitude stars are listed among the principal navigational stars of the almanac. These are Bellatrix, just west of Betelgeuse; Alnilam, the middle star (actually, a spiral nebula) in the belt; Elnath, in *Taurus;* and Adhara, part of a triangle in *Canis Major*, and just south of Sirius.

Nearly on the meridian far to the south, the brilliant Canopus, second brightest star, is visible only to observers in the United States south of latitude 37½°, thus excluding most of those in the United States. This star is part of the constellation *Carina* (the keel).

THE SOUTH POLAR SKY

2126   While the south polar sky (Star Chart 6, fig. 2126) contains a number of bright stars, a person who travels to the Southern Hemisphere for the first time is likely to be disappointed by the absence of any striking configuration of stars similar to those with

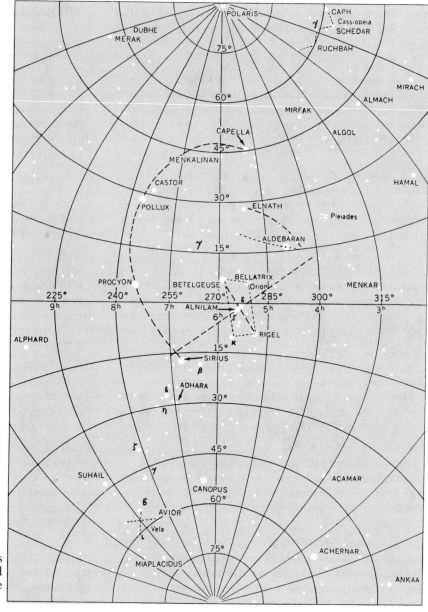

Fig. 2124. Star Chart 5. The winter sky as seen at 2200 LMT on 21 January. Hold the chart overhead with the top of the page toward the north.

which he or she is familiar. The famed *Southern Cross* (*Crux*) is far from an impressive constellation and such a poor cross it might easily be overlooked if two of its stars were not of the first magnitude. A somewhat similar "false cross" in the constellation *Vela* may be easily mistaken for the *Southern Cross*.

Canopus is almost due south of Sirius. The constellation *Carina*, of which Canopus is a part, was originally a part of a larger constellation, *Argo* (the ship), which is now generally divided into *Carina* (the keel), *Puppis* (the stern), *Pyxis* (the mariner's compass), and *Vela* (the sails). Navigational stars included in *Argo* are, besides first-magnitude Canopus, Avior (part of the "false cross"), and Miaplacidus, all second-magnitude stars.

Counterclockwise from Canopus is the false cross and then *Crux*, the true *Southern Cross*. Acrux and Gacrux are listed among the principal navigational stars of the almanac. This constellation also contains the first-magnitude star (Crucis, also known as Mimosa. Although not one of the fifty-seven daily stars, Mimosa has its monthly data listed in the star table following the star charts in the *Nautical Almanac*.

CENTAURUS

2127 Two more good first-magnitude stars lie in nearby *Centaurus* (the centaur). These are Rigil Kentaurus and Hadar. Near *Centaurus* and in a counter-

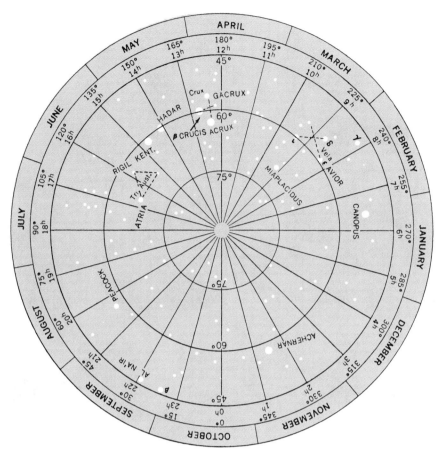

Fig. 2126. Star Chart 6, the south polar region. Hold the chart toward the south at 2200 LMT with the name of the current month at the top.

clockwise direction around the pole is Atria, a commonly used navigational star in *Triangulum Australe.*

The half of the south polar region thus far described has a relatively large number of first- and second-magnitude stars. This area is actually a continuation of the bright area around *Orion,* as can be seen by referring to Star Chart 5. In the remaining section of the south polar region, there are relatively few navigational stars, and they are in faint and poorly defined constellations. Second-magnitude Peacock in *Pavo* (the peacock) and first-magnitude Achernar in *Eridanus* (the river) are good navigational stars; the others are seldom used.

STAR IDENTIFICATION BY COMPUTER

2128   There are a number of software programs available that can be used to find celestial bodies. One of them, introduced in article 2005 and discussed in more detail in subsequent chapters, is STELLA (System to Estimate Latitude and Longitude Astronomically) developed by the U.S. Naval Observatory for Navy use. (Note: The following discussion pertains to the Windows Version 2.0 of STELLA. Also note that STELLA

is not available for use by the general public as of this writing.)

Once STELLA has been loaded into a PC, you need only enter an initial fix and then go to the drop-down menu under "Task" and select "Sight Planning." You will then be given two choices. One option is for "Sky Chart" and the other is for "Selected Stars."

Sky Chart

2129   If you select the "Sky Chart" option, you will see a dialog box on your screen (see fig. 2129a). The dialog box gives you the option of selecting morning or evening twilight and then to either specify a date or use the current one. You also have the option of selecting a time other than twilight. Once you have made these selections, a polar coordinate diagram will appear similar to the one in figure 2129b (Note: Contrast and colors will be different on an actual computer screen.)

Displayed at the correct azimuth will be all the visible navigational stars, identified by the same numbers used in the *Nautical Almanac.* Any planets that are visible are also shown, using a letter abbre-

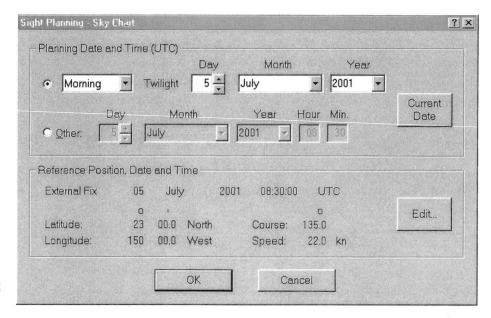

Fig. 2129a. Sky chart dialog box in STELLA program.

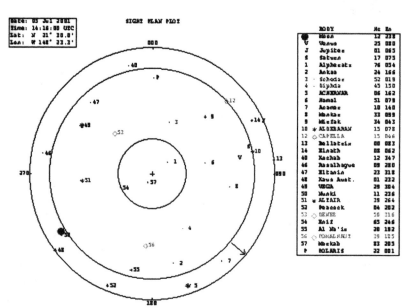

Fig. 2129b. STELLA polar coordinate diagram.

viation (*V* for Venus, *S* for Saturn, etc.) Open diamond symbols point out the three stars with separations in azimuth that make them suitable for a three-star fix. Symbols for the remaining stars are indicted by a large asterisk (indicating stars brighter than 0.5 magnitude), a small asterisk (indicating a star in the range 1.5 to 0.5 magnitude), and single dots (for stars fainter than 2.0 magnitude). If visible at the time selected, the Sun and Moon are shown by their appropriate astronomical symbols.

Placing your cursor over the symbols on the chart will immediately highlight the name of the body on a list to the right of the diagram, along with its altitude and azimuth. Similarly, placing your cursor

over one of the bodies on the list will simultaneously highlight the object on the polar coordinate display.

The list to the right of the polar diagram provides the correspondence of star numbers, symbols and common star names. The table also correlates names of solar system objects with the symbols used in the diagram. Names in all capital letters signify stars brighter than magnitude 1.5. Azimuths and altitudes for all objects are given to the nearest degree to assist identification.

In the example shown, the stars Capella, Deneb, and Fomalhaut are suitable for a three-star fix. Also available are Schedar, Diphda, Aldebaran, and

Altair. A full Moon appears near the star Nunki in the Southwest. Venus, Jupiter, and Saturn are all toward the East and in a single 15° sector of azimuth. Nevertheless, Venus is at a good altitude and brilliant and might be a good sextant target. Jupiter and Elnath (14) are so close that their identifications overlap.

Since corrections are all included in another selectable STELLA task—the "Sight Reduction" selection from the drop down menu—the Moon and planets are as easy to use as the stars.

On a color monitor, all information is displayed against a black background. Reference position, date and time, together with the plot altitude circles and table column heads, are in white. If the monitor colors are in good adjustment, most stars and all solar system objects are presented in light blue. An added feature of STELLA is that the program will recommend the seven best stars for sighting for the date and time selected (weather conditions notwithstanding). Of the seven, those recommended for a three-star fix appear yellow, as do their open diamond symbols; the remaining four recommended stars and their symbols are in red. If the mouse is pointed to an object on the plot or in the table, the rectangular highlight will show as iridescent red.

Selected Stars

2130   Like the "Sky Chart" option, the "Selected Stars" option first requires you to choose the time you wish to make your observations using the dialog box that will appear. Once you have made that choice, each of the visible bodies will appear in tabular form, listing the altitude and azimuth for each at four minute intervals for one hour's time starting with the beginning of twilight (or the time you specified) as shown in figure 2130.

STELLA advances the vessel's position to the time on the first line of the table, which in the example above is near the beginning of morning twilight. Star data are given at four-minute intervals, which is almost equivalent to a 1° increase in the Local Hour Angle of Aries. Time (UTC) for the tabulated data is shown in the first column. (Note: the table shown is shortened as indicated by the series of periods; an actual table generated by STELLA would include additional four-minute entries to cover the entire one-hour period.) The next seven columns give the altitude and azimuth for seven stars, with those recommended for a three-star fix having a diamond above the star name at the top of the column. In the far right column there is an indicator of available natural light at each time. The word Day indicates daylight, CTw indicates civil twi-

```
                        o    ,
              Lat:   N 21 30.0
              Long:  W148 23.3
              Ht:        0 ft.
```

05 Jul 2001

	Schedar	CAPELLA <>	ALDEBARAN	Diphda	FOMALHAUT <>	ALTAIR	DENEB <>	
UTC	Hc Zn	Hc Zn	Hc Zn	Hc Zn	Hc Zn	Hc Zn	Hc Zn	
h m	o , o	o , o	o , o	o , o	o , o	o , o	o , o	
1416	51 43 019	15 20 046	15 15 078	45 11 150	38 41 185	38 56 264	50 22 316	
1420	52 01 018	16 00 046	16 10 078	45 38 151	38 35 186	38 00 264	49 43 316	
1424	52 18 017	16 41 046	17 05 079	46 05 153	38 28 188	37 04 265	49 03 315	NTw
1428	52 33 016	17 21 047	18 00 079	46 30 154	38 20 189	36 08 265	48 24 315	NTw
1432	52 49 015	18 02 047	18 55 079	46 54 155	38 11 190	35 13 266	47 44 315	NTw
..	. .	. .	. .	. .	. .	. .	. .	
1516	54 42 006	25 36 048	29 02 082	50 00 170	35 26 201	24 57 270	40 14 312	CTw

SUN, MOON, PLANETS

05 Jul 2001

	Aries	Sun	Moon 100% ill.	Venus -4.1 mag.	Mars -2.1 mag.	Jupiter -1.9 mag.	Saturn +0.1 mag.	
UTC	LHA	Hc Zn	Hc Zn	Hc Zn	Hc Zn	Hc Zn	Hc Zn	
h m	o	o , o	o , o	o , o	o , o	o , o	o , o	
1416	349		11 42 238	25 18 080		00 38 065	17 12 075	M
1420	350		10 56 239	26 13 080		01 29 066	18 06 075	M
1424	351		10 09 239	27 09 081		02 20 066	19 00 075	M
..	.		. .	. .		. .	. .	
1516	004	-00 53 065	-00 09 244	39 08 084		13 35 070	30 49 079	M

Fig. 2130. Tabular listing of altitudes and azimuths in STELLA.

light, and NTw indicates nautical twilight. A blank space signifies night.

The lower half of the table resembles the upper half, but gives altitude (Hc) and azimuth (Zn) for the Sun, Moon, and navigational planets. Again the UTC appears in the first column; the second column has the Local Hour Angle of Aries. Because these two quantities increase at slightly different rates, two consecutive values of the (rounded) LHA Aries may be the same or may differ by up to 2°. Names of the navigational objects are at the top of each of the next six columns. For the Moon, the percentage of its disk that is illuminated by sunlight corresponds to the first time listed in the time column. Any change through one hour would be imperceptible, except during an eclipse. Magnitudes of the planets are found directly under their names.

If numerical data for the Sun, a planet, or the Moon are missing from a column in the body of the table, the object or its upper limb is below the horizon, making it unavailable for use. However, coordinates of the Sun are given through civil twilight. If Venus or Jupiter is within 10° of the Sun, or if Mars or Saturn is within 15° of the Sun, the words "near Sun" appear in place of Hc and Zn. For the chosen date, time, and location of the example shown, there are no Hc or Zn entries for the Sun until near the end of the table, and there are no entries for Mars at all indicating that it remains below the horizon for the time selected.

Information on solar and lunar eclipses is also given in this table. If the letter S appears in the last (rightmost) column, then a solar eclipse is in progress. Similarly, an M indicates a lunar eclipse. During partial phases of an eclipse and during an annular solar eclipse, the Sun and Moon may be available for navigational use, and their Hc and Zn are tabulated. When an eclipse becomes total, the word "eclipse" appears in place of altitude and azimuth data. In the table above, the Moon's hemisphere facing the Earth is 100 percent illuminated, making it a full Moon. However, the table shows that a lunar eclipse is in progress. Taking into account that the Moon's coordinates are tabulated, you can know that the eclipse is partial, not total; the Moon is still visible.

The example table above also shows that Venus is brilliant. It is in the good range for sextants, as is Saturn, although not nearly so bright. Jupiter is bright but near the horizon. An unfavorable feature of the planet distribution in this example is the small spread in azimuth.

Chapter 22

The Sextant

The sextant is one of the basic "tools" of celestial navigation. It is used to make a highly precise and accurate measurement of the angle between two lines of sight from the observer, one to a celestial body and the other to the horizon; this pure angular measurement made in a vertical plane is called *sextant altitude* and is identified by the abbreviation *hs*. It is used to measure angles of the Sun, Moon, planets, and stars. Once certain corrections have been made, the reading becomes *apparent altitude* (ha). Further corrections refine that to the *observed altitude* (Ho) that is ultimately compared to a *computed altitude* (Hc).

In this chapter, the term "sextant" will be used for the standard marine sextant; other types will be specifically identified when discussed.

DEVELOPMENT OF THE SEXTANT

2201   The first successful instrument developed for measuring the altitude of celestial bodies while at sea was the *cross-staff*. It was unique for its time in that it measured altitude from the sea horizon; its disadvantage was that it required the user to look at the horizon *and* at the body at the same time. This must have been quite a feat, particularly when the body was well above the horizon; an experienced navigator, however, could for the first time determine the altitude of a body at sea with an accuracy of about one degree.

In 1590, the *backstaff*, or *Davis quadrant*, shown in figure 2201, was invented by John Davis; this was a great advancement over the cross-staff. To use this newer instrument the observer turned his back on the Sun and aligned a shadow cast by the Sun with the horizon. Later designs of this instrument were fitted with a mirror so as to make possible observations of bodies other than the Sun.

Today's *sextant* is an instrument designed to permit measurement of the angle between the lines of sight to two objects with great precision. It derives its name from the Latin *sextans*, meaning the sixth part, because its arc is approximately one-sixth of a circle; because of the optical principle used in its construction, it can measure angles up to about 120°, or twice the value of the arc itself. Quintants and octants are similar instruments, named for the lengths of their arcs, but today it is the general practice to refer to all such instruments as sextants, regardless of the precise lengths of their arcs.

The optical principle of the sextant was first described by Sir Isaac Newton. However, its importance was not realized, and the information was long forgotten until it was applied to celestial navigation.

The double-reflecting principle of the sextant, described hereafter, was independently rediscovered in 1730 by Hadley in England and Godfrey in Philadelphia; it made possible a high standard of accuracy in celestial navigation.

COMPONENTS OF A SEXTANT

2202   A typical sextant is illustrated in figure 2202a with the principal parts labeled as follows:

A. The *frame*, on which the other parts are mounted. The frame is normally made of brass, but some "lightweight" models are aluminum alloy. There are also less expensive models in which the frame is made of specially reinforced plastic material.

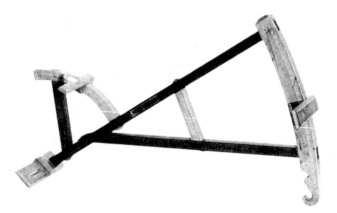

Fig. 2201. A Davis quadrant, 1775.

B. The *limb* is the lower part of the frame and carries the *arc* (B´) graduated in degrees. The arc may be inscribed directly on the limb, or it may be inscribed on a separate plate permanently attached to the limb. The outer edge of the limb is cut into teeth, which are engaged by the threads of the *tangent screw* (not visible) to hold the setting when an observation is taken.

C. The *index arm* is pivoted at the center of curvature of the arc and is free to swing around it. Its lower end carries an *index mark* to indicate the reading in degrees on the arc.

D. The *micrometer drum* is used to make fine adjustments of the index arm. It is mounted on a shaft, having a helical pinion gear at the other end called the *tangent screw*. This tangent screw engages the teeth cut into the limb, and one full turn moves the index arm by one half-degree on the arc, thus changing the observed altitude by one whole degree. The micrometer drum is generally graduated in minutes of arc. On some models there is only a single index mark for the micrometer drum, and fractions of a minute can only be estimated between graduations for whole minutes. On other models there is a *vernier scale*, which permits readings to be taken to 0.1´ (see fig. 2202b). The *release levers* (D´) are spring-loaded clamps that hold the tangent screw against the teeth of the limb. When squeezed together, these levers disengage the tangent screw and allow the index arm to be moved easily along the arc to roughly the desired setting (which is then refined by use of the micrometer drum after pressure on these levers is released).

E. The *index mirror* is mounted at the upper end of the index arm directly over its pivot point; it is perpendicular to the plane of the limb and moves with the index arm.

F. The *horizon glass* is mounted on the frame. It, too, is precisely perpendicular to the plane of the limb. When the index arm is set to exactly 0°, the horizon glass is parallel to the index mirror. The "traditional" horizon glass is divided vertically into halves by a line parallel to the plane of the limb. The half nearer the frame is silvered as a mirror; the other half is clear optical glass. This arrangement permits the user to see the body and the horizon at the same time, side by side.

A newer type is a horizon glass uniformly coated in a manner similar to that of a "one-way" mirror. The horizon can be seen all across the glass, as can the reflected image of the body. This type is a little easier to use and is often preferred by beginners, but the tradeoff is a reduction in the amount of light that gets through; for this reason, some seasoned professionals prefer the older type.

G. The *telescope* is mounted with its axis parallel to the plane of the limb. The magnification of the telescope permits the observer to judge contact between the celestial body and the sea horizon more exactly than is possible with the unaided eye, and it often makes it possible to pick up the image of a star when it cannot be seen by the naked eye. Telescopes are adjustable for the characteristics of the individual observer's eye. And on some models, the telescope can be moved toward or away from the frame as conditions warrant.

H. The *index shade glasses* are of optically ground glass mounted perpendicular to the arc, and are pivoted so that they can be swung into or out of the line of sight between the index and horizon mirrors. Two types of index shade glasses are employed on sextants. The first is a variable density polarizing filter; the second consists of four or more shade glasses of neutral tint and increasing density. The shade glasses are employed when making observations of the Sun, and sometimes when observing a bright planet or star above a dimly lighted horizon.

I. The *horizon shades* are similar to the index shades, but of lesser density, and serve to reduce the glare of reflected sunlight on the horizon when necessary.

J. The *handle*, usually made of wood or plastic, is mounted on the frame at a location and angle for good balance and easy grip with the right hand. Some sextants provide for night lighting of the index marks of both the arc and the micrometer drum; the batteries for such lights are within the handle.

(Note: The term "limb" has two meanings in celestial navigation. As described here, it is a part of the

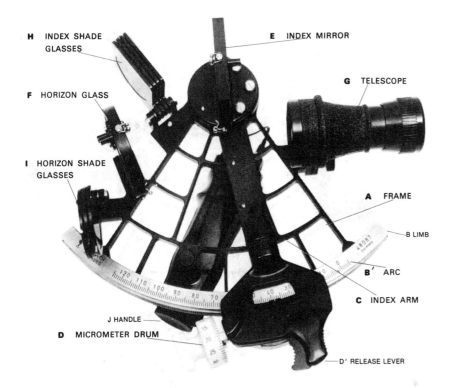

H INDEX SHADE GLASSES

E INDEX MIRROR

G TELESCOPE

F HORIZON GLASS

I HORIZON SHADE GLASSES

A FRAME

B LIMB

B' ARC

C INDEX ARM

J HANDLE

D MICROMETER DRUM

D' RELEASE LEVER

Fig. 2202a. Component parts of a typical sextant.

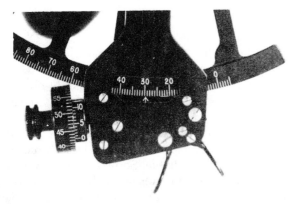

Fig. 2202b. Marine sextant, showing arc, micrometer drum, and vernier scale.

sextant. But the same term applies to sightings on large bodies [Sun and Moon]. In this case it is usually accompanied by the word "upper" or "lower" [as in "lower limb"] and describes the upper or lower edge of the body. When making a sextant observation of the Sun or Moon, you will bring the upper or lower edge to align with the horizon as described later. The term "limb" is preferred to "edge" in celestial navigation.)

Optical Principles of a Sextant

2203 The optics of a sextant are based on a system of double reflection in that the image of the observed body is reflected from the upper, or index,

mirror to the lower, or horizon, mirror, and thence into the field of view of the telescope, where it is brought into coincidence with the sea horizon, which is seen through the clear portion of the horizon mirror. The principle of optics involved is stated: The angle between the first and last directions of a ray of light that has undergone two reflections in the same plane is twice the angle that the two reflecting surfaces make with each other. This principle can be demonstrated by geometry as illustrated in figure 2203. Angle a in the figure, the difference between first and last reflection, equals twice angle b, the angle between the reflecting surfaces. Angle c equals angle d, and angle e equals angle f, the angles of incidence and reflection, respectively, of the index and horizon mirrors.

TYPES OF SEXTANTS

2204 There are many different kinds of sextants. The vast majority are similar to the one described above with only moderate variations. There are, however, other types that may be encountered.

The *bubble sextant* has long been used by aerial navigators for celestial observations. Sometimes called an *artificial horizon sextant*, the vertical is established in these instruments by bringing the center of the observed body into coincidence with the center of a free-floating bubble. Most aviation sextants are fitted with an averaging device. This

Fig. 2203. The optical principle of a sextant.

provides the determination of a mean of observations made over a considerable period of time, usually two minutes. On later models, the observation may be discontinued at any time after the first thirty seconds and the average altitude determined. It is usually desirable, however, to use the full one- or two-minute observation series, as it is assumed that this will at least cover the complete period of natural oscillation of the aircraft in pitch and roll.

The aircraft bubble sextant is difficult to use aboard most surface vessels, particularly in a seaway, because of the different kinds of motion encountered. Useful results, however, have been obtained with them aboard large vessels and partially surfaced submarines. For civilian use, artificial horizons (bubble devices) are available from some sextant manufacturers for attachment to their instruments.

Considerable experimentation has been conducted with sextants fitted with gyroscopic artificial horizon systems. The advantages of such a system are obvious but are offset by the considerable expense.

The great advantage of an artificial horizon sextant is that it permits observations of celestial bodies when the sea horizon is obscured by darkness, fog, or haze. But the accuracy obtainable with the bubble sextant lies in the range of minutes of arc, rather than the *tenths of minutes* obtained with a marine sextant using the natural horizon.

Night-vision telescopes that use an electronic unit to amplify the small amount of ambient light at night can be adapted to sextants for night observations. Again, expense is a tradeoff that may have to be considered.

For navigators whose requirements are less demanding, less-expensive models of lesser precision and accuracy are available. Some sextants are made of very stable plastic materials with optics of good, but lesser, quality than those of metal sextants (see fig. 2204). Such a sextant, sometimes carried as a backup to a more refined instrument, can have a micrometer drum and read angles to a precision of 0.2′ with fully acceptable accuracy for ordinary navigation yet cost one-tenth or less of the price of a first-line sextant.

There are also very simple plastic instruments often referred to as "practice" or "lifeboat" sextants. These operate on the same basic principles, but lack such features as a drum vernier, adjustable mirrors, and telescope. Such sextants serve their intended purposes, however, and are relatively inexpensive.

SEXTANT OBSERVATIONS

2205   Altitude observations of celestial bodies are made in the plane perpendicular to the celestial horizon, along the vertical circle passing through

Fig. 2204. Sextant with a plastic frame.

the body. They are measured upward from the visible, or sea horizon, and corrections are applied to adjust the sextant altitude to read as though the observed angle had been measured from the Earth's center, upward from the celestial horizon. The plane of the visible horizon may, for all practical purposes, be considered to be parallel to the celestial horizon and even coincident with it. Figure 2205a illustrates the principle of a celestial altitude measurement. As already mentioned, the altitude of a body above the visible horizon, as read from the sextant before any corrections are made, is termed the *sextant altitude* (hs).

To make an observation, you should stand facing the body, holding the sextant vertically in your right hand, and center the horizon in your field of view. Squeeze the release levers and move the index arm until the body also appears in the field of view.

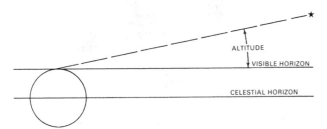

Fig. 2205a. An altitude measurement.

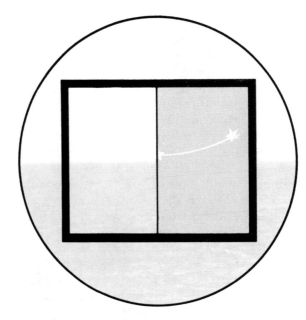

Fig. 2205b. Swinging the arc.

Allow the tangent screw to engage the teeth on the arc, and turn the micrometer drum until the horizon and the body are in precise coincidence.

Next, tilt the sextant slightly from side to side slowly to determine that you are holding the sextant vertically to ensure an accurate measurement. This rotation about the axis of the line of sight causes the body to swing like a pendulum across the horizon and is called *swinging the arc* (see fig. 2205b). The lowest point indicated on this arc marks the correct position for the sextant; again turn the micrometer drum until the body makes contact with the horizon at the bottom of its swing. At this instant, note the time and read off and record the sextant altitude.

With practice, it is easy to determine when the body is on the vertical except for high altitudes. The eye tends to extend the line of the sea horizon into the mirrored portion of the sea horizon, and the arc of the reflected image appears not only in the mirrored half but also somewhat into the clear half as well.

Skill in obtaining accurate altitudes comes only with practice. Some individuals are markedly more accurate observers than others, but experiments conducted for the Office of Naval Research clearly indicate that the accuracy of even the best observers tends to increase with practice. Each of five observers made over three thousand sextant observations, and for each observer the mean of his second thousand observations was better than his first thousand, and that of the third thousand showed still further improvement.

As a novice observer, you may encounter difficulty in obtaining sights that yield satisfactory lines of position. Working with an experienced navigator will probably improve your technique, but *practice* is the key. It may be helpful for you to make a string of ten or more observations of the same body in a period of less than three minutes. These sights should then be plotted on a large sheet of plotting paper, using a horizontal scale of one inch to ten seconds of time, and a vertical scale of one inch to one minute of arc, if possible. A "curve of best fit" is then drawn through the string. The divergence of the individual sights from this line will tend to indicate the magnitude of the observer's random errors; the random error of a single sight is the greatest hazard to the accuracy of celestial navigation. Where accuracy is required, a single observation should not be relied on to obtain a line of position. It is far better practice to take at least three sights of each body, and for maximum accuracy an even greater number of observations should be made and graphed as described above (because the body's altitude is constantly changing at a varying rate, simple averaging cannot be used). An altitude and time combination that lies on or near the best fit curve can then be selected as the sight to be reduced for the LOP. Nearly always, a curve faired in by eye will suffice for any round of sights on a single body. For a least-squares fit by mathematics, a parabolic model, although not exact, works well and is especially valuable for bodies transiting the meridian during the round of sights. The larger number of sights taken over a reasonable period of time, the better should be the results.

Reading a Sextant

2206   To read the sextant altitude (hs), the position of the arm's index mark against the scale of degrees on the arc is first read. In figure 2202b, the index mark is located between 29° and 30°, indicating that the altitude will be 29° plus the reading of minutes and tenths obtained from the micrometer drum and its vernier respectively. The index mark for the micrometer drum is the zero mark on the vernier. In the figure, it is between the drum markings for 42' and 43', indicating that the altitude will be 42' plus the number of tenths obtained from the vernier. To read the vernier, the two graduations that line up most perfectly indicate the correct reading. In the figure, this is 5, indicating a reading of 0.5'. The complete "hs" reading in this case would be 29° 42.5'.

Considerable care and simple logic must be exercised in reading the micrometer drum if the index

mark for the index arm is very close to a graduation on the arc. If, for example, that index mark were apparently right opposite the 30° mark on the arc (see fig. 2206), and the micrometer drum read 57' and some tenths, then the true reading for the sextant would be 29° 57', *not* 30° 57'. Similar care must be used in reading the micrometer drum when the vernier scale is at its upper end near 8 or 9 tenths.

Sun Observations

2207   As described earlier, the sextant is fitted with index shade glasses, either of the variable-density polarizing type, or neutrally tinted filters of varying degrees of density. To determine the degree of density best suited to the observer's eye under existing conditions, it is usually best to first look at the Sun through the *darkest* index shade; if this dims the image too much, the next lighter shade should be tried. It should be noted that sometimes the best results are achieved by using two of the lighter filters, rather than a single dark one. When a polarizing filter is used, it should be set to *full dark* before looking at the Sun; the rotatable portion can then be turned to lighten the image until the eye sees the image comfortably and clearly.

On a calm day, when the Sun is low in altitude, the sea short of the horizon may reflect the sunlight so glaringly that it is desirable to employ a horizon shade. The most desirable shade must again be selected by trial and error.

After the proper shade or shades are selected, the observer sets the index arm to 0°, faces the Sun, and proceeds as described above until the Sun's *lower limb* (bottom edge) is on the horizon; during this process the arc must be swung to establish the vertical. At most altitudes, the best results are obtained by observing the Sun's lower limb; however, at alti-

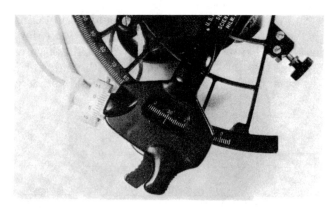

Fig. 2206. A U.S. Navy sextant showing the index mark opposite the 30° mark. The correct angle is 29° 57', not 30° 57'.

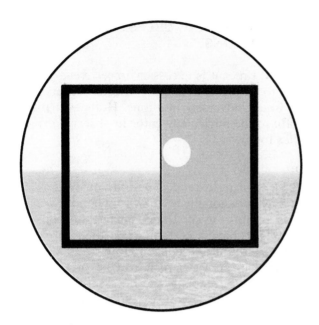

Fig. 2207. Observing the Sun, lower limb.

tudes below about 5°, it is more desirable to observe the *upper limb*. In this case, the correction for *irradiation effect* should be applied to the sextant altitude, in addition to other corrections. (Note: These corrections will be discussed later in this chapter.) The procedure for observing the Sun's upper limb is much the same as for the lower limb. Figure 2207 shows the Sun's lower limb on the horizon, as seen through a sextant telescope.

When practicing with the sextant, a neophyte navigator should begin by observing the Sun at local apparent noon (LAN). In most latitudes, the Sun changes altitude but little for a period of several minutes before and after LAN. The procedures for the determination of the time of LAN are covered in a later chapter. A string of twelve or more observations should be made, as rapidly as possible, and the altitudes noted. After each sight, the micrometer drum should be moved so that the Sun's image initially appears alternately above and below the horizon. It should then be brought to the horizon, and the arc swung until the Sun's image is brought into coincidence with the horizon on the vertical. When you are able to obtain a consistent string of altitudes at LAN, you should then take a series of sights in the afternoon or morning when the Sun's altitude is changing rapidly.

Moon Observations

2208   Observations of the Moon are made in the same manner as those of the Sun. Because of the various phases of the Moon, upper limb observa-

tions are made about as frequently as those of the lower limb. Accurate observations of the Moon can only be obtained if the upper or lower limb is brought to the horizon. This is not always possible, because of the Moon's phase and its position in the sky.

Carefully made Moon observations, obtained during daylight hours, under good observational conditions, yield excellent LOPs. If the Moon is observed at night, it may be desirable to shade its image somewhat, so that the horizon will not be obscured by the Moon's brilliance; nighttime observations of the Moon, using a moonlit horizon, are generally less accurate than daytime sights or those taken at morning and evening twilight because the horizon is less distinct at night than during twilight periods.

Star and Planet Observations

2209   Observations of stars and planets are made at twilight so that both the body and the horizon are visible. More experience in the use of the sextant is required to obtain good twilight sights than is needed in daylight. This is chiefly because a star appears only as a point of light in the sextant telescope (and a planet as little more), rather than as a body of considerable size, like the Sun and Moon. In addition, the stars and planets fade out in the morning as the horizon brightens; in the evening this condition is reversed, and in either twilight it is sometimes difficult to obtain a good star image and a well-defined horizon at the same time.

Three methods of bringing the star (or planet) and the horizon together are possible. The first is to bring the star's image down to the horizon, the second is to bring the horizon up to the star, and the third is to predetermine the approximate altitude and azimuth of the selected star. Of the three methods, the third is usually the most satisfactory, as it often permits locating the star before it can be seen by the unaided eye.

Bringing a Star or Planet Down

2210   To employ the first method, set the sextant to 0° and then look through it directly at the star (or planet). You will see it as a double image. Slowly push the index arm forward, while moving the sextant itself downward, keeping the image of the body in the field of the telescope. When the horizon appears in the field, allow the micrometer drum to engage the teeth on the arc. Final contact between body and horizon is made by means of turning the drum, while swinging the arc to establish the vertical.

Some observers, when using a sextant with a small optical field of view, prefer to remove the telescope from the sextant while bringing the star down. The telescope should always be reinstalled before the altitude is read in order to obtain maximum accuracy.

Bringing the Horizon Up

2211 The second method is sometimes employed when the horizon is bright, and the star (or planet) is dim. To bring the horizon up to the star, the sextant is set at approximately 0°, and then held inverted in the left hand. Looking through the clear portion of the horizon glass, the line of sight is then directed at the body as shown in figure 2211. The index arm is next adjusted until the horizon appears in the field of view and is then allowed to lock to the arc, the sextant is righted, and the altitude determined in the usual way.

Using Precomputed Altitudes

2212 The best procedure for star observations, in most cases, is to determine in advance the approximate altitude and azimuth of the stars to be observed, by means of a star finder, such as the "Star Finder and Identifier" 2102-D or the STELLA program (see chapter 21). Predetermination of the approximate altitude permits full use to be made of the sextant telescope, which will usually make it possible to sight a star when it cannot be seen with the naked eye. Stars can thus be located at evening twilight, while the horizon is still clearly defined, and can be observed in the morning after they have faded from view of the unaided eye.

When using this method, the altitude of the body to be observed is taken from the star finder, and set on the sextant. The observer then faces in the direction of the body's azimuth, usually determined by sighting over a gyro repeater or magnetic compass, and directs his or her line of sight at the horizon. After locating the star, its altitude is determined in the regular manner.

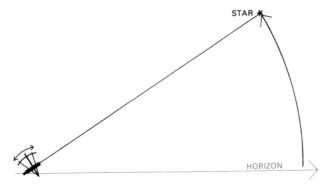

Fig. 2211. Using a sextant inverted.

NOTES REGARDING CELESTIAL OBSERVATIONS

2213 At times it is necessary to seize every opportunity to obtain one or more celestial observations, even under adverse conditions. Hints that may be helpful to the novice navigator in observing various bodies follow.

Sun

2214 During extended periods of overcast, the Sun may occasionally break through, appearing for only a minute or so. Under such conditions it is advisable to have a sextant set to the approximate altitude, with the telescope mounted, and located in a convenient spot where it can be picked up instantly if the Sun appears. If necessary, you should be prepared to note your own time of observation rather than using another person for this. At times the Sun shows through thin overcast, but its image is not sharply defined. It can nevertheless supply a helpful line of position.

Excellent running fixes can be obtained by making an observation when the Sun bears about 45° east of the meridian, following with a conventional noon sight, and then taking a third observation when the Sun bears about 45° west of the meridian.

Low-altitude sights of the Sun (i.e., altitudes of 5° or less) can be extremely helpful at times, and under most observational conditions will yield lines of position accurate to 2 miles or less when carefully corrected. When making low-altitude Sun sights, the upper limb will usually yield better observations than the lower.

Moon

2215 Observations of the Moon can often be used for valuable daytime fixes when made in conjunction with observations of the Sun. When Moon sights are to be taken at night, it is advisable to make them from a point as low in the ship as possible. This vantage will minimize errors caused by cloud shadows, which can shade the true horizon and make the Moon appear below its true position, causing the sextant altitude to read higher than it should.

Planets

2216 Venus can frequently be observed with a sextant during daylight, particularly when its altitude is greater than that of the Sun, and it is not too close to the latter in azimuth.

To locate Venus during daylight, its position (declination and angle relative to Aries) should be carefully plotted on the "Star Finder and Identifier"

2102-D or located via STELLA or some other comparable program. The latter is then set in the regular manner for the time of the desired observation and the corresponding DR position, and the approximate altitude and azimuth are read off.

Fixes based on sights of the Sun, Moon, and Venus made during daylight hours should be employed whenever possible.

The other planets (Mars, Jupiter, and Saturn), which are not as brilliant as Venus, are ordinarily observed only at twilight. Their positions may also be plotted on the Star Finder, to aid in locating them in the sky. Twilight observation techniques, applicable to planets as well as stars, are described in the following section.

Stars

2217 When the Star Finder or STELLA is used, altitudes and azimuths of twelve or more stars, preferably with altitudes of 20° or more, should be listed in advance for the time of twilight. It is desirable to list considerably more stars than will actually be observed, since clouds may prevent some of the chosen stars from being visible at twilight.

The visibility of a star at twilight depends primarily on its magnitude and on its altitude. If two stars are of equal magnitude and have the same azimuth, the star with the higher altitude will appear to be the brighter. Because of the polarization of the Sun's light rays, stars situated at 90° to the Sun's azimuth will appear to be slightly brighter than stars of the same magnitude and altitude having nearly the same azimuth as the Sun or lying about 180° from it.

The visibility of stars also depends on the sextant's mirrors, and on the quality and magnification of the telescope. The mirrors must be of a size that permits use of the full angular field of view of the telescope; the larger the mirror, the larger is the bundle of light rays transmitted to the observer's eye, which is another way of saying the brighter will be the star's reflected image. In addition, the greater the magnification of the telescope, the more easily can the star be located against a bright sky; full daylight observations have been made of Sirius (Mag. –1.6) and Arcturus (Mag. 0.2) with a sextant fitted with a 20-power telescope; typically, however, sextant telescopes are only 2 to 7 power. A higher-power telescope is not necessarily advantageous, because unsteadiness of the observer's hands can make sighting very difficult. Although higher power results in light magnification, it reduces the field of view and makes it more difficult to keep the star in the field, particularly with vessel motion such as on a small craft. Further, the higher the power of a tel-

escope, the greater its weight. Although some navigators consider weight useful in steadying the instrument, it can add to muscular fatigue, with a resulting increase in shakiness. A 3- or 4-power telescope with a 21- or 28-mm objective (front) lens is a good overall choice for star observations.

Often the position of the telescope, relative to the sextant frame, may be adjusted to fit varying conditions of illumination at twilight. Some sextant telescopes are not permanently fixed in relation to the frame, and their axis may be moved in or out. This is generally true of sextants with small mirrors, which have less light-gathering power. When the telescope is moved as close as possible to the frame, the maximum amount of light is reflected from the elevated field of view. Conversely, when it is moved out from the frame, more light is transmitted from the horizon, and less from the sky. With a dim horizon, the telescope is moved out to the end of its travel. When the horizon is very dim, it may even be desirable to use a pale index filter when observing a brilliant star or planet; this will facilitate obtaining an accurate contact between the body and the horizon. A navigator should experiment in positioning the telescope in order to obtain the optimum balance of lighting between the body and the horizon. It should be noted that a telescope with good light-gathering powers will permit the observer to see a sharply defined horizon, when it appears less distinct to the naked eye.

It is, of course, desirable to observe stars against a sharply defined horizon, which implies a fairly bright sky. At evening twilight, the eastern horizon will fade first; as a general rule, therefore, it is best to observe stars situated to the eastward first. At morning twilight, the eastern horizon will brighten first and so it makes sense to first observe those stars generally toward the east. With experience, a navigator should be able to determine the most desirable sequence of star observation, balancing off the various factors involved, such as star magnitude and altitude and horizon lighting.

With a sextant telescope of good magnification and optical characteristics, it is possible to observe stars at any time on a clear night. However, the observer's vision must be completely dark adapted. Using a sextant fitted with a 6-power prismatic telescope, having an objective lens 30 mm in diameter will generally yield the best results for these observations.

SEXTANT ERRORS, CORRECTIONS, AND ADJUSTMENTS

2218 There are a number of factors that can produce errors or that require corrections when taking sextant observations. Some are dealt with by the use of measurements and compensations, others are corrected through the use of available tables in almanacs, and others require adjustments to the sextant itself.

Once your actual sextant altitude (hs) has been corrected as discussed below, it yields a more accurate altitude called by convention the *observed altitude* and abbreviated *Ho*.

Instrument Error

2219   The sextant, being an optical-mechanical instrument, cannot be manufactured totally error free. When a sextant is assembled by the manufacturer, it is tested for *fixed instrument errors*, and the combined values are recorded on a certificate attached to the inside of the sextant case. The error is usually listed for each 10° of the arc. Some manufacturers merely certify the instruments to be free of errors "for practical use." This implies that the error nowhere exceeds approximately 10 seconds of arc. In modern precision sextants, these nonadjustable errors are small and may usually be ignored. Specifications for the Navy Mark II sextant require that no errors be greater than 35 seconds of arc. Since this exceeds a half minute of arc, or half a mile on the Earth's surface, correction should be applied to the sextant reading for any errors approaching this magnitude.

The correction for these errors is called the *instrument correction* (I) and is included by the manufacturer on the certificate in the sextant box. It varies with the angle, may be either *positive* or *negative*, and is applied to *all* observations made with that particular sextant.

Perpendicularity of Mirrors

2220   The sextant should occasionally be checked to see that the mirrors are perpendicular to the sextant frame; that is, the index mirror must be perpendicular to the plane of the instrument. This alignment is checked by setting the movable arm near the middle of the arc. Hold the sextant horizontally and look obliquely into the index mirror from the end of the instrument. The reflected image of the arc should now be in line with the arc itself. Should the two not be in line (see fig. 2220a) this can be corrected by rotating a small screw in the center of the frame of the index mirror. Again, some sextants have two adjusting screws, one of which must first be loosened and then the other tightened. Other sextants use only one adjusting screw, which moves the mirror against retaining springs. The tangent screw is adjusted until the reflected and direct images of the horizon appear

as a straight line with the sextant in a vertical position. The sextant is then turned or rocked around the line of sight; the reflected horizon and the direct horizon should remain in exact alignment, as in figure 2220b. If they do not, as in figure 2220c, the horizon glass needs adjustment to make it perpendicular to the plane of the limb. On the Navy Mark II sextant, two additional adjusting screws (see fig. 2220d) are used to move the mirror frame assembly. Care must be used to loosen one before tightening the other. On sextants where the mirror is adjusted within the frame, the adjusting screw farthest away from the sextant frame is used (fig. 2220e). When the mirror is properly adjusted, the horizon will appear as a straight line while the sextant is rotated around the line of sight.

Index Error and Correction

2221   Index error should be determined each time the sextant is used. In the daytime, this is usu-

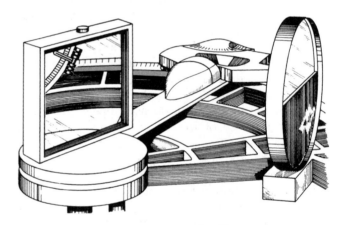

Fig. 2220a. Checking perpendicularity of index mirror; here the mirror is not perpendicular.

Fig. 2220b. Horizon glass perpendicular to the sextant frame.

Fig. 2220c. Here the horizon glass is not perpendicular to the frame.

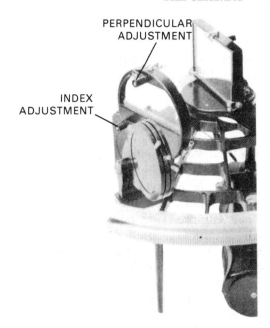

Fig. 2220e. Adjusting screws, Plath sextant.

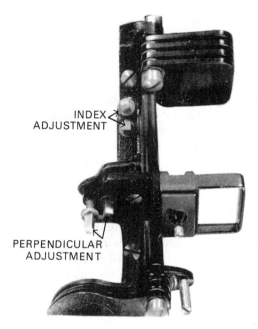

Fig. 2220d. Adjusting screws, Navy Mark II sextant.

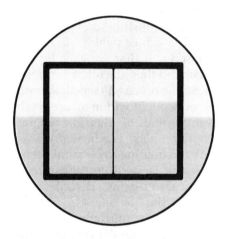

Fig. 2221a. Sextant set at zero, with index error.

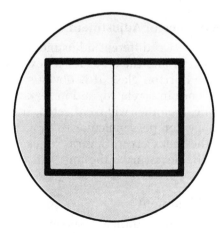

Fig. 2221b. Sextant set at zero, horizon in alignment as seen through sextant telescope.

ally done by an observation of the horizon. The index arm is first set at exactly 0° 00.0′ and with the sextant held in a vertical position, the horizon is observed. In nearly all instances, the horizon will not appear as a continuous line in the direct and reflected views (see fig. 2221a). The micrometer drum is adjusted until the reflected and direct images of the horizon are brought into coincidence, forming a straight, unbroken line, as shown in figure 2221b. This operation should be repeated several times, the reflected image of the horizon being alternately brought down and up to the direct image. The value of the index error is read in minutes and/or tenths after each alignment, and the average of the readings is taken.

The *index correction* (IC) to be applied to an observed sextant angle is simply the index error *with the sign reversed.* If the error is positive—the micrometer drum reads more than 0.0′—the sign of the correction is negative. Conversely, if the drum reads less than 0.0′, the error is negative and the sign of the correction is positive. For example, if the average reading of the micrometer drum is 58.5′, the error is –1.5′ and the IC is +1.5′. When the error is negative, it is sometimes said to be "off the arc," conversely, when positive it is "on the arc."

Index error is caused by a lack of perfect parallelism between the index mirror and horizon glass when the sextant is set at 0°. This lack of parallelism causes a greater error in observation than would a slight error in the perpendicularity of the mirrors.

If the index error is small, less than about 4.0′, it is best not to try to remove it. If you choose to eliminate or reduce excessive index error, the *horizon glass* must be adjusted. On a Mark II Navy sextant the mirror is fixed within the mirror frame; adjustment is accomplished by moving the mirror frame by means of two adjusting screws, as shown in figure 2220d. This adjustment is a trial and error process; one screw is first loosened by a small fraction of a turn, and then the other is tightened by an equal amount; the process is repeated until the error is removed, or brought within an acceptable limit.

With several brands of other fine commercial sextants, the horizon glass is adjusted within the mirror frame. When holding the sextant vertically, only the upper screw is used, as illustrated in figure 2220e. The procedure just described is followed except that only the one adjusting screw is turned slightly; this moves the mirror against the mounting springs. When the sextant is properly adjusted, the horizon will appear as in figure 2221b with the sextant reading zero.

Proper Sequence of Adjustment

2222   Since two different adjustments—one for perpendicularity and the other for index error—are made on the horizon glass, it is obvious that these adjustments are interrelated, and in making adjustment for one, the other will be affected. It is important to adjust for perpendicularity first, and then check for the index error. Several series of adjustments may be necessary if the mirror is badly misaligned.

Telescope Alignment

2223   If extreme difficulty is encountered in bringing a star down to the horizon, it is possible that the sextant has a collimation error, which means the line of sight of the telescope is not parallel to the plane of the sextant limb. This is usually difficult to adjust onboard ship, but there is a quick practical check to determine if the telescope is out of alignment. The sextant is held in a horizontal position in the left hand, with the horizon glass toward the observer and the index arm set near 0°. The observer looks into the index mirror, holding the sextant in such a position that the reflected image of the centerline of the horizon mirror is directly in line with the actual centerline. In this position it should be possible to see straight through the telescope, the line of sight being the same as the path of light rays of a star when an observation is being made. If the telescope is out of alignment, the observer will be unable to look straight through it (see fig. 2223). Some sextants have adjusting screws on the telescope for adjusting the line of sight, but it is better to have this done in an optical shop if possible.

Personal Error

2224   After all adjustable errors have been reduced or eliminated insofar as possible, the sextant will probably still retain some residual, variable, adjustable error as well as a small fixed nonadjustable instrument error. Additionally, a small variable error called *personal error* may often be produced as a result of the eye of the observer acting in conjunction with the optical system of the sextant. This might be different for the Sun and Moon than for planets and stars, it might vary with the degree of fatigue of the observer, and/or it might change with the altitude being measured (high altitudes are usually harder to measure than lower ones). For these reasons, a personal error should be approached with caution. However, if a relatively constant personal error persists, and experience

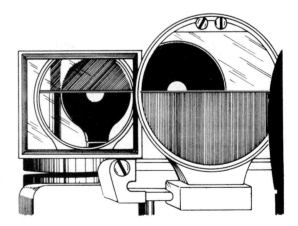

Fig. 2223. Checking telescope alignment.

indicates that observations are improved by applying a correction to remove its effect, better results might be obtained by this procedure than by attempting to eliminate it from one's observations. The *personal correction* (PC) is the determined personal error with the sign reversed.

Dip of the Horizon (D)

2225 Dip of the horizon is customarily referred to merely as *dip* and its correction is usually symbolized on sight forms as *D*. The D correction is required because of the height of the observer's eye above the level of the sea.

Celestial altitudes obtained with the marine sextant are measured relative to the visible, or sea, horizon. Because the Earth is a spheroid, the higher the observer is situated above the surface, the more depressed the visible horizon will be below the celestial horizon or true horizontal at his eye. Figure 2225 shows two observers sharing a common zenith and observing the same star. The observer at *A″* is situated considerably higher than the observer at *A′*. The observers' height of eye is greatly exaggerated in the figure for illustrative purposes. It is obvious that the star's hs will be considerably larger for the observer at *A″*, than that the latter for the one at *A′*, and will have a larger hs than she or he would at the point *A*, on the water surface directly beneath her or him. The value of the dip may be defined as the excess over 90° of the angular distance from observer's zenith to his visible horizon, which is perpendicular to the zenith-nadir line. The D correction must be made for this excess. As the magnitude of the correction depends upon the observer's height above the water, it is sometimes called the "height of eye correction." Not obvious in the figure is the slight curvature of light paths from the horizon to the observer's eye. This curvature, which

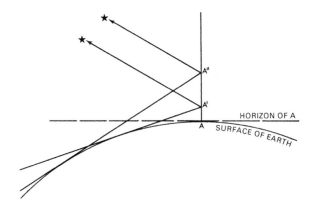

Fig. 2225. Dip increases with greater height of eye above the water's surface.

results from local refraction by Earth's atmosphere, has the effect of reducing the numerical value of dip and of increasing the distance to the sea horizon.

The D correction is always *negative*, and is applied to all celestial altitude observations made by marine sextant. Its application to the hs corrects the latter to the value it would have if the visible horizon were a plane passing through the eye of the observer and perpendicular to the line of his zenith.

Apparent Altitude (ha)

2226 For purposes of routine navigation, corrections to the sextant altitude can be applied in any order using the hs as entering argument in the various correction tables. Where greater accuracy is desired, however, or at low altitudes where small changes in altitude can result in significant changes in the correction, the order of applying the corrections is important. To obtain maximum accuracy, the four corrections so far discussed—for nonadjustable instrument error (I), index error (IC), dip (D), and personal error (PE) if applicable—are first applied to the hs. The hs so corrected becomes the ha (for apparent altitude), and its value is used when entering tables to obtain the corrections discussed in the following articles. (Note: In some books you may see the term "rectified altitude" [hr] used instead.) Once the ha has been established as an intermediate step, other corrections can then be applied.

Refraction (R)

2227 Refraction is caused by the bending of a light ray as it passes from a medium of one density into one of a different density. The increasingly dense layers of Earth's atmosphere cause the rays to be bent more and more downward in the vertical plane, as they approach the surface. Refraction, therefore, causes every heavenly body to appear higher than its actual position, as shown in figure 2227 (exaggerated for emphasis). The only exception to this occurs when the body is at the observer's zenith, when the light rays are traveling vertically and there is no refraction.

The lower a body is located in altitude, the more atmosphere its light rays will penetrate in reaching the observer, and the greater, therefore, will be the refraction. The effect of refraction on sextant altitude increases progressively with lower altitudes until the celestial body disappears below the visible horizon. In fact, when the Sun's upper limb appears tangent to the horizon at sunrise or sunset, its upper limb is actually below the celestial horizon. But be aware that given sufficient height of eye, ha may

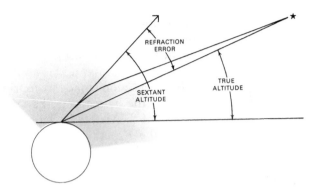

Fig. 2227. Atmospheric refraction causes light rays to bend.

also become *negative*, and make the refraction effect even more pronounced. Although the standard or mean refraction tables in the *Nautical Almanac* do not list a value for any negative ha, they may be extended by extrapolation. Alternatively, the values may be calculated by the formulas given for the purpose under the heading of "Methods and Formulae for Direct Computation" under "Sight Reduction Procedures" in the *Nautical Almanac*.

The refractive effect is not absolutely constant but varies with changes in the distribution of density within the atmosphere.

The R correction is always *negative*, and it is applied to all celestial altitude observations. It is obtained from the *Nautical Almanac*, but in some cases it is not applied independently but is incorporated into the "altitude correction" obtained from the almanac (see below).

Air Temperature (T) and Atmospheric Pressure (B) Corrections

2228 The R correction varies slightly with normal changes in the density of the atmosphere; that density, in turn, depends upon the air temperature and atmospheric pressure. The refraction correction table given in the *Nautical Almanac* is based on a standard or average atmospheric density, with a temperature of 50° Fahrenheit (10° C) and atmospheric pressure of 29.83 inches (1010 mb). An additional table of corrections is given in the almanac to permit further correction for variations of temperature and pressure from the selected norms. The T (temperature) and B (barometric) corrections are ordinarily not required, except for low-altitude observations, unless temperature and pressure vary materially from the standard values. All observations at altitudes of 10° or less should be corrected for temperature and barometric pressure.

The *combined T and B* correction may be *positive* or *negative* and is applied to all observations when conditions require it, in addition to the usual R correction. When applied to the ha, the sextant altitude is corrected to the value it would have under conditions of a standard atmospheric density. Note that the entering argument for the lower part of the T & B Correction Table in the *Nautical Almanac* is *ha* not *hs*. As with its mean refraction tables, the *Nautical Almanac* T & B Correction Table does not list values for negative altitudes; but the table may be extended by extrapolation or by computation as suggested in article 2227.

Semidiameter Correction (SD)

2229 The values of Greenwich hour angle and declination tabulated in all almanacs are for the centers of the various celestial bodies. Because an observer using a marine sextant cannot readily determine the center of the Sun or Moon, she or he measures the altitude of one of the *limbs* (upper or lower) of these two bodies. The *semidiameter* (SD) is the angular distance between the limb of the Sun or Moon and the center, as illustrated in figure 2229. If a lower limb observation is made, the SD must be added to the hs to obtain the altitude of the center of the body; conversely, it is subtracted if the upper limb is observed.

The semidiameter varies with the distance of the body from the observer. The Moon is comparatively near the Earth, and the changes in its distance as it revolves about the Earth have a comparatively large effect on its SD. At certain times, the Moon's SD may change significantly from day to day. The Sun is much more distant, and the eccentricity of the Earth's orbit has a less pronounced effect on the Sun's SD, which varies between about 15.8' and 16.3'.

The SD correction is applied only to observations of the Sun and Moon; it is not applicable to observations of stars or planets, as they have no significant apparent diameter when viewed through telescopes

a—altitude of upper limb
b—altitude of center body
c—altitude of lower limb

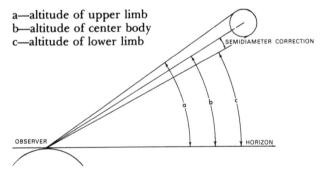

Fig. 2229. Semidiameter correction for Sun or Moon (not to scale).

normally used with sextants. (Note: Venus is an exception, but rather than by semidiameter, it is covered by a related *phase* correction explained below.) When the SD is applied, the altitude is corrected to the value it would have if the center of the body had been observed.

Augmentation (A)

2230 The semidiameter of a body varies with its distance from the observer's eye. Other conditions being constant, its distance when at zero altitude is greater than when it is at the zenith, the difference in distance being equal to the Earth's radius (see fig. 2230). As Earth's radius is extremely small in comparison to the distance to the Sun, any correction for the difference in distance due to the observer's position on Earth, which is termed *augmentation,* is not of practical significance in Sun sights. Augmentation for a planet would vary with the relative positions in the orbits of that body and the Earth, but again the effect is too small to be considered.

As a result of the comparative nearness of the Moon, however, its augmentation from the observer's horizon to his zenith is about 0.3′ at mean lunar distance. No separate correction for augmentation need be applied, however, because allowance for it has been made in the Moon correction tables of the *Nautical Almanac.*

Phase (F)

2231 The planets go through phases that are much like those of the Moon. A planet's phase is not obvious to the unaided eye, but a telescope increases the phase effect and affects the positioning of a planet on the horizon by an observer using a sextant. In the case of Venus, these phases can be significant and a correction is required as explained

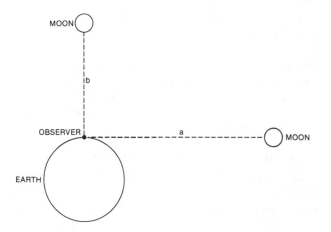

Fig. 2230. Correction for augmentation; distance *a* is greater than *b*. (Not to scale.)

below. The phase correction is similar to the semidiameter correction for the Sun and Moon but much smaller. When applied to ha, the sextant altitude is corrected to the value it would have if the center of the planet had been observed.

Irradiation (J)

2232 Irradiation is the name applied to the optical illusion that causes the apparent size of a bright or light-colored object in juxtaposition with a darker one to appear larger than it actually is; conversely, a darker one appears smaller. Thus, when the sky is considerably brighter than the water, the horizon appears depressed. The apparent diameter of the Sun is increased slightly by irradiation, and the brighter stars appear to have a measurable diameter. Altitudes of the Sun's lower limb should not be affected, for the irradiation effects on the Sun and on the horizon are in the same direction and effectively cancel out. The effect on the upper limb of the Sun, however, is opposite to that on the horizon, and a subtractive correction would be applicable. Quantitatively, it decreases with increasing telescope magnification, and with increasing altitudes. Irradiation corrections are seldom, if ever, calculated and applied in practical surface navigation, primarily because they are small, variable, and not accurately predictable.

Parallax (P)

2233 *Parallax* is the difference in the direction of an object at a finite distance when viewed simultaneously from two different positions. It enters into the sextant altitude corrections because the actual altitude observed with a sextant (hs) is measured from near the Earth's surface, but the observed altitude (Ho) determined through additional corrections to hs is calculated as though from the Earth's center. Since the Moon is the celestial body nearest the Earth, parallax has its greatest effect on lunar observations.

The effect of parallax is illustrated in figure 2233. If the Moon is directly overhead, that is, with an altitude of 90°, there is no parallax, because its direction in space is the same from the center of the Earth as from the observer. As the Moon decreases in altitude its direction from the observer begins to differ with its direction from the Earth's center, and the difference in direction increases continuously until the Moon sets. The same effect, of course, occurs in reverse when a body is rising. At altitude 0°, it is called *horizontal parallax* (HP).

In addition to increasing as altitude decreases, parallax increases as distance to a celestial body

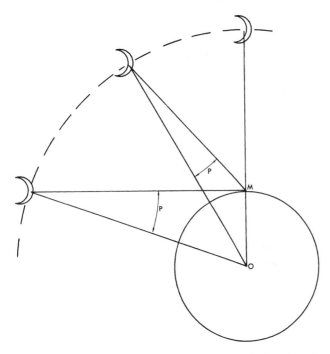

Fig. 2233. The parallax correction varies with the altitude of the observed body. (Not to scale.)

decreases. Venus and Mars, when close to the Earth, are also appreciably affected by parallax. The Sun is only slightly affected, its HP being always less than 0.15 minutes of arc. All other celestial bodies are too far from the Earth to require correction for parallax when observed with a sextant.

The correction for parallax is always positive, and is applied only to observations of the Moon, Sun, Venus, and Mars. Its effect is to correct the sextant altitude to the value it would have if the observer were at the center of the Earth. Parallax for the Sun is included with other corrections such as those for refraction and semidiameter in the Altitude Correction Tables found just inside the front cover (pages A2 and A3) of the *Nautical Almanac*. For the Moon, the value of horizontal parallax is tabulated hourly in the daily pages of the *Nautical Almanac* and is then used as an entering argument in the Altitude Correction Tables for the Moon found on the inside back covers of the *Nautical Almanac*. The star tables are used for the planets, but an additional correction for parallax is required for Venus and Mars and is included in the tables on page A2 of the *Nautical Almanac* as discussed below.

The foregoing discussion of geocentric parallax assumes a spherical shape for the Earth. This is a reasonable assumption that simplifies calculations, while keeping them within acceptable ranges of accuracy. For a spherical Earth, altitude parallax varies very nearly as the cosine of the apparent altitude. However, in a special section of the *Nautical*

Almanac called "Methods and Formulae for Direct Computation," under the larger section entitled "Sight Reduction Procedures," you can find a pair of equations that may be used to calculate the parallax in altitude for observers on an oblate Earth.

APPLYING CORRECTIONS FROM THE *NAUTICAL ALMANAC*

2234   After corrections have been applied for instrument error (I) and index correction (IC), other corrections for values discussed above must be applied, using tables found in the *Nautical Almanac*. On the inside front cover, the left-hand page is labeled "A2" and is titled "Altitude Correction Tables 10°–90°—Sun, Stars, Planets" (see fig. 2234); on the right-hand page (labeled "A3") are other, similar tables that cover 0°–10°. The A2 page also includes the "DIP" table used for height of eye corrections. For convenience, the A2 tables are also reproduced on one side of a special heavy paper, nearly full-page size bookmark provided with the almanac, but the A3 tables are not.

The table labeled "Sun" *combines the corrections for refraction, semidiameter,* and *parallax.* The one marked "Stars and Planets" covers *refraction only* because semidiameter and parallax are not necessary for the majority of these sights. Because Venus and Mars do require an additional correction for parallax, additional corrections for them are also provided on the A2 page.

Note that several of these tables are *critical-value* tables in that the tabulated values are found on "steps" half a line between the entering arguments. If the entering argument is an exact tabulated value, the correction on the half-line *above* it should be used.

Height of Eye Correction

2235   Using the table labeled "DIP," enter with your height of eye in either meters or feet. Be sure to include your own height with that of the ship's bridge or wherever else you are standing when taking your sightings. Looking at the DIP table in figure 2234 you can see that your D correction should be –4.6′ for a height of eye 22.5 feet. If your height is 4 meters, the D correction is –3.5′.

Correcting Observations of the Sun

2236   Using the table labeled "Sun" in the Altitude Correction Tables found inside the front cover of the *Nautical Almanac* (on either page A2 or A3 depending upon the apparent altitude of the Sun), you are able to take care of the necessary corrections for refraction, semidiameter, and parallax all

A2 ALTITUDE CORRECTION TABLES 10°–90°—SUN, STARS, PLANETS

SUN (OCT.–MAR. | APR.–SEPT.)

OCT.–MAR. App. Alt.	Lower Limb / Upper Limb	APR.–SEPT. App. Alt.	Lower Limb / Upper Limb
9 34	+10.8 −21.5	9 39	+10.6 −21.2
9 45	+10.9 −21.4	9 51	+10.7 −21.1
9 56	+11.0 −21.3	10 03	+10.8 −21.0
10 08	+11.1 −21.2	10 15	+10.9 −20.9
10 21	+11.2 −21.1	10 27	+11.0 −20.8
10 34	+11.3 −21.0	10 40	+11.1 −20.7
10 47	+11.4 −20.9	10 54	+11.2 −20.6
11 01	+11.5 −20.8	11 08	+11.3 −20.5
11 15	+11.6 −20.7	11 23	+11.4 −20.4
11 30	+11.7 −20.6	11 38	+11.5 −20.3
11 46	+11.8 −20.5	11 54	+11.6 −20.2
12 02	+11.9 −20.4	12 10	+11.7 −20.1
12 19	+12.0 −20.3	12 28	+11.8 −20.0
12 37	+12.1 −20.2	12 46	+11.9 −19.9
12 55	+12.2 −20.1	13 05	+12.0 −19.8
13 14	+12.3 −20.0	13 24	+12.1 −19.7
13 35	+12.4 −19.9	13 45	+12.2 −19.6
13 56	+12.5 −19.8	14 07	+12.3 −19.5
14 18	+12.6 −19.7	14 30	+12.4 −19.4
14 42	+12.7 −19.6	14 54	+12.5 −19.3
15 06	+12.8 −19.5	15 19	+12.6 −19.2
15 32	+12.9 −19.4	15 46	+12.7 −19.1
15 59	+13.0 −19.3	16 14	+12.8 −19.0
16 28	+13.1 −19.2	16 44	+12.9 −18.9
16 59	+13.2 −19.1	17 15	+13.0 −18.8
17 32	+13.3 −19.0	17 48	+13.1 −18.7
18 06	+13.4 −18.9	18 24	+13.2 −18.6
18 42	+13.5 −18.8	19 01	+13.3 −18.5
19 21	+13.6 −18.7	19 42	+13.4 −18.4
20 03	+13.7 −18.6	20 25	+13.5 −18.3
20 48	+13.8 −18.5	21 11	+13.6 −18.2
21 35	+13.9 −18.4	22 00	+13.7 −18.1
22 26	+14.0 −18.3	22 54	+13.8 −18.0
23 22	+14.1 −18.2	23 51	+13.9 −17.9
24 21	+14.2 −18.1	24 53	+14.0 −17.8
25 26	+14.3 −18.0	26 00	+14.1 −17.7
26 36	+14.4 −17.9	27 13	+14.2 −17.6
27 52	+14.5 −17.8	28 33	+14.3 −17.5
29 15	+14.6 −17.7	30 00	+14.4 −17.4
30 46	+14.7 −17.6	31 35	+14.5 −17.3
32 26	+14.8 −17.5	33 20	+14.6 −17.2
34 17	+14.9 −17.4	35 17	+14.7 −17.1
36 20	+15.0 −17.3	37 26	+14.8 −17.0
38 36	+15.1 −17.2	39 50	+14.9 −16.9
41 08	+15.2 −17.1	42 31	+15.0 −16.8
43 59	+15.3 −17.0	45 31	+15.1 −16.7
47 10	+15.4 −16.9	48 55	+15.2 −16.6
50 46	+15.5 −16.8	52 44	+15.3 −16.5
54 49	+15.6 −16.7	57 02	+15.4 −16.4
59 23	+15.7 −16.6	61 51	+15.5 −16.3
64 30	+15.8 −16.5	67 17	+15.6 −16.2
70 12	+15.9 −16.4	73 16	+15.7 −16.1
76 26	+16.0 −16.3	79 43	+15.8 −16.0
83 05	+16.1 −16.2	86 32	+15.9 −15.9
90 00		90 00	

STARS AND PLANETS

App. Alt.	Corrn
9 56	−5.3
10 08	−5.2
10 20	−5.1
10 33	−5.0
10 46	−4.9
11 00	−4.8
11 14	−4.7
11 29	−4.6
11 45	−4.5
12 01	−4.4
12 18	−4.3
12 35	−4.2
12 54	−4.1
13 13	−4.0
13 33	−3.9
13 54	−3.8
14 16	−3.7
14 40	−3.6
15 04	−3.5
15 30	−3.4
15 57	−3.3
16 26	−3.2
16 56	−3.1
17 28	−3.0
18 02	−2.9
18 38	−2.8
19 17	−2.7
19 58	−2.6
20 42	−2.5
21 28	−2.4
22 19	−2.3
23 13	−2.2
24 11	−2.1
25 14	−2.0
26 22	−1.9
27 36	−1.8
28 56	−1.7
30 24	−1.6
32 00	−1.5
33 45	−1.4
35 40	−1.3
37 48	−1.2
40 08	−1.1
42 44	−1.0
45 36	−0.9
48 47	−0.8
52 18	−0.7
56 11	−0.6
60 28	−0.5
65 08	−0.4
70 11	−0.3
75 34	−0.2
81 13	−0.1
87 03	0.0
90 00	

App. Alt. — Additional Corrn

VENUS

Jan. 1-Jan. 29
47 + 0.2

Jan. 30-Feb. 26
46 + 0.3

Feb. 27-Mar. 14
11 + 0.4
41 + 0.5

Mar. 15-Mar. 23
6 + 0.5
20 + 0.6
31 + 0.7

Mar. 24-Apr. 19
4 + 0.6
12 + 0.7
22 + 0.8

Apr. 20-Apr. 28
6 + 0.5
20 + 0.6
31 + 0.7

Apr. 29-May 13
11 + 0.4
41 + 0.5

May 14-June 8
46 + 0.3

June 9-July 23
47 + 0.2

July 24-Dec. 31
42 + 0.1

MARS

Jan. 1-Nov. 12
60 + 0.1

Nov. 13-Dec. 31
41 + 0.2
75 + 0.1

DIP

Ht. of Eye (m)	Corrn	Ht. of Eye (ft)	Ht. of Eye (m)	Corrn
2.4	−2.8	8.0	1.0	−1.8
2.6	−2.9	8.6	1.5	−2.2
2.8	−3.0	9.2	2.0	−2.5
3.0	−3.1	9.8	2.5	−2.8
3.2	−3.2	10.5	3.0	−3.0
3.4	−3.3	11.2	See table	
3.6	−3.4	11.9		
3.8	−3.5	12.6		
4.0	−3.6	13.3	(m)	
4.3	−3.7	14.1	20	−7.9
4.5	−3.8	14.9	22	−8.3
4.7	−3.9	15.7	24	−8.6
5.0	−4.0	16.5	26	−9.0
5.2	−4.1	17.4	28	−9.3
5.5	−4.2	18.3		
5.8	−4.3	19.1	30	−9.6
6.1	−4.4	20.1	32	−10.0
6.3	−4.5	21.0	34	−10.3
6.6	−4.6	22.0	36	−10.6
6.9	−4.7	22.9	38	−10.8
7.2	−4.8	23.9		
7.5	−4.9	24.9	40	−11.1
7.9	−5.0	26.0	42	−11.4
8.2	−5.1	27.1	44	−11.7
8.5	−5.2	28.1	46	−11.9
8.8	−5.3	29.2	48	−12.2
9.2	−5.4	30.4	(ft)	
9.5	−5.5	31.5	2	−1.4
9.9	−5.6	32.7	4	−1.9
10.3	−5.7	33.9	6	−2.4
10.6	−5.8	35.1	8	−2.7
11.0	−5.9	36.3	10	−3.1
11.4	−6.0	37.6	See table	
11.8	−6.1	38.9		
12.2	−6.2	40.1	(ft)	
12.6	−6.3	41.5	70	−8.1
13.0	−6.4	42.8	75	−8.4
13.4	−6.5	44.2	80	−8.7
13.8	−6.6	45.5	85	−8.9
14.2	−6.7	46.9	90	−9.2
14.7	−6.8	48.4	95	−9.5
15.1	−6.9	49.8		
15.5	−7.0	51.3	100	−9.7
16.0	−7.1	52.8	105	−9.9
16.5	−7.2	54.3	110	−10.2
16.9	−7.3	55.8	115	−10.4
17.4	−7.4	57.4	120	−10.6
17.9	−7.5	58.9	125	−10.8
18.4	−7.6	60.5		
18.8	−7.7	62.1	130	−11.1
19.3	−7.8	63.8	135	−11.3
19.8	−7.9	65.4	140	−11.5
20.4	−8.0	67.1	145	−11.7
20.9	−8.1	68.8	150	−11.9
21.4		70.5	155	−12.1

App. Alt. = Apparent altitude = Sextant altitude corrected for index error and dip.
For daylight observations of Venus, see page 260.

Fig. 2234. *Nautical Almanac* correction tables for the Sun, stars, and planets at altitudes between approximately 10° and 90°.

at once, because all three have been factored in to these tables. The corrections are arranged in two columns, titled "Oct.–Mar." and "Apr.–Sept.," to incorporate the change in the Sun's semidiameter throughout the year (see fig. 2234).

Example: A navigator observes the upper limb of the Sun with a marine sextant on 5 June with a height of eye of 48 feet. The sextant reading is 51° 58.4′. The instrument correction is –0.2′ and the sextant has an index error of 2.2′ "off the arc."

Required: Ho at the time of observation using the *Nautical Almanac.*

Solution: (1) Record I and IC; in this case, they are –0.2′ and +2.2′ (+2.0′).

(2) Enter the *Nautical Almanac* "DIP" table with height of eye; extract and record the D correction; in this case, it is –6.7′.

(3) Determine the net correction (–4.7′) and apply it to hs (51° 58.4′) to obtain ha (51° 53.7′).

(4) Using ha, enter the Altitude Correction Table

for the SUN (inside front cover of the *Nautical Almanac*), using the appropriate column (Apr.–Sept., Upper Limb); extract the combined correction for refraction, parallax, and semidiameter; in this case, –16.6′ (see fig. 2234).

(5) Algebraically add this correction to ha to obtain Ho.

Answer: Ho 51° 37.1′.

To achieve maximum accuracy, you may apply these corrections *individually*, using the more precise value for semidiameter for the specific date as obtained from the daily pages of the *Almanac*. Because the Sun table yields results that are a close approximation, this more detailed procedure is rarely used in practical navigation. However, for those who want the additional accuracy, the steps to follow are:

1. Apply I, IC, and D corrections to hs to obtain ha.
2. With the apparent altitude thus found, extract the refraction correction from the "Stars and Planets" correction table from page A2 (or from the bookmark). Remember that this table covers refraction only.
3. Turn to the appropriate date in the daily pages and find the SD value on the lower right page; this correction is positive for lower limb sights and negative for upper limb sights.
4. For altitudes below 65°, apply a positive correction of 0.1′ for parallax (P).

Correcting Observations of a Star

2237   In addition to the I, IC, and D corrections, star observations require only a correction for refraction, R; semidiameter and parallax are not required. Refraction is found in the appropriate column of the Altitude Correction Tables on the inside front cover of the *Nautical Almanac*, headed "Stars and Planets" (see fig. 2234).

Example: A navigator observes the star Zubenelgenubi with a marine sextant from a height of eye of 12 meters. The sextant altitude is 64° 52.7′, and the instrument has an index error of 1.7′ "off the arc"; the certificate inside the sextant's box indicates that "this instrument is free of errors for practical use," so there is no applicable instrument correction.

Required: Ho at the time of observation.

Solution: (1) Since there is no I error, record only the IC correction (+1.7′).

(2) Enter the *Nautical Almanac* "DIP" table with height of eye, and extract and record the D correction. In this case it is –6.1′.

(3) Determine the net correction (–4.4′) and apply it to hs (64° 52.7′) to obtain ha (64° 48.3′).

(4) Using ha, enter the Altitude Correction Tables found in the inside front cover of the *Nautical Almanac* and, using the column for "Stars and Planets," extract the refraction correction, in this case –0.5′, and apply it algebraically to ha.

Answer: Ho 64° 47.8′.

Correcting Observations of Jupiter and Saturn

2238   Because of their comparatively great distance from the Earth, the planets Jupiter and Saturn do not require corrections for semidiameter and parallax, and so their altitude correction may therefore be treated as those for stars in the ordinary practice of navigation.

Correcting Observations of Venus and Mars

2239   Observations of Venus and Mars besides being corrected for I, IC, D, and R (as for Jupiter, Saturn, and the stars) should be corrected for parallax. For Venus, a phase correction (which is related to semidiameter) is applied in addition to the other corrections. The parallax correction is listed in the table of Additional Corrections on the inside front cover of the *Nautical Almanac* (see fig. 2234). Those who want to see how P changes smoothly, rather than abruptly by 0.1-minute steps as shown in the additional correction tables, may consult the Explanation section which follows the daily pages of the *Nautical Almanac*. The phase correction (now applicable only to Venus among the planets) is accommodated more subtly in that an allowance for it is included the tabulations of Venus's Greenwich hour angle and declination found in the daily pages. Accordingly, you may disregard this tiny, automatically applied correction, except as a reminder that you need not attempt to observe a limb of Venus as you would when sighting the Sun or Moon. You should focus instead on the apparent optical center of Venus.

Example: During morning twilight on 5 June, a navigator with a marine sextant observes the planet Venus from a height of eye of 16.5 meters. The sextant altitude is 41° 17.6′, the instrument has an IC of –0.5′, and there is no I correction necessary.

Required: Ho at the time of observation.

Solution: (1) Record the IC. In this case, it is –0.5′.

(2) Enter the "DIP" table with the height of eye and extract and record the D correction. In this case, it is –7.1′.

(3) Determine the net correction (–7.6′) and apply it to hs (41° 17.6′) to obtain ha (41° 10.0′).

(4) Enter the *Nautical Almanac* page A2 and use the Altitude Correction Tables on the inside front cover of the Nautical Almanac in the column labeled "Stars and Planets," using the left-hand col-

umn with the ha to extract the refraction correction, which is –1.1′.

(5) Enter the right-hand column of "Stars and Planets" and extract the additional correction for phase and parallax, in this case +0.3′.

(6) Determine the net correction (–0.8′) to ha and apply it algebraically to determine Ho.

Answer: Ho 41° 09.2′.

Correcting Observations of the Moon

2240 The Altitude Correction Tables for observations of the Moon are found on the inside back cover and the facing page of the *Nautical Almanac,* as shown in part in figure 2240. These tables combine the corrections for refraction, semidiameter, parallax, and augmentation.

To correct observations of the Moon, the I, IC, and D corrections are applied to the sextant altitude. The upper portion of the Moon correction tables are then entered with the apparent altitude thus obtained, and the first correction is found under the appropriate altitude heading. The Moon's HP (horizontal parallax) is next obtained from the daily pages of the *Almanac* for the time of the observation. HP is the entering argument to obtain the second correction from the lower portion of the tables. These tables are entered in the same vertical column as was used to obtain the first correction. Two values are listed in each column under the headings L and U for each tabulated value of HP; the L value is for observations of the Moon's lower limb, and the U for those of the upper limb. The second correction is extracted under the appropriate heading. It should be noted that as HP is tabulated in increments of 0.3′, it is desirable to interpolate

for nontabulated values of HP when obtaining the second correction.

Both the first and second corrections are *added* to the apparent altitude of all Moon observations, but for observations of the upper limb, 30.0′ is to be subtracted from the sum of the corrections.

Example: A navigator observes the lower limb of the Moon with a marine sextant from a height of eye of 7.6 meters. The sextant reading is 56° 39.7′; there is no instrument or index error. The HP from the daily pages of the *Nautical Almanac* for the day concerned is found to be 57.6′.

Required: Ho for the time of observation.

Solution: (1) Record the I and IC. In this case there is neither.

(2) Enter the *Nautical Almanac* "DIP" table with height of eye, and extract and record the D correction (–4.9′).

(3) Apply the D correction to hs to obtain ha of 56° 34.8′.

(4) Enter the upper portion of the *Nautical Almanac* "Moon" table with ha and extract and record the first correction. In this case it is +41.8′.

(5) Follow down the altitude column used in (4) above, and extract and record from the lower portion of the "Moon" table the L correction for the HP found on the daily page. In this case HP is 57.6′ and L is +4.9′.

(6) Sum the corrections (+46.7′) and apply algebraically to ha to obtain Ho.

Answer: Ho 57° 21.5′.

Correcting for Nonstandard Refraction

2241 The refraction corrections included in the various Altitude Correction Tables in the *Nautical*

ALTITUDE CORRECTION TABLES 35°–90°—MOON

App. Alt.	35°–39° Corrⁿ	40°–44° Corrⁿ	45°–49° Corrⁿ	50°–54° Corrⁿ	55°–59° Corrⁿ	60°–64° Corrⁿ	65°–69° Corrⁿ	70°–74° Corrⁿ	75°–79° Corrⁿ	80°–84° Corrⁿ	85°–89° Corrⁿ	App. Alt.
00	35 56·5	40 53·7	45 50·5	50 46·9	55 43·1	60 38·9	65 34·6	70 30·1	75 25·3	80 20·5	85 15·6	00
10	56·4	53·6	50·4	46·8	42·9	38·8	34·4	29·9	25·2	20·4	15·5	10
20	56·3	53·5	50·2	46·7	42·8	38·7	34·3	29·7	25·0	20·2	15·3	20
30	56·2	53·4	50·1	46·5	42·7	38·5	34·1	29·6	24·9	20·0	15·1	30
40	56·2	53·3	50·0	46·4	42·5	38·4	34·0	29·4	24·7	19·9	15·0	40
50	56·1	53·2	49·9	46·3	42·4	38·2	33·8	29·3	24·5	19·7	14·8	50
00	36 56·0	41 53·1	46 49·8	51 46·2	56 42·3	61 38·1	66 33·7	71 29·1	76 24·4	81 19·6	86 14·6	00
10	55·9	53·0	49·7	46·0	42·1	37·9	33·5	29·0	24·2	19·4	14·5	10
20	55·8	52·8	49·5	45·9	42·0	37·8	33·4	28·8	24·1	19·2	14·3	20
30	55·7	52·7	49·4	45·8	41·8	37·7	33·2	28·7	23·9	19·1	14·1	30
40	55·6	52·6	49·3	45·7	41·7	37·5	33·1	28·5	23·8	18·9	14·0	40
50	55·5	52·5	49·2	45·5	41·6	37·4	32·9	28·3	23·6	18·7	13·8	50

H.P.	L	U	L	U	L	U	L	U	L	U	L	U	L	U	L	U	L	U	L	U	L	U	H.P.
	′	′	′	′	′	′	′	′	′	′	′	′	′	′	′	′	′	′	′	′	′	′	
57·0	4·3	3·2	4·3	3·3	4·3	3·3	4·4	3·4	4·4	3·4	4·5	3·5	4·5	3·5	4·6	3·6	4·7	3·6	4·7	3·7	4·8	3·8	57·0
57·3	4·6	3·4	4·6	3·4	4·6	3·4	4·6	3·5	4·7	3·5	4·7	3·6	4·8	3·6	4·8	3·6	4·8	3·7	4·9	3·7	4·8	3·7	57·3
57·6	4·9	3·6	4·9	3·6	4·9	3·6	4·9	3·6	4·9	3·6	4·9	3·6	4·9	3·6	5·0	3·6	5·0	3·6	5·0	3·6	4·9	3·6	57·6
57·9	5·2	3·7	5·2	3·7	5·2	3·7	5·2	3·7	5·1	3·6	5·1	3·6	5·1	3·6	5·1	3·6	5·1	3·6	5·1	3·6	5·1	3·6	57·9
58·2	5·5	3·9	5·5	3·8	5·5	3·8	5·4	3·8	5·4	3·7	5·4	3·7	5·3	3·7	5·3	3·6	5·2	3·6	5·2	3·5	5·2	3·5	58·2

Fig. 2240. *Nautical Almanac* correction tables for Moon observations.

Almanac are based on an air temperature of 50° F (10° C), and an atmospheric pressure of 29.83 inches of mercury (1010 millibars). When atmospheric conditions vary from these standard values, the light from celestial bodies is refracted to a greater or lesser value than is stated in the tables.

Additional corrections for nonstandard conditions of refraction are given in the *Nautical Almanac*, page A4, which is reproduced in figure 2241. It is entered at the top with the temperature, and a line is projected down vertically until it intersects with a horizontal line drawn in from the appropriate point on the pressure scale. The intersection of these two lines will fall within one of the diagonal lettered zones; the name of this letter establishes the vertical correction column to be

used. Using the apparent altitude as the entering argument, the additional refraction correction is then found.

Except under extreme conditions, it is not necessary to use this table for altitudes above 10°. However, due to the extremely rapid change in the value of the refraction at very low altitudes, this table should always be used for correcting observations of 10° or less. Interpolation may be desirable at extremely low altitudes.

Example: A sextant observation of 7° is taken under conditions of air temperature +20° C and barometric pressure 1010 millibars.

Required: The additional correction for refraction.

Solution: (1) Turn to page A4 in the *Nautical Almanac*.

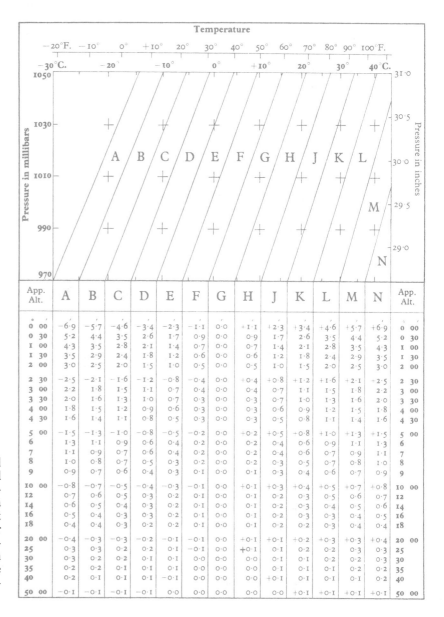

Fig. 2241. *Nautical Almanac* additional refraction corrections for nonstandard conditions. The graph is entered with values of temperature and pressure to find a "zone letter," A to L. Using the apparent altitude (sextant altitude corrected for dip) and column for appropriate zone letter, the proper correction is taken from the table. This correction is applied to the apparent altitude *in addition to* the corrections for standard conditions.

App. Alt.	A	B	C	D	E	F	G	H	J	K	L	M	N	App. Alt.
0 00	−6·9	−5·7	−4·6	−3·4	−2·3	−1·1	0·0	+1·1	+2·3	+3·4	+4·6	+5·7	+6·9	0 00
0 30	5·2	4·4	3·5	2·6	1·7	0·9	0·0	0·9	1·7	2·6	3·5	4·4	5·2	0 30
1 00	4·3	3·5	2·8	2·1	1·4	0·7	0·0	0·7	1·4	2·1	2·8	3·5	4·3	1 00
1 30	3·5	2·9	2·4	1·8	1·2	0·6	0·0	0·6	1·2	1·8	2·4	2·9	3·5	1 30
2 00	3·0	2·5	2·0	1·5	1·0	0·5	0·0	0·5	1·0	1·5	2·0	2·5	3·0	2 00
2 30	−2·5	−2·1	−1·6	−1·2	−0·8	−0·4	0·0	+0·4	+0·8	+1·2	+1·6	+2·1	−2·5	2 30
3 00	2·2	1·8	1·5	1·1	0·7	0·4	0·0	0·4	0·7	1·1	1·5	1·8	2·2	3 00
3 30	2·0	1·6	1·3	1·0	0·7	0·3	0·0	0·3	0·7	1·0	1·3	1·6	2·0	3 30
4 00	1·8	1·5	1·2	0·9	0·6	0·3	0·0	0·3	0·6	0·9	1·2	1·5	1·8	4 00
4 30	1·6	1·4	1·1	0·8	0·5	0·3	0·0	0·3	0·5	0·8	1·1	1·4	1·6	4 30
5 00	−1·5	−1·3	−1·0	−0·8	−0·5	−0·2	0·0	+0·2	+0·5	+0·8	+1·0	+1·3	+1·5	5 00
6	1·3	1·1	0·9	0·6	0·4	0·2	0·0	0·2	0·4	0·6	0·9	1·1	1·3	6
7	1·1	0·9	0·7	0·6	0·4	0·2	0·0	0·2	0·4	0·6	0·7	0·9	1·1	7
8	1·0	0·8	0·7	0·5	0·3	0·2	0·0	0·2	0·3	0·5	0·7	0·8	1·0	8
9	0·9	0·7	0·6	0·4	0·3	0·1	0·0	0·1	0·3	0·4	0·6	0·7	0·9	9
10 00	−0·8	−0·7	−0·5	−0·4	−0·3	−0·1	0·0	+0·1	+0·3	+0·4	+0·5	+0·7	+0·8	10 00
12	0·7	0·6	0·5	0·3	0·2	0·1	0·0	0·1	0·2	0·3	0·5	0·6	0·7	12
14	0·6	0·5	0·4	0·3	0·2	0·1	0·0	0·1	0·2	0·3	0·4	0·5	0·6	14
16	0·5	0·4	0·3	0·3	0·2	0·1	0·0	0·1	0·2	0·3	0·3	0·4	0·5	16
18	0·4	0·4	0·3	0·2	0·2	0·1	0·0	0·1	0·2	0·2	0·3	0·4	0·4	18
20 00	−0·4	−0·3	−0·3	−0·2	−0·1	−0·1	0·0	+0·1	+0·1	+0·2	+0·3	+0·3	+0·4	20 00
25	0·3	0·3	0·2	0·2	0·1	−0·1	0·0	+0·1	0·1	0·2	0·2	0·3	0·3	25
30	0·3	0·2	0·2	0·1	0·1	0·0	0·0	0·0	0·1	0·1	0·2	0·2	0·3	30
35	0·2	0·2	0·1	0·1	0·1	0·0	0·0	0·0	0·1	0·1	0·1	0·2	0·2	35
40	0·2	0·1	0·1	0·1	−0·1	0·0	0·0	0·0	+0·1	0·1	0·1	0·1	0·2	40
50 00	−0·1	−0·1	−0·1	−0·1	0·0	0·0	0·0	0·0	0·0	+0·1	+0·1	+0·1	+0·1	50 00

(2) Using the upper diagram of the table, locate the intersection of 20° C and 1010 millibars; we find that it lies in the "J" zone.

(3) In the table below, follow down the J column to the line for an altitude of 7°, the value is found to be +0.4′.

Answer: Additional refraction correction is +0.4′.

CORRECTIONS USING THE *AIR ALMANAC*

2242 The *Air Almanac* can be used to obtain corrections for each of the categories of possible error discussed in the preceding sections, but the *Nautical Almanac* is generally preferred in marine navigation because of the greater precision of the tabulated corrections. In the *Air Almanac,* the refraction correction for all bodies is extracted from the same refraction table; see figure 2242. When applicable, the effects of semidiameter, augmentation, phase, and parallax must be separately reckoned using data in the daily pages, and combined with the extracted refraction correction to form the total correction to ha for each body observed. An additional adjustment to the resulting line of position, necessitated by the Coriolis effect on a fast-moving aircraft, is also required in air navigation; tables for this correction are also contained in the *Air Almanac.*

More on the *Air Almanac* is found in chapter 24.

SUMMARY OF EFFECTS AND CORRECTIONS

2243 The various effects on observations and applicable corrections are summarized in figure

CORRECTIONS TO BE APPLIED TO SEXTANT ALTITUDE

REFRACTION

To be subtracted from sextant altitude (referred to as observed altitude in A.P. 3270)

R_0	Height above sea level in units of 1 000 ft.												R_0	$R = R_0 \times f$
	0	5	10	15	20	25	30	35	40	45	50	55		f
	Sextant Altitude													0·9 1·0 1·1 1·2
														R
0	90	90	90	90	90	90	90	90	90	90	90	90	0	0 0 0 0
1	63	59	55	51	46	41	36	31	26	20	17	13	1	1 1 1 1
2	33	29	26	22	19	16	14	11	9	7	6	4	2	2 2 2 2
3	21	19	16	14	12	10	8	7	5	4	2 40	1 40	3	3 3 3 4
4	16	14	12	10	8	7	6	5	3 10	2 20	1 30	0 40	4	4 4 4 5
5	12	11	9	8	7	5	4 00	3 10	2 10	1 30	0 39	+0 05	5	5 5 5 6
6	10	9	7	5 50	4 50	3 50	3 10	2 20	1 30	0 49	+0 11	−0 19	6	5 6 7 7
7	8 10	6 50	5 50	4 50	4 00	3 00	2 20	1 50	1 10	0 24	−0 11	−0 38	7	6 7 8 8
8	6 50	5 50	5 00	4 00	3 10	2 30	1 50	1 20	0 38	+0 04	−0 28	−0 54	8	7 8 9 10
9	6 00	5 10	4 10	3 20	2 40	2 00	1 30	1 00	0 19	−0 13	−0 42	−1 08	9	8 9 10 11
10	5 20	4 30	3 40	2 50	2 10	1 40	1 10	0 35	+0 03	−0 27	−0 53	−1 18	10	9 10 11 12
12	4 30	3 40	2 50	2 20	1 40	1 10	0 37	+0 11	−0 16	−0 43	−1 08	−1 31	12	11 12 13 14
14	3 30	2 50	2 10	1 40	1 10	0 34	+0 09	−0 14	−0 37	−1 00	−1 23	−1 44	14	13 14 15 17
16	2 50	2 10	1 40	1 10	0 37	+0 10	−0 13	−0 34	−0 53	−1 14	−1 35	−1 56	16	14 16 18 19
18	2 20	1 40	1 20	0 43	+0 15	−0 08	−0 31	−0 52	−1 08	−1 27	−1 46	−2 05	18	16 18 20 22
20	1 50	1 20	0 49	+0 23	−0 02	−0 26	−0 46	−1 06	−1 22	−1 39	−1 57	−2 14	20	18 20 22 24
25	1 12	0 44	+0 19	−0 06	−0 28	−0 48	−1 09	−1 27	−1 42	−1 58	−2 14	−2 30	25	22 25 28 30
30	0 34	+0 10	−0 13	−0 36	−0 55	−1 14	−1 32	−1 51	−2 06	−2 21	−2 34	−2 49	30	27 30 33 36
35	+0 06	−0 16	−0 37	−0 59	−1 17	−1 33	−1 51	−2 07	−2 23	−2 37	−2 51	−3 04	35	31 35 38 42
40	−0 18	−0 37	−0 58	−1 16	−1 34	−1 49	−2 06	−2 22	−2 35	−2 49	−3 03	−3 16	40	36 40 44 48
45		−0 53	−1 14	−1 31	−1 47	−2 03	−2 18	−2 33	−2 47	−2 59	−3 13	−3 25	45	40 45 50 54
50		−1 10	−1 28	−1 44	−1 59	−2 15	−2 28	−2 43	−2 56	−3 08	−3 22	−3 33	50	45 50 55 60
55			−1 40	−1 53	−2 09	2 24	−2 38	−2 52	−3 04	−3 17	−3 29	−3 41	55	49 55 60 66
60				−2 03	−2 18	−2 33	−2 46	−3 01	−3 12	−3 25	−3 37	−3 48	60	54 60 66 72
							−2 53	−3 07	−3 19	−3 31	−3 42	−3 53		

f	0	5	10	15	20	25	30	35	40	45	50	55	f	0·9 1·0 1·1 1·2
	Temperature in °C.													f
0·9	+47	+36	+27	+18	+10	+3	−5	−13					0·9	Where R_0 is
1·0	+26	+16	+6	−4	−13	−22	−31	−40	For these heights no				1·0	less than 10′
1·1	+5	−5	−15	−25	−36	−46	−57	−68	temperature correction				1·1	or the height
1·2	−16	−25	−36	−46	−58	−71	−83	−95	is necessary, so use				1·2	greater than
	−37	−45	−56	−67	−81	−95			$R = R_0$					35 000 ft. use $R = R_0$

Fig. 2242. *Air Almanac* corrections for refractions, all bodies.

2243. It should be clear from the previous discussions that some are more significant than others.

In some of the following chapters, you will encounter these corrections again and see how they are found and used.

STELLA

2244 As discussed in the previous chapter, the U.S. Navy's STELLA (System to Estimate Latitude and Longitude Astronomically) software program greatly streamlines much of the celestial navigation process. This is certainly true in the case of sextant corrections.

When using STELLA (Version 2.0 for Windows) to enter a sextant observation, you must select "Sight Reduction" from the "Task" drop-down menu and then choose "Record Observations." A dialog box will appear (see fig. 2244a).

Notice that the dialog title bar states that this is the first observation and that several of the boxes are blank. For subsequent sights, most of the boxes will contain data and may not have to be filled in again. STELLA keeps track of the number of sights recorded. The maximum the program will accept for a single fix is 25.

A default date is shown in the dialog. Day of the month is highlighted and ready to be changed, if necessary. You can enter the Day, Month, and Year directly, or use the Current Date button. (Caution: Computer clocks can drift and become inaccurate. Use the Current Date button with care, especially

near midnight. Be certain the date wanted is the UTC [Greenwich] date.) Enter the time of day, including seconds, that the sight was taken. Be certain the time is in UTC.

Enter the time difference (UT1 – UTC = DUT1) in seconds and tenths. As discussed in chapter 23, UT1 – UTC (= DUT1) is a time difference, an offset from the precise time (UTC) transmitted by time broadcast services and displayed by GPS receivers. UT1 is the time scale that carries a ship under the stars, and it depends upon the variable rotation rate of the Earth. STELLA requires the difference between the two time scales in order to refer an observation precisely to a vessel's geographic position. There are several ways to obtain the difference UT1 – UTC for input to the program (see article 2306). Because DUT1 is never allowed to exceed ±0.9 seconds, if the value of DUT1 cannot be determined for input to the *Record Observations* dialog, the "UT1 – UTC" box can be set to zero. The correction affects longitude and is negligible for DUT1 between ±0.2 seconds, so when DUT1 is not applied to observations, the maximum error in a fix on that account will be 0.2′ in longitude for a numerical value of DUT1 between 0.7 sec. and 0.9 sec.

The program accepts observations of the Sun, Moon, navigational planets, Polaris, any of the 57 navigational stars, and a set of additional stars. You can specify an observed body by opening the Body list box and scrolling until the observed body appears and then selecting it. Alternatively, you may type in the first letter(s) of the body you want and

Correction	Symbol	Sign	Increases with	Bodies*	Sextants*	Source
Instrument	I	±	changing altitude	S, M, P, ☆	M, A	sextant box
Index	IC	±	constant	S, M, P, ☆	M, A	measurement
Personal	PC	±	constant	S, M, P, ☆	M, A	measurement
Dip	D	–	higher height of eye	S, M, P, ☆	M	almanacs
Sea-air temp. diff.	S	±	greater temp. diff.	S, M, P, ☆	M	computation
Refraction	R	–	lower altitude	S, M, P, ☆	M, A	almanacs
Air temp.	T	±	greater diff. from 50° F	S, M, P, ☆	M, A	almanacs, table 23 H. O. 9
Atmospheric pressure	B	±	greater diff. from 29.83 in. mercury	S, M, P, ☆	M, A	Nautical Almanac table 24 H. O. 9
Irradiation	J	–	constant	S	M, A	Nautical Almanac
Semidiameter	SD	±	lesser dist. from earth	S, M	M, A	almanacs
Phase	F	±	phase	P	M, A	Nautical Almanac
Augmentation	A	±	higher altitude	M	M, A	Nautical Almanac
Parallax	P	±	lower altitude	S, M, P	M, A	almanacs

* Bodies: S refers to sun, M to moon, P to planets, ☆ to stars.
* Sextants: M refers to Marine, A to artificial horizon.

Fig. 2243. Summary of sextant corrections.

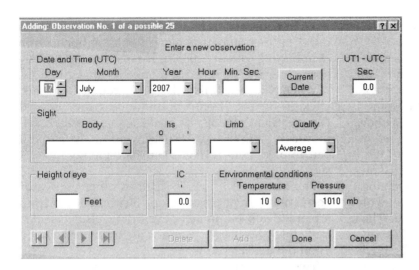

Fig. 2244a. Entering a sextant observation using STELLA.

the list will automatically scroll to the word that most closely matches the first few letters that have been typed (e.g., typing "ald" will scroll the Body list to "Aldebaran"). Stars listed in the Body field in all capital letters are ones that are brighter than 1.5 magnitude.

Enter the altitude of the observed body in the "hs" boxes (in degrees and minutes of altitude) as read directly from the sextant. Do not apply any index correction to the sextant reading before entering it.

The "Limb" box is active only when the observed body is the Sun or Moon. You can specify the observed limb by clicking the box and selecting the one you want ("upper," "lower," or "none"). Or, if you are using the Tab key, the limb will appear in reverse color and you can type u, l, or n for upper, lower, and none.

The "Quality" box is always active and accepts an elementary assessment of the sight. The assessment might include such physical factors as atmosphere steadiness, vessel motion, cloud obscuration, etc. The Quality entry is an opportunity to weight, statistically, a sight that will be used, with other sights, in a fix solution. Specify quality by clicking the box and selecting "Good," "Average," or "Poor." As with the Limb choices, you can also Tab to the box and enter the initials g, a, or p.

The "Height of eye" box may already contain a number, even when the first sight is being entered. If the existing number does not represent the height of eye above the water line when the sight was taken, enter the correct height in *feet*.

Enter the sextant Index Correction in the "IC" box.

The "Temperature" and "Pressure" boxes contain default (standard) values. If the values are very close to what the thermometer and barometer read at the time that the sight was taken, the two boxes may be ignored. However, when there are significant differences between the actual and standard conditions, you should enter the actual temperature and pressure. That will cause the program to compute and apply a value for refraction that ensures your sight is correctly represented in the form of an LOP. Temperature must be entered in *degrees Celsius* and pressure in *millibars*.

When you have completed all necessary data entries, two buttons at the bottom of the dialog become active, "Add" and "Done." The "Add" button records a sight, then clears the dialog for another sight to be entered. If you have only one sight to record, or if it is the last of a round, use the "Add" button. "Done" without an "Add" closes the dialog without recording dialog contents. After the last sight has been entered and recorded, use "Add," then "Done" to exit the dialog. This will ensure that your last sight was recorded into STELLA's ongoing log and can then be included in computing a fix.

There are four additional buttons, at the bottom and left of the dialog, that become active once observations are in the Log. They allow you to access and modify details of observations previously recorded, by using Sight Recorder as an editor. The inner buttons space forward and backward through the series of observations. The outer buttons bring up the first and last of the observation series. Those four buttons are not active until at least one sight has been recorded. If an error was made while entering sights during a particular Adding session, the sights may be removed by first scrolling to them with the arrow keys in the lower left corner of the dialog box and then pressing the Remove button. (The Add button changes to a Remove button when the arrows are used).

Figure 2244b shows a completed dialog box for an observation of the Moon's lower limb.

Dealing with the first or only sight takes the most effort in the Record Observations dialog. For all other sights in a round, if the "Add" button is used, the program will clear the time of day ("Hour," "Min.," and "Sec."), "Body," and "hs" boxes. Other boxes will contain either the data you put there, or default data.

For the second and all other sights in a round, you may find that you only need to complete the dialog by giving it the time of an observation, the name of the observed object, and the sextant altitude. The program assumes that other data are constant throughout a round. That is, you have observed from the same height, the "UT1 - UTC" value has not changed, and the thermometer and barometer readings have been steady. For example, figure 2244c shows the dialog ready to accept the second sight of a round.

You should examine the boxes containing "held-over" entries, and pay particular attention to the "Limb" and "Quality" boxes. If those are not strictly correct for the sight being entered, change them.

When you are finished with a round of sights, clicking on the "Done" button closes the "Record Observations" dialog. All of the sights are then displayed in STELLA's Worksheet window, where you can immediately review them individually or as a set.

The beauty of STELLA is that no other entries or corrections are necessary and arithmetical errors are practically eliminated. Everything else needed is built into the program and is incorporated, based upon the entries you make.

Two entries that may prove troublesome are pressure in millibars and temperature in degrees Celsius, since many American instruments still read in inches of mercury and degrees Fahrenheit. Conversion tables found in *Bowditch* are helpful when at

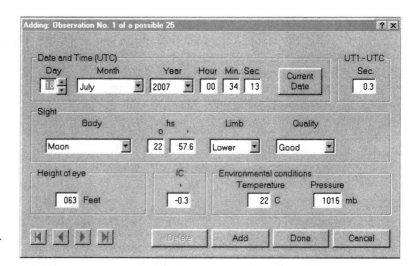

Fig. 2244b. A completed STELLA dialog box for an observation of the Moon's lower limb.

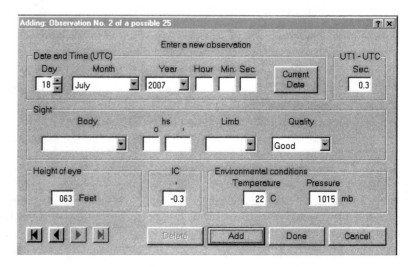

Fig. 2244c. STELLA dialog box ready to accept the next sight of a round of observations.

hand. Simple but sufficiently precise conversion formulas for use in entering these data are:

Bm = 33.864 Bi
where Bm is barometric pressure in millibars and Bi is pressure in inches
and C = 5/9 (F − 32°)
where F is degrees Fahrenheit, and C is degrees Celsius.

After entering more than one observation, you may then select "Compute Fix" from the options provided when "Sight Reduction" is chosen from the "Task" drop down menu. The program will then use the entered observations to compute a fix that can be plotted on a chart or entered into an electronic charting system.

CARE OF A SEXTANT

2245 The modern marine sextant is a well-built, very precise optical instrument capable of rendering many years of service if it is properly maintained. Its usefulness can be greatly impaired, however, by careless handling or neglect. If a sextant is ever dropped, some error is almost certain to be introduced into subsequent sightings.

When not in use, the sextant should always be kept in its case, and the case itself should be securely stowed in a location free from excessive heat, dampness, and vibration. In particular, the sextant should never be left unattended and unsecured on the chartroom table or any other high place. When outside its case, a sextant should be held or carried by its handle—never by the telescope, limb, or index arm. To prevent losing this important (and expensive) instrument overboard, it is a sensible practice (required in the Royal Navy) to keep a lanyard attached to both the instrument and the person using the sextant.

Next to careless handling, moisture is the greatest enemy of a sextant. The mirrors and lens should always be wiped off before a series of observations, because fogged optics make it very difficult to pick up dimmer stars; any moisture should also be wiped off before a sextant is placed back into its box after use. Lens paper should be used—cloth of any type tends to attract and retain dust particles that could scratch the mirror or lens surface; in particular, never use silk. Moisture in the sextant case can be controlled, at least partially, by keeping in the case a small bag of a desiccant, usually silica gel; the bag should occasionally be dehumidified by placing it in a moderately hot oven for a few hours.

If the sextant is normally stowed in an air-conditioned space and the ship is operating in a humid climate, condensation may form on the mirror and lens surfaces when the sextant is brought out into the humid air. Therefore, it is a good practice to bring the sextant *in its case* out into the open an hour or so before use. By allowing it time to adjust to the temperature difference before exposing it to the humid air, condensation is less likely to form.

Lubrication is important, but must not be overdone. The teeth of the tangent screw and those on the limb should always be kept lightly coated with a thin film of oil. The graduations on an arc that is bare, polished metal should be protected with a thin film of petroleum jelly.

Chapter 23　　　　Time

The single indispensable element of all forms of navigation, from dead reckoning to celestial to the most advanced forms of satellite navigation, is *time*. In some instances—such as the determination of tides and currents, or celestial navigation—it is *actual time* (an instant or moment of time, commonly called "clock" time) that is needed. Under other circumstances—dead reckoning, for example, or advancing a line of position in piloting—it is *elapsed time* (a time interval) that is required, and the accuracy of clock time is of less importance. But whichever kind it is, a navigator lives constantly with time.

This chapter will first consider time in general terms, and then its specific applications to celestial navigation. Other uses of time data occur in nearly every chapter of this book.

BASICS OF TIME

2301　Most forms of time are based on the rotation of the Earth in relation to various celestial bodies. Because of the different rates of motion, these various forms of time may differ in the lengths of their standard unit, the day, which represents one rotation of the Earth relative to the reference body, whatever that may be.

The Solar Day

2302　The Sun is the reference body most commonly used by man, and is the one principally used by the navigator; the period of the Earth's rotation relative to the Sun is called the *solar day*. The *solar year* is based on the period of the Earth's revolution about the Sun, which requires approximately 365 1/4 days. The *common year* is 365 days in length. In years exactly divisible by four, such as 1984 and 1988 (known as *leap years*), an additional day—29 February—is usually inserted to adjust the calendar to the actual period of revolution. As the fraction in this period is not exactly one-quarter of a day—it is some eleven minutes fourteen seconds less—years ending in two zeros (1900, 2100) are not leap years, unless they are exactly divisible by 400 as are the years 2000 and 2400.

The other units of time—month, week, hour, minute, and second—have origins deep in man's history. The ancient Egyptians used the rising of certain stars or star-groups to divide their calendar into ten-day periods. Such stars, or star-groups, rose successively at intervals of roughly forty minutes, and so approximately twelve of them could be seen on any night. From this, the night was divided into twelve hours and the entire day became twenty-four hours. The division of hours into sixty minutes of sixty seconds each was a development of the ancient Babylonian culture.

In the "metric system," which comprises the International System of Units (SI) along with some other units not strictly a part of SI, the *second* is the basic unit of time. Contrary to the usage for larger values of many metric units, prefixes such as *kilo* and *mega* are not customarily used for longer periods of time. Instead, the customary units of minute, hour, day, and year are acceptable in the metric system, and find very wide use. For shorter periods of time, the metric prefixes such as *milli*, *micro*, and *nano* are used (*microsecond*, for example).

The month is now an arbitrary, irregular unit of time, but it was originally based upon the Moon's period of revolution around the Earth. The week, as a quarter of a month, was derived from the Moon's four phases.

Apparent Solar Time vs. Mean Solar Time

2303   Apparent solar time was originally read from a Sun dial. Unfortunately, the speed of the apparent rotation of the Sun around the Earth, actually caused by the rotation of the Earth on its axis, is *not* constant; as a result, the length of the *apparent day* varies throughout the year. This variation results, in part, from the fact that the revolution of the Earth around the Sun is in an elliptical orbit and is not at a constant speed. A second cause of the variation in the length of a day is the tilt of the axis of the Earth's rotation with respect to its plane of revolution around the Sun (see fig. 2303a), causing the apparent yearly path of the Sun to be along the ecliptic.

The irregularities of apparent solar time resulted in numerous difficulties as civilization advanced and technology became more complex. To overcome these problems of a nonuniform rate, *mean solar time* was developed. This is based on a fictitious Sun, termed the *mean Sun*, that has an hour circle moving westward along the celestial equator at a *constant* rate (see fig. 2303b). Mean solar time is nearly equal to the average apparent solar time

and is the time used in everyday life, kept by the great majority of timepieces; for mariners, it is the time kept by ships' chronometers and used in almanacs for tabulating the position of celestial bodies.

Equation of Time

2304   The difference in length between any apparent and mean day is never as great as a minute, but the effect is cumulative and oscillatory. As a result, the difference between apparent time and mean solar time may amount to approximately a quarter-hour at certain times of the year. This difference between mean and apparent time is called the *equation of time*. Values are tabulated in the *Nautical Almanac* for 00 and 12 hours each day and are found on the bottom right half of the right-hand daily pages; there is no comparable tabulation in the *Air Almanac*.

For navigational purposes, daily values of the equation of time are often used for the determination of time of local apparent noon (see article 2801).

Upper and Lower Transit of Celestial Bodies

2305   In order to discuss some of the finer points of time, it is helpful to understand some basic terms and concepts regarding celestial motion. It is instructive to realize that the GPs of celestial bodies are moving across the face of the Earth at the rate of 15 degrees per minute—that's 900 knots at the equator. The term *transit* is used to describe the instant a celestial body crosses a given meridian. You will remember that a meridian on the Earth is a great circle, passing through the Earth's geographical poles, at any given position. Transit is often associated with the crossing of a celestial body in relation to an observer's *local* meridian, but it is also used in relation to others, such as the Greenwich meridian.

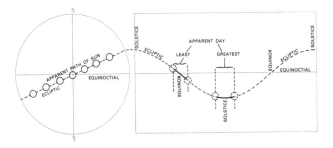

Fig. 2303a. Variation in the length of an apparent day due to the obliquity of the ecliptic.

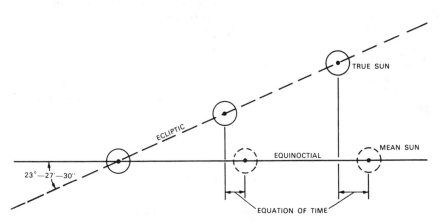

Fig. 2303b. Relationship of mean time to solar time.

The passage of a celestial body across the upper branch (the half in the observer's hemisphere) of the observer's meridian is called *upper transit;* in figure 2305, the Sun at *M* is shown at upper transit. Depending on the observer's latitude and the body's declination, at this instant the body is either due north or due south of the observer (or, in rare cases, directly overhead). The passage of a celestial body across the lower branch of an observer's meridian is called *lower transit;* in figure 2305, the Sun is also shown at lower transit, at *m.* At this instant, the body will be either directly to the north, or south, or directly below the observer, at the nadir, again depending on the latitude and the body's declination. Bodies visible at the observer's position will be above the horizon at upper transit; the majority will be below the horizon at lower transit. *Circumpolar stars* are those that are above the horizon for both the upper and lower transits at the latitude of the observer.

At all times, one half of the Earth is in sunlight, and the other is in darkness. The Sun will be in upper transit on the central meridian of the half that is in sunlight, and it will be *midday* (noon, local time) at that meridian; when on the lower branch of the same meridian the Sun will be in lower transit; at that instant it will be *midnight.* Lower transit of the mean Sun simultaneously marks the end of one day (24-00-00) and the beginning of the next (00-00-00). For the observer, whose upper branch includes

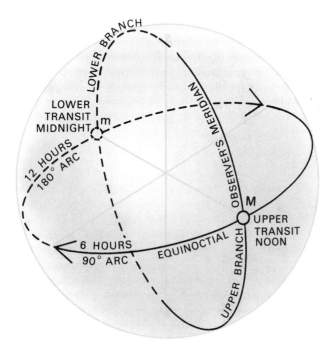

Fig. 2305. Upper and lower transit.

M in figure 2305, this instant occurs when the mean Sun is at *m.*

As the mean Sun is considered to complete a revolution of 360° of arc about the Earth in exactly twenty-four hours, it is evident that in one hour it will have traveled through 15°. In six hours it will have traveled through 90°, and so on. Thus, there is a definite relationship between time and longitude; this relationship will be discussed in more detail below.

TYPES OF TIME

2306 In a perfect world, there would be one system of timekeeping for all purposes, but the reality is that there are several types in use depending upon the intended purpose and the means used to keep the time.

Ephemeris Time (or its succeeding *dynamical time*) is used by astronomers but has no particular purpose in navigation.

Sidereal Time uses the first point of Aries (vernal equinox) as the celestial reference point. Because the Earth revolves around the Sun, and because the direction of the Earth's rotation and revolution are the same, the Earth completes a rotation in less time (by less than four minutes) than with respect to the Sun. Also during its revolution about the Sun, the Earth makes one complete rotation more with respect to the stars than to the Sun. This accounts for the 1° westward shift of the stars each night and means that sidereal days are shorter than solar days (as are sidereal hours, minutes, and seconds). The ratio of the length of a mean solar day to that of a mean sidereal day is 1.00273791:1.

For a very long time, *Greenwich Mean Time* (GMT) was the main standard for navigation. GMT is mean solar time measured with reference to the meridian of Greenwich, 0° longitude. The mean Sun transits the lower branch of the meridian of Greenwich at GMT 00-00-00 and again at 24-00-00 (which is concurrently 00-00-00 of the following day); the mean Sun transits the upper branch at 12-00-00. The choice of the meridian of Greenwich as the reference meridian for time is convenient, because it is also the reference meridian used in reckoning longitude. (Note: Occasionally, you may encounter "GCT" for *Greenwich Civil Time.* This is merely another term for GMT and is equivalent in every sense.)

GMT has been replaced to a large extent by *UT,* which stands for *Universal Time.* This can be a bit confusing and requires some explanation. To begin with, the invention of the atomic clock has improved and, at the same time, complicated matters. Atomic clocks are based on the frequency of vibrations of excited atoms of specific elements (cesium, for example). These clocks, as you might guess, are extremely accurate, which one would think is a pure blessing. However, when dealing with astronomical phenomena (including celestial navigation), a complication is introduced because the Earth's motion is not constant. As a result, we find that some distinctions are necessary.

Civil time—that which is used for day-to-day time in business, government, and so on—is based upon atomic time, and the standard for that is kept by the U.S. Naval Observatory. This time is independent of the spatial relationship of the Earth to the surrounding universe and is used as the time standard for electronic navigation systems such as GPS and radio broadcast time signals. Used in this way, it is known as *UTC*. The abbreviation is sometimes referred to as "Universal Time Constant" but this is a reference to an older system; the applicable term is now "Universal Time, Coordinated."

Another form of universal time that *does* account for the motions of the Earth is determined directly from astronomical observations and is called *UT0* (the last figure is a zero, not the letter "o"). When UT0 is corrected for the very minute motion of the geographic poles (caused by movement of the Earth's crust relative to the axis of rotation) it becomes *UT1*. This time is not uniform like atomic time (though the variations are very small) and no clock can keep it accurately. Also, it is difficult to predict for more than a few months at time. Nonetheless, a vessel's position with respect to celestial bodies is more accurately related to UT1 than to UTC.

To further complicate matters, when UT1 is corrected for the mean seasonal variations in the Earth's rotations, it becomes *UT2*. This distinction is of more importance to astronomers than to navigators.

As a navigator, you should realize that UT1 and GMT are essentially the same and that often the abbreviation *UT* is used (instead of the more specific UT1) as equivalent to GMT. While it can be useful to know these distinctions, the bottom line is that *for navigational purposes, you may consider UT and GMT as equivalent.* When using the *Nautical Almanac* you will find UT used as the entering argument (older navigators will remember that GMT or GCT used to be the entering argument). The Navy's STELLA program uses UTC as its standard except for its ephemeral (almanac) data, which uses UT (UT1)

and can be extracted separately from the program's other functions.

Because the actual time differences involved in these different kinds of time are so small—the worst case scenario would result in a positional error of two-tenths of a mile at or near the equator—it is generally acceptable to think of UTC and GMT as equivalent in most cases. On some occasions, however, it may be desirable to account for the differences. STELLA, for example, requires this difference as one of the entries you must make when using its "Record Observations" task. To be responsive to the needs of users requiring greater accuracy, information is included in UTC broadcasts for adjustment to UT1. This increment, called DUT1, may be either positive or negative and is measured in tenths of a second. Sometimes (as when you are using the STELLA program), you will see DUT1 expressed as "UT1−UTC." This notation signifies the difference between UT1 and UTC.

Because STELLA requires the difference between the two time scales in order to refer an observation precisely to a vessel's geographic position, there are several ways to obtain the difference UT1−UTC for input to the program. It is coded into many radio broadcast time signals. The U. S. Naval Observatory also makes it available on the Internet at usno.navy.mil or in paper bulletin format available by mail. The latest DUT1 value, for use with STELLA, is also posted at http://aa.usno.navy.mil/AA/DoD/software/stella/updates/ut1_utc.html. A value obtained from any of these sources can be used without significant error for 30 days or more.

When obtaining time information using broadcast signals, you should be aware of certain conventions. To prevent DUT1 corrections from getting out of hand, UTC is changed by occasional adjustments of exactly one second—called a *leap second*. These adjustments are inserted into UTC whenever needed to keep UTC time signals within ±0.9 second of UT1 at all times. Ordinarily, a positive leap second is required about once a year, usually at the end of December or June, depending upon how the Earth's rotation rate is changing for that year.

Again, for navigational purposes, you are safe in considering GMT and UT as equivalent.

Local Mean Time (LMT) vs. Zone Time (ZT)

2307 Just as Greenwich Mean Time is mean solar time measured with reference to the meridian of Greenwich, so *Local Mean Time* (LMT) is mean solar time measured with reference to a given local meridian.

Local Mean Time was the standard generally used after the introduction of time based on a mean Sun, and every city kept time based on the mean Sun's transit of its meridian. As a result, a number of different standards were used in comparatively small geographic areas. Before the days of modern electronic communications, and when physical travel was at the speed of a man, a horse, or the flow of a river, such disparities in time over relatively small areas were of no real importance. When electrical and mechanical developments made communications essentially instantaneous and transportation quite rapid, the differences in local times could no longer be tolerated. This led to the introduction of *Zone Time* to straighten out the confusion caused by the multiplicity of different Local Mean Times in a given area. In Zone Time, all the places in a specified "zone" or band of longitude keep the same time, based on the Local Mean Time of a single designated meridian, frequently the central meridian of the zone. Timepieces are reset only when moving into an adjoining time zone; they are advanced an hour if travel is to the east, and retarded an hour if to the west.

Zone Description

2308   As a general rule, these time zones are laid out so that they are not excessively wide; therefore, at no given place in the zone will the ZT vary greatly from the LMT, and the time will be in reasonably good agreement with the motions of the Sun. At sea, the zones are usually equal bands of longitude 15° in width. On land, the boundaries between adjacent zones are generally irregular, reflecting political boundaries and commercial influences, but the zones usually approximate the same 15° width, and usually use the corresponding central meridian as standard.

In general, the central meridians selected for time zones are longitudes that are exact multiples of 15°. There are twenty-four of these central or "standard" meridians, each one hour apart, and the longitude boundaries of each zone are $7\frac{1}{2}°$ on either side of the zone's standard meridian, as shown in figure 2308a. For any one of several reasons, a ship at sea may elect to keep its clocks on a zone other than the one in which it is geographically located. For example, in the Falklands War, the British forces stayed on Zulu time even though the Falkland Islands straddle the central meridian of time zone Q (ZD +4), while Argentina, which lies mostly *west* of the Falklands, nevertheless kept Zone Time P (ZD +3).

The *zone description* (ZD) of a zone is the adjustment to be applied to the time of that zone to obtain GMT (or UT). For example, between longitudes $7\frac{1}{2}°$ east and $7\frac{1}{2}°$ west, the ZD is zero, and GMT will be used throughout the zone. In the zone bordered by longitudes 7° 30′ E and 22° 30′ E, the standard meridian is longitude (l) 15° E. ZT in this zone will differ from GMT by one hour, and the zone being *east* of the meridian of Greenwich, the ZT will read one hour *later*. Therefore, one hour is *subtracted* from ZT to obtain GMT. The ZD of any zone in *west* longitude is *plus*. The numerical value of the adjustment for a zone can be determined by dividing the longitude of its standard meridian by 15°. Thus, the zone having longitude 135° W as its standard meridian will have a ZD of +9, the zone having longitude 75° E as its standard meridian will have a ZD description of −5.

The ZD at a given position can be similarly determined. The longitude of the place is divided by 15°, and the whole number of the quotient is determined. If the remainder is less than 7° 30′, the whole number quotient establishes the numerical

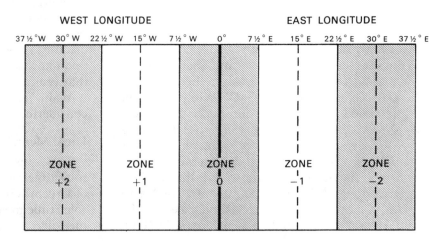

Fig. 2308a. Time zone boundaries.

value of the ZD; if it is greater than 7° 30′, the numerical value of the ZD is one more than the whole number of the quotient. Thus, in longitude 37° 25.4′ W, the ZD will be +2, while in longitude 37° 43.6′, the ZD will be +3. These calculations refer to positions at sea where the zone boundaries are uniform; ashore, care must be taken with similar computations due to the frequently irregular boundaries of time zones.

Letter designations have been assigned to each time zone and are used primarily by the U.S. Armed Forces in communications and operational planning for identification of the ZT in the various zones. These zone-descriptive letters have been widely adopted by other government and private activities. GMT, which is Zone Time at Greenwich, is designated by the letter Z. Zones to the east of Greenwich are designated alphabetically in order of increasing east longitude, commencing with A and ending with M; the letter J is not used. Zones to the west of Greenwich are similarly designated, commencing with N, and ending with Y for the zone with ZD +12. It should be noted that the 15°-wide zone centered on the 180th meridian is divided into two parts. The half in east longitude has a ZD of −12 and is designated by the letter M, and the half

in west longitude is lettered Y and has a ZD of +12 (see fig. 2308b). This division of the zone having the 180th meridian as its standard is necessitated by the convention of the *International Date Line*. As a further, but practical, complication, the Date Line itself deviates from the 180th meridian in several places by as much as 7.5 degrees, both eastward and westward. Coordinates of the corner points of the International Date Line are tabulated in the *Nautical Almanac*.

The zone-description letters may be added to the four-digit statement of time. For example, a vessel off the East Coast of the United States, keeping Eastern Standard Time (EST) could refer to the time of an event, as "1715R"—R (Romeo) being the designator for zone +5 which is EST. In communications involving ships or activities in different time zones, it is common to use Z, which is popularly known as "Zulu Time," (because "Zulu" is the international phonetic alphabet equivalent for the letter Z).

The military system of including a date with the time is frequently useful. This is accomplished by *prefixing* the time group with two digits that indicate the date of the current month. Thus "121725Z" would indicate a *date/time* of GMT 1725 on the

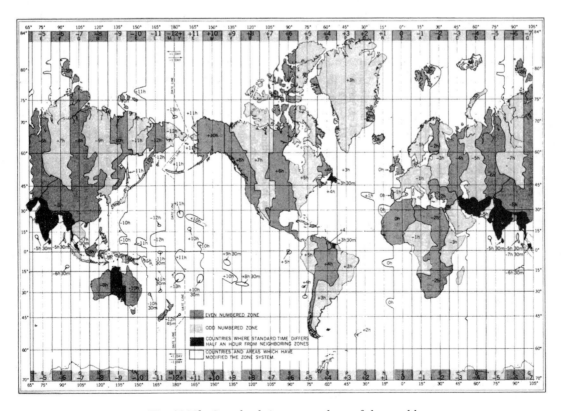

Fig. 2308b. Standard time zone chart of the world.

twelfth of the current month. If a month other than the current one is to be described, the date/time group with the appropriate designator is used, and the name of the desired month is added as a *suffix*. If a year other than the current one is to be indicated, it is indicated after the month. Therefore, if the date/time example previously used were for May 2003, the full group would read 121725Z May 03.

Variations in Zone Description; Standard and Daylight Time

2309   Zone Time, based on uniform 15° bands of longitude, is a convenience at sea, but it can lead to complications on shore. For example, a city, or group of cities closely related by business ties, might lie astride the dividing line between zones. To avoid inconvenience to commerce and everyday life, such a territorial entity will often keep a single time that does not fully agree with the uniform zone system just described; boundaries between adjacent zones become quite irregular in many areas. This form of modified Zone Time is called *standard time*. In the 48 contiguous states of the U.S., it is designated as Eastern, Central, Mountain, or Pacific standard time. The "central" meridians of these zones are the 75°, 90°, 105°, and 125° of west longitude, respectively; the boundaries may be more or less than 7¹/₂° from a central meridian. Similarly, a nation which overlaps into two or three time zones may choose to keep one single ZT throughout its territory, thus eliminating any time difference problem within the country (see fig. 2308b).

Some places, for convenience, maintain a standard time that results in a ZD that is not a whole hour. The *Nautical Almanac* and *Air Almanac*, under the heading "Standard Times," tabulate the zone descriptions used in many areas of the world; the list is corrected as new countries come into existence or changes in standard time are made, but there may be a lag of several years in the publication of such corrections. (Among other reasons for the lag, almanacs must be published many months in advance.)

Daylight Time (DT), also called *Daylight Saving Time* (DST) or *summer time*, is another variation of Zone Time. As a result of the early rising of the Sun in summer, a certain amount of daylight would be "lost" to most people if the ZD were not adjusted. To avoid this loss, in many areas it is customary to adopt the time of the next adjacent zone to the *east*, during the period DT is in effect. This results in sunrise and sunset occurring one hour later by the clock. Along the East Coast of the United States,

where the ZD is usually +5, during daylight time, the ZD becomes +4. Similarly, a place using a ZD of −9 might, in summer, advance its time so that the ZD becomes −10.

Changing Time and Date at Sea

2310   When a vessel passes from one time zone into the next, it enters an area where it is desirable to keep a ZT differing by one hour from the previous one; if travel is toward the west, the ZT of the new zone will be one hour earlier than that of the old, and the ship's clocks would be set back one hour. If travel were eastward, the reverse would be true, and the clocks would be advanced one hour.

When a new time zone is about to be entered, a ship's navigator notifies the captain, who makes the decision as to the time that clocks will be reset throughout the vessel. On smaller craft, such as yachts, the procedure is less formal, but essentially the same. Zone Time is used as a matter of convenience, and the time that a change is made is selected with this in mind, to cause the minimal dislocation to the vessel's routine. The ZD does not change until the ZT is changed.

The International Date Line

2311   A vessel moving to the west sets its clocks back one hour in each new time zone; in a circumnavigation of the Earth, it would therefore "lose" twenty-four hours. Conversely, if it were moving around the world in an easterly direction it would "gain" twenty-four hours in circling the globe. A method adjusting for the day lost or gained is necessary, and this is accomplished by the use of the International Date Line, which follows the 180° meridian, with some offsets so that it does not bisect an inhabited area. The adjustment to the date is made at some convenient time before or after the vessel crosses the date line. If a vessel has been proceeding *east*, its clocks have been steadily advanced, and this is compensated for by *retarding* the date one day. Conversely, a vessel traveling *west* has been setting back its clocks, and so the date needs to be *advanced* one day. Note that the date change is in the *opposite* direction to the hour changes. A convenient mnemonic for remembering this is "If it's Sunday in San Francisco, it's Monday in Manila." This date change is made by every vessel crossing the date line, regardless of the length of the voyage.

The change of date accounts for the two zone descriptions associated with the 15° band of longitude centered on the 180th meridian. That part of the zone in west longitude has a ZD of (+12), and that part in east longitude has a ZD of (−12). The ZT is the same throughout the zone, but the date is *one day later* in the half that is in east longitude than it is in the half that is in west longitude. For example, aboard a ship in longitude 175° W at 0900 ZT on 3 February, GMT is determined to be 2100, 3 February, by applying the ZD of (+12). At the same instant, onboard a ship in longitude 175° E, ZT is 0900 on 4 February; by applying the ZD (−12), GMT is also found to be 2100, 3 February.

The date line is used as a convenience, just as Zone Time is used as a convenience, and the change of date is made in the area of the date line at a time when the ship's routine will be disturbed as little as possible. Frequently, it is convenient to change the date at the midnight falling closest to the time the ship crosses the date line. However, it would generally be considered undesirable either to repeat a Sunday or a holiday, or to drop one. Under such conditions, ships have found it convenient to operate for a period using a ZD of either (+13), or (−13). Regardless of when the line is crossed, the *sign* of the ZD remains unchanged until the date is changed.

In summary, all changes in time and date are made solely for the purpose of convenience. The chosen Zone Time and date used onboard ship are of comparatively little importance in themselves; what is important is that the navigator be able to determine the time and date at Greenwich (UT), so that she or he can obtain the coordinates of celestial bodies from the almanac. Also, navigators should remember that the day that is added or subtracted when crossing the date line has *no effect* on the Greenwich date.

TIME DIAGRAMS

2312   The transits of celestial bodies and the resultant time-arc relationships are, for navigational purposes, generally sketched on a *time diagram* as in figure 2312. This is a most useful aid in visualizing any time and date problem; a navigator should be thoroughly familiar with the preparation and use of such a diagram.

Essentially, it is a simple sketch showing the relative positions of the meridians and hour circles involved in a particular problem. It consists of a circle representing the equator, straight lines from the center to the circumference representing the meridians and hour circles of the problem, and appropriate labels. In this book, time diagrams are always considered to be viewed from a point in space beyond the *South* Pole. East is thus in a clockwise, and west in a counterclockwise direction; all celes-

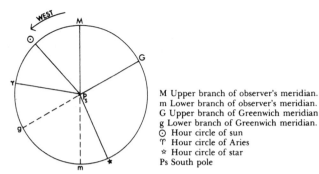

M Upper branch of observer's meridian.
m Lower branch of observer's meridian.
G Upper branch of Greenwich meridian.
g Lower branch of Greenwich meridian.
☉ Hour circle of sun
♈ Hour circle of Aries
☆ Hour circle of star
Ps South pole

Fig. 2312. Elements of a time diagram.

tial bodies are therefore considered to revolve in a counterclockwise direction about the circle. Time problems in this book are illustrated with the use of a time diagram prepared in this manner. The basic elements of the time diagram are shown in figure 2312.

By convention, the observer's meridian is always drawn vertically, with the upper branch, *M*, shown as a solid line extending upward from the center. The lower branch, *m*, is shown as a broken line extended downward. In problems in which it is necessary to distinguish between Local Mean Time and Zone Time, the *M-m* line represents the observer's meridian, and a *Z-z* line represents the central meridian of the time zone; these meridians will usually be quite close together. In the majority of cases, the central meridian of the zone is not necessary and is omitted. The approximate Zone Time (ZT) at *M* is shown by drawing in the hour circle of the Sun for the time in question. In figure 2312, the Sun is shown at approximately 1500.

Time and Longitude

2313   The mean Sun circles the Earth's 360° of longitude in twenty-four hours, moving from east to west. In *one hour*, it passes over 1/24 of the Earth's meridians, or 15°. In *one minute* it covers 1/60 of 15°, or 15 minutes of arc; in *four seconds* of time it covers one minute of arc, and in *one second*, it covers 0.25′ of arc.

The time-arc relationship may be summarized in tabular form.

Time	Arc
24 hours	360°
1 hour	15°
1 minute	15′
4 seconds	1′
1 second	0.25′

Because the mean Sun moves constantly from east to west, Local Mean Time always reads *later* at places to the observer's *east,* and *earlier* at those to his or her *west.*

In doing any arithmetical calculations with time, but especially when subtracting, a navigator must be mentally alert to the fact that there are sixty, not one hundred minutes in an hour, and sixty seconds in a minute. In more technical terminology, time functions in a *sexagesimal* rather than *decimal* system. One gets so used to decimal calculations that it is very easy to slip up on this "60" situation when "borrowing" or "carrying" (that is, in regrouping) sexagesimal units.

In the interconversion of time and arc, a navigator is aided by a conversion table published in the *Nautical Almanac,* an extract of which is shown in figure 2313a. A generally comparable table is included in each volume of the NOS *Tide Tables* and *Tidal Current Tables.*

It is also helpful to write out all times in the hh ss mm format, always using 24-hour time. For example, noon on a given day would be written as 12 00 00 (for 12 hours, no minutes and no seconds. Three and a half minutes after four in the afternoon would be written as 16 03 30, and so on.

The relationship between time and longitude can be used to determine the difference in Local Mean Time between places in different longitudes. It is more easily visualized using a time diagram. For example, from the U.S. Naval Observatory in Washington, D.C. at longitude 77° 04′ W, consider a ship in the Mediterranean at longitude 19° 58′ E, and the lighthouse at Point Loma, California, at longitude 117° 15′ W. These meridians are shown in figure 2313b, which depicts the Earth on a time diagram and makes their relationships to one another much clearer than when trying to keep it straight in your head. West, the direction of the Sun's motion, is in a counterclockwise direction. Ps-G represents the meridian of Greenwich, Ps-S that of the ship, Ps-N that of the Naval Observatory, and Ps-L that of the lighthouse. It can be seen from the diagram that the difference in longitude between the ship and the observatory is 97° 02′, since 19° 58′ E + 77° 04′ W = 97° 02′, and the difference between the observatory and the lighthouse is 40° 11′, since 117° 15′ W − 77° 04′ W = 40° 11′. Converting these differences in longitude to time, we find that the difference in local time between the ship and the observatory is 6 hours, 28 minutes, and 08 seconds, and the difference between the observatory and the lighthouse is 2 hours, 40 minutes, and 44 seconds. Because of the Sun's westerly motion, it is always later at the ship than at the other two positions. For example, when the Local Mean Time at the observatory is 12-00-00, as shown by the Sun over the meridian Ps-N in figure 2313b, the Local Mean Time at the ship is 18-28-08, and that at the lighthouse it is 09-19-16. If subtracting a time difference results in a change of date, it is convenient to add twenty-four hours to the numerically smaller time in making the computation. For example, if the local time at the Naval Observatory were 01-00-00 and it were desired to find the then Local Mean Time at the Point Loma Lighthouse, 2-40-44 to the west, it is convenient to consider *0100 of today* as 0100 + 2400, or *2500* of the *preceding day.* Then it is 25-00-00 minus 2-40-44 = 22-19-16, the *preceding day* at the lighthouse.

Using Time Diagrams

2314 Because UT is used in the *Nautical Almanac,* STELLA, and other sources of ephemeral

0°–59°		60°–119°		120°–179°		180°–239°		240°–299°		300°–359°			0′·00		0′·25		0′·50		0′·75	
°	h m	°	h m	°	h m	°	h m	°	h m	°	h m	′	m s	m s	m s	m s
0	0 00	60	4 00	120	8 00	180	12 00	240	16 00	300	20 00	0	0 00	0 01	0 02	0 03
1	0 04	61	4 04	121	8 04	181	12 04	241	16 04	301	20 04	1	0 04	0 05	0 06	0 07
2	0 08	62	4 08	122	8 08	182	12 08	242	16 08	302	20 08	2	0 08	0 09	0 10	0 11
3	0 12	63	4 12	123	8 12	183	12 12	243	16 12	303	20 12	3	0 12	0 13	0 14	0 15
4	0 16	64	4 16	124	8 16	184	12 16	244	16 16	304	20 16	4	0 16	0 17	0 18	0 19
5	0 20	65	4 20	125	8 20	185	12 20	245	16 20	305	20 20	5	0 20	0 21	0 22	0 23
6	0 24	66	4 24	126	8 24	186	12 24	246	16 24	306	20 24	6	0 24	0 25	0 26	0 27
7	0 28	67	4 28	127	8 28	187	12 28	247	16 28	307	20 28	7	0 28	0 29	0 30	0 31
8	0 32	68	4 32	128	8 32	188	12 32	248	16 32	308	20 32	8	0 32	0 33	0 34	0 35
9	0 36	69	4 36	129	8 36	189	12 36	249	16 36	309	20 36	9	0 36	0 37	0 38	0 39
10	0 40	70	4 40	130	8 40	190	12 40	250	16 40	310	20 40	10	0 40	0 41	0 42	0 43
11	0 44	71	4 44	131	8 44	191	12 44	251	16 44	311	20 44	11	0 44	0 45	0 46	0 47
12	0 48	72	4 48	132	8 48	192	12 48	252	16 48	312	20 48	12	0 48	0 49	0 50	0 51
13	0 52	73	4 52	133	8 52	193	12 52	253	16 52	313	20 52	13	0 52	0 53	0 54	0 55
14	0 56	74	4 56	134	8 56	194	12 56	254	16 56	314	20 56	14	0 56	0 57	0 58	0 59

Fig. 2313a. *Nautical Almanac* table "Conversion of Arc to Time" (extract).

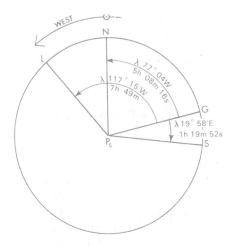

Fig. 2313b. The difference in time between places is equal to the difference in their longitudes, converted into time units.

data, and celestial problems cannot be solved without their help, the navigator must be able to convert times for their proper use. Time diagrams are a proven method for preventing confusion and consequent errors. Since UT is essentially equivalent to GMT and because there is a direct relationship between time and longitude, the Greenwich meridian is shown on the diagram at an angular distance appropriate for the observer's longitude, east or clockwise from *M* if you are in west longitude, and west of *M*, if your longitude is east. The upper branch of the Greenwich meridian is drawn as a solid line and is labeled *G*, and the lower branch as a broken line and labeled *g*.

Since the Sun is the basis of GMT as well as ZT, the approximate GMT can also be determined from a time diagram. In the left-hand time diagram in figure 2314, with the observer at longitude 60° W, the Sun is approximately 90° west of the upper branch of the observer's meridian, *M*, and 150° or 10 hours west of the upper branch of the Greenwich meridian *G*; the GMT is therefore approximately 2200.

Similarly, in the diagram at the right with the observer at longitude 15° E, the Sun is about 90° or six hours west of the local meridian *M*, but it is only 75° or five hours west of the upper branch of the Greenwich meridian *G*; the GMT is therefore about 1700. In this case, the Sun will be at *g* in seven hours, which will signal the start of the next day for Greenwich.

A difference in dates is readily apparent when a time diagram is used, because the dates at two meridians are always different *if the Sun's hour circle falls between the lower branches of the Greenwich meridian and the observer's meridian;* the meridian whose *lower* branch is to the west of the Sun's hour circle will have the earlier date.

ZONE TIME VS. GREENWICH MEAN TIME

2315   Zone Time differs from Greenwich Mean Time by the zone description.

To convert ZT to GMT, apply the ZD to ZT with the *sign as shown.*

To convert GMT to ZT, apply the ZD to GMT with the *opposite sign* (also called *reversed sign*).

These conversions are illustrated in the following examples:

Example 1: Your ship is at longitude 156° 19.5′ E when you observe the Sun at 16-36-14 ZT on 26 April.

Required: GMT and date at the time of the observation.

Solution: First record the name of the body, the date based on ZT, and the ZT of the observation. Then sketch on a time diagram the relative positions of the observer, Greenwich, and the Sun, to assist in visualizing the problem. Next, note the ZD of the time being kept aboard the vessel (longitude divided by 15° as described in article 2308). The ZD is −10 ("minus" because the observer is in east longitude; "10" because 156° 10.5′ ÷ 15° = 10, with a

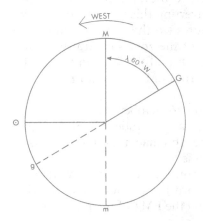

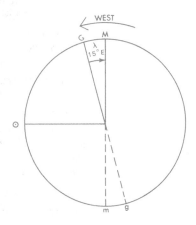

Fig. 2314. East and west longitude shown on a time diagram.

remainder of less than 7° 30´). Then apply the ZD to ZT in accordance with its sign to determine GMT. Finally, record the date at Greenwich, which in this case is the same as the local date (see fig. 2315a.)

Answer: GMT 06-36-14 on 26 April.

Example 2: You are at longitude 83°17.9' W when you observe the star Arcturus at 19-15-29 ZT on 14 June.

Required: GMT and date at the time of the observation.

Solution: First record the name of the body, the date based upon ZT, and the ZT. Then sketch on a time diagram the relative positions of the observer, Greenwich, and the Sun, to assist in visualizing the problem. Next, note the ZD (if necessary, dividing the longitude by 15°, to the nearest whole number). The ZD is +6 ("plus" because the observer is in west longitude; "6" because 83° 17.9' ÷ 15° = 5, with remainder more than 7° 30'). Then apply the ZD to ZT in accordance with its sign to determine GMT. Finally, record the date at Greenwich, which in this case is one day later than the local date—the Sun having passed the Greenwich lower meridian (g) signaling the start of a new date there; it has not passed the lower branch of the local meridian that changes the local date (see fig. 2315b).

Answer: GMT 01-15-29 on 15 June.

The relationship between Zone Time and Greenwich Mean Time can also be remembered by the following phrases:

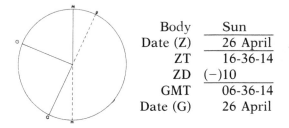

Body	Sun
Date (Z)	26 April
ZT	16-36-14
ZD	(−)10
GMT	06-36-14
Date (G)	26 April

Fig. 2315a. Time diagram: zone time vs. GMT (example 1).

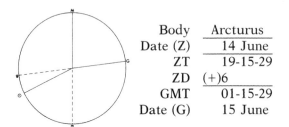

Body	Arcturus
Date (Z)	14 June
ZT	19-15-29
ZD	(+)6
GMT	01-15-29
Date (G)	15 June

Fig. 2315b. Time diagram: zone time vs. GMT (example 2).

Longitude west, Greenwich time best
Longitude east, Greenwich time least

in which "best" means greater and "least" means lesser.

ZONE TIME VS. LOCAL MEAN TIME

2316 *Local Mean Time* (LMT) differs from Zone Time by the difference of longitude (DLo), expressed as time, between the meridian of the observer and the standard meridian of the zone. Local Mean Time is primarily of interest to the navigator in determining the Zone Time of phenomena such as sunrise and set, and moonrise and set.

If you are *east* of the central meridian of your zone, the phenomenon will occur for you *before* it will happen at the zone's central meridian. Conversely, if you are *west* of the standard meridian, the phenomenon will occur *later*, and LMT at your position will be earlier than ZT.

The following examples will serve to clarify the use of LMT, and its relationship to ZT.

Example 1: As the navigator of a vessel at longitude 117° 19.4' W you determine from the almanac that sunrise is at LMT 0658 on 26 October. (The times of phenomena such as sunrise are given in the almanacs only to the nearest minute, which is fully adequate for practical navigation.)

Required: ZT of sunrise and local date.

Solution: First, record the name of the phenomenon, the date based on LMT, and the LMT of the event. Then sketch on a time diagram the relative positions of the observer, the Sun, and the central meridian of the time zone (Z-z), to assist in visualizing the problem. Next, determine the difference in longitude (DLo) between the meridian of the observer and the central meridian of the zone, and convert to units of time, to the nearest minute. In this example the central meridian of the zone is 120° W (nearest whole multiple of 15°) and DLo equals 2° 40.6'. Converting this value to time units, DLo equals 11 minutes (to the nearest minute). As the observer is east of the zone's central meridian, ZT is earlier than LMT, and the DLo, in time units, must be subtracted from LMT to obtain ZT (see fig. 2316a).

Answer: ZT 0647 on 26 October.

Example 2: While at longitude 38° 58.5' E you determine from the almanac that moonset is at LMT 2347 on 26 January.

Required: ZT of moonset, including local date.

Solution: First record the phenomenon, the date based upon LMT, and the LMT of the phenomenon.

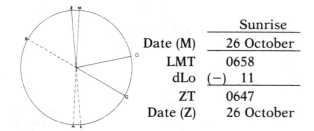

	Sunrise
Date (M)	26 October
LMT	0658
dLo	(−) 11
ZT	0647
Date (Z)	26 October

Fig. 2316a. Time diagram: zone time vs. local mean time (example 1).

Then sketch on a time diagram the relative positions of the observer, the central meridian of the zone, and the Sun, to assist in visualizing the problem. Next, determine the difference of longitude between the meridian of the observer and that of the central meridian of the zone and convert to time units, to the nearest minute. In this case, the central meridian of the zone is 45° E and DLo equals 6° 01.5′. Converting this to time units, DLo equals twenty-four minutes (to the nearest minute). Since the observer is west of the central meridian, the ZT of moonset is later than LMT, and the DLo value must be added to LMT to obtain ZT.

Finally, record the date in the zone, which in this case is one day later than the date based upon LMT (see fig. 2316b).

Answer: ZT 0011 on 27 January.

In the practice of modern navigation, the only times that the navigator will need to convert ZT to LMT (or vice versa) are when he or she is computing the time of sunrise, sunset, moonrise, moonset, or upper solar transit, and chooses this convenient method of doing so.

CHRONOMETERS

2317   Time of day is used in many aspects of navigation, but nowhere is it more important than in the determination of longitude. The keeping of accurate time at sea was impossible until the invention of the

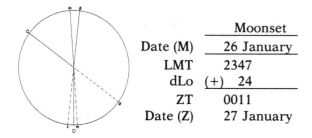

	Moonset
Date (M)	26 January
LMT	2347
dLo	(+) 24
ZT	0011
Date (Z)	27 January

Fig. 2316b. Time diagram: zone time vs. local mean time (example 2).

chronometer by John Harrison in the early eighteenth century; voyages had to be sailed using techniques that accommodated the lack of knowledge of the vessel's longitude. Hour or sand glasses were satisfactory for rough dead reckoning, but were useless for sustained time keeping. Probably the best shipboard timekeeper before the eighteenth century was the compass. Many compasses were designed especially for this purpose, with a vertical pin at the center of the card. The compass card was, in effect, a sundial, and the pin was the gnomon.

The invention of the chronometer represented a tremendous breakthrough in navigation because it was sufficiently accurate to permit determining longitude afloat. The sextant offered both convenience and accuracy in measuring altitudes, not only of the Sun, but also of the Moon, planets, and stars. Until about 1880, it was the general practice to compute position by the time-sight method. A latitude was obtained from an observation of Polaris or of the Sun's transit. This latitude was carried forward by dead reckoning and used in determining longitude by a subsequent observation; latitude and longitude were both calculated, rather than being determined from plotting lines of position (LOPs) on a chart, as is done today.

A traditional chronometer is a very accurate spring-driven timepiece, usually about 4 or 5 inches in diameter, mounted in a heavy brass case, which is supported in gimbals in a wooden case. The gimbals take up much of the ship's motion, so that the chronometer remains in a nearly horizontal position. The wooden case is usually mounted in a very heavily padded second case, designed to give maximum protection against shock and sudden fluctuation of temperature. Chronometers are usually fitted with a detent escapement, and they beat, or tick, half-seconds, as compared to the five beats per second of most watches. This slow beat is of great convenience when comparing the instrument with radio time signals or other timepieces.

The great majority of chronometers have a twelve-hour dial (see fig. 2317); a few instruments have been produced that have a twenty-four-hour face. A "winding indicator," showing how many hours have elapsed since the instrument was wound, is universally employed. Most chronometers will run for fifty-six hours before running down, although some eight-day models have been produced. However, *it is essential that the instrument be wound at the same time every day.*

Marine chronometers are almost invariably set to GMT (UT); they may, however, be adjusted to keep sidereal time. They are never reset aboard a vessel;

Fig. 2317. A mechanical chronometer (Hamilton).

once the chronometer is started, the setting of the hands is not changed until it is removed for cleaning and overhaul. Because of the design of the escapement, a fully wound mechanical chronometer will not start of its own accord. When a chronometer is to be started, the hands are set to the appropriate hour and minute of UT. When the elapsed seconds of UT agree with the second hand on the chronometer, the chronometer case is given a brisk horizontal turn through about 45°, and immediately turned back to its original position; this will start the movement.

The time indicated by a chronometer is chronometer time (C).

No mechanical chronometer may be expected to keep sufficiently accurate UT for navigational purposes over an extended period of time, say weeks or months, without some change in its error. Since it is not to be reset aboard your vessel, its error, which is almost certain to change with passing days, must be carefully tracked so that it may be appropriately applied to the chronometer reading to ascertain the correct UT. The rate of change of chronometer error is usually expressed as seconds and tenths of seconds per twenty-four-hour day, and labeled "gaining" or "losing." The error rate for a quality chronometer will be almost linear unless it is subjected to unusual shocks or abuse. Temperature is the main factor affecting fine timepieces; in general, their rates will increase with rising temperatures.

Quartz Chronometers

2318   A development of modern science is the quartz chronometer, in which a tiny quartz crystal is used to stabilize the frequency of an electronic oscillator. The stability of these newer chronome-

ters far surpasses that of older mechanical designs; kept at a reasonably constant temperature, they are capable of maintaining an excellent rate, with the better models having a deviation of less than 0.01 second from their average daily rate that should not exceed 0.2 second per day. Many models have a sweep-second hand that can be advanced or retarded electronically in increments of one-tenth or one-hundredth of a second while the chronometer is running.

These quartz chronometers are powered by small "flashlight" batteries and thus do not require winding. They are highly resistant to shock and vibration and do not require gimbals; they may be mounted in a traditional box or on a bulkhead.

Quartz Wristwatches

2319   A quartz-crystal-controlled movement is now used in a large percentage of wristwatches, replacing the tuning-fork technique, which was the first advancement from basic mechanical designs. Although the accuracy achieved will probably not be as great as that of a quartz chronometer, the daily rate will often be quite stable and adequate for practical navigation, especially if a few precautions are taken. A uniform "environment" should be established for the watch, such as always wearing it, or always *not* wearing it and keeping it in the same protected place, or wearing it a consistent number of hours each day. Before such a timepiece is used for navigation, its time should be regularly compared to time of known accuracy (radio time signals or a chronometer) for a sufficiently long period to establish both the amount and stability of its rate.

A useful feature found on many quartz wristwatches is an indication of the day of the month. If such a calendar watch is set to Greenwich time *and date*, one calculation (and possible error) can be eliminated. Care must be taken with ordinary watch dials as to whether GMT is between 00 and 12 or between 13 and 24 hours, but this is easily worked out mentally by adding the ZD to the hours of local time. (Many watches with digital dials can be set to show time in the 24-hour system.) Some watches may require a manual adjustment at the end of month having fewer than thirty-one days in it, but many that show the date by month and day accomplish this automatically. But beware of twenty-nine-day Februarys in leap years.

ATOMIC TIME STANDARDS ABOARD SHIP

2320   Some U.S. naval vessels, particularly nuclear-powered, missile-launching submarines, are equipped with one or more cesium- or rubidium-beam devices for time information that are orders of magnitude more precise than mechanical or quartz chronometers. With onboard time data of such extreme accuracy, equipment and systems can be synchronized independently with signals received from land-based or satellite transmitters.

The time signal received by *GPS* receivers (see chapter 17) is based on atomic frequency clocks and is therefore extremely accurate. GPS time can safely be used in nautical navigation, either as a primary source or as a check on others.

ERRORS IN TIMEPIECES

2321 Suppose the timepiece you are using has a known error. If the error (E) is *fast* (F), meaning that the time indicated is later than the correct time, the amount of error must be *subtracted* to obtain the correct time. If the error is *slow* (S), meaning that the time indicated is earlier than the correct time, the amount of error must be *added* to obtain the correct time.

Because time is often measured with a watch, particularly when making celestial observations, this difference between the indication of a timepiece and the correct time is often called *watch error* (WE) and is often recorded as such on celestial sight forms.

Chronometer Error

2322 The difference between chronometer time and GMT at any instant is called *chronometer error* (CE), labeled (F) or (S) as the chronometer is fast or slow on the correct (Greenwich) time. Since chronometers are not reset aboard ship, the accumulated error may become quite large. This is not important if the error is accurately known.

Chronometer error is usually determined by means of a radio time signal (see below). The chronometer may be compared directly, or a *comparing watch* (explained below) may be used to avoid moving the chronometer.

Rate Calculations

2323 The nearly constant rate (stated as either *gaining* or *losing*) of a fine chronometer is its most important feature, as it makes safe navigation possible on a long voyage without dependence on time signals. While the rate should be as small as possible, its consistency is more important. A timepiece rate is determined by comparison with radio signals obtained several days apart.

COMPARING WATCH

2324 A comparing watch is a watch employed to time celestial observations, and to assist in checking a chronometer against a radio time signal. It is also sometimes called a *hack watch*. A good quality *split-second timer* makes the best comparing watch. It has two sweep second hands, one directly below the other, which can be started and stopped together, by means of a push button usually mounted in the center of the winding stem. A second push button stops only the lower of the two sweep hands, permitting an accurate readout. When this button is pushed again, the stopped hand catches up with the running hand. These watches are also fitted with a small dial to indicate the elapsed time after the continuously running sweep hand was started.

Lacking a split-second timer, any watch with a sweep second hand makes an acceptable comparing watch, as it facilitates reading time to the nearest second. A standard stopwatch may be used to advantage for this purpose, but should not be used for any extended period of time, as such units generally have low long-term accuracy.

Every watch used as a comparing watch should be checked regularly to determine whether it runs free of appreciable error for the period of its normal maximum use; ordinarily this period would be about sixty minutes.

A comparing watch can also be used in the determination of chronometer error and rate.

TIMING CELESTIAL OBSERVATIONS

2325 The coordinates of celestial bodies are tabulated with respect to GMT and date; it is therefore necessary that the navigator know the GMT and Greenwich date of each celestial observation. This knowledge is gained most simply by using a timepiece set precisely to GMT, and noting the time at the instant of each observation. This is far superior to using a watch set either to zone or chronometer time, as it both speeds the operation, and reduces the hazard of error.

A split-second timer, or lacking such, a stopwatch, should be used for celestial observations. The watch should, if possible, be started against a radio time signal (see article 2326), using the tick that marks any exact minute; the GMT and Greenwich date at which the watch was started should be noted. If a radio time signal is unavailable, the watch should be started against the best chronometer. To do this, the local time zone description is applied to the ship's time to determine the Greenwich date, and whether the time there is A.M. or P.M. The updated chronometer error is then determined. The chronometer error must be applied to the chronometer time, *with the opposite sign,* in order to obtain GMT. With the error known, the watch is started at the proper time. This procedure is illustrated in the following example.

Morning star observations are to be obtained, and the recorder's watch is to be started on a five-minute increment of GMT. The ship's clocks are set to Zone –10 time. Calculations are shown in figure 2325. Be aware that the chronometer may be reading P.M. but not letting that fact on to the casual observer.

TIME SIGNALS

2326 *Radio time signals,* often called "time ticks," are broadcast from many stations throughout the world. Complete information on the time signals of all countries is given in *Radio Navigational Aids* (NIMA Publications No. 117A and 117B), and in various publications of the U.S. Naval Observatory and the National Institute of Standards and Technology, an activity of the Department of Commerce.

The signals most commonly used by United States vessels are broadcast from the Bureau of Standards radio stations WWV at Fort Collins, Col-

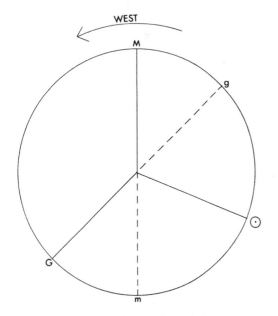

Fig. 2325. Time diagram for a celestial observation using a stopwatch.
Ship's time and date: 0543 (–10), 7 April
GMT time and date: 1943, 6 April
Chronometer error: + (fast) 2 min, 41.5 sec
At GMT 19-45-00, a chronometer with a 12-hour dial will read 7 hours, 47 minutes, 41.5 seconds, and the comparing watch is started at this reading.

orado, and from WWVH on the island of Kauai, Hawaii. These signals have an accuracy far greater than is required for ordinary navigation.

Stations WWV and WWVH

2327 Stations WWV and WWVH broadcast time signals continuously during each day on various frequencies ranging from 2.5 to 20 MHz. The selection of frequency for best reception will depend on the time of day, and on atmospheric conditions. As a general rule, the 15 MHz band is satisfactory during the daylight hours, while the 5 MHz band is usually better at night. During times in the sunspot cycle when radio propagation conditions are favorable, WWV transmits on 20 MHz; this frequency is particularly useful at long distances from the station. Double-sideband AM modulation is used on all frequencies.

Each second is marked by an audible "tick" (a 5-millisecond pulse, audio frequency of 1000 Hz at WWV and 1200 Hz at WWVH); however, the 29th and 59th seconds are not marked by a tick. Once each minute, time is announced by voice in the last 15 seconds of the minute. The two stations are distinguished by a female voice from WWVH at 15 seconds before the minute, and a male voice from WWV at 7½ seconds before the minute. The time is stated as Coordinated Universal Time (UTC), which for ordinary navigational purposes can be used as GMT. The format of the time announcement is the same from both stations; for example, just before 0310 UTC, the announcement, which is recorded, would be, "At the tone, three hours, ten minutes, Coordinated Universal Time."

The first pulse of each minute is longer, 800 milliseconds, for emphasis. The first pulse of each *hour* is further emphasized by being of a higher frequency (1500 Hz). The exact time is indicated by the *beginning* of each pulse. Pulses are transmitted in exact synchronization by WWV and WWVH, but propagation delays may result in their being received very slightly out of step if both stations are being heard at the same time.

Audio Tones

2328 In alternate minutes during most of each hour, 500 or 600 Hz audio tones are broadcast. A 440 Hz tone, the musical note *A* above middle *C*, is broadcast once each hour. In addition to being a musical standard, the 440 Hz tone can be used to provide a marker for chart recorders or other automated devices.

There are "silent periods" with no tone modulation. The carrier frequency, however, continues, as do the seconds pulses and the time announcements. On WWV, no audio tones are broadcast at 45 through 51 minutes after each hour, and additionally there are no audio tones for minutes 29 and 59. On WWVH, no audio tones are broadcast for minutes 00 and 30.

High Seas Weather Information

2329 Weather information about major storms in the Atlantic and eastern North Pacific are broadcast in voice from WWV at 8, 9, and 10 minutes after each hour. Similar storm warnings covering the eastern and central North Pacific are given from WWVH at 48, 49, and 50 minutes after each hour. An additional segment (at 11 minutes after the hour on WWV and at 51 minutes on WWVH) may be used when there are unusually widespread storm conditions. These brief messages are designed to tell mariners of storm threats in their areas. If there are no warnings in the designated areas, the broadcasts will so indicate. The ocean areas involved are those for which the U.S. has warning responsibility under international agreement. The regular times of issue by the National Weather Service are 0500, 1100, 1700, and 2300 UTC for WWV and 0000, 0600, 1200, and 1800 UTC for WWVH. These broadcasts by WWV and WWVH also contain information regarding radio propagation forecasts, geophysical alerts, and official announcements by federal agencies.

Using WWV and WWVH Time Signals

2330 The signals broadcast from WWV and WWVH are in a very useful form for the navigator. The tick transmitted every second is most useful for starting a stopwatch accurately. By beating every second with the incoming signal for about the final 15 seconds of the minute, with a little practice one can start a stopwatch without a readable error—that is, with an error of less than one-fifth of a second.

If UT1 accuracy is required, the DUT1 correction may be noted and applied. This correction, in units of 0.1 second to a maximum of 0.9 second, is encoded into the broadcasts by using double ticks or pulses after the start of each minute. The 1st through the 8th ticks, when doubled, indicate a "plus" correction; doubled 9th through 16th ticks indicate a "minus" correction. For example, if the 1st, 2d, and 3d ticks are doubled, the correction is "plus" 0.3 seconds: UT1 = UTC + 0.3; if UTC is 08-45-17, then UT1 is 08-45-17.3. If the 9th, 10th, 11th, and 12th seconds had been doubled, the correction would have been a "minus" 0.4 second and, in the above example, UT1 = 08-45-16.6.

Time Signals from Other Nations

2331 Continuous time signals are also broadcast by the Canadian station CHU near Ottawa, Ontario, on 3,330, 7,335, and 14,670 kHz. Voice announcements of the upcoming minute and hour of Eastern Standard Time (ZD 5) are made in both English and French. The 29th second tick is omitted, as are the 51st to 59th; during this latter period the voice announcement is made. The zero second pulse of each minute is one-half second long; the start of an hour is identified by a pulse of one full second length followed by 12 seconds of silence. The modulation is single-sideband, AM-compatible (A3H) in order that the signals may be heard on either single-sideband or double-sideband receivers. These transmissions can be very useful to vessels off the Atlantic Coast of North America.

Many other foreign nations around the world broadcast time signals on a wide variety of frequencies and schedules; identifying information is given in some cases by Morse code and in other instances by voice. Details will be found in Pub. No. 117; changes are published in *Notices to Mariners*. Another source of information on time signal broadcasts is the U.S. Naval Observatory *Time Service Publication, Series 1*.

Chapter 24

Ephemeral Data

Following a consideration of time, that most important ingredient of navigation, the next logical subject is a review of sources of ephemeral data. Without this data, the navigator cannot solve the celestial triangle, since knowing the GP of a body is essential to the process. The most commonly known sources of ephemeral data are the "almanacs." These volumes are sources of astronomical data such as Greenwich Hour Angle (GHA) and declination (Dec.) for celestial bodies at any given instant of time. Almanacs also provide much other information—such as times of sunrise and twilight—that is necessary and useful in celestial navigation.

Although the *Air Almanac* will be discussed in this chapter, primary attention will be given to the *Nautical Almanac*, which is normally the choice of a marine navigator. A discussion of the ephemeral data in the U.S. Navy's STELLA (System to Estimate Latitude and Longitude Astronomically) program will appear at the end of the chapter along with a brief mention of other sources that are available.

THE DEVELOPMENT OF ALMANACS

2401 The sixteenth-century Danish astronomer Tycho Brahe spent over twenty years making accurate observations of the heavenly bodies. On the data he amassed, Johannes Kepler based his laws of motion, which are the foundations both of modern astronomy and celestial navigation. The earliest compilations of astronomical calculations for nautical purposes date from the fifteenth century and were published privately by individuals. The first official nautical ephemeris or almanac was published by the French in 1687; this was followed by the British *Nautical Almanac* in 1765 for the year 1767. In 1852, the United States Nautical Almanac Office published the first *American Ephemeris and Nautical Almanac* for the year 1855; this volume has appeared annually since then. In 1858, the *American Nautical Almanac* was published, the sections of primary interest only to astronomers being omitted.

In 1933, the *Air Almanac* was first published in the United States. It was considered revolutionary at the time, because Greenwich Hour Angle was substituted for Right Ascension. It was discontinued in 1934, but produced again in 1937 by the Royal Greenwich Observatory in somewhat modified form, and published in the United States by Weems System of Navigation. In 1941, the U.S. Naval Observatory resumed publication of the *Air Almanac* in the United States.

The British and American editions of the *Nautical Almanac*, which are now identical in content, are produced jointly by Her Majesty's Nautical Almanac Office, Royal Greenwich Observatory, and by the Nautical Almanac Office of the U.S. Naval Observatory, but are printed separately in the United States and Britain. The *Nautical Almanac* is prepared to the general requirements of the British Admiralty and the United States Navy, but, of course, meets well the needs of other surface vessel navigators; its purpose is to provide, in convenient form, the astronomical data required for the practice of celestial navigation at sea.

The *Nautical Almanac* is also published, with minor modifications, by a number of foreign nations using their language for page headings, explanatory text, and notes.

NAUTICAL ALMANAC

2402 A "List of Contents" appears on the back cover for quick reference. Each *Nautical Almanac* comes with a special bookmark, printed on heavy paper, that reproduces several useful observation tables on one side and lists the so-called navigational stars (those most often used by navigators) on the reverse (indexed alphabetically and by their assigned number, which is correlated to their SHAs).

Tables used in correcting sextant observations (for Dip and Altitude Correction) are provided on the inside covers of the *Almanac*. These values do not change as a function of time as do the ephemeral data. Their uses are explained in chapter 22.

In the opening pages are a number of useful compilations of information and data. There are calendars listing holidays, major phases of the Moon (new, full, and first and last quarter), and Julian dates. There are also solar eclipse diagrams and planet notes (explaining when they can be seen, their proximity to one another, etc.) with an accompanying diagram (showing their times of meridian passage).

The bulk of the *Almanac* consists of the daily pages, which provide the main data necessary to establish the GPs of celestial bodies. These data consist principally of Greenwich Hour Angle (GHA) and declination (Dec.) of the celestial bodies for any instant of time (UT). In general, these data are presented to the nearest one-tenth minute of arc, and one second of time.

Following the daily pages is a section titled "Explanation" with much useful information about how the information contained in the *Almanac* is compiled and how it may be used. Included are such things as standards of accuracy and an explanation of how the current year's *Almanac* may be adapted for use in the following year.

Tables of standard times and star charts that assist in the identification of celestial bodies are also included as described in chapter 21.

Following the star charts is a section that lists all of the fifty-seven navigational stars as well as 116 others that may occasionally be used for navigational purposes. They are listed in ascending order of SHA and include both their SHA and declination for each month of the year, as well as their magnitude and the constellation in which they can be found. No interpolation is needed, and the data can be used in the same way as for the selected stars on the daily pages.

Next is a section titled "Polaris (Pole Star) Tables" that are used for determining latitude from sextant altitude. The tables provided can also be used to obtain an azimuth to Polaris.

Following the Polaris tables is a section that covers sight reduction procedures based on both mathematical computation and on some included tables. These will be explained in more detail in chapter 25.

The last pages of the *Almanac* are tinted yellow for easy location and include a table that can be used for converting arc to time as well as multiple pages of "Increments and Corrections" that are used for interpolation of the hourly data on the daily pages. Finally, there is a "Table for Interpolating Sunrise, Moonrise, Etc." and an "Index to Selected Stars" that is identical to the one on the special bookmark.

Daily Pages

2403 The basic ephemeral data for all navigational bodies of interest to a mariner covering a three-day period are presented on pairs of white facing pages of the *Nautical Almanac*. The left-hand pages tabulate data for the stars and navigational planets. The right-hand pages present the ephemeral data for the Sun and Moon, together with the times of twilight, sunrise, sunset, moonrise, and moonset. Sample *Almanac* pages are shown as figures 2403a and 2403b.

The top of each page (both left and right) is marked with the dates covered and the extreme left-hand column of each page contains the dates, days of the week, and the hours of UT for the three days. It should be noted that the date is that at Greenwich and may, therefore be one day earlier or later than the local date at the navigator's position.

Left-Hand Pages

2404 As can be seen in figure 2403a, the left-hand page for each set of three days gives, for each hour, the GHA of Aries and the GHA and declination of the navigational planets—Venus, Mars, Jupiter, and Saturn. Also on this page, in the lower right corner, is a tabulation of the SHA of each planet and the time of its meridian passage, and separately, the time of meridian passage of ♈. Next to the planets' names at the top of their data columns is a number representing their magnitude (brightness).

A list of fifty-seven selected stars is also provided, arranged in alphabetical order together with their SHA and declination. These are the prime navigational stars, selected for their magnitude and distribution in the heavens, and are the ones most frequently observed by a navigator.

UT	ARIES GHA	VENUS −4.0 GHA	VENUS Dec	MARS +1.7 GHA	MARS Dec	JUPITER −1.9 GHA	JUPITER Dec	SATURN +0.1 GHA	SATURN Dec	STARS Name	SHA	Dec
d h	° ′	° ′	° ′	° ′	° ′	° ′	° ′	° ′	° ′		° ′	° ′
19 00	236 29.5	148 33.3	N24 54.3	153 22.2	N24 13.1	131 12.4	N22 55.8	161 52.4	N21 21.4	Acamar	315 25.3	S40 17.8
01	251 31.9	163 32.4	54.4	168 22.8	13.2	146 14.3	55.7	176 54.6	21.5	Achernar	335 33.6	S57 13.4
02	266 34.4	178 31.6	54.5	183 23.5	13.3	161 16.3	55.7	191 56.7	21.5	Acrux	173 18.9	S63 06.9
03	281 36.8	193 30.8 ..	54.7	198 24.1 ..	13.4	176 18.2 ..	55.6	206 58.8 ..	21.6	Adhara	255 19.7	S28 58.6
04	296 39.3	208 29.9	54.8	213 24.8	13.5	191 20.2	55.6	222 00.9	21.6	Aldebaran	290 59.8	N16 30.8
05	311 41.8	223 29.1	54.9	228 25.4	13.5	206 22.2	55.5	237 03.1	21.6			
06	326 44.2	238 28.2	N24 55.0	243 26.1	N24 13.6	221 24.1	N22 55.5	252 05.2	N21 21.7	Alioth	166 27.8	N55 57.1
07	341 46.7	253 27.4	55.2	258 26.7	13.7	236 26.1	55.4	267 07.3	21.7	Alkaid	153 05.2	N49 18.3
08	356 49.2	268 26.6	55.3	273 27.4	13.8	251 28.0	55.4	282 09.5	21.7	Al Na'ir	27 54.6	S46 56.9
S 09	11 51.6	283 25.7 ..	55.4	288 28.0 ..	13.9	266 30.0 ..	55.4	297 11.6 ..	21.8	Alnilam	275 55.6	S 1 12.1
U 10	26 54.1	298 24.9	55.5	303 28.7	14.0	281 32.0	55.3	312 13.7	21.8	Alphard	218 04.7	S 8 40.2
N 11	41 56.6	313 24.0	55.6	318 29.3	14.1	296 33.9	55.3	327 15.8	21.9			
D 12	56 59.0	328 23.2	N24 55.7	333 30.0	N24 14.2	311 35.9	N22 55.2	342 18.0	N21 21.9	Alphecca	126 18.0	N26 42.4
A 13	72 01.5	343 22.3	55.8	348 30.6	14.3	326 37.8	55.2	357 20.1	21.9	Alpheratz	357 52.8	N29 05.9
Y 14	87 03.9	358 21.5	56.0	3 31.3	14.3	341 39.8	55.1	12 22.2	22.0	Altair	62 16.6	N 8 52.3
15	102 06.4	13 20.7 ..	56.1	18 31.9 ..	14.4	356 41.7 ..	55.1	27 24.4 ..	22.0	Ankaa	353 24.5	S42 17.6
16	117 08.9	28 19.8	56.2	33 32.6	14.5	11 43.7	55.0	42 26.5	22.0	Antares	112 36.7	S26 26.3
17	132 11.3	43 19.0	56.3	48 33.2	14.6	26 45.7	55.0	57 28.6	22.1			
18	147 13.8	58 18.1	N24 56.4	63 33.9	N24 14.7	41 47.6	N22 54.9	72 30.7	N21 22.1	Arcturus	146 03.4	N19 10.3
19	162 16.3	73 17.3	56.5	78 34.5	14.8	56 49.6	54.9	87 32.9	22.2	Atria	107 45.9	S69 01.9
20	177 18.7	88 16.4	56.6	93 35.2	14.9	71 51.5	54.8	102 35.0	22.2	Avior	234 22.0	S59 31.2
21	192 21.2	103 15.6 ..	56.7	108 35.8 ..	14.9	86 53.5 ..	54.8	117 37.1 ..	22.2	Bellatrix	278 41.7	N 6 21.1
22	207 23.7	118 14.8	56.8	123 36.5	15.0	101 55.5	54.7	132 39.3	22.3	Betelgeuse	271 11.1	N 7 24.4
23	222 26.1	133 13.9	56.9	138 37.1	15.1	116 57.4	54.7	147 41.4	22.3			
20 00	237 28.6	148 13.1	N24 57.0	153 37.8	N24 15.2	131 59.4	N22 54.7	162 43.5	N21 22.3	Canopus	264 00.5	S52 42.0
01	252 31.1	163 12.2	57.1	168 38.4	15.3	147 01.3	54.6	177 45.6	22.4	Capella	280 47.9	N46 00.0
02	267 33.5	178 11.4	57.2	183 39.1	15.4	162 03.3	54.6	192 47.8	22.4	Deneb	49 37.3	N45 17.0
03	282 36.0	193 10.5 ..	57.3	198 39.7 ..	15.4	177 05.2 ..	54.5	207 49.9 ..	22.5	Denebola	182 42.4	N14 33.6
04	297 38.4	208 09.7	57.4	213 40.4	15.5	192 07.2	54.5	222 52.0	22.5	Diphda	349 04.8	S17 58.5
05	312 40.9	223 08.9	57.5	228 41.0	15.6	207 09.1	54.4	237 54.1	22.5			
06	327 43.4	238 08.0	N24 57.6	243 41.7	N24 15.7	222 11.1	N22 54.4	252 56.3	N21 22.6	Dubhe	194 02.0	N61 44.6
07	342 45.8	253 07.2	57.6	258 42.3	15.8	237 13.1	54.3	267 58.4	22.6	Elnath	278 24.0	N28 36.6
08	357 48.3	268 06.3	57.7	273 42.9	15.8	252 15.0	54.3	283 00.5	22.6	Eltanin	90 49.7	N51 29.1
M 09	12 50.8	283 05.5 ..	57.8	288 43.6 ..	15.9	267 17.0 ..	54.2	298 02.7 ..	22.7	Enif	33 55.7	N 9 52.9
O 10	27 53.2	298 04.7	57.9	303 44.2	16.0	282 18.9	54.2	313 04.8	22.7	Fomalhaut	15 33.6	S29 36.6
N 11	42 55.7	313 03.8	58.0	318 44.9	16.1	297 20.9	54.1	328 06.9	22.8			
D 12	57 58.2	328 03.0	N24 58.1	333 45.5	N24 16.2	312 22.8	N22 54.1	343 09.0	N21 22.8	Gacrux	172 10.5	S57 07.7
A 13	73 00.6	343 02.1	58.2	348 46.2	16.2	327 24.8	54.0	358 11.2	22.8	Gienah	176 01.2	S17 33.3
Y 14	88 03.1	358 01.3	58.2	3 46.8	16.3	342 26.8	54.0	13 13.3	22.9	Hadar	148 59.9	S60 23.2
15	103 05.6	13 00.4 ..	58.3	18 47.5 ..	16.4	357 28.7 ..	53.9	28 15.4 ..	22.9	Hamal	328 11.0	N23 28.2
16	118 08.0	27 59.6	58.4	33 48.1	16.5	12 30.7	53.9	43 17.5	22.9	Kaus Aust.	83 55.1	S34 23.0
17	133 10.5	42 58.8	58.5	48 48.8	16.6	27 32.6	53.9	58 19.7	23.0			
18	148 12.9	57 57.9	N24 58.5	63 49.4	N24 16.6	42 34.6	N22 53.8	73 21.8	N21 23.0	Kochab	137 18.3	N74 08.9
19	163 15.4	72 57.1	58.6	78 50.1	16.7	57 36.5	53.8	88 23.9	23.1	Markab	13 47.2	N15 12.8
20	178 17.9	87 56.2	58.7	93 50.7	16.8	72 38.5	53.7	103 26.0	23.1	Menkar	314 24.5	N 4 05.8
21	193 20.3	102 55.4 ..	58.8	108 51.4 ..	16.9	87 40.4 ..	53.7	118 28.2 ..	23.1	Menkent	148 17.6	S36 23.0
22	208 22.8	117 54.6	58.8	123 52.0	16.9	102 42.4	53.6	133 30.3	23.2	Miaplacidus	221 42.0	S69 43.8
23	223 25.3	132 53.7	58.9	138 52.7	17.0	117 44.3	53.6	148 32.4	23.2			
21 00	238 27.7	147 52.9	N24 59.0	153 53.3	N24 17.1	132 46.3	N22 53.5	163 34.6	N21 23.2	Mirfak	308 53.5	N49 52.0
01	253 30.2	162 52.0	59.0	168 54.0	17.2	147 48.3	53.5	178 36.7	23.3	Nunki	76 08.9	S26 17.6
02	268 32.7	177 51.2	59.1	183 54.6	17.2	162 50.2	53.4	193 38.8	23.3	Peacock	53 32.6	S56 43.5
03	283 35.1	192 50.3 ..	59.2	198 55.3 ..	17.3	177 52.2 ..	53.4	208 40.9 ..	23.4	Pollux	243 38.6	N28 01.4
04	298 37.6	207 49.5	59.2	213 55.9	17.4	192 54.1	53.3	223 43.1	23.4	Procyon	245 09.1	N 5 13.2
05	313 40.0	222 48.7	59.3	228 56.6	17.5	207 56.1	53.3	238 45.2	23.4			
06	328 42.5	237 47.8	N24 59.4	243 57.2	N24 17.5	222 58.0	N22 53.2	253 47.3	N21 23.5	Rasalhague	96 14.3	N12 33.4
07	343 45.0	252 47.0	59.4	258 57.9	17.6	238 00.0	53.2	268 49.4	23.5	Regulus	207 52.8	N11 57.4
08	358 47.4	267 46.1	59.5	273 58.5	17.7	253 01.9	53.1	283 51.6	23.5	Rigel	281 20.8	S 8 12.0
T 09	13 49.9	282 45.3 ..	59.5	288 59.2 ..	17.8	268 03.9 ..	53.1	298 53.7 ..	23.6	Rigil Kent.	140 03.3	S60 50.7
U 10	28 52.4	297 44.5	59.6	303 59.8	17.8	283 05.8	53.0	313 55.8	23.6	Sabik	102 22.3	S15 43.7
E 11	43 54.8	312 43.6	59.6	319 00.5	17.9	298 07.8	53.0	328 57.9	23.7			
S D 12	58 57.3	327 42.8	N24 59.7	334 01.1	N24 18.0	313 09.7	N22 52.9	344 00.1	N21 23.7	Schedar	349 51.1	N56 32.7
A 13	73 59.8	342 41.9	59.7	349 01.8	18.0	328 11.7	52.9	359 02.2	23.7	Shaula	96 33.4	S37 06.3
Y 14	89 02.2	357 41.1	59.8	4 02.4	18.1	343 13.6	52.8	14 04.3	23.8	Sirius	258 41.7	S16 43.2
15	104 04.7	12 40.3 ..	59.8	19 03.1 ..	18.2	358 15.6 ..	52.8	29 06.4 ..	23.8	Spica	158 40.2	S11 10.4
16	119 07.2	27 39.4	59.9	34 03.7	18.2	13 17.5	52.7	44 08.6	23.8	Suhail	222 59.1	S43 26.7
17	134 09.6	42 38.6	59.9	49 04.4	18.3	28 19.5	52.7	59 10.7	23.9			
18	149 12.1	57 37.7	N25 00.0	64 05.0	N24 18.4	43 21.4	N22 52.7	74 12.8	N21 23.9	Vega	80 44.6	N38 46.9
19	164 14.5	72 36.9	00.0	79 05.7	18.4	58 23.4	52.6	89 14.9	24.0	Zuben'ubi	137 14.8	S16 03.1
20	179 17.0	87 36.1	00.1	94 06.3	18.5	73 25.3	52.6	104 17.1	24.0		SHA	Mer. Pass.
21	194 19.5	102 35.2 ..	00.1	109 07.0 ..	18.6	88 27.3 ..	52.5	119 19.2 ..	24.0	Venus	270 44.5	14 08
22	209 21.9	117 34.4	00.2	124 07.6	18.7	103 29.3	52.5	134 21.3	24.1	Mars	276 09.2	13 45
23	224 24.4	132 33.5	00.2	139 08.3	18.7	118 31.2	52.4	149 23.5	24.1	Jupiter	254 30.8	15 10
Mer. Pass. 8 08.8		v −0.8 d 0.1		v 0.6 d 0.1		v 2.0 d 0.0		v 2.1 d 0.0		Saturn	285 14.9	13 07

Fig. 2403a. Left-hand daily page of the *Nautical Almanac* (typical).

All tabulations are in degrees, minutes, and tenths of minutes of arc.

At the bottom of each column of data for a planet are the v and d values for that body; because these values change slowly, a single entry is given for the three-day period covered by that page.

The v *and* d *values are factors for use with the interpolation tables,* called "Increments and Corrections" tables (on the yellow-tinted pages in the back of the *Almanac*). These tables are used to interpolate for intermediate times, since the entries on the daily pages are only for whole-hour values of GMT (UT). The v corrections serve as supplements to the GHA increments, in that they allow for the *changes* in the continuing hourly rates of increase of GHA. The v values as printed on the left-hand daily page for the planets are the three-day average amount in arc by which the hourly increase in GHA departs from the basic, or reference, hourly rate assumed in the almanac interpolation tables. The respective d values for planets (and incidentally for the Sun) are the three-day average *full amount* in arc by which the declination of the particular body changes during each hour as shown on the white, daily page. Interpolation by use of the Increments and Corrections tables and the v and d values in conjunction with them is explained further in articles 2406 and 2408.

Right-Hand Pages

2405   As illustrated in figure 2403b, data for the Sun and Moon are presented on the right-hand page, with GHA and Dec., tabulated to one-tenth minute of arc for each hour. For the Moon, additional values, namely, those of the horizontal parallax (HP) and of v and d, are tabulated for each hour. The Moon's rate of change of GHA and Dec. varies considerably. For the Sun, v is not necessary and its d is given only once at the bottom of the page for the three-day period.

Additionally, the right-hand pages provide data on sunrise and sunset, moonrise and moonset, and the beginnings and endings of both nautical and civil twilight.

At bottom-left is a value for the semidiameter (SD) of the Sun that covers the three-day period. Next to it is a d value for the Sun that also covers the entire three-day period. To the right of that are three values of semidiameter (SD) for the Moon; they are in sequential order for the three days covered by the almanac page. In the lower-right corner are data for each day covering the equation of time, the meridian passage of the Sun and Moon, and the age and phase of the Moon, as well as the percentage of the Moon's disk that can be seen. While the little diagram shows the phase of the Moon roughly as it would be seen in the sky, the *percentage* figures under the percentage sign (%) are a more quantitative description of the Moon's appearance. If you think of the Moon as a circular disk against the sky, then the ratio of the area illuminated by direct sunlight to total area of the disk, multiplied by 100, is the percentage of the disk apparently illuminated. At new Moon, 0% of the Moon is illuminated, as seen from Earth; at first and last quarters, 50% is illuminated, and at full Moon, 100%. During crescent phases, 0–50% is illuminated, and during gibbous phases, it is 50–100%. Also, scanning a column of percentage illuminated will indicate whether the Moon is waxing or waning.

Interpolation

2406   To establish the GHA and declination of a body, for a specific time of observation other than an exact whole hour of UT, it is necessary to interpolate, that is, calculate intermediate values between those that appear in the hourly tabulation. For the intermediate time, stated as minutes and seconds past the whole hour printed in the tables, GHA and Dec. are assumed to increase at uniform rates. This assumption is not strictly correct, but the errors involved are negligible for the stars, and the v and d corrections found on the daily pages are applied for greater accuracy when using bodies within the solar system.

To interpolate for time, including adjustments for the v and d factors, you must turn to the yellow-tinted tables near the back of the *Almanac* labeled "Increments and Corrections." A sample page is shown in figure 2406. The computations are based on standard reference rates of motion of the heavenly bodies about the Earth. For GHAs, these rates are 15° per hour for the Sun and planets, 15° 02.46′ for Aries, and 14° 19.0′ for the Moon. The values of the correction for v are then based on the excesses of the actual hourly motions beyond these adopted reference values. The reference rate of change for Dec. is *zero*. The d correction, then, accounts for the entire increment of declination to be applied to the hourly value of declination tabulated on the daily page.

Note that the tinted tables are arranged with a whole-minute value in the upper left corner within each table (36 and 37 minutes are shown in figure 2406). Down the left side of each minute table are whole-second arguments. The time interpolations to the nearest second are found by moving across the table to the appropriate entry for the body being used. For example, the interpolated value for 36

MAY 19, 20, 21 (SUN., MON., TUES.)

UT	SUN GHA	SUN Dec	MOON GHA	v	Dec	d	HP
d h	° ′	° ′	° ′	′	° ′	′	′
19 00	180 53.9	N19 40.9	95 23.9	8.0	N19 58.9	9.2	58.6
01	195 53.9	41.5	109 50.9	8.1	19 49.7	9.4	58.6
02	210 53.8	42.0	124 18.0	8.1	19 40.3	9.4	58.6
03	225 53.8 ..	42.6	138 45.1	8.2	19 30.9	9.7	58.6
04	240 53.8	43.1	153 12.3	8.2	19 21.2	9.7	58.6
05	255 53.8	43.6	167 39.5	8.2	19 11.5	9.8	58.7
06	270 53.7	N19 44.2	182 06.7	8.3	N19 01.7	10.0	58.7
07	285 53.7	44.7	196 34.0	8.4	18 51.7	10.1	58.7
08	300 53.7	45.2	211 01.4	8.4	18 41.6	10.2	58.7
S 09	315 53.6 ..	45.8	225 28.8	8.4	18 31.4	10.3	58.8
U 10	330 53.6	46.3	239 56.2	8.5	18 21.1	10.4	58.8
N 11	345 53.6	46.9	254 23.7	8.5	18 10.7	10.5	58.8
D 12	0 53.6	N19 47.4	268 51.2	8.6	N18 00.2	10.7	58.8
A 13	15 53.5	47.9	283 18.8	8.6	17 49.5	10.8	58.8
Y 14	30 53.5	48.5	297 46.4	8.7	17 38.7	10.8	58.9
15	45 53.5 ..	49.0	312 14.1	8.7	17 27.9	11.0	58.9
16	60 53.4	49.5	326 41.8	8.8	17 16.9	11.1	58.9
17	75 53.4	50.1	341 09.6	8.8	17 05.8	11.2	58.9
18	90 53.4	N19 50.6	355 37.4	8.8	N16 54.6	11.3	58.9
19	105 53.3	51.1	10 05.2	8.9	16 43.3	11.4	59.0
20	120 53.3	51.6	24 33.1	9.0	16 31.9	11.5	59.0
21	135 53.3 ..	52.2	39 01.1	8.9	16 20.4	11.6	59.0
22	150 53.2	52.7	53 29.0	9.1	16 08.8	11.7	59.0
23	165 53.2	53.2	67 57.1	9.0	15 57.1	11.8	59.0
20 00	180 53.2	N19 53.8	82 25.1	9.2	N15 45.3	11.9	59.1
01	195 53.1	54.3	96 53.3	9.1	15 33.4	12.0	59.1
02	210 53.1	54.8	111 21.4	9.2	15 21.4	12.1	59.1
03	225 53.1 ..	55.3	125 49.6	9.3	15 09.3	12.1	59.1
04	240 53.0	55.9	140 17.9	9.3	14 57.2	12.3	59.1
05	255 53.0	56.4	154 46.2	9.3	14 44.9	12.4	59.2
06	270 53.0	N19 56.9	169 14.5	9.4	N14 32.5	12.5	59.2
07	285 52.9	57.4	183 42.9	9.4	14 20.0	12.5	59.2
08	300 52.9	58.0	198 11.3	9.4	14 07.5	12.6	59.2
M 09	315 52.9 ..	58.5	212 39.7	9.5	13 54.9	12.8	59.2
O 10	330 52.8	59.0	227 08.2	9.6	13 42.1	12.8	59.2
N 11	345 52.8	19 59.5	241 36.8	9.5	13 29.3	12.9	59.3
D 12	0 52.8	N20 00.0	256 05.3	9.7	N13 16.4	12.9	59.3
A 13	15 52.7	00.6	270 34.0	9.6	13 03.5	13.1	59.3
Y 14	30 52.7	01.1	285 02.6	9.7	12 50.4	13.1	59.3
15	45 52.7 ..	01.6	299 31.3	9.7	12 37.3	13.2	59.3
16	60 52.6	02.1	314 00.0	9.8	12 24.1	13.3	59.4
17	75 52.6	02.6	328 28.8	9.8	12 10.8	13.4	59.4
18	90 52.5	N20 03.1	342 57.6	9.8	N11 57.4	13.5	59.4
19	105 52.5	03.7	357 26.4	9.9	11 43.9	13.5	59.4
20	120 52.5	04.2	11 55.3	9.9	11 30.4	13.6	59.4
21	135 52.4 ..	04.7	26 24.2	9.9	11 16.8	13.6	59.4
22	150 52.4	05.2	40 53.1	10.0	11 03.2	13.8	59.5
23	165 52.4	05.7	55 22.1	10.0	10 49.4	13.8	59.5
21 00	180 52.3	N20 06.2	69 51.1	10.0	N10 35.6	13.8	59.5
01	195 52.3	06.7	84 20.1	10.0	10 21.8	14.0	59.5
02	210 52.2	07.3	98 49.1	10.1	10 07.8	14.0	59.5
03	225 52.2 ..	07.8	113 18.2	10.1	9 53.8	14.0	59.5
04	240 52.2	08.3	127 47.3	10.2	9 39.8	14.2	59.6
05	255 52.1	08.8	142 16.5	10.1	9 25.6	14.1	59.6
06	270 52.1	N20 09.3	156 45.6	10.2	N 9 11.5	14.3	59.6
07	285 52.0	09.8	171 14.8	10.3	8 57.2	14.3	59.6
T 08	300 52.0	10.3	185 44.1	10.2	8 42.9	14.3	59.6
U 09	315 52.0 ..	10.8	200 13.3	10.3	8 28.6	14.4	59.6
E 10	330 51.9	11.3	214 42.6	10.3	8 14.2	14.5	59.6
S 11	345 51.9	11.8	229 11.9	10.3	7 59.7	14.5	59.7
D 12	0 51.8	N20 12.3	243 41.2	10.3	N 7 45.2	14.6	59.7
A 13	15 51.8	12.9	258 10.5	10.3	7 30.6	14.6	59.7
Y 14	30 51.8	13.4	272 39.8	10.4	7 16.0	14.7	59.7
15	45 51.7 ..	13.9	287 09.2	10.4	7 01.3	14.7	59.7
16	60 51.7	14.4	301 38.6	10.4	6 46.6	14.7	59.7
17	75 51.6	14.9	316 08.0	10.4	6 31.9	14.8	59.7
18	90 51.6	N20 15.4	330 37.4	10.4	N 6 17.1	14.9	59.8
19	105 51.5	15.9	345 06.8	10.5	6 02.2	14.8	59.8
20	120 51.5	16.4	359 36.3	10.5	5 47.4	15.0	59.8
21	135 51.5 ..	16.9	14 05.8	10.4	5 32.4	14.9	59.8
22	150 51.4	17.4	28 35.2	10.5	5 17.5	15.0	59.8
23	165 51.4	17.9	43 04.7	10.5	N 5 02.5	15.0	59.8
	SD 15.8	d 0.5	SD 16.0		16.2		16.3

Lat.	Twilight Naut.	Twilight Civil	Sunrise	Moonrise 19	20	21	22
°	h m	h m	h m	h m	h m	h m	h m
N 72	□	□	□	□	09 38	12 09	14 27
N 70	□	□	□	07 22	10 06	12 21	14 29
68	////	////	01 18	08 13	10 27	12 31	14 30
66	////	////	02 03	08 44	10 44	12 38	14 31
64	////	00 18	02 32	09 07	10 57	12 45	14 32
62	////	01 30	02 54	09 25	11 08	12 51	14 32
60	////	02 04	03 12	09 40	11 18	12 56	14 33
N 58	00 16	02 28	03 26	09 53	11 26	13 00	14 33
56	01 21	02 47	03 39	10 04	11 33	13 04	14 34
54	01 52	03 03	03 50	10 14	11 40	13 07	14 34
52	02 15	03 16	03 59	10 22	11 46	13 10	14 35
50	02 33	03 28	04 08	10 30	11 51	13 13	14 35
45	03 07	03 51	04 26	10 46	12 02	13 19	14 36
N 40	03 31	04 10	04 41	10 59	12 11	13 24	14 37
35	03 50	04 25	04 53	11 11	12 19	13 28	14 37
30	04 06	04 37	05 04	11 20	12 26	13 32	14 38
20	04 30	04 58	05 22	11 37	12 38	13 39	14 39
N 10	04 49	05 16	05 38	11 52	12 49	13 44	14 39
0	05 05	05 31	05 53	12 05	12 58	13 50	14 40
S 10	05 19	05 45	06 08	12 19	13 08	13 55	14 41
20	05 33	06 00	06 23	12 33	13 18	14 01	14 42
30	05 46	06 15	06 41	12 50	13 30	14 07	14 43
35	05 53	06 24	06 51	13 00	13 37	14 11	14 43
40	06 00	06 33	07 03	13 10	13 44	14 15	14 44
45	06 08	06 44	07 16	13 23	13 53	14 20	14 45
S 50	06 17	06 57	07 33	13 39	14 04	14 26	14 46
52	06 21	07 03	07 43	13 46	14 09	14 28	14 46
54	06 25	07 09	07 50	13 54	14 14	14 31	14 47
56	06 29	07 16	07 59	14 03	14 20	14 34	14 47
58	06 34	07 24	08 11	14 13	14 27	14 38	14 48
S 60	06 39	07 32	08 23	14 24	14 34	14 42	14 48

Lat.	Sunset	Twilight Civil	Twilight Naut.	Moonset 19	20	21	22
°	h m	h m	h m	h m	h m	h m	h m
N 72	□	□	□	□	04 16	03 33	03 04
N 70	□	□	□	04 37	03 45	03 19	02 59
68	22 41	////	////	03 46	03 23	03 07	02 54
66	21 53	////	////	03 13	03 05	02 57	02 51
64	21 23	////	////	02 49	02 50	02 49	02 48
62	21 01	22 27	////	02 30	02 38	02 45	02 45
60	20 43	21 52	////	02 14	02 27	02 36	02 43
N 58	20 28	21 27	////	02 01	02 18	02 30	02 40
56	20 15	21 08	22 36	01 49	02 10	02 25	02 38
54	20 04	20 52	21 52	01 39	02 02	02 21	02 37
52	19 55	20 38	21 40	01 30	01 56	02 17	02 35
50	19 46	20 26	21 22	01 22	01 50	02 13	02 34
45	19 28	20 03	20 47	01 04	01 37	02 05	02 31
N 40	19 13	19 44	20 23	00 50	01 26	01 58	02 28
35	19 00	19 29	20 03	00 38	01 17	01 53	02 26
30	18 49	19 16	19 48	00 27	01 09	01 47	02 24
20	18 31	18 55	19 23	00 08	00 55	01 38	02 20
N 10	18 15	18 37	19 04	24 42	00 42	01 30	02 17
0	18 00	18 22	18 48	24 31	00 31	01 23	02 14
S 10	17 45	18 08	18 33	24 19	00 19	01 15	02 10
20	17 30	17 53	18 20	24 06	00 06	01 07	02 07
30	17 12	17 38	18 07	23 52	24 58	00 58	02 03
35	17 02	17 29	18 00	23 43	24 52	00 52	02 01
40	16 50	17 19	17 53	23 33	24 46	00 46	01 58
45	16 36	17 09	17 45	23 22	24 39	00 39	01 55
S 50	16 20	16 56	17 36	23 08	24 30	00 30	01 52
52	16 12	16 50	17 32	23 01	24 26	00 26	01 50
54	16 03	16 44	17 28	22 54	24 21	00 21	01 48
56	15 53	16 37	17 23	22 46	24 16	00 16	01 46
58	15 42	16 29	17 18	22 37	24 10	00 10	01 44
S 60	15 29	16 20	17 13	22 26	24 04	00 04	01 41

Day	SUN Eqn. of Time 00ʰ	SUN Eqn. of Time 12ʰ	SUN Mer. Pass.	MOON Mer. Pass. Upper	MOON Mer. Pass. Lower	Age	Phase
d	m s	m s	h m	h m	h m	d	%
19	03 36	03 34	11 56	18 18	05 51	07	46
20	03 33	03 31	11 56	19 11	06 45	08	58
21	03 29	03 27	11 57	20 02	07 36	09	69

Fig. 2403b. Right-hand daily page of the *Nautical Almanac* (typical).

36ᵐ s	SUN PLANETS ° '	ARIES ° '	MOON ° '	v or Corrⁿ d ' '	v or Corrⁿ d ' '	v or Corrⁿ d ' '
00	9 00·0	9 01·5	8 35·4	0·0 0·0	6·0 3·7	12·0 7·3
01	9 00·3	9 01·7	8 35·6	0·1 0·1	6·1 3·7	12·1 7·4
02	9 00·5	9 02·0	8 35·9	0·2 0·1	6·2 3·8	12·2 7·4
03	9 00·8	9 02·2	8 36·1	0·3 0·2	6·3 3·8	12·3 7·5
04	9 01·0	9 02·5	8 36·4	0·4 0·2	6·4 3·9	12·4 7·5
05	9 01·3	9 02·7	8 36·6	0·5 0·3	6·5 4·0	12·5 7·6
06	9 01·5	9 03·0	8 36·8	0·6 0·4	6·6 4·0	12·6 7·7
07	9 01·8	9 03·2	8 37·1	0·7 0·4	6·7 4·1	12·7 7·7
08	9 02·0	9 03·5	8 37·3	0·8 0·5	6·8 4·1	12·8 7·8
09	9 02·3	9 03·7	8 37·5	0·9 0·5	6·9 4·2	12·9 7·8
10	9 02·5	9 04·0	8 37·8	1·0 0·6	7·0 4·3	13·0 7·9
11	9 02·8	9 04·2	8 38·0	1·1 0·7	7·1 4·3	13·1 8·0
12	9 03·0	9 04·5	8 38·3	1·2 0·7	7·2 4·4	13·2 8·0
13	9 03·3	9 04·7	8 38·5	1·3 0·8	7·3 4·4	13·3 8·1
14	9 03·5	9 05·0	8 38·7	1·4 0·9	7·4 4·5	13·4 8·2
15	9 03·8	9 05·2	8 39·0	1·5 0·9	7·5 4·6	13·5 8·2
16	9 04·0	9 05·5	8 39·2	1·6 1·0	7·6 4·6	13·6 8·3
17	9 04·3	9 05·7	8 39·5	1·7 1·0	7·7 4·7	13·7 8·3
18	9 04·5	9 06·0	8 39·7	1·8 1·1	7·8 4·7	13·8 8·4
19	9 04·8	9 06·2	8 39·9	1·9 1·2	7·9 4·8	13·9 8·5
20	9 05·0	9 06·5	8 40·2	2·0 1·2	8·0 4·9	14·0 8·5
21	9 05·3	9 06·7	8 40·4	2·1 1·3	8·1 4·9	14·1 8·6
22	9 05·5	9 07·0	8 40·6	2·2 1·3	8·2 5·0	14·2 8·6
23	9 05·8	9 07·2	8 40·9	2·3 1·4	8·3 5·0	14·3 8·7
24	9 06·0	9 07·5	8 41·1	2·4 1·5	8·4 5·1	14·4 8·8
25	9 06·3	9 07·7	8 41·4	2·5 1·5	8·5 5·2	14·5 8·8
26	9 06·5	9 08·0	8 41·6	2·6 1·6	8·6 5·2	14·6 8·9
27	9 06·8	9 08·2	8 41·8	2·7 1·6	8·7 5·3	14·7 8·9
28	9 07·0	9 08·5	8 42·1	2·8 1·7	8·8 5·4	14·8 9·0
29	9 07·3	9 08·7	8 42·3	2·9 1·8	8·9 5·4	14·9 9·1
30	9 07·5	9 09·0	8 42·6	3·0 1·8	9·0 5·5	15·0 9·1
31	9 07·8	9 09·2	8 42·8	3·1 1·9	9·1 5·5	15·1 9·2
32	9 08·0	9 09·5	8 43·0	3·2 1·9	9·2 5·6	15·2 9·2
33	9 08·3	9 09·8	8 43·3	3·3 2·0	9·3 5·7	15·3 9·3
34	9 08·5	9 10·0	8 43·5	3·4 2·1	9·4 5·7	15·4 9·4
35	9 08·8	9 10·3	8 43·8	3·5 2·1	9·5 5·8	15·5 9·4
36	9 09·0	9 10·5	8 44·0	3·6 2·2	9·6 5·8	15·6 9·5
37	9 09·3	9 10·8	8 44·2	3·7 2·3	9·7 5·9	15·7 9·6
38	9 09·5	9 11·0	8 44·5	3·8 2·3	9·8 6·0	15·8 9·6
39	9 09·8	9 11·3	8 44·7	3·9 2·4	9·9 6·0	15·9 9·7
40	9 10·0	9 11·5	8 44·9	4·0 2·4	10·0 6·1	16·0 9·7
41	9 10·3	9 11·8	8 45·2	4·1 2·5	10·1 6·1	16·1 9·8
42	9 10·5	9 12·0	8 45·4	4·2 2·6	10·2 6·2	16·2 9·9
43	9 10·8	9 12·3	8 45·7	4·3 2·6	10·3 6·3	16·3 9·9
44	9 11·0	9 12·5	8 45·9	4·4 2·7	10·4 6·3	16·4 10·0
45	9 11·3	9 12·8	8 46·1	4·5 2·7	10·5 6·4	16·5 10·0
46	9 11·5	9 13·0	8 46·4	4·6 2·8	10·6 6·4	16·6 10·1
47	9 11·8	9 13·3	8 46·6	4·7 2·9	10·7 6·5	16·7 10·2
48	9 12·0	9 13·5	8 46·9	4·8 2·9	10·8 6·6	16·8 10·2
49	9 12·3	9 13·8	8 47·1	4·9 3·0	10·9 6·6	16·9 10·3
50	9 12·5	9 14·0	8 47·3	5·0 3·0	11·0 6·7	17·0 10·3
51	9 12·8	9 14·3	8 47·6	5·1 3·1	11·1 6·8	17·1 10·4
52	9 13·0	9 14·5	8 47·8	5·2 3·2	11·2 6·8	17·2 10·5
53	9 13·3	9 14·8	8 48·0	5·3 3·2	11·3 6·9	17·3 10·5
54	9 13·5	9 15·0	8 48·3	5·4 3·3	11·4 6·9	17·4 10·6
55	9 13·8	9 15·3	8 48·5	5·5 3·3	11·5 7·0	17·5 10·6
56	9 14·0	9 15·5	8 48·8	5·6 3·4	11·6 7·1	17·6 10·7
57	9 14·3	9 15·8	8 49·0	5·7 3·5	11·7 7·1	17·7 10·8
58	9 14·5	9 16·0	8 49·2	5·8 3·5	11·8 7·2	17·8 10·8
59	9 14·8	9 16·3	8 49·5	5·9 3·6	11·9 7·2	17·9 10·9
60	9 15·0	9 16·5	8 49·7	6·0 3·7	12·0 7·3	18·0 11·0

37ᵐ s	SUN PLANETS ° '	ARIES ° '	MOON ° '	v or Corrⁿ d ' '	v or Corrⁿ d ' '	v or Corrⁿ d ' '
00	9 15·0	9 16·5	8 49·7	0·0 0·0	6·0 3·8	12·0 7·5
01	9 15·3	9 16·8	8 50·0	0·1 0·1	6·1 3·8	12·1 7·6
02	9 15·5	9 17·0	8 50·2	0·2 0·1	6·2 3·9	12·2 7·6
03	9 15·8	9 17·3	8 50·4	0·3 0·2	6·3 3·9	12·3 7·7
04	9 16·0	9 17·5	8 50·7	0·4 0·3	6·4 4·0	12·4 7·8
05	9 16·3	9 17·8	8 50·9	0·5 0·3	6·5 4·1	12·5 7·8
06	9 16·5	9 18·0	8 51·1	0·6 0·4	6·6 4·1	12·6 7·9
07	9 16·8	9 18·3	8 51·4	0·7 0·4	6·7 4·2	12·7 7·9
08	9 17·0	9 18·5	8 51·6	0·8 0·5	6·8 4·3	12·8 8·0
09	9 17·3	9 18·8	8 51·9	0·9 0·6	6·9 4·3	12·9 8·1
10	9 17·5	9 19·0	8 52·1	1·0 0·6	7·0 4·4	13·0 8·1
11	9 17·8	9 19·3	8 52·3	1·1 0·7	7·1 4·4	13·1 8·2
12	9 18·0	9 19·5	8 52·6	1·2 0·8	7·2 4·5	13·2 8·3
13	9 18·3	9 19·8	8 52·8	1·3 0·8	7·3 4·6	13·3 8·3
14	9 18·5	9 20·0	8 53·1	1·4 0·9	7·4 4·6	13·4 8·4
15	9 18·8	9 20·3	8 53·3	1·5 0·9	7·5 4·7	13·5 8·4
16	9 19·0	9 20·5	8 53·5	1·6 1·0	7·6 4·8	13·6 8·5
17	9 19·3	9 20·8	8 53·8	1·7 1·1	7·7 4·8	13·7 8·6
18	9 19·5	9 21·0	8 54·0	1·8 1·1	7·8 4·9	13·8 8·6
19	9 19·8	9 21·3	8 54·3	1·9 1·2	7·9 4·9	13·9 8·7
20	9 20·0	9 21·5	8 54·5	2·0 1·3	8·0 5·0	14·0 8·8
21	9 20·3	9 21·8	8 54·7	2·1 1·3	8·1 5·1	14·1 8·8
22	9 20·5	9 22·0	8 55·0	2·2 1·4	8·2 5·1	14·2 8·9
23	9 20·8	9 22·3	8 55·2	2·3 1·4	8·3 5·2	14·3 8·9
24	9 21·0	9 22·5	8 55·4	2·4 1·5	8·4 5·3	14·4 9·0
25	9 21·3	9 22·8	8 55·7	2·5 1·6	8·5 5·3	14·5 9·1
26	9 21·5	9 23·0	8 55·9	2·6 1·6	8·6 5·4	14·6 9·1
27	9 21·8	9 23·3	8 56·2	2·7 1·7	8·7 5·4	14·7 9·2
28	9 22·0	9 23·5	8 56·4	2·8 1·8	8·8 5·5	14·8 9·3
29	9 22·3	9 23·8	8 56·6	2·9 1·8	8·9 5·6	14·9 9·3
30	9 22·5	9 24·0	8 56·9	3·0 1·9	9·0 5·6	15·0 9·4
31	9 22·8	9 24·3	8 57·1	3·1 1·9	9·1 5·7	15·1 9·4
32	9 23·0	9 24·5	8 57·4	3·2 2·0	9·2 5·8	15·2 9·5
33	9 23·3	9 24·8	8 57·6	3·3 2·1	9·3 5·8	15·3 9·6
34	9 23·5	9 25·0	8 57·8	3·4 2·1	9·4 5·9	15·4 9·6
35	9 23·8	9 25·3	8 58·1	3·5 2·2	9·5 5·9	15·5 9·7
36	9 24·0	9 25·5	8 58·3	3·6 2·3	9·6 6·0	15·6 9·8
37	9 24·3	9 25·8	8 58·5	3·7 2·3	9·7 6·1	15·7 9·8
38	9 24·5	9 26·0	8 58·8	3·8 2·4	9·8 6·1	15·8 9·9
39	9 24·8	9 26·3	8 59·0	3·9 2·4	9·9 6·2	15·9 9·9
40	9 25·0	9 26·5	8 59·3	4·0 2·5	10·0 6·3	16·0 10·0
41	9 25·3	9 26·8	8 59·5	4·1 2·6	10·1 6·3	16·1 10·1
42	9 25·5	9 27·0	8 59·7	4·2 2·6	10·2 6·4	16·2 10·1
43	9 25·8	9 27·3	9 00·0	4·3 2·7	10·3 6·4	16·3 10·2
44	9 26·0	9 27·5	9 00·2	4·4 2·8	10·4 6·5	16·4 10·3
45	9 26·3	9 27·8	9 00·5	4·5 2·8	10·5 6·6	16·5 10·3
46	9 26·5	9 28·1	9 00·7	4·6 2·9	10·6 6·6	16·6 10·4
47	9 26·8	9 28·3	9 00·9	4·7 2·9	10·7 6·7	16·7 10·4
48	9 27·0	9 28·6	9 01·2	4·8 3·0	10·8 6·8	16·8 10·5
49	9 27·3	9 28·8	9 01·4	4·9 3·1	10·9 6·8	16·9 10·6
50	9 27·5	9 29·1	9 01·6	5·0 3·1	11·0 6·9	17·0 10·6
51	9 27·8	9 29·3	9 01·9	5·1 3·2	11·1 6·9	17·1 10·7
52	9 28·0	9 29·6	9 02·1	5·2 3·3	11·2 7·0	17·2 10·8
53	9 28·3	9 29·8	9 02·4	5·3 3·3	11·3 7·1	17·3 10·8
54	9 28·5	9 30·1	9 02·6	5·4 3·4	11·4 7·1	17·4 10·9
55	9 28·8	9 30·3	9 02·8	5·5 3·4	11·5 7·2	17·5 10·9
56	9 29·0	9 30·6	9 03·1	5·6 3·5	11·6 7·3	17·6 11·0
57	9 29·3	9 30·8	9 03·3	5·7 3·6	11·7 7·3	17·7 11·1
58	9 29·5	9 31·1	9 03·6	5·8 3·6	11·8 7·4	17·8 11·1
59	9 29·8	9 31·3	9 03·8	5·9 3·7	11·9 7·4	17·9 11·2
60	9 30·0	9 31·6	9 04·0	6·0 3·8	12·0 7·5	18·0 11·3

Fig. 2406. *Nautical Almanac,* Increments and Corrections page (typical).

minutes and fifteen seconds for GHA of the Sun or one of the planets is 9 degrees, 3.8 minutes.

Continuing across the table, you see an adjoining table of three pairs of columns with separate entries for the *v* and *d* values that you obtained from the daily pages. Enter the table by moving down the left sides of the columns under the "*v* or *d*" heading until you reach the value of *v* or *d* obtained from the daily pages. Right next to it, you find the correction to be applied. For example, in figure 2403b the *d* value for the Sun (found at the foot of the Sun column) is 0.3. This value in the "Increments and Corrections" table shown in figure 2406 would show a correction of 0.2 for both the 36- and 37-minute tables. (See article 2408 for additional discussion of the use of these tables.) No mystery need attend how the *v* and *d* corrections are computed. They are merely the *v* and *d* values multiplied by the fraction of an hour that has gone by at the midpoint of the minute for which calculated. In corroboration of this relationship, one may multiply the various *v* and *d* values in the 37-minute table in figure 2406 by the fraction $^{37.5}/_{60}$ and compare the results against the corresponding corrections as printed. As for the increments printed on the tinted pages for each second, they are computed in much the same way; that is, the base, or reference, hourly GHA rate is multiplied by the fraction of an hour that has elapsed for each cumulative second within the hour.

Correction Standards

2407   The daily-page tabulated values of GHA and Dec. are, in most cases, correct to the nearest one-tenth minute of arc; the one exception being the Sun's GHA, which is deliberately adjusted by as much as 0.15′ to reduce the error caused by omitting the *v* correction. The largest imprecision that can occur in GHA or Dec. of any body other than the Sun or Moon, is less than 0.2′; it may reach 0.25′ for the GHA of the Sun, and 0.3′ for the Moon. These are extremes; in actual use, you may expect less than 10 percent of the values of GHA and Dec. to have errors greater than 0.1′.

Errors in altitude corrections are generally of the same order as those for GHA and Dec., because they result from the addition of several quantities each rounded to 0.1′. While rarely the case, the *actual* values of dip and refraction at low altitudes may, in extreme atmospheric conditions, differ considerably from the mean values shown in the tables of the *Nautical Almanac*.

The values of the time arguments used in the *Almanac* are UT1 (see article 2306). This may differ from radio broadcast time signals, which are in UTC, by up to 0.9 second of time; step adjustments of exactly one second are made as required to prevent this difference from exceeding 0.9 seconds. Those who require the reduction of observations to a precision of better than one second of time must apply a correction, DUT1, which normally can be determined from the radio broadcast, to each time of observation. Alternatively, the DUT1 correction may be applied to the longitude reduced from the uncorrected time in accordance with the table below:

Correction to Time Signals	Correction to Longitude
–09^s to –0.7^s	0.2′ to east
–0.6^s to –0.3^s	0.1′ to east
–0.2^s to +0.2^s	No correction
+0.3^s to +0.6^s	0.1′ to west
+0.7^s to +0.9^s	0.2′ to west

Use of the *Nautical Almanac*

2408   GHA and declination data are usually extracted from the *Almanac* in the order indicated by figure 2408. The time of an observation is expressed as a day and an hour, followed by minutes and seconds. The tabular values of GHA and Dec., and, where necessary, the corresponding values of *v* and *d*, are taken directly from the daily pages for the day and hour of UT (GMT). For star sights, GHA ♈, SHA, and Dec. are also taken from the daily pages.

Turning to the table of Increments and Corrections in the rear of the *Almanac*, find the appropriate table for the *minutes* component of your observation; note that figure 2406 shows the Increments and Corrections tables for 36 and 37 minutes (as indicated by the number in the upper left-hand corner of each half-page table shown). Once you have the appropriate *minute* column, move down the left-hand side, below the minute indicator, to find the appropriate entry for the *seconds* of your time of observation; as you can see, there are entries for 00 through 60 seconds as you might expect. Moving across from the second you have selected, stop in the column headed by the kind of observation you made; the first column would be the obvious choice if you had sighted the Sun or a planet, the second column (Aries) is used for stars, and the third column is for Moon observations.

The increment in minutes and seconds of UT is taken from the line for the number of seconds, and the column for the body concerned. The *v* correction is taken from the right-hand portion of the

Body	SUN	MOON	DENEBOLA	MARS
Date (G)	5 JUN	5 JUN	5 JUN	5 JUN
GMT	13-36-35	09-37-08	23-36-56	23-37-22
GHA (h)	15° 24.0'	83° 49.6'	239° 15.1'	211° 05.1'
Incre (m/s)	9° 08.8'	8° 51.6'	9° 15.5'	9° 20.5'
V/V Corr	—	7.6/ +4.8'		0.7/ +0.4'
SHA			183° 01.3'	—
Total GHA	24° 32.8'	92° 46.0'	431° 31.9'	220° 26.0'
± 360°			71° 31.9'	
Tab Dec	N 22° 34.0'	S 14° 25.0'	N14° 41.9'	N10° 26.9'
d/d Corr	+0.3'/ 0.2	7.6/ –4.8	—	+0.7'/ + 0.4
True Dec	N22° 34.2'	S 14° 20.2'	N 14° 41.9'	N 10° 27.3'

Fig. 2408. Tabular solutions for GHA and declination using *Nautical Almanac.*

table for the same UT minutes opposite the *v* value taken from the daily pages. Both increment and *v* corrections are to be added to the GHA value extracted from the daily page for the whole hour, except for Venus when its *v* value is prefixed with a minus sign; it must then be subtracted. Negative *v* values for Venus are rare, but important when they occur.

For the Dec. there is no increment tabulated against the seconds within a minute of UT, but a *d* correction is applied in much the same way as for *v*. Values of *d* on the daily pages are not marked "+" or "–"; the sign must be determined by observing the trend (increasing or decreasing) of the Dec. values straddling the time of your observation.

Figure 2408 illustrates the determination and recording of data for the Sun, Moon, Mars, and the star Denebola. The data have been extracted from the daily pages illustrated in figures 2403a and 2403b, and the Increments and Corrections page shown in figure 2406. Step-by-step explanations are provided below.

Solution for the Sun

2409 The use of the *Nautical Almanac* will be illustrated first by the extraction of data for an observation of the Sun.

Assume you are located at approximately L30° N, 60° W on 5 June ZT 09-36-35 (+4). Having taken an observation of the Sun, you need to determine its GHA and Dec. from the *Nautical Almanac.* You would accomplish this by the following steps:

1. Determine UT by adding the ZD to the ZT; UT is thus 13-36-35.
2. On the right-hand page, which includes the data on 5 June (fig. 2403b), find the column headed UT and find the line for the whole hour "13" of the day indicated as "5 Sunday."

3. Follow across this line to the column for the Sun; read and record the value for GHA (15° 24.0') and Dec. (N22° 34.0'); note from previous (N22° 33.7') and following (N22° 34.3') values that the Dec. is *increasing;* this tells you that the sign of the *d* correction will be +.
4. At the bottom of the Dec. column, read and record the *d* value (0.3').
5. Turn to the yellow pages for Increments and Corrections and find the page that includes values for 36 minutes of UT as indicated at the top of the page (fig. 2406); find the line for 35 seconds and follow across to the Sun/Planets column; read and record the GHA increment (9° 08.8').
6. In the column for *v* and *d* corrections, find the line for a *d* value of 0.3'; the *d* correction is read and recorded (0.2'); the sign is determined to be + because the declination values in the daily tables were increasing when going from 13 to 14 hours on 5 June.
7. Add the GHA increment to the value of GHA for 13 hours UT on 5 June: 15° 24.0' + 9° 08.8' = 24° 32.8'; this is the GHA of the Sun at the time of observation.
8. Add the *d* correction to the value of Dec. for 13 hours UT on 5 June: N22° 34.0' + 0.2 = N22° 34.2'; this is the declination of the Sun at the time of observation.

Solution for Other Bodies

2410 Referring to figure 2408 and the above procedure for determining GHA and Dec. for the Sun, a similar procedure is followed for the other bodies. Following through the problems it will be noted that there is both a *v* and *d* correction for the Moon in addition to the correction for minutes and seconds of time after the whole hour of UT. The south declination of the Moon was decreasing with time (Moon moving northward), resulting in the *d* correction being minus. In the Denebola problem, the GHA ♈ plus SHA star produced a GHA Denebola of 431° 31.9′ with the result that 360° was subtracted to produce a GHA of 71° 31.9′. For the Mars observation, the north declination was increasing with time and the sign of the *d* correction was therefore +. In both the Mars and Moon observations, the declination was changing toward the north. In the first case, there was an increase in N Dec., and in the latter there was a decrease of S Dec.

Nautical Almanac: Summary

2411 The coordinates of celestial bodies are tabulated in the *Nautical Almanac* with respect to Universal Time (UT), which is, for nautical navigation needs, the same as Greenwich Mean Time (GMT). Using the UT of an observation, the navigator extracts the GHA and Dec. of the body observed. These data are very important because they establish the GP of the body being observed, and this in turn provides one vertex of the navigational triangle.

The GHAs of the Sun, Moon, planets, and Aries are tabulated in the *Nautical Almanac* for each hour of UT, and tables of increments permit interpolation for the minutes and seconds of an observation. A small *v* correction factor applying to the GHA is also shown on the daily pages for the planets (at the bottom of the column) and for the Moon (alongside each entry of GHA). The sum of the tabulated GHA, together with the increment for excess minutes and seconds, and the value of the *v* correction (where applicable) for these minutes and seconds, is the GHA of the body at the time of observation. The SHA of the star is taken from the *Nautical Almanac* without interpolation. The SHA of a star is added to the GHA of Aries to obtain the star's GHA.

The declinations of the Sun, Moon, and planets are also tabulated in the daily pages of the *Nautical Almanac* for UT, along with a *d* factor. The correction to the declination for *d* is obtained from the table of increments for the minutes and seconds in excess of the tabulated value. The declination of a star is taken from the *Nautical Almanac* without any correction.

In practice, you should obtain *all* the necessary values of GHA and Dec., plus associated data, from the daily pages during one book opening. Then turn to the "Increments and Corrections" tables for the remaining data. This procedure materially shortens the time required to reduce observations.

AIR ALMANAC

2412 The *Air Almanac* contains basically the same data as the *Nautical Almanac*. The *Air Almanac* arrangement was designed primarily for the use of aviators, and is accordingly more convenient for a fast solution; however, the tradeoff is that small inaccuracies result for some bodies. It is popular with many navigators on yachts and small craft, but its use is not recommended when maximum precision and accuracy are required. The same may be said for the *Nautical Almanac* when STELLA is available.

The *Air Almanac* gives ephemeral data for each ten minutes of UT (GMT) on the daily pages, and because of the greater number of tabulations, it cannot conveniently be bound as a single volume covering an entire year. It is issued twice a year, each volume covering a six-month period of time. Two pages, the front and back of a single sheet, cover one calendar day (figs. 2312a and 2412b). Thus, at any one opening, the left-hand page contains the tabulation of data for every 10 minutes of time from 12 hours 0 minutes UT (GMT) to 23 hours 50 minutes of one day. Data from 0 hours 0 minutes to 11 hours 50 minutes of the *following* day are presented on the right-hand page. The daily data include GHA and Dec. of the Sun, the GHA of Aries, and the GHA and Dec. of the Moon and of the three planets most suitable for observation at that time. All are given to the nearest 1′. The volumes are bound with plastic rings to enable the user to tear out the daily pages for more convenient use. Notice that a full Greenwich day of ephemeral data appears on one leaf, A.M. on one side, P.M. on the other. In addition, these daily pages give the time of moonrise and moonset, the Moon's parallax in altitude (shown as "Moon's P. in A."), the semidiameter of the Sun and Moon, and the latter's "age" (i.e., the number of days since the last new Moon). At the bottom of each column of data (except GHA ♈), an hourly rate of change is given (shown as simply "Rate").

On the inside of the front cover there is a table to permit ready interpolation of GHA of the Sun, Aries, and planets on the one hand, and of the Moon on the other, for elapsed time increments between the 10-minute tabulated values of GHA. This table is repeated on a flap that can be folded out from the book. Both of these tables state arc to the nearest whole minute. For greater precision there is also included in the white section in the back of the *Air Almanac* a separate page for the interpolation of GHA Sun and one for inter-

(DAY 156) GREENWICH A. M.   JUNE 5 (SUNDAY)

GMT	☉ SUN GHA	Dec.	ARIES GHA ♈	VENUS−4.1 GHA	Dec.	MARS 1.3 GHA	Dec.	SATURN 0.6 GHA	Dec.	☽ MOON GHA	Dec.
00 00	180 25.5	N22 30.4	253 18.4	225 38	N 8 57	225 49	N10 12	118 04	N18 00	313 54	S15 29
10	182 55.5	30.5	255 48.8	228 08		228 19		120 34		316 18	28
20	185 25.5	30.5	258 19.2	230 38		230 49		123 05		318 42	27
30	187 55.4 ·	30.6	260 49.6	233 08 ·		233 19 · ·		125 35 · ·		321 07 ·	25
40	190 25.4	30.6	263 20.0	235 38		235 49		128 06		323 31	24
50	192 55.4	30.6	265 50.4	238 08		238 20		130 36		325 55	23
01 00	195 25.4	N22 30.7	268 20.9	240 38	N 8 57	240 50	N10 13	133 06	N18 00	328 20	S15 22
10	197 55.4	30.7	270 51.3	243 08		243 20		135 37		330 44	21
20	200 25.4	30.8	273 21.7	245 38		245 50		138 07		333 08	20
30	202 55.3 ·	30.8	275 52.1	248 08 ·		248 20 · ·		140 38 · ·		335 33 ·	19
40	205 25.3	30.9	278 22.5	250 38		250 50		143 08		337 57	17
50	207 55.3	30.9	280 52.9	253 08		253 20		145 38		340 21	16
02 00	210 25.3	N22 31.0	283 23.3	255 38	N 8 58	255 50	N10 13	148 09	N18 00	342 46	S15 15
10	212 55.3	31.0	285 53.7	258 08		258 21		150 39		345 10	14
20	215 25.2	31.1	288 24.1	260 38		260 51		153 09		347 34	13
30	217 55.2 ·	31.1	290 54.6	263 08 ·		263 21 · ·		155 40 · ·		349 59 ·	12
40	220 25.2	31.2	293 25.0	265 39		265 51		158 10		352 23	10
50	222 55.2	31.2	295 55.4	268 09		268 21		160 41		354 47	09
03 00	225 25.2	N22 31.3	298 25.8	270 39	N 8 59	270 51	N10 14	163 11	N17 59	357 12	S15 08
10	227 55.2	31.3	300 56.2	273 09		273 21		165 41		359 36	07
20	230 25.1	31.3	303 26.6	275 39		275 51		168 12		2 00	06
30	232 55.1 ·	31.4	305 57.0	278 09 ·		278 21 · ·		170 42 · ·		4 25 ·	05
40	235 25.1	31.4	308 27.4	280 39		280 52		173 12		6 49	03
50	237 55.1	31.5	310 57.8	283 09		283 22		175 43		9 13	02
04 00	240 25.1	N22 31.5	313 28.3	285 39	N 8 59	285 52	N10 15	178 13	N17 59	11 38	S15 01
10	242 55.0	31.6	315 58.7	288 09		288 22		180 43		14 02	15 00
20	245 25.0	31.6	318 29.1	290 39		290 52		183 14		16 26	14 59
30	247 55.0 ·	31.7	320 59.5	293 09 ·		293 22 · ·		185 44 · ·		18 51 ·	58
40	250 25.0	31.7	323 29.9	295 39		295 52		188 15		21 15	56
50	252 55.0	31.8	326 00.3	298 09		298 22		190 45		23 40	55
05 00	255 25.0	N22 31.8	328 30.7	300 39	N 9 00	300 53	N10 15	193 15	N17 59	26 04	S14 54
10	257 54.9	31.9	331 01.1	303 09		303 23		195 46		28 28	53
20	260 24.9	31.9	333 31.5	305 39		305 53		198 16		30 53	51
30	262 54.9 ·	31.9	336 01.9	308 09 ·		308 23 · ·		200 46 · ·		33 17 ·	50
40	265 24.9	32.0	338 32.4	310 40		310 53		203 17		35 41	49
50	267 54.9	32.0	341 02.8	313 10		313 23		205 47		38 06	48
06 00	270 24.8	N22 32.1	343 33.2	315 40	N 9 01	315 53	N10 16	208 18	N17 59	40 30	S14 47
10	272 54.8	32.1	346 03.6	318 10		318 23		210 48		42 55	45
20	275 24.8	32.2	348 34.0	320 40		320 53		213 18		45 19	44
30	277 54.8 ·	32.2	351 04.4	323 10 ·		323 24 · ·		215 49 · ·		47 43 ·	43
40	280 24.8	32.3	353 34.8	325 40		325 54		218 19		50 08	42
50	282 54.8	32.3	356 05.2	328 10		328 24		220 49		52 32	41
07 00	285 24.7	N22 32.4	358 35.6	330 40	N 9 01	330 54	N10 17	223 20	N17 59	54 57	S14 39
10	287 54.7	32.4	1 06.1	333 10		333 24		225 50		57 21	38
20	290 24.7	32.4	3 36.5	335 40		335 54		228 21		59 45	37
30	292 54.7 ·	32.5	6 06.9	338 10 ·		338 24 · ·		230 51 · ·		62 10 ·	36
40	295 24.7	32.5	8 37.3	340 40		340 54		233 21		64 34	34
50	297 54.6	32.6	11 07.7	343 10		343 24		235 52		66 59	33
08 00	300 24.6	N22 32.6	13 38.1	345 40	N 9 02	345 55	N10 17	238 22	N17 59	69 23	S14 32
10	302 54.6	32.7	16 08.5	348 10		348 25		240 52		71 47	31
20	305 24.6	32.7	18 38.9	350 40		350 55		243 23		74 12	29
30	307 54.6 ·	32.8	21 09.3	353 11 ·		353 25 · ·		245 53 · ·		76 36 ·	28
40	310 24.6	32.8	23 39.8	355 41		355 55		248 24		79 01	27
50	312 54.5	32.9	26 10.2	358 11		358 25		250 54		81 25	26
09 00	315 24.5	N22 32.9	28 40.6	0 41	N 9 02	0 55	N10 18	253 24	N17 59	83 49	S14 24
10	317 54.5	33.0	31 11.0	3 11		3 25		255 55		86 14	23
20	320 24.5	33.0	33 41.4	5 41		5 56		258 25		88 38	22
30	322 54.5 ·	33.0	36 11.8	8 11 ·		8 26 · ·		260 55 · ·		91 03 ·	21
40	325 24.4	33.1	38 42.2	10 41		10 56		263 26		93 27	19
50	327 54.4	33.1	41 12.6	13 11		13 26		265 56		95 52	18
10 00	330 24.4	N22 33.2	43 43.0	15 41	N 9 03	15 56	N10 19	268 27	N17 59	98 16	S14 17
10	332 54.4	33.2	46 13.4	18 11		18 26		270 57		100 40	16
20	335 24.4	33.3	48 43.9	20 41		20 56		273 27		103 05	14
30	337 54.4 ·	33.3	51 14.3	23 11 ·		23 26 · ·		275 58 · ·		105 29 ·	13
40	340 24.3	33.4	53 44.7	25 41		25 56		278 28		107 54	12
50	342 54.3	33.4	56 15.1	28 11		28 27		280 58		110 18	10
11 00	345 24.3	N22 33.5	58 45.5	30 41	N 9 04	30 57	N10 19	283 29	N17 59	112 43	S14 09
10	347 54.3	33.5	61 15.9	33 11		33 27		285 59		115 07	08
20	350 24.3	33.5	63 46.3	35 42		35 57		288 30		117 32	07
30	352 54.2 ·	33.6	66 16.7	38 12 ·		38 27 · ·		291 00 · ·		119 56 ·	05
40	355 24.2	33.6	68 47.1	40 42		40 57		293 30		122 21	04
50	357 54.2	33.7	71 17.6	43 12		43 27		296 01		124 45	03
Rate	14 59.9	N0 00.3		15 00.3	N0 00.6	15 00.7	N0 00.7	15 02.3	S0 00.1	14 26.3	N0 07.3

Moonrise table:

Lat.	Moonrise	Diff.
N	h m	m
72	01 02	−11
70	00 26	+03
68	00 00	08
66	23 57	07
64	23 46	10
62	23 36	11
60	23 28	13
58	23 20	14
56	23 14	15
54	23 08	16
52	23 03	17
50	22 58	18
45	22 47	19
40	22 39	20
35	22 31	21
30	22 24	23
20	22 13	24
10	22 03	26
0	21 54	27
10	21 44	28
20	21 34	30
30	21 22	31
35	21 16	32
40	21 08	33
45	20 59	35
50	20 48	36
52	20 43	37
54	20 38	38
56	20 32	39
58	20 25	40
60	20 17	41
S		

Moon's P. in A.

Alt.	+ Corr	Alt.	+ Corr
0		54	34
10	59	55	33
14	58	56	32
18	57	58	32
21	56	59	31
23	55	60	30
25	54	61	29
28	53	62	28
30	52	63	27
31	51	64	26
33	50	65	25
35	49	66	24
36	48	67	23
38	47	68	22
40	46	69	21
41	45	70	20
42	44	71	19
44	43	72	18
45	42	73	17
47	41	74	16
48	40	75	15
49	39	76	14
50	38	77	13
52	37	78	12
53	36	79	11
54	35	80	10
55	34		

Sun SD 15.8
Moon SD 16'
Age 18d

Fig. 2412a. *Air Almanac*, right-hand daily page (typical).

polation of GHA ♈, each giving values precise to 0.1' of arc. A star index of the fifty-seven navigational stars in alphabetical order with their magnitudes, SHA, and Dec. to nearest minute of arc is given, covering their average position for the six-month period of the *Air Almanac*. For those desiring greater precision, or for stars other than the fifty-seven principal ones, separate tables are included in the white section giving SHA and Dec. of 173 stars to 0.1' of arc for each month of the period covered. They are listed in ascending order of SHA. The value of SHA is combined with

(DAY 156) GREENWICH P. M.   JUNE 5 (SUNDAY)

GMT	SUN GHA	SUN Dec.	ARIES GHA ϒ	VENUS−4.1 GHA	VENUS Dec.	MARS 1.3 GHA	MARS Dec.	SATURN 0.6 GHA	SATURN Dec.	MOON GHA	MOON Dec.
12 00	0 24.2	N22 33.7	73 48.0	45 42	N 9 04	45 57	N10 20	298 31	N17 59	127 10	S14 01
10	2 54.2	33.8	76 18.4	48 12		48 28		301 01		129 34	14 00
20	5 24.2	33.8	78 48.8	50 42		50 58		303 32		131 59	13 59
30	7 54.1 ·	33.9	81 19.2	53 12 ·		53 28 ·		306 02 ·		134 23 ·	57
40	10 24.1	33.9	83 49.6	55 42		55 58		308 33		136 47	56
50	12 54.1	34.0	86 20.0	58 12		58 28		311 03		139 12	55
13 00	15 24.1	N22 34.0	88 50.4	60 42	N 9 05	60 58	N10 21	313 33	N17 59	141 36	S13 54
10	17 54.1	34.0	91 20.8	63 12		63 28		316 04		144 01	52
20	20 24.0	34.1	93 51.3	65 42		65 58		318 34		146 25	51
30	22 54.0	34.1	96 21.7	68 12 ·		68 28 ·		321 04 ·		148 50 ·	50
40	25 24.0	34.2	98 52.1	70 42		70 59		323 35		151 14	48
50	27 54.0	34.2	101 22.5	73 12		73 29		326 05		153 39	47
14 00	30 24.0	N22 34.3	103 52.9	75 42	N 9 06	75 59	N10 21	328 36	N17 59	156 03	S13 46
10	32 54.0	34.3	106 23.3	78 12		78 29		331 06		158 28	44
20	35 23.9	34.4	108 53.7	80 43		80 59		333 36		160 52	43
30	37 53.9 ·	34.4	111 24.1	83 13 ·		83 29 ·		336 07 ·		163 17 ·	42
40	40 23.9	34.4	113 54.5	85 43		85 59		338 37		165 41	40
50	42 53.9	34.5	116 24.9	88 13		88 29		341 07		168 06	39
15 00	45 23.9	N22 34.5	118 55.4	90 43	N 9 06	91 00	N10 22	343 38	N17 59	170 30	S13 38
10	47 53.8	34.6	121 25.8	93 13		93 30		346 08		172 55	36
20	50 23.8	34.6	123 56.2	95 43		96 00		348 39		175 20	35
30	52 53.8 ·	34.7	126 26.6	98 13 ·		98 30 ·		351 09 ·		177 44 ·	34
40	55 23.8	34.7	128 57.0	100 43		101 00		353 39		180 09	32
50	57 53.8	34.8	131 27.4	103 13		103 30		356 10		182 33	31
16 00	60 23.7	N22 34.8	133 57.8	105 43	N 9 07	106 00	N10 23	358 40	N17 59	184 58	S13 30
10	62 53.7	34.9	136 28.2	108 13		108 30		1 10		187 22	28
20	65 23.7	34.9	138 58.6	110 43		111 00		3 41		189 47	27
30	67 53.7 ·	34.9	141 29.1	113 13 ·		113 31 ·		6 11 ·		192 11 ·	26
40	70 23.7	35.0	143 59.5	115 43		116 01		8 42		194 36	24
50	72 53.7	35.0	146 29.9	118 13		118 31		11 12		197 00	23
17 00	75 23.6	N22 35.1	149 00.3	120 43	N 9 08	121 01	N10 23	13 42	N17 59	199 25	S13 22
10	77 53.6	35.1	151 30.7	123 13		123 31		16 13		201 49	20
20	80 23.6	35.2	154 01.1	125 44		126 01		18 43		204 14	19
30	82 53.6 ·	35.2	156 31.5	128 14 ·		128 31 ·		21 13 ·		206 39 ·	17
40	85 23.6	35.3	159 01.9	130 44		131 01		23 44		209 03	16
50	87 53.5	35.3	161 32.3	133 14		133 31		26 14		211 28	15
18 00	90 23.5	N22 35.3	164 02.8	135 44	N 9 08	136 02	N10 24	28 45	N17 59	213 52	S13 13
10	92 53.5	35.4	166 33.2	138 14		138 32		31 15		216 17	12
20	95 23.5	35.4	169 03.6	140 44		141 02		33 45		218 41	11
30	97 53.5 ·	35.5	171 34.0	143 14 ·		143 32 ·		36 16 ·		221 06 ·	09
40	100 23.5	35.5	174 04.4	145 44		146 02		38 46		223 30	08
50	102 53.4	35.6	176 34.8	148 14		148 32		41 16		225 55	06
19 00	105 23.4	N22 35.6	179 05.2	150 44	N 9 09	151 02	N10 25	43 47	N17 58	228 20	S13 05
10	107 53.4	35.7	181 35.6	153 14		153 32		46 17		230 44	04
20	110 23.4	35.7	184 06.0	155 44		156 03		48 48		233 09	02
30	112 53.4 ·	35.7	186 36.4	158 14 ·		158 33 ·		51 18 ·		235 33 ·	01
40	115 23.3	35.8	189 06.9	160 44		161 03		53 48		237 58	13 00
50	117 53.3	35.8	191 37.3	163 14		163 33		56 19		240 23	12 58
20 00	120 23.3	N22 35.9	194 07.7	165 44	N 9 09	166 03	N10 25	58 49	N17 58	242 47	S12 57
10	122 53.3	35.9	196 38.1	168 14		168 33		61 19		245 12	55
20	125 23.3	36.0	199 08.5	170 45		171 03		63 50		247 36	54
30	127 53.3 ·	36.0	201 38.9	173 15 ·		173 33 ·		66 20 ·		250 01 ·	53
40	130 23.2	36.1	204 09.3	175 45		176 03		68 51		252 26	51
50	132 53.2	36.1	206 39.7	178 15		178 34		71 21		254 50	50
21 00	135 23.2	N22 36.1	209 10.1	180 45	N 9 10	181 04	N10 26	73 51	N17 58	257 15	S12 48
10	137 53.2	36.2	211 40.6	183 15		183 34		76 22		259 39	47
20	140 23.2	36.2	214 11.0	185 45		186 04		78 52		262 04	46
30	142 53.1 ·	36.3	216 41.4	188 15 ·		188 34 ·		81 22 ·		264 29 ·	44
40	145 23.1	36.3	219 11.8	190 45		191 04		83 53		266 53	43
50	147 53.1	36.4	221 42.2	193 15		193 34		86 23		269 18	41
22 00	150 23.1	N22 36.4	224 12.6	195 45	N 9 11	196 04	N10 26	88 54	N17 58	271 42	S12 40
10	152 53.1	36.5	226 43.0	198 15		198 35		91 24		274 07	39
20	155 23.0	36.5	229 13.4	200 45		201 05		93 54		276 32	37
30	157 53.0 ·	36.5	231 43.8	203 15 ·		203 35 ·		96 25 ·		278 56 ·	36
40	160 23.0	36.6	234 14.2	205 45		206 05		98 55		281 21	34
50	162 53.0	36.6	236 44.7	208 15		208 35		101 25		283 46	33
23 00	165 23.0	N22 36.7	239 15.1	210 45	N 9 11	211 05	N10 27	103 56	N17 58	286 10	S12 31
10	167 53.0	36.7	241 45.5	213 15		213 35		106 26		288 35	30
20	170 22.9	36.8	244 15.9	215 45		216 05		108 56		290 59	29
30	172 52.9 ·	36.8	246 46.3	218 16 ·		218 35 ·		111 27 ·		293 24 ·	27
40	175 22.9	36.9	249 16.7	220 46		221 06		113 57		295 49	26
50	177 52.9	36.9	251 47.1	223 16		223 36		116 28		298 13	24
Rate	14 59.9	N0 00.3		15 00.3	N0 00.6	15 00.7	N0 00.7	15 02.2	S0 00.1	14 27.4	N0 08.2

Moonset / Diff.

Lat.	Moon-set	Diff.
N	h m	m
72	05 35	70
70	06 10	56
68	06 35	51
66	06 54	47
64	07 09	45
62	07 22	43
60	07 33	41
58	07 42	40
56	07 50	39
54	07 58	38
52	08 04	37
50	08 10	37
45	08 22	35
40	08 33	34
35	08 42	33
30	08 49	32
20	09 03	30
10	09 14	29
0	09 25	28
10	09 36	27
20	09 47	25
30	10 00	24
35	10 07	22
40	10 16	22
45	10 26	21
50	10 38	19
52	10 43	19
54	10 49	18
56	10 56	17
58	11 03	16
60	11 12	15
S		

Moon's P. in A.

Alt	+Corr	Alt	+Corr
0			
7	59	54	34
12	58	55	33
16	57	56	32
19	56	57	31
22	55	58	30
24	54	60	29
27	53	61	28
29	52	62	27
31	51	63	26
32	50	64	25
34	49	65	24
36	48	66	23
38	47	67	22
39	46	68	21
41	45	69	20
42	44	70	19
43	43	71	18
45	42	72	17
46	41	73	16
47	40	74	15
49	39	75	14
50	38	76	13
51	37	77	12
53	36	78	11
54	35	79	10
55	34	80	

Sun SD 15.'8
Moon SD 16'
Age 19d

Fig. 2412b. *Air Almanac*, left-hand daily page (typical).

GHA ϒ from the daily pages, to obtain GHA of the star.

Additional Tables

2413 Various other tables, sky diagrams, and other data are included in the back of the book. As far as possible they are arranged in inverse order of use; for instance, the more commonly used data, such as refraction and dip corrections, are placed directly inside the back cover, where they are more easily located. A table is included in the back pages of the volume to assist in interpolating the time of moonrise and moonset for longitude.

Use of the *Air Almanac*

2414 Sample daily pages from the *Air Almanac* are shown in figures 2412a and 2412b; for comparison purposes, these are for dates included in the period covered by the sample pages from the *Nautical Almanac*. The table for interpolation of GHA is shown as figure 2414a.

Figure 2414b illustrates the extraction of data from the *Air Almanac* for various bodies. Again, for comparison purposes, the same bodies and times

STARS, JAN.—JUNE

No.	Name		Mag.	S.H.A.	Dec.
				° '	° '
7*	Acamar		3·1	315 39	S. 40 24
5*	Achernar		0·6	335 47	S. 57 21
30*	Acrux		1·1	173 39	S. 62 58
19	Adhara	†	1·6	255 34	S. 28 57
10*	Aldebaran	†	1·1	291 21	N. 16 28
32*	Alioth		1·7	166 44	N. 56 05
34*	Alkaid		1·9	153 20	N. 49 26
55	Al Na'ir		2·2	28 18	S. 47 04
15	Alnilam	†	1·8	276 14	S. 1 13
25*	Alphard	†	2·2	218 23	S. 8 34
41*	Alphecca	†	2·3	126 34	N. 26 47
1*	Alpheratz	†	2·2	358 12	N. 28 58
51*	Altair	†	0·9	62 35	N. 8 48
2	Ankaa		2·4	353 43	S. 42 26
42*	Antares	†	1·2	113 00	S. 26 23
37*	Arcturus	†	0·2	146 20	N. 19 18
43	Atria		1·9	108 26	S. 68 59
22	Avior		1·7	234 29	S. 59 26
13	Bellatrix	†	1·7	279 01	N. 6 20
16*	Betelgeuse	†	0·1-1·2	271 31	N. 7 24
17*	Canopus		−0·9	264 08	S. 52 41
12*	Capella		0·2	281 15	N. 45 59
53*	Deneb		1·3	49 50	N. 45 12
28*	Denebola	†	2·2	183 01	N. 14 42
4*	Diphda	†	2·2	349 23	S. 18 07
27*	Dubhe		2·0	194 25	N. 61 52
14	Elnath	†	1·8	278 47	N. 28 35
47	Eltanin		·2·4	90 59	N. 51 29
54*	Enif	†	2·5	34 14	N. 9 46
56*	Fomalhaut	†	1·3	15 54	S. 29 45
31	Gacrux		1·6	172 31	S. 56 59
29*	Gienah	†	2·8	176 20	S. 17 25
35	Hadar		0·9	149 26	S. 60 16
6*	Hamal	†	2·2	328 32	N. 23 21
48	Kaus Aust.		2·0	84 20	S. 34 24
40*	Kochab		2·2	137 18	N. 74 15
57	Markab	†	2·6	14 06	N. 15 05
8*	Menkar	†	2·8	314 44	N. 4 00
36	Menkent		2·3	148 39	S. 36 16
24*	Miaplacidus		1·8	221 45	S. 69 38
9*	Mirfak		1·9	309 20	N. 49 47
50*	Nunki	†	2·1	76 32	S. 26 19
52*	Peacock		2·1	54 02	S. 56 48
21*	Pollux	†	1·2	244 01	N. 28 05
20*	Procyon	†	0·5	245 28	N. 5 17
46*	Rasalhague	†	2·1	96 32	N. 12 35
26*	Regulus	†	1·3	208 12	N. 12 05
11*	Rigel	†	0·3	281 38	S. 8 14
38*	Rigil Kent.		0·1	140 29	S. 60 44
44	Sabik	†	2·6	102 44	S. 15 42
3*	Schedar		2·5	350 12	N. 56 25
45*	Shaula		1·7	96 59	S. 37 05
18*	Sirius	†	−1·6	258 58	S. 16 41
33*	Spica	†	1·2	159 00	S. 11 03
23*	Suhail		2·2	223 12	S. 43 21
49*	Vega		0·1	80 57	N. 38 46
39	Zuben'ubi	†	2·9	137 35	S. 15 57

*Stars used in H.O. 249 (A.P. 3270) Vol. 1.
†Stars that may be used with Vols. 2 and 3.

INTERPOLATION OF G.H.A.

Increment to be added for intervals of G.M.T. to G.H.A. of: Sun, Aries (♈) and planets; Moon

SUN, etc.		MOON	SUN, etc.		MOON	SUN, etc.		MOON
m s	° '	m s	m s	° '	m s	m s	° '	m s
00 00	0 00	00 00	03 17	0 50	03 25	06 37	1 40	06 52
01	0 01	00 02	21	0 51	03 29	41	1 41	06 56
05	0 02	00 06	25	0 52	03 33	45	1 42	07 00
09	0 03	00 10	29	0 53	03 37	49	1 43	07 04
13	0 04	00 14	33	0 54	03 41	53	1 44	07 08
17	0 05	00 18	37	0 55	03 45	06 57	1 45	07 13
21	0 06	00 22	41	0 56	03 49	07 01	1 46	07 17
25	0 07	00 26	45	0 57	03 54	05	1 47	07 21
29	0 08	00 31	49	0 58	03 58	09	1 48	07 25
33	0 09	00 35	53	0 59	04 02	13	1 49	07 29
37	0 10	00 39	03 57	1 00	04 06	17	1 50	07 33
41	0 11	00 43	04 01	1 01	04 10	21	1 51	07 37
45	0 12	00 47	05	1 02	04 14	25	1 52	07 42
49	0 13	00 51	09	1 03	04 19	29	1 53	07 46
53	0 14	00 55	13	1 04	04 23	33	1 54	07 50
00 57	0 15	01 00	17	1 05	04 27	37	1 55	07 54
01 01	0 16	01 04	21	1 06	04 31	41	1 56	07 58
05	0 17	01 08	25	1 07	04 35	45	1 57	08 02
09	0 18	01 12	29	1 08	04 39	49	1 58	08 06
13	0 19	01 16	33	1 09	04 43	53	1 59	08 11
17	0 20	01 20	37	1 10	04 48	07 57	2 00	08 15
21	0 21	01 24	41	1 11	04 52	08 01	2 01	08 19
25	0 22	01 29	45	1 12	04 56	05	2 02	08 23
29	0 23	01 33	49	1 13	05 00	09	2 03	08 27
33	0 24	01 37	53	1 14	05 04	13	2 04	08 31
37	0 25	01 41	04 57	1 15	05 08	17	2 05	08 35
41	0 26	01 45	05 01	1 16	05 12	21	2 06	08 40
45	0 27	01 49	05	1 17	05 17	25	2 07	08 44
49	0 28	01 53	09	1 18	05 21	29	2 08	08 48
53	0 29	01 58	13	1 19	05 25	33	2 09	08 52
01 57	0 30	02 02	17	1 20	05 29	37	2 09	08 56
02 01	0 31	02 06	21	1 21	05 33	41	2 10	09 00
05	0 32	02 10	25	1 22	05 37	45	2 11	09 04
09	0 33	02 14	29	1 23	05 41	49	2 12	09 09
13	0 34	02 18	33	1 24	05 46	53	2 13	09 13
17	0 35	02 22	37	1 25	05 50	08 57	2 14	09 17
21	0 36	02 27	41	1 26	05 54	09 01	2 15	09 21
25	0 37	02 31	45	1 27	05 58	05	2 16	09 25
29	0 38	02 35	49	1 28	06 02	09	2 17	09 29
33	0 39	02 39	53	1 29	06 06	13	2 18	09 33
37	0 40	02 43	05 57	1 30	06 10	17	2 19	09 38
41	0 41	02 47	06 01	1 31	06 15	21	2 20	09 42
45	0 42	02 51	05	1 32	06 19	25	2 21	09 46
49	0 43	02 56	09	1 33	06 23	29	2 22	09 50
53	0 44	03 00	13	1 34	06 27	33	2 23	09 54
02 57	0 45	03 04	17	1 35	06 31	37	2 24	09 58
03 01	0 46	03 08	21	1 36	06 35	41	2 25	10 00
05	0 47	03 12	25	1 37	06 39	45	2 26	
09	0 48	03 16	29	1 38	06 44	49	2 27	
13	0 49	03 20	33	1 39	06 48	53	2 28	
17	0 50	03 25	37	1 40	06 52	09 57	2 29	
03 21		03 29	06 41		06 56	10 00	2 30	

Fig. 2414a. *Air Almanac*, tables on inside front cover.

Body	SUN	MOON	DENEBOLA	MARS
Date (G)	5 JUN	5 JUN	5 JUN	5 JUN
GMT	13-36-35	09-37-08	23-36-56	23-37-22
GHA (h + 10ᵐ)	22° 54'	91° 03'	246° 46'	218° 35'
Incre (m/s)	1° 39'	1° 43'	1° 44'	1° 51'
SHA	—	—	183° 01'	—
Total GHA	24° 33'	92° 46'	431° 31'	220° 26'
± 360°			71° 31'	
Tab Dec	N 22° 34'	S14° 21'	N14° 42'	N 10° 27'

Fig. 2414b. Tabular solutions for GHA and declination, *Air Almanac.*

are used as were illustrated in figure 2408 for the *Nautical Almanac.*

For example, assume you are under way on 5 June and observe the Sun at ZT 09-36-35 (+4). To obtain the data needed, you should proceed as follows:

1. Determine UT by adding ZD to ZT; UT is 13-36-35.
2. Locate the page that includes the second half of 5 June; locate the line for the hour and next lesser 10-minute interval (13 30).
3. Follow across this line to the column headed "Sun"; read and record the GHA (22° 54.0') and the Dec. (N22° 34.1').
4. Turn to the table for "Interpolation of GHA" on the inside front cover of the *Almanac* (fig. 2414a) and pick out incremental correction in "Sun, etc." column for 6 minutes and 35 seconds (1° 39' appears as the figure between 33 seconds and 37 seconds). This is a quickly used table of critical values to the nearest 1'; if a value to 0.1' is needed, there are also interpolation tables for GHA Sun and GHA Aries in the white pages at the back of the *Air Almanac.*
5. Add the increment of GHA to the value from the daily page: 22° 54.0' + 1° 39' = 24° 33'; this is the GHA of the Sun for the time of observation.

It should be noted here that the *Air Almanac,* with entries for each 10 minutes of time, permits the GHA of the Sun to be found more accurately than with the *Nautical Almanac* (unless special procedures are used with the latter). The reason for this is that the *Nautical Almanac,* with tabulated data only for each whole hour, lists GHA adjusted by as much as 0.15' to minimize the error caused by ignoring any *v* correction.

In the *Air Almanac,* tabulated declination is always used without interpolation; the tabular value for the GMT (UT) immediately *before* the time of observation is the declination used (unless the sight is taken exactly at a tabulated time). In this example, then, the declination is N22° 34.1'.

The other examples used in figure 2414b can be compared by extracting in a similar manner the data from the example pages provided.

TIMES OF CELESTIAL PHENOMENA

2415 Almanac data are not used only for determining the GP of observed celestial bodies. They are also used to determine the times of celestial phenomena such as the rising and setting of celestial bodies and the time of twilight.

Sunrise is defined as the first appearance of the Sun's *upper limb* above the visible horizon; similarly, sunset is the disappearance of the upper limb below the visible horizon. The times of moonrise and moonset are similarly determined, by contact of the upper limb with the horizon.

Twilight is the period before sunrise when darkness is giving way to daylight, and after sunset when the opposite is true. The importance of twilight is that you can see the stars and planets and simultaneously have a visible horizon to use for measuring their altitudes. By convention, three kinds of twilight are defined: *civil, nautical,* and *astronomical.* They are defined by their darker limits occurring when the Sun's center is 6°, 12°, and 18°, respectively, below the celestial horizon. Astronomical twilight is beyond the usual concern of the nautical navigator, but the other two are of regular concern and are listed in the almanacs. The duration of twilight is chiefly a function of the observer's latitude, increasing with an increase in latitude.

In the *Nautical Almanac,* the UT of sunrise and sunset, and of the beginnings of morning and endings of evening civil and nautical twilight, are tabulated for every three-day period at various latitudes along the meridian of Greenwich (0°l), the second of the three days being the reference day. The UT of moonrise and moonset for 0° longitude are similarly tabulated in a separate column for each day.

The Local Mean Time (LMT) of sunrise, sunset, and twilight for a given date and latitude are practically the same in any longitude. This relative stability derives mainly from the slow rate of change of the Sun's declination and from the nearly constant rate of increase of its GHA. As a result, the solar phenomena at any given latitude tend to progress around the Earth at a nearly constant rate of about 15 degrees or 900 minutes of arc per hour. Notice that near the equinoxes, when the declination of the Sun is changing quickly—as much as 1 minute of arc per hour—the change in tabulated times of sunrise, sunset, and so on is much greater from one three-day period to the next than at other times of the year, especially on dates near the solstices. The Moon has much greater variability in its apparent motion, and so its rising and setting need to be tabulated daily, and interpolation made for longitude if different from that of Greenwich.

In the back of each volume of the *Air Almanac,* tables will be found giving the times of sunrise and sunset and the darker limits of civil twilight; times of moonrise and moonset are given on the daily pages. Additionally, the *Tide Tables* (published by the National Ocean Service) include tables for the LMT of sunrise and sunset, with a convenient table for the conversion of LMT to ZT; moonrise and moonset in the *Tide Tables* are tabulated daily for specific cities rather than by latitude.

Time of Sunrise and Sunset

2416   The UT of sunrise and sunset for the middle day of the three days covered by each page opening in the *Nautical Almanac* is tabulated to the nearest minute of time for selected intervals of latitude from 72° N to 60° S. An extract from this table is shown in figure 2416a. The tabulated times are generally used to obtain the ZT of the phenomena by either of two possible methods. The UT of sunrise or sunset may be considered to be its LMT, and therefore its ZT on the standard meridian of any zone. To obtain the ZT of the phenomenon at your vessel's location, it is only necessary to convert the difference of longitude between the standard meridian and the vessel into time, adding this difference if the vessel is west of the standard meridian and subtracting if it is east. Each degree of longitude will be equivalent to 4 minutes of time, and each 15' of longitude 1 minute of time. The same result can be obtained by taking from the table the UT at the required latitude, and applying to this the longitude converted to time, to give the UT of the phenomenon at the local meridian, and finally applying the zone description with the sign reversed. Interpolation for latitude is made by means of a table near the back of the *Nautical Almanac;* a portion of this is reproduced in figure 2416b. When more precise times of sunrise and sunset are desired, they may be obtained by interpolating for the correct day, in addition to the regular interpolation for latitude.

At times, in high latitudes, the Sun remains continuously either below or above the horizon. In the former case, a blacked-in rectangle appears in place of a time; in the latter, the rectangle is not blacked-in. These symbols are seen in figure 2416a where

Lat.	Sunset	Twilight		Moonset			
		Civil	Naut.	3	4	5	6
°	h m	h m	h m	h m	h m	h m	h m
N 72	▢	▢	▢	▮	03 02	05 35	07 40
N 70	▢	▢	▢	02 35	04 17	06 10	08 00
68	▢	▢	▢	03 26	04 54	06 35	08 16
66	23 01	////	////	03 58	05 21	06 54	08 29
64	22 07	////	////	04 22	05 41	07 09	08 39
62	21 36	////	////	04 41	05 58	07 22	08 48
60	21 12	22 41	////	04 56	06 11	07 33	08 56
N 58	20 54	22 03	////	05 09	06 23	07 42	09 03
56	20 38	21 37	////	05 21	06 33	07 50	09 08
54	20 25	21 17	22 48	05 31	06 42	07 58	09 14
52	20 13	21 00	22 13	05 40	06 50	08 04	09 18
50	20 03	20 46	21 48	05 47	06 57	08 10	09 23
45	19 42	20 18	21 07	06 04	07 12	08 22	09 32
N 40	19 25	19 57	20 38	06 18	07 25	08 33	09 40
35	19 10	19 40	20 16	06 30	07 36	08 42	09 46
30	18 58	19 25	19 58	06 40	07 45	08 49	09 52
20	18 37	19 01	19 30	06 57	08 01	09 03	10 02
N 10	18 19	18 42	19 08	07 13	08 15	09 14	10 11
0	18 02	18 24	18 50	07 27	08 28	09 25	10 19
S 10	17 45	18 08	18 34	07 41	08 40	09 36	10 27
20	17 27	17 51	18 19	07 56	08 54	09 47	10 35
30	17 07	17 33	18 03	08 13	09 10	10 00	10 45
35	16 55	17 23	17 55	08 23	09 19	10 07	10 50
40	16 42	17 12	17 46	08 35	09 29	10 16	10 57
45	16 26	16 59	17 36	08 48	09 41	10 26	11 04
S 50	16 07	16 44	17 25	09 04	09 56	10 38	11 12
52	15 57	16 37	17 20	09 12	10 02	10 43	11 16
54	15 47	16 30	17 15	09 21	10 09	10 49	11 21
56	15 35	16 21	17 10	09 30	10 18	10 56	11 26
58	15 21	16 12	17 03	09 41	10 28	11 03	11 31
S 60	15 05	16 01	16 56	09 53	10 38	11 12	11 37

Day	SUN			MOON			
	Eqn. of Time		Mer. Pass.	Mer. Pass.		Age	Phase
	00ʰ	12ʰ		Upper	Lower		
	m s	m s	h m	h m	h m	d	
3	02 02	01 57	11 58	01 12	13 43	16	
4	01 52	01 47	11 58	02 13	14 43	17	◗
5	01 42	01 37	11 58	03 12	15 39	18	

Fig. 2416a. Portion of a daily page from the *Nautical Almanac* showing evening phenomena.

TABLES FOR INTERPOLATING SUNRISE, MOONRISE, ETC.
TABLE I—FOR LATITUDE

Tabular Interval			Difference between the times for consecutive latitudes																
10°	5°	2°	5m	10m	15m	20m	25m	30m	35m	40m	45m	50m	55m	60m	1h05m	1h10m	1h15m	1h20m
0 30	0 15	0 06	0	0	1	1	1	1	1	2	2	2	2	2	0 02	0 02	0 02	0 02
1 00	0 30	0 12	0	1	1	2	2	3	3	3	4	4	4	5	05	05	05	05
1 30	0 45	0 18	1	1	2	3	3	4	4	5	5	6	7	7	07	07	07	07
2 00	1 00	0 24	1	2	3	4	5	5	6	7	7	8	9	10	10	10	10	10
2 30	1 15	0 30	1	2	4	5	6	7	8	9	9	10	11	12	12	13	13	13
3 00	1 30	0 36	1	3	4	6	7	8	9	10	11	12	13	14	0 15	0 15	0 16	0 16
3 30	1 45	0 42	2	3	5	7	8	10	11	12	13	14	16	17	18	18	19	19
4 00	2 00	0 48	2	4	6	8	9	11	13	14	15	16	18	19	20	21	22	22
9 00	4 30	1 48	4	9	13	18	22	27	31	35	39	43	47	52	0 55	0 58	1 01	1 04
9 30	4 45	1 54	5	9	14	19	24	28	33	38	42	47	51	56	1 00	1 04	1 08	1 12
10 00	5 00	2 00	5	10	15	20	25	30	35	40	45	50	55	60	1 05	1 10	1 15	1 20

Table I is for interpolating the L.M.T. of sunrise, twilight, moonrise, etc., for latitude. It is to be entered, in the appropriate column on the left, with the difference between true latitude and the nearest tabular latitude which is *less* than the true latitude; and with the argument at the top which is the nearest value of the difference between the times for the tabular latitude and the next higher one; the correction so obtained is applied to the time for the tabular latitude; the sign of the correction can be seen by inspection. It is to be noted that the interpolation is not linear, so that when using this table it is essential to take out the tabular phenomenon for the latitude *less* than the true latitude.

TABLE II—FOR LONGITUDE

Long. East or West	Difference between the times for given date and preceding date (for east longitude) or for given date and following date (for west longitude)						1h +			1h +								
	10m	20m	30m	40m	50m	60m	10m	20m	30m	40m	50m	60m	2h10m	2h20m	2h30m	2h40m	2h50m	3h00m
0	0	0	0	0	0	0	0	0	0	0	0	0	0 00	0 00	0 00	0 00	0 00	0 00
10	0	1	1	1	1	2	2	2	2	3	3	3	04	04	04	04	05	05
20	1	1	2	2	3	3	4	4	5	6	6	7	07	08	08	09	09	10
30	1	2	2	3	4	5	6	7	7	8	9	10	11	12	12	13	14	15
40	1	2	3	4	6	7	8	9	10	11	12	13	14	16	17	18	19	20
50	1	3	4	6	7	8	.0	11	12	14	15	17	0 18	0 19	0 21	0 22	0 24	0 25
60	2	3	5	7	8	10	12	13	15	17	18	20	22	23	25	27	28	30
70	2	4	6	8	10	12	14	16	17	19	21	23	25	27	29	31	33	35
80	2	4	7	9	11	13	16	18	20	22	24	27	29	31	33	36	38	40
90	2	5	7	10	12	15	17	20	22	25	27	30	32	35	37	40	42	45
100	3	6	8	11	14	17	19	22	25	28	31	33	0 36	0 39	0 42	0 44	0 47	0 50
110	3	6	9	12	15	18	21	24	27	31	34	37	40	43	46	49	0 52	0 55
120	3	7	10	13	17	20	23	27	30	33	37	40	43	47	50	53	0 57	1 00
130	4	7	11	14	18	22	25	29	32	36	40	43	47	51	54	0 58	1 01	1 05
140	4	8	12	16	19	23	27	31	35	39	43	47	51	54	0 58	1 02	1 06	1 10
150	4	8	13	17	21	25	29	33	38	42	46	50	0 54	0 58	1 03	1 07	1 11	1 15
160	4	9	13	18	22	27	31	36	40	44	49	53	0 58	1 02	1 07	1 11	1 16	1 20
170	5	9	14	19	24	28	33	38	42	47	52	57	1 01	1 06	1 11	1 16	1 20	1 25
180	5	10	15	20	25	30	35	40	45	50	55	60	1 05	1 10	1 15	1 20	1 25	1 30

Fig. 2416b. *Nautical Almanac*, tables for interpolating the times of rising and setting of the Sun and Moon, and of twilight.

Table II is for interpolating the L.M.T. of moonrise, moonset and the Moon's meridian passage for longitude. It is entered with longitude and with the difference between the times for the given date and for the preceding date (in east longitudes) or following date (in west longitudes). The correction is normally *added* for west longitudes and *subtracted* for east longitudes, but if, as occasionally happens, the times become earlier each day instead of later, the signs of the corrections must be reversed.

the Sun does not set in high latitudes, and where the Moon, at extreme latitudes, did not come above the horizon on 3 June.

To determine the time at a latitude between those tabulated, enter Table I and follow the instructions listed below the table. Note that the correction table is not linear and that information from the daily pages is always taken for the tabulated latitude *smaller* than the actual latitude. The entering arguments are:

Latitude difference between the next smaller tabulated latitude and the actual one.

Time difference between the times of the occurrence at the tabulated latitudes that straddle the latitude for which the information is desired.

The latitude interval between tabular entries for sunrise and sunset varies with the latitude concerned, being 10° near the equator, 5° in midlatitudes, and 2° in higher latitudes. Table I has a separate column at the left for each of these intervals. The *latitude difference* between the actual latitude and the *smaller* tabulated latitude is determined and used to select the appropriate line of Table I. For example, if the interval between tabulated latitudes is 2°, and the latitude for which the information is desired is 0° 24' greater than the smaller tabulated latitude, the "Tabular Interval" column headed 2° is entered and 0° 24' is found on the fourth line down. If the tabular interval were 5°, a latitude difference of 0° 24' would be located approximately on the second line down; if it were 10°, this same latitude difference would be located approximately on the first line down. The *time difference* is used to determine the column of Table I that is to be used; the time correction is taken directly from the table, with interpolation if necessary to obtain the time of the phenomenon to the nearest minute. The correction thus obtained is applied to the UT of the phenomenon for the *smaller* tabulated latitude, as originally extracted from the daily pages; the sign of the correction is determined by inspection.

To this sum (or difference), the longitude converted from arc to time is applied as previously described, to obtain the ZT of the phenomenon for the latitude and longitude.

Assume you are at latitude 41° 34.1′ N, longitude 16° 46.1′ W and want to determine the ZT of sunset on 5 June. Using the *Nautical Almanac* (figs. 2416a and 2416b), proceed as explained in the notes beneath Table I (fig. 2416b) as follows:

1. Enter the appropriate daily page of the *Nautical Almanac* (fig. 2416a) and extract and record the LMT of sunset for the next *lesser* tabulated latitude. In this case, the next lesser latitude is 40° N and the LMT of sunset at that latitude is 1925.

2. Note the difference of latitude between the tabulated values above and below the latitude for which information is desired, and the difference in the times of the phenomenon between these latitudes including its sign. In this instance, the tabular interval is 5° and the time difference is +17ᵐ (1925 at Lat. 40° N and 1042 at Lat. 45° N).

3. Enter Table I of "Tables for Interpolating Sunrise, Moonrise, etc." (fig. 2416b) and obtain the correction to the tabulated LMT. In this example, the latitude difference, 41° 34.1′ minus 40° 00.0′ or 1° 34.1′, is applied to the column for Tabular Interval of 5° (because that was the interval used in the daily page).

4. Moving down that column until you reach the appropriate entry for the difference between the tabulated and actual latitude (in this case, 1° 30′ would be the appropriate entry for the entering argument of the latitude difference of 1° 34.1′), you then move across that line in the table to the intersection of the nearest values above and below the time difference (in this case, 15 m and 20 m).

5. You can then interpolate the time difference (the straddling entries in the table are 4 and 6). Interpolating to the nearest minute, you determine the correction to be +5ᵐ·

6. Apply this correction to the LMT for the lesser tabulated latitude (40° N) to obtain the LMT of sunset at the given latitude (41° 34.1′ N). For this example, the LMT of sunset at Lat. 41° 34.1′ N is 1925 + 5 = 1930

7. Finally, convert this time to ZT. Your actual position (16° 46.1′ W) differs from the central meridian (15° W) of your time zone by 1° 46.1′. Using the "Conversion of Arc to Time" table to convert this difference in longitude to time and rounding to the nearest minute, you find a difference of +7

minutes. Adding that to the time of sunset determined above (1930), you get a Zone Time of 1937.

The above example used tabulated data directly from the *Nautical Almanac* without correction for the fact that 5 June is not the center date of the *Almanac* pages for "June 3, 4, 5," and also without correction for the difference in longitude between the vessel and Greenwich. While this procedure will yield a time of sunrise or sunset sufficiently accurate for most purposes, a more precise determination of the times of these phenomena is sometimes needed. Corrections can be calculated in accordance with procedures explained in the *Nautical Almanac*. In the above example, because of the time of year and latitude, such a correction is negligible; in months near the equinoxes and at high latitudes, corrections can be as much as six to eight minutes.

The procedure for obtaining the time of sunrise from the *Nautical Almanac* is the same as that explained above for sunset.

Procedures for using the *Air Almanac* to find the time of sunset are illustrated in the following example for the same date and position (5 June at lat. 41° 34′ N, long. 16° 46′ W). Refer to figure 2416c for this example.

The tabular data for sunrise, sunset, and civil twilight are given in the "white pages" of the *Air Almanac* at three-day intervals for the longitude of Greenwich and latitude intervals of 10°, 5°, or 2°, similar to the *Nautical Almanac*. These figures may be used for other longitudes without correction. The nearest date is used but the actual latitude is interpolated. Looking at the *Air Almanac* data, you can see that the times for the straddling latitudes (40°N and 45°N are 1924 and 1941). The LMT of sunset at latitude 41° 34′ N is found by interpolation to be 1930. Adjusting for longitude, the ZT is 1937 (1930 + 7ᵐ for 1° 46′ longitude west of zone central meridian).

Note that in this example the ZT of sunset is the same whether the *Air Almanac* or the *Nautical Almanac* is used. In some instances, slight differences will occur between the results obtained from the use of the two procedures, but these are of negligible practical significance.

Time of Twilight

2417 As already discussed, morning and evening twilight are very important times of the day in celestial navigation because they are the only periods during which a fix may be obtained by nearly simultaneous lines of position from observations of a number of celestial bodies. At the darker limit of

SUNSET

Lat.	May 17	20	23	26	29	June 1	4	7	10	13	16	19	22	25	28	July 1
	h m	h m	h m	h m	h m	h m	h m	h m	h m	h m	h m	h m	h m	h m	h m	h m
N 72	□	□	□	□	□	□	□	□	□	□	□	□	□	□	□	□
70	□	□	□	□	□	□	□	□	□	□	□	□	□	□	□	□
68	22 18	22 37	23 01	23 43	□	□	□	□	□	□	□	□	□	□	□	□
66	21 39	21 51	22 04	22 17	22 30	22 44	22 58	23 14	23 32	□	□	□	□	□	□	23 46
64	21 12	21 22	21 31	21 40	21 49	21 58	22 06	22 13	22 20	22 25	22 29	22 31	22 32	22 32	22 30	22 26
62	20 51	20 59	21 07	21 15	22	28	21 34	21 40	21 45	21 48	21 51	21 53	21 54	21 54	21 53	21 51
N 60	20 35	20 42	20 48	20 55	21 01	21 06	21 11	21 16	21 20	21 23	21 25	21 27	21 28	21 28	21 27	21 25
58	21	27	33	38	20 43	20 48	20 53	20 57	21 00	21 03	21 05	21 06	21 07	21 07	21 06	21 06
56	20 09	14	20	24	29	33	37	41	20 44	20 46	20 48	20 50	20 50	20 51	20 50	20 49
54	19 58	20 03	20 08	13	17	21	24	27	30	32	34	35	36	36	36	35
52	49	19 54	19 58	20 02	20 06	09	13	15	18	20	22	23	24	24	24	23
N 50	19 41	19 45	19 49	19 53	19 56	20 00	20 02	20 05	20 07	20 09	20 11	20 12	20 13	20 13	20 13	20 13
45	24	27	30	33	36	19 39	19 41	19 43	19 45	19 47	19 49	19 50	19 50	19 51	19 51	19 50
40	19 09	12	15	18	20	22	24	26	28	29	30	31	32	33	33	33
35	18 58	19 00	19 02	19 04	19 06	19 08	19 10	19 12	13	14	16	16	17	18	18	18
30	47	18 49	18 51	18 53	18 54	18 56	18 58	18 59	19 00	19 01	19 03	19 03	19 04	19 05	19 05	19 05
N 20	18 29	18 31	18 32	18 33	18 34	18 35	18 37	18 38	18 39	18 40	18 41	18 41	18 42	18 43	18 43	18 43
N 10	14	15	16	16	17	18	19	19	20	21	22	22	23	24	24	25
0	18 00	18 00	18 00	18 01	18 01	18 01	18 02	18 02	18 03	18 03	18 04	18 05	18 05	18 06	18 07	18 07
S 10	17 46	17 45	17 45	17 45	17 45	17 45	17 45	17 46	17 46	17 46	17 47	17 47	17 48	17 49	17 49	17 50
20	31	30	29	28	28	28	28	28	28	28	29	30	30	31	32	32
S 30	17 14	17 12	17 11	17 10	17 09	17 08	17 07	17 07	17 07	17 07	17 07	17 08	17 08	17 09	17 10	17 11
35	17 04	17 02	17 00	16 59	16 57	16 56	16 56	16 55	16 55	16 55	16 55	16 55	16 56	16 57	16 58	16 59
40	16 53	16 51	16 48	46	45	43	42	41	41	41	41	41	42	42	43	45
45	40	37	34	32	30	28	27	25	25	24	24	24	25	26	27	28
50	24	20	17	14	11	09	16 07	16 05	16 04	16 04	16 03	16 03	16 04	16 05	16 06	16 08
S 52	16 16	16 12	16 09	16 05	16 02	16 00	15 58	15 56	15 55	15 54	15 53	15 53	15 54	15 55	15 56	15 58
54	16 08	16 04	16 00	15 56	15 53	15 50	47	45	44	43	42	42	43	44	45	47
56	15 59	15 54	15 49	45	42	38	36	33	32	30	30	30	30	31	33	35
58	48	43	38	33	29	25	22	19	17	15 16	15 15	15 15	15 15	15 17	18	20
S 60	15 36	15 30	15 24	15 19	15 14	15 10	15 06	15 03	15 00	14 59	14 58	14 57	14 58	14 59	15 01	15 03

Fig. 2416c. *Air Almanac,* Sunset Tables.

nautical twilight, when the Sun's center is 12° below the celestial horizon, the horizon is usually only dimly visible, except to an observer with dark-adapted vision, or who is using a telescope of superior light-gathering power. At the darker limit of civil twilight, when the Sun's center is 6° below the celestial horizon, the bright stars are readily discernible to the practiced eye, and the horizon is clearly defined (weather conditions permitting). This is approximately the mid-time of the period during which star observations should ordinarily be made.

The time of the darker limit of civil or nautical twilight is obtained from the *Nautical Almanac* in the same manner that sunrise and sunset data are obtained. The UT of the phenomenon at the closest tabulated latitude is taken from the daily pages, interpolation for latitude is made in Table I, and the ZT of the phenomenon at the desired latitude is then obtained by applying the longitude in time.

When twilight lasts all night, as happens at times in high latitudes, the symbol //// is shown in lieu of a time; see the higher latitudes of figure 2416a.

For example, to find the ZT of the ending of civil twilight on 5 June at latitude 41° 36.0' N, longitude 16° 54.0' W using the *Nautical Almanac,* you would:

1. Enter the appropriate daily page of the *Nautical Almanac* (fig. 2416a) and extract and record the LMT for the end of civil twilight for the next lesser tabulated latitude. In this case, the next lesser latitude is 40° and the LMT at that latitude is 1957.

2. Note the difference between the tabulated values of latitude north or south of the latitude for which the information is desired, and the difference in time of the phenomenon between these tabulated latitudes, and determine its sign. In this case the tabular interval is 5° and the time difference is $+21^m$ (1957 at 40° N and 2018 at 45° N.)

3. Enter Table I (fig. 2416b) and obtain the correction to LMT. This is found by moving down the column on the left marked 5° Tabular Interval until you reach the 1° 30' line, since the difference in actual latitude (41° 36.0' N) and next lesser tabulated latitude (40° N) is 1° 36'. Next, move across to the intersection of the column headed by the nearest figure to the time differ-

ence (21^m); in this case, the appropriate column is headed by 20^m and the intersection yields a correction of 6 minutes. You know this correction to be positive (+) because the tabulated entries for civil twilight were increasing between 40° and 45° N.

4. Apply this correction to the LMT of the lesser latitude (40°) to obtain the LMT at the desired latitude, and convert this time to ZT. In this example, the LMT of the end of civil twilight at latitude 41° 36.0′ N is 1957 + 6 = 2003.

5. Finally, convert this time to ZT. Your actual position (16° 54.0′ W) differs from the central meridian (15° W) of your time zone by 1° 54.0′. Using the "Conversion of Arc to Time" table to convert this difference in longitude to time and rounding to the nearest minute, you find a difference of +8 minutes. Adding that to the time of sunset determined above (2003), you get a Zone Time of 2011.

The procedures for finding the ending of nautical twilight, or the beginning of civil or nautical twilight, are similar to the example shown above.

The beginning or ending of civil twilight can also be found using the *Air Almanac* by following the instructions contained in that publication; the procedures are generally the same as those for sunrise or sunset explained above.

Time of Moonrise and Moonset

2418 The times of moonrise and moonset are found by first interpolating for the latitude at which they are required, as was done with the Sun. However, because the times of moonrise and moonset differ considerably from day to day, there must be a second interpolation for longitude, and at any longitude other than 0° these phenomena will fall somewhere between the times tabulated for consecutive days on the 0° meridian. The relatively high accelerations of the Moon's declination and GHA are what necessitate interpolation for longitude when finding times of moonrise and moonset. These phenomena do not normally progress around the Earth at a nearly constant rate for as long as three days, or even for one day, and certainly not at the 15-degree-per-hour rate as often assumed for the Sun. Fortunately, despite the nonconstant rates involved, linear interpolation for longitude over any single twenty-four-hour period in predicting moonrise and moonset will nearly always suffice. In the rare instances when it is thought not to suffice, calculation first of what the Ho of the Moon should be at the observer's position when its upper-limb ha is zero, followed by calculation of the corresponding

meridian angle (t), and finally calculating the time at which the Moon should have that meridian angle, will give the time of the Moon's rising or setting. Seldom is such precision of prediction worth the effort, but understanding the process of achieving it will improve your understanding of how the Moon and other celestial bodies appear to behave.

Always remember that the tabulated times of moonrise and moonset are their times at the longitude of Greenwich (0° l); an observer in east longitude will experience each phenomenon before it occurs at 0° longitude. The UT (GMT) of moonrise and moonset in *east* longitude is found by interpolating between the tabulated time for the given day and the tabulated time for the *preceding* day. For *west* longitude, the UT at a given meridian is found by interpolating between the tabulated time for the given day and the tabulated time for the *following* day. (It is for this reason that the *Nautical Almanac* shows moonrise and moonset times for *four* days—the three days of the daily page plus the next day.)

Before interpolating for longitude, however, the times of the required phenomenon on the two days involved must first be interpolated for the required latitude using Table I, "Tables for Interpolating Sunrise, Moonrise, Etc." (fig. 2416b). The interpolation for longitude is then made using Table II. UT is converted to ZT in the usual manner.

For example, if you wanted to find the ZT of moonset on 5 June at latitude 41° 12.4′ N, longitude 15° 17.1′ W using the *Nautical Almanac*, you would:

1. Enter the appropriate daily page of the *Nautical Almanac* and extract and record, for the next smaller tabulated latitude, the LMT of the phenomenon at the Greenwich meridian on the given date. In this case, the LMT at Greenwich, tabulated for latitude 40° N is 0833 on 5 June.

2. Extract the equivalent time on the *preceding day if in east longitude*, or on the *following day if in west longitude*. In this example, the LMT at Greenwich, again using 40° N, is 0940 on 6 June, the later day being taken since the position for which information is desired is in west longitude.

3. Determine the interval between tabulated values of latitude on either side of the one for which information is desired, and the time difference and its sign between the tabulated LMT at each of these latitudes for each of the two days involved. In this case, the tabular interval for both days is 5°, and the difference in time is –11^m on 5 June and –8^m on 6 June.

4. Enter Table I and obtain the correction for latitude to the tabulated LMT at the longitude of

Greenwich. The correction is –2^m on 5 June, and –2^m on 6 June.

5. Apply these corrections to the lesser tabulated latitude (40°), thus completing interpolation to the nearest minute of time for the exact latitude on each day. In this case, the LMT at the longitude of Greenwich at latitude 41° 12.4′ N is 0831 on 5 June and 0938 on 6 June.

6. To interpolate for longitude, enter Table II with the longitude (east or west) in the left-hand column, and the difference between the LMT at each date in the line at the top of the table. In this case, the longitude is approximately 15° and the time difference is 1^{h}07^m (0938 – 0831). Obtain the correction from the table, using eye interpolation as necessary. In this case, the correction to the nearest minute is 3^m.

7. Apply the correction to the LMT of the phenomenon on the date for which the information is desired, in such a way that the time determined falls between the LMT at Greenwich on the two dates in question. In most cases, this will mean that the correction is added if the longitude is west, and subtracted if it is east. In this case, the correction is added, making the LMT of moonset at the observer's meridian 0834 (since 0831 + 3 = 0834) on 5 June.

8. Finally, convert this LMT to ZT; 0834 + 1^m (correction for 0° 17.1′ of longitude west of zone central meridian) = 0835.

The procedure for obtaining the time of moonrise from the *Nautical Almanac* is the same as explained above for moonset.

Calculations for the local times of moonrise and moonset can also be done using the *Air Almanac*. On each daily page (figs. 2412a and 2412b) there are data for the 0° longitude occurrence at various latitudes, plus a column headed "Diff.," which gives the half-way difference in order to correct for a longitude other than Greenwich. The correction to be applied to the tabulated GMT (UT) of moonrise or moonset is given in Table F4 located on the flap headed "Interpolation of Moonrise, Moonset for Longitude" (fig. 2418). This table is entered with Diff. and longitude, and the correction, selected without interpolation, is applied with the sign indicated.

For example, if you wanted to determine the ZT of moonset at latitude 41° 12′ N, longitude 15° 17′ W using the *Air Almanac* you would:

1. Using the exact date and interpolating for latitude, find the time to be 0830 and the difference 34 minutes.
2. Using the nearest Table F4 arguments, Long. 20°, find the difference of 30^m. Because the difference

F4 INTERPOLATION OF MOONRISE, MOONSET

FOR LONGITUDE

Add if longitude *west*
Subtract if longitude *east*

Longi-tude	Diff.*					
	05	10	15	20	25	30
*	m	m	m	m	m	m
0	00	00	00	00	00	00
20	01	01	02	02	03	03
40	01	02	03	04	06	07
60	02	03	05	07	08	10
80	02	04	07	09	11	13
100	03	06	08	11	14	17
120	03	07	10	13	17	20
140	04	08	12	16	19	23
160	04	09	13	18	22	27
180	05	10	15	20	25	30

Fig. 2418. *Air Almanac*, Table F4 for interpolating time of moonrise and moonset (extract).

is positive and the longitude is west, the correction is additive; the LMT is 0830 + 3 = 0833.

3. The ZT is 0833 + 1 (for longitude 17′ west of central meridian) = 0834.

Note that this differs from the time found from the *Nautical Almanac* by one minute, a difference of no practical significance.

The Moon appears to make a revolution about the Earth in a period averaging 24^{h}50^m; that is to say that moonrise and moonset occur, *on the average*, about fifty minutes later on successive days. However, any given period may vary considerably from the average. Under certain conditions moonrise may even occur twice during a single day, or may not occur at all. If moonrise occurs twice on the same day, both times are tabulated in the *Nautical Almanac* and *Air Almanac*; for example, "0002/2355." If moonrise does not occur before midnight of a day, it may be tabulated for that day, but, for example, as 2413, rather than as 0013. This over-extended clock time means that moonrise at the tabulated latitude will not occur at all on the stated day, but at 0013 on the next day. This phenomenon can occur earlier on successive days. Considerable care must be exercised in interpolation.

Determining Times of Phenomena for a Moving Vessel

2419 In the preceding articles, the methods of obtaining the times of various phenomena have been considered for a specific fixed position. More typical, however, is the need to determine the time of such an event for a moving vessel.

To obtain the required time, first examine the vessel's DR track with respect to the tabulated latitudes and UT in the *Nautical Almanac*. Select the tabulated latitude nearest the DR position for the approximate time of the phenomenon and note the tabulated UT. This UT is treated as ZT—for example, a tabulated UT 1144 is considered as ZT 1144 and the DR position for this time is determined by plot. Since LMT for any location and ZT seldom differ by more than 30 minutes, this assumption is sufficiently accurate for the initial DR. Using the latitude and longitude of this position, determine the ZT of the phenomenon as previously described; this is termed the *first estimate*.

Next, a revised DR position is determined for the time just found. Then the time of the phenomenon is recalculated for the latitude and longitude of the revised DR position; this is the *second estimate*.

Ordinarily, this second estimate will give an acceptably accurate time for the phenomenon. If, however, the two DR positions should prove to differ considerably in longitude, a new determination of the first estimate should be made.

Usually at sea, the maximum obtainable precision is required only for the time of sunrise and sunset; ordinarily, 2 or 3 minutes leeway are permissible in predicting the times of other phenomena. The "Tables for Interpolating Sunrise, Moonrise, Etc.," in the back of the *Nautical Almanac* are used, and longitude to the nearest 15′ may be used in converting to time, that is, to the nearest minute.

Sunset Calculation for a Moving Vessel

2420   On 5 June, the 1600 DR position of a ship is Lat. 33° 23.3′ N, Long. 65° 19.4′ W. The vessel is on course 255°, speed 20 knots. To find the ZT of sunset to the nearest whole number, using the *Nautical Almanac*, you would proceed as follows:

1. By examination of the DR plot (fig. 2420) and the almanac (fig. 2403b), you note that in the band of latitude between 30° N and 35° N, sunset will occur at some time after 1858. At that time, the tabulated latitude nearest to your DR is 35° N. Note that for this latitude, sunset occurs at 1910; also note that for latitude 30° N, sunset occurs at 1858, or 12 minutes earlier.
2. Next, plot your expected DR position for 1910 (fig. 2420); this turns out to be latitude 33° 06.9′ N, longitude 66° 32.6′ W.
3. Using this DR position, compute the time of sun-

set by entering the table on the daily page for latitude 30° and extracting the time of 1858. The latitude correction from Table I is +8^m and the correction for difference in longitude between the DR and the central meridian of the time zone is +26 minutes (dLo of 6° 32.6′). Adding 1858 + 8 + 26 results in a ZT of 1932 as the *first estimate*.

4. Plot the 1932 DR position, finding it to be Lat. 33° 05.0′ N, Long 66° 41.0′ W; now the difference in longitude from the central meridian (computed to the nearest 15′ of arc) is 6° 45′, resulting in a recomputed value for dLo correction of +27 minutes. The ZT is adjusted for this additional minute and 1933 is the *second estimate* and is your ZT of sunset.

Problems involving the times of sunrise, moonrise, moonset, and twilight for a moving ship are solved in a similar manner.

Moonrise Calculation for a Moving Vessel

2421   Moonrise or moonset calculations are similar. For example, on the evening of 5 June, a ship's 2000 DR position is latitude 16° 52.6′ N, longitude 62° 19.4′ W (fig. 2421). The course is 063°, speed 20 knots. To find the ZT of moonrise on the night of 5–6 June, using the *Nautical Almanac*:

1. Inspect the moonrise tables (fig. 2403b) for latitudes 10° N and 20° N, to see that the time of

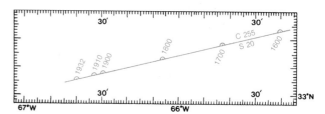

Fig. 2420. Plot for determination of ZT of sunset for a moving vessel.

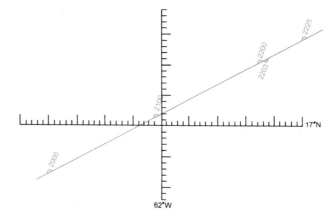

Fig. 2421. Plot for determination of ZT of moonrise for a moving vessel.

moonrise will be approximately 2203 on 5 June. For latitude 10° N and longitude 0°, the time of moonrise will be 2203. The DR position for this time is plotted (fig. 2421) and found to be latitude 17° 11.2' N, longitude 61° 41.2' W.

2. Next, calculate the time of moonrise for this position as the first estimate; this is 2225.

3. Plot the ship's DR position for the time of the first estimate and find it to be latitude 17° 14.5' N, longitude 61° 34.4' W.

4. Recalculate the time of moonrise for this revised DR position using the same procedures as in obtaining the first estimate; this gives the second estimate of moonrise as 2224.

EPHEMERAL DATA IN STELLA

2422 The U.S. Naval Observatory's STELLA program includes ephemeral data covering the years 1970 to 2010. The reason that the data go so far back is that many textbooks and courses rely on old data for examples; including the old data allows STELLA to be used to work those examples.

A word of caution, however: When comparing manual solutions of problems with STELLA solutions, one should be aware that some small differences are to be expected. Positions of celestial bodies used by the program are more accurate than their positions in almanacs. Another factor involves the relative rigor of mathematical procedures. STELLA uses no compromises of the kind that are necessary with tables and procedures to make the manual process tractable. Even so, if textbook examples and problem sets are accurately solved by traditional methods, there should be no *large* differences when answers are compared to the results given by STELLA.

To obtain ephemeral data from STELLA, you should click on the "Task" menu and then select "Almanac." You will then be presented with four choices:

Sun/Moon/Aries
Planets
Stars
All

Sun/Moon/Aries

2423 If you select "Sun/Moon/Aries" (Task → Almanac → Sun/Moon/Aries) you will see the dialog box shown in figure 2423a.

Select the "Current Date" button or manually enter the date you wish to use ("10 July 2003" in the example shown). Select the desired time by filling in the appropriate boxes ("0402" in the example shown).

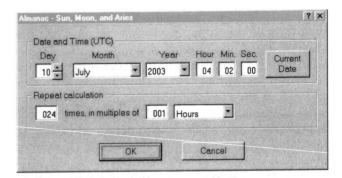

Fig. 2423a. STELLA dialog box for obtaining Sun, Moon, and Aries ephemeral data.

Also choose how many times you want the data presented and the interval; in the example, the default of 24 times in multiples of one hour is selected. You can obtain immediate help for any specific item in the dialog by highlighting the item and pressing the F1 key; or, click the question mark on the far right side of the dialog title bar, move the mark to the item and click again. Once you have made your selections, select "OK" and you will obtain the desired data.

For example, if you wanted to construct an almanac of the Sun, Moon, and Aries covering the period 0402 to 0411 on 8 April 2007 at three-minute intervals, you would enter those parameters as described above. Note that to complete the specification, the first entry in the "Repeat calculation" section of the dialog will be 4 (the number of calculated data lines). The second box will contain 3 (specifying the multiple of units). In the third box, units of minutes will be selected. The requested almanac will appear as shown in figure 2423b.

Note that the data provided are all that you would need for the various functions of celestial navigation: GHA and declination for the Sun along with its semidiameter (S.D.); the same for the Moon, along with its horizontal parallax and an indication of its percent of illumination; and the GHA of Aries.

Planets

2424 Selecting "Planets" (Task → Almanac → Planets) yields virtually the same dialog box as the one used for "Sun/Moon/Aries," and the procedures are identical.

Stars

2425 If you select "Stars" (Task → Almanac → Stars) from the drop-down menu, the dialog box that appears is similar to the one for "Sun, Moon, Aries" except that there is no "Repeat calculation" function.

The program supplies a default time of day that it takes from the last recorded position in STELLA's

ALMANAC

2007 Apr 8 (Sun)

SUN/MOON/ARIES

UT	SUN , S.D. = 16.0		MOON					ARIES	
	GHA	Dec.	GHA	Dec.	H.P.	S.D.	Ill.	GHA	
h m	° ,	° ,	° ,	° ,	,	,	%	° ,	
04 02	239 59.4	N07 02.5	0 20.2	S28 03.5	55.1	15.0	75	256 32.6	
04 05	240 44.4	N07 02.6	1 03.6	S28 03.6	55.1	15.0	75	257 17.7	
04 08	241 29.4	N07 02.6	1 47.0	S28 03.8	55.1	15.0	75	258 02.8	
04 11	242 14.4	N07 02.7	2 30.4	S28 03.9	55.1	15.0	75	258 47.9	

Fig. 2423b. Resulting STELLA almanac data.

Log (either a fix or a DR). You may want to enter a different starting time of day. Be certain the time you enter is in UT. As with the "Sun, Moon, and Aries" selection, you can enter the day, month, and year directly, or use the "Current Date" button. Caution: computer clocks can drift and become inaccurate. Use the "Current Date" button with care, especially near midnight. Be certain the date entered is the correct UT (GMT) date. After all data have been specified correctly, click "OK" or press the "Enter" key. STELLA will generate the almanac. Coordinates of the stars and Aries will be listed once, for the exact time specified in the dialog.

For example, for the date and time shown in the dialog above, a *part* of the complete tabulation generated by STELLA is shown in figure 2425b as it would be displayed on your computer screen.

Note that besides the GHA of Aries for the date selected, the program actually provides the Sidereal Hour Angle, Greenwich Hour Angle, and declination of all fifty-seven of the navigational stars plus

Polaris—only a sample is shown above (leaving out the stars numbered 4 through 56). Note also that for Ankaa and Polaris, the GHA apparently does not equal the GHA of Aries plus the SHA of the star as listed. This aberration occurs because STELLA rounds off after adding addends of greater precision than the prescribed format can show in print.

All

2426 If you select "All" (Task→Almanac→All) the dialog box resembles the one for "Stars" except that there is no choice of time (only date), and it provides a combination of the data shown in the examples above. Once you select a date and click on "OK," you will obtain an hourly tabulation, at one-hour intervals, beginning at 0000 UT with coordinates for the Sun, Moon, Aries, and the planets. The program also provides the coordinates of all the navigational stars and Polaris at 1200 UT on the specified date.

Rise, Set, and Transit Task

2427 In the paper *Nautical Almanac*, sunrise, sunset, moonrise, moonset, and twilight information is included on the daily pages with other celestial information. To obtain this information when using STELLA, as well as the times that celestial bodies will transit a meridian, you must go to the separate task called "Rise, Set, and Transit."

Once you have selected this task from the dropdown menu, you will be given the choice of "Underway" or "Fixed Site."

The *Underway* function calculates and displays

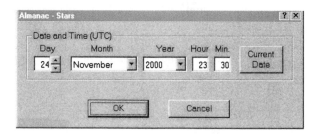

Fig. 2425a. STELLA dialog box for obtaining star ephemeral data.

h m
2000 Nov 24 (Fri) 23 30 UT

NAVIGATIONAL STARS

° ,
GHA of ARIES = 56 43.2

NAME	No.	SHA	GHA	Dec.
		° ,	° ,	° ,
Alpheratz	1	357 53.6	54 36.8	N29 05.8
Ankaa	2	353 25.1	50 08.4	S42 18.3
Schedar	3	349 51.5	46 34.7	N56 32.7
. . .	..	. . .	. . .	. . .
Markab	57	13 48.1	70 31.3	N15 12.7
Polaris	--	321 26.7	18 10.0	N89 16.1

Fig. 2425b. Star data from STELLA.

rise, transit, set, twilight, and related data for the Sun. Except for twilight, it also provides similar data for the Moon. The information is particularly useful for navigating a vessel under way because the program advances vessel position while tracking the Sun and Moon so that the events are predicted to occur relative to instantaneous positions of the moving vessel.

For a vessel in port, or for other stationary locations, the *Fixed Site* function calculates Sun or Moon events for a sequence of dates under user control. That option is most useful for planning activities for extended periods when a vessel is in port.

Even though the Rise/Set/Transit functions include twilight information, you need not use this task separately if you are planning to take star sights at twilight. This information is also included in STELLA's Sight Planning task.

Underway Function

2428   When you select the Underway function from the menu (Task→Rise/Set/Twilight→Fixed Site), the dialog box shown in figure 2428a appears.

In order for the Underway function to work, a Fix or DR position must be available in the program Log before using this function. It will appear in the dialog box as "Reference Position, Date, and Time." As you can see, that position can be changed by clicking on the "Edit" button.

A default date is shown in the dialog. Day of the month is highlighted and ready to be changed, if necessary. You can enter the day, month, and year directly, or use the "Current Date" button.

The "Time Zone" area of the dialog offers some flexibility. On that account there are some factors to consider. For straightforward use, and since the date is expressed in UTC, the Time Zone boxes may be left at the default values. You will not have to choose East or West; the buttons will be inactive. If event times are needed for the time zone in which the vessel is operating, then identify the number of hours East or West of the Prime Meridian (Greenwich, England) that apply to the coordinates of the approximate location for which you are calculating the events. Enter that number in the Hour box. The Min. box is to accommodate certain locations that have a time zone offset of thirty or forty-five minutes. If the location is in the Western Hemisphere, choose the West option button. If the location is in the Eastern Hemisphere, choose East.

You may decide to specify a remote location, yet want the times of events expressed in your local or other time. For example, if you want sunrise and sunset for San Diego, California, but expressed in Eastern Standard Time, you would enter 05 for Hour and 00 for Min. in the Time Zone boxes, followed by choosing the West option button. Note that, when Daylight Saving Time is in use, you would need to enter 04, not 05.

The "Height of Eye" box can normally be ignored. Setting the height of eye parameter will yield a slightly more accurate result; not setting it will cause a small, rounding difference in the rise and set times, but it does not affect the time of transits. If an entry is made, it should be in feet and refers to the height above the sea surface.

In "Body" area of the dialog you choose, using the option buttons, whether you want the rise and set times for the Sun or for the Moon. STELLA will do only one at a time.

In the "Reference Position, Date and Time" area, STELLA takes the data from its Log and will use them

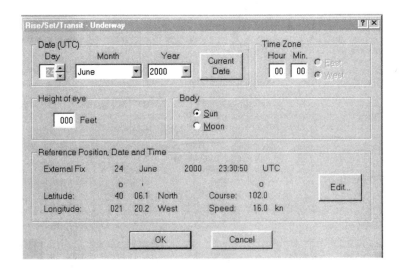

Fig. 2428a. STELLA dialog box for underway task.

to compute the Sun and Moon events while simultaneously advancing vessel position. The reference data can be for the last recorded fix. Or the data can be for the latest DR position in the Log, provided there was a course or speed change at the time of the DR. If any of the reference data, date, time, position, or motion are not correct, calculated events will be incorrect.

You may encounter circumstances that call for a temporary revision of the vessel track. Vessel position and motion can be partly or completely changed by using the "Edit" button, provided for such cases. Changing any or all of the reference data is permitted, but the changes do not affect the program Log.

For example, assume that on 22 June 2000 at 1841 and 30 seconds a fix has been obtained and recorded in the STELLA Log as follows: Latitude N42° 0.9', Longitude W040° 02.1'. Course = 094°; Speed = 16 kn. The ship is keeping +2 hours on UTC for scheduling watches. To determine the time of sunrise, sunset, and so on, the appropriate data would be entered and STELLA would provide the output shown in figure 2428b.

At the top of the table is a summary of all reference data used to perform the calculation. In the time column of the table all events are stated in local time because the 02 hour West offset was introduced into the dialog. Note the Zn/Hc data. They indicate the azimuth (Zn) reckoned from North for rise and set, and the altitude (Hc) above the Southern horizon at transit.

To determine lunar events, the same dialog box is used, but the Moon option button must be selected. The results would appear as in figure 2428c.

Note that the final column in the table also provides useful information. It gives the percentage of the Moon's disk illuminated by sunlight, indicating

that the Moon should be easily visible in daylight and that it is waning.

The "Edit" function can be used to change course and speed or enter new position information, such as a waypoint. The dialog box shown in figure 2428d appears, giving you access to the appropriate data.

When the *OK* command button is selected, the original, main dialog returns. In the example shown, the user entered a new waypoint. It now shows the waypoint as the reference position. But the type of reference position is now labeled as "User-defined," because the edited position is neither a fix nor a DR position.

Selecting the *OK* button produces the data shown in figure 2428e.

Note that the following symbols may appear in the tables of rise, set, and transit produced by STELLA:

N	Altitude at transit is measured from the northern horizon.
S	Altitude at transit is measured from the southern horizon.
****	No event. The body is continuously above the horizon.
- - - -	No event. The body is continuously below the horizon or the twilight limit.
????	The event is indeterminate.
////	Twilight lasts all night.

Fixed Site Function

2429   When you select the Fixed Site function from the drop-down menu (Task→Rise/Set/Twilight→Fixed Site), the dialog box shown in figure 2429a appears.

The setup for this dialog box is similar to the one

```
                    UNDERWAY
                       Sun

                Reference Position
                                o     ,
     Date: 22 Jun 2000      Lat:   N 42 00.9
            h  m  s         Long:  W040 02.1
     Time: 18 41 30 UTC     Ht:         0 ft.
                             o
                Course:  094.0

                 Speed:  16.0 kn.

             Tabular Time + 02h 00m = UTC

Event                   Time     Zn/Hc      Lat          Long
                         h m       o        o    ,        o    ,
Beg. Naut. Twi.   23 Jun 0332     ---     N41 48.8     W036 10.4
Beg. Civ. Twi.    23 Jun 0415     ---     N41 48.0     W035 55.0
Rise              23 Jun 0449     057     N41 47.4     W035 43.0
Transit (LAN)     23 Jun 1215     72S     N41 39.1     W033 04.7
Set               23 Jun 1940     303     N41 30.8     W030 26.9
End Civ. Twi.     23 Jun 2013     ---     N41 30.2     W030 15.2
End Naut. Twi.    23 Jun 2055     ---     N41 29.4     W030 00.1
```

Fig. 2428b. Sunrise, twilight, and other data yielded by STELLA.

```
                          UNDERWAY
                            Moon

                      Reference Position
                                          o     ,
        Date: 22 Jun 2000        Lat:    N 42 00.9
              h  m  s            Long:   W040 02.1
        Time: 18 41 30 UTC       Ht:        56 ft.
                                          o
                      Course: 094.0
                      Speed:  16.0 kn.

                  Tabular Time + 02h 00m = UTC

Event            Time      Zn/Hc    Lat          Long       Ill.
                 h m        o        o    ,        o    ,    %
Rise      22 Jun 2354      106      N41 52.8    W037 27.8    69
Transit   23 Jun 0514       37S     N41 46.9    W035 33.9    67
Set       23 Jun 1042      257      N41 40.8    W033 37.7    65
Rise      23 Jun 2348      100      N41 26.2    W028 59.1    60
Transit   24 Jun 0524       42S     N41 19.9    W027 00.3    58
Set       24 Jun 1108      263      N41 13.5    W024 59.0    55
```

Fig. 2428c. Lunar events from STELLA.

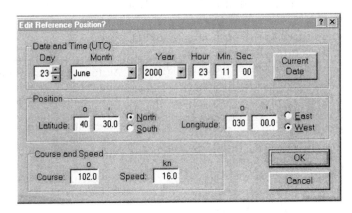

Fig. 2428d. STELLA's edit function.

```
                          UNDERWAY
                            Sun

                      Reference Position
                                          o     ,
        Date: 23 Jun 2000        Lat:    N 41 30.0
              h  m  s            Long:   W030 00.0
        Time: 23 11 00 UTC       Ht:         0 ft.
                                          o
                      Course: 102.0
                      Speed:  16.0 kn.

                  Tabular Time + 00h 00m = UTC

Event                  Time      Zn/Hc    Lat          Long
                       h m        o        o    ,        o    ,
Beg. Naut. Twi.  24 Jun 0503     ---      N41 10.5    W027 58.1
Beg. Civ. Twi.   24 Jun 0545     ---      N41 08.1    W027 43.4
Rise             24 Jun 0619     057      N41 06.3    W027 32.0
Transit (LAN)    24 Jun 1342      73S     N40 41.7    W024 59.3
Set              24 Jun 2104     302      N40 17.2    W022 28.5
End Civ. Twi.    24 Jun 2136     ---      N40 15.4    W022 17.5
End Naut. Twi.   24 Jun 2217     ---      N40 13.1    W022 03.6
Beg. Naut. Twi.  25 Jun 0438     ---      N39 52.0    W019 54.1
Beg. Civ. Twi.   25 Jun 0519     ---      N39 49.7    W019 40.2
Rise             25 Jun 0551     058      N39 47.9    W019 29.4
Transit (LAN)    25 Jun 1311      74S     N39 23.5    W017 01.0
Set              25 Jun 2028     301      N38 59.3    W014 34.4
End Civ. Twi.    25 Jun 2059     ---      N38 57.5    W014 23.9
End Naut. Twi.   25 Jun 2139     ---      N38 55.3    W014 10.7
```

Fig. 2428e. Data resulting from STELLA edit function.

for the underway function. However, instead of taking the initial position from STELLA's ongoing log, there are boxes for entry of a latitude and longitude position and a box for selecting how many times (on successive days) you want the data repeated. Note that all of the dialog boxes in the above illustration contain default entries (except for time zone). This signifies that there is position information in the STELLA Log. If the Day, Month, and Year are "1 Jan. 2000," and the other dialog boxes contain no data, there may be no active program Log.

After completing the dialog and checking the entries for accuracy, click OK or press the Enter key. STELLA will display the table of Sun or Moon rise, set, and transit events in the Worksheet window. For example, if you wanted to compute a four-day table of moonrise, moonset, and transit in Eastern Standard Time beginning 17 December 2000 for Latitude N35° 43.3', Longitude W082° 33.5', you would make the appropriate entries in the dialog box and obtain the data shown in figure 2429b.

The leftmost column of data gives the dates as specified in the example. However, note that the first event time under the Rise column is for 16 December. That is because moonrise occurs shortly before midnight beginning the seventeenth and there is no rise on the seventeenth. The Moon rises shortly after 0000 hours on 18 December.

The column headed "Ill." provides the percent of the Moon's surface facing the Earth that is illuminated. For this example, the run of data from one event to the next indicates that the Moon's phase is waning, and last quarter occurs in the evening of 17 December.

The symbols used with this data are the same as those used with the underway function as described above.

Differences Between the *Nautical Almanac* and STELLA

2430 When you create an almanac using STELLA, the display will look similar to the daily pages of the printed *Nautical Almanac*. However, some differences will be obvious. One of the most obvious is that navigators who are used to the paper *Nautical Almanac* are accustomed to having rising, setting, and twilight data on the same page as the hourly positions of the Sun and Moon. As discussed above, when STELLA executes the *Almanac* task for Sun and Moon positions, only those positions and GHA of Aries are displayed. Rise, Set, and Transit (and twilight) are treated as a separate task in the STELLA program, and it produces phenomena times for the user's position (fixed or underway) without any necessity of adjusting the data for actual Latitude and Longitude by table lookup or arithmetic.

The data on the Moon includes a fraction of the Moon's visible disk that is illuminated (Ill.), given as a percentage. As explained in the discussion of the *Nautical Almanac* above, the percentage of the Moon's disk illuminated is a more quantitative description of the Moon's appearance than its phase. If the Moon is thought of as a circular disk against the sky, then the ratio of the area illuminated by direct sunlight to total area, multiplied by 100, is the percentage of the Moon's face illuminated. At new Moon, 0 percent of the Moon is illuminated, as seen from Earth; at first and last quarters, 50 percent is illuminated, and at full Moon, 100 percent. During crescent phases, 0 to 50 percent is illuminated; and during gibbous phases, it is 50 to 100 percent. The percent illuminated corresponding to each time and position is a more refined quantity than is the phase symbol or percentage provided in the *Nautical Almanac*. Consequently, the Moon phase symbol and Age of the Moon are not produced by the STELLA

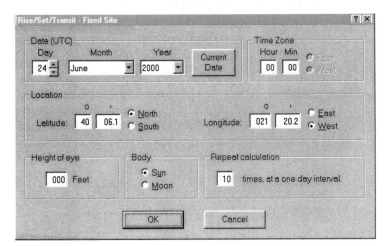

Fig. 2429a. STELLA fixed site function.

```
                        FIXED SITE
                           Moon
                            o    ,
                      Lat:   N 35 43.3
                      Long:  W082 33.5

                      Ht:        0 ft.

                 Tabular Time + 05h 00m = UTC

        Date           Rise   Ill.    Transit Ill.      Set   Ill.

                     d  h m    %     d  h m   %      d  h m    %
        17 Dec 2000  16 2328  59     17 0610  56     17 1244  53
        18 Dec 2000  18 0033  48     18 0659  45     18 1317  42
        19 Dec 2000  19 0136  37     19 0746  34     19 1348  32
        20 Dec 2000  20 0238  27     20 0832  24     20 1419  22
```

Fig. 2429b. Data from STELLA's fixed site function.

Almanac task. Both the phase of the Moon and its correct orientation with respect to the navigator can be found on the display generated by the Sky Chart option under the Task "Sight Planning," if the Moon is above the horizon at the time and the location is specified. If necessary, scanning the "% Ill." column of almanac data given by STELLA will reveal whether the Moon is waxing or waning.

Since users can direct STELLA to generate an almanac at virtually any time interval (seconds, minutes, etc.), the familiar v and d quantities that appear on the printed pages are not displayed. They are never needed while using STELLA.

Under the Planets option, STELLA displays positions of the navigational planets, with their magnitudes. The tabulations will also look familiar, but not identical, to the printed almanac. The quantities v and d are omitted for the reasons given above.

In the printed *Nautical Almanac*, the fifty-seven navigational stars are listed alphabetically by their popular names on the left-hand pages. In the STELLA display they are listed in increasing numerical order. As a consequence, the stars appear in *decreasing order* of Sidereal Hour Angle and Greenwich Hour Angle. The exception is Polaris, which has no number. Polaris is listed by STELLA but is not found on the left-hand pages of the *Nautical Almanac*. (Note: Polaris *is* listed in the *Nautical Almanac*'s list of 173 stars.)

If numerical comparisons are made between a STELLA generated almanac and corresponding pages of the *Nautical Almanac*, some differences will be noted in the final digits of some quantities. In most cases, the differences are due to the effects of rounding final numerical results that are produced by independent methods of computation. An exception to this will be found in the Greenwich Hour Angle of the Sun, for which a constant difference of 0.1' should be expected during certain times of the year. (Rounding effects may randomly increase the difference to 0.2'.) This is because a deliberate offset is introduced into the Sun's GHA in the printed book for the purpose of eliminating the need to apply a v correction from the "Increments and Corrections" table. Occasionally, small differences not due to rounding may be noticed in the coordinates of Venus, at or near times of inferior conjunction. Since Venus cannot be observed during such intervals, the differences are of no consequence.

OTHER SOURCES OF EPHEMERAL DATA

2431   Commercial products, such as *Reed's Almanacs*, the Celesticomp calculator, and the Cap'n software program are all reliable sources of ephemeral data. Other sources, such as the U.S. Naval Observatory's *Astronomical Almanac* are also excellent sources of data but their scientific orientation for professional astronomers make them much less practical for navigational purposes.

Chapter 25   Sight Reduction

Once an observation of an identified celestial body has been made with a sextant at a precise and accurate time, and the proper corrections made from tabulated data in an almanac, the problem still remains of converting this information into a line of position. This process is termed *sight reduction,* and there is a variety of methods by which it can be accomplished.

This chapter will continue the step-by-step progression toward a complete celestial navigation solution by considering computational and tabular methods of sight reduction. These include some mathematical methods, the use of tables found in NIMA publications 229, 249, the *Nautical Almanac,* the Ageton method, and the STELLA computer program.

EARLY METHODS

2501 The most widely used sight reduction method in the nineteenth century and well into the twentieth was the *time sight*. A latitude line was obtained by means of an observation of Polaris, or the transit of the Sun or of some other body. This latitude line was advanced to the time of an observation of a body located well to the east or west of the observer. The body most frequently used was the Sun. With this assumed latitude, a longitude was calculated, originally in units of time, which gave the time sight its name. The accuracy of the time sight obviously depended on the accuracy of the assumed latitude and upon accurate timekeeping.

In 1875, Marcq St.-Hilaire conceived the altitude intercept method of solution, a system the U.S. Navy soon adopted. For sight reduction by this method, the "cosine-haversine" equations were used for computed altitude and azimuth and remained in general use in the U.S. Navy until other simplified methods were developed early in the twentieth century. These became known as the "short methods," and led to a succession of publications known by their publication numbers and/or by their creators' names. The Weems *Line of Position Book,* and the Dreisenstok tables published by the Hydrographic Office as H.O. 208, and H.O. 211 by Ageton were among the most successful and are still used by some navigators. These two H.O. publications are no longer in print, but the Dreisenstok and Ageton tables can be obtained from commercial sources. Those navigators who still hold on to their copies of the 1977/1981 editions of *Bowditch* will find the Ageton tables in Volume II as Table 35. Readers of this book who wish to obtain Ageton tables may find them at the Naval Institute's web site, www.navalinstitute.org/navtable.

A modification of the Ageton tables also resulted in a set of condensed, or "compact," Ageton tables that are well suited for small-craft or lifeboat use. The only mathematical skill these demand of the user is the ability to add, subtract, and interpolate. They are convenient, in that one small volume permits solution for virtually any latitude, any declination, and any altitude.

In more recent times, the computations that go into solving the sight reduction problem have been incorporated into specially designed calculators such as the Celesticomp series and into computer programs such as the U.S. Navy's STELLA and the commercially available Cap'n (Computerized American Practical Navigator) program, both of which run on standard PCs.

SIGHT REDUCTION EQUATIONS

2502 While there are many variations, the classic equations for calculating a computed altitude and an azimuth angle for celestial observations are:

$$\sin H = \sin L \sin d + \cos L \cos d \cos LHA$$

$$\tan Z = \frac{\cos d \sin LHA}{\cos H}$$

where H is computed altitude
  L is latitude
  d is declination
  LHA is local hour angle
  Z is azimuth angle

These equations—or equations derived from them or by similar means—are also used for the development of procedures and programs for sight reduction using computers or electronic calculators.

An interesting and enlightening discussion of the mathematics involved in sight reduction (with examples) can be found in the *Nautical Almanac* near the back of the book in a section titled "Sight Reduction Procedures: Methods and Formulae for Direct Computation."

INSPECTION TABLES

2503 To avoid lengthy calculations (and the inherent risk of error), or as a means of checking these calculations, navigators often rely upon the so-called inspection tables—so called because altitude and azimuth are extracted for a given latitude, meridian angle, and declination by inspection, requiring no calculation other than some simple interpolation. These tables are much larger and heavier than the Dreisenstok and Ageton tables because they consist of vast numbers of precomputed solutions.

The *Sight Reduction Tables for Marine Navigation*, NIMA Pub. No. 229, are used today by surface navigators of the U.S. Navy, Coast Guard, Merchant marine, and many private yachtsmen. *Sight Reduction Tables for Air Navigation*, Pub. No. 249, was originally designed for air navigation but is today popular with some marine navigators, especially small craft operators. Since 1989, the Nautical Almanac has included a set of concise tables that can be used with about the same degree of accuracy as those found in Pub. No. 249.

REDUCTION BY PUB. NO. 229

2504 The set of tables titled *Sight Reduction Tables for Marine Navigation* are generally referred to as Pub. 229 or Pub. No. 229 (and sometimes by their former number, H.O. 229) and yield precomputed altitudes and azimuths. The publication of these tables is a joint U.S.–British project involving the U.S. Naval Oceanographic Office, the U.S. Naval Observatory, and the Royal Greenwich Observatory.

Pub. No. 229 tables are published in six volumes, arranged by latitude. Each volume contains data for a 16° band of latitude, good for either north or south, with an overlap of 1° between volumes; for example, latitude 30° appears in both Volumes 2 and 3. In each volume, the latitudes are separated into two nonoverlapping "zones" as shown below.

Vol. No.	First Zone of Latitude	Second Zone of Latitude
1	0°–7°	8°–15°
2	15°–22°	23°–30°
3	30°–37°	38°–45°
4	45°–52°	53°–60°
5	60°–67°	68°–75°
6	75°–82°	83°–90°

Pub. No. 229 is primarily intended to be used with an *assumed position* (AP). The latitude of this position is the integral degree *nearest* the vessel's DR or EP latitude; its longitude is artificially selected to give a whole degree of local hour angle within 30′ of the vessel's DR or EP longitude. This procedure is used to fit the format of these tables that present all combinations of latitude, local hour angle (measured westward from the observer's celestial meridian through 360°), and declination at uniform whole degree intervals of each argument. These tables may, however, also be used for reduction from a DR position, and directions for this procedure are given in each volume.

Using the assumed position method, Pub. No. 229 provides computed altitudes (Hc) correct to the nearest 0.1′ when all corrections are employed, and azimuth angles to 0.1°. Among today's tables it is unique, in that it offers both the maximum degree of precision required by the navigator and also permits the reduction of an observation of *any* navigational body, at *any* altitude, including those of negative value; there are no limitations of latitude, hour angle, or declination.

Entering Arguments

2505 To use Pub. No. 229, you need three entering arguments: latitude, LHA, and declination. With these three quantities you can use the tables to solve your navigational triangle and provide an LOP.

Before entering the tables you must determine whether your latitude and declination are of the *same* or *contrary* names (i.e., if both are north or both are south, they have the *same* names; if one is north and the other south, they have *contrary* names). This determination is important in deciding which part of the table you will use.

Latitude

2506 To begin, you should select the volume that includes the assumed latitude (a Lat. *or* aL). As mentioned above, you should assume your latitude to be a whole degree quantity that is closest to your DR position (or your estimated position). For example, if your DR position was 37° 29.8′ N 122° 37.3′ E when you took your first sight, you would use an assumed latitude of 37° as one of your entering arguments. In most cases, all the assumed positions will lie along the same assumed parallel of latitude. The exception occurs when a ship moves closer to an adjoining whole degree while observations are being made. In the example above, a ship heading northward might have a new DR latitude of 37° 30.1′ N by the time the navigator took the last sight; in this case, the appropriate assumed latitude for the second sight would be 38° instead of the 37° assumed latitude used for the first sight.

Upon opening the volume of Pub. No. 229 you have selected, you will note that the book is divided

roughly in half, with the first eight degrees of latitude in the front of the book (heading the table's *columns*) and the second half of the book containing the other eight degrees of latitude coverage. For example, in figure 2506, you can see that the columns are headed by whole degrees of latitude from 30° to 37°. This figure is an abstract from the Pub. No. 229 volume covering latitudes 30° to 45° inclusive, so you would expect to find latitudes 38° to 45° covered in the second half of the book.

LHA

2507 Once you have selected the right volume and located the appropriate half of the volume for your assumed latitude, your next entering argument is LHA. The pages of the book are organized according to quantities of LHA, each page representing two values of LHA that when added together equal 360°. For example, in figure 2506, the selected page has LHAs of 34° and 326° indicated prominently at the top of the page. Facing pages repeat the same values. As you might expect, the values of LHA are from "0°, 360°" to "90°, 270°" and these values are repeated in the first and second halves of the book in order to accommodate all latitudes as explained above.

To determine the LHA you must combine the GHA of the observed body with an assumed longitude (aλ). You should deliberately assume a longi-

34°, 326° L.H.A.   LATITUDE **SAME** NAME AS DECLINATION   N. Lat. { L.H.A. greater than 180°......Zn=Z / L.H.A. less than 180°............Zn=360°−Z

Dec.	30° Hc	d	Z	31° Hc	d	Z	32° Hc	d	Z	33° Hc	d	Z	34° Hc	d	Z	35° Hc	d	Z	36° Hc	d	Z	37° Hc	d	Z	Dec.
0	45 53.2	+42.8	126.5	45 17.1	+43.7	127.4	44 40.4	+44.5	128.2	44 03.0	+45.3	128.9	43 25.0	+46.0	129.7	42 46.4	+46.7	130.4	42 07.3	+47.4	131.1	41 27.6	+48.0	131.7	0
1	46 36.0	42.3	125.5	46 00.8	43.2	126.4	45 24.9	44.0	127.2	44 48.3	44.8	128.0	44 11.0	45.6	128.8	43 33.1	46.3	129.5	42 54.7	47.0	130.2	42 15.6	47.7	130.9	1
2	47 18.3	41.7	124.5	46 44.0	42.6	125.4	46 08.9	43.4	126.2	45 33.1	44.2	127.1	44 56.6	45.1	127.9	44 19.4	45.9	128.6	43 41.7	46.6	129.4	43 03.3	47.3	130.1	2
3	48 00.0	41.1	123.4	47 26.6	42.0	124.3	46 52.3	43.0	125.2	46 17.4	43.8	126.1	45 41.7	44.6	126.9	45 05.3	45.4	127.7	44 28.3	46.2	128.5	43 50.6	46.9	129.3	3
4	48 41.1	40.5	122.3	48 08.6	41.5	123.3	47 35.3	42.4	124.2	47 01.2	43.3	125.1	46 26.3	44.2	126.0	45 50.7	45.0	126.8	45 14.5	45.7	127.6	44 37.5	46.5	128.4	4
5	49 21.6	+39.8	121.2	48 50.1	+40.8	122.2	48 17.7	+41.7	123.1	47 44.5	+42.7	124.1	47 10.5	+43.6	125.0	46 35.7	+44.5	125.8	46 00.2	+45.3	126.7	45 24.0	+46.1	127.5	5
6	50 01.4	39.0	120.0	49 30.9	40.1	121.1	48 59.4	41.2	122.1	48 27.2	42.1	123.0	47 54.1	43.0	123.9	47 20.2	43.9	124.9	46 45.5	44.8	125.7	46 10.1	45.6	126.6	6
7	50 40.4	38.4	118.9	50 11.0	39.4	119.9	49 40.6	40.5	120.9	49 09.3	41.5	121.9	48 37.1	42.5	122.9	48 04.1	43.4	123.8	47 30.3	44.3	124.7	46 55.7	45.2	125.6	7
8	51 18.8	37.5	117.6	50 50.4	38.7	118.7	50 21.1	39.8	119.8	49 50.8	40.8	120.8	49 19.6	41.9	121.8	48 47.5	42.9	122.8	48 14.6	43.8	123.7	47 40.9	44.6	124.7	8
9	51 56.3	36.7	116.4	51 29.1	37.9	117.5	51 00.9	39.0	118.6	50 31.6	40.2	119.7	50 01.5	41.2	120.7	49 30.4	42.2	121.7	48 58.4	43.2	122.7	48 25.5	44.1	123.7	9
10	52 33.0	+35.8	115.1	52 07.0	+37.1	116.3	51 39.9	+38.3	117.4	51 11.8	+39.4	118.5	50 42.7	+40.5	119.6	50 12.6	+41.6	120.6	49 41.6	+42.5	121.6	49 09.6	+43.6	122.6	10
11	53 08.8	35.0	113.8	52 44.1	36.2	115.0	52 18.2	37.5	116.1	51 51.2	38.7	117.3	51 23.2	39.8	118.4	50 54.2	40.8	119.5	50 24.1	42.0	120.5	49 53.2	42.9	121.6	11
12	53 43.8	34.0	112.4	53 20.3	35.3	113.6	52 55.7	36.6	114.9	52 29.9	37.8	116.0	52 03.0	39.0	117.2	51 35.0	40.2	118.3	51 06.1	41.2	119.4	50 36.1	42.3	120.5	12
13	54 17.8	32.9	111.0	53 55.6	34.4	112.3	53 32.3	35.7	113.5	53 07.7	37.0	114.8	52 42.0	38.3	116.0	52 15.2	39.4	117.1	51 47.3	40.6	118.3	51 18.4	41.7	119.4	13
14	54 50.7	31.9	109.6	54 30.0	33.4	110.9	54 08.0	34.7	112.2	53 44.7	36.1	113.4	53 20.3	37.3	114.7	52 54.6	38.7	115.9	52 27.9	39.8	117.1	52 00.1	40.9	118.2	14
15	55 22.6	+30.9	108.1	55 03.4	+32.3	109.4	54 42.7	+33.8	110.8	54 20.8	+35.2	112.1	53 57.6	+36.5	113.4	53 33.3	+37.7	114.6	53 07.7	+39.0	115.8	52 41.0	+40.2	117.0	15
16	55 53.5	29.6	106.6	55 35.7	31.2	108.0	55 16.5	32.7	109.3	54 56.0	34.1	110.7	54 34.1	35.6	112.0	54 11.0	36.9	113.3	53 46.7	38.2	114.5	53 21.2	39.4	115.8	16
17	56 23.1	28.5	105.0	56 06.9	30.0	106.4	55 49.2	31.6	107.8	55 30.1	33.1	109.2	55 09.7	34.5	110.6	54 47.9	36.0	111.9	54 24.9	37.3	113.2	54 00.6	38.6	114.5	17
18	56 51.6	27.2	103.4	56 36.9	28.9	104.9	56 20.8	30.5	106.3	56 03.2	32.0	107.8	55 44.2	33.5	109.2	55 23.9	34.9	110.5	55 02.2	36.3	111.9	54 39.2	37.7	113.2	18
19	57 18.8	25.9	101.8	57 05.8	27.6	103.3	56 51.3	29.2	104.8	56 35.2	30.9	106.2	56 17.7	32.5	107.7	55 58.8	34.0	109.1	55 38.5	35.4	110.5	55 16.9	36.7	111.8	19
85	34 06.1	−48.7	3.4	35 06.0	−48.7	3.4	36 05.9	−48.7	3.5	37 05.8	−48.7	3.5	38 05.7	−48.6	3.6	39 05.6	−48.6	3.6	40 05.5	−48.6	3.7	41 05.3	−48.4	3.7	85
86	33 17.4	49.1	2.7	34 17.3	49.0	2.7	35 17.2	48.9	2.7	36 17.1	48.9	2.8	37 17.1	48.9	2.8	38 17.0	48.9	2.8	39 16.9	48.8	2.9	40 16.9	48.8	2.9	86
87	32 28.3	49.2	2.0	33 28.3	49.2	2.0	34 28.3	49.2	2.0	35 28.2	49.2	2.1	36 28.2	49.1	2.1	37 28.1	49.1	2.1	38 28.1	49.1	2.1	39 28.1	49.1	2.2	87
88	31 39.1	49.5	1.3	32 39.1	49.5	1.3	33 39.1	49.5	1.3	34 39.0	49.4	1.4	35 39.0	49.4	1.4	36 39.0	49.4	1.4	37 39.0	49.4	1.4	38 39.0	49.4	1.4	88
89	30 49.6	49.6	0.7	31 49.6	49.6	0.7	32 49.6	49.6	0.7	33 49.6	49.6	0.7	34 49.6	49.6	0.7	35 49.6	49.6	0.7	36 49.6	49.6	0.7	37 49.6	49.6	0.7	89
90	30 00.0	−49.8	0.0	31 00.0	−49.8	0.0	32 00.0	−49.8	0.0	33 00.0	−49.8	0.0	34 00.0	−49.9	0.0	35 00.0	−49.9	0.0	36 00.0	−49.9	0.0	37 00.0	−49.9	0.0	90
	30°			31°			32°			33°			34°			35°			36°			37°			

34°, 326° L.H.A.   LATITUDE **SAME** NAME AS DECLINATION

Fig. 2506. Pub. No. 229, typical "same name" page (extract).

tude that when applied to the GHA of the body being observed, will yield a *whole degree* of LHA; this assumed longitude (aλ) must lie within 30 minutes of arc of the best estimate of the ship's actual longitude at the time of the observation. Keep in mind that you will be adding east longitudes and subtracting west longitudes when combining with the GHA. When a number of celestial bodies are observed at about the same time, as in a round of star sights, a different longitude will have to be assumed for each body. The longitudes assumed should all fall within a span of about 60 minutes, except in higher latitudes, when the vessel's course and speed result in a rapid change of longitude and the period required to obtain the observations is protracted.

In the example above, the DR longitude was 122° 37.3′ E. If the GHA for the observed body that you obtained from the Nautical Almanac was 097° 27.2′, then you would use an assumed longitude of 122° 32.8′, because when *added* (because it is *east*) to the GHA you would get the needed whole degree LHA of 220° (122° 32.8′ + 097° 27.2′ = 220°).

If your longitude had been west instead of east, you would have used a value that, when subtracted, would yield a whole degree of LHA. For example, if your DR longitude had been 14° 40.4′ W and the GHA to your observed body had been 304° 57.7′, then you would use an assumed longitude of 14°

57.7′ to obtain an LHA of 290° (304° 57.7′ – 14° 57.7′ = 290).

Once you have determined these values, you must then find the correct page in Pub. No. 229 that covers the latitude and LHA combination you have determined.

Declination

2508 Having found the correct page for your entering arguments of latitude and LHA, you will note that the table *columns* are headed by latitudes as described above, and the table *rows* are labeled with whole degrees of declination. Find the appropriate assumed latitude column—making sure that you are in the appropriate "name" section; that is, use the portion of the table labeled "Latitude Same Name as Declination" (see fig. 2506) if both your assumed latitude and the declination of the body are north or if both are south; use the portion labeled "Latitude Contrary Name to Declination" (see fig. 2508) if that is the case.

The Results

2509 You will see by observing the subcolumn headings that the intersection of latitude and declination yields (Hc) and an azimuth angle (Z). Also included, between the Hc and Z, is a "d" factor; this is a convenience listing that tells you the difference between the tabulated altitude (Hc) on that line and

LATITUDE **CONTRARY** NAME TO DECLINATION   L.H.A. 34°, 326°

Dec.	30° Hc	d	Z	31° Hc	d	Z	32° Hc	d	Z	33° Hc	d	Z	34° Hc	d	Z	35° Hc	d	Z	36° Hc	d	Z	37° Hc	d	Z	Dec.
0	45 53.2	43.3	126.5	45 17.1	44.1	127.4	44 40.4	44.9	128.2	44 03.0	45.7	128.9	43 25.0	46.4	129.7	42 46.4	47.0	130.4	42 07.3	47.7	131.1	41 27.6	48.3	131.7	0
1	45 09.9	43.9	127.5	44 33.0	44.7	128.3	43 55.5	45.4	129.1	43 17.3	46.1	129.8	42 38.6	46.7	130.5	41 59.4	47.5	131.2	41 19.6	48.1	131.9	40 39.3	48.7	132.5	1
2	44 26.0	44.3	128.5	43 48.3	45.0	129.3	43 10.1	45.8	130.0	42 31.2	46.4	130.7	41 51.9	47.2	131.4	41 11.9	47.7	132.0	40 31.5	48.4	132.7	39 50.6	48.9	133.3	2
3	43 41.7	44.9	129.4	43 03.3	45.5	130.2	42 24.3	46.2	130.9	41 44.8	46.9	131.5	41 04.7	47.5	132.2	40 24.2	48.1	132.8	39 43.1	48.8	133.4	39 01.7	49.3	134.0	3
4	42 56.9	45.2	130.4	42 17.8	45.9	131.0	41 38.1	46.5	131.7	40 57.9	47.2	132.4	40 17.2	47.8	133.0	39 36.1	48.4	133.6	38 54.5	49.0	134.2	38 12.4	49.5	134.8	4
5	42 11.7	–45.6	131.2	41 31.9	46.6	131.9	40 51.6	47.0	132.6	40 10.7	47.5	133.2	39 29.4	48.1	133.8	38 47.7	48.7	134.4	38 05.5	49.2	134.9	37 22.9	49.7	135.5	5
6	41 26.1	46.0	132.1	40 45.6	46.6	132.8	40 04.6	47.2	133.4	39 23.2	47.8	134.0	38 41.3	48.4	134.6	37 59.0	49.0	135.1	37 16.3	49.5	135.7	36 33.2	50.0	136.2	6
7	40 40.1	46.4	133.0	39 59.0	47.0	133.6	39 17.4	47.6	134.2	38 35.4	48.2	134.8	37 52.9	48.7	135.3	37 10.0	49.2	135.9	36 26.8	49.7	136.4	35 43.2	50.2	136.9	7
8	39 53.7	46.7	133.8	39 12.0	47.3	134.4	38 29.8	47.9	135.0	37 47.2	48.4	135.5	37 04.2	49.0	136.1	36 20.8	49.5	136.6	35 37.1	50.0	137.1	34 53.0	50.5	137.5	8
9	39 07.0	47.0	134.6	38 24.7	47.6	135.2	37 41.9	48.1	135.7	36 58.8	48.7	136.3	36 15.2	49.2	136.8	35 31.3	49.7	137.3	34 47.1	50.2	137.7	34 02.5	50.6	138.2	9
10	38 20.0	–47.4	135.4	37 37.1	–47.9	136.0	36 53.8	–48.5	136.5	36 10.1	–49.0	137.0	35 26.0	–49.4	137.5	34 41.6	–49.9	137.9	33 56.9	–50.4	138.4	33 11.9	–50.8	138.8	10
11	37 32.6	47.6	136.2	36 49.2	48.2	136.7	36 05.3	48.7	137.2	35 21.1	49.2	137.7	34 36.6	49.7	138.2	33 51.7	50.2	138.6	33 06.5	50.6	139.1	32 21.1	51.1	139.5	11
12	36 45.0	48.0	136.9	36 01.0	48.5	137.4	35 16.6	49.0	137.9	34 31.9	49.5	138.4	33 46.9	49.9	138.8	33 01.5	50.3	139.3	32 15.9	50.8	139.7	31 30.0	51.2	140.1	12
13	35 57.0	48.2	137.7	35 12.5	48.7	138.2	34 27.6	49.2	138.6	33 42.4	49.6	139.1	32 57.0	50.1	139.5	32 11.2	50.6	139.9	31 25.1	50.9	140.3	30 38.8	51.3	140.7	13
14	35 08.8	48.4	138.4	34 23.8	49.0	138.9	33 38.4	49.4	139.3	32 52.8	49.9	139.8	32 06.8	50.3	140.2	31 20.6	50.7	140.6	30 34.2	51.2	140.9	29 47.5	51.6	141.3	14
15	34 20.4	–48.8	139.1	33 34.8	–49.2	139.6	32 49.0	–49.6	140.0	32 02.9	–50.1	140.4	31 16.5	–50.5	140.8	30 29.9	–50.9	141.2	29 43.0	–51.3	141.5	28 55.9	–51.6	141.9	15
16	33 31.6	48.9	139.8	32 45.6	49.4	140.3	31 59.4	49.9	140.7	31 12.8	50.2	141.1	30 26.0	50.6	141.4	29 39.0	51.1	141.8	28 51.7	51.4	142.1	28 04.3	51.8	142.5	16
17	32 42.7	49.2	140.5	31 56.2	49.6	140.9	31 09.5	50.0	141.3	30 22.6	50.5	141.7	29 35.4	50.9	142.1	28 47.9	51.2	142.4	28 00.3	51.6	142.7	27 12.5	52.0	143.0	17
18	31 53.5	49.4	141.2	31 06.6	49.8	141.6	30 19.5	50.2	142.0	29 32.1	50.6	142.3	28 44.5	51.0	142.7	27 56.7	51.4	143.0	27 08.7	51.7	143.3	26 20.5	52.1	143.6	18
19	31 04.1	49.6	141.9	30 16.8	50.0	142.2	29 29.3	50.4	142.6	28 41.5	50.8	142.9	27 53.5	51.2	143.3	27 05.3	51.5	143.6	26 17.0	51.9	143.9	25 28.4	52.2	144.2	19
85	25 49.1	+50.5	3.1	26 49.0	+50.6	3.1	27 48.9	+50.6	3.2	28 48.8	+50.6	3.2	29 48.7	+50.7	3.2	30 48.7	+50.6	3.3	31 48.6	+50.7	3.3	32 48.5	+50.7	3.3	85
86	26 39.6	50.4	2.5	27 39.6	50.3	2.5	28 39.5	50.4	2.5	29 39.4	50.5	2.6	30 39.4	50.2	2.6	31 39.3	50.5	2.6	32 39.3	50.5	2.7	33 39.2	50.5	2.7	86
87	27 30.0	50.1	1.9	28 29.9	50.2	1.9	29 29.9	50.2	1.9	30 29.9	50.2	1.9	31 29.8	50.2	2.0	32 29.8	50.3	2.0	33 29.8	50.3	2.0	34 29.7	50.3	2.0	87
88	28 20.1	50.1	1.3	29 20.1	50.1	1.3	30 20.1	50.1	1.3	31 20.1	50.1	1.3	32 20.1	50.0	1.3	33 20.1	50.0	1.3	34 20.1	50.0	1.4	35 20.0	50.1	1.4	88
89	29 10.2	49.8	0.6	30 10.2	49.8	0.6	31 10.2	49.8	0.7	32 10.2	49.8	0.7	33 10.1	49.9	0.7	34 10.1	49.9	0.7	35 10.1	49.9	0.7	36 10.1	49.9	0.7	89
90	30 00.0	+49.6	0.0	31 00.0	+49.6	0.0	32 00.0	+49.6	0.0	33 00.0	+49.6	0.0	34 00.0	+49.6	0.0	35 00.0	+49.6	0.0	36 00.0	+49.6	0.0	37 00.0	+49.6	0.0	90

| | 30° | 31° | 32° | 33° | 34° | 35° | 36° | 37° | |

S. Lat. { L.H.A. greater than 180°...... Zn=180°–Z
{ L.H.A. less than 180°.......... Zn=180°+Z

LATITUDE **SAME** NAME AS DECLINATION   L.H.A. 146°, 214°

Fig. 2508. Pub. No. 229, typical "contrary name" page (extract).

the one for the next higher degree of declination (on the next line down). The sign of this value is indicated (at every fifth entry) and is determined by the trend of Hc values—it will be positive if the Hc values are increasing, and negative if they are decreasing, as declination increases. This "d" value is used for interpolation, as explained below.

Interpolation

2510 Realizing that you entered the tables in Pub. No. 229 with only the whole degree of declination, it is usually necessary to refine both the Hc and the Z you obtained by interpolating for the difference between the whole degree value and the actual value of declination. To accomplish this, some interpolations can be done mentally without resorting to calculations or tables, but for less obvious interpolations you may find the new value mathematically or by using the interpolation tables that are provided on the pages inside the front and back covers of each volume. Both the mathematical and tabular methods are described below; while each will yield satisfactory results, using both serves as a good check for errors.

Mathematical Interpolation of Hc

2511 To interpolate the actual value of Hc by calculation, multiply the d value provided in the table by the amount that the actual declination exceeds the integral (whole degree) degree of declination that you used to enter the main body of the tables—this excess is often called the "declination increment" (Dec. Inc.)—and divide the result by 60 (to measure the whole-degree increment in *minutes* of arc). Add the resulting value to the Hc value extracted for the whole degree to get the *actual* Hc corresponding to the exact declination. Beware that the sign of the Hc increment is sometimes negative.

For example, if you had entered Pub. No. 229 with an assumed latitude of 34° N, an LHA of 326°, and a declination of 17° 28.7′ N, you would find the following values at the appropriate intersection of the 34° latitude column and the 17° declination row (see fig. 2506):

Hc	55° 09.7′
d	+34.5′
Z	110.6°

Applying the interpolation formula described above, you would calculate as follows using d from the table and the difference (Dec. Inc.) between the whole degree of declination used to enter the table (17) and the actual declination value (17° 28.7′):

$$\frac{d \times \text{Dec. Inc.}}{60} = \text{Hc correction}$$

$$\frac{34.5 \times 28.7}{60} = \text{Hc correction} = 16.5'$$

Hc correction + Hc (tabulated) = actual Hc
16.5′ + 55° 09.7′ = 55° 26.2′

Tabular Interpolation of Hc

2512 An alternative method for determining the actual (interpolated) value of Hc is to use the interpolation tables provided on the inside covers of Pub. No. 229. The tables inside the front cover are used for values 0.0′ through 31.9′ and those inside the back cover are used for values 28.0′ through 59.9′. (Note the convenient overlap.)

Portions of the interpolation tables are shown in figure 2512. The main argument in entering these tables is the excess Dec. Inc. of the actual declination over the integral (whole) degree of declination that you used to enter the main body of the tables. Values of Dec. Inc. are tabulated in the vertical column at the left-hand edge of each table. The other argument used with the interpolation table is the tabulated altitude difference (d), which must be separated into two parts, the first being a multiple of 10′ (10′, 20′, 30′, 40′, or 50′), and the second being the remainder in units and tenths, in the range 0.0′ to 9.9′.

Using the same example as in the mathematical interpolation above, if you had entered Pub. No. 229 with an assumed latitude of 34° N, an LHA of 326°, and a declination of 17° 28.7′, you would find the following values at the appropriate intersection of the 34° column and the 17° declination row (see fig. 2506):

Hc	55° 09.7
d	+34.5
Z	110.6

To refine the Hc, you would interpolate for the declination increment by going to the interpolation table and finding the row under "Dec. Inc." corresponding to this difference. In this case, because the declination was 17° 28.7′, and you entered the main table with a whole degree value of 17°, the declination increment (Dec. Inc.) is obviously 28.7′.

Having located the row labeled "28.7" (see fig. 2512), next use the d value (+34.5) to move across the row and stop at the intersection of the corresponding "tens" value—in this case, you would stop at the 30′ column (corresponding to the "3" in the tens column of 34.5)—and extract the value found there—in this case, it is 14.4.

INTERPOLATION TABLE

Dec. Inc.	10'	20'	30'	40'	50'	Dec.	0'	1'	2'	3'	4'	5'	6'	7'	8'	9'	Double Second Diff. and Corr.
28.0	4.6	11.3	14.0	18.6	23.3	.0	0.0	0.5	0.9	1.4	1.9	2.4	2.8	3.3	3.8	4.3	0.8
28.1	4.7	9.3	14.0	18.7	23.4	.1	0.0	0.5	1.0	1.5	1.9	2.4	2.9	3.4	3.8	4.3	2.4 .01
28.2	4.7	9.4	14.1	18.8	23.5	.2	0.1	0.6	1.0	1.5	2.0	2.5	2.9	3.4	3.9	4.4	4.0 .02
28.3	4.7	9.4	14.1	18.9	23.6	.3	0.1	0.6	1.1	1.6	2.0	2.5	3.0	3.5	3.9	4.4	5.6 .03
28.4	4.7	9.5	14.2	18.9	23.7	.4	0.2	0.7	1.1	1.6	2.1	2.6	3.0	3.5	4.0	4.5	7.2 .04
28.5	4.8	9.5	14.3	19.0	23.8	.5	0.2	0.7	1.2	1.7	2.1	2.6	3.1	3.6	4.0	4.5	8.8 .05 / 10.4 .06
28.6	4.8	9.5	14.3	19.1	23.8	.6	0.3	0.8	1.2	1.7	2.2	2.7	3.1	3.6	4.1	4.6	12.0 .07
28.7	4.8	9.6	14.4	19.2	23.9	.7	0.3	0.8	1.3	1.8	2.2	2.7	3.2	3.7	4.1	4.6	13.6 .08
28.8	4.8	9.6	14.4	19.2	24.0	.8	0.4	0.9	1.3	1.8	2.3	2.8	3.2	3.7	4.2	4.7	15.2 .09
28.9	4.9	9.7	14.5	19.3	24.1	.9	0.4	0.9	1.4	1.9	2.3	2.8	3.3	3.8	4.2	4.7	16.8 .10
34.0	5.6	11.3	17.0	22.6	28.3	.0	0.0	0.6	1.1	1.7	2.3	2.9	3.4	4.0	4.6	5.2	0.8
34.1	5.7	11.3	17.0	22.7	28.4	.1	0.1	0.6	1.2	1.8	2.4	2.9	3.5	4.1	4.7	5.2	2.5 .01
34.2	5.7	11.4	17.1	22.8	28.5	.2	0.1	0.7	1.3	1.8	2.4	3.0	3.6	4.1	4.7	5.3	4.1 .02
34.3	5.7	11.4	17.1	22.9	28.6	.3	0.2	0.7	1.3	1.9	2.5	3.0	3.6	4.2	4.8	5.3	5.8 .03
34.4	5.7	11.5	17.2	22.9	28.7	.4	0.2	0.8	1.4	2.0	2.5	3.1	3.7	4.3	4.8	5.4	7.4 .04
34.5	5.8	11.5	17.3	23.0	28.8	.5	0.3	0.9	1.4	2.0	2.6	3.2	3.7	4.3	4.9	5.5	9.1 .05 / 10.7 .06
34.6	5.8	11.5	17.3	23.1	28.8	.6	0.3	0.9	1.5	2.1	2.6	3.2	3.8	4.4	4.9	5.5	12.3 .07
34.7	5.8	11.6	17.4	23.2	28.9	.7	0.4	1.0	1.6	2.1	2.7	3.3	3.9	4.4	5.0	5.6	14.0 .08
34.8	5.8	11.6	17.4	23.2	29.0	.8	0.5	1.0	1.6	2.2	2.8	3.3	3.9	4.5	5.1	5.6	15.6 .09
34.9	5.9	11.7	17.5	23.3	29.1	.9	0.5	1.1	1.7	2.2	2.8	3.4	4.0	4.5	5.1	5.7	17.3 .10 / 18.9 .11
35.0	5.8	11.6	17.5	23.3	29.1	.0	0.0	0.6	1.2	1.8	2.4	3.0	3.5	4.1	4.7	5.3	20.6 .12
35.1	5.8	11.7	17.5	23.4	29.2	.1	0.1	0.7	1.2	1.8	2.4	3.0	3.6	4.2	4.8	5.4	22.2 .13
35.2	5.8	11.7	17.6	23.4	29.3	.2	0.1	0.7	1.3	1.9	2.5	3.1	3.7	4.3	4.9	5.4	23.9 .14
35.3	5.9	11.8	17.6	23.5	29.4	.3	0.2	0.8	1.4	2.0	2.5	3.1	3.7	4.3	4.9	5.5	25.5 .15
35.4	5.9	11.8	17.7	23.6	29.5	.4	0.2	0.8	1.4	2.0	2.6	3.2	3.8	4.4	5.0	5.6	27.2 .16
35.5	5.9	11.8	17.8	23.7	29.6	.5	0.3	0.9	1.5	2.1	2.7	3.3	3.8	4.4	5.0	5.6	28.8 .17
35.6	5.9	11.8	17.8	23.7	29.7	.6	0.4	0.9	1.5	2.1	2.7	3.3	3.9	4.5	5.1	5.7	30.4 .18
35.7	6.0	11.9	17.9	23.8	29.8	.7	0.4	1.0	1.6	2.2	2.8	3.4	4.0	4.6	5.1	5.7	32.1 .19
35.8	6.0	12.0	17.9	23.9	29.9	.8	0.5	1.1	1.7	2.2	2.8	3.4	4.0	4.6	5.2	5.8	33.7 .20
35.9	6.0	12.0	18.0	24.0	30.0	.9	0.5	1.1	1.7	2.3	2.9	3.5	4.1	4.7	5.3	5.9	35.4 .21
36.0	6.0	12.0	18.0	24.0	30.0	.0	0.0	0.6	1.2	1.8	2.4	3.0	3.6	4.3	4.9	5.5	0.8
36.1	6.0	12.0	18.0	24.0	30.1	.1	0.1	0.7	1.3	1.9	2.5	3.1	3.7	4.3	4.9	5.5	2.5 .01
36.2	6.0	12.0	18.1	24.1	30.1	.2	0.1	0.7	1.3	1.9	2.6	3.2	3.8	4.4	5.0	5.6	4.2 .02
36.3	6.0	12.1	18.1	24.2	30.2	.3	0.2	0.8	1.4	2.0	2.6	3.2	3.8	4.4	5.0	5.7	5.9 .03
36.4	6.1	12.1	18.2	24.3	30.3	.4	0.2	0.9	1.5	2.1	2.7	3.3	3.9	4.5	5.1	5.7	7.6 .04
36.5	6.1	12.2	18.3	24.3	30.4	.5	0.3	0.9	1.5	2.1	2.7	3.3	4.0	4.6	5.2	5.8	9.3 .05 / 11.0 .06
36.6	6.1	12.2	18.3	24.4	30.5	.6	0.4	1.0	1.6	2.2	2.8	3.4	4.0	4.6	5.2	5.8	12.7 .07
36.7	6.1	12.3	18.4	24.5	30.6	.7	0.4	1.0	1.6	2.3	2.9	3.5	4.1	4.7	5.3	5.9	14.4 .08
36.8	6.2	12.3	18.4	24.6	30.7	.8	0.5	1.1	1.7	2.3	2.9	3.5	4.1	4.7	5.4	6.0	16.1 .09
36.9	6.2	12.3	18.5	24.6	30.8	.9	0.5	1.2	1.8	2.4	3.0	3.6	4.2	4.8	5.4	6.0	17.8 .10
42.0	7.0	14.0	21.0	28.0	35.0	.0	0.0	0.7	1.4	2.1	2.8	3.5	4.2	5.0	5.7	6.4	1.0
42.1	7.0	14.0	21.0	28.0	35.1	.1	0.1	0.8	1.5	2.2	2.9	3.6	4.3	5.0	5.7	6.4	3.0 .01
42.2	7.0	14.0	21.1	28.1	35.1	.2	0.1	0.8	1.6	2.3	3.0	3.7	4.4	5.1	5.8	6.5	4.9 .02
42.3	7.0	14.1	21.1	28.2	35.2	.3	0.2	0.9	1.6	2.3	3.0	3.8	4.5	5.2	5.9	6.6	6.9 .03
42.4	7.1	14.1	21.2	28.3	35.3	.4	0.3	1.0	1.7	2.4	3.1	3.8	4.5	5.2	5.9	6.6	8.9 .04
42.5	7.1	14.2	21.3	28.3	35.4	.5	0.4	1.1	1.8	2.5	3.2	3.9	4.6	5.3	6.0	6.7	10.8 .05
42.6	7.1	14.2	21.3	28.4	35.5	.6	0.4	1.1	1.8	2.5	3.3	4.0	4.7	5.4	6.1	6.8	12.8 .06
42.7	7.1	14.3	21.4	28.5	35.6	.7	0.5	1.2	1.9	2.6	3.3	4.0	4.7	5.4	6.2	6.9	14.8 .07
42.8	7.2	14.3	21.4	28.6	35.7	.8	0.6	1.3	2.0	2.7	3.4	4.1	4.8	5.5	6.2	6.9	16.7 .08
42.9	7.2	14.3	21.4	28.6	35.8	.9	0.6	1.3	2.1	2.8	3.5	4.2	4.9	5.6	6.3	7.0	18.7 .09
43.0	7.1	14.3	21.5	28.6	35.8	.0	0.0	0.7	1.4	2.2	2.9	3.6	4.3	5.1	5.8	6.5	20.7 .10
43.1	7.2	14.3	21.5	28.7	35.9	.1	0.1	0.8	1.5	2.2	3.0	3.7	4.4	5.1	5.9	6.6	22.7 .11
43.2	7.2	14.4	21.6	28.8	36.0	.2	0.1	0.9	1.6	2.3	3.0	3.7	4.5	5.2	5.9	6.7	24.6 .12
43.3	7.2	14.4	21.6	28.9	36.1	.3	0.2	0.9	1.7	2.4	3.1	3.8	4.6	5.3	6.0	6.7	26.6 .13
43.4	7.2	14.5	21.7	28.9	36.2	.4	0.3	1.0	1.7	2.5	3.2	3.9	4.6	5.4	6.1	6.8	28.6 .14
43.5	7.3	14.5	21.8	29.0	36.3	.5	0.4	1.1	1.8	2.5	3.3	4.0	4.7	5.4	6.2	6.9	30.5 .15
43.6	7.3	14.5	21.8	29.1	36.3	.6	0.4	1.1	1.9	2.6	3.3	4.0	4.8	5.5	6.2	7.0	32.5 .16
43.7	7.3	14.6	21.9	29.2	36.4	.7	0.5	1.2	2.0	2.7	3.4	4.1	4.9	5.6	6.3	7.0	34.5 .17
43.8	7.3	14.6	21.9	29.2	36.5	.8	0.6	1.3	2.0	2.8	3.5	4.2	4.9	5.7	6.4	7.1	36.4 .18
43.9	7.4	14.7	22.0	29.3	36.6	.9	0.7	1.4	2.1	2.8	3.6	4.3	5.0	5.7	6.5	7.2	

The Double-Second-Difference correction (Corr.) is always to be added to the tabulated altitude.

Fig. 2512. Pub No. 229, Interpolation Table (extract).

Next move over to the portion of the table marked "Units" that is directly adjacent to the Dec. Inc. value you just used and locate the appropriate units column—in this case, the column marked "4'" would be the appropriate one (corresponding to the "4" in the d value of "34.5"). Then move vertically within that column until you find the intersection marked .5 (corresponding to the ".5" component of the d value of "34.5")—in figure 2512 you can see that a value of 2.1 is found at that intersection. Note that each whole minute of Dec. Inc. has its own block of ten rows for its use across all the tens-and-units columns; it is important to stay in the right block. Adding the two extracted values, 14.4 and 2.1, gives you a total value of 16.5 (the same value arrived at by calculation in the mathematical interpolation above) that can then be added to the Hc value you found in the main table for 17° to get the actual computed altitude (Hc) for declination 17° 28.7′:

Hc correction + Hc (tabulated) = actual Hc
16.5′ + 55° 09.7′ = 55° 26.2′

This interpolation table is a great convenience to the navigator. Its use may occasionally lead to a small error in the Hc not exceeding 0.1′, but such error is acceptable in the course of ordinary navigation. Again, beware of possible negative values of the correction.

Double-second Difference

2513 About 1 percent of the time, another correction is needed. The linear interpolation tables are sufficiently accurate for altitudes below 60°, but above that figure, the accuracy of linear interpolation decreases, and an additional difference correction will be necessary for some, though not all, reductions. The interpolation tables are designed to permit, where required, correction for the effect of this difference, thereby allowing full precision to be obtained in the computed altitude. The technique used for these additional corrections is known as applying the *double-second difference* (DSD). The corrections are listed in the form of boxed tables of critical values at the right side of each half-page panel of figures in the interpolation table and are labeled at the top of the block "Double Second Diff. and Corr." (see fig. 2512). To alert the user in those cases in which second differences are significant, that is, where omission of the correction for second difference might cause an error in excess of 0.25′ in the calculated altitude, the value of d is printed in the main table in italics, and is followed by a dot. In figure 2513 you can see that the d value for latitude 75° and declination 68° is so labeled (italics and a dot) and would require a double-second difference correction, while the d value for 67° just above it would not.

An example of using the double-second difference correction would be as follows. Using figure 2513,

29°, 331° L.H.A.   LATITUDE SAME NAME AS DECLINATION

N. Lat. { L.H.A. greater than 180°...Zn = Z / L.H.A. less than 180°........Zn = 360° − Z }

Dec.	75° Hc	d	Z	76° Hc	d	Z	77° Hc	d	Z	78° Hc	d	Z	79° Hc	d	Z	80° Hc	d	Z	81° Hc	d	Z	82° Hc	d	Z	Dec.
0	13 05.0	+59.5	150.2	12 12.9	+59.6	150.3	11 20.8	+59.6	150.4	10 28.6	+59.7	150.5	9 36.4	+59.7	150.5	8 44.1	+59.8	150.6	7 51.8	+59.9	150.7	6 59.5	+59.9	150.8	0
1	14 04.5	59.5	150.0	13 12.5	59.6	150.1	12 20.4	59.7	150.3	11 28.3	59.7	150.4	10 36.1	59.8	150.5	9 43.9	59.8	150.5	8 51.7	59.8	150.6	7 59.4	59.8	150.7	1
65	76 11.4	+50.4	120.9	75 39.1	+52.4	124.2	75 04.0	+54.0	127.3	74 26.4	+55.4	130.2	73 46.7	+56.4	132.8	73 04.9	+57.3	135.2	72 21.5	+58.0	137.5	71 36.6	+58.5	139.5	65
66	77 01.8	49.0	118.5	76 31.5	51.2	122.2	75 58.0	53.1	125.6	75 21.8	54.6	128.7	74 43.1	55.9	131.6	74 02.2	57.0	134.2	73 19.5	57.7	136.6	72 35.1	58.4	138.8	66
67	77 50.8	47.3	115.9	77 22.7	49.9	119.9	76 51.1	52.1	123.6	76 16.4	53.9	127.0	75 39.0	55.4	130.2	74 59.2	56.5	133.0	74 17.2	57.5	135.6	73 33.5	58.2	138.0	67
68	78 38.1	45.1	112.8	78 12.6	48.3	117.3	77 43.2	50.9	121.4	77 10.3	53.0	125.1	76 34.4	54.6	128.5	75 55.7	56.0	131.7	75 14.7	57.1	134.5	74 31.7	57.9	137.1	68
69	79 23.2	42.5	109.4	79 00.9	46.2	114.3	78 34.1	49.2	118.8	78 03.3	51.8	122.9	77 29.0	53.8	126.7	76 51.7	55.4	130.1	76 11.8	56.6	133.3	75 29.6	57.6	136.1	69
70	80 05.7	+39.4	105.4	79 47.1	+43.6	110.8	79 23.3	+47.3	115.8	78 55.1	+50.3	120.4	78 22.8	+52.7	124.6	77 47.1	+54.6	128.4	77 08.4	+56.2	131.8	76 27.2	+57.3	134.9	70
71	80 45.1	35.4	100.9	80 30.7	40.5	106.8	80 10.6	44.8	112.3	79 45.4	48.4	117.4	79 15.5	51.4	122.1	78 41.7	53.7	126.4	78 04.6	55.4	130.2	77 24.5	56.8	133.6	71
72	81 20.5	30.6	95.7	81 11.2	36.4	102.1	80 55.4	41.7	108.3	80 33.8	46.0	114.0	80 06.9	49.6	119.2	79 35.4	52.4	124.0	79 00.0	54.6	128.3	78 21.3	56.2	132.1	72
73	81 51.1	24.8	89.8	81 47.6	31.6	96.7	81 37.1	37.6	103.5	81 19.8	42.9	109.9	80 56.5	47.3	115.8	80 27.8	50.8	121.2	79 54.6	53.5	126.0	79 17.5	55.5	130.3	73
74	82 15.9	18.2	83.2	82 19.2	25.6	90.6	82 14.7	32.6	98.0	82 02.7	39.0	105.1	81 43.8	44.3	111.7	81 18.6	48.7	117.8	80 48.1	52.0	123.3	80 13.0	54.6	128.1	74
89	75 52.0	52.0	2.0	76 52.0	52.0	2.1	77 51.9	51.9	2.3	78 51.9	51.9	2.5	79 51.8	51.8	2.8	80 51.7	51.7	3.1	81 51.6	51.6	3.4	82 51.5	51.5	3.9	89
90	75 00.0	-52.9	0.0	76 00.0	-52.9	0.0	77 00.0	-53.0	0.0	78 00.0	-53.0	0.0	79 00.0	-53.1	0.0	80 00.0	-53.1	0.0	81 00.0	-53.2	0.0	82 00.0	-53.3	0.0	90
	75°			76°			77°			78°			79°			80°			81°			82°			

29°, 331° L.H.A.   LATITUDE SAME NAME AS DECLINATION

Fig. 2513. Portion of a page from Pub. No. 229 with entries requiring a double-second difference correction.

enter the main tables with L76° N, LHA 29°, and Dec. 69° 28.4′ N. Note that the value of d corresponding to the whole degree of declination in the main table is 46.2′. Because it is printed in italics and followed by a dot, a double-second difference correction is required. Looking at the lines just above and below in this table, you note that the value of d, for Dec. 68° (one line above the selected entry) is 48.3′, and for Dec. 70° (one line below) it is 43.6′. The difference of these values is 4.7′. Going to the column at the right of the Interpolation Table (see fig. 2512), headed "Double Second Diff. and Corr.," find the box corresponding to the "Dec. Inc." of 28.4 and enter this section with the 4.7′ difference, to obtain the correction of 0.3′ by noting that 4.7 falls between 4.0 and 5.6. *This correction is always additive* and is added to the other interpolated value that you would find as described above, which in this case would amount to 21.9′ by arithmetic or 21.8′ by interpolation table.

Mathematical Interpolation of Azimuth Angle

2514   The value of the azimuth angle (Z) can also change significantly with each degree of declination. Interpolation of azimuth angle may also be interpolated for the actual value of the declination to improve accuracy, based upon the difference in declination between the whole degree quantities found in the main table.

Interpolating Z by calculation is virtually the same as the method used for interpolating Hc. First extract from the main tables of Pub. No. 229 the values of Z for the whole degrees above and below the actual declination—call this value the "Z diff." (for Z difference). It is equivalent to the d factor for Hc but

is not supplied in the tables. Multiply that figure by the Dec. Inc. and divide the product by 60 just as you did when interpolating for Hc. The resulting equation can be expressed as

$$\frac{\text{Z diff.} \times \text{Dec. Inc.}}{60} = \text{Z correction}$$

The sign of Z diff. is determined by inspection of the tables; if the values of Z are increasing, the sign is positive, and if they are decreasing, Z diff. is negative.

For example, if you were in the vicinity of latitude 75° N and you determined an observed body to have a declination of 69° 35.0′ N and a local hour angle of 29°, you would first go to the main tables of Pub. No. 229 (see fig. 2513) and determine that the Z values for the two straddling, whole-degree declination values (69° and 70°) are 109.4° and 105.4°, respectively. The difference in these two Z values (Z diff.) is 4.0 and is determined to be a negative quantity because an inspection of the table shows that the Z quantities are diminishing as declination increases. Multiplying −4.0 by the declination difference (35.0) and then dividing by 60, because the difference is measured over 60′ of arc (69° to 70°), yields a Z correction of −2.3′ as indicated:

$$\frac{\text{Z diff.} \times \text{Dec. Inc.}}{60} = \text{Z correction}$$

$$\frac{-4.0 \times 35.0}{60} = -2.3$$

Applying that difference to the Z obtained for the entering whole degree:

109.4 (Tabulated Z) – 2.3 (Interpolated difference [calculated]) = 107.1 (Actual Z)

Converting the azimuth angle to a true azimuth using the appropriate rule (360° – Z) for N latitude and LHA less than 180° yields an azimuth of 248. For plotting a celestial LOP, precision in azimuth to the nearest half-degree is adequate, and so use of DSD for azimuth determination is not necessary.

Tabular Interpolation of Z

2515   To interpolate the azimuth angle (Z) by using the tables provided inside the covers of Pub. No. 229, substitute the difference between the two tabulated azimuth angles (Z diff.) as your secondary argument (equivalent to the d factor you used when interpolating the Hc value).

Using the figures in the above example, you would enter the left side of the interpolation table with Dec. Inc. (35.0), just as when interpolating Hc. Next move across the table using the Z diff. factor (see fig. 2512). Because the Z diff. in this case is only –4.0°, it is not necessary to include the "tens" factor which is zero. Moving to the "units" section of the table, find the correction corresponding to the 4.0 figure, which is "2.4." As you can see, this figure is one tenth of a degree different from the 2.3 figure derived by calculation above. This is an acceptable difference, but remember to apply the minus sign where appropriate, as here.

As with the calculated interpolation, this tabular interpolation would be combined with the Z figure extracted from the main table to determine the actual azimuth angle corresponding to the actual declination.

109.4 (Tabulated Z) – 2.4 (Interpolated difference [tabular]) = 107.0 (Actual Z)

Using the Results

2516   You will recall that solving the navigational triangle and ultimately plotting your solution as an LOP requires:
1. comparing the observed altitude (Ho) with a computed altitude (Hc) to determine their difference, called an *altitude intercept* (a) (so that you will know whether your LOP should be plotted *toward* the observed body or *away* from it).
2. determining the direction (*azimuth* or *Zn*) in which the geographical position (GP) of the body being observed bears from the assumed position (AP) of the observer, so that an LOP may be plotted perpendicular to it.

By providing you the computed altitude (Hc) and azimuth angle (Z) corresponding to the entering arguments, Pub. No. 229 gives you what you need to accomplish these steps.

Determining Intercept

2517   To determine the intercept (a) for plotting the resulting lines of position, the Hc you obtain from Pub. No. 229 is compared to the observed altitude (Ho). This intercept must be defined as being toward or away from the observed body (in the direction of the determined azimuth or in the direction of its reciprocal).

As explained earlier, a lesser observed altitude places the circle of equal altitude, and therefore the resulting LOP, farther from the GP of the body than does a larger altitude. Accordingly, if Hc is greater than Ho, the actual position from which the observation was made would be farther from the GP of the body than is the assumed position. Similarly, if Ho is the greater, the actual position would be nearer the GP. The intercept you have gleaned from Pub. No. 229 should always be labeled accordingly, using the suffix "T" (toward) or "A" (away), to make clear in which direction to measure. The phrase "Computed Greater Away" (remembered by the mnemonic "Coast Guard Academy") helps you to remember this rule as does the acronym "HoMoTo" for "Ho More Toward."

Determining Azimuth

2518   Note that the entering arguments (LHA, Lat., and Dec.) in Pub. No. 229 are *not* designated as north or south, east or west. The reason for this is illustrated in figure 2518a, where four navigational triangles are shown on the surface of the Earth. The Pub. 229 tables are designed such that each of these triangles is covered by the same portion of the tables. The fact that four triangles can be solved by using one set of entering arguments obviously makes it possible to save considerable space in an inspection table.

In each of the four triangles, the assumed position (AP) is at the same latitude (either north or south of the equator). If the numerical value of the latitude of the AP is assumed to be 33°, then the side of the triangle between the AP and the pole in *each* triangle, the colatitude, is equal to an arc of 57°. Similarly, the GP in each triangle is at the same latitude, (numerically equal to the a declination) say 14° (on the same side of the equator as the AP), making the polar distance in each triangle equal to 76°. Further, the four triangles illustrated are constructed so that the angular distance from the meridian of the AP to

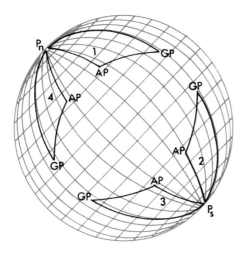

Fig. 2518a. Four numerically equal celestial triangles.

the meridian of the GP is equal in each case, making the numerical value of meridian angle, t, the same in all four triangles. With the two corresponding sides and the included angle of all the triangles being numerically equal, the values of computed altitude and azimuth angle obtained by solving each triangle will be respectively the same in each. Using LHA = 34°, Lat. = 33°, and Dec. = 14°, you can obtain the numerical value of Hc (53° 44.7′) and Z (113.4°) from the tabular extract of figure 2506 as the same for all four triangles.

Note that in each of the four triangles illustrated, the AP and GP are on the same side of the equator—both north or both south. In these cases, the latitude and declination are said to have the *same name*. When the latitude and declination lie on opposite sides of the equator, they are said to have *contrary names*. Solutions are provided for both sets of triangles by means of the tables being divided into two parts, "Latitude Same Name as Declination" and "Latitude Contrary Name to Declination." Figures 2518b and 2518c show a sample pair of left-hand and right-hand pages from Pub. No. 229. For each opening of the tables of Pub. No. 229, the left-hand page is always limited to tabulations for declination and latitude of the *same* name. On the upper portion of the right-hand page are stated the tabulations for declination and latitude of *contrary* name; in the lower portions of these right-hand pages are given tabulations for the supplementary values of LHA, those from 90° to 270° (t zero through 90°), for declinations of the same name as latitude. The upper and lower sections of each right-hand page are separated by horizontal lines in each column of data (causing a stair-step appearance); these are known as the *Contrary-Same Lines*, or C-S Lines,

and indicate the degree of declination in which the celestial horizon occurs (where the altitude reaches zero).

Since each of the solutions obtained from the tables can apply to multiple triangles, the names north and south (for latitude and declination) or east and west (for meridian angle) are omitted in the tabulation, and must be supplied by the navigator as appropriate for the particular triangle being solved.

Remembering that the azimuth is the direction of the GP from the AP, the azimuth angle (Z) obtained from the table must be converted to true azimuth (Zn) to be conveniently usable on a chart. The Zn differs for each triangle, since the true direction of the GP from the AP is different in each case. Referring to figure 2518a, you can see that the Z in the first triangle is N and E (i.e., the reference pole is North and the direction of the GP from the AP is east); Zn therefore equals Z. In the second triangle, the Z is S and E, since the reference pole is South and the direction of GP from AP is east; in this case you must subtract Z from 180° to get Zn. In the third triangle, Z is S and W, so Zn equals 180° + Z. In the fourth triangle, Z is N and W; Zn therefore equals 360° − Z. Rules for making these conversions using LHA are repeated on every set of facing pages in Pub. No. 229—rules for north latitudes (LHA greater than 180° means that Zn and Z are equal, and LHA less than 180° requires Z to be subtracted from 360° in order to obtain Zn) are on the left-hand page at the top, near the spine of the book; rules for south latitudes (LHA greater than 180° means that Z must be subtracted from 180°, and LHA less than 180° requires Z to be added to 180° in order to obtain Zn) are on the right-hand page, at the bottom, near the spine of the book (see figs. 2518b and 2518c).

Plotting the LOP

2519   Once you have determined the altitude and azimuth, you are ready to plot your LOP by using your assumed position (AP) as a reference point, drawing an azimuth line through it and constructing your LOP perpendicular to the azimuth either toward or away from the GP of the observed celestial body. This process is explained in detail in chapter 26.

Possible Errors from Use of an AP

2520   Pub. No. 229, when used with an assumed position, offers sight reductions that are mathematically accurate. However, as with any sight reduction method designed for use with an assumed posi-

Dec.	30° Hc	d	Z	31° Hc	d	Z	32° Hc	d	Z	33° Hc	d	Z	34° Hc	d	Z	35° Hc	d	Z	36° Hc	d	Z	37° Hc	d	Z	Dec.
°	° ′	′	°	° ′	′	°	° ′	′	°	° ′	′	°	° ′	′	°	° ′	′	°	° ′	′	°	° ′	′	°	°
0	42 18.1	+40.3	121.7	41 46.2	+41.2	122.5	41 13.7	+42.0	123.2	40 40.5	+42.9	123.9	40 06.7	+43.7	124.6	39 32.3	+44.5	125.3	38 57.4	+45.1	126.0	38 21.8	+45.9	126.6	0
1	42 58.4	39.7	120.7	42 27.4	40.7	121.5	41 55.7	41.6	122.2	41 23.4	42.4	123.0	40 50.4	43.2	123.7	40 16.8	44.0	124.4	39 42.5	44.8	125.1	39 07.7	45.5	125.8	1
2	43 38.1	39.2	119.7	43 08.1	40.1	120.5	42 37.3	41.0	121.3	42 05.8	41.9	122.0	41 33.6	42.8	122.8	41 00.8	43.6	123.5	40 27.3	44.4	124.3	39 53.2	45.2	124.9	2
3	44 17.3	38.6	118.6	43 48.2	39.6	119.5	43 18.3	40.5	120.3	42 47.7	41.4	121.1	42 16.4	42.3	121.9	41 44.4	43.1	122.6	41 11.7	44.0	123.4	40 38.4	44.7	124.1	3
4	44 55.9	38.0	117.5	44 27.8	39.0	118.4	43 58.8	40.0	119.3	43 29.1	40.9	120.1	42 58.7	41.8	120.9	42 27.5	42.7	121.7	41 55.7	43.5	122.5	41 23.1	44.4	123.2	4
5	45 33.9	+37.3	116.4	45 06.8	+38.3	117.3	44 38.8	+39.4	118.2	44 10.0	+40.4	119.1	43 40.5	+41.3	119.9	43 10.2	+42.2	120.7	42 39.2	+43.1	121.5	42 07.5	+43.9	122.3	5
6	46 11.2	36.7	115.3	45 45.1	37.8	116.2	45 18.2	38.8	117.1	44 50.4	39.8	118.0	44 21.8	40.7	118.9	43 52.4	41.7	119.7	43 22.3	42.5	120.6	42 51.4	43.4	121.4	6
7	46 47.9	35.9	114.2	46 22.9	37.0	115.1	45 57.0	38.1	116.1	45 30.2	39.1	117.0	45 02.5	40.2	117.9	44 34.1	41.1	118.7	44 04.8	42.1	119.6	43 34.8	43.0	120.4	7
8	47 23.8	35.2	113.0	46 59.9	36.4	114.0	46 35.1	37.5	114.9	46 09.3	38.6	115.9	45 42.7	39.6	116.8	45 15.2	40.6	117.7	44 46.9	41.5	118.6	44 17.8	42.5	119.5	8
9	47 59.0	34.5	111.8	47 36.3	35.6	112.8	47 12.6	36.7	113.8	46 47.9	37.9	114.8	46 22.3	38.9	115.7	45 55.8	40.0	116.7	45 28.4	41.0	117.6	45 00.3	41.9	118.5	9
10	48 33.5	+33.6	110.5	48 11.9	+34.9	111.6	47 49.3	+36.1	112.6	47 25.8	+37.1	113.6	47 01.2	+38.3	114.6	46 35.8	+39.3	115.6	46 09.4	+40.4	116.5	45 42.2	+41.4	117.4	10
11	49 07.1	32.8	109.3	48 46.8	34.0	110.4	48 25.4	35.2	111.4	48 02.9	36.5	112.5	47 39.5	37.6	113.5	47 15.1	38.7	114.5	46 49.8	39.8	115.5	46 23.6	40.8	116.4	11
12	49 39.9	31.9	108.0	49 20.8	33.2	109.1	49 00.6	34.5	110.2	48 39.4	35.7	111.3	48 17.1	36.9	112.3	47 53.8	38.0	113.3	47 29.6	39.1	114.4	47 04.4	40.1	115.3	12
13	50 11.8	31.1	106.7	49 54.0	32.4	107.8	49 35.1	33.7	108.9	49 15.1	34.9	110.0	48 54.0	36.1	111.1	48 31.8	37.3	112.2	48 08.7	38.4	113.2	47 44.5	39.6	114.2	13
14	50 42.9	30.0	105.3	50 26.4	31.4	106.5	50 08.8	32.7	107.7	49 50.0	34.1	108.8	49 30.1	35.3	109.9	49 09.1	36.6	111.0	48 47.1	37.7	112.1	48 24.1	38.8	113.1	14
15	51 12.9	+29.1	104.0	50 57.8	+30.5	105.2	50 41.5	+31.9	106.3	50 24.1	+33.2	107.5	50 05.4	+34.5	108.7	49 45.7	+35.7	109.8	49 24.8	+37.0	110.9	49 02.9	+38.2	112.0	15
16	51 42.0	28.0	102.6	51 28.3	29.5	103.8	51 13.4	30.9	105.0	50 57.3	32.3	106.2	50 39.9	33.7	107.4	50 21.4	35.0	108.5	50 01.8	36.2	109.7	49 41.1	37.4	110.8	16
17	52 10.0	27.0	101.1	51 57.8	28.5	102.4	51 44.3	29.9	103.6	51 29.6	31.3	104.8	51 13.6	32.7	106.1	50 56.4	34.0	107.2	50 38.0	35.4	108.4	50 18.5	36.6	109.6	17
18	52 37.0	25.9	99.7	52 26.3	27.4	100.9	52 14.2	28.9	102.2	52 00.9	30.4	103.5	51 46.3	31.8	104.7	51 30.4	33.2	105.9	51 13.4	34.5	107.1	50 55.1	35.8	108.3	18
19	53 02.9	24.7	98.2	52 53.7	26.3	99.5	52 43.1	27.9	100.8	52 31.3	29.3	102.1	52 18.1	30.8	103.3	52 03.6	32.2	104.6	51 47.9	33.6	105.8	51 30.9	35.0	107.0	19
20	53 27.6	+23.6	96.6	53 20.0	+25.2	98.0	53 11.0	+26.7	99.3	53 00.6	+28.3	100.6	52 48.9	+29.7	101.9	52 35.8	+31.3	103.2	52 21.5	+32.6	104.5	52 05.9	+34.0	105.7	20
21	53 51.2	22.3	95.1	53 45.2	23.9	96.5	53 37.7	25.6	97.8	53 28.9	27.1	99.1	53 18.6	28.7	100.5	53 07.1	30.2	101.8	52 54.1	31.7	103.1	52 39.9	33.1	104.4	21
22	54 13.5	21.1	93.5	54 09.1	22.8	94.9	54 03.3	24.4	96.3	53 56.0	26.0	97.6	53 47.3	27.6	99.0	53 37.3	29.1	100.3	53 25.8	30.7	101.7	53 13.0	32.1	103.0	22
23	54 34.6	19.8	91.9	54 31.9	21.4	93.3	54 27.7	23.1	94.7	54 22.0	24.8	96.1	54 14.9	26.4	97.5	54 06.4	28.0	98.9	53 56.5	29.5	100.2	53 45.1	31.1	101.6	23
24	54 54.4	18.4	90.3	54 53.3	20.2	91.7	54 50.8	21.9	93.1	54 46.8	23.6	94.5	54 41.3	25.3	95.9	54 34.4	26.8	97.3	54 26.0	28.5	98.7	54 16.2	30.0	100.1	24
25	55 12.8	+17.0	88.6	55 13.5	+18.8	90.1	55 12.7	+20.5	91.5	55 10.4	+22.2	92.9	55 06.6	+23.9	94.4	55 01.2	+25.7	95.8	54 54.5	+27.2	97.2	54 46.2	+28.9	98.6	25
26	55 29.8	15.7	86.9	55 32.3	17.4	88.4	55 33.2	19.2	89.8	55 32.6	21.0	91.3	55 30.5	22.7	92.7	55 26.9	24.4	94.2	55 21.7	26.1	95.6	55 15.1	27.7	97.1	26
27	55 45.5	14.2	85.2	55 49.7	16.0	86.7	55 52.4	17.8	88.2	55 53.6	19.6	89.6	55 53.2	21.3	91.1	55 51.3	23.0	92.6	55 47.8	24.8	94.1	55 42.8	26.5	95.5	27
28	55 59.7	12.7	83.5	56 05.7	14.6	85.0	56 10.2	16.4	86.4	56 13.2	18.1	87.9	56 14.5	20.0	89.4	56 14.3	21.8	90.9	56 12.6	23.5	92.4	56 09.3	25.2	93.9	28
29	56 12.4	11.2	81.7	56 20.3	13.0	83.2	56 26.6	14.9	84.7	56 31.3	16.7	86.2	56 34.5	18.5	87.7	56 36.1	20.3	89.2	56 36.1	22.1	90.8	56 34.5	23.9	92.3	29
30	56 23.6	+ 9.7	80.0	56 33.3	+11.5	81.4	56 41.5	+13.3	83.0	56 48.0	+15.3	84.5	56 53.0	+17.1	86.0	56 56.4	+18.9	87.5	56 58.2	+20.7	89.1	56 58.4	+22.5	90.6	30
31	56 33.3	8.2	78.2	56 44.8	10.0	79.7	56 54.8	11.9	81.2	57 03.3	13.7	82.7	57 10.1	15.5	84.2	57 15.3	17.4	85.8	57 18.9	19.3	87.3	57 20.9	21.1	88.9	31
32	56 41.5	6.5	76.4	56 54.8	8.5	77.9	57 06.7	10.3	79.4	57 17.0	12.1	80.9	57 25.6	14.1	82.4	57 32.7	15.9	84.0	57 38.2	17.8	85.6	57 42.0	19.6	87.1	32
33	56 48.0	5.0	74.6	57 03.3	6.8	76.0	57 17.0	8.6	77.6	57 29.1	10.6	79.1	57 39.7	12.4	80.6	57 48.6	14.4	82.2	57 56.0	16.2	83.8	58 01.6	18.1	85.4	33
34	56 53.0	3.4	72.7	57 10.1	5.2	74.2	57 25.6	7.1	75.7	57 39.7	8.9	77.2	57 52.1	10.9	78.8	58 03.0	12.7	80.4	58 12.2	14.6	82.0	58 19.7	16.6	83.6	34
35	56 56.4	+ 1.8	70.9	57 15.3	+ 3.6	72.4	57 32.7	+ 5.5	73.9	57 48.6	+ 7.4	75.4	58 03.0	+ 9.2	76.9	58 15.7	+11.1	78.5	58 26.8	+13.1	80.1	58 36.3	+15.0	81.7	35
36	56 58.2	+ 0.2	69.1	57 18.9	2.0	70.5	57 38.2	3.8	72.0	57 56.0	5.6	73.5	58 12.2	7.5	75.1	58 26.8	9.5	76.6	58 39.9	11.4	78.2	58 51.3	13.3	79.9	36
37	56 58.4	− 1.5	67.2	57 20.9	+ 0.3	68.7	57 42.0	2.1	70.1	58 01.6	4.0	71.7	58 19.7	5.9	73.2	58 36.3	7.8	74.8	58 51.3	9.7	76.3	59 04.6	11.7	78.0	37
38	56 56.9	3.0	65.4	57 21.2	− 1.3	66.8	57 44.1	+ 0.5	68.3	58 05.6	2.4	69.8	58 25.6	4.2	71.3	58 44.1	6.1	72.8	59 01.0	8.0	74.4	59 16.3	10.0	76.1	38
39	56 53.9	4.7	63.6	57 19.9	2.9	65.0	57 44.6	− 1.1	66.4	58 08.0	+ 0.6	67.9	58 29.8	2.5	69.4	58 50.2	4.4	70.9	59 09.0	6.3	72.5	59 26.3	8.2	74.1	39
40	56 49.2	− 6.2	61.8	57 17.0	− 4.5	63.1	57 43.5	− 2.8	64.5	58 08.6	− 1.0	66.0	58 32.3	+ 0.8	67.5	58 54.6	+ 2.6	69.0	59 15.3	+ 4.5	70.6	59 34.5	+ 6.5	72.2	40
41	56 43.0	7.8	59.9	57 12.5	6.2	61.3	57 40.7	4.5	62.7	58 07.6	2.8	64.1	58 33.1	− 0.9	65.6	58 57.2	+ 0.9	67.1	59 19.8	2.8	68.6	59 41.0	4.6	70.2	41
42	56 35.2	9.3	58.1	57 06.3	7.7	59.4	57 36.2	6.1	60.8	58 04.8	4.4	62.2	58 32.2	2.7	63.6	58 58.1	− 0.8	65.1	59 22.6	+ 1.0	66.7	59 45.6	3.0	68.2	42
43	56 25.9	10.9	56.3	56 58.6	9.4	57.6	57 30.1	7.7	58.9	58 00.4	6.0	60.3	58 29.5	4.3	61.7	58 57.3	2.6	63.2	59 23.6	− 0.7	64.7	59 48.6	+ 1.1	66.2	43
44	56 15.0	12.4	54.6	56 49.2	10.9	55.8	57 22.4	9.3	57.1	57 54.4	7.7	58.4	58 25.2	6.1	59.8	58 54.7	4.3	61.2	59 22.9	2.5	62.7	59 49.7	− 0.7	64.3	44
45	56 02.6	−13.9	52.8	56 38.3	−12.4	54.0	57 13.1	−10.9	55.3	57 46.7	− 9.4	56.6	58 19.1	− 7.7	57.9	58 50.4	− 6.0	59.3	59 20.4	− 4.3	60.8	59 49.0	− 2.5	62.3	45
46	55 48.7	15.3	51.1	56 25.9	13.9	52.2	57 02.2	12.5	53.5	57 37.3	10.9	54.7	58 11.4	9.3	56.0	58 44.4	7.8	57.4	59 16.1	6.1	58.8	59 46.5	4.3	60.3	46
47	55 33.4	16.8	49.4	56 12.0	15.4	50.5	56 49.7	14.0	51.7	57 26.4	12.5	52.9	58 02.1	11.0	54.2	58 36.6	9.4	55.5	59 10.0	7.7	56.9	59 42.2	6.0	58.3	47
48	55 16.6	18.1	47.7	55 56.6	16.8	48.8	56 35.7	15.5	49.9	57 13.9	14.1	51.1	57 51.1	12.6	52.3	58 27.2	11.0	53.6	59 02.3	9.5	54.9	59 36.2	7.9	56.3	48
49	54 58.5	19.5	46.0	55 39.8	18.3	47.1	56 20.2	16.9	48.1	56 59.8	15.5	49.3	57 38.5	14.2	50.5	58 16.2	12.7	51.7	58 52.8	11.2	53.0	59 28.3	9.5	54.4	49
50	54 39.0	−20.8	44.4	55 21.5	−19.5	45.4	56 03.3	−18.3	46.4	56 44.3	−17.1	47.5	57 24.3	−15.7	48.7	58 03.5	−14.3	49.9	58 41.6	−12.8	51.1	59 18.8	−11.3	52.4	50
51	54 18.2	22.0	42.7	55 02.0	21.0	43.7	55 45.0	19.8	44.7	56 27.2	18.5	45.8	57 08.6	17.2	46.9	57 49.2	15.8	48.0	58 28.8	14.4	49.2	59 07.5	12.9	50.4	51
52	53 56.2	23.3	41.2	54 41.0	22.2	42.1	55 25.2	21.1	43.1	56 08.7	19.9	44.1	56 51.4	18.6	45.1	57 33.4	17.4	46.2	58 14.4	16.0	47.4	58 54.6	14.6	48.6	52
53	53 32.9	24.5	39.6	54 18.8	23.4	40.5	55 04.1	22.3	41.4	55 48.8	21.2	42.4	56 32.8	20.1	43.4	57 16.0	18.9	44.5	57 58.4	17.5	45.6	58 40.0	16.2	46.7	53
54	53 08.4	25.6	38.1	53 55.4	24.7	38.9	54 41.8	23.7	39.8	55 27.6	22.6	40.7	56 12.7	21.5	41.7	56 57.1	20.2	42.7	57 40.9	19.1	43.8	58 23.8	17.8	44.9	54
55	52 42.8	−26.8	36.6	53 30.7	−25.8	37.4	54 18.1	−24.8	38.2	55 05.0	−23.9	39.1	55 51.2	−22.8	40.0	56 36.9	−21.7	41.0	57 21.8	−20.5	42.0	58 06.0	−19.3	43.1	55
56	52 16.0	27.8	35.1	53 04.9	27.0	35.9	53 53.3	26.1	36.7	54 41.1	25.1	37.5	55 28.4	24.0	38.4	56 15.2	23.0	39.3	57 01.3	21.9	40.3	57 46.7	20.7	41.3	56
57	51 48.2	28.9	33.7	52 37.9	28.0	34.4	53 27.2	27.2	35.1	54 16.0	26.2	35.9	55 04.4	25.4	36.8	55 52.2	24.4	37.7	56 39.4	23.3	38.6	57 26.0	22.2	39.5	57
58	51 19.3	29.8	32.3	52 09.9	29.1	32.9	53 00.0	28.2	33.7	53 49.8	27.4	34.4	54 39.0	26.5	35.2	55 27.8	25.6	36.0	56 16.1	24.6	36.9	57 03.8	23.6	37.8	58
59	50 49.5	30.8	30.9	51 40.8	30.1	31.5	52 31.8	29.3	32.2	53 22.4	28.6	32.9	54 12.5	27.7	33.7	55 02.2	26.8	34.4	55 51.5	25.9	35.3	56 40.2	24.9	36.1	59
60	50 18.7	−31.7	29.5	51 10.7	−31.0	30.1	52 02.5	−30.4	30.8	52 53.8	−29.5	31.4	53 44.8	−28.8	32.1	54 35.4	−27.9	32.9	55 25.6	−27.1	33.7	56 15.3	−26.2	34.5	60
61	49 47.0	32.7	28.2	50 39.7	32.0	28.8	51 32.1	31.3	29.4	52 24.3	30.6	30.0	53 16.0	29.8	30.7	54 07.5	29.1	31.4	54 58.5	28.3	32.1	55 49.1	27.4	32.9	61
62	49 14.3	33.4	26.9	50 07.7	32.8	27.4	51 00.8	32.2	28.0	51 53.7	31.6	28.6	52 46.2	30.9	29.2	53 38.4	30.2	29.9	54 30.2	29.4	30.6	55 21.7	28.6	31.3	62
63	48 40.9	34.3	25.6	49 34.9	33.7	26.1	50 28.6	33.1	26.7	51 22.1	32.5	27.2	52 15.3	31.9	27.8	53 08.2	31.2	28.4	54 00.8	30.5	29.1	54 53.1	29.8	29.8	63
64	48 06.6	35.0	24.4	49 01.2	34.6	24.9	49 55.5	34.0	25.4	50 49.6	33.4	25.9	51 43.4	32.8	26.4	52 37.0	32.2	27.0	53 30.3	31.5	27.6	54 23.3	30.8	28.3	64
65	47 31.6	−35.8	23.2	48 26.6	−35.3	23.6	49 21.5	−34.8	24.1	50 16.2	−34.3	24.6	51 10.6	−33.7	25.1	52 04.8	−33.1	25.6	52 58.8	−32.5	26.2	53 52.5	−31.9	26.8	65
66	46 55.8	36.5	22.0	47 51.3	36.0	22.4	48 46.7	35.6	22.9	49 41.9	35.1	23.3	50 36.9	34.6	23.8	51 31.7	34.0	24.3	52 26.3	33.5	24.8	53 20.6	32.9	25.4	66
67	46 19.3	37.2	20.9	47 15.3	36.8	21.2	48 11.1	36.3	21.6	49 06.8	35.9	22.1	50 02.3	35.4	22.5	50 57.7	34.9	23.0	51 52.8	34.4	23.5	52 47.7	33.8	24.0	67
68	45 42.1	37.8	19.7	46 38.5	37.4	20.1	47 34.8	37.0	20.5	48 30.9	36.6	20.8	49 26.9	36.1	21.3	50 22.8	35.8	21.7	51 18.4	35.2	22.2	52 13.9	34.7	22.6	68
69	45 04.3	38.5	18.6	46 01.1	38.1	19.0	46 57.8	37.8	19.3	47 54.3	37.3	19.7	48 50.8	37.0	20.0	49 47.0	36.5	20.4	50 43.2	36.1	20.9	51 39.2	35.6	21.3	69
70	44 25.8	−39.1	17.5	45 23.0	−38.8	17.8	46 20.0	−38.4	18.2	47 17.0	−38.1	18.5	48 13.8	−37.6	18.9	49 10.5	−37.2	19.2	50 07.1	−36.8	19.6	51 03.6	−36.5	20.0	70
71	43 46.7	39.6	16.5	44 44.2	39.3	16.8	45 41.6	39.0	17.1	46 38.9	38.6	17.4	47 36.2	38.4	17.7	48 33.3	38.0	18.0	49 30.3	37.7	18.4	50 27.1	37.2	18.8	71
72	43 07.1	40.2	15.5	44 04.9	39.9	15.7	45 02.6	39.6	16.0	46 00.3	39.4	16.3	46 57.8	39.0	16.6	47 55.3	38.7	16.9	48 52.6	38.3	17.2	49 49.9	38.0	17.5	72
73	42 26.9	40.7	14.4	43 25.0	40.5	14.7	44 23.0	40.2	14.9	45 20.9	39.9	15.2	46 18.8	39.6	15.4	47 16.6	39.3	15.7	48 14.3	39.0	16.0	49 11.9	38.7	16.4	73
74	41 46.2	41.2	13.4	42 44.5	40.9	13.7	43 42.8	40.7	13.9	44 41.0	40.5	14.1	45 39.2	40.2	14.4	46 37.3	40.0	14.6	47 35.3	39.7	14.9	48 33.2	39.4	15.2	74
75	41 05.0	−41.7	12.5	42 03.6	−41.5	12.7	43 02.1	−41.3	12.9	44 00.5	−41.0	13.1	44 59.0	−40.8	13.3	45 57.3	−40.5	13.5	46 55.6	−40.3	13.8	47 53.8	−40.0	14.1	75
76	40 23.3	42.1	11.5	41 22.1	42.0	11.7	42 20.8	41.7	11.9	43 19.5	41.5	12.1	44 18.2	41.4	12.3	45 16.8	41.2	12.5	46 15.3	40.9	12.7	47 13.8	40.6	13.0	76
77	39 41.2	42.6	10.6	40 40.1	42.4	10.8	41 39.1	42.3	10.9	42 38.0	42.1	11.1	43 36.8	41.8	11.3	44 35.6	41.6	11.5	45 34.4	41.4	11.7	46 33.2	41.3	11.9	77
78	38 58.6	43.0	9.7	39 57.7	42.8	9.8	40 56.8	42.6	10.0	41 55.9	42.5	10.1	42 55.0	42.4	10.3	43 54.0	42.2	10.5	44 53.0	42.0	10.6	45 51.9	41.8	10.8	78
79	38 15.6	43.4	8.8	39 14.9	43.3	8.9	40 14.2	43.2	9.1	41 13.4	43.0	9.2	42 12.6	42.8	9.3	43 11.8	42.7	9.5	44 11.0	42.5	9.6	45 10.1	42.3	9.8	79
80	37 32.2	−43.7	7.9	38 31.6	−43.6	8.0	39 31.0	−43.5	8.1	40 30.4	−43.4	8.3	41 29.8	−43.3	8.4	42 29.1	−43.1	8.5	43 28.5	−43.0	8.7	44 27.8	−42.9	8.8	80
81	36 48.5	44.2	7.1	37 48.0	44.0	7.2	38 47.5	43.9	7.3	39 47.0	43.8	7.4	40 46.5	43.7	7.5	41 46.0	43.6	7.6	42 45.5	43.5	7.7	43 44.9	43.3	7.8	81
82	36 04.3	44.5	6.2	37 04.0	44.4	6.3	38 03.6	44.3	6.4	39 03.2	44.2	6.5	40 02.8	44.1	6.6	41 02.4	44.0	6.7	42 02.0	43.9	6.8	43 01.6	43.8	6.9	82
83	35 19.8	44.8	5.4	36 19.6	44.8	5.5	37 19.3	44.7	5.5	38 19.0	44.6	5.6	39 18.7	44.5	5.7	40 18.4	44.4	5.8	41 18.1	44.3	5.9	42 17.8	44.2	6.0	83
84	34 35.0	45.1	4.6	35 34.8	45.0	4.6	36 34.6	45.0	4.7	37 34.4	44.9	4.8	38 34.2	44.8	4.8	39 34.0	44.8	4.9	40 33.8	44.7	5.0	41 33.6	44.7	5.0	84
85	33 49.9	−45.4	3.8	34 49.8	−45.4	3.8	35 49.6	−45.3	3.9	36 49.5	−45.3	3.9	37 49.4	−45.3	4.0	38 49.2	−45.2	4.0	39 49.1	−45.2	4.1	40 48.9	−45.1	4.2	85
86	33 04.5	45.7	3.0	34 04.4	45.7	3.0	35 04.3	45.6	3.1	36 04.2	45.6	3.1	37 04.1	45.5	3.2	38 04.0	45.5	3.2	39 03.9	45.4	3.2	40 03.8	45.4	3.3	86
87	32 18.8	46.0	2.2	33 18.7	46.0	2.3	34 18.7	46.0	2.3	35 18.6	45.9	2.3	36 18.6	45.9	2.3	37 18.5	45.8	2.4	38 18.5	45.9	2.4	39 18.4	45.8	2.4	87
88	31 32.8	46.3	1.5	32 32.7	46.2	1.5	33 32.7	46.2	1.5	34 32.7	46.2	1.5	35 32.7	46.2	1.5	36 32.7	46.2	1.6	37 32.6	46.1	1.6	38 32.6	46.1	1.6	88
89	30 46.5	46.5	0.7	31 46.5	46.5	0.7	32 46.5	46.5	0.7	33 46.5	46.5	0.8	34 46.5	46.5	0.8	35 46.5	46.5	0.8	36 46.5	46.5	0.8	37 46.5	46.5	0.8	89
90	30 00.0	−46.7	0.0	31 00.0	−46.8	0.0	32 00.0	−46.8	0.0	33 00.0	−46.8	0.0	34 00.0	−46.8	0.0	35 00.0	−46.8	0.0	36 00.0	−46.8	0.0	37 00.0	−46.8	0.0	90
	30°			31°			32°			33°			34°			35°			36°			37°			

Fig. 2518b. Sample left-hand page from Pub. No. 229.

LATITUDE CONTRARY NAME TO DECLINATION L.H.A. 39°, 321°

Dec.	30°			31°			32°			33°			34°			35°			36°			37°			Dec.
	Hc	d	Z	Hc	d	Z	Hc	d	Z	Hc	d	Z	Hc	d	Z	Hc	d	Z	Hc	d	Z	Hc	d	Z	
°	° ′	′	°	° ′	′	°	° ′	′	°	° ′	′	°	° ′	′	°	° ′	′	°	° ′	′	°	° ′	′	°	°
0	42 18.1	-40.8	121.7	41 46.2	-41.7	122.5	41 13.7	-42.5	123.2	40 40.5	-43.3	123.9	40 06.7	-44.1	124.6	39 32.3	-44.8	125.3	38 57.4	-45.6	126.0	38 21.8	-46.2	126.6	0
1	41 37.3	41.4	122.7	41 04.5	42.1	123.4	40 31.2	43.0	124.1	39 57.2	43.7	124.8	39 22.6	44.4	125.5	38 47.5	45.2	126.2	38 11.8	45.8	126.8	37 35.6	46.5	127.4	1
2	40 55.9	41.7	123.6	40 22.4	42.6	124.4	39 48.2	43.3	125.0	39 13.5	44.1	125.7	38 38.2	44.9	126.4	38 02.3	45.5	127.0	37 26.0	46.2	127.6	36 49.1	46.9	128.2	2
3	40 14.2	42.3	124.6	39 39.8	43.0	125.3	39 04.9	43.8	125.9	38 29.4	44.5	126.6	37 53.3	45.2	127.2	37 16.8	45.9	127.8	36 39.8	46.6	128.4	36 02.2	47.1	129.0	3
4	39 31.9	42.6	125.5	38 56.8	43.4	126.2	38 21.1	44.2	126.8	37 44.9	44.9	127.4	37 08.1	45.5	128.0	36 30.9	46.2	128.6	35 53.2	46.8	129.2	35 15.1	47.4	129.8	4
5	38 49.3	-43.1	126.4	38 13.4	-43.8	127.1	37 36.9	-44.5	127.7	37 00.0	-45.2	128.3	36 22.6	-45.8	128.9	35 44.7	-46.5	129.4	35 06.4	-47.1	130.0	34 27.7	-47.7	130.5	5
6	38 06.2	43.5	127.3	37 29.6	44.2	127.9	36 52.4	44.8	128.5	36 14.8	45.5	129.1	35 36.8	46.2	129.7	34 58.2	46.7	130.2	34 19.3	47.4	130.7	33 40.0	48.0	131.2	6
7	37 22.7	43.8	128.2	36 45.4	44.6	128.8	36 07.6	45.2	129.3	35 29.3	45.8	129.9	34 50.6	46.5	130.4	34 11.5	47.1	131.0	33 31.9	47.6	131.5	32 52.0	48.2	132.0	7
8	36 38.9	44.3	129.0	36 00.8	44.8	129.6	35 22.4	45.6	130.2	34 43.5	46.2	130.7	34 04.1	46.7	131.2	33 24.4	47.3	131.7	32 44.3	47.9	132.2	32 03.8	48.4	132.7	8
9	35 54.6	44.5	129.9	35 16.0	45.2	130.4	34 36.8	45.8	131.0	33 57.3	46.4	131.5	33 17.4	47.0	132.0	32 37.1	47.6	132.4	31 56.4	48.1	132.9	31 15.4	48.7	133.4	9
10	35 10.1	-44.9	130.7	34 30.8	-45.5	131.2	33 51.0	-46.1	131.7	33 10.9	-46.7	132.2	32 30.4	-47.3	132.7	31 49.5	-47.8	133.2	31 08.3	-48.3	133.6	30 26.7	-48.8	134.0	10
11	34 25.2	45.2	131.5	33 45.3	45.9	132.0	33 04.9	46.4	132.5	32 24.2	47.0	133.0	31 43.1	47.5	133.4	31 01.7	48.0	133.9	30 20.0	48.6	134.3	29 37.9	49.1	134.7	11
12	33 40.0	45.5	132.3	32 59.4	46.0	132.8	32 18.5	46.6	133.3	31 37.2	47.2	133.7	30 55.6	47.7	134.1	30 13.7	48.3	134.6	29 31.4	48.8	135.0	28 48.8	49.2	135.4	12
13	32 54.5	45.8	133.1	32 13.4	46.4	133.5	31 31.9	46.9	134.0	30 50.0	47.4	134.4	30 07.9	48.0	134.8	29 25.4	48.5	135.3	28 42.6	48.9	135.6	27 59.6	49.4	136.0	13
14	32 08.7	46.0	133.8	31 27.0	46.6	134.3	30 45.0	47.2	134.7	30 02.6	47.7	135.1	29 19.9	48.2	135.5	28 36.9	48.6	135.9	27 53.7	49.1	136.3	27 10.2	49.6	136.7	14
15	31 22.7	-46.3	134.6	30 40.4	-46.8	135.0	29 57.8	-47.4	135.4	29 14.9	-47.9	135.8	28 31.7	-48.3	136.2	27 48.3	-48.9	136.6	27 04.6	-49.4	136.9	26 20.6	-49.8	137.3	15
16	30 36.4	46.6	135.3	29 53.6	47.1	135.8	29 10.4	47.6	136.1	28 27.0	48.1	136.5	27 43.4	48.6	136.9	26 59.4	49.0	137.2	26 15.2	49.4	137.6	25 30.8	49.9	137.9	16
17	29 49.8	46.8	136.1	29 06.5	47.3	136.5	28 22.8	47.8	136.8	27 38.9	48.2	137.2	26 54.8	48.8	137.6	26 10.4	49.2	137.9	25 25.8	49.7	138.2	24 40.9	50.0	138.5	17
18	29 03.0	47.0	136.8	28 19.2	47.6	137.2	27 35.0	48.0	137.5	26 50.7	48.5	137.9	26 06.0	48.9	138.2	25 21.2	49.4	138.5	24 36.1	49.7	138.8	23 50.9	50.2	139.1	18
19	28 16.0	47.2	137.5	27 31.6	47.7	137.9	26 47.0	48.2	138.2	26 02.2	48.7	138.5	25 17.1	49.1	138.8	24 31.8	49.5	139.2	23 46.4	50.0	139.4	23 00.7	50.4	139.7	19
20	27 28.8	-47.5	138.2	26 43.9	-47.9	138.5	25 58.8	-48.3	138.9	25 13.5	-48.8	139.2	24 28.0	-49.2	139.5	23 42.3	-49.6	139.8	22 56.4	-50.0	140.0	22 10.3	-50.4	140.3	20
21	26 41.3	47.6	138.9	25 56.0	48.1	139.2	25 10.5	48.6	139.5	24 24.7	48.9	139.8	23 38.8	49.4	140.1	22 52.7	49.8	140.4	22 06.4	50.2	140.6	21 19.9	50.6	140.9	21
22	25 53.7	47.8	139.6	25 07.9	48.3	139.9	24 21.9	48.7	140.2	23 35.8	49.2	140.5	22 49.4	49.5	140.7	22 02.9	50.0	141.0	21 16.2	50.3	141.2	20 29.3	50.7	141.5	22
23	25 05.9	48.1	140.2	24 19.6	48.4	140.5	23 33.2	48.8	140.8	22 46.6	49.2	141.1	21 59.9	49.7	141.3	21 12.9	50.0	141.6	20 25.9	50.5	141.8	19 38.6	50.8	142.0	23
24	24 17.8	48.1	140.9	23 31.2	48.6	141.2	22 44.4	49.0	141.4	21 57.4	49.4	141.7	21 10.2	49.8	141.9	20 22.9	50.2	142.2	19 35.4	50.5	142.4	18 47.8	50.9	142.6	24
25	23 29.7	-48.4	141.5	22 42.6	-48.7	141.8	21 55.4	-49.2	142.1	21 08.0	-49.6	142.3	20 20.4	-49.9	142.5	19 32.7	-50.3	142.8	18 44.9	-50.7	143.0	17 56.9	-51.0	143.2	25
26	22 41.3	48.5	142.2	21 53.9	48.9	142.4	21 06.2	49.3	142.7	20 18.4	49.6	142.9	19 30.5	50.0	143.1	18 42.4	50.3	143.3	17 54.2	50.7	143.5	17 05.9	51.0	143.7	26
27	21 52.8	48.6	142.8	21 05.0	49.1	143.1	20 16.9	49.4	143.3	19 28.8	49.8	143.5	18 40.5	50.2	143.7	17 52.1	50.5	143.9	17 03.5	50.8	144.1	16 14.9	51.2	144.3	27
28	21 04.2	48.8	143.5	20 15.9	49.1	143.7	19 27.5	49.5	143.9	18 39.0	49.9	144.1	17 50.3	50.2	144.3	17 01.6	50.6	144.5	16 12.7	50.9	144.6	15 23.7	51.2	144.8	28
29	20 15.4	48.9	144.1	19 26.8	49.3	144.3	18 38.0	49.6	144.5	17 49.1	50.0	144.7	17 00.1	50.3	144.9	16 11.0	50.7	145.0	15 21.8	51.0	145.2	14 32.5	51.4	145.3	29
30	19 26.5	-49.0	144.7	18 37.5	-49.4	144.9	17 48.4	-49.8	145.1	16 59.1	-50.1	145.3	16 09.8	-50.4	145.4	15 20.3	-50.7	145.6	14 30.8	-51.1	145.7	13 41.1	-51.3	145.9	30
31	18 37.5	49.1	145.3	17 48.1	49.5	145.5	16 58.6	49.8	145.7	16 09.0	50.1	145.8	15 19.4	50.6	146.0	14 29.6	50.9	146.1	13 39.7	51.1	146.3	12 49.8	51.5	146.4	31
32	17 48.4	49.3	145.9	16 58.6	49.6	146.1	16 08.8	49.9	146.2	15 18.9	50.3	146.4	14 28.8	50.5	146.6	13 38.7	50.8	146.7	12 48.6	51.2	146.8	11 58.3	51.5	146.9	32
33	16 59.1	49.3	146.5	16 09.0	49.6	146.7	15 18.9	50.1	146.8	14 28.6	50.3	147.0	13 38.3	50.7	147.1	12 47.9	51.0	147.2	11 57.4	51.3	147.4	11 06.8	51.5	147.5	33
34	16 09.8	49.5	147.1	15 19.4	49.8	147.3	14 28.8	50.1	147.4	13 38.3	50.4	147.5	12 47.6	50.7	147.7	11 56.9	51.0	147.8	11 06.1	51.3	147.9	10 15.3	51.7	148.0	34
35	15 20.3	-49.5	147.7	14 29.6	-49.9	147.8	13 38.7	-50.1	148.0	12 47.9	-50.5	148.1	11 56.9	-50.8	148.2	11 05.9	-51.1	148.3	10 14.8	-51.4	148.4	9 23.6	-51.6	148.5	35
36	14 30.8	49.7	148.3	13 39.7	49.9	148.4	12 48.6	50.3	148.5	11 57.4	50.6	148.6	11 06.1	50.8	148.7	10 14.8	51.2	148.8	9 23.4	51.4	148.9	8 32.0	51.7	149.0	36
37	13 41.1	49.7	148.8	12 49.8	50.1	149.0	11 58.3	50.3	149.1	11 06.8	50.6	149.2	10 15.3	50.9	149.3	9 23.6	51.1	149.4	8 32.0	51.5	149.5	7 40.3	51.7	149.5	37
38	12 51.4	49.8	149.4	11 59.7	50.0	149.5	11 08.0	50.4	149.6	10 16.2	50.7	149.7	9 24.4	51.0	149.8	8 32.5	51.3	149.9	7 40.5	51.5	150.0	6 48.6	51.8	150.0	38
39	12 01.6	49.8	150.0	11 09.7	50.2	150.1	10 17.6	50.4	150.2	9 25.5	50.7	150.3	8 33.4	51.0	150.4	7 41.2	51.2	150.4	6 49.0	51.5	150.5	5 56.8	51.8	150.5	39
40	11 11.8	-49.9	150.6	10 19.5	-50.2	150.7	9 27.2	-50.5	150.7	8 34.8	-50.7	150.8	7 42.4	-51.0	150.9	6 50.0	-51.3	151.0	5 57.5	-51.5	151.0	5 05.0	-51.8	151.1	40
41	10 21.9	50.0	151.1	9 29.3	50.2	151.2	8 36.7	50.5	151.3	7 44.1	50.8	151.4	6 51.4	51.1	151.4	5 58.7	51.3	151.5	5 06.0	51.6	151.5	4 13.2	51.8	151.6	41
42	9 31.9	50.0	151.7	8 39.1	50.3	151.8	7 46.2	50.6	151.8	6 53.3	50.9	151.9	6 00.3	51.1	151.9	5 07.4	51.4	152.0	4 14.4	51.6	152.0	3 21.4	51.9	152.1	42
43	8 41.9	50.1	152.3	7 48.8	50.4	152.3	6 55.6	50.6	152.4	6 02.4	50.8	152.4	5 09.2	51.1	152.5	4 16.0	51.4	152.5	3 22.8	51.6	152.5	2 29.5	51.8	152.6	43
44	7 51.8	50.1	152.8	6 58.4	50.4	152.9	6 05.0	50.6	152.9	5 11.6	50.9	153.0	4 18.1	51.1	153.0	3 24.6	51.3	153.0	2 31.2	51.7	153.1	1 37.7	51.9	153.1	44
45	7 01.7	-50.2	153.4	6 08.0	-50.4	153.4	5 14.4	-50.7	153.5	4 20.7	-50.9	153.5	3 27.0	-51.2	153.5	2 33.3	-51.4	153.5	1 39.5	-51.6	153.6	0 45.8	-51.9	153.6	45
46	6 11.5	50.2	153.9	5 17.6	50.4	154.0	4 23.7	50.7	154.0	3 29.8	51.0	154.0	2 35.8	51.2	154.0	1 41.9	51.5	154.1	0 47.9	-51.6	154.1	0 06.1	+51.8	25.9	46
47	5 21.3	50.2	154.5	4 27.2	50.5	154.5	3 33.0	50.7	154.5	2 38.8	50.9	154.6	1 44.6	51.1	154.6	0 50.4	-51.4	154.6	0 03.7	+51.7	25.4	0 57.9	51.9	25.4	47
48	4 31.1	50.3	155.0	3 36.7	50.5	155.0	2 42.3	50.7	155.1	1 47.9	51.0	155.1	0 53.5	51.2	155.1	0 01.0	+51.4	24.9	0 55.4	51.6	24.9	1 49.8	51.9	24.9	48
49	3 40.8	50.2	155.6	2 46.2	50.5	155.6	1 51.6	50.8	155.6	0 56.9	50.9	155.6	0 02.3	-51.2	155.6	0 52.4	51.4	24.4	1 47.0	51.7	24.4	2 41.7	51.8	24.4	49
50	2 50.6	-50.3	156.1	1 55.7	-50.5	156.1	1 00.8	-50.7	156.1	0 06.0	-51.0	156.1	0 48.9	+51.2	23.9	1 43.8	+51.4	23.9	2 38.7	+51.6	23.9	3 33.5	+51.8	23.9	50
51	2 00.3	50.3	156.7	1 05.2	50.5	156.7	0 10.1	-50.8	156.7	0 45.0	+51.0	23.3	1 40.1	51.2	23.3	2 35.2	51.4	23.4	3 30.3	51.6	23.4	4 25.3	51.8	23.4	51
52	1 10.0	50.3	157.2	0 14.7	-50.6	157.2	0 40.7	+50.7	22.8	1 36.0	50.9	22.8	2 31.3	51.1	22.8	3 26.6	51.3	22.8	4 21.9	51.5	22.9	5 17.1	51.8	22.9	52
53	0 19.7	-50.3	157.7	0 35.9	+50.5	22.3	1 31.4	50.7	22.3	2 26.9	51.0	22.3	3 22.4	51.2	22.3	4 17.9	51.4	22.3	5 13.4	51.6	22.4	6 08.9	51.8	22.4	53
54	0 30.6	+50.3	21.7	1 26.4	50.5	21.7	2 22.1	50.7	21.7	3 17.9	50.9	21.7	4 13.6	51.1	21.8	5 09.3	51.3	21.8	6 05.0	51.5	21.8	7 00.7	51.7	21.9	54
55	1 20.9	+50.3	21.2	2 16.9	+50.5	21.2	3 12.8	+50.7	21.2	4 08.8	+50.9	21.2	5 04.7	+51.1	21.2	6 00.6	+51.3	21.3	6 56.5	+51.5	21.3	7 52.4	+51.7	21.4	55
56	2 11.2	50.3	20.6	3 07.4	50.5	20.6	4 03.5	50.7	20.7	4 59.7	50.8	20.7	5 55.8	51.1	20.7	6 51.9	51.3	20.8	7 48.0	51.5	20.8	8 44.1	51.6	20.9	56
57	3 01.5	50.3	20.1	3 57.9	50.4	20.1	4 54.2	50.7	20.1	5 50.5	50.9	20.2	6 46.9	51.0	20.2	7 43.2	51.2	20.2	8 39.5	51.4	20.3	9 35.7	51.6	20.3	57
58	3 51.8	50.2	19.5	4 48.3	50.5	19.6	5 44.9	50.6	19.6	6 41.4	50.8	19.6	7 37.9	51.0	19.7	8 34.4	51.2	19.7	9 30.9	51.3	19.8	10 27.3	51.6	19.8	58
59	4 42.0	50.3	19.0	5 38.8	50.4	19.0	6 35.5	50.6	19.0	7 32.2	50.8	19.1	8 28.9	50.9	19.1	9 25.6	51.1	19.2	10 22.2	51.3	19.2	11 18.9	51.5	19.3	59
60	5 32.3	+50.1	18.4	6 29.2	+50.3	18.5	7 26.1	+50.5	18.5	8 23.0	+50.7	18.5	9 19.8	+50.9	18.6	10 16.7	+51.1	18.7	11 13.5	+51.3	18.7	12 10.4	+51.4	18.8	60
61	6 22.4	50.2	17.9	7 19.5	50.4	17.9	8 16.6	50.5	18.0	9 13.7	50.7	18.0	10 10.7	50.9	18.1	11 07.8	51.0	18.1	12 04.8	51.2	18.2	13 01.8	51.4	18.2	61
62	7 12.6	50.1	17.3	8 09.9	50.3	17.4	9 07.1	50.5	17.4	10 04.4	50.6	17.5	11 01.6	50.8	17.5	11 58.8	51.0	17.6	12 56.0	51.1	17.6	13 53.2	51.3	17.7	62
63	8 02.7	50.1	16.8	9 00.2	50.2	16.8	9 57.6	50.4	16.9	10 55.0	50.6	16.9	11 52.4	50.7	17.0	12 49.8	50.9	17.0	13 47.1	51.1	17.1	14 44.5	51.2	17.2	63
64	8 52.8	50.0	16.2	9 50.4	50.2	16.3	10 48.0	50.3	16.3	11 45.6	50.5	16.4	12 43.1	50.7	16.4	13 40.7	50.8	16.5	14 38.2	51.0	16.6	15 35.7	51.1	16.6	64
65	9 42.8	+50.0	15.7	10 40.6	+50.1	15.7	11 38.3	+50.3	15.8	12 36.1	+50.4	15.8	13 33.8	+50.6	15.9	14 31.5	+50.7	15.9	15 29.2	+50.9	16.0	16 26.8	+51.1	16.1	65
66	10 32.8	49.9	15.1	11 30.7	50.0	15.1	12 28.6	50.2	15.2	13 26.5	50.4	15.3	14 24.4	50.5	15.3	15 22.2	50.7	15.4	16 20.1	50.8	15.5	17 17.9	50.9	15.6	66
67	11 22.7	49.8	14.5	12 20.7	50.0	14.6	13 18.8	50.1	14.6	14 16.9	50.2	14.7	15 14.9	50.4	14.8	16 12.9	50.6	14.8	17 10.9	50.7	14.9	18 08.8	50.9	15.0	67
68	12 12.5	49.8	14.0	13 10.7	49.9	14.0	14 08.9	50.1	14.1	15 07.1	50.2	14.1	16 05.3	50.3	14.2	17 03.5	50.4	14.3	18 01.6	50.6	14.4	18 59.7	50.8	14.4	68
69	13 02.3	49.7	13.4	14 00.6	49.9	13.4	14 59.0	50.0	13.5	15 57.3	50.1	13.6	16 55.6	50.3	13.6	17 53.9	50.4	13.7	18 52.2	50.6	13.8	19 50.5	50.7	13.9	69
70	13 52.0	+49.6	12.8	14 50.5	+49.7	12.9	15 49.0	+49.8	12.9	16 47.4	+50.0	13.0	17 45.9	+50.1	13.1	18 44.3	+50.3	13.1	19 42.8	+50.4	13.2	20 41.2	+50.5	13.3	70
71	14 41.6	49.5	12.2	15 40.2	49.7	12.3	16 38.8	49.8	12.3	17 37.4	50.0	12.4	18 36.0	50.1	12.5	19 34.6	50.2	12.6	20 33.2	50.3	12.6	21 31.7	50.4	12.7	71
72	15 31.1	49.4	11.6	16 29.9	49.5	11.7	17 28.6	49.7	11.8	18 27.4	49.8	11.8	19 26.1	49.9	11.9	20 24.8	50.0	12.0	21 23.5	50.1	12.1	22 22.1	50.3	12.1	72
73	16 20.5	49.4	11.1	17 19.4	49.5	11.1	18 18.3	49.6	11.2	19 17.2	49.6	11.2	20 16.0	49.8	11.3	21 14.8	49.9	11.4	22 13.6	50.1	11.5	23 12.4	50.2	11.5	73
74	17 09.9	49.2	10.5	18 08.9	49.3	10.5	19 07.9	49.4	10.6	20 06.8	49.6	10.6	21 05.8	49.7	10.7	22 04.7	49.8	10.8	23 03.7	49.9	10.9	24 02.6	50.0	10.9	74
75	17 59.1	+49.1	9.9	18 58.2	+49.2	9.9	19 57.3	+49.3	10.0	20 56.4	+49.4	10.0	21 55.5	+49.5	10.1	22 54.5	+49.7	10.2	23 53.6	+49.7	10.3	24 52.6	+49.9	10.3	75
76	18 48.2	49.0	9.3	19 47.4	49.1	9.3	20 46.6	49.2	9.4	21 45.8	49.3	9.4	22 45.0	49.4	9.5	23 44.2	49.5	9.6	24 43.3	49.7	9.6	25 42.5	49.7	9.7	76
77	19 37.2	48.9	8.6	20 36.5	49.0	8.7	21 35.8	49.1	8.8	22 35.1	49.2	8.8	23 34.4	49.3	8.9	24 33.7	49.4	9.0	25 33.0	49.4	9.0	26 32.2	49.6	9.1	77
78	20 26.1	48.7	8.0	21 25.5	48.8	8.1	22 24.9	48.9	8.1	23 24.3	49.0	8.2	24 23.7	49.1	8.3	25 23.1	49.1	8.3	26 22.4	49.3	8.4	27 21.8	49.3	8.5	78
79	21 14.8	48.6	7.4	22 14.3	48.7	7.5	23 13.8	48.8	7.5	24 13.3	48.9	7.6	25 12.8	48.9	7.6	26 12.2	49.1	7.7	27 11.7	49.1	7.8	28 11.1	49.2	7.8	79
80	22 03.4	+48.5	6.8	23 03.0	+48.5	6.8	24 02.6	+48.6	6.9	25 02.2	+48.6	6.9	26 01.7	+48.8	7.0	27 01.3	+48.8	7.0	28 00.8	+48.9	7.1	29 00.3	+49.0	7.2	80
81	22 51.9	48.3	6.1	23 51.5	48.4	6.2	24 51.2	48.4	6.2	25 50.8	48.5	6.3	26 50.5	48.6	6.3	27 50.1	48.7	6.4	28 49.7	48.8	6.5	29 49.3	48.8	6.5	81
82	23 40.2	48.1	5.5	24 39.9	48.2	5.5	25 39.6	48.3	5.6	26 39.3	48.4	5.6	27 39.1	48.3	5.7	28 38.8	48.4	5.7	29 38.5	48.5	5.8	30 38.1	48.6	5.8	82
83	24 28.3	48.0	4.8	25 28.1	48.0	4.9	26 27.9	48.1	4.9	27 27.7	48.1	5.0	28 27.4	48.2	5.0	29 27.2	48.3	5.1	30 27.0	48.3	5.1	31 26.7	48.4	5.2	83
84	25 16.3	47.8	4.2	26 16.1	47.9	4.2	27 16.0	47.9	4.2	28 15.8	47.9	4.3	29 15.6	48.0	4.3	30 15.5	48.0	4.4	31 15.3	48.1	4.4	32 15.1	48.1	4.5	84
85	26 04.1	+47.6	3.5	27 04.0	+47.6	3.5	28 03.9	+47.6	3.6	29 03.7	+47.8	3.6	30 03.6	+47.8	3.6	31 03.5	+47.8	3.7	32 03.4	+47.8	3.7	33 03.2	+47.9	3.8	85
86	26 51.7	47.4	2.8	27 51.6	47.4	2.8	28 51.5	47.5	2.9	29 51.5	47.5	2.9	30 51.4	47.5	2.9	31 51.3	47.6	3.0	32 51.2	47.6	3.0	33 51.1	47.7	3.0	86
87	27 39.1	47.2	2.1	28 39.0	47.3	2.2	29 39.0	47.2	2.2	30 39.0	47.2	2.2	31 38.9	47.3	2.2	32 38.9	47.3	2.2	33 38.8	47.4	2.3	34 38.8	47.3	2.3	87
88	28 26.3	47.0	1.4	29 26.3	46.9	1.4	30 26.2	47.0	1.5	31 26.2	47.0	1.5	32 26.2	47.0	1.5	33 26.2	47.0	1.5	34 26.2	47.0	1.5	35 26.1	47.1	1.5	88
89	29 13.3	46.7	0.7	30 13.2	46.8	0.7	31 13.2	46.8	0.7	32 13.2	46.8	0.7	33 13.2	46.8	0.8	34 13.2	46.8	0.8	35 13.2	46.8	0.8	36 13.2	46.8	0.8	89
90	30 00.0	+46.5	0.0	31 00.0	+46.5	0.0	32 00.0	+46.5	0.0	33 00.0	+46.5	0.0	34 00.0	+46.5	0.0	35 00.0	+46.5	0.0	36 00.0	+46.5	0.0	37 00.0	+46.5	0.0	90
	30°			31°			32°			33°			34°			35°			36°			37°			

S. Lat. { L.H.A. greater than 180°......Zn=180°−Z
L.H.A. less than 180°............Zn=180°+Z

LATITUDE SAME NAME AS DECLINATION L.H.A. 141°, 219°

Fig. 2518c. Sample right-hand page from Pub. No. 229.

tion, which tabulates latitude and meridian hour angle by integral degrees, the resulting lines of position may be somewhat in error under certain conditions. These errors tend to arise when the intercepts are long or the ship's actual position is far from the azimuth lines; they are caused by plotting the intercept and the line of position as rhumb lines on the chart, rather than as arcs of a great and a small circle, respectively. These errors are not sufficiently large to require consideration in the ordinary practice of navigation at sea. But for those who wish to correct for these small differences, the following explanation and corrective is useful when using Pub. No. 229.

It has been found that for any given distance between the true and assumed position, the maximum perpendicular distance from the true position to the plotted line of position is roughly proportional to the tangent of the altitude. The error tends to increase with the altitude of the body, and it is roughly proportional to the square of the difference between the true and assumed positions. Other factors being equal, the error decreases as the latitude increases. In the vicinity of the equator, for an altitude of 75° and a true position differing in both latitude and longitude by 30′ from the assumed position, the error will not exceed 1.0 mile; at latitude 60° near the equator, the error will not exceed .05 mile. If the difference in both latitude and longitude between the true and assumed positions is reduced to 20′, the errors quoted above would be reduced by more than half.

The introductory pages of each volume of Pub. No. 229 include a "Table of Offsets," linear distances that can be drawn at right angles to a straight line of position (LOP). These result in a series of points that can be connected to form a better approximation of the arc of the *small* circle of equal altitude, the true LOP. Usually, the desired approximation of the arc can be obtained by drawing a straight line through pairs of offset points. The lengths of these offsets depend upon the altitude and the distance of the offset point from the intercept line (azimuth line).

Solution by Pub. No. 229 from a DR Position

2521   Pub. No. 229 can also be used for the reduction of an observation using the dead reckoning (DR) position rather than an assumed position (AP); this procedure, however, is more complex and difficult and is rarely used. In principle, the method is the measurement of the difference in radii of two circles of equal altitude corresponding to the altitudes of the celestial body from two positions at the same time. One circle passes through the AP (selected, as usual, for whole degrees of latitude and LHA), and the second circle passes through the DR position (or other position from which the computed altitude is desired).

A graphic procedure is followed in which the Hc and intercept are first calculated in the usual way, followed by an offset correction to the plot. Full instructions on this procedure are given in the introductory pages of each volume. This method will give very satisfactory results except when plotting on a Mercator chart in high latitudes.

Other Uses of Pub. No. 229

2522   The tables of Pub. No. 229 can also be used in a number of secondary procedures. These include great-circle sailing problems (see article 3113), the solution of general spherical triangles, star identification (see article 2106), and the determination of compass error (see article 2902). Instructions for all of these procedures are given in the introductory pages of Pub. No. 229, together with several illustrative examples.

REDUCTION BY PUB. NO. 249

2523   Another set of precomputed tables bears the name *Sight Reduction Tables for Air Navigation*, now designated as NIMA Pub. No. 249. As their name implies, these tables were designed for use by air navigators. Modern aircraft navigation systems have largely obviated the use of celestial navigation by aviators, but Pub. No. 249 is still used by many mariners, particularly by small craft operators who like its relative ease of use and the fact that it requires little stowage space and who know that the degree of accuracy is consistent with their ability to get good sights on craft that are particularly subject to abrupt vessel motion.

Volume I, Selected Stars

2524   Pub. No. 249 tables are published in three volumes. Similar to Pub. No. 229, they are inspection tables designed for use with an assumed position, but they differ from Pub. 229 in that altitude is stated only to the nearest whole minute of arc, and azimuth values are stated only to the nearest whole degree. The first volume is designed for use with certain selected stars on a worldwide basis; all integral degrees of latitude, from 89° north to 90° south are included. The arguments for entering the tables in Volume I are the nearest whole degree of latitude, specified as north or south, LHA Aries, and the name of the star observed. LHA ♈ is obtained by applying to GHA ♈ an assumed longitude (within 30′ of DR or EP longitude) that will yield a whole degree of LHA ♈. From these entering arguments, a calculated altitude (Hc) and a *true azimuth* (Zn), rather than an azimuth angle (Z), are obtained.

For each degree of latitude and of LHA ♈, seven stars are tabulated (see fig. 2524). These seven stars have been specifically selected for best results and the group will therefore differ in different parts of the table. The names of first-magnitude stars are printed in capital letters; those of second and third magnitude are in upper and lowercase letters. These stars are selected primarily for good distribution in azimuth, for their magnitude and altitude, and for continuity in latitude and hour angle. Of these seven stars, those that are considered best suited for a three-star fix are identified by a solid diamond symbol. Tabulated altitude and azimuth of the selected stars also permits the use of this publication as a starfinder by presetting the sextant and observing in the tabulated direction.

The stars for which data are given in Volume I of Pub. No. 249 have continual slight changes in sidereal hour angle and declination due to the precession and nutation of the Earth's axis of rotation. Editions of this publication contain tabulated data for a specific year and an auxiliary table (Table 5) for corrections to be applied to an LOP or fix for years other than the base year. Editions are currently published every five years, but to provide for some overlap and extension, the table of corrections

covers a span of eight or more years. Each edition is designated with an *epoch year*, a multiple of five, and may be used for that year (and possibly another) without correction. For example, the basic tables of the Epoch 2005.0 edition may be used without correction for the years 2004 and 2006. The tables of corrections cover the years 2001 through 2009, but the basic data can be used without correction over the span 2002–2007 with errors no greater than 2 miles.

Volume I has other auxiliary tables including altitude corrections for change in position of the observer (primarily for airborne observers), and change in position of the body between time of observation and fix. Polaris latitude and azimuth tables are provided, as well as a table of GHA ♈ that eliminates the need for an *Air Almanac*. Another auxiliary table facilitates conversion between arc and time units.

Volumes II and III

2525 Volumes II and III of Pub. No. 249 are generally similar in format to Pub. No. 229, except that Hc is tabulated only to the nearest whole minute and Z to the nearest whole degree. Both volumes list declination by integral degrees, but only for 0° to 29°; this covers all bodies of our solar system. These volumes are not epoch-limited as is Volume I, for they use as entering arguments the LHA and declination of the body, not LHA ♈ and the name of the star.

Volume I will normally be used for reducing star sights, although stars with Dec. of 29° or less can

LAT 42°N

LHA ♈	Hc Zn	Hc Zn	Hc Zn	Hc Zn	Hc Zn	Hc Zn	Hc Zn
	◆Alpheratz	ALTAIR	Nunki	◆ANTARES	ARCTURUS	◆Alkaid	Kochab
270	17 41 067	48 59 136	20 33 167	18 23 202	37 34 262	46 28 302	51 20 341
271	18 22 067	49 29 137	20 43 168	18 06 203	36 50 263	45 51 303	51 05 341
272	19 03 068	49 59 139	20 52 169	17 49 203	36 06 264	45 13 303	50 51 341
273	19 45 068	50 28 140	21 00 170	17 31 204	35 21 265	44 36 303	50 36 341
274	20 26 069	50 56 141	21 07 171	17 12 205	34 37 265	43 59 303	50 22 341
275	21 08 069	51 23 143	21 14 172	16 53 206	33 52 266	43 21 304	50 07 340
276	21 50 070	51 50 144	21 20 173	16 33 207	33 08 267	42 44 304	49 52 340
277	22 32 071	52 15 146	21 25 174	16 12 208	32 23 267	42 08 304	49 37 340
278	23 14 071	52 40 147	21 29 175	15 51 209	31 39 268	41 31 305	49 21 340
279	23 56 072	53 04 149	21 33 176	15 30 210	30 54 269	40 54 305	49 06 340
280	24 39 072	53 26 150	21 36 177	15 07 210	30 10 270	40 18 305	48 51 340
281	25 21 073	53 48 152	21 38 178	14 44 211	29 25 270	39 41 306	48 35 340
282	26 04 073	54 08 153	21 39 179	14 21 212	28 40 271	39 05 306	48 20 339
283	26 47 074	54 28 155	21 40 180	13 57 213	27 56 272	38 29 306	48 04 339
284	27 30 075	54 46 157	21 40 181	13 33 214	27 11 272	37 53 306	47 48 339
	◆Mirfak	Alpheratz	◆ALTAIR	Rasalhague	◆ARCTURUS	Alkaid	Kochab
285	13 22 033	28 13 075	55 03 158	55 07 219	26 27 273	37 17 307	47 32 339
286	13 47 033	28 56 076	55 19 160	54 38 220	25 42 273	36 42 307	47 16 339
287	14 11 034	29 39 076	55 34 162	54 09 222	24 58 274	36 06 307	47 00 339
288	14 36 034	30 22 077	55 47 163	53 39 223	24 13 275	35 31 308	46 44 339
289	15 01 035	31 06 077	55 59 165	53 08 225	23 29 275	34 56 308	46 28 339
290	15 27 035	31 49 078	56 10 167	52 36 226	22 44 276	34 21 309	46 12 339
291	15 53 036	32 33 079	56 20 169	52 04 227	22 00 277	33 46 309	45 56 339
292	16 19 036	33 17 079	56 28 170	51 31 229	21 16 277	33 11 309	45 40 339

Fig. 2524. Pub. No. 249, Volume I (extract).

be used with Volume II and Volume III; 28 of the 57 selected stars fall into this category. Volume II covers latitudes 0° to 39°, and Volume III covers latitudes 40° to 89°. A portion of a page from Volume II is reproduced in figure 2525a. The entering arguments are a whole degree of latitude (without name in these volumes), a whole degree of declination of same or contrary name to the latitude, and a whole degree of LHA. The tabulated values of LHA provide for negative altitudes because of the large value of dip when aircraft are operating at high altitudes; this feature of Pub. No. 249 permits the observation of bodies below the celestial horizon.

For each single set of entering arguments, the tables yield an altitude expressed to the nearest whole minute of arc, under the heading "Hc." Adjoining this, under the heading "d," is a value with sign, which is the difference in minutes between the tabulated altitude and the altitude for a declination one degree higher, but at the same latitude and for the same LHA. The third item, under the heading "Z," is the azimuth angle (not Zn as in Volume I). The rules for converting Z to Zn are given on each page.

As with Pub. No. 229, the Hc must be interpolated for greater accuracy. This can be done mathematically using the same equations as described above—the difference in declination multiplied by the difference in Hc (the d factor provided in the table) and the result divided by 60. Or you may use the table provided in the back of the volume (see fig. 2525b); enter the left most column with the difference of Hc (d) and find the value intersecting the column headed by the difference in declination (in minutes). The sign of the value is determined by the values provided in the main table.

THE AGETON METHOD

2526   A volume titled *Dead Reckoning Altitude and Azimuth Tables* was formerly published as H.O. 211 and the included tables were once included in *Bowditch*. Commonly called "the Ageton tables" after their designer, they are no longer available from government sources. Some commercial publishers still produce these tables, and they are available in their entirety at the U.S. Naval Institute web site, www.navalinstitute.org/navtable.

The Ageton tables consist of a single table of log secants and log cosecants ($\times$ 100,000), stated for each 0.5′ of arc. They are suitable for worldwide use with any declination and for any altitude. As their title implies, they are intended for use from a DR position. A partial page is shown in figure 2526a.

What makes the Ageton method work is that two right triangles are formed by dropping a perpendicular from the celestial body to the celestial meridian of the observer. The right angle falls on the celestial meridian at a point that may lie either inside or outside the navigational triangle. The right triangles are then solved for altitude and azimuth angle from equations derived from Napier's rules.

In figure 2526b the navigational triangle is shown with the parts of the triangle lettered. In right triangle *PMX*, t and d are known. *R* may be found from equation (1). Knowing *R* and d, *K* may be found by equation (2). *K* is then combined algebraically with *L* to obtain *K* ~ *L*.

In triangle *ZMX*, sides *R* and *K* ~ *L* are now known. Hc may be found by equation (3). The azimuth angle, Z, is computed by equation (4).

All equations are in terms of secants and cose-

DECLINATION (19°-29°) CONTRARY NAME TO LATITUDE

LHA	19° Hc	d	Z	20° Hc	d	Z	21° Hc	d	Z	22° Hc	d	Z	23° Hc	d	Z	24° Hc	d	Z	25° Hc	d	Z	26° Hc	d	Z	27° Hc	d	Z	28° Hc	d	Z	29° Hc	d	Z	LHA
14	36 18	58	164	35 20	58	164	34 22	58	164	33 24	58	164	32 26	58	165	31 28	59	165	30 29	59	165	29 31	58	166	28 33	59	166	27 34	58	166	26 36	59	166	346
13	36 32	58	165	35 34	58	165	34 36	59	165	33 37	58	166	32 39	59	166	31 40	58	166	30 42	59	166	29 43	59	167	28 44	58	167	27 46	58	167	26 47	58	167	347
12	36 45	58	166	35 47	59	166	34 48	59	166	33 49	58	167	32 51	59	167	31 52	59	167	30 53	59	167	29 54	58	168	28 56	59	168	27 57	59	168	26 58	59	168	348
11	36 57	59	167	35 58	59	167	34 59	59	167	34 00	58	168	33 02	59	168	32 03	59	168	31 04	59	168	30 05	59	169	29 06	59	169	28 07	59	169	27 08	59	169	349
10	37 08	59	168	36 09	59	168	35 10	59	169	34 11	59	169	33 12	59	169	32 13	60	169	31 14	59	170	30 14	59	170	29 15	59	170	28 16	59	170	27 16	59	170	350
9	37 18	60	169	36 18	59	170	35 19	59	170	34 20	59	170	33 21	59	170	32 22	59	170	31 22	59	170	30 23	59	171	29 24	60	171	28 24	59	171	27 25	59	171	351
8	37 27	60	171	36 27	59	171	35 28	60	171	34 28	59	171	33 29	59	171	32 30	60	171	31 30	59	172	30 31	60	172	29 31	59	172	28 32	60	172	27 32	59	172	352
7	37 34	59	172	36 35	60	172	35 35	59	172	34 36	60	172	33 36	59	172	32 37	60	172	31 37	59	173	30 38	60	173	29 38	59	173	28 38	59	173	27 39	60	173	353
6	37 41	59	173	36 42	60	173	35 42	60	173	34 42	59	173	33 43	60	173	32 43	60	174	31 43	59	174	30 44	60	174	29 44	60	174	28 44	60	174	27 44	59	174	354
5	37 47	59	174	36 47	60	174	35 47	59	174	34 48	60	174	33 48	60	175	32 48	60	175	31 48	59	175	30 49	60	175	29 49	60	175	28 49	60	175	27 49	60	175	355
4	37 52	60	175	36 52	60	175	35 52	60	175	34 52	60	176	33 52	60	176	32 52	60	176	31 53	60	176	30 53	60	176	29 53	60	176	28 53	60	176	27 53	60	176	356
3	37 55	60	176	36 55	60	177	35 55	59	177	34 56	60	177	33 56	60	177	32 56	60	177	31 56	60	177	30 56	60	177	29 56	60	177	28 56	60	177	27 56	60	177	357
2	37 58	60	178	36 58	60	178	35 58	60	178	34 58	60	178	33 58	60	178	32 58	60	178	31 58	60	178	30 58	60	178	29 58	60	178	28 58	60	178	27 58	60	178	358
1	38 00	60	179	37 00	60	179	36 00	60	179	35 00	60	179	34 00	60	179	33 00	60	179	32 00	60	179	31 00	60	179	30 00	60	179	29 00	60	179	28 00	60	179	359
0	38 00	-60	180	37 00	-60	180	36 00	-60	180	35 00	-60	180	34 00	-60	180	33 00	-60	180	32 00	-60	180	31 00	-60	180	30 00	-60	180	29 00	-60	180	28 00	-60	180	360

DECLINATION (19°-29°) CONTRARY NAME TO LATITUDE   LAT 33°

Fig. 2525a. Pub. No. 249, Volume II (extract).

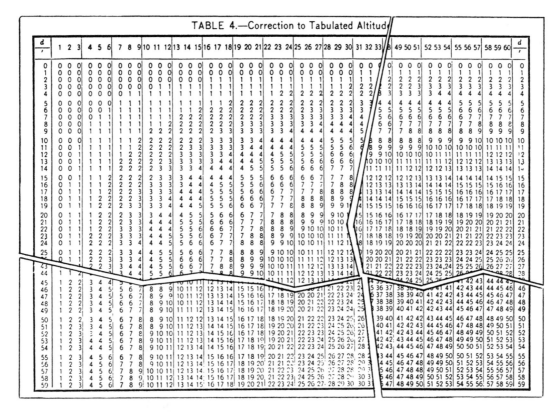

Fig. 2525b. Portion of Table 4, Volume II of Pub. No. 249 (extract).

cants (whose logarithms are never negative). The table is arranged in parallel A and B columns; the A columns containing log cosecants multiplied by 100,000, and the B columns log secants multiplied by 100,000 (to reduce the need for decimals). This design greatly simplifies the necessary calculations. The tradeoff in these tables is that the user must enter them twice for each LOP.

The tabulation of functions for every half-minute of arc throughout the table is employed so that, in ordinary use, interpolation will not be necessary. If the entry value is midway between two tabular values, use the smaller of the two; the difference in results is not significant, but this procedure will ensure consistency in reductions.

"Compact" Ageton Tables

2527 As noted earlier, the Ageton tables have been condensed to create a pamphlet of only thirty small pages. These tables are compact; they list only whole degrees in columns and whole minutes in rows, reducing them to one-fourth the tabulated entries (see fig. 2527a). They actually cover only nine pages; the remaining pages contain instructions and other explanatory material. The overall size of the booklet containing these compact tables

was deliberately chosen to make the publication fit into the lid of a typical sextant case.

Use of the compact tables decreases the accuracy of the position determined, but not to a degree of practical significance in the high-seas navigation of small vessels or for emergency use in survival craft. An example of the use of the compact tables is shown in figure 2527b. The input data are the same as for the preceding example by the Ageton Method and the differences in this particular case are slight: less than 1 mile in intercept and less than 0.05 degree in azimuth.

CONCISE SIGHT REDUCTION TABLES IN THE *NAUTICAL ALMANAC*

2528 Since 1989, the *Nautical Almanac* has included a set of concise sight reduction tables to be used when more extensive tables or computer programs are not available. These tables, like Pubs. 229 and 249, are intended for use with an assumed position and for plotting LOPs by azimuth and altitude intercept. There are two tables. The first, called "Sight Reduction Table," is the main table and occupies 30 pages. The second, called "Auxiliary Table," covers only two facing

′	22° 30′ A	B	23° 00′ A	B	23° 30′ A	B	24° 00′ A	B	24° 30′ A	B	′
10	41412	3491	40516	3651	39641	3815	38786	3983	37951	4155	20
	41397	3494	40501	3654	39626	3818	38772	3986	37937	4158	
11	41382	3496	40486	3657	39612	3821	38758	3989	37924	4161	19
	41367	3499	40471	3659	39597	3824	38744	3992	37910	4164	
12	41352	3502	40457	3662	39583	3826	38730	3995	37896	4167	18
	41337	3504	40442	3665	39569	3829	38716	3998	37882	4170	
13	41322	3507	40427	3667	39554	3832	38702	4000	37869	4173	17
	41307	3509	40413	3670	39540	3835	38688	4003	37855	4176	
14	41291	3512	40398	3673	39525	3838	38674	4006	37841	4179	16
	41276	3515	40383	3676	39511	3840	38660	4009	37828	4182	
15	41261	3517	40368	3678	39497	3843	38645	4012	37814	4185	15
	41246	3520	40354	3681	39482	3846	38631	4015	37800	4187	
16	41231	3523	40339	3684	39468	3849	38617	4017	37786	4190	14
	41216	3525	40324	3686	39454	3851	38603	4020	37773	4193	
17	41201	3528	40310	3689	39439	3854	38589	4023	37759	4196	13
	41186	3531	40295	3692	39425	3857	38575	4026	37745	4199	
18	41171	3533	40280	3695	39411	3860	38561	4029	37732	4202	12
	41156	3536	40266	3697	39396	3863	38547	4032	37718	4205	
19	41141	3539	40251	3700	39382	3865	38533	4035	37704	4208	11
	41126	3541	40236	3703	39368	3868	38520	4037	37691	4211	
20	41111	3544	40222	3705	39353	3871	38506	4040	37677	4214	10
	41096	3547	40207	3708	39339	3874	38492	4043	37663	4217	
21	41081	3549	40192	3711	39325	3876	38478	4046	37650	4220	9
	41066	3552	40178	3714	39311	3879	38464	4049	37636	4222	
22	41051	3555	40163	3716	39296	3882	38450	4052	37623	4225	8
	41036	3557	40149	3719	39282	3885	38436	4055	37609	4228	
23	41021	3560	40134	3722	39268	3888	38422	4057	37595	4231	7
	41006	3563	40119	3725	39254	3890	38408	4060	37582	4234	
24	40991	3565	40105	3727	39239	3893	38394	4063	37568	4237	6
	40976	3568	40090	3730	39225	3896	38380	4066	37554	4240	
25	40961	3571	40076	3733	39211	3899	38366	4069	37541	4243	5
	40946	3573	40061	3735	39197	3902	38352	4072	37527	4246	
26	40931	3576	40046	3738	39182	3904	38338	4075	37514	4249	4
	40916	3579	40032	3741	39168	3907	38324	4078	37500	4252	
27	40902	3581	40017	3744	39154	3910	38311	4080	37486	4255	3
	40887	3584	40003	3746	39140	3913	38297	4083	37473	4258	

Fig. 2526a. Pub. No. 9 (*Bowditch*), Volume II (1981), Table 35 (extract).

pages, and is used to modify the results obtained from the first table. The data needed for solution by this method are whole-degree values of assumed latitude and of LHA, and the actual declination, but only the first two of these are used directly as entering arguments. Declination is combined with a respondent from the first table for use as an arugument for entering the same table a second time.

As in the Ageton method, compactness is achieved in part by dividing the navigational triangle into two right spherical triangles, but with the difference that the perpendicular dividing them is dropped from the zenith to the hour circle of the celestial body, rather than from that body to the observer's celestial meridian. A result is that the azimuth angle is split into two typically unequal parts that must be solved for separately, then carefully combined to form the azimuth angle and the azimuth. Several entries in the tables are required for each complete celestial solution, but they employ and yield angles in sexagesimal units with-out the use of logarithms, and they have the distinct advantage of being immediately available within the covers of the *Nautical Almanac*.

Use of these concise reduction tables seems complicated on your first encounter with them, but detailed instructions with example problems are provided in the *Nautical Almanac* and they become easy to use after repeated use. Rules for determining the signs of arguments are provided at the top of each table page and the familiar rules for converting Z to Zn are included at the bottom. Altitudes greater than 80° should be avoided when using these tables. The accuracy of these tables is roughly equivalent to that of Pub. No. 249.

SIGHT REDUCTION USING STELLA

2529 As with the other processes of celestial navigation, the U.S. Naval Observatory's STELLA (System to Estimate Latitude and Longitude Astronomically) program can be effectively used for sight reduction without tables or manual computation.

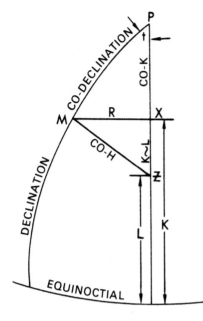

P. Pole

Z. Zenith of observer. The azimuth (angle PZM) is also called Z.

M. Heavenly body observed.

L. Latitude of observer.

d. Declination of body M.

t. (or LHA). Local hour angle of body M.

H. Altitude of body M.

R. Perpendicular let fall from M on PZ. This is an auxiliary part.

X. Intersection of R with PZ.

K. Arc from X to the equinoctial. This is an auxiliary part introduced to facilitate solution.

The following equations have been derived:

From triangle PMX—

1. $\csc R = \csc t \sec d$.

2. $\csc K = \dfrac{\csc d}{\sec R}$

From triangle ZMX—

3. $\csc HC = \sec R \sec (K \sim L)$.

4. $\csc Z = \dfrac{\csc R}{\sec Hc}$

Fig. 2526b. The celestial triangle as solved by the Ageton method.

t AND K ARE BOTH GREATER OR BOTH LESS THAN 90°.
Z IS LESS THAN 90° ONLY WHEN K HAS THE SAME NAME AND IS GREATER THAN L.

	A 20° B B 110° A		A 21° B B 111° A		A 22° B B 112° A		A 23° B B 113° A		A 24° B B 114° A		
00	46595	2701	44567	2985	42642	3283	40812	3597	39069	3927	60
01	560	706	534	990	611	289	782	603	040	933	59
02	525	711	501	995	580	294	753	608	012	938	58
03	491	715	463	999	549	299	723	613	38984	944	57
04	456	720	436	3004	518	304	693	619	955	950	56
05	46422	2724	44403	3009	42486	3309	40664	3624	38927	3955	55
06	387	729	370	014	455	314	634	630	899	961	54
07	353	734	337	019	424	319	604	635	871	966	53
08	318	738	305	024	393	324	575	640	842	972	52
09	284	743	272	029	362	330	545	646	814	978	51
10	46249	2748	44239	3034	42331	3335	40516	3651	38786	3983	50
11	215	752	207	038	300	340	486	657	758	989	49
12	181	757	174	043	269	345	457	662	730	995	48
13	146	762	142	048	238	350	427	667	702	4000	47
14	112	766	109	053	207	355	398	673	674	006	46
15	46078	2771	44077	3058	42176	3360	40368	3678	38646	4012	45
16	043	776	044	063	145	366	339	684	618	018	44
17	009	780	012	068	115	371	310	689	589	023	43
18	45975	785	43979	073	084	376	280	695	562	029	42
19	941	790	947	078	053	381	251	700	534	035	41
20	45907	2794	43915	3083	42022	3386	40222	3706	38506	4040	40
21	873	799	882	088	41992	392	192	711	478	046	39
22	839	804	850	093	961	397	163	716	450	052	38
23	805	808	818	097	930	402	134	722	422	058	37
24	771	813	785	102	899	407	105	727	394	063	36
25	45737	2818	43753	3107	41869	3412	40076	3733	38366	4069	35
26	703	822	721	112	838	418	046	738	338	075	34
27	669	827	689	117	808	423	017	744	311	080	33
28	635	832	657	122	777	428	39988	749	283	086	32
29	601	837	625	127	747	433	959	755	255	092	31

Fig. 2527a. Condensed Ageton tables (extract).

However, the sight reduction process is virtually invisible to the STELLA user because the program incorporates the computational and/or tabular part of the process into its two tasks: *Record Observations* and *Compute Fix*. You will remember from chapter 22 that if you select "Sight Reduction" from the Task menu, you will be given the choice of selecting one or the other of these subtasks. As the titles suggest, you would use the first task to record your sextant observations into STELLA and then use the second to compute a fix. The processes explained in this chapter are incorporated into the algorithms that make STELLA function, so that you, as the navigator, do not need to do anything other

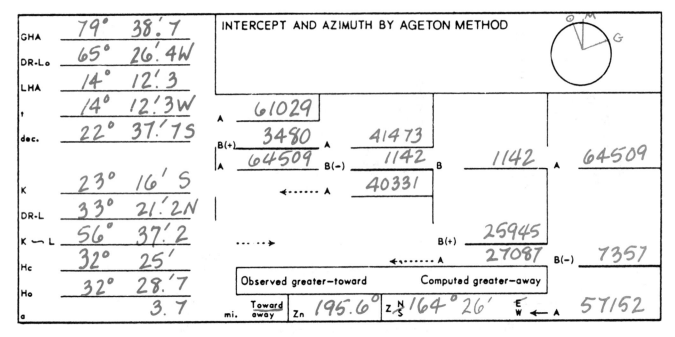

Fig. 2527b. Form with sight reduction using condensed Ageton tables.

than record your observations and let the computer convert this information into the LOPs and fixes that you are seeking. The "Compute Fix" task dis-plays the results both graphically and in table form. Strip form representations of each observation are also available should you desire them.

Chapter 26

Celestial Lines of Position

After the actions described in the preceding chapters have been completed, and you have acquired values of altitude intercept and azimuth, the task remains to use this information to determine your position. Although a sight reduction will always yield a circular line of position, this cannot be used directly except in the case of extremely high altitude observations. In practice, nautical navigators plot only a minute fraction of that circle, an arc so short that it can be considered a straight line in the vicinity of your DR position.

The purpose of this chapter is to explain the techniques whereby celestial altitudes are converted into celestial lines of position (LOP), and how fixes and running fixes are obtained from such lines. Celestial lines of position are usually plotted on special charts called *plotting sheets*. In the interest of simplification, however, the term *chart* will be used throughout this chapter whenever referring to a plot.

Some of the material in this chapter has already been explained elsewhere in the book, but it is repeated here by way of summation since the previous chapters have been leading up to this point where numbers gleaned from sextants, almanacs, tables, and so on are at last converted to plotted positions on charts.

LINES OF POSITION

2601 An American, Captain Thomas H. Sumner, discovered the line of position in 1837. Due to thick weather when approaching the English coast, he had been unable to obtain any observations. About 10:00 A.M. the Sun broke through, and he measured an altitude that he reduced to obtain the longitude. However, the latitude he used for the reduction was in doubt, so he solved for longitude twice more, each time using a different latitude. After plotting the three positions on a chart, he was surprised to find that a straight line could be drawn through them. He correctly deduced that his position must lie somewhere along this line, which happened to pass through a light off the English coast. He turned the ship and sailed along that line until the light appeared, thus establishing his position exactly. Sumner's discovery of the line of position was a great step forward in celestial navigation. Its greatest weakness lay in the fact that to obtain such a line of position, a sight had to be worked at least twice, using different latitudes.

In 1875, Commander Marcq de St.-Hilaire of the French Navy introduced the altitude difference, or intercept method, which has become the basis of virtually all present-day celestial navigation. In this method, the altitude and azimuth of a body are calculated for a given instant of time and for a location where the vessel is assumed to be. The difference between the altitude as observed by sextant and the calculated altitude is then determined; this difference, which is called the intercept (a), will be in minutes of arc.

A line is then drawn through the position, corresponding in direction to the calculated azimuth. The intercept is next laid off along the azimuth line, 1 nautical mile being equal to 1 minute of arc. It is measured toward the body if the observed altitude is greater than the calculated, and away if it is less. All that remains is to draw the line of position at right angles to the azimuth line.

TERRESTRIAL AND CELESTIAL LOPS COMPARED

2602 In piloting, a navigator may obtain a line of position in any of several ways; usually such lines represent bearings of a landmark or aid to navigation. In celestial navigation, a line of position is a small segment of a circle, which represents distance in nautical miles from the geographical position (GP) of the observed body; it is analogous to the circular LOP obtained from a radar range in piloting. This distance is obtained by converting the altitude of the observed body into miles on the surface of the Earth; this distance must then be transformed into a line of position that can be plotted on the appropriate chart. Both celestial and terrestrial lines of position are used in essentially the same manner, and may be advanced or retired as required; usually they are advanced to the time of the last observation so as to result in a common time for two or more LOPs taken in sequence rather than simultaneously.

LABELING CELESTIAL LOPS AND FIXES

2603 A neat, carefully labeled plot of navigational information is a prime characteristic of a good navigator. All lines of position and fixes should be drawn and labeled in such a way that no doubt ever exists as to their meaning. The illustrations in this chapter are all drawn and labeled in conformance with the standards that have been generally agreed upon by various U.S. instructional activities. These standards are:

Assumed position or geographical position. Assumed positions (AP) and geographical positions (GP) used with an LOP are always marked by an encircled dot and may be labeled "AP" or "GP," as appropriate. They are numbered consecutively if more than one appears on a plot.

Advanced AP or GP. The direction and distance that an AP or GP is advanced is always shown by a solid line or lines, the end point of which is encircled but not labeled. This is the advanced AP or GP from which an advanced LOP is plotted.

Azimuth line. The direction of the LOP from the AP used to plot the line is always shown by a broken line extending from the AP to the LOP, as indicated by the magnitude and direction of the intercept; no labels are used.

Line of position. A line of position, whether a straight line or an arc, is always shown by a solid line and labeled with the name of the body "below" the line. The ship's time of the observation may be labeled "above" the LOP, or may be omitted to reduce chart clutter if the time is close to that shown at the fix. If the LOP has been advanced or retired for a running fix, the time of observation and the time to which it has been adjusted are both shown if time labels are being used; for example, "1210–1420" for a 1210 line of position advanced to 1420.

Fix. The position found by a fix is encircled and labeled with the time placed horizontally; the word "fix" is understood and should not be labeled. If a small polygon is formed by an inexact intersection of more than two lines, an encircled dot may be added to indicate the position considered to be the fix.

Running fix. The position found by a running fix is marked in the same manner as a fix, but is labeled as to its special nature; for example, "1628 R Fix" placed horizontally.

LINES OF POSITION FROM HIGH-ALTITUDE OBSERVATIONS

2604 As previously discussed, the radius of a circle of equal altitude is equal to the coaltitude, or 90° minus the altitude. If a body is observed at a very high altitude, the radius will be small, and the resulting circle of equal altitude can be plotted directly on a chart. The center of this circle will be the GP of the body, and the radius will equal the coaltitude. In practice, only that portion of the circle that lies in the vicinity of the ship's DR position need be drawn.

While this type of celestial plotting has the advantage of not requiring the use of an assumed position (AP) and the calculations accompanying it—thereby allowing a direct plot of the result of the observation—this direct method of plotting is not suitable for most celestial observations for two reasons. First, the radii of most circles of equal altitude are very long. For example, for an altitude of 50°, the coaltitude, and therefore the radius, is 40°, which equals 2,400 nautical miles; and for an altitude of 20°, the radius is 4,200 nautical miles. A chart that would permit plotting radii of such magnitudes would be of such small scale that it would not yield the precision in position required in practical navigation.

Second, distortion is apparent on the commonly used Mercator projection, and it increases with the latitude of the GP. The distortion of such a circle is illustrated in figure 2604a; it would be exceedingly difficult to draw such a line.

If, however, the body is very high in altitude, the coaltitude will be small enough to plot on a naviga-

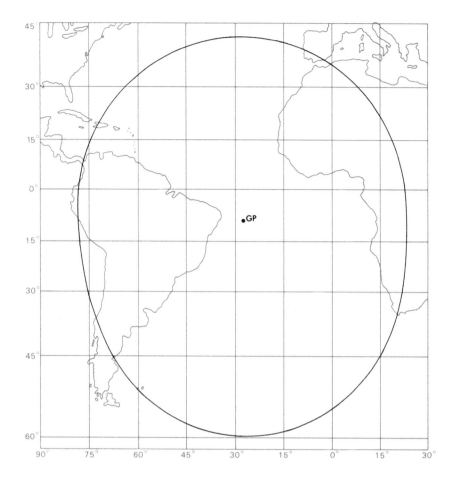

Fig. 2604a. Circle of equal altitude plotted on a Mercator chart.

tional chart, and the distortion will be negligible. There is no precise answer as to how great the altitude should be to permit direct plotting as a "high-altitude observation." One obvious determination is whether the GP and your position will both fit on the chart in use. Typically, all sights with an observed altitude of 87° or more are classed as high-altitude observations and the resulting LOP is plotted directly; the radius in this case would not exceed 180 miles.

Example: The 1137 DR position of an observer is L 5° 30′ N, l 139° 57.7′ E, at which time he determines the observed altitude (Ho) of the Sun to be 88° 14.5′. The GP of the Sun for this time is determined from an almanac to be L 7° 14.9′ N, l 140° 26.2′ E.

Required: The plot of the 1137 LOP.

Solution: See figure 2604b.

(1) Plot and label the 1137 DR position and the GP, using the latitudes and longitudes given.

(2) Since the radius of the circle of equal altitude equals the coaltitude, subtract the observed altitude from 90°, and convert the difference into minutes of arc, which equal nautical miles.

	90° 00.0′
Ho	88° 14.5′
Radius	1° 45.5′ = 105.5 miles

(3) Using a radius of 105.5 miles (shown by the broken line), construct an arc with the GP as the center, drawing only that segment that lies in the vicinity of the DR position. (4) Label the resulting line of position as shown, except for the radius shown in this figure, which is normally not drawn or labeled.

LOP BASED UPON ASSUMED POSITIONS

2605 The great majority of celestial observations are made at altitudes that do not permit direct plotting as described above; for these, a different method must be employed. This method is usually based on the use of an assumed position (AP), and the solution of the navigational triangle associated with it.

It has been stated that the navigational triangle may be defined by the AP, the elevated pole, and the GP of the body. By solving that triangle, the altitude

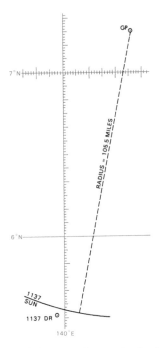

Fig. 2604b. Plot of the LOP from a high-altitude observation.

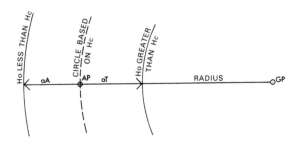

Fig. 2605b. The difference in the radii of the two circles of equal altitude is equal to the difference between the coaltitudes obtained from Ho and Hc.

If the altitude (Ho) obtained by the observer at M is greater than the altitude computed (Hc) by solving the triangle, the observer must be closer to the GP than is the AP; if it is less, he must be farther away. Also, the difference in the radii of the two circles of equal altitude, as illustrated in figure 2605b, is equal to the difference between the coaltitudes obtained from Ho and Hc, respectively. The difference is the intercept (a) and is expressed in nautical miles, which equals the difference expressed in minutes of arc.

Plotting the LOP

2606   As has been explained, plotting a celestial LOP requires the following:

Position of the AP
Azimuth of the body (Zn)
Intercept (a)

As explained in previous chapters, in solving the triangle, the value of the azimuth angle (Z) is obtained and is used to determine the true direction or azimuth (Zn) of the body's GP from the AP (unless Zn is found directly as with Pub. No. 249, Volume I). If the Ho is greater than the Hc, a line representing Zn is plotted from the AP *toward* the GP; if the Hc is the greater, the line will be plotted as the reciprocal of Zn, or *away* from the GP.

The intercept (a) lies along a partial radius of a circle of equal altitude. The length of (a) in miles is equal to the difference between Ho and Hc in minutes of arc. This distance is measured from the AP in the direction of Zn if Ho is greater than Hc and labeled "T" for "toward." If Hc is the greater, the intercept distance is plotted along the reciprocal of the azimuth and is marked "A" for "away." While it is important for you to understand *why* this works, a check on your logic can be found in the two convenient memory aids "Coast Guard Academy" and "HoMoTo." Coast Guard Academy uses the first letters to indicate that if the *Computed* altitude (Hc) is *Greater*, then the LOP must be plotted *Away* from

and azimuth of the body at the AP at the time of observation may be computed. In figure 2605a, the circle represents the circle of equal altitude for an observer at M, and the point AP is the assumed position selected for the particular observation. By solving the triangle containing AP, the navigator determines the length of the side AP–GP, or coaltitude, which is the radius of the circle of equal altitude through the AP (not shown in figure 2605a).

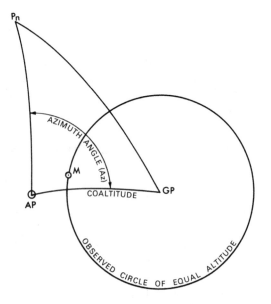

Fig. 2605a. A circle of equal altitude and the navigational triangle associated with one AP.

the GP of the observed body (in the direction of the azimuth's reciprocal). HoMoTo simply reminds us that if the observed altitude (Ho) is *More* than the computed altitude (Hc), then the LOP must be plotted *To*ward the GP of the observed body (in the direction of the azimuth).

The line of position on which the observer is located is perpendicular to the radius line. Although this LOP is actually an arc of a circle of equal altitude, for most observations, the radius of this circle is so large that the curvature of the LOP is not significant. Except for those LOPs resulting from very high altitude observations, celestial LOPs may be drawn as straight lines. The resulting error inherent in this convention is insignificant in the ordinary practice of navigation. Figure 2606a, which shows the relationships among the AP, GP, coaltitude, and circle of equal altitude, also illustrates the approximation made by using a straight line rather than an arc for plotting a celestial LOP. If a more precise solution is required, the circle can be closely approximated by plotting "offsets" from the straight LOP as explained in the introductory pages to any volume of NIMA Pub. No. 229.

The following example will illustrate that portion of a navigator's work that has just been discussed. The actual plot, as laid down on the chart, is shown in figure 2606b. Note that only two lines are drawn—the dashed line, from the AP, which represents the intercept; and the heavy line, which is the LOP. The latter is labeled in accordance with standard practice, the ship's time of the observation being shown above, and the name of the body observed below. In normal practice, the intercept is not labeled; the time may be omitted from the LOP if it is used for a fix that is labeled with time.

Example: At 0623 a navigator determines the Ho of the star Procyon to be 12° 37.4′. Selecting a point at L 35° 00.0′ S and l 76° 27.1′ W as his assumed position, he computes Hc to be 12° 17.4′ and Zn to be 329.2°.

Required: The plot of the 0623 celestial LOP.
Solution: See figure 2606b.

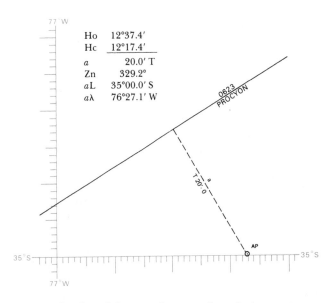

Fig. 2606b. Plot of the LOP from a celestial observation.

(1) Plot the AP, using the aL and al given.

(2) By comparing the Hc and Ho, determine the intercept (a) to be 20.0 miles from the AP.

(3) Because the Ho is greater than the Hc, the LOP will be constructed *toward* the GP, that is, in the direction of the azimuth (329.2°) rather than in the direction of its reciprocal.

(4) From the AP draw a broken line toward the direction of the GP, in the direction indicated by Zn (329.2°).

(5) Measure the distance of the intercept along this line (20.0 miles)

(6) At the point so determined, construct a perpendicular.

(7) This perpendicular is the 0623 LOP; label it with the time of the observation above the LOP and with the name of the body below the LOP, as shown in figure 2606b.

THE CELESTIAL FIX

2607 In piloting, a navigator can fix his position by taking bearings of two or more landmarks or other aids to navigation in rapid succession. For practical purposes, it is generally assumed that these bearings are taken simultaneously, and no adjustment of the lines of position is required. In celestial navigation, observations cannot be taken as rapidly as in piloting, with the result that the lines of position obtained usually must be adjusted for the relatively few minutes of travel of the ship between sights. This means that what is termed a *fix* in celestial navigation is actually constructed using the principles of the running fix used in piloting, since lines of

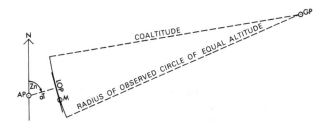

Fig. 2606a. Plot of the same LOP from the AP and from the GP.

position are advanced or retired to a common time. It is customary to consider the position resulting from observations obtained during a single round of sights as a "fix," with the term *running fix* being reserved for a position obtained from observations separated by a more lengthy period of time, typically more than 30 minutes.

Except when the high-altitude technique is used, each celestial line of position requires an AP (which in some procedures may be the DR position), a segment of the radius (in the direction determined by Zn) equal in length to an intercept (a), and the actual LOP constructed perpendicular to the Zn line at the point found by using (a). If three successive celestial observations are taken with small time intervals between them, the resulting APs with their associated lines of position can readily be plotted. To obtain a celestial fix, however, each would have to be advanced or retired to the time desired for the fix, making proper allowance for the travel of the ship during the intervening time. This could be done, as in piloting, by moving each LOP for the correct distance and direction. Because of the larger number of lines required to plot a celestial fix in this manner in a comparatively small area of the chart or plotting sheet, many navigators prefer to *advance the AP rather than the line of position*, thereby plotting the LOP only once. This is the method that will be used throughout this book and is illustrated in the following examples:

Example: The 0515 DR position of a ship on course 176°, speed 14.5 knots, is L 35° 09.2′ S, l 119° 13.7′ E. About this time the navigator observes the stars Antares, Acrux, and Regulus, with the following results:

Body	Antares	Acrux	Regulus
Time	0515	0519	0525
a	20.3 T	18.1 T	7.0 A
Zn	093.6°	189.5°	311.0°
aL	35° 00.0′ S	35° 00.0′ S	35° 00.0′ S
al	118° 56.0′ E	119° 17.9′ E	119° 27.9′ E

Required: The plot of the 0525 celestial fix.
Solution: See figure 2607a.
(1) Plot the 0515 DR position and the DR track from 0515 to 0525.
(2) Plot the DR position for the time of each observation.
(3) Plot the AP of the earlier sight (Antares) and advance it in the direction and for the distance corresponding to the travel of the ship between the

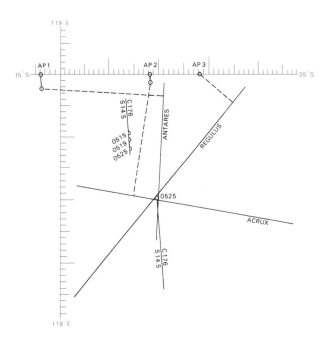

Fig. 2607a. A fix determined from three celestial LOPs.

0515 DR position and the 0525 DR position (2.4 miles in direction 176°).

(4) From the advanced AP so obtained, plot the 0515–0525 LOP, labeling it as shown. (Note that the line joining the original AP and the advanced AP is plotted as a solid line, and that the advanced AP is *not* labeled).

(5) Next, plot the AP of Acrux and advance it in the direction and for the distance the ship has traveled between 0519 and 0525 (1.4 miles in direction 176°).

(6) Plot and label the 0519–0525 Acrux LOP from the advanced AP.

(7) Finally, plot the AP for the Regulus sight, and from it plot the 0525 Regulus LOP. (Note that this final AP does not need to be advanced because it was the final sight and was actually taken at the "advanced" time of 0525.)

Answer: The intersection of the three lines of position (or the center of the small triangle so formed) is the 0525 fix. (Note that to reduce the clutter of the plot, times are omitted on the individual LOPs and are shown only for the DR positions and the final fix.)

When a *change of course or speed* occurs between the times of the observations used in plotting a fix, the procedure used for advancing or retiring a line of position is the same as that used in piloting. This is illustrated in the following example:

Example: The 0500 DR position of a ship on course 250°, speed 20 knots, is L 35° 11.0′ N, l 78° 17.0′ W. At 0535 course is changed to 190°. During morning twilight the navigator observes two bodies with results as follows:

Body	Deneb	Venus
Time	0525	0550
A	8.1 A	5.3 T
Zn	058.5°	123.9°
aL	35° 00.0′ N	35° 00.0′ N
al	78° 09.0′ W	78° 27.5′ W

Required: The plot of the 0550 celestial fix.

Solution: See figure 2607b.

(1) Plot the 0500 DR position and the DR track until 0550, indicating the DR position for the time of each observation.

(2) Plot the AP of the earlier sight (Deneb) and advance it in the direction and for the distance corresponding to the travel of the ship between the 0525 DR position and the 0550 DR position (7.3 miles in direction 213.4°, as shown by the broken line marked "CMG" for "course made good").

(3) From the advanced AP so obtained, plot the 0525–0550 LOP, labeling it as shown. (4) Plot an AP of the Venus sight, and from it plot the 0550 LOP.

Answer: The intersection of the two lines of position is the 0550 fix.

A fix obtained using the results of *high-altitude observations* is plotted in a manner similar to that described above, except that the GP of the body (not the AP of the observer) is advanced or retired as

necessary. The method of advancing a high-altitude celestial line of position by advancing its GP is explained in the following example.

Example: The 1200 DR position of a ship on course 270°, speed 20.0 knots, is L 23° 20.0′ N, l 75° 08.4′ W. About this time, the navigator observes the Sun twice, with the following results:

Body	Sun	Sun
Time	1154	1206
Ho	88° 33.6′	88°00.8′
L GP	22° 07.7′ N	22° 07.7′ N
l GP	74° 04.2′ W	77° 04.2′ W

Required: The plot of the 1206 fix.

Solution: (See fig. 2607c.)

(1) Plot the DR track from 1154 to 1206, indicating the 1154 and 1206 DR positions.

(2) Plot the 1154 position of the Sun's GP, and advance it for the direction and distance from the 1154 DR position to the 1206 DR position (4.0 miles in direction 270°).

(3) Determine the radius of the observed circle of equal altitude about the GP by subtracting the Ho from 90° 00.0′. The radius is 86.4 miles (since 90° 00.0′ – 88° 33.6′ = 1° 26.4′ = 86.4 miles).

(4) With this radius, and using the advanced GP as the center, swing an arc through the area containing the DR position. This is the 1154–1206 line of position, and is labeled as shown.

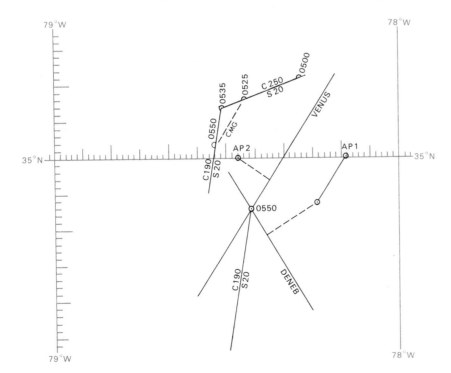

Fig. 2607b. A celestial fix with a change of course between observations.

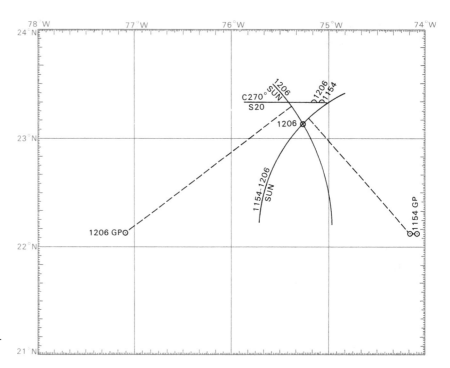

Fig. 2607c. A celestial fix using high altitude observations.

(5) Plot the 1206 GP of the Sun, and determine the radius of the circle of equal altitude about it by subtracting the Ho from 90° 00.0′. The radius is 119.2 miles (since 90° 00.0′ − 88° 00.8′ = 1° 59.2′ = 119.2 miles).

(6) With this radius, and using the 1206 GP as a center, swing an arc through the area containing the DR position.

Answer: The intersection of the two lines of position is the 1206 fix.

Note that there are two possible intersections of two circles of equal altitude, only one of which is shown. In all ordinary circumstances, the intersection nearer the DR position is the fix. In the case shown in Figure 2607c, there is no doubt as to the correct intersection, as the body passed to the south of the observer, and the intersection to the north of the GPs used must be the fix. Where doubt exists and the navigator is unable to determine which intersection to use, commence a DR track from both positions, and assume that the ship is on the DR track that is the more dangerous until confirmation is obtained.

RUNNING CELESTIAL FIX

2608 When the times of the observations used are separated by a considerable interval (more than 30 minutes in a normal situation), the result is a *celestial running fix* (R Fix). The observations may be of different bodies or successive sights of the same body. Since the time elapsed between observations used to obtain a running fix is usually at least an hour, and frequently considerably longer, the LOP obtained from the earlier observation is plotted for the information it provides. The *LOP is then advanced* (rather than its AP) to the time of the later observation to establish the R fix, using the same methods employed in establishing a running fix in piloting.

There is no absolute limit on the maximum time interval between observations used for a celestial running fix. This must be left to the discretion of the navigator who must give consideration to how accurately he thinks he knows his course and speed made good during that time interval. In most instances, however, three hours might be considered a practical limit.

It should be noted that in summer, when the Sun transits at high altitudes, it changes azimuth very rapidly before and after transit; excellent running fixes may thus be obtained within reasonable periods of time.

Example: The 0930 DR position of a ship on course 064°, speed 18.0 knots, is L 33° 06.4′ N, l 146° 24.5′ W. The navigator observes the Sun twice during the morning, with the results as follows:

Body	Sun	Sun
Time	0942	1200
A	6.2 A	27.9 A
Zn	134.2°	182.5°
aL	33° 00.0′ N	33° 00.0 N
al	146° 24.9′ W	145° 38.0′ W

Required: The plot of the 1200 running fix.

Solution: See figure 2608a.

(1) Plot the 0930 DR position, and the DR track to 1200, indicating the 0942 and the 1200 DR positions.

(2) Plot the AP with its associated LOP for 0942.

(3) Advance the LOP for the distance and direction from the 0942 DR position to the 1200 DR position (41.4 miles in direction 064°), and label it as shown.

(4) Plot the AP and from it the LOP for the 1200 Sun observation, labeling it as shown.

Answer: The intersection of the 0942–1200 LOP and the 1200 LOP is the 1200 running fix. (In this plot, the time is labeled on the 0942 LOP and on the 0942–1200 advanced LOP to ensure proper identification.)

When a *change of course or speed* occurs between the times of the observations used for obtaining a running celestial fix, the procedures used are the same as those employed in advancing the first LOP to obtain a running fix in piloting.

Using the same observations as in the previous example, the following example illustrates how a running fix is obtained when both course and speed are changed between observations:

Example: The 0930 DR position of a ship on course 064°, speed 18.0 knots, is L 33° 06.4′ N, l 146° 24.5′ W. At 1100 course is changed to 030°, and speed is reduced to 13.5 knots. During the morning, the navigator observes the Sun twice, with results as tabulated in the previous example.

Required: The plot of the 1200 running fix.

Solution: See figure 2608b.

(1) Plot the 0930 DR position and the DR track to 1200, indicating the 0942 and the 1200 DR positions.

(2) Plot the 0942 LOP and advance it for the distance and direction from the 0942 DR position to the 1200 DR position (35.4 miles in the direction 052°). Label it as shown.

(3) Plot and label the 1200 LOP. The intersection of the 0942–1200 LOP and the 1200 LOP is the 1200 running fix.

Where a current of known set and drift exists, the position of a running fix may be adjusted to allow for the effect of the current during the time elapsed between the first and second observation.

Errors in Running Celestial Fixes

2609 Many of the errors possible in the running celestial fix are the same as those for the terrestrial running fix. However, the magnitude of the errors tends to be greater in the celestial fix because:

1. The celestial LOP is rarely as accurate as the terrestrial LOP.

2. Information on set and draft is not available at sea to the same degree of accuracy as is usual along a coast or in pilot waters.

3. In celestial navigation, the time required to obtain the running fix is usually longer than that required in piloting; therefore errors in courses and distances made good affect the accuracy to a greater extent.

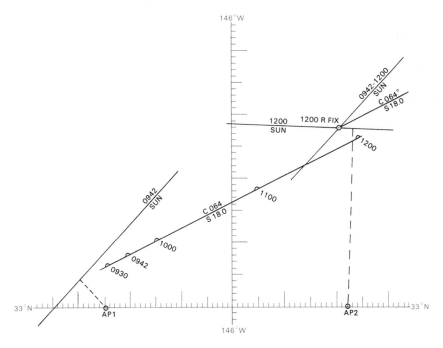

Fig. 2608a. A celestial running fix.

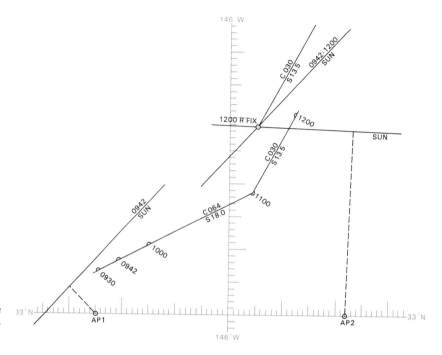

2608b. A celestial running fix with change of course and speed between observations.

These problems notwithstanding, the celestial running fix may be the only information available is some circumstances, and it is always useful as a check against other sources of navigational information.

FIXES COMBINING CELESTIAL AND OTHER LOPS

2610 A line of position, however obtained, is merely an indication of likely positions of a vessel, and must be crossed with one or more other LOPs to fix the position. A major objective of all forms of navigation is the determination of position—so that the ship or craft can safely and efficiently be directed from where it is to the desired destination.

As a navigator you should, therefore, use any and all lines of position that you can obtain.

Therefore, you might cross a Loran line with an LOP obtained from a celestial body. In a like manner, when making a landfall you might cross a celestial or some other LOP with a depth curve shown on your chart, determining by echo sounder the time that the curve was crossed. When only one LOP is obtainable at sea, a sounding or series of soundings may be helpful in determining the general area of the vessel's position.

All LOPs will not be of the same order of accuracy, but with experience a navigator will learn to evaluate the resulting fix. *It is vital that no opportunity be lost to acquire information that may be helpful in determining the vessel's position.*

Chapter 27

The Complete Celestial Solution

The complete solution for a typical celestial navigation sight involves the identification of the body to be observed, the use of a sextant to measure altitude, the accurate determination of the time of the sight, the use of an almanac to extract data, and some method of sight reduction to obtain a line of position, which is then plotted and combined with other LOPs to determine a fix.

In chapter 20 ("Introduction to Celestial Navigation"), you were introduced to the process of basic celestial navigation and provided with a summarized list of the steps involved for obtaining an LOP by means of an observation. Each of those steps was explained in greater detail in subsequent chapters as follows:

(1) Identify and locate the celestial body or bodies you are going to use. For the Sun or Moon, this process is obviously a simple matter, but for a star or planet, you will need some assistance from special charts, almanacs, devices, or software. (See chapter 21, "Identification of Celestial Bodies.")

(2) Using a sextant and timepiece, take your sightings and record them, in both altitude and time (plus, preferably, their approximate azimuths). (See chapters 22, "The Sextant," and 23, "Time.")

(3) Determine the actual position of each celestial body sighted at the time of its sighting. This is accomplished by using an almanac or other source of ephemeral data, which will give you the body's GP in celestial coordinates that can be translated to a terrestrial position. (See chapter 24, "Ephemeral Data.")

(4) Determine your assumed position. As mentioned above, this is based upon your DR but will be refined for convenience when using sight reduction tables. The AP will give you an assumed latitude and longitude to work with. (See chapter 25, "Sight Reduction.")

(5) Enter the sight reduction tables with the local hour angle, declination, and latitude (all deduced from the ephemeral and assumed position data) to obtain the computed altitude and azimuth. (See chapter 25, "Sight Reduction.")

(6) Comparing the computed altitude with the observed altitude, and using the azimuth, plot an LOP. (See chapter 26, "Celestial Lines of Position.")

Using the information presented in those chapters, we will now bring them together. The first method presented involves the use of a sight form using the *Nautical Almanac* and Pub. No. 229. Subsequently, other methods will be discussed, including using the *Air Almanac* and Pub. No. 249, as well as Ageton and STELLA (System to Estimate Latitude and Longitude Astronomically).

COMPLETE SOLUTIONS FOR CELESTIAL OBSERVATIONS USING A SIGHT FORM

2701 Each block of the sight form used in this book to reduce sights using the *Nautical Almanac* and Pub. No. 229 is listed below with a brief explanation of how each item is used and a reference to the relevant articles should you require more detail or further explanation. Using this list as your guide while studying the sight forms and examples following should make the process clear.

Body Record the name of the body being observed. If your observation was an upper-limb or a lower-limb one, note it here. (For "limb" see arts. 2202 and 2229.)

IC Apply the IC (index correction) based upon your determined index error; that is, reverse the sign of your index error to get the appropriate index correction. (See art. 2221.)

Dip (Ht.) Enter your height of eye and find the appropriate dip correction as determined from the *Nautical Almanac*. Table on page A2 inside the front cover (and on the bookmark provided) includes a "Dip" table to be used for this purpose. (See art. 2225.)

Sum Add the values of IC and Dip and record this figure.

hs After making your observation, record the actual reading from your sextant here. (See art. 2205.)

ha Applying the "Sum" figure (of IC and Dip) to the hs figure above will give you the apparent altitude. (See art. 2226.)

Alt. corr. Altitude corrections from 10 to 90° for the Sun, stars, and planets are found in table A2 inside the front cover of the *Nautical Almanac* on the left-hand page (and on the bookmark provided). Altitude corrections from 0 to 10° for the Sun, stars, and planets are found inside the front cover of the *Nautical Almanac* on the *right*-hand page, A3. Be sure to use the "Stars and Planets" portion of the table or the "Sun" portion as appropriate, and enter with the apparent altitude (ha). Altitude corrections for the Moon are found on the inside *back* cover of the *Nautical Almanac* (0–35° on the left-hand page and 35–90° on the right-hand page). (See arts. 2234, 2236 [Sun], 2237 [Star], 2238/2239 [Planets], and 2240 [Moon].)

Add'l. Used only for Venus and Mars observations to counter the effects of parallax. Obtain the additional correction from the right-hand column of the "Stars and Planets" portion of the Altitude Correction Tables on page A2 (inside cover) of the *Nautical Almanac* (also available on the special bookmark provided with the *Almanac*). (See arts. 2233 and 2239.)

H.P. Used for Moon observations only. First obtain the Horizontal Parallax value from the daily pages of the *Nautical Almanac* (in the column headed by "H.P."). Then go to the H.P. portion (lower half) of the Altitude Correction Tables for the Moon on the inside back cover of the *Nautical Almanac*. Be sure to use the appropriate column for lower (L) or Upper (U) limb, and to use the extra 30′ subtracted for upper limb. (See arts. 2233 and 2240.)

Corr. to ha Sum of Alt. corr., Add'l, and H.P. corrections. Applied to ha above to determine Ho (observed altitude) below.

Ho (Obs. Alt.) Derived from ha and corrections above. (See art. 2218.)

Date Enter the local date.

DR Lat. Enter your dead-reckoned latitude. (See chapter 9.)

DR Long. Enter your dead-reckoned longitude. (See chapter 9.)

Obs. Time The actual (local) watch time that this observation was made.

WE (S+, F–) Record watch error, making the correction positive (+) if the timepiece you used in making your observations is running slow and making it negative (-) if the timepiece is running fast. (See art. 2321.)

ZT Apply the correction for watch error to the watch time of observation to get the corrected Zone (local) Time.

ZD (W+, E–) Enter the zone description with a plus sign if your DR position is in west longitude or a negative sign if it is east. (See art. 2308.)

GMT Apply the zone description to the Zone Time to obtain the Greenwich Mean Time. Remember that this time may also be expressed as Universal Time (UT). (See art. 2306.)

Date (GMT) Add or subtract a day if necessary after applying the zone description.

Tab GHA / v Enter the appropriate daily pages of the *Nautical Almanac* to obtain the appropriate Greenwich Hour Angle. Each of the planets, the Sun, and the Moon, has its own column of GHA listings for each whole hour of GMT (UT) for the days covered. For stars, you must record the GHA of Aries (♈) here (and later combine it with the individual star's sidereal hour angle as discussed below). In each case, you must locate the appropriate whole hour of your observation in the left-most column (marked "UT") of the page being used, making certain that you are using the figures for the appropriate date.

The "v" factor is the amount in arc by which GHA departs from the basic hourly rate used in the almanac interpolation table and applies only to planet and Moon sights. For the planets it is found at the bottom of each plant's column on the left-hand daily pages. For the Moon, it is found as a separate column entry on the right-hand daily pages between the whole-hour entries for GHA and Dec. The sign of v is always positive with the exception of Venus, which can sometimes be negative. (For GHA, see arts. 2007, 2402, 2404, and 2408. For "v," see arts. 2404, 2405, and 2406.)

GHA inc. Turning to the Increments and Corrections Table in the yellow pages near the back of the *Almanac*, find the appropriate increments of

GHA for the minutes and seconds of the GMT. (See arts. 2402, 2406, and 2408.)

SHA or v corr. f your observed body is a star, obtain its sidereal hour angle from the appropriate daily page of the *Nautical Almanac* (left-hand page, far-right column).

Find the "v corr." values (Moon and planets only) in the right-hand half of the Increments and Corrections Table in the *Nautical Almanac;* enter with the v factor obtained from the daily pages and find the v correction adjacent to it. (For SHA see arts. 2007, 2408, and 2411. For "v corr." see arts. 2404, 2405, 2406, and 2408.)

GHA Total the values in the three boxes above (Tab GHA, GHA inc., and either SHA or v corr. as appropriate) to determine the Greenwich hour angle.

360° if needed Apply 360° to the GHA if necessary to keep it within the conventional range.

aλ (–W, +E) Select an assumed longitude by choosing a figure close to your DR longitude that, when applied (added if east, subtracted if west) to the GHA, will yield a whole degree of LHA (local hour angle). (See arts. 2504 and 2507.)

LHA Combine the GHA and aλ to obtain a whole-degree local hour angle.

Tab Dec. / d Obtain the tabulated declination from the appropriate daily page of the *Almanac* (left-hand for planets and stars, right-hand for the Sun and Moon). The d values are the amount in arc by which declination changes during each hour. Find d values for planets and the Sun at the bottom of each one's daily page column of data. Find hourly d values for the Moon listed as a separate column between "Dec." and "H.P." Stars do not require a d value. (For Tab Dec. see arts. 2007, 2404, 2405, and 2408. For d, see arts. 2404, 2405, and 2406.)

d corr. (+ or –) Find the "d corr." values (Sun, Moon, and planets only) in the right-hand half of the Increments and Corrections Table in the *Nautical Almanac;* enter with the d factor obtained from the daily pages and find the d correction adjacent to it. Values of d on the daily pages are not marked "+" or "–"; the sign must be determined by observing the trend (increasing or decreasing) of the Dec. values straddling the time of your observation in the daily pages. (For "d corr." see arts. 2404, 2405, 2406, and 2408.)

True Dec. For star sights, merely repeat the Tab Dec. from above. For Sun, Moon, and planet observations, apply the "d corr." to the Tab Dec. to obtain the true declination.

a Lat. (N or S) Choose the whole degree of latitude that is closest to your DR position. Note whether the latitude and declination have the "same" or "contrary" names (N or S). (See arts. 2504 and 2506.)

Dec. inc./(±)d Determine the declination increment by simply recording the amount by which the True Declination exceeds the whole degree. Obtain the d factor (along with the Hc and Z) by entering Pub. No. 229 with the latitude (assumed), LHA, and true declination; extract the value from the column labeled "d" (from the row determined by your entering argument of Dec.) and recording the appropriate sign. (For "Dec. inc." see art. 2512. For this "d" see art. 2509.)

Hc (Tab. Alt.) Obtain the tabulated altitude (Hc) (along with the d factor and Z) by entering Pub. No. 229 with the latitude (assumed), LHA, and true declination. (See art. 2509.)

tens/DS Diff. Using the Interpolation Table found in the inside covers of Pub. No. 229, determine the "tens" portion of the interpolation. Record the double-second difference if applicable (dot and italics used with "d" in the main 229 table). (For "tens" see arts. 2510 and 2512. For "DS Diff" see art. 2513.)

Units/DS corr. Using the Interpolation Table found in the inside covers of Pub. No. 229, determine the "units" portion of the interpolation. Record the double-second difference correction if applicable. (For "units" see arts. 2510 and 2512. For "DS corr." see art. 2513.)

Tot. corr. (±) Combine the corrections recorded in the "tens," "units," and "DS corr." boxes above.

Hc (Comp. Alt.) Apply the "Tot. corr." value to the "HC (Tab. Alt.)" to determine the computed altitude.

Ho (Obs. Alt.) Repeat the observed altitude value determined earlier and recorded above in a box of the same name.

a (Intercept) Determine the altitude intercept by comparing Hc and Ho above. Also note whether the value is to be applied toward (T) or away (A). If Ho is greater than Hc, the intercept is toward and vice versa. (See arts. 2516 and 2517.)

Z Obtain the azimuth angle (along with the Hc and d factor) by entering Pub. No. 229 with the latitude (assumed), LHA, and true declination. (See art. 2505–2509.)

Zn (° T) Using the rules provided on the main pages of Pub. No. 229, convert the azimuth angle to true azimuth (see art. 2518):

(If latitude is north and LHA > 180°, then Zn = Z.

If latitude is north and LHA < 180°, then Zn = 360 - Z.

If latitude is south and LHA > 180°, then Zn = 180 - Z.

If latitude is south and LHA < 180°, then Zn = 180 + Z.)

It should be apparent that you will save time, and perhaps reduce the possibility of error, if you extract the pertinent data for all bodies from the daily pages of the *Nautical Almanac* at one page opening, when working multiple sights for a fix. Similarly, the *v* and *d* corrections, as well as the increments of GHA for minutes and seconds for each body, should be obtained at a single use of the Increments and Corrections Table.

You will note that GMT and UT are used interchangeably (see article 2306) in the discussion below. While UT is used in the *Nautical Almanac* as an entering argument, GMT is used in the sight form because its relationship to GHA and so on is clearer than is UT.

Be careful not to confuse the "d" factors that appear twice. One usage is for the difference of declination that applies to the *Almanac,* while the other applies to the difference in Hc values found in Pub. No. 229. The corrections for the former are found in the Increments and Corrections Table in the back of the *Nautical Almanac,* and the corrections for the latter are found by using the Interpolation Table inside the front and back covers of Pub. No. 229.

Selections from a Typical Day's Work

2702 The examples presented here represent typical portions of a single day's work in celestial navigation. The computations are shown on a typical work form (see figs. 2702a and 2702b). Modifications to these forms may be made, and each individual navigator should develop a format that is best suited to her or him. The lines of position and resultant fix from the observations are shown as a plot in figures 2702c and 2702d.

For the examples that follow, assume you are navigator on a salvage tug accompanying a partially disabled tanker; the course is 288°, speed 6.8 knots. At 0400 (time zone +1) on 5 June, the ship's DR position is Lat. 41° 02.8′ N, Long. 14° 38.0′ W.

Complete Solution for Star Observations

2703 Referring to article 2701, use the sight form in figure 2702a as you read through the following discussion of converting your star sights to LOPs.

Using your 2102-D Star Finder, you determine that observations of Alkaid and Capella should yield useful LOPs.

Assume that you made two sextant observations of these stars, measuring the sextant altitude of each as follows:

Body	Time	Sextant Altitude
Alkaid	20-03-06	77° 39.3′
Capella	20-04-08	15° 27.0′

Your DR position at the time of the observations was Lat. 41° 34.8′ N and Long. 17° 00.5′ W, the watch used is known to be 10 seconds fast, your sextant has an index *error* of –0.2′, and your height of eye is 21 feet.

Using your sight form, enter the names of the stars in the appropriate boxes at the top and record your actual observations in the "hs" boxes.

Using the index error determined for your sextant, enter the index *correction* (IC) on the form and then the Dip correction as determined from the *Nautical Almanac* for your height of eye. These values will not change for the two observations. Apply these (and any corrections for instrument or personal errors) to each hs to obtain ha.

Find the altitude correction for each star sight in the "Stars and Planets" column on page A2 on the inside front cover (or on the bookmark) of the *Nautical Almanac* and record them in the sight form box marked "Alt. Corr." Because the "Add'l" correction only applies to Mars and Venus, that box on the sight form should be left blank. The same is true for the next box (H.P), which applies only to the Moon.

Bring down the alt. corr. value and write it in the box labeled "Corr. to ha" since there are no other corrections to be included from above. Add this box to the ha above and write the algebraic sum in the box labeled "Ho (Obs Alt)."

Next, record your DR position and fill in the boxes relating to time and date (Date, Obs. Time, WE, ZT, and ZD) to arrive at the correct GMT and date for each star sight.

Enter the appropriate daily pages of the *Nautical Almanac* to obtain the GHA of Aries at the whole hours of GMT, as well as the SHA and the declination of the stars for that same day. No "v" correction is necessary since these are star sights.

Turning to the Increments and Corrections Table, obtain the increments for minutes and seconds in the "Aries" column and enter them in the "GHA incr'mt" boxes for the two stars.

Add the tabulated GHA of Aries, the SHA of the stars, and the GHA inc. to obtain the stars' GHAs at the time of observation.

For each star, select an assumed longitude that

Sight Reduction using Pub. 229

Body	ALKAID			CAPELLA		
IC	+ 0.2		-	+ 0.2		-
Dip (Ht 21 ')		4.4			4.4	
Sum		- 4.2			-4.2	
hs	77	39.3		15	27.0	
ha	77	35.1		15	22.8	
Alt. Corr		0.2			3.5	
Add'l.						
H.P. ( )						
Corr. to ha		-0.2			-3.5	
Ho (Obs Alt)	77	34.9		15	19.3	
Date	5 JUN			5 JUN		
DR Lat	41	34.8 N		41	34.8 N	
DR Long	17	00.5 W		17	00.5 W	
Obs. Time	20-03-06			20-04-08		
WE (S+, F-)		-10 F			-10 F	
ZT	20-02-56			20-03-58		
ZD (W+, E-)	+1			+1		
GMT	21-02-56			21-03-58		
Date (GMT)	5 JUN			5 JUN		
Tab GHA v	209	10.1		209	10.1	
GHA incr'mt.	0	44.1		0	59.7	
SHA or v Corr.	153	20.0		281	15.0	
GHA	363	14.2		491	24.8	
±360 if needed				131	24.8	
aλ (-W, +E)	17	14.2	W	17	24.8	W
LHA	346			114		
Tab Dec d	N 49	25.7		N 45	58.9	
d Corr (+ or -)						
True Dec	N 49	25.7		N 45	58.4	
a Lat (N or S)	42 N Same Cont.			42 N Same Cont.		
Dec Inc (±)d	25.7	-32.0		58.4	+42.6	
Hc (Tab. Alt.)	77	58.6		15	02.1	
tens DS Diff.	-12.9	6.9		+38.9		
units DS Corr.	- 0.8	+ 0.4		+ 2.5	+	
Tot. Corr. (+ or -)	-13.3			+41.4		
Hc (Comp. Alt.)	77	45.3		15	43.5	
Ho (Obs. Alt.)	77	34.9		15	19.3	
a (Intercept)	10.4	A		24.2	A	
Z	N 47.9 E			N 41.2 W		
Zn (°T)	047.9°			318.8°		

Fig. 2702a. Sight reductions using Pub. No. 229; stars.

will yield a whole degree of LHA when added to the GHA. Record it and the resulting LHA in the appropriate boxes for each star.

Use the Tab Dec. values as your true declinations (True Dec.) since no d correction is required for stars.

Enter a whole-degree assumed latitude based upon your DR latitude. Record the declination increment (Dec. inc.) for each sight. Note that the assumed longitudes for the two stars are different but the assumed latitudes in this instance are the same.

Entering Pub. No. 229 with integral degrees of local hour angle (LHA), assumed latitude (a Lat), and declination (True Dec.), obtain the tabulated altitude (Hc), d and its sign, and the azimuth angle (Z) for each star. Increments to these tabulated altitudes are then taken from the Interpolation Table in Pub. No. 229 and entered in the tens and units boxes. A double-second difference correction (DS corr.) is necessary for the Alkaid observation (the d value in Pub. No. 229 was listed in italics and had a dot next to it) but not for Capella. These values are then totaled (in the "Tot. Corr." box) and applied to the Hc (Tab. Alt.) to determine the Hc (Comp. Alt.).

Determine the altitude intercepts by comparing the Hc and Ho for each star. Convert Z to Zn.

Using the intercepts and azimuths determined, a line of position can be constructed on a chart relative to each AP for each of the above observations, resulting in a 2004 fix as shown in figure 2702c. Note that for both observations—Alkaid and Capella—the resultant intercepts are *away* from the GPs of the bodies, requiring the LOPs to be constructed as perpendiculars to the reciprocals of the true azimuths. As you can see, the 2004 fix, as determined by the intersection of the LOPs, is about 6 miles northwest of the 2004 DR. In this plot the travel of the salvage tug in the 62 seconds between star observations was ignored.

Complete Solution for a Planet Observation

2704   Much of the process for a planet observation is the same, but there are some important differences. Assume that you observed Venus at 0417 and 21 seconds on 5 June. Your DR position at that time was Lat. 41° 03.4′ N and Long. 14° 40.4′ W. The watch error is 8 seconds fast. Your height of eye is again 21 feet. The reading on your sextant when you took the sight was 21° 13.4′ and your sextant continues to have an index error of –0.2′. To convert this information into an LOP, you would fill out your sight form as shown in figure 2702b.

When observing a planet, you first measure the sextant altitude of the center of the body and record it along with the time and date of the observation. The same values of index correction (IC) and Dip would apply to this observation as for the star sights and would be applied to hs to get ha. Next, deter-

Sight Reduction using Pub. 229

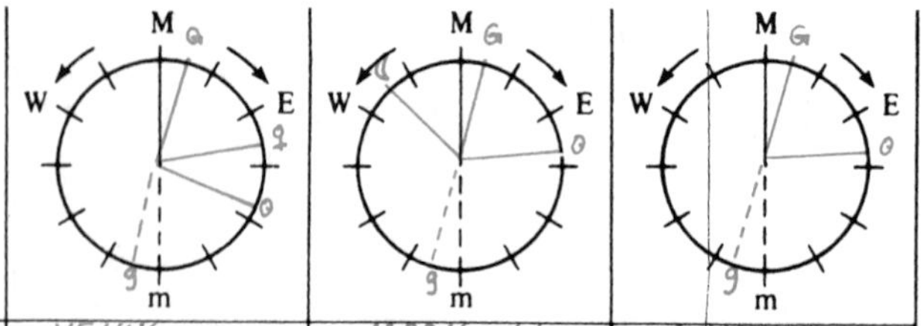

Body	VENUS		MOON LL		SUN LL	
IC	+0.2	-	+0.2	-	+0.2	-
Dip (Ht 21 ')		4.4		4.4		4.4
Sum		-4.2		-4.2		-4.2
hs	21	13.4	18	56.0	19	17.5
ha	21	09.2	18	51.8	19	13.3
Alt. Corr		2.5	62.4			
Add'l.	03					
H.P. ( )			7.2	(59.5')		
Corr. to ha		-2.2	+1	09.6	+	13.3
Ho (Obs Alt)	21	07.0	20	01.4	19	26.6
Date	5 JUN		5 JUN		5 JUN	
DR Lat	41	03.4 N	41	07.9 N	41	07.9 N
DR Long	14	40.4 W	14	58.7 W	14	58.7 W
Obs. Time	04-17-21		06-24-43		06-25-23	
WE (S+, F-)	-8F		-8F		-8F	
ZT	04-17-13		06-24-35		06-25-15	
ZD (W+, E-)	+1		+1		+1	
GMT	05-17-13		07-24-35		07-25-15	
Date (GMT)	5 JUN		5 JUN		5 JUN	
Tab GHA v	300 39.3	+0.4	54 56.7	+7.4	285	24.7
GHA incr'mt.	4	18.3	5	52.0	6	18.8
SHA or v Corr.		0.1		3.0		
GHA	304	57.7	60	51.7	291	43.5
±360 if needed						
aλ (-W, +E)	14	57.7 W	14	51.7 W	14	43.5 W
LHA	290		46		277	
Tab Dec d	N8 59.6	+0.6	S14 39.9	-7.4	N22 32.4	+0.3
d Corr (+ or -)		+0.2		-3.0		+0.1
True Dec	N8	59.8	S14	36.9	N22	32.5
a Lat (N or S)	41 N	Same Cont.	41 N	Same Cont.	41 N	Same Cont.
Dec Inc (±)d	59.8	+39.2	36.9	-49.0	32.5	+36.4
Hc (Tab. Alt.)	20	17.9	20	29.2	19	19.9
tens DS Diff.	29.9		-24.6		16.3	
units DS Corr.	9.1	+	-5.5	+	3.5	+
Tot. Corr. (+ or -)		+39.0		-30.1		+19.8
Hc (Comp. Alt.)	20	56.9	19	59.1	19	39.7
Ho (Obs. Alt.)	21	07.0	20	01.4	19	26.6
a (Intercept)	10.1	A/T	2.3	A/T	13.1	A/T
Z	N	96.4 E	N	132.2 W	N	76.8 E
Zn (°T)	096.4°		227.8°		076.8°	

Fig. 2702b. Sight reductions using Pub. No. 229; planet, Moon, and Sun.

mine and record the altitude correction for refraction from the "Stars and Planets" column of Table A2 or the bookmark. Because this is the planet Venus, you must also include an "Add'1" value from the right-hand section of the table; both values are applied to ha to yield the observed altitude (Ho).

Next record your DR position and fill in the boxes relating to time and date (Date, Obs. Time, WE, ZT, and ZD) to arrive at the correct GMT and date for the sight.

Enter the appropriate daily pages of the *Nautical Almanac* to obtain the GHA and declination at the whole hours of GMT. Also find the v and d values at the bottom of the column and record them. The v

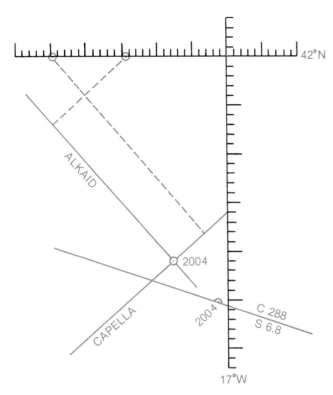

Fig. 2702c. Plot of LOPs from sight reductions of figure 2702a.

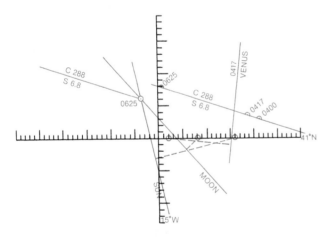

Fig. 2702d. Plot of LOPs from sight reductions of figure 2702b.

value will have a sign (+ or –), but the d value's sign must be determined by observing the trend of the Dec. values from hour to hour. In this example the declination in the table is increasing, so the sign of d will be positive.

Turning to the appropriate Increments and Corrections Table, obtain the increments of GHA for minutes and seconds, and the corrections to GHA and declination for the v and d values, respectively. Applying these values to those obtained from the

daily pages, obtain the GHA and Dec. of the planet at the time of observation.

Select an assumed longitude that will yield a whole degree of LHA when applied to the GHA. Record it and the resulting LHA in the appropriate boxes.

Enter a whole-degree assumed latitude based upon your DR latitude. Note that this assumed latitude is different from the one used in the later star sights because some time had passed and the DR latitude changed sufficiently to require a different whole-degree of latitude.

Entering Pub. No. 229 with the integral degrees of LHA, a Lat, and Dec., extract the tabular value for computed altitude (Hc), d and its sign, and Z. Correct Z by interpolation for the actual value of declination. Find the correction to the tabulated Hc for Dec. inc. and d in the Interpolation Table of Pub. No. 229 using the portion of the table that is inside the *back* cover, since the Dec. inc. value (59.8) is greater than 31.9. No double-second difference correction need be applied since the d value is not printed in italics nor followed by a dot. These corrections give the computed altitude, Hc, for the exact declination of the body.

Compare this corrected Hc with Ho to determine the intercept. Convert the azimuth angle to azimuth. Complete the reduction by using Zn and a, then plot the LOP from the AP (see fig. 2702d).

Complete Solution for a Moon Observation

2705 Assume you made an observation of the Moon at time 06-24-43 on 5 June and obtained a sextant altitude of 18° 56.0′. Your DR position was Lat. 41° 07.9′ N, Long. 14° 58.7′ W. Your watch remains 8 seconds fast, your height of eye and IC are as before (21 feet and +0.2′, respectively).

When observing the Moon, you must use either the upper or lower limb and be sure to record which. In this case, your observation was made on the lower limb and is so indicated in the "Body" box of the sight form, next to the name.

Many other aspects of the process are the same as when sighting a star or planet, but there are some important differences. No "Add'l" correction is required but a correction for horizontal parallax (H.P.) *is* used along with an "Alt. Corr" to arrive at the final observed altitude (Ho).

A "v Corr." is required for Moon sight reduction and is obtained by first extracting a v factor from the daily pages of the *Nautical Almanac*, where it is found as a separate column entry on the right-hand page between the whole-hour entries for GHA and Dec. The sign of v is always positive with Moon sights. This factor is then used to enter the right-hand portion of the Increments and Corrections Table to find the v corr.

As with other sights, the results are turned into an LOP and plotted as shown in figure 2702d.

Complete Solution for a Sun Observation

2706 If you observed the lower limb of the Sun at 06-25-23 (watch error 8 seconds fast) on 5 June and obtained a sextant altitude of 19° 17.5′ using the same DR (Lat. 41° 07.9′ N, Long. 14° 58.7′ W) as the Moon observation (since they were taken at nearly the same time), you would fill in the sight form as shown in figure 2702b.

Ordinarily, the ha is corrected to Ho by means of the Sun portion of the Altitude Correction Tables on the inside front cover of the *Nautical Almanac*, which include corrections for nominal values of semidiameter, refraction, and parallax. The value thus obtained would be entered in the "Alt. Corr" box. In this example, however, the alternative method discussed in article 2236 was used. This entails using the semidiameter (SD) found at the bottom of the Sun column in the daily pages of the *Nautical Almanac* together with the value of the refraction correction found under the heading "Stars and Planets" portion of the Altitude Correction Tables and an additional correction of +0.1′ for parallax to be used for an altitude of 65° or less. These corrections were combined and entered in the "Corr. to ha" box and applied to ha to obtain Ho.

No v correction is required for Sun observations so both the "v" and "v Corr." portions of the sight form are not used. SHA is also not required, so that box is left empty. All other items in the sight form are used in the same manner as with other observations.

With the resulting intercept and azimuth, you may plot an LOP from the assumed position used as shown in figure 2702d.

The 0625 fix in figure 2702d is based upon the LOPs obtained from the Moon and Sun observations. The AP for the Moon LOP was not advanced because of the short interval between observations and the slow speed of the vessel. Although not shown in the figure, the Venus LOP could have been advanced as a further check on the vessel's position.

REDUCTION BY PUB. NO. 249

2707 As has been noted before, some navigators prefer the greater ease and speed gained through the use of the *Air Almanac* and Pub. No. 249, accepting the lesser degree of precision of the results.

Actually, either almanac could be used with either set of sight reduction tables, but in typical practice, the *Nautical Almanac* is normally paired with Pub. No. 229 and the *Air Almanac* with Pub. No. 249.

To illustrate the use of the *Air Almanac* and Pub. No. 249 tables, several of the same observations used in the preceding articles will be reduced by that method.

The *Air Almanac* has been described in chapter 24, and the Pub. No. 249 tables in chapter 25. Here attention will be focused on their use, with particular reference to the differences between these procedures and those of the *Nautical Almanac*/Pub. No. 229 method. Comparisons will be made of the results obtained by using the two different methods.

Reduction of a Star Observation by *Air Almanac*/Pub. No. 249

2708 In the reduction of a star observation, the navigator uses the *Air Almanac* as before to find the dip and refraction corrections and combines them with the IC and the sextant reading to obtain Ho to the nearest minute.

If the star observed is not one of the seven current "selected stars" for use in Volume I of Pub. No. 249, the procedure is the same as previously discussed for Volumes II and III of that publication.

If, however, the star *is* one of those "selected stars," the unique procedure of Volume I can be employed. These tables are entered with whole degrees of latitude and LHA of Aries, and the name of the star. Values of Hc and Zn can be read directly and the intercept and Zn obtained with great ease and speed.

Note that when Volume I can be used, no incremental corrections of any kind within it are required. After the LHA ♈ and assumed latitude have been determined, a simple table "look-up" is all that is necessary to find Hc and Zn. The tabular value of LHA is carried to the tenth of a minute, and this degree of precision is correspondingly used in the value of assumed longitude. The assumed latitude is simply the whole degree of latitude nearest the DR position of the vessel at the time of the sight. The GHA can also be found from Pub. No. 249 without the use of either almanac. Values are taken from its table 4 for the month and year, the hour of the day, and the minutes of the hour; these three values are added together to get the GHA ♈ to the nearest whole minute of arc.

For example, on 5 June, the 2004 DR position of the vessel is 41° 34.8′ N, Long. 17° 00.5′ W. At 20-04-08 watch time, a sight was taken on the star Capella. The height of eye was 21 feet, the IC was +0.2′, and

Body	CAPELLA	
IC	+0.2	
Dip		4
Sum		-4
Hs	15	27
Ha	15	23
Alt Corr.		-4
Ho (obs alt.)	15	19
Date	5 JUN 77	
DR Lat	41	34.8 N
DR Long	17	00.5 W
Obs Time	20 -04-08	
WE (S+, F-)		-10 F
ZT	20 -03 -58	
ZD (W+, E-)	+1	
GMT	21 - 03 - 58	
Date (GMT)	5 JUN 77	
Tab GHA γ	209	10
GHA incr'mt.	1	00
GHA γ	210	10
Aλ (-W, +E)	17	10
LHA γ	193	
A Lat	42 N	
Hc	15	35
Ho	15	19
a T A	16 ⊼ A	
Zn	319°	
P&N Corr.	2 mi 120°	

Fig. 2708a. Sight reductions using Pub. No. 249, Volume I.

the watch error was 10 seconds fast. The sextant reading was 15° 27′. Using this information and the sight form shown in figure 2708a, you can solve for

an LOP in much the same manner as when using the *Nautical Almanac* and Pub. No. 229.

The line of position calculated in this manner is subject to a correction for the effects upon the tabulated altitude of progressive changes in the declination and SHA of the star due to the precession of the equinoxes and nutation. As discussed in article 2524, such a correction should be included if the year of the observation is other than the base year of the tables used. Corrections are given in table 5 of Pub. No. 249, Volume I, for two years before the base year and for five years afterward. In this case, the year of the sight was not the base year but three years later, necessitating a "P&N" (for "precession and nutation") correction. For the appropriate year, Table 5 is entered for the nearest values of LHA and latitude (180° and N40° in this case); interpolation is not used. In the example above, the line of position should be adjusted 2 miles, 120° when plotted. (If several lops were determined, a single P&N correction could be applied to the *fix*, rather than to each LOP individually.) The P&N correction is applicable *only* to sight reductions made with Volume I of Pub. No. 249.

Note that although the Zn can be compared directly with the solution by Pub. No. 229 (article 2703), the intercept value cannot be directly compared, as it is drawn from a different assumed position. Figure 2708b shows the LOP as produced by the two methods; the difference is apparent, but slight, and of no particular significance in navigation.

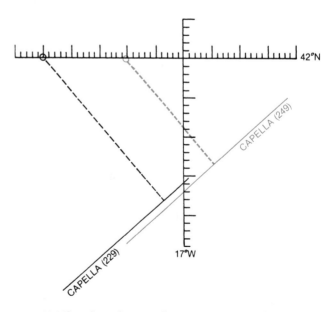

Fig. 2708b. Plot of LOPs from reductions of the same sight by Pub. No. 229 and by Pub. No. 249, Volume I.

Reduction of a Planet Observation by *Air Almanac*/Pub. No. 249

2709 Assume you observed Venus at 0417 and 21 seconds on 5 June. The DR position of the vessel is Lat. 41° 03.4′ N, Long. 14° 40.4′ W. Your watch is 8 seconds fast, your height of eye is 21 feet, and your sextant requires an IC of +0.2′. The observed sextant altitude is 21° 13′. Referring to figure 2709, you can see the steps required in reducing a planet observation to an LOP using the *Air Almanac* and Pub. No. 249.

Enter the IC and the dip correction (found on the inside back cover of the *Air Almanac*). When obtaining the refraction correction, be sure to use the left-hand column "0" for 0 feet elevation above the Earth's surface rather than the ones provided for air observations. Find the refraction correction on the page facing the inside back cover and enter the correction in the "R" box. (Note that the sextant altitude and its corrections are summed to the nearest minute rather than tenth of a minute.)

Next locate the applicable daily page and then the line for the GMT just before the time of observation, remembering that tabular entries in the *Air Almanac* are for each 10 minutes of GMT. The values of GHA and declination are taken from the inside front cover; the same column is used for the Sun, Aries, and planets, with a different column for the Moon. The GHA of the body is the sum of the angles from the daily page and the increment.

Select an assumed position (AP) that has a whole degree of latitude, and a longitude that will yield a whole degree of LHA when combined with the GHA of the body.

Volume II or III of Pub. No. 249 is selected as determined by the ship's latitude. The appropriate volume is entered with integral degrees of latitude, declination, and LHA; values are obtained for Hc and *d* to the nearest minute and Z to the nearest degree; the declination correction is obtained from Table 5 at the back of the volume and is applied to Hc with the proper sign.

The comparison of corrected Hc and Ho to obtain the intercept (a) and the conversion of Z to Zn are the same as when using Pub. No. 229.

Reduction of a Moon Observation by *Air Almanac*/Pub. No. 249

2710 In using the *Air Almanac* for reduction of a Moon observation, you would proceed as above for the IC, dip, and refraction corrections. From the daily pages, obtain GHA and declination. Semidiameter is read from the box at the lower right corner of the daily page and entered on the form; this is

Body	VENUS		MOON LL	
IC	+0.2		+0.2	
Dip (Ht.21′)		−4		−4
R		−2		−3
S.D.			+16	
Sum		−6		+9
hs	21	13	18	56
P in A (Moon)				+56
Ho	21	07	20	01
Date	5 JUN		5 JUN	
DR Lat	41	03.4 N	41	07.9 N
DR Long	14	40.4 W	14	58.7 W
Obs Time	04-17-21		06-24-43	
WE		−8F		−8F
ZT	04-17-13		06-24-35	
ZD	+1		+1	
GMT	05-17-13		07-24-35	
Date (GMT)	5 JUN		5 JUN	
Tab GHA	303	09	59	45
GHA incrmt	1	48	1	06
SHA				
GHA	304	57	60	51
± 360				
a λ (− W, + E)	14	57	14	51
LHA	290		46	
Tab Dec	N 9	00	S 14	37
a Lat	41 N	S C	41 N	S C
Dec Inc	00		37	−49
Tab Hc	20	57	20	29
Dec corr		00		−30
Hc	20	57	19	59
Ho	21	07	20	01
a		10 ᴬ/T		2 ᴬ/T
Z	N 96 E		N 132 W	
Zn	096°		228°	

Fig. 2709. Sight reductions using Pub. No. 249, Volume I.

combined with the first three corrections to obtain a value that is used to enter the critical value table "Moon's P in A" to get the correction for parallax. This final correction is added to obtain Ho of the Moon's center from observation of its lower limb.

(Remember to subtract 30 minutes of arc when the Moon's upper limb is used.)

The tabular value of GHA for the Moon is incremental for the balance of time beyond the tabular entry (using a value from the column headed "Moon"); no correction is required to the tabulated declination. An AP is determined as before, so as to give an integral value of LHA when the longitude is subtracted (W) or added (E). Volume II or III of Pub. No. 249 is now used to determine tabular Hc, which is corrected for d. Intercept and Zn are found in the usual manner.

Here again, compare the results of this reduction with those obtained from the *Nautical Almanac*/Pub. No. 229 solution. The differences are slight and without significance in high-seas navigation.

Reduction of a Sun Observation by *Air Almanac*/Pub No. 249

2711   The procedures for determining the Ho of the Sun are basically the same as those just described for the Moon, except that there is no parallax correction ("P in A") to the sextant altitude. The procedures for GHA, declination, and LHA are the same for the Sun as for the Moon. Although the increments of GHA for the Sun are the same as for planets and Aries, those for the Moon are tabulated against a special entry column of time.

REDUCTION BY AGETON METHOD

2712   Because of the greater time and effort required, the Ageton method is now seldom used as a primary procedure for sight reduction. The fully qualified navigator should, however, be competent in its use. This method uses the DR position rather than an assumed position, and the intercept distance is thus a relatively direct measure of the accuracy of the DR position. The Ageton method has a considerable advantage for small craft or lifeboat use, as multiple large volumes such as those of Pub. No. 229 are not required. Use of the "compact" Age-

,	22° 30'		23° 00'		23° 30'		24° 00'		24° 30'		,
	A	B	A	B	A	B	A	B	A	B	
10	41412	3491	40516	3651	39641	3815	38786	3983	37951	4155	20
	41397	3494	40501	3654	39626	3818	38772	3986	37937	4158	
11	41382	3496	40486	3657	39612	3821	38758	3989	37924	4161	19
	41367	3499	40471	3659	39597	3824	38744	3992	37910	4164	
12	41352	3502	40457	3662	39583	3826	38730	3995	37896	4167	18
	41337	3504	40442	3665	39569	3829	38716	3998	37882	4170	
13	41322	3507	40427	3667	39554	3832	38702	4000	37869	4173	17
	41307	3509	40413	3670	39540	3835	38688	4003	37855	4176	
14	41291	3512	40398	3673	39525	3838	38674	4006	37841	4179	16
	41276	3515	40383	3676	39511	3840	38660	4009	37828	4182	
15	41261	3517	40368	3678	39497	3843	38645	4012	37814	4185	15
	41246	3520	40354	3681	39482	3846	38631	4015	37800	4187	
16	41231	3523	40339	3684	39468	3849	38617	4017	37786	4190	14
	41216	3525	40324	3686	39454	3851	38603	4020	37773	4193	
17	41201	3528	40310	3689	39439	3854	38589	4023	37759	4196	13
	41186	3531	40295	3692	39425	3857	38575	4026	37745	4199	
18	41171	3533	40280	3695	39411	3860	38561	4029	37732	4202	12
	41156	3536	40266	3697	39396	3863	38547	4032	37718	4205	
19	41141	3539	40251	3700	39382	3865	38533	4035	37704	4208	11
	41126	3541	40236	3703	39368	3868	38520	4037	37691	4211	
20	41111	3544	40222	3705	39353	3871	38506	4040	37677	4214	10
	41096	3547	40207	3708	39339	3874	38492	4043	37663	4217	
21	41081	3549	40192	3711	39325	3876	38478	4046	37650	4220	9
	41066	3552	40178	3714	39311	3879	38464	4049	37636	4222	
22	41051	3555	40163	3716	39296	3882	38450	4052	37623	4225	8
	41036	3557	40149	3719	39282	3885	38436	4055	37609	4228	
23	41021	3560	40134	3722	39268	3888	38422	4057	37595	4231	7
	41006	3563	40119	3725	39254	3890	38408	4060	37582	4234	
24	40991	3565	40105	3727	39239	3893	38394	4063	37568	4237	6
	40976	3568	40090	3730	39225	3896	38380	4066	37554	4240	
25	40961	3571	40076	3733	39211	3899	38366	4069	37541	4243	5
	40946	3573	40061	3735	39197	3902	38352	4072	37527	4246	
26	40931	3576	40046	3738	39182	3904	38338	4075	37514	4249	4
	40916	3579	40032	3741	39168	3907	38324	4078	37500	4252	
27	40902	3581	40017	3744	39154	3910	38311	4080	37486	4255	3
	40887	3584	40003	3746	39140	3913	38297	4083	37473	4258	

Fig. 2712a. Sample Ageton Table (extract).

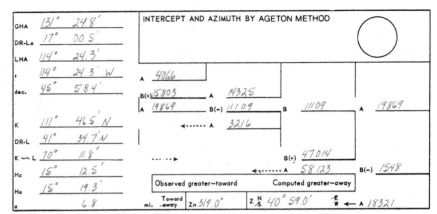

Fig. 2712b. Sight reduction by Ageton method.

ton method tables will result in an even further saving of weight and space with little loss of accuracy. (Note: The Ageton tables are available to readers of this book at the U.S. Naval Institute's web site, www.navalinstitute.com.)

Sextant corrections and almanac data are determined as before, and time calculations are made in the same manner. The Ageton table (see fig. 2712a) is entered for the various angular values, recording the entry for *A* or *B*, or both, as appropriate; note carefully the instruction "When LHA (E or W) is *greater* than 90°, take *K* from *bottom* of table." A simple rough sketch of the navigational triangle goes far in helping to understand the rules given in the Ageton tables.

The GHA of the body is entered on the form, and from this is subtracted the DR longitude to obtain the LHA and angle t. The *A* value for t is found in the tables and entered on the form. The value of declination is entered, followed by both the *B* and *A* values. Addition, as shown on the form, yields an *A* value (which is copied again in the fourth column); the corresponding *B* value is located in the tables and entered in columns 2 and 3. Further additions and subtractions are carried out, ending in a value for Hc and Z from which an intercept (a) and azimuth (Zn) can be derived.

A single reduction is shown here to illustrate the complete solution by the Ageton method; an observation of the star Capella is selected as a typical example.

Example: On 5 June, the 2004 DR position of the ship is Lat. 41° 34.7′ N, Long. 17° 01.0′ W. At 20-40-08 (watch is 10 seconds fast), the star Capella is observed from height of eye of 21 feet with a sextant having an IC of +0.2. The sextant reading is 15° 27.0′.

Required: The a and Zn using the *Nautical Almanac* and the Ageton method of reduction.

Solution: The following data are extracted from

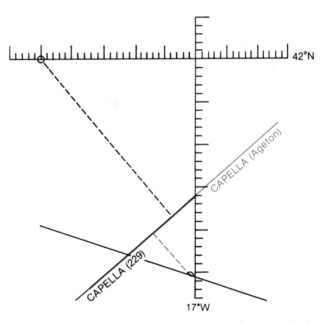

Fig. 2712c. Plot of LOPs from reductions of same sight by Pub. No. 229 and by the Ageton method.

the *Nautical Almanac* and are the same as those used in previous examples:

Ho	15° 19.3′
GHA	131° 24.8′
Dec.	N 45° 58.4′

The solution by the Ageton method is shown in figure 2712b.

Note that the intercept value obtained from the Ageton method is quite different from that resulting from reduction by Pub. No. 229 or 249. This results, of course, from the use of the DR position rather than an assumed position selected for convenience. Sight reduction by the Ageton method can be readily compared to the results of the other methods only by means of a plot of the corresponding LOPs; see figure 2712c.

STELLA

2713 The use of the U.S. Naval Observatory's STELLA has been covered in some detail in earlier chapters. Once STELLA is loaded into a computer it can be used for virtually all celestial navigation functions. Using a running log method of keeping track of positions and various entries, the key to individual actions is in the use of the "Task" drop-down menu. Once selected, you are presented with a variety of options that include "Sight Planning," "Almanac," and "Sight Reduction." While all of these tasks can be used for various peripheral functions, the most important of these for reducing celestial observations to LOPs is the "Sight Reduction" task, which incorporates many of the functions described in the preceding chapters and makes the process very simple indeed. When selected, this task offers two sub-options: "Record Observations" and "Compute Fix." Having determined which bodies you wish to observe (using the very useful "Sight Planning" task if desired), you simply select "Record Observations" and enter the date, time, name of the body, sextant altitude (hs), limb (if a Sun or Moon sight), height of eye, and index correction (IC) for each observation made. If you choose, you may also refine your sights by choosing a quality (good, average, or poor) and entering the existing temperature and barometric pressure; or you may elect to use the defaults for these entries. You may enter up to 25 different observations. Once all your observations have been entered, you may have the computer provide a fix simply by selecting the "Compute Fix" option from the "Sight Reduction" task. You will then be asked to make a selection of "Time of First Observation," "Average Time of Observations," or "Time of Last Observation."

The "Compute Fix" function calculates and displays lines of position (LOPs). More importantly, it solves for a celestial fix using the LOPs and displays the results both graphically and in table form. Strip form representations of each observation are also available. If a sufficient number of sights, spread over time, are logged, the "Compute Fix" task will include solutions for course, speed, track made good, speed made good, set and drift. It allows you to tailor a set of observations and to accept or reject a fix. You direct the process and decide whether the final result is acceptable.

A detailed discussion of this and other STELLA capabilities is beyond the scope of this book, but for those with access to the program, the information given here should get you started in using the program. A *user's manual* is available on the CD in both PDF and Microsoft Word versions; you may refer to it directly or print it out for handy reference. (Note: As previously mentioned, as of this writing, the STELLA program is listed as LIMDIS [limited distribution] and is not available to the general public.)

Relying upon STELLA or other commercially available computer programs is not only acceptable but advisable, but as a serious nautical navigator, you will want to understand what is behind the dialog boxes and displays that appear on your screen. Use computer programs as very useful tools but not as substitutes for knowledge and understanding of the celestial navigation process. And be prepared to do without them in an emergency.

Chapter 28

Latitude and Longitude Observations

Not only can "ordinary" celestial sights be taken and reduced to fix a vessel's position relative to her DR track, but there are also "special" observations that can be made for the specific determination of latitude or longitude. These are taken for particular positions of the body observed and are reduced to an LOP by shorter, simpler procedures than are used for the complete solution as discussed in previous chapters. A sight taken when the celestial body is either due north or due south of the observer that yields an LOP extending in an east-west direction, is termed a *latitude line*. A longitude observation is obtained when the observed body is either east or west of the observer. The resulting LOP is a called a *longitude line*; it extends in a north-south direction, as does a meridian.

Latitude lines will be considered primarily in this chapter, as they have much in their favor—a celestial body changes altitude very slowly at transit, except at very high altitudes. Ordinarily, an experienced observer can obtain a considerable number of consecutive observations of a transiting body that will be almost identical in altitude. When one of these observations is reduced, great reliance can be placed on its accuracy.

Any celestial body will yield a latitude line when observed at or sufficiently near transit. The two bodies most commonly used for latitude LOPs, however, are the Sun and Polaris. Polaris is not often observed at transit, but it is always "sufficiently near." The Sun transits the observer's meridian at *local apparent noon* (LAN); the LAN observation is extremely important in navigation, chiefly because it can usually be relied upon to yield the most dependable celestial LOP of the day. The Sun should be observed at LAN as a matter of routine aboard every vessel.

DETERMINING THE TIME OF LAN

2801 To predict the time of LAN accurately, while the Sun is still well to your east, enter the *Nautical Almanac* for the appropriate day and find the tabulated GHA of the Sun that is nearest to, but still *east of*, the DR longitude, and note the GMT hour of this entry. Then turn to your chart and, for this GMT, determine the difference of longitude in minutes between the Sun's GHA and the vessel's longitude at that same hour of GMT in the *Nautical Almanac*. This difference is the current *meridian angle east* (tE). The next step is to determine the instant when the Sun's hour circle will coincide with the vessel's meridian of longitude. One way of performing this step, which establishes the predicted time of LAN, is accomplished by combining the rate of the Sun's rate of change of longitude with that of the vessel. The Sun changes longitude at an almost uniform rate of 15°, or 900', per hour. The rate of the vessel's change of longitude per hour is usually determined by measurement on the chart.

If the vessel is steaming toward the east, its hourly rate of change of longitude is added to that of the Sun (a meeting situation); if it is steaming west, the rate of change is subtracted from that of the Sun (an overtaking situation).

All that remains is to divide the meridian angle east expressed in arc minutes, as found above, by the combined rate of change of longitude. The answer, which will be in decimals of an hour, should be determined to three significant places. Multiplied by 60, minutes and decimals of minutes are obtained; the latter may be converted to seconds by again multiplying by 60. The answer will be mathematically correct to about four seconds; when added to the hour of GMT obtained from the *Nautical Almanac*, it will give the predicted GMT of the Sun's transit (LAN) at the vessel's position. Any error in DRl will, of course, affect the accuracy. The zone description may be employed to convert the GMT of LAN to ship's time. The above procedure can conveniently be written as the following equation.

Interval to LAN = *tE in minutes of arc*
900' arc ± ship's movement in longitude '/hour

This procedure is illustrated in the following example.

Example: On 5 June, as the navigator of a ship proceeding on course 281°, speed 11.5 knots, you plan to observe the Sun at LAN. At 1145 (+1), you note that the 1200 DR position will be Lat. 41° 17.7' N, Long. 20° 51.6' W.

Required: The ZT of transit of the Sun.

Solution: (See fig. 2801.) The ship's 1200 DR longitude will be 20° 51.6' W. Entering the *Nautical Almanac* with this value and for this date, 5 June, find the nearest, but lesser, GHA of the Sun; this is 15° 24.0' for 1300 GMT, which is 1200 ship's time. (If the longitude had been east, it would have been subtracted from 360° to get the angular distance west of Greenwich for entry into the *Nautical Almanac*.)

The difference in longitude between the ship and the Sun at 1200 (+1) equals 20° 51.6' minus 15° 24.0' or 5° 27.6'. This value is used for tE.

By inspection of the plot of the ship's DR longitude for 1200 and 1300 (fig. 2801) the hourly change of longitude, in minutes of arc, is found to be 15.0'. This change is in a *westerly* direction; it will therefore be subtracted from the Sun's hourly change, which is 900' per hour. The net hourly rate of change is 900' minus 15.0', or 885.0' per hour. The value of tE is next divided by this net rate, 327.6 ÷ 885.0', to find the time, in decimal fractions of an hour, after 1200 ship's time, at which transit will occur. The answer, rounded off, is 0.37; in minutes 0.37 ÷ 60 = 22.2 minutes or 22 minutes 12 seconds. This is added to 1200 (+1) to get the time of transit, or LAN.

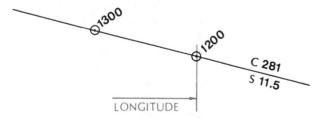

Fig. 2801. Plot for calculating the time of LAN.

Answer: 12-22-12 ZT.

Alternate Method of Determining LAN

2802 The time of local apparent noon can also be predicted from calculations using the time of meridian passage of the Sun as tabulated for each day on the right-hand pages of the *Nautical Almanac* (see fig. 2802). This time is given for the meridian of Greenwich, but the rate of change is so slight that it can be used as the Local Mean Time (LMT) at any longitude on the same date without significant error.

Obtain the tabulated value of meridian passage from the *Nautical Almanac;* this is usable as LMT. Then plot the DR position of the vessel for that time in Zone Time (ZT), which is the LMT at the central meridian of the time zone being used. Next determine the longitude difference between the DR position and the central meridian of the time zone, and convert it to time units. This time difference is applied to the LMT of meridian passage, *adding* if the DR position is *west* of the central meridian, subtracting if it is east. The time thus obtained is but a first estimate of ZT of transit of the Sun.

If the vessel is moving, further computation is required. Plot a new DR position for the first estimate of the ZT of LAN as determined above. Using this new DR longitude, compute a new ZT correction to the tabulated LMT of meridian passage; this is the second estimate of the ZT of LAN and is usually usable for making observations. Rarely is a third estimate needed.

This procedure is illustrated using the same situation as in the prior method.

Example: On 5 June, as the navigator of a ship proceeding on course 281°, speed 11.5 knots, you plan to observe the Sun at local apparent noon.

Required: The ZT of transit of the Sun.

Solution: Determine from the *Nautical Almanac* the LMT of meridian passage, which is 1158. Determine by plot that the ship's longitude at that Zone Time will be 20° 51.1' W. This is 5° 51.1' west of the central meridian of the (+1) time zone; converted to time units, this difference in longitude is 23^m24^s; rounded to 23 minutes and added to 1158, the first estimate becomes 1221.

The DR longitude for 1221 ZT is 20° 56.9' W. The time difference for 5° 56.9' is 23^m48^s This is rounded to 24 minutes and added to 1158, giving 1222.

Answer: 1222 ZT.

Note that this procedure computes values to the nearest minute only, consistent with the *Nautical Almanac* tabulations of the time of meridian pas-

JUNE 3, 4, 5 (FRI., SAT., SUN.)

UT (d h)	SUN GHA	SUN Dec	MOON GHA	v	MOON Dec	d	HP
3 00	180 30.4	N22 16.2	342 44.5	3.6	S18 46.2	12	61.1
01	195 30.3	16.5	357 07.1	3.6	18 45.0	12	61.1
02	210 30.2	16.8	11 29.7	3.7	18 43.8	14	61.1
03	225 30.1 ··	17.1	25 52.4	3.7	18 42.4	15	61.0
04	240 30.0	17.4	40 15.1	3.7	18 40.9	17	61.0
05	255 29.9	17.7	54 37.8	3.8	18 39.2	18	61.0
06	270 29.8	N22 18.1	69 00.6	3.8	S18 37.4	19	61.0
07	285 29.7	18.4	83 23.4	3.9	18 35.5	21	61.0
08	300 29.6	18.7	97 46.3	3.9	18 33.4	22	60.9
F 09	315 29.5 ··	19.0	112 09.2	3.9	18 31.2	23	60.9
R 10	330 29.4	19.3	126 32.1	4.1	18 28.9	25	60.9
I 11	345 29.3	19.6	140 55.2	4.0	18 26.4	26	60.9
D 12	0 29.2	N22 19.9	155 18.2	4.1	S18 23.8	27	60.8
A 13	15 29.1	20.2	169 41.3	4.2	18 21.1	29	60.8
Y 14	30 29.0	20.5	184 04.5	4.2	18 18.2	30	60.8
15	45 28.9 ··	20.8	198 27.7	4.3	18 15.2	31	60.8
16	60 28.8	21.1	212 51.0	4.4	18 12.1	33	60.7
17	75 28.7	21.4	227 14.4	4.4	18 08.8	34	60.7
18	90 28.6	N22 21.7	241 37.8	4.5	S18 05.4	35	60.7
19	105 28.5	22.0	256 01.3	4.5	18 01.9	37	60.7
20	120 28.4	22.3	270 24.8	4.6	17 58.2	37	60.6
21	135 28.3 ··	22.6	284 48.4	4.7	17 54.5	39	60.6
22	150 28.2	22.9	299 12.1	4.7	17 50.6	40	60.6
23	165 28.1	23.2	313 35.8	4.8	17 46.6	42	60.5
4 00	180 28.0	N22 23.5	327 59.6	4.9	S17 42.4	42	60.5
01	195 27.9	23.8	342 23.5	4.9	17 38.2	44	60.5
02	210 27.8	24.1	356 47.4	5.1	17 33.8	45	60.5
03	225 27.7 ··	24.4	11 11.5	5.1	17 29.3	46	60.4
04	240 27.6	24.7	25 35.6	5.1	17 24.7	48	60.4
05	255 27.5	25.0	39 59.7	5.3	17 19.9	48	60.4
06	270 27.4	N22 25.3	54 24.0	5.3	S17 15.1	50	60.3
07	285 27.3	25.6	68 48.3	5.4	17 10.1	50	60.3
S 08	300 27.1	25.9	83 12.7	5.4	17 05.1	52	60.3
A 09	315 27.0 ··	26.1	97 37.1	5.6	16 59.9	53	60.2
T 10	330 26.9	26.4	112 01.7	5.6	16 54.6	54	60.2
U 11	345 26.8	26.7	126 26.3	5.7	16 49.2	56	60.2
R 12	0 26.7	N22 27.0	140 51.0	5.8	S16 43.6	56	60.1
D 13	15 26.6	27.3	155 15.8	5.9	16 38.0	57	60.1
A 14	30 26.5	27.6	169 40.7	6.0	16 32.3	58	60.1
Y 15	45 26.4 ··	27.9	184 05.7	6.0	16 26.5	60	60.0
16	60 26.3	28.2	198 30.7	6.1	16 20.5	60	60.0
17	75 26.2	28.4	212 55.8	6.2	16 14.5	62	60.0
18	90 26.1	N22 28.7	227 21.0	6.3	S16 08.3	63	59.9
19	105 26.0	29.0	241 46.3	6.4	16 02.1	63	59.9
20	120 25.9	29.3	256 11.7	6.5	15 55.8	65	59.9
21	135 25.8 ··	29.6	270 37.2	6.5	15 49.3	65	59.8
22	150 25.7	29.9	285 02.7	6.7	15 42.8	66	59.8
23	165 25.5	30.1	299 28.4	6.7	15 36.2	68	59.8
5 00	180 25.4	N22 30.4	313 54.1	6.8	S15 29.4	68	59.7
01	195 25.3	30.7	328 19.9	6.9	15 22.6	69	59.7
02	210 25.2	31.0	342 45.8	7.0	15 15.7	70	59.6
03	225 25.1 ··	31.3	357 11.8	7.1	15 08.7	70	59.6
04	240 25.0	31.5	11 37.9	7.2	15 01.7	72	59.6
05	255 24.9	31.8	26 04.1	7.2	14 54.5	73	59.5
06	270 24.8	N22 32.1	40 30.3	7.4	S14 47.2	73	59.5
07	285 24.7	32.4	54 56.7	7.4	14 39.9	74	59.5
08	300 24.6	32.6	69 23.1	7.5	14 32.5	75	59.4
S 09	315 24.5 ··	32.9	83 49.6	7.6	14 25.0	76	59.4
U 10	330 24.4	33.2	98 16.2	7.7	14 17.4	76	59.3
N 11	345 24.2	33.5	112 42.9	7.8	14 09.8	78	59.3
D 12	0 24.1	N22 33.7	127 09.7	7.9	S14 02.0	78	59.3
A 13	15 24.0	34.0	141 36.6	8.0	13 54.2	79	59.2
Y 14	30 23.9	34.3	156 03.6	8.0	13 46.3	79	59.2
15	45 23.8 ··	34.5	170 30.6	8.2	13 38.4	80	59.1
16	60 23.7	34.8	184 57.8	8.2	13 30.4	82	59.1
17	75 23.6	35.1	199 25.0	8.3	13 22.2	81	59.1
18	90 23.5	N22 35.4	213 52.3	8.4	S13 14.1	83	59.0
19	105 23.4	35.6	228 19.7	8.5	13 05.8	83	59.0
20	120 23.3	35.9	242 47.2	8.6	12 57.5	83	58.9
21	135 23.1 ··	36.2	257 14.8	8.7	12 49.2	85	58.9
22	150 23.0	36.4	271 42.5	8.8	12 40.7	85	58.8
23	165 22.9	36.7	286 10.3	8.8	12 32.2	85	58.8
	S.D. 15.8	d 0.3	S.D. 16.6		16.4		16.1

Moonrise

Lat.	Twilight Naut.	Twilight Civil	Sunrise	3	4	5	6
N 72				■	01 33	01 02	00 50
N 70				24 18	00 18	00 26	00 28
68				23 40	24 00	00 00	00 11
66			01 00	23 13	23 40	24 09	24 09
64		////	01 51	22 52	23 24	23 46	24 02
62			02 22	22 35	23 11	23 36	23 55
60		01 18	02 45	22 21	22 59	23 28	23 50
N 58		01 55	03 04	22 09	22 49	23 20	23 45
56		02 20	03 19	21 59	22 41	23 14	23 40
54	01 11	02 40	03 32	21 49	22 33	23 08	23 36
52	01 45	02 56	03 44	21 41	22 26	23 03	23 33
50	02 09	03 11	03 54	21 34	22 20	22 58	23 30
45	02 50	03 39	04 15	21 18	22 06	22 47	23 22
N 40	03 19	04 00	04 32	21 05	21 55	22 39	23 16
35	03 41	04 17	04 46	20 54	21 46	22 31	23 11
30	03 59	04 32	04 59	20 44	21 37	22 24	23 07
20	04 26	04 55	05 20	20 27	21 23	22 13	22 59
N 10	04 48	05 15	05 38	20 13	21 10	22 03	22 52
0	05 06	05 32	05 55	19 59	20 58	21 54	22 45
S 10	05 22	05 49	06 11	19 45	20 46	21 44	22 39
20	05 38	06 05	06 29	19 31	20 33	21 34	22 32
30	05 53	06 23	06 49	19 14	20 19	21 22	22 24
35	06 01	06 33	07 01	19 04	20 10	21 16	22 19
40	06 10	06 44	07 14	18 53	20 01	21 08	22 14
45	06 20	06 57	07 30	18 40	19 49	20 59	22 08
S 50	06 31	07 12	07 50	18 24	19 36	20 48	22 00
52	06 36	07 19	07 59	18 17	19 29	20 43	21 57
54	06 41	07 26	08 09	18 08	19 22	20 38	21 53
56	06 47	07 35	08 21	17 59	19 14	20 32	21 49
58	06 53	07 44	08 35	17 48	19 05	20 25	21 44
S 60	07 00	07 55	08 51	17 36	18 55	20 17	21 39

Moonset

Lat.	Sunset	Twilight Civil	Twilight Naut.	3	4	5	6
N 72				■	03 02	05 35	07 40
N 70				02 35	04 17	06 10	08 00
68	23 01			03 26	04 54	06 35	08 16
66	22 07	////	////	03 58	05 21	06 54	08 29
64	21 36	////	////	04 22	05 41	07 09	08 39
62	21 12	22 41		04 41	05 58	07 22	08 48
60	20 54	22 03		04 56	06 11	07 33	08 56
N 58	20 54	22 03		05 09	06 23	07 42	09 03
56	20 38	21 37		05 21	06 33	07 50	09 08
54	20 25	21 17	22 48	05 31	06 42	07 58	09 14
52	20 13	21 00	22 13	05 40	06 50	08 04	09 18
50	20 03	20 46	21 48	05 47	06 57	08 10	09 23
45	19 43	20 18	21 07	06 04	07 12	08 22	09 32
N 40	19 25	19 57	20 38	06 18	07 25	08 33	09 40
35	19 10	19 40	20 16	06 30	07 36	08 42	09 46
30	18 58	19 25	19 58	06 40	07 45	08 49	09 52
20	18 37	19 01	19 30	06 57	08 01	09 03	10 02
N 10	18 19	18 42	19 08	07 13	08 15	09 14	10 11
0	18 02	18 24	18 50	07 27	08 28	09 25	10 19
S 10	17 45	18 08	18 34	07 41	08 40	09 36	10 27
20	17 27	17 51	18 19	07 56	08 54	09 47	10 35
30	17 07	17 33	18 03	08 13	09 10	10 00	10 45
35	16 55	17 23	17 55	08 23	09 19	10 07	10 50
40	16 42	17 12	17 46	08 35	09 29	10 16	10 57
45	16 26	16 59	17 36	08 48	09 41	10 26	11 04
S 50	16 07	16 44	17 25	09 04	09 56	10 38	11 12
52	15 57	16 37	17 20	09 12	10 02	10 43	11 16
54	15 47	16 30	17 15	09 21	10 10	10 49	11 21
56	15 21	16 12	17 03	09 41	10 28	11 03	11 31
58	15 21	16 12	17 03	09 41	10 28	11 03	11 31
S 60	15 05	16 01	16 56	09 53	10 38	11 12	11 37

Day	SUN Eqn. of Time 00h	SUN Eqn. of Time 12h	SUN Mer. Pass.	MOON Mer. Pass. Upper	MOON Mer. Pass. Lower	Age	Phase
3	02 02	01 57	11 58	01 12	13 43	16	
4	01 52	01 47	11 58	02 13	14 43	17	◗
5	01 42	01 37	11 58	03 12	15 39	18	

Fig. 2802. *Nautical Almanac*, right-hand daily page (typical).

sage. This is sufficiently precise, as the time of LAN will be used only as the approximate center time for a series of observations.

A determination of the time of LAN is especially necessary when a vessel is running on a generally northerly or southerly course at speed. For a vessel proceeding towards the south, for example, the Sun will continue to increase its altitude for a considerable period *after* it actually has crossed the ship's meridian, and an observation made at the moment when it reaches its maximum altitude will yield a latitude that may be considerably in error.

Under most conditions, however, the Sun will appear to "hang" for an appreciable period of time near LAN; that is, it will not change perceptibly in altitude. To obtain a latitude line at LAN, you should start observing about two minutes before the time of transit, and continue to obtain sights until the altitude has unmistakably begun to decrease. The average of the three or four highest altitudes can be used for the reduction (or a graph can be plotted of altitude vs. time). On a northerly or southerly course several altitudes may be taken before and after that calculated time of transit to ensure that an unpredictable random error did not occur in the sight taken at the time of transit.

SOLUTION OF MERIDIAN ALTITUDES

2803 While meridian altitudes may be solved routinely by means of the inspection tables such as Pub. No. 229, using an assumed latitude, LHA 0°, and a tabulated declination as entering arguments, such tables are not necessary to obtain a solution.

The method of solution is the same for all celestial bodies observed on the upper branch of the meridian; at that instant each azimuth is precisely 000.0°, or 180.0°. In terms of the navigational triangle, it is a special case, in that the elevated pole, the observer's zenith, and the celestial body are all on the same great circle, the meridian, the vertical circle, and the hour circle of interest all coincide. The LOP obtained from a meridian observation is an arc of parallel of latitude.

The example used here is the transit of the Sun, as it is the most frequently observed body, but any celestial body observed when precisely on the navigator's meridian may be used, and the method of reduction would be the same as outlined here for the Sun.

The semicircle in figure 2803 represents that half of the observer's meridian extending from the north point to the south point of his celestial horizon; it is also occupied by a celestial body (in this case the Sun) at the instant of transit. In this diagram, Z represents the observer's zenith, Q the equator, P_n the North Pole (here the elevated pole), N and S the north and south points of the observer's horizon, respectively, and the circled dot the Sun on the meridian. The angle z is the zenith distance of the Sun, that is, 90° minus the observed altitude; L, Dec., and Ho are the observer's latitude, the declination, and the observed altitude, respectively. The same sort of labeling is used in all the diagrams on the plane of the observer's meridian.

Zenith Distance (z)

2804 In reductions to the meridian, *z is named for the direction of the observer from the body;* that is, if the observer is south of the body, z is named *south.* The latitude may then be obtained by applying the angular value of z to the declination, adding the two if they are of the same name, and subtracting the smaller from the larger if the names are contrary. The latitude will have the same name as the remainder; for example, if z is 42° N and the declination is 18° S, the latitude equals 42° N minus 18° S, or 24° N.

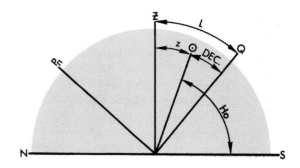

Fig. 2803. Lat. = z + Dec.

Figure 2803 is drawn for an observer in north latitude, who is north of the Sun; the observer's altitude of the Sun at transit is 71°. The z, therefore, is 90° minus 71°, or 19° N. The Sun's declination at the time of transit is 21° N. As the declination is north, and as the observer is north of the Sun, z and Dec. are added (19° N + 21° N) to give the observer's latitude, 40° N. Figure 2804a illustrates a case where the observer's latitude and the declination are of opposite name. The Ho is 40°, and the Sun is north of the observer, giving a z of 50° S, and the declination is 20° N. In this case Dec. is subtracted from the z (50° S – 20° N) to yield a latitude of 30° S.

Figure 2804b shows Lat. and Dec. of the same name, but Dec. greater than Lat. The Dec. is 21° N; Ho is 78°, giving a z of 12° S. Therefore, z is sub-

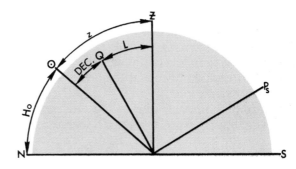

Fig. 2804a. Lat. = z – Dec.

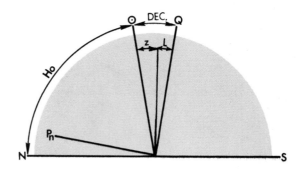

Fig. 2804b. Lat. = Dec. – z.

tracted from Dec. (21° N – 12° S) to yield a latitude of 9° N.

The procedure for the determination of latitude from an observation of the Sun at LAN can be summarized in the following two rules:

1. If the zenith distance and declination are of the *same* name, they are added; the *sum* is the latitude of the observer.
2. If the zenith distance and declination are of *contrary* name, the smaller value is *subtracted* from the larger; the *difference* is the latitude, with the sign of the larger value.

Use of a diagram on the plane of the meridian obviates the need for remembering these rules.

Solutions for Lower-branch Meridian Altitudes

2805 When a body is observed at *lower transit,* on the lower branch of the meridian, the solution differs from that for the upper branch, in that polar distance (p) is used, rather than z; p is the angular distance of the body from the pole or 90° minus Dec. At lower transit, the observer's latitude is equal to the observed altitude plus the polar distance, or L = Ho + p. In figure 2805, a star with a declination of 50° N is observed at lower transit at an Ho of 20°. L therefore equals 20° + 40°, or 60° N.

LATITUDE FROM A POLARIS OBSERVATION

2806 The latitude of a place is equal to the altitude of the elevated pole, as illustrated in figure 2806. Both the latitude of the observer, *QOZ,* and the altitude of the pole, *NOPn,* equal 90° minus *PnOZ.* Thus, if a star were located exactly at each celestial pole, the corrected altitude of the star would equal the observer's latitude.

No readily observed star is located exactly at either pole, but Polaris is less than a degree from the

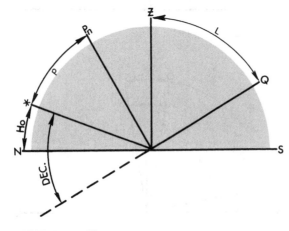

Fig. 2805. Lat. = Ho + p.

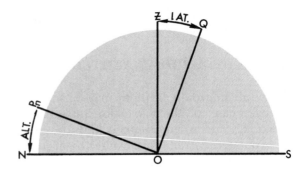

Fig. 2806. Latitude equals the altitude of the elevated pole.

north celestial pole. Like all stars, it alternately transits the upper and lower branches of each celestial meridian in completing its diurnal circle. Twice during every 24 hours, as it moves in its diurnal circle, Polaris is at the same altitude as the pole, and at that moment no correction would be required to its observed altitude to obtain latitude. At all other times a correction, constantly changing in value, must be applied. The value for any instant may be obtained from the Polaris Tables in the *Nautical Almanac,* the entering argument being LHA ^. The correction is tabulated in three parts; the first is the basic correction applicable under all conditions. This correction, designated "a_0" in the *Nautical Almanac,* compensates for the component of the distance between the position of Polaris in its diurnal circle and the north celestial pole, measured along the observer's celestial meridian. The second correction (a_1) is for the DR latitude of the observer, and corrects for the angle at which one views the star's diurnal circle. The third correction (a_2) is for the date and corrects for the small variations in the SHA and Dec. of the star in the course of a year.

SOLUTION OF A POLARIS OBSERVATION BY *NAUTICAL ALMANAC*

2807 A latitude LOP can be obtained from an observation of Polaris by using only the *Nautical Almanac* (or *Air Almanac*) to reduce the observation.

The three Polaris correction tables comprise three white pages before the Sight Reduction Procedures that the precede the tinted pages in the *Nautical Almanac.* A portion of these tables, showing the arrangement of the three corrections a_0, a_1, and a_2, is reproduced in figure 2807a (the year of the table, normally shown on the top line, has been deleted from this extract). It must be borne in mind that *these three corrections are in addition to the usual corrections applied to all sextant observations to obtain Ho.*

POLARIS (POLE STAR) TABLES
FOR DETERMINING LATITUDE FROM SEXTANT ALTITUDE AND FOR AZIMUTH

L.H.A. ARIES	240°–249°	250°–259°	260°–269°	270°–279°	280°–289°	290°–299°	300°–309°	310°–319°	320°–329°	330°–339°	340°–349°	350°–359°
	a_0	a_0	a_0	a_0	a_0	a_0	a_0	a_0	a_0	a_0	a_0	a_0
0	1 43·5	1 38·9	1 33·1	1 26·2	1 18·5	1 10·2	1 01·5	0 52·7	0 44·1	0 36·0	0 28·5	0 22·0
1	43·1	38·4	32·4	25·5	17·7	09·3	1 00·6	51·9	43·3	35·2	27·8	21·4
2	42·7	37·8	31·8	24·7	16·9	08·4	0 59·7	51·0	42·5	34·4	27·1	20·8
9	39·4	33·7	26·9	19·3	11·0	02·4	53·6	45·0	36·8	29·2	22·6	17·0
10	1 38·9	1 33·1	1 26·2	1 18·5	1 10·2	1 01·5	0 52·7	0 44·1	0 36·0	0 28·5	0 22·0	0 16·5
Lat.	a_1	a_1	a_1	a_1	a_1	a_1	a_1	a_1	a_1	a_1	a_1	a_1
0	0·5	0·4	0·3	0·3	0·2	0·2	0·2	0·2	0·2	0·3	0·4	0·4
10	·5	·4	·4	·3	·3	·2	·2	·2	·3	·3	·4	·5
20	·5	·5	·4	·4	·3	·3	·3	·3	·3	·4	·4	·5
30	·5	·5	·5	·4	·4	·4	·4	·4	·4	·4	·5	·5
66	·7	·8	·8	0·9	1·0	1·0	1·0	1·0	0·9	·9	·8	·7
68	0·7	0·8	0·9	1·0	1·0	1·1	1·1	1·1	1·0	0·9	0·9	0·8
Month	a_2	a_2	a_2	a_2	a_2	a_2	a_2	a_2	a_2	a_2	a_2	a_2
Jan.	0·4	0·5	0·5	0·5	0·5	0·5	0·6	0·6	0·6	0·7	0·7	0·7
Feb.	·4	·4	·4	·4	·4	·4	·4	·5	·5	·5	·6	·6
Mar.	·4	·3	·3	·3	·3	·3	·3	·3	·3	·4	·4	·5
Apr.	0·5	0·4	0·4	0·3	0·3	0·3	0·2	0·2	0·2	0·3	0·3	0·3
May	·6	·5	·5	·4	·4	·3	·3	·2	·2	·2	·2	·2
June	·8	·7	·6	·6	·5	·4	·4	·3	·3	·3	·2	·2
July	0·9	0·8	0·8	0·7	0·7	0·6	0·5	0·5	0·4	0·4	0·3	0·3
Aug.	·9	·9	·9	·8	·8	·8	·7	·7	·6	·5	·5	·4
Sept.	·9	·9	·9	·9	·9	·9	·9	·8	·8	·7	·7	·6
Oct.	0·8	0·8	0·9	0·9	0·9	0·9	0·9	0·9	0·9	0·9	0·8	0·8
Nov.	·6	·7	·8	·8	·9	·9	1·0	1·0	1·0	1·0	1·0	1·0
Dec.	0·5	0·6	0·6	0·7	0·8	0·8	0·9	1·0	1·0	1·0	1·0	1·0

Latitude = Apparent altitude (corrected for refraction) $-1° + a_0 + a_1 + a_2$

The table is entered with L.H.A. Aries to determine the column to be used; each column refers to a range of 10°. a_0 is taken, with mental interpolation, from the upper table with the units of L.H.A. Aries in degrees as argument; a_1, a_2 are taken, without interpolation, from the second and third tables with arguments latitude and month respectively. a_0, a_1, a_2 are always positive. The final table gives the azimuth of *Polaris*.

Fig. 2807a. *Nautical Almanac,* Polaris Tables (extract).

As with any body, the sextant altitude is obtained, and the time and date are recorded. The index error is checked and recorded.

Given the GMT and Greenwich date, the appropriate pages of the almanac are entered, and the GHA ♈ is obtained. The DR longitude at the time of observation is applied (subtract west, add east) to get LHA ♈. Note that ordinarily the DR, not some other assumed position, is used.

To solve a Polaris observation for latitude, find the value of LHA ♈ in the column headings across the top of the Polaris correction tables; these headings are in groups of 10°. Then follow down that column until opposite the single-degree value of LHA ♈ as tabulated in the left-most column; the exact value for a_0 is then found for the minutes of LHA ♈ by interpolation. Staying in the same vertical column, find the value of a_1 in the next lower part of the table for the tabulated latitude nearest the DR, without interpolation. Next, find the a_2 correction in the same column for the current month, in the third part of the table, again without interpolation.

The arrangement of the tables is such that these three corrections are always *positive* (additive), *but an additional constant of 1° negative is finally applied* to determine the total correction to Ho to obtain the latitude at the time of the observation. The net correction can be negative in some instances.

Customarily, the navigator uses the latitude thus obtained to draw a latitude LOP. If his DR longitude is reasonably accurate, this latitude line will yield acceptable accuracy. If there is considerable uncertainty as to the vessel's longitude, the azimuth of Polaris should be determined. This will be found at the bottom of the Polaris tables, the two entering arguments being the nearest 10° of LHA ♈, and the nearest tabulated latitude; no interpolation is required. The LOP is then drawn through the computed latitude and the DR longitude, perpendicular to this azimuth. Alternatively, the latitude may be determined or each of two longitudes that straddle the DR position, and the two points so found joined by a straight line to form the LOP.

Example: Find the latitude at the time of observation using the *Nautical Almanac.*

Answer: Lat. 41° 00.8′. (Example data and the solution are shown in figure 2807b.)

SOLUTION OF A POLARIS OBSERVATION BY *AIR ALMANAC*

2808 An observation of Polaris can also be reduced for a latitude line of position by use of the Polaris table for latitude in the *Air Almanac.*

The table lists Q corrections against critical values of LHA ♈ (which is found from GHA ♈ and DR

longitude in the usual manner). The respondent Q value is applied to the corrected sextant altitude to directly yield the latitude.

Example: During morning twilight on 5 June, at approximately 0352 (+1), you observe Polaris. The ship's DR position is Lat. 41° 02.5′ N, Long. 14° 36.9′ W. The sextant has an IC of +0.2; the watch is 8 seconds fast; the height of eye is 21 feet. The sextant altitude at 03-52-16 watch time is 41° 14′.

Required: The latitude at the time of observation, using the *Air Almanac.*

Answer: Lat. 41° 01′ N. (Solution is shown in figure 2808.)

Note that this value, to the nearest whole minute of latitude, is essentially the same as that obtained to the nearest tenth of a minute by use of the *Nautical Almanac;* several fewer steps were required by use of the *Air Almanac.*

OBSERVATIONS FOR LONGITUDE

2809 Longitude observations were in general use until the altitude difference or intercept method, devised in 1875 by Marcq de St.-Hilaire, was accepted. The longitude obtained was predicated on a latitude which had usually been obtained from a LAN Sun observation, and carried forward or back by DR. The calculated longitude therefore could be accurate only if the DR latitude was accurate. Sub-

IC	0.2	
Dip (Ht.21′)		4.4
Sum		-4.2
hs	41	14.2
ha	41	-10.0
Alt. Corr		- 1.1
TB (hs < 10°)		
Ho	41	08.9
Date	5 JUN	77
DR Lat.	41°	02.5 N
DR Long	14°	36.9′W
Obs time	03-52-16	
WE (S+, F−)		8F
ZT	03-52-08	
ZD (W+, E−)	+1	
GMT	04-52-08	
Date (GMT)	5 JUN 77	
Tab GHA ♈	313	28.3
GHA Incrmt	13	04.1
GHA ♈	326	32.4
DR Long	14	36.9 W
LHA ♈	311	55.5
a₀	**51.1**	
a₁	0.5	
a₂	0.3	
Add'n'l		60.0
Sub total	51.9	60.0
Corr to Ho		- 8.1
Ho	41	08.9
Lat	41°	00.8 N
True Az		
Gyro Brg		
Gyro Error		

Fig. 2807b. Calculation of latitude from a Polaris observation using the *Nautical Almanac.*

IC	+ 0.2	−	
Dip (Ht.21′)		4	
Sum		- 3.8	
hs	41 - 14		
ha	41 -10		
Alt Corr		- 1	
TB (hs < 10°)			
Ho	41° 09′		
Date	5 JUN 77		
DR Lat	41° 02.5′ N		
DR Long	14° 36.9′ W		
Obs time	03-52-16		
WE	8F		
ZT	03-52-08		
ZD	+1		
GMT	04-52-08		
Date GMT	5 JUN 77		
Tab GHA ♈	326 · 00		
Incrmt	0 32		
GHA ♈	326 32		
DR Long	14 37		
LHA ♈	311 55		
Q	−8		
Ho	41 09		
Lat.	41° 01′ N		

Fig. 2808. Calculation of latitude from a Polaris observation using the *Air Almanac.*

sequently, as the accuracy of the chronometers was improved, celestial bodies were observed, when possible, on the *prime vertical*, that is, when their azimuth was exactly 090.0° or 270.0°; this method yielded considerably increased accuracy, but still depended to some extent on accuracy of latitude.

Currently, observations intended solely to yield longitude are seldom required or made. If one is to be made, a convenient method involves the use of an inspection table, usually Pub. No. 229, to predict an opportune observation time. Pub. No. 229, may be entered with values of latitude and declination, and the LHA determined for the time at which the azimuth equals 90.0° (or 270.0°). The GMT at which this LHA, converted to GHA by applying DR longitude, occurs can then be obtained from the *Nautical Almanac.* For the best results, interpolation should be made for t, Dec., and L. The process is feasible but laborious, and consequently is not often done. Nonetheless, to make observations of bodies on the prime vertical as the opportunities present themselves is good practice; a reliable longitude line is always valuable. Bodies not on the prime vertical can also be used by sight reduction to yield computed longitude, but with decreasing accuracy as their departure from the prime vertical increases.

OBSERVATIONS ON THE BEAM, BOW, AND STERN

2810 Observations made directly on the beam are helpful in determining whether the ship is on the desired track line, while observations obtained dead ahead or astern show how far she has advanced. The Sun is the body most commonly used in making such observations. Here, again, Pub. No. 229 may be used to advantage. It is entered with the appropriate latitude and declination, and the desired azimuth angle (in relation to the ship's head, stern, or beam) is found in the body of the table. The time of the observation is then predicted as for a longitude observation, by making use of the LHA as found in Pub. No. 229.

Chapter 29

Compass Checks at Sea

In the previous chapters, compass error was addressed by reference to visible landmarks and aids to navigation. It is not necessary, however, to have such relatively close objects at hand. Compass error on the high seas can be determined from azimuth observations of various celestial bodies, but the Sun is the body most frequently used. For ease and reliability of measurements, azimuth observations should be made when the Sun is low in altitude, preferably less than 20°.

For U.S. naval vessels, regulations require that compasses be checked at least once a day. Prudent navigators often make compass checks at least *twice* a day whenever possible. A check should be made immediately if there is any reason to suppose that a compass has been damaged or is malfunctioning.

Thus far, the celestial navigation portion of this book has been concerned with the solution of navigational triangles to obtain LOPS and fix the position of the vessel. This chapter considers the solution of a navigational triangle to determine true azimuth, and from it, the compass error at sea.

AZIMUTH OBSERVATION

2901   Azimuth observations of celestial bodies are made by azimuth circle, bearing circle, or similar device. As discussed earlier, an azimuth circle is an instrument whose principal components are a small, hinged, concave mirror and a shielded prism that is located on the ring opposite the mirror. When such an instrument is used to observe the Sun's azimuth, it is fitted over a gyrocompass repeater, or the bowl of a magnetic compass, and aligned so that the prism is between the mirror and the Sun. When the hinged mirror is properly

adjusted in the plane of the vertical circle of the Sun, a thin, vertical beam of sunlight is cast upon a slit in the prism shield and reflected downward onto the compass card. The line of sunlight on the card indicates the compass azimuth of the Sun at that time. Two leveling bubbles are provided on the azimuth circle, to aid in keeping the instrument horizontal for measuring an accurate compass azimuth.

An azimuth observation of a star or planet is made through the sight vanes of an azimuth circle or bearing circle, in a manner similar to that used for observing a terrestrial bearing. The Moon may be observed for azimuth using either the mirror-prism method or the sight-vane method. Partly because of the difficulty in seeing the leveling bubbles during darkness, azimuth observations are most often accomplished using the Sun. A pelorus can also be used to determine the azimuth measurements, although generally with less accuracy.

In practice, you observe the azimuth of a celestial body and note the time of the observation. You then solve the navigational triangle appropriate for your position and determine the true azimuth of the body at the time of the observation. The difference between the true and observed azimuths, properly labeled E or W, is the compass error.

In general, the lower the celestial body, the more accurate the azimuth observation. For most practical purposes, azimuth precision of one-half degree is sufficient.

EXACT AZIMUTH BY INSPECTION TABLES

2902   The inspection tables for sight reduction, Pub. No. 229, make excellent azimuth tables. Pub.

No. 249 tables can also be used for obtaining exact azimuths, but not as precisely, because the azimuths are tabulated only to the nearest whole degree.

When Pub. No. 229 is used to determine true azimuth for the purpose of checking the compass, triple linear interpolation usually is made in order to obtain the required accuracy. The d values in Pub. No. 229 apply only to *altitude,* not to azimuth.

Example: The azimuth of the Sun is observed at 06-25-42 on 5 June. The 0625 position has been fixed at Lat. 41° 06.1' N, Long. 15° 03.1' W. The azimuth obtained by using a gyro repeater is 076.0°.

Required: Gyro error, using Pub. No. 229 to obtain exact true azimuth.

Solution: (See fig. 2902a.) It is first necessary to determine the exact values of LHA, Dec., and L for the instant of observation of the azimuth. These values are determined in the same manner as when working a sight, except that the *actual* position of the ship is used rather than an assumed position. Thus the DR longitude, 15° 03.1' W, is used to determine the exact value of LHA at the time of observation. The exact value of Dec. is found to be N22° 32.5' by use of the *Nautical Almanac* in the usual manner. The DR latitude is taken as the exact value of L at the time of observation. (If a fix obtained from observations and complete reductions at about this time shows the DR position to be significantly in error, the more accurate values of DR Lat. and Long. based on the fix nearest in time should be used whether the fix occurs before or after the azimuth observation.)

With the exact values of LHA, Dec., and L determined, the appropriate page of Pub. No. 229 is entered for the "tab" values, those tabulated entering arguments *nearest* to the exact values. In this case, they are LHA 277, Dec. N23°, and L41° N. With these "tab" values as entering arguments, the corresponding tabulated azimuth angle (Z) 76.4° is recorded (see fig. 2902b). This value of Z is the *tabulated* ("tab") value, to which the corrections resulting from the necessary interpolations are applied to obtain the azimuth angle for the exact values of LHA, Dec., and L at the moment of observation. Interpolation is made separately for the difference between each of these exact values and its corresponding "tab" value of LHA, Dec., and L; the algebraic sum of the resulting corrections is then applied to the value of tab Z to obtain the exact azimuth angle at the moment of observation. It is sufficiently accurate to reduce these corrections to the nearest tenth of a degree.

An interpolation is made between LHA 277° (Z 76.4°) and LHA 276° (Z 75.8°). The change in Z is –0.6° for a change in LHA of 1° (60'); this is known as the "Z diff." Since the exact value of LHA is 276° 47.1', or 12.9' less than the "tab" value of LHA, the difference in the value of Z corresponding to this difference in LHA is 12.9 divided by 60 (0.215) of the difference for a 1° change in LHA. Thus the "corr," which is the correction to apply to the value

EXACT AZIMUTH USING Pub. 229

Body	☉			
DR L	41° 06.1' N			
DR λ	15° 03.1' W			
Date (L)	5 JUN			
ZT	06 - 25 - 42			
ZD (+ or -)	+1			
GMT	07 - 25 - 42			
Date (G)	5 JUN			
Tab GHA	285° 24.7'			
Inc'mt	6° 25.5'			
GHA	291° 50.2'			
DR λ	- 15° 03.1' W			
LHA	276° 47.1			

		Deg	d(+/-)
Tab Dec	N22° 32.4'		+ 0.2'
d corr	+ 0.1'		
Dec	N22° 32.5'		

	EXACT		Z DIFF.	CORR.
	Deg	Min	(+ or -)	(+ or -)
LAT	41	06.1	+ 0.3	0.0
LHA	276	47.1	- 0.6	- 0.1
DEC	22	32.5	+ 0.8	+ 0.4

Total (±)	+ 0.3
Tab Z	76.4
Exact Z	76.7
Exact Zn	076.7
Gyro/Compass Brg	076.0
Gyro/Compass Error	0.7 E

NORTH LAT

LHA greater than 180° . . . . Zn = Z
LHA less than 180° . . . . Zn = 360° - Z

SOUTH LAT

LHA greater than 180° . . . . Zn = 180° - Z
LHA less than 180° . . . . Zn = 180° + Z

Fig. 2902a. Determination of exact azimuth and gyro error using Pub. No. 229.

N. Lat. {L.H.A. greater than 180°......Zn=Z / L.H.A. less than 180°...........Zn=360°−Z}

Dec.	38° Hc	d	Z	39° Hc	d	Z	40° Hc	d	Z	41° Hc	d	Z
°	° ′	′	°	° ′	′	°	° ′	′	°	° ′	′	°
0	5 30.7	+37.0	94.3	5 26.1	+37.9	94.4	5 21.4	+38.7	94.5	5 16.6	+39.5	94.6
1	6 07.7	37.0	93.5	6 04.0	37.8	93.6	6 00.1	38.7	93.7	5 56.1	39.5	93.8
2	6 44.7	37.0	92.7	6 41.8	37.8	92.9	6 38.8	38.5	93.0	6 35.6	39.4	93.1
3	7 21.7	36.8	91.9	7 19.6	37.6	92.1	7 17.3	38.5	92.2	7 15.0	39.2	92.3
4	7 58.5	36.8	91.2	7 57.2	37.6	91.3	7 55.8	38.4	91.4	7 54.2	39.3	91.6
5	8 35.3	+36.6	90.4	8 34.8	+37.5	90.5	8 34.2	+38.3	90.7	8 33.5	+39.1	90.8
6	9 11.9	36.6	89.6	9 12.3	37.4	89.7	9 12.5	38.2	89.9	9 12.6	39.0	90.0
7	9 48.5	36.4	88.7	9 49.7	37.3	88.9	9 50.7	38.2	89.1	9 51.6	38.9	89.3
8	10 24.9	36.3	87.9	10 27.0	37.1	88.1	10 28.9	37.9	88.3	10 30.5	38.8	88.5
9	11 01.2	36.2	87.1	11 04.1	37.1	87.3	11 06.8	37.9	87.5	11 09.3	38.7	87.7
10	11 37.4	+36.1	86.3	11 41.2	+36.9	86.5	11 44.7	+37.7	86.7	11 48.0	+38.6	86.9
11	12 13.5	35.9	85.5	12 18.1	36.7	85.7	12 22.4	37.6	85.9	12 26.6	38.4	86.2
12	12 49.4	35.7	84.7	12 54.8	36.6	84.9	13 00.0	37.5	85.1	13 05.0	38.3	85.4
13	13 25.1	35.6	83.9	13 31.4	36.5	84.1	13 37.5	37.3	84.3	13 43.3	38.1	84.6
14	14 00.7	35.4	83.0	14 07.9	36.3	83.3	14 14.8	37.1	83.5	14 21.4	38.0	83.8
15	14 36.1	+35.3	82.2	14 44.2	+36.1	82.5	14 51.9	+37.0	82.7	14 59.4	+37.8	83.0
16	15 11.4	35.0	81.4	15 20.3	35.9	81.6	15 28.9	36.7	81.9	15 37.2	37.6	82.2
17	15 46.4	34.9	80.5	15 56.2	35.7	80.8	16 05.6	36.6	81.1	16 14.8	37.4	81.4
18	16 21.3	34.6	79.7	16 31.9	35.5	80.0	16 42.2	36.4	80.2	16 52.2	37.3	80.5
19	16 55.9	34.5	78.8	17 07.4	35.3	79.1	17 18.6	36.2	79.4	17 29.5	37.0	79.7
20	17 30.4	+34.2	78.0	17 42.7	+35.1	78.3	17 54.8	+35.9	78.6	18 06.5	+36.8	78.9
21	18 04.6	34.0	77.1	18 17.8	34.9	77.4	18 30.7	35.8	77.7	18 43.3	36.6	78.1
22	18 38.6	33.7	76.2	18 52.7	34.6	76.6	19 06.5	35.5	76.9	19 19.9	36.4	77.2
23	19 12.3	33.5	75.4	19 27.3	34.4	75.7	19 42.0	35.3	76.0	19 56.3	36.1	76.4
24	19 45.8	33.3	74.5	20 01.7	34.1	74.8	20 17.3	35.0	75.2	20 32.4	35.9	75.5
25	20 19.1	+32.9	73.6	20 35.8	+33.9	73.9	20 52.3	+34.7	74.3	21 08.3	+35.6	74.7
26	20 52.0	32.7	72.7	21 09.7	33.6	73.1	21 27.0	34.5	73.4	21 43.9	35.4	73.8
27	21 24.7	32.4	71.8	21 43.3	33.3	72.2	22 01.5	34.1	72.6	22 19.3	35.0	72.9
28	21 57.1	32.1	70.9	22 16.6	33.0	71.3	22 35.6	33.9	71.7	22 54.3	34.8	72.1
29	22 29.2	31.8	70.0	22 49.6	32.7	70.4	23 09.5	33.6	70.8	23 29.1	34.5	71.2
30	23 01.0	+31.5	69.1	23 22.3	+32.3	69.5	23 43.1	+33.3	69.9	24 03.6	+34.1	70.3
31	23 32.5	31.1	68.1	23 54.6	32.1	68.5	24 16.4	32.9	69.0	24 37.7	33.8	69.4
32	24 03.6	30.8	67.2	24 26.7	31.6	67.6	24 49.3	32.6	68.0	25 11.5	33.5	68.5
33	24 34.4	30.4	66.3	24 58.3	31.4	66.7	25 21.9	32.2	67.1	25 45.0	33.2	67.5
34	25 04.8	30.1	65.3	25 29.7	31.0	65.7	25 54.1	31.9	66.2	26 18.2	32.7	66.6
35	25 34.9	+29.7	64.3	26 00.7	+30.6	64.8	26 26.0	+31.5	65.2	26 50.9	+32.5	65.7
36	26 04.6	29.3	63.4	26 31.3	30.2	63.8	26 57.5	31.1	64.3	27 23.4	32.0	64.7
37	26 33.9	28.9	62.4	27 01.5	29.8	62.9	27 28.6	30.8	63.3	27 55.4	31.6	63.8
38	27 02.8	28.5	61.4	27 31.3	29.4	61.9	27 59.4	30.3	62.3	28 27.0	31.2	62.8
39	27 31.3	28.1	60.4	28 00.7	29.0	60.9	28 29.7	29.8	61.4	28 58.2	30.8	61.8
40	27 59.4	+27.6	59.4	28 29.7	+28.5	59.9	28 59.5	+29.5	60.4	29 29.0	+30.3	60.9
41	28 27.0	27.2	58.4	28 58.2	28.1	58.9	29 29.0	29.0	59.4	29 59.3	29.9	59.9
42	28 54.2	26.7	57.4	29 26.3	27.6	57.9	29 58.0	28.5	58.4	30 29.2	29.4	58.9
43	29 20.9	26.2	56.4	29 53.9	27.1	56.9	30 26.5	28.0	57.3	30 58.6	29.0	57.9
44	29 47.1	25.8	55.4	30 21.0	26.7	55.8	30 54.5	27.6	56.3	31 27.6	28.4	56.8
45	30 12.9	+25.3	54.3	30 47.7	+26.1	54.8	31 22.1	+27.0	55.3	31 56.0	+28.0	55.8
46	30 38.2	24.7	53.3	31 13.8	25.7	53.7	31 49.1	26.6	54.2	32 24.0	27.4	54.7
47	31 02.9	24.2	52.2	31 39.5	25.1	52.7	32 15.7	25.9	53.2	32 51.4	26.9	53.7
48	31 27.1	23.7	51.1	32 04.6	24.5	51.6	32 41.6	25.5	52.1	33 18.3	26.3	52.6
49	31 50.8	23.1	50.0	32 29.1	24.0	50.5	33 07.1	24.9	51.0	33 44.6	25.8	51.5
50	32 13.9	+22.6	49.0	32 53.1	+23.5	49.4	33 32.0	+24.3	49.9	34 10.4	+25.1	50.5
51	32 36.5	22.0	47.9	33 16.6	22.8	48.3	33 56.3	23.7	48.8	34 35.5	24.6	49.4
52	32 58.5	21.4	46.8	33 39.4	22.3	47.2	34 20.0	23.1	47.7	35 00.1	24.0	48.2
53	33 19.9	20.8	45.6	34 01.7	21.6	46.1	34 43.1	22.5	46.6	35 24.1	23.3	47.1
54	33 40.7	20.2	44.5	34 23.3	21.0	45.0	35 05.6	21.8	45.5	35 47.4	22.7	46.0
55	34 00.9	+19.5	43.4	34 44.3	+20.4	43.9	35 27.4	+21.2	44.3	36 10.1	+22.1	44.8
56	34 20.4	18.9	42.2	35 04.7	19.7	42.7	35 48.6	20.5	43.2	36 32.2	21.3	43.7
57	34 39.3	18.3	41.1	35 24.4	19.0	41.5	36 09.1	19.9	42.0	36 53.5	20.7	42.5
58	34 57.6	17.6	39.9	35 43.4	18.4	40.4	36 29.0	19.2	40.9	37 14.2	20.0	41.3
59	35 15.2	16.9	38.8	36 01.8	17.7	39.2	36 48.2	18.4	39.7	37 34.2	19.2	40.2
60	35 32.1	+16.2	37.6	36 19.5	+17.0	38.0	37 06.6	+17.7	38.5	37 53.4	+18.5	39.0
61	35 48.3	15.5	36.4	36 36.5	16.2	36.8	37 24.3	17.0	37.3	38 11.9	17.8	37.8
62	36 03.8	14.8	35.2	36 52.7	15.5	35.6	37 41.3	16.3	36.1	38 29.7	17.0	36.5
63	36 18.6	14.1	34.0	37 08.2	14.8	34.4	37 57.6	15.5	34.9	38 46.7	16.2	35.3
64	36 32.7	13.3	32.8	37 23.0	14.0	33.2	38 13.1	14.7	33.6	39 02.9	15.5	34.1
65	36 46.0	+12.6	31.6	37 37.0	+13.3	32.0	38 27.8	+14.0	32.4	39 18.4	+14.6	32.8
66	36 58.6	11.9	30.4	37 50.3	12.5	30.7	38 41.8	13.1	31.1	39 33.0	13.8	31.6
67	37 10.5	11.0	29.1	38 02.8	11.7	29.5	38 54.9	12.3	29.9	39 46.8	13.0	30.3
68	37 21.5	10.3	27.9	38 14.5	10.9	28.3	39 07.2	11.6	28.6	39 59.8	12.1	29.0
69	37 31.8	9.6	26.6	38 25.4	10.1	27.0	39 18.8	10.6	27.4	40 11.9	11.3	27.8
70	37 41.4	+8.7	25.4	38 35.5	+9.3	25.7	39 29.4	+9.9	26.1	40 23.2	+10.5	26.5
71	37 50.1	7.9	24.2	38 44.8	8.4	24.5	39 39.3	9.0	24.8	40 33.7	9.5	25.2
72	37 58.0	7.1	22.9	38 53.2	7.7	23.2	39 48.3	8.1	23.5	40 43.2	8.7	23.9
73	38 05.1	6.3	21.6	39 00.9	6.7	21.9	39 56.4	7.3	22.2	40 51.9	7.8	22.6
74	38 11.4	5.5	20.4	39 07.6	6.0	20.7	40 03.7	6.5	20.9	40 59.7	6.9	21.3
75	38 16.9	+4.7	19.1	39 13.6	+5.1	19.4	40 10.2	+5.5	19.6	41 06.6	+6.0	19.9
76	38 21.6	3.9	17.8	39 18.7	4.3	18.1	40 15.7	4.7	18.3	41 12.6	5.1	18.6
77	38 25.5	3.0	16.6	39 23.0	3.4	16.8	40 20.4	3.7	17.0	41 17.7	4.2	17.3
78	38 28.5	2.2	15.3	39 26.4	2.5	15.5	40 24.1	2.9	15.7	41 21.9	3.2	16.0
79	38 30.7	1.4	14.0	39 28.9	1.7	14.2	40 27.0	2.0	14.4	41 25.1	2.3	14.6
80	38 32.1	+0.5	12.7	39 30.6	+0.8	12.9	40 29.0	+1.1	13.1	41 27.4	+1.5	13.3
81	38 32.6	−0.3	11.5	39 31.4	−0.1	11.6	40 30.1	+0.2	11.8	41 28.9	+0.4	12.0
82	38 32.3	1.2	10.2	39 31.3	0.9	10.3	40 30.3	−0.6	10.5	41 29.3	−0.4	10.6
83	38 31.1	1.9	8.9	39 30.4	1.8	9.0	40 29.7	1.6	9.2	41 28.9	1.4	9.3
84	38 29.2	2.8	7.6	39 28.6	2.6	7.7	40 28.1	2.5	7.8	41 27.5	2.3	8.0
85	38 26.4	−3.7	6.3	39 26.0	−3.5	6.4	40 25.6	−3.3	6.5	41 25.2	−3.2	6.6
86	38 22.7	4.4	5.1	39 22.5	4.3	5.1	40 22.3	4.3	5.2	41 22.0	4.1	5.3
87	38 18.3	5.3	3.8	39 18.2	5.3	3.8	40 18.0	5.1	3.9	41 17.9	5.1	4.0
88	38 13.0	6.1	2.5	39 12.9	6.0	2.6	40 12.9	6.0	2.6	41 12.8	5.9	2.6
89	38 06.9	6.9	1.3	39 06.9	6.9	1.3	40 06.9	6.9	1.3	41 06.9	6.9	1.3
90	38 00.0	−7.7	0.0	39 00.0	−7.7	0.0	40 00.0	−7.7	0.0	41 00.0	−7.8	0.0
	38°			39°			40°			41°		

42° Hc	d	Z	43° Hc	d	Z	44° Hc	d	Z	45° Hc	d	Z	Dec.
° ′	′	°	° ′	′	°	° ′	′	°	° ′	′	°	°
5 11.8	+40.3	94.7	5 06.8	+41.1	94.8	5 01.8	+41.8	94.9	4 56.6	+42.6	95.0	0
5 52.1	40.2	94.0	5 47.9	41.0	94.1	5 43.6	41.7	94.2	5 39.2	42.5	94.3	1
6 32.3	40.1	93.2	6 28.9	40.9	93.3	6 25.3	41.7	93.4	6 21.7	42.4	93.5	2
7 12.4	40.1	92.5	7 09.8	40.9	92.6	7 07.0	41.7	92.7	7 04.1	42.4	92.8	3
7 52.5	40.0	91.7	7 50.7	40.8	91.8	7 48.7	41.5	92.0	7 46.5	42.3	92.1	4
8 32.5	+40.0	91.0	8 31.5	+40.7	91.1	8 30.2	+41.5	91.3	8 28.8	+42.3	91.4	5
9 12.5	39.8	90.2	9 12.2	40.6	90.4	9 11.7	41.4	90.5	9 11.1	42.1	90.7	6
9 52.3	39.7	89.4	9 52.8	40.5	89.6	9 53.1	41.3	89.8	9 53.2	42.1	90.0	7
10 32.0	39.6	88.7	10 33.3	40.4	88.9	10 34.4	41.2	89.1	10 35.3	41.9	89.2	8
11 11.6	39.5	87.9	11 13.7	40.3	88.1	11 15.6	41.1	88.3	11 17.2	41.9	88.5	9
11 51.1	+39.4	87.1	11 54.0	+40.2	87.4	11 56.7	+40.9	87.6	11 59.1	+41.7	87.8	10
12 30.5	39.2	86.4	12 34.2	40.0	86.6	12 37.6	40.9	86.8	12 40.8	41.6	87.0	11
13 09.7	39.1	85.6	13 14.2	39.9	85.8	13 18.5	40.7	86.1	13 22.4	41.5	86.3	12
13 48.8	39.0	84.8	13 54.1	39.8	85.1	13 59.2	40.5	85.3	14 03.9	41.4	85.6	13
14 27.8	38.8	84.0	14 33.9	39.6	84.3	14 39.7	40.4	84.6	14 45.3	41.2	84.8	14
15 06.6	+38.6	83.2	15 13.5	+39.4	83.5	15 20.1	+40.3	83.8	15 26.5	+41.0	84.1	15
15 45.2	38.5	82.5	15 52.9	39.3	82.7	16 00.4	40.1	83.0	16 07.5	40.9	83.3	16
16 23.7	38.2	81.7	16 32.2	39.1	81.9	16 40.5	39.9	82.2	16 48.4	40.7	82.5	17
17 01.9	38.1	80.8	17 11.3	38.9	81.2	17 20.4	39.7	81.5	17 29.1	40.6	81.8	18
17 40.0	37.9	80.0	17 50.2	38.7	80.4	18 00.1	39.6	80.7	18 09.7	40.3	81.0	19
18 17.9	+37.7	79.2	18 28.9	+38.5	79.5	18 39.7	+39.3	79.9	18 50.0	+40.2	80.2	20
18 55.6	37.4	78.4	19 07.4	38.3	78.7	19 19.0	39.1	79.1	19 30.2	39.9	79.4	21
19 33.0	37.2	77.6	19 45.7	38.1	77.9	19 58.1	38.9	78.3	20 10.1	39.8	78.6	22
20 10.2	37.0	76.7	20 23.8	37.9	77.1	20 37.0	38.7	77.5	20 49.9	39.5	77.8	23
20 47.2	36.8	75.9	21 01.7	37.6	76.3	21 15.7	38.4	76.6	21 29.4	39.2	77.0	24
21 24.0	+36.5	75.1	21 39.3	+37.3	75.4	21 54.1	+38.2	75.8	22 08.6	+39.1	76.2	25
22 00.5	36.2	74.2	22 16.6	37.1	74.6	22 32.3	38.0	75.0	22 47.7	38.8	75.4	26
22 36.7	35.9	73.3	22 53.7	36.8	73.7	23 10.3	37.6	74.1	23 26.5	38.5	74.6	27
23 12.6	35.7	72.5	23 30.5	36.5	72.9	23 47.9	37.4	73.3	24 05.0	38.2	73.7	28
23 48.3	35.3	71.6	24 07.0	36.2	72.0	24 25.3	37.1	72.4	24 43.2	37.9	72.9	29
24 23.6	+35.0	70.7	24 43.2	+35.9	71.1	25 02.4	+36.8	71.6	25 21.1	+37.7	72.0	30
24 58.6	34.7	69.8	25 19.1	35.6	70.3	25 39.2	36.4	70.7	25 58.8	37.3	71.2	31
25 33.3	34.4	68.9	25 54.7	35.3	69.4	26 15.6	36.2	69.8	26 36.1	37.0	70.3	32
26 07.7	34.1	68.0	26 30.0	34.9	68.5	26 51.8	35.8	68.9	27 13.1	36.7	69.4	33
26 41.8	33.6	67.1	27 04.9	34.6	67.5	27 27.6	35.4	68.0	27 49.8	36.3	68.5	34
27 15.4	+33.3	66.1	27 39.5	+34.2	66.6	28 03.0	+35.1	67.1	28 26.1	+36.0	67.6	35
27 48.7	32.9	65.2	28 13.7	33.8	65.7	28 38.1	34.7	66.2	29 02.1	35.6	66.7	36
28 21.6	32.6	64.3	28 47.5	33.4	64.8	29 12.8	34.3	65.3	29 37.7	35.2	65.8	37
28 54.2	32.1	63.3	29 20.9	33.0	63.8	29 47.1	33.9	64.3	30 12.9	34.8	64.8	38
29 26.3	31.7	62.3	29 53.9	32.6	62.8	30 21.0	33.5	63.4	30 47.7	34.4	63.9	39
29 58.0	+31.2	61.4	30 26.5	+32.1	61.9	30 54.5	+33.1	62.4	31 22.1	+33.9	62.9	40
30 29.2	30.8	60.4	30 58.6	31.7	60.9	31 27.6	32.6	61.4	31 56.0	33.5	62.0	41
31 00.0	30.3	59.4	31 30.3	31.3	59.9	32 00.2	32.1	60.4	32 29.5	33.1	61.0	42
31 30.3	29.9	58.4	32 01.6	30.7	58.9	32 32.3	31.7	59.4	33 02.6	32.6	60.0	43
32 00.2	29.3	57.3	32 32.3	30.3	57.9	33 04.0	31.2	58.4	33 35.2	32.0	59.0	44
32 29.5	+28.9	56.3	33 02.6	+29.7	56.9	33 35.2	+30.6	57.4	34 07.2	+31.6	58.0	45
32 58.4	28.3	55.3	33 32.3	29.3	55.8	34 05.8	30.1	56.4	34 38.8	31.0	56.9	46
33 26.7	27.8	54.2	34 01.6	28.6	54.8	34 35.9	29.6	55.3	35 09.8	30.5	55.9	47
33 54.5	27.2	53.2	34 30.2	28.2	53.7	35 05.5	29.0	54.3	35 40.3	30.0	54.8	48
34 21.7	26.7	52.1	34 58.4	27.5	52.6	35 34.5	28.5	53.2	36 10.3	29.3	53.8	49
34 48.4	+26.0	51.0	35 25.9	+27.0	51.5	36 03.0	+27.8	52.1	36 39.6	+28.8	52.7	50
35 14.4	25.5	49.9	35 52.9	26.3	50.4	36 30.8	27.3	51.0	37 08.4	28.1	51.6	51
35 39.9	24.8	48.8	36 19.2	25.7	49.3	36 58.1	26.6	49.9	37 36.5	27.5	50.5	52
36 04.7	24.2	47.7	36 44.9	25.1	48.2	37 24.7	26.0	48.8	38 04.0	26.9	49.4	53
36 28.9	23.6	46.5	37 10.0	24.4	47.1	37 50.7	25.3	47.6	38 30.9	26.2	48.2	54
36 52.5	+22.9	45.4	37 34.4	+23.8	45.9	38 16.0	+24.6	46.5	38 57.1	+25.5	47.1	55
37 15.4	22.2	44.2	37 58.2	23.0	44.8	38 40.6	23.9	45.3	39 22.6	24.7	45.9	56
37 37.6	21.5	43.0	38 21.2	22.4	43.6	39 04.5	23.2	44.1	39 47.3	24.1	44.7	57
37 59.1	20.8	41.9	38 43.6	21.6	42.4	39 27.7	22.4	42.9	40 11.4	23.3	43.5	58
38 19.9	20.0	40.7	39 05.2	20.9	41.2	39 50.1	21.8	41.7	40 34.7	22.6	42.3	59
38 39.9	+19.3	39.5	39 26.1	+20.1	40.0	40 11.9	+20.9	40.5	40 57.3	+21.7	41.1	60
38 59.2	18.6	38.2	39 46.2	19.3	38.8	40 32.8	20.1	39.3	41 19.0	21.0	39.8	61
39 17.8	17.7	37.0	40 05.5	18.5	37.5	40 52.9	19.4	38.0	41 40.0	20.1	38.6	62
39 35.5	17.0	35.8	40 24.0	17.8	36.3	41 12.3	18.5	36.8	42 00.1	19.3	37.3	63
39 52.5	16.2	34.5	40 41.8	16.9	35.0	41 30.8	17.6	35.5	42 19.4	18.5	36.1	64
40 08.7	+15.3	33.3	40 58.7	+16.0	33.8	41 48.4	+16.8	34.2	42 37.9	+17.5	34.8	65
40 24.0	14.5	32.0	41 14.7	15.2	32.5	42 05.2	16.0	33.0	42 55.4	16.7	33.5	66
40 38.5	13.6	30.7	41 29.9	14.4	31.2	42 21.2	15.0	31.7	43 12.1	15.7	32.1	67
40 52.1	12.8	29.5	41 44.3	13.4	29.9	42 36.2	14.1	30.3	43 27.8	14.9	30.8	68
41 04.9	12.0	28.2	41 57.7	12.6	28.6	42 50.3	13.2	29.0	43 42.7	13.9	29.5	69
41 16.9	+11.0	26.9	42 10.3	+11.6	27.3	43 03.5	+12.3	27.7	43 56.6	+12.9	28.1	70
41 27.9	10.1	25.5	42 21.9	10.8	25.9	43 15.8	11.3	26.3	44 09.5	11.9	26.8	71
41 38.0	9.3	24.2	42 32.7	9.8	24.6	43 27.1	10.4	25.0	44 21.4	11.0	25.4	72
41 47.3	8.3	22.9	42 42.5	8.8	23.3	43 37.5	9.4	23.6	44 32.4	10.0	24.0	73
41 55.6	7.4	21.6	42 51.3	7.9	21.9	43 46.9	8.4	22.3	44 42.4	8.9	22.6	74
42 03.0	+6.4	20.2	42 59.2	+6.9	20.6	43 55.3	+7.4	20.9	44 51.3	+7.9	21.2	75
42 09.4	5.5	18.9	43 06.1	6.0	19.2	44 02.7	6.5	19.5	44 59.2	6.9	19.8	76
42 14.9	4.6	17.6	43 12.1	5.0	17.8	44 09.2	5.4	18.1	45 06.1	5.9	18.4	77
42 19.5	3.6	16.2	43 17.1	4.0	16.5	44 14.6	4.4	16.7	45 12.0	4.8	17.0	78
42 23.1	2.7	14.9	43 21.1	3.0	15.1	44 19.0	3.4	15.3	45 16.8	3.8	15.6	79
42 25.8	+1.7	13.5	43 24.1	+2.1	13.7	44 22.4	+2.4	14.0	45 20.6	+2.7	14.2	80
42 27.5	+0.8	12.1	43 26.2	1.0	12.3	44 24.8	1.3	12.6	45 23.3	1.6	12.8	81
42 28.3	−0.2	10.8	43 27.2	+0.1	11.0	44 26.1	+0.3	11.2	45 24.9	+0.6	11.3	82
42 28.1	1.2	9.4	43 27.3	−1.0	9.6	44 26.4	−0.7	9.8	45 25.5	−0.4	9.9	83
42 26.9	2.1	8.1	43 26.3	1.9	8.2	44 25.7	1.7	8.4	45 25.1	1.6	8.5	84
42 24.8	−3.1	6.7	43 24.4	−2.9	6.8	44 24.0	−2.8	7.0	45 23.5	−2.6	7.1	85
42 21.7	4.0	5.4	43 21.5	3.9	5.5	44 21.2	3.8	5.6	45 20.9	3.6	5.7	86
42 17.7	4.9	4.0	43 17.6	4.9	4.1	44 17.4	4.8	4.2	45 17.3	4.7	4.2	87
42 12.8	6.0	2.7	43 12.7	5.9	2.7	44 12.6	5.8	2.8	45 12.6	5.8	2.8	88
42 06.8	6.8	1.3	43 06.8	6.8	1.4	44 06.8	6.8	1.4	45 06.8	6.8	1.4	89
42 00.0	−7.8	0.0	43 00.0	−7.8	0.0	44 00.0	−7.8	0.0	45 00.0	−7.8	0.0	90
42°			43°			44°			45°			

83°, 277° L.H.A. LATITUDE SAME NAME AS DECLINATION

Fig. 2902b. Page from Pub. No. 229, Volume III.

of tab Z because of the difference between the exact value of LHA and the tab value, is equal to –0.6° × 0.215 or –0.1°.

An interpolation for declination is made between 23° (Z76.4°) and 22° (Z77.2°) in the same manner as above: 77.2° – 76.4° = +0.8° (Z diff); the exact declination is 60' – 32.5' = 27.5' less than the tab declination of 23°; the correction is +0.8 × 0.458 (27.5 divided by 60) = +0.4°.

A similar interpolation is made for latitude between 41° (Z76.4°) and 42° (Z76.7); 76.4° = +0.3°; the exact latitude is 6.1' greater than the tab latitude of 41°; the correction is +0.3 × 0.102 (6.1 divided by 60) = 0.0'.

By applying the algebraic sum of the LHA, Dec., and L corrections, as determined above, to the tab Z, the exact azimuth angle at the moment of observation is found to be N76.7° E, which converts to a Zn of 076.7°. The gyro error is found by comparing this exact azimuth with that obtained by observation, 076.0°. Thus 076.7 minus 076.0 equals 0.7°; as the compass is "least" (lesser in value than the true value), the error is "east."

Answer: Gyro error is 0.7° E.

Note that although exact azimuth is calculated to the nearest tenth of a degree, if the gyro repeater used for taking the bearing is graduated only in whole degrees, and readings are not possible to a greater precision than a half degree, then gyro error in the above example should more properly be stated as 0.5° E.

In solving problems for exact azimuth using Pub. No. 229, the multiplication of the fractional amount by the amount of the "diff" to obtain the appropriate correction can be accomplished readily by establishing a proportion with dividers on a log scale of speed or distance, such as is found on some charts and on Maneuvering Board forms. In establishing the fractions involved, remember that the denominator of the fractional part of LHA, Dec., and L is always 60', for the tabulated entering arguments of LHA, Dec., and L are always 1° apart.

As noted above, the other set of commonly used inspection tables, Pub. No. 249, will yield azimuths only to whole degrees. This level of precision is adequate for checking the gross accuracy of magnetic compasses in yachts and other small vessels.

AZIMUTH BY AMPLITUDE

2903 When using an azimuth to check a compass, a body at low altitude is most desirable, for it is both easy to observe and gives the most accurate results. An amplitude observation is one made when the center of the observed body is on either the celestial or visible horizon, that is, it is in the act of rising or setting. If the visible horizon is used, a correction is applied to the observation in order to obtain the corresponding amplitude when the center of the body is on the celestial horizon—the condition when Ho equals zero. The Sun is the body most frequently observed in obtaining an amplitude. However, the Moon, a planet, or a bright star having a declination not exceeding 24° may also be used. (Higher declinations fall outside the domain of the *Bowditch* amplitude tables.) The measurement of amplitudes should be avoided in high latitudes. Diurnal circles at high latitudes are so nearly parallel to the horizon that small errors in recognizing the instant of rising or setting cause large errors in the amplitude.

Amplitude may be defined as the horizontal angular distance measured N or S from the prime verti-

TABLE 22
Amplitudes

Latitude	Declination													Latitude
	18°0	18°5	19°0	19°5	20°0	20°5	21°0	21°5	22°0	22°5	23°0	23°5	24°0	
°	°	°	°	°	°	°	°	°	°	°	°	°	°	°
0	18.0	18.5	19.0	19.5	20.0	20.5	21.0	21.5	22.0	22.5	23.0	23.5	24.0	0
10	18.3	18.8	19.3	19.8	20.3	20.8	21.3	21.8	22.4	22.9	23.4	23.9	24.4	10
15	18.7	19.2	19.7	20.2	20.7	21.3	21.8	22.3	22.8	23.3	23.9	24.4	24.9	15
20	19.2	19.7	20.3	20.8	21.3	21.9	22.4	23.0	23.5	24.0	24.6	25.1	25.6	20
25	19.9	20.5	21.1	21.6	22.2	22.7	23.3	23.9	24.4	25.0	25.5	26.1	26.7	25
30	20.9	21.5	22.1	22.7	23.3	23.9	24.4	25.0	25.6	26.2	26.8	27.4	28.0	30
32	21.4	22.0	22.6	23.2	23.8	24.4	25.0	25.6	26.2	26.8	27.4	28.0	28.7	32
34	21.9	22.5	23.1	23.7	24.4	25.0	25.6	26.2	26.9	27.5	28.1	28.7	29.4	34
36	22.5	23.1	23.7	24.4	25.0	25.7	26.3	26.9	27.6	28.2	28.9	29.5	30.2	36
38	23.1	23.7	24.4	25.1	25.7	26.4	27.1	27.7	28.4	29.1	29.7	30.4	31.1	38
40	23.8	24.5	25.2	25.8	26.5	27.2	27.9	28.6	29.3	30.0	30.7	31.4	32.1	40
41	24.2	24.9	25.6	26.3	26.9	27.6	28.3	29.1	29.8	30.5	31.2	31.9	32.6	41
42	24.6	25.3	26.0	26.7	27.4	28.1	28.8	29.5	30.3	31.0	31.7	32.5	33.2	42
43	25.0	25.7	26.4	27.2	27.9	28.6	29.3	30.1	30.8	31.6	32.3	33.0	33.8	43
44	25.4	26.2	26.9	27.6	28.4	29.1	29.9	30.6	31.4	32.1	32.9	33.7	34.4	44

Fig. 2903a. Table 22, Amplitudes, from Pub. No. 9, *Bowditch* (extract).

TABLE 23

Correction of Amplitude as Observed on the Visible Horizon

Latitude	Declination													Latitude
	0°	2°	4°	6°	8°	10°	12°	14°	16°	18°	20°	22°	24°	
°	°	°	°	°	°	°	°	°	°	°	°	°	°	°
0	0.0	0.0	0.0	0.0	0.0	0.0	0.0	0.0	0.0	0.0	0.0	0.0	0.0	0
10	0.1	0.1	0.1	0.1	0.1	0.1	0.1	0.1	0.1	0.1	0.1	0.1	0.1	10
15	0.2	0.2	0.2	0.2	0.2	0.2	0.2	0.2	0.2	0.2	0.2	0.2	0.2	15
20	0.3	0.3	0.3	0.3	0.3	0.3	0.3	0.3	0.3	0.3	0.3	0.3	0.3	20
25	0.3	0.3	0.3	0.3	0.3	0.4	0.3	0.3	0.3	0.3	0.3	0.3	0.3	25
30	0.4	0.4	0.4	0.4	0.5	0.4	0.4	0.4	0.4	0.4	0.4	0.5	0.5	30
32	0.4	0.4	0.4	0.4	0.5	0.4	0.4	0.4	0.4	0.4	0.5	0.5	0.5	32
34	0.5	0.5	0.5	0.5	0.5	0.5	0.5	0.5	0.5	0.5	0.5	0.5	0.5	34
36	0.5	0.5	0.5	0.5	0.5	0.5	0.5	0.5	0.6	0.5	0.6	0.6	0.6	36
38	0.6	0.6	0.6	0.6	0.6	0.6	0.6	0.6	0.6	0.6	0.6	0.6	0.6	38
40	0.6	0.6	0.6	0.6	0.6	0.6	0.6	0.6	0.6	0.6	0.7	0.7	0.7	40
42	0.6	0.6	0.6	0.6	0.7	0.7	0.7	0.7	0.7	0.7	0.7	0.7	0.7	42
44	0.7	0.7	0.7	0.6	0.6	0.7	0.7	0.7	0.8	0.8	0.8	0.8	0.9	44
46	0.7	0.7	0.7	0.7	0.7	0.8	0.8	0.8	0.8	0.8	0.8	0.9	0.9	46
48	0.8	0.8	0.8	0.8	0.8	0.8	0.8	0.8	0.9	0.9	1.0	1.0	1.0	48

Fig. 2903b. Table 23, Correction of Amplitude as Observed on the Visible Horizon from Pub. No. 9, *Bowditch* (extract).

cal to the body on the celestial horizon. It is given the *prefix* "E" (east) if the body is rising, and W (west) if it is setting; the *suffix* is "N" if the body rises or sets north of the prime vertical, as it does with a northerly declination, and "S" if it rises or sets south of the prime vertical, having a southerly declination.

If a body is observed when its center is on the celestial horizon, the amplitude may be taken directly from Table 22 in *Bowditch* (see fig. 2903a).

When observing amplitudes of the Sun or Moon with a height of eye typical of larger ships' bridges, two assumptions can be made that will yield results sufficiently accurate for practical purposes. The first is that when the *Sun's lower limb* is about two-thirds of a diameter above the *visible* horizon, its center is on the *celestial* horizon. The second is that when the *Moon's upper limb* is on the *visible* horizon, its center is on the *celestial* horizon. This apparent anomaly is due to the Sun's parallax being very small (0.1′) as compared to the refraction, which at this altitude amounts to about 34.5′; whereas the Moon's parallax is large (between 54.0′ and 61.5′, depending on the date), while the refraction remains is about 34.5′ (actually, slightly greater numerically, since ha is negative from a positive height of eye).

Planets or stars are on the celestial horizon when they are about one *Sun* diameter, or some 32.0′ above the visible horizon.

If a body is observed on the *visible* horizon, the *observed* value is corrected by a value taken from Table 23 in *Bowditch* (see fig. 2903b), according to the following rules: For the *Sun*, a *planet*, or a *star*, apply the correction to the observed amplitude in the direction away from the elevated pole, thus increasing the azimuth angle; for the *Moon*, apply

half the correction *toward* the elevated pole. Notice that *increasing* the azimuth angle will sometimes *increase* the amplitude and sometimes *decrease* it. The entering arguments for both tables are latitude and declination. Table 23 was computed for a height of eye of 41 feet (12.5 m), but may be used for other ordinary shipboard heights of eye without significant error.

Application of the rules just given corrects the visible-horizon amplitude reading to what would have been taken with the body on the celestial horizon. If desired, the correction from Table 23 can be applied in the reversed direction to the Table 22 value, for direct comparison with the uncorrected observed value. This is the procedure used if amplitude or azimuth is desired when the celestial body is on the visible horizon.

Example: The DR latitude of a ship is 41° 03.8′ N when the declination of the Sun is N22° 31.9′. The Sun, when centered on the visible horizon, bears 059.5° by gyro, giving a compass amplitude of E30.5° N (090° – 59.5°).

Required: The gyro error.

Solution: By interpolation in Tables 22 and 23 (figs. 2903a and 2903b).

True amplitude (altitude 0°)	E30.5° N (Table 22)
Correction	0.7° (Table 23),
	E31.2° N

Zn	058.8°
Compass	059.5°
Error	0.7° W (Compass best, error west.)

Answer: Gyro error is 0.7° W. (Roundable to 0.5° west)

A computer or electronic calculator can be used instead of the *Bowditch* tables. If the observation is made when the center of the body is on the celestial horizon using the procedures given above for the Sun and Moon (no Table 23 correction required), true amplitude (A) can be found from the equation:

$$A = \sin^{-1}\left(\frac{\sin d}{\cos L}\right)$$

If the body is observed when its center is on the visible horizon, the equation is:

$$A = \sin^{-1}\left(\frac{\sin d - \sin L \sin(-0.7)}{\cos L \cos(-0.7)}\right)$$

where –0.7° is the value for the altitude of the body used in the preparation of Table 23. When the declination is of contrary name, it too should be considered negative in this last equation. Since sin A = cos Z, this same equation may be used for calculating azimuth angle directly, without reference to the amplitude.

AZIMUTH FROM POLARIS OBSERVATION

2904   The true azimuth of Polaris is tabulated in the *Nautical Almanac* for northern latitudes up to 65°. Polaris, the "north star," is always within about 2° of true north at this and lower northern latitudes, and observations of it provide a convenient means of checking the compass, with little interpolation needed. An extract from the *Nautical Almanac* Polaris azimuth table, which appears in the almanac at the bottom of the Polaris latitude tables, is shown in figure 2904.

The entering arguments in the *Nautical Almanac* azimuth table for Polaris are: (1) LHA ♈ and (2) latitude (at intervals of 5°, 10°, or 20°). Interpolation by eye is made if necessary.

Example: The navigator of a ship at Lat. 41° 39.2′ N, Long. 17° 07.6′ W observes Polaris when the GHA ♈ is 210° 25.3′. The observed azimuth by gyro repeater (GB) is 359.0°.

Required: Gyro error by Polaris, using *Nautical Almanac* Polaris Table.

Solution: Using the exact DR longitude (note that an assumed position is *not* used), determine the LHA ♈ for the time of observation. Turn to the three pages of Polaris tables located just before the Sight Reduction Procedures that precede the tinted pages in the *Nautical Almanac*, and locate the column heading encompassing the computed value of LHA ♈. In this case, it occurs on the second page of the Polaris tables, an extract of which is shown in figure 2904. (In this figure the azimuth tables appear directly below the columnar headings, whereas the azimuth portion of the tables is actually at the extreme bottom of the table.) Using the column with a heading of LHA ♈ 190°–199°, follow down the column to the appropriate latitude. Using interpolation by eye for latitude, the value of 359.7° is found; this is the true azimuth of Polaris. The gyro error is determined by comparing this with the azimuth observed by gyro repeater.

DR Lat.	41° 39.2′ N
DR Long.	17° 07.6′ W
GHA ♈	210° 25.3′
DR Long.	17° 07.6′ W
LHA ♈	193° 17.7′ W
Zn	359.7° (from table)
GB	359.0°
GE	0.7° E

Answer: Gyro error 0.7° E. (Roundable to 0.5 east.)

In practice, it is difficult to observe Polaris accurately for azimuth unless the vessel is in a lower latitude, because of the difficulty of observing accurate azimuths at higher altitudes; this difficulty is increased if the vessel is rolling. However, Polaris serves as a useful check on the compass any time it

POLARIS (POLE STAR) TABLES
FOR DETERMINING LATITUDE FROM SEXTANT ALTITUDE AND FOR AZIMUTH

L.H.A. ARIES	120°–129°	130°–139°	140°–149°	150°–159°	160°–169°	170°–179°	180°–189°	190°–199°	200°–209°	210°–219°	220°–229°	230°–239°
Lat.						AZIMUTH						
0°	359·2	359·2	359·2	359·3	359·4	359·5	359·6	359·7	359·9	0·0	0·2	0·3
20	359·1	359·1	359·2	359·2	359·3	359·5	359·6	359·7	359·9	0·0	0·2	0·3
40	358·9	358·9	359·0	359·1	359·2	359·3	359·5	359·7	359·9	0·0	0·2	0·4
50	358·7	358·7	358·8	358·9	359·0	359·2	359·4	359·6	359·8	0·1	0·3	0·5
55	358·5	358·6	358·7	358·8	358·9	359·1	359·3	359·6	359·8	0·1	0·3	0·5
60	358·3	358·4	358·5	358·6	358·8	359·0	359·2	359·5	359·8	0·1	0·4	0·6
65	358·0	358·1	358·2	358·4	358·6	358·8	359·1	359·4	359·7	0·1	0·4	0·7

Fig. 2904. Polaris azimuth table from *Nautical Almanac* (extract).

can be observed, because an azimuth observation of approximately 000° indicates that the compass is reasonably free of error. Conning officers are well advised to glance at Polaris often as a measure of situational awareness.

CURVE OF MAGNETIC AZIMUTHS

2905   The deviation of a magnetic compass on various headings is determined by *swinging ship*. During the process of swinging ship at sea, it is desirable to be able to obtain the magnetic azimuth of the Sun at any moment, without the delay that would result if it were necessary to determine each azimuth by triple interpolation from the tables. For this reason, it is common practice to determine *in advance* the magnetic azimuths at intervals during the period of swing, and to plot these against time on cross-section paper, fairing a curve through the points. The curve can be constructed by means of azimuths from Pub. No. 229.

To construct the curve, the navigator first determines the true azimuth for the approximate mid-time of the period during which the vessel is to be swung. During the time devoted to swinging the ship, the latitude, and declination remain practically constant, and the only one of the three entering arguments to change appreciably is meridian angle. Since meridian angle changes at the nearly constant rate of 1° for each four minutes of time, the azimuth at a time four minutes before or after the mid-time of the swing can be obtained by entering Pub. No. 229 with the same values of Dec. and L as used before but with an LHA value 1° greater or less, and applying the same correction to the tabulated value as that used for the mid-time. In practice, the change in azimuth in four minutes (1° of LHA) is usually quite small, and good results are

obtained by determining the azimuth in steps of eight minutes (2° steps of LHA). Thus, having determined the correction to the tabulated azimuth for the mid-time of the swing, the navigator has only to enter Pub. No. 229 with the same values of declination and latitude, and a meridian angle two degrees greater or less, and apply the previously found correction to the tabulated Z to determine the true Z eight minutes earlier or later. A series of such computations provides values of true azimuth (from the azimuth angles) at intervals throughout the swing. By converting these values to magnetic azimuths, the navigator can plot them on cross-section paper and fair a curve through the points, from which the magnetic azimuth can be taken at any time during the period. The above method will provide acceptable accuracy if the total time period is not overly long or close to the time of LAN. For more accurate results, the determination of a separate correction for each solution is recommended.

Example: A ship is to be swung between 1630 and 1730 ZT to determine magnetic compass deviation. The 1700 DR is Lat. 41° 28.3′ N, Long. 16° 34.2′ W. The variation in the area is 14° 32′ W.

Required: A curve of magnetic azimuths for use during the swing.

Solution: Determine the correction to tabulated azimuth angle and the true azimuth for the mid-time of the swing. The correction to tabulated azimuth angle is +0.7° and the true azimuth is 277.6°. Record this information on the middle line of a form such as that shown in figure 2905a, and then record ZT at eight-minute intervals before and after the mid-time to provide for the full period of the swing. In this case the time range is 1628 to 1732. Next to each ZT, record LHA at that time. Since the Sun is setting for the period of the swing, LHA increases with time in this situation, from

ZT	LHA	Tab	Tab Z	Corr	Z	Zn	Var	Mag Zn
	°	°	°		°	°		°
1628	65.8	66	86.6	↑	N 87.3 W	272.7	↑	287.2
1636	67.8	68	85.4		86.1	273.9		288.4
1644	69.8	70	84.2		84.9	275.1		289.6
1652	71.8	72	82.9		83.6	276.4		290.9
1700	73.8	74	81.7	+ 0.7°	82.4	277.6	14.5° W	292.1
1708	75.8	76	80.5		81.2	278.8		293.3
1716	77.8	78	79.3		80.0	280.0		294.5
1724	79.8	80	78.2		78.9	281.1		295.6
1732	81.8	82	77.0	↓	77.7	282.3	↓	296.8

Fig. 2905a. Table of magnetic azimuths.

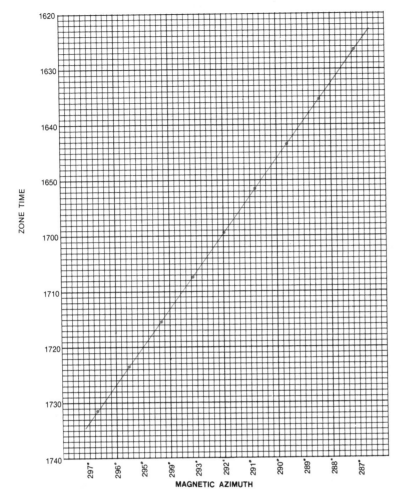

Fig. 2905b. A curve of magnetic azimuths.

65.8° to 81.8°. Take the nearest whole degree of value, which is the tab LHA value in each case. Then obtain the tabulated Z from Pub. No. 229 for each tab LHA and the constant values of Lat. and Dec. (which are 41° N and N23°, respectively, in this case), and apply the correction for the mid-time (+0.7° in this example) to each tabulated Z to obtain the exact Z for each ZT. Next, convert each Z to Zn and apply the variation for the locality to determine the magnetic azimuth of the Sun at each ZT. Finally, plot the magnetic azimuths against Zone Time on cross-section paper.

Answer: See figure 2905b.

AZIMUTHS BY DIAGRAM

2906 Various azimuth diagrams have been produced over the years, to permit a graphic determination of azimuth; the Weir diagram was long used by the Navy. Currently the most commonly used azimuth diagram is that designed by Armistead Rust, a portion of which is reproduced in figure 2906 at much-reduced scale.

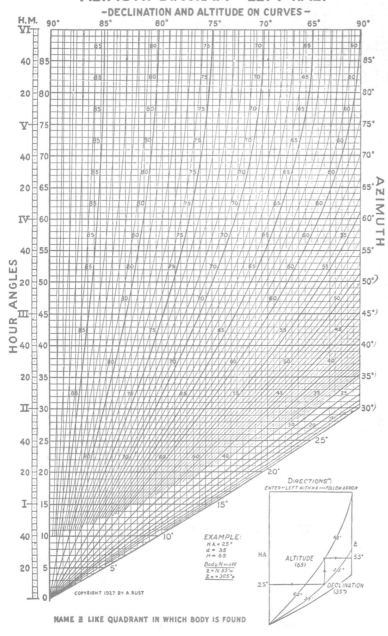

Fig. 2906. Armistead Rust azimuth diagram, left half; declination and altitude on the curves.

Chapter 30

The Practice of Celestial Navigation

The proper practice of celestial navigation on the high seas is of great importance even in this era of advanced electronic systems. Electronic equipment, on the vessel or at shore-based stations, may become unreliable or fail entirely; it must, by definition, rely upon a power source; some may also rely upon an external input of information to initialize a subsequent flow of positional data. Even with an electronic system functioning apparently normally, it is prudent to check it periodically from an independent source, and celestial navigation is ideal for that purpose.

In this chapter, navigation will be summarized for a passage on the high sea, out of sight of landmarks and aids to navigation, where celestial techniques are most useful.

THE DAY'S WORK IN CELESTIAL NAVIGATION

3001 Details of a navigating team's work during a day at sea will vary with the navigator and the ship, as well as with other factors, but a typical *minimum* "day's work" during good weather might include the following over a period of twenty-four hours:

1. Plot of dead reckoning throughout the period.
2. Computation of the time of the beginning of morning civil twilight; preparation of a list of stars and planets in favorable positions for observation at that time, with the approximate azimuth and altitude of each body.
3. Observation of selected celestial bodies and the solution of these observations for a fix during morning twilight.
4. Determining azimuths of the Sun to determine compass error.
5. Observation of the Sun for a morning Sun line (and of the Moon and Venus, if available).
6. Observation of the Sun at LAN (and of the Moon if it is available) to obtain a ZT 1200 position (running fix or fix), or observations as near LAN as possible in the event of overcast.
7. Observation of the Sun for an afternoon Sun line (and of Venus and the Moon, if available).
8. Computation of the time of the ending of evening civil twilight, and preparation of a list of stars and planets in favorable positions for observation at that time, with the approximate altitude and azimuth of each body.
9. Observations of the celestial bodies selected and solution of the observations for a fix during evening twilight. If only one or two bodies can be obtained, the afternoon Sun line can be advanced and combined with the evening stars for a running fix.

Notes on the Day's Work

3002 Venus can frequently be observed in the morning, when it is well west of and higher than the Sun. Similarly, it can be observed in the afternoon, if it is well east of, and therefore considerably higher than the Sun.

When the Sun is high at transit, it is changing rapidly in azimuth. This rapidity permits excellent short-interval running fixes to be obtained by combining late morning and early afternoon Sun lines with LAN.

During prolonged periods of overcast, the Sun does at times break through for a short time. Under such conditions, an observer should be ready to obtain an observation without delay. The Sun should be observed even if it is veiled by thin cirrus;

rarely does such blurring of the Sun's limb cause an error of as much as one minute of arc.

MORNING TWILIGHT OBSERVATIONS

3003 The LMTs of the beginning of morning nautical and civil twilights, and of sunrise, are tabulated in the *Nautical Almanac* or they may be obtained using STELLA (see article 2427). These should be used to assist you in planning for morning twilight observations. Do this by determining the time at which civil twilight begins (see articles 2415–2417), and obtaining LHA for that time. By setting your Star Finder (see chapter 21) for that LHA, you can determine the approximate altitudes and azimuths of celestial bodies that will be visible at that time. STELLA can also be used as an indicator of available and best-located stars (see article 2128).

Absent STELLA, a table like that shown in figure 3003 is useful in preparing to observe celestial bodies during twilight, as it is of great assistance in locating bodies in both azimuth and altitude. In addition, it permits the selection of bodies with a distribution of azimuths that will be particularly helpful.

In general, the bodies selected should be well distributed in azimuth. Good practice calls for observing a minimum of five bodies; six or seven are more desirable so that the minimum will still be available if on later reduction one or more yield poor results due to misidentification or poor altitude data. Of the several sights, four should be reduced, and the resulting LOPs should be advanced for the run between observations. If the resulting quadrangle is of reasonable size, its center is taken as the position of the fix; if not, the other observations are reduced to obtain data for a better position. However, when all the bodies observed lie within 180° of azimuth, the *bisector method*, described in article 3018, should be used in establishing the fix, which may be *external* rather than *internal*.

The table should include many more bodies than the navigator expects to observe, as some may be obscured by cloud cover. Bodies in the altitude range between 15° and 65° are, in general, the most satisfactory to observe. The most desirable bodies for observation should be marked by asterisks on the star table, to signify that they are the first choice for observation, as is shown in figure 3003. The marked stars should have good distribution in azimuth and should be at good altitudes for observation. Polaris, which should be observed, both for an LOP and a check on the compass, is not on the list, as its azimuth will be within about a degree of north, and its altitude will be about the same as the DR latitude, for observers in the northern hemisphere.

Rate of Change of Altitude

3004 When there is broken cloud cover, considerable time is often consumed in obtaining observations of a round of stars. As daylight increases, the stars become increasingly difficult to locate, particularly with the naked eye, and allowance must be made for the change in their altitudes. Bodies to the east or west will change altitude much more rapidly than those to the north or south; for example, in the list, Alpheratz, with an azimuth near 090° at twilight, will be increasing in altitude at a rate of about 11.3' per minute of time, while Dubhe will be decreasing in altitude at a rate of only about 3.1'. Alpheratz, therefore, could well have moved out of the field of view of the sextant telescope, if no allowance were made for its motion. The rate of change of altitude in a minute of time may be obtained by the equation:

$$\Delta H \text{ per minute} = 15 \times \cos \text{Lat.} \times \sin Z$$

where Z is the azimuth angle of the body (or its supplement). This equation was used in preparing the nomogram shown in figure 3004, which can also be helpful.

During morning twilight, the eastern horizon is the first to become sharply defined, and as a general rule, bodies in that direction are observed first. This procedure may be modified by the brightness of a particular body, which may make it visible in the

Star	Magnitude	H		Zn
		°	'	°
Capella	0.2	10	45	036.4
*Mirfak	1.9	27	25	046.2
Schedar	2.5	52	22	047.9
Hamal	2.2	25	50	081.1
*Alpheratz	2.2	50	55	093.0
Diphda	2.2	12	00	127.2
Formalhaut	1.3	14	22	155.2
*Enif	2.5	57	43	161.3
Nunki	2.1	16	18	210.6
*Altair	0.9	53	49	212.9
*Ralsahague	2.1	36	11	254.5
Vega	0.1	61	49	278.1
*Alphecca	2.3	22	21	287.0
Deneb	1.3	84	07	314.2
Alkaid	1.9	19	33	318.8
Alioth	1.7	18	21	330.4
*Kochab	2.2	38	21	339.5
Dubhe	2.0	15	51	345.9

Fig. 3003. Morning stars, DR Lat. 41° 02.6' N, Long. 14° 37.1' W. Civil twilight 0354.

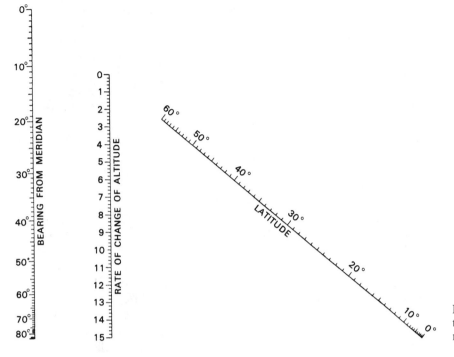

Fig. 3004. Nomogram for determining the change in altitude of a body per minute of time.

east for some time after all other bodies are hidden from view by the approaching daylight. Conversely, it may be desirable to observe a relatively dim star to the westward as soon as the horizon is clear under it, as it may otherwise be lost to view. In general, the later a star or planet is observed during morning twilight, the more accurate will be its LOP, as the observation will then be made with a more sharply defined horizon. The inexperienced navigator must, however, guard against waiting too long, as the body may then be too faint to see, or too high or too low for reliable observation. For this reason, it is often desirable to make an observation of a body as soon as conditions permit, and then a second one of the same body as late as possible.

No difficulty should be experienced in identifying the bodies observed during morning twilight, as the navigator usually has ample opportunity to study them before horizon visibility makes the taking of sights possible. If any doubt does exist, its azimuth should be noted and recorded for possible use in identifying the body later.

In checking the index error of the sextant, one should use a moderately bright star before making the observations, or the clearest part of the horizon after making them.

DAYLIGHT OBSERVATIONS

3005   The usual observations made at sea each day include two azimuths made for compass checks.

The Sun is the body most frequently used for this purpose; the most accurate observations can be made when it is rising or setting, as it is then moving comparatively slowly in azimuth, is easy to observe in a nearly horizontal direction, and minimal error is introduced by any tilt in the azimuth circle. Under conditions where it is very difficult to obtain accurate azimuths with an azimuth circle, it is wise to make an amplitude observation.

Venus and the Moon should be observed whenever possible in conjunction with the Sun to obtain a forenoon fix.

Noon Fix

3006   If only one morning Sun sight is to be made, it should be taken with two thoughts in mind. One is that the resulting LOP is to be advanced to noon to obtain a running fix, and the other is that the LAN observation will yield a latitude line, or an approximate latitude line in the event that the Sun cannot be observed exactly at LAN. It is desirable that the two LOPs intersect at an angle of 45° or more. On the other hand, the morning Sun observation should not be obtained so early that there can be much error due to uncertainty as to the ship's speed and course in advancing it to noon. The two factors depend on the latitude of the observer and the Sun's declination. Pub. No. 229 can be used to determine the rate of change of the Sun's azimuth, and therefore how long before noon the observation should be made.

LAN should be observed as a matter of routine aboard all vessels. Because the Sun is not changing altitude perceptibly when near LAN, and the horizon is usually sharply defined, it often offers the most accurate celestial line of position of the day.

In addition to the LAN sight, it may be desirable to obtain a Sun line at exactly ZT 1200, so that it will not have to be adjusted to determine the ZT 1200 position. Many Navy navigators prefer to make an observation at about ZT 1145, so that it and the morning Sun line can be advanced to 1200, and the running fix at that time determined and submitted with the noon position report at 1200. Accuracy of the official noon position usually being more important than its punctual reporting, it is usually determined after LAN (whether before or after 1200 ZT) if dependent on celestial means.

The conditions governing the afternoon Sun-line observations are similar to those that apply to the morning Sun line. A longitude line in the afternoon is useful for determining the time at which to make evening twilight observations, and since in mid-latitudes it generally will be taken rather late in the afternoon, it affords a good speed check for a vessel on an easterly or westerly course.

The above discussion is based upon the assumption that good weather prevails, and that you can observe the Sun at any time. If the sky is overcast, you should not ignore the possibility of obtaining an LOP at any time when the Sun might be visible. With skillful use of the sextant shade glasses, the Sun often can be observed even when behind thin clouds.

If the Moon can be observed during daylight, its LOP should be crossed with a Sun line obtained at the same time, unless the two bodies are at nearly the same or reciprocal azimuths. Venus can often be seen during daylight, when it is higher in altitude than the Sun, if the navigator knows its approximate altitude and azimuth. Mars and Jupiter can sometimes be seen in daylight as well, but less frequently than Venus.

Low-Altitude Sun Sights

3007 Observations of the Sun in the altitude range of 0° to 5° have acquired a reputation for unreliability that they do not wholly deserve. Refraction is somewhat uncertain at low altitudes; however, except under very unusual atmospheric conditions, such sights usually yield acceptable results.

Low-altitude Sun sights must be corrected in detail. The fixed sextant error, the IC, and the dip are applied to the sextant altitude (hs) before the refraction correction is taken from the Stars and

Planets column on page A3 of the *Nautical Almanac*. The resulting ha may actually be negative, in which case the refraction correction may be obtained by extrapolation. The semidiameter is taken from the daily pages of an almanac, and +0.1′ is used as the parallax correction. The "Additional Corrections" to the Altitude Correction Tables should also be used for all low-altitude observations.

For some observers, the upper limb of the Sun at low altitude is both easier to observe and somewhat more accurate in results than is the lower limb.

High-Altitude Sun Sights

3008 Observations of the Sun at altitudes greater than 80°+ are generally difficult to obtain accurately because of the difficulty of establishing the vertical. A compensatory advantage, however, is the near absence of observational error from refraction.

When the Sun's declination is near the vessel's latitude, morning Sun observations make possible the determination of longitude with considerable accuracy. This accurate longitude, in turn, makes possible a highly accurate prediction of the time of local apparent noon, and a high altitude LAN observation can frequently be made with great accuracy, through use of the averaging or curve-fairing technique.

Shortly before LAN, an azimuth circle is placed on a gyro repeater on the side of the bridge on which the Sun will transit and is aligned with the north-south points of the gyro repeater card. The sextant index arm is set to the expected altitude at LAN, and the observer then steps back from the pelorus and places himself so that the azimuth circle vanes are in line when seen through the horizon glass of the sextant. The Sun's altitude is obtained for LAN when its image is in contact with the horizon at a point directly above the vanes.

Such a high-altitude LAN observation can be of considerable value, for under such conditions all other Sun lines obtained during the day will lie generally in a north-south direction, and cross only at small angles when advanced or retired one to another in attempts at obtaining a running fix.

Care should be taken in plotting very high altitude observations, those with sextant altitudes of roughly 87°or more. The curvature of the circular line of position becomes so great that a straight line is not a satisfactory approximation. In such cases, it is preferable to plot the LOP as an entire circle using the geographical position (GP) of the body as the center and the zenith distance (90° − Ho) as the radius. This graphic solution eliminates the need for sight reduction tables. Two circular LOPs can be drawn for observations separated by a short period of time; the DR position will guide the navigator as to which of the two possible intersections should be used for the fix.

Sea-Air Temperature Differences

3009 A difference between the sea surface temperature and that of the air in contact with it tends to affect the value of the dip correction. This correction is calculated for "standard conditions," and these are distorted when the air in contact with the sea is warmed or cooled by the water. The resulting error is not serious when a number of bodies well distributed in azimuth are observed, as it may generally be assumed that the anomaly is the same for all azimuths and will apply equally to all the bodies observed.

When only the Sun is available for observation, as is usually the case in daytime, this anomaly can affect the accuracy of the LOP. This same difficulty applies for several bodies if they all are located in too limited a sector of azimuth; however, in such a case, the use of bisectors (see article 3018) is helpful.

For best results in measuring its surface temperature, sea water should be picked up in a dip bucket at some point well forward in the vessel; this is normally done on yachts and smaller ships, but larger vessels often use as a convenient (but risky) proxy, the intake water temperature as measured in the engine room. However obtained, the water temperature is compared with the dry-bulb air temperature measured at the level where the observations are made. The correction is subtractive when the air is colder than the water (i.e., the sextant altitude will be too great), and additive when the water is colder than the air. This correction should be used only when experienced judgment indicates that it will result in improved observations.

EVENING TWILIGHT OBSERVATIONS

3010 Evening twilight observations are similar to those of morning twilight, with the important difference that there is little opportunity to identify bodies by their appearance in advance of taking sights. Under these conditions, prior computation of the approximate altitude and azimuth is particularly helpful in locating the proper bodies; the azimuth of a body that has been observed, but not positively identified, should always be noted.

In the evening, the stars and planets in the east are usually observed first, subject to their brightness, as that area of the sky darkens first.

NIGHT OBSERVATIONS

3011 Star observations can be made successfully on clear nights, provided the observer's vision is dark-adapted and the sextant telescope and mirrors have reasonably good optical qualities. With dark-adapted vision, and using a sextant fitted with a prismatic telescope having a 30-mm objective lens and a magnification of 6x, one can obtain satisfactory star fixes. The 6x30 telescope is acceptable for night use, but the 7x50 is superior, for it has about twice the light-gathering power of the 6x30.

Light-amplification or night-vision telescopes developed as sniper scopes for the Army will, when mounted on a sextant, provide a view of the horizon on a dark night.

When observing bright stars or planets with a dim horizon, it is often advisable to use a pale Sun shade to reduce the body's brilliance. Many sextants have an *astigmatizing shade* that can be helpful under such conditions. This shade is a prism that elongates the image of a star into a thin horizontal line.

There is considerable risk of obtaining a false altitude when observing a brilliant Moon, or a star or planet near the Moon in azimuth, for the Moon's glisten may give a false horizon. This risk is reduced if such observations are made from a point as low as possible in the ship. It is also wise to check the horizon under the Moon through a 7x50 binocular to see if the illuminated water is actually at the horizon.

ACCURACY OF CELESTIAL LOPS AND FIXES

3012 The accuracy of an LOP obtained by celestial navigation is only rarely equal to that of the average LOP obtained in piloting. Ordinarily, therefore, a navigator should consider a single celestial LOP to be accurate only within 1 to 2 miles in either direction. Errors can be introduced in altitude measurement, timing, computation, or plotting. With experience and the cultivation of sound judgment in such matters, a navigator will be able to accurately evaluate sights and decide which ones are reliable and which are not. Obviously, the accuracy of celestial observations increases with practice. Expert observers, under good conditions, can expect a multiple star fix to yield a position that will be accurate within a quarter of a mile.

Analysis of Uncertainties

3013 The following discussion of the theory of errors may be helpful in evaluating positioning data.

A fix or running fix in celestial navigation is determined by two or more lines of position, each of which may be in error. If two lines are crossed at an angle of 90° and each has a possible error of 2 miles, the situation illustrated in figure 3013a results.

The navigator selects the point where LOP *A-B* intersects LOP *X-Y* as his fix, but if each line is in error by 2 miles, he will be at one of the corners shown by the broken lines, 2.8 miles from his fix. If one of the lines is in error by 2 miles and the other is without error, his actual position will be at the intersection of one of the solid lines and one of the broken lines, 2.0 miles from his fix.

If two lines are crossed at an angle of 30° and each has a possible error of 2 miles, the situation illustrated in figure 3013b results. The navigator selects the point where LOP *A-B* intersects LOP *C-D* as his fix, but if each line is in error by 2 miles, he will be at one of the corners of the parallelogram shown by the broken lines, either 2.1 or 7.7 miles from his fix. If one of the lines is in error by 2 miles and the other is without error, his actual position will be at the intersection of one of the solid lines and one of the broken lines, or 4.0 miles from his fix.

From the above discussion it can be seen that, when two lines of position are obtained, the navigator may place the most confidence in the resulting fix when the lines intersect at angles of 90°, or nearly 90°, all other factors being equal. A 90° intersection in a *running fix*, however, may not give as reliable a position as can be obtained from two lines of a *fix* that cut at a smaller angle, because of the possible inexactness in advancing the earlier LOP for a running fix.

Use of Multiple LOPs

3014   Whenever possible, a navigator should use at least three lines of position to obtain a fix. If these lines intersect at angles of 60° and each has a possible error of 2 miles, the situation illustrated in figure 3014 results. The navigator selects the point where the three lines intersect as his fix, but if each line is subject to error of up to 2 miles, his actual position may be anywhere within the shaded hexagon of the figure, at a maximum distance of 2.3 miles from the plotted fix.

The accuracy of a fix is not materially increased by plotting more than four lines of position *if* the lines can be relied on to be equally accurate *and* are approximately evenly distributed in azimuth. In practice, the usable stars are never perfectly located in azimuth, and five or more lines will usually yield a better idea of the most probable position than will three. When the bodies observed all lie within a 180° sector of azimuth, bisectors, which are discussed in article 3018, should be drawn and used.

In figure 3014, the three solid lines are shown intersecting at a point. In practice, they rarely do, and the navigator takes the center of the small figure usually formed as being his fix. The point selected is equidistant from all sides of the figure. It can be determined geometrically or by computation, but in normal practice the navigator estimates it by eye. The size of the figure obtained is not necessarily an indication of the accuracy of the fix.

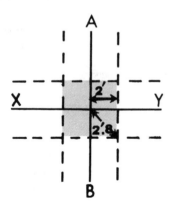

Fig. 3013a. Possible error in a fix from two lines of position differing in azimuth by 90° if each LOP has a possible error of two miles.

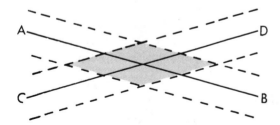

Fig. 3013b. Possible error in a fix from two lines of position differing in azimuth by 30° if each LOP has a possible error of two miles.

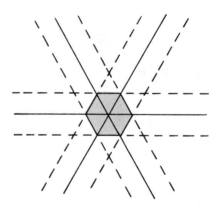

Fig. 3014. Possible error in a fix from three lines of position differing in azimuth by 120° if each LOP has a possible error of two miles.

Constant Error

3015 When a navigator can select three or more bodies to be observed for a fix (as when observing stars), he can guard against a constant error in altitude by observing bodies at equal intervals of azimuth. A constant error in altitude causes all lines of position to be in error by the same amount and in the same direction, relative to the bodies being observed. When bodies are observed at equal intervals of azimuth, a constant error will either increase or decrease the size of the figure formed when the lines are plotted, but will have no effect on the center of the figure. Thus, three stars differing in azimuth by 120° (*not* 60°), or four stars differing by 90° should be observed, or five stars differing by 72°, and so on. Theoretically, a four-star fix from bodies differing in azimuth by 90° (as N, S, E, and W) should produce only two lines of position, but in all probability a small rectangle will be the result; the center of the rectangle, determined by eye, can be taken as the fix.

Random Error

3016 The factor that has the greatest effect on a single observation is usually random error. The reliability of an individual line of position can be considerably improved by making several observations of the same body and averaging the times and altitudes before solving for an LOP; this tends to average out the random errors. Alternatively, if five or more observations of the same body are taken in quick succession, and its azimuth is noted by gyro, the accuracy of the individual observations may by determined by comparing the change of altitude between observations; the rate of change in altitude per second of time being equal to 0.25 arc minute × cos Latitude × the sine of the azimuth angle of the body. If the rate of change is steady for several sights, one of these should be selected for reduction. This equation may be solved very rapidly with an electronic calculator or computer.

An alternate method is to make three observations in quick succession and to solve and plot each one. If two LOPs are then in close agreement and a third differs considerably, it is usually safe to assume that the correct LOP lies midway between the two lines that are in agreement. This method is not as tedious as it may at first seem, particularly if solutions are made on a form with multiple columns, for usually the only differences in the solutions are in minutes and seconds of time and the resulting differences in GHA and al. Ordinarily, multiple sight reductions of the same body are lim-

ited to Sun lines, since the several bodies observed for a twilight fix serve as a check on each other.

In fixing or estimating the position of a ship, the navigator should not ignore the DR or EP, as these positions are based on other navigational information that may be more or less accurate than a given LOP. A DR or EP should be considered a *circle* with radius equal to the navigator's estimate of its accuracy, if knowledge of course and speed are considered to be equally good. If the navigator believes that one of these is known more accurately than the other, the DR or EP should be considered an *ellipse*, with its minor axis extending in the direction indicated by the more accurately known quantity and its major axis extending in the direction indicated by the less accurately known quantity.

From the above, it can be seen that the interpretation of celestial lines of position can be a complex subject, one that calls for sound judgment on the part of an experienced navigator.

Mistakes

3017 The above discussion of "errors" does *not* cover "mistakes." *Errors* of navigation are usually either constant or random inaccuracies of the input data used. In contrast, a *mistake* is a blunder, a completely invalid figure resulting from an incorrect procedure, misreading of an instrument, taking a wrong value from a table, and so on. Mistakes vary widely and have no systematic basis, thus no mathematical or graphic analysis can be made of them. The only "cure" is constant attention to detail and thorough checking of procedures. A large mistake is usually readily apparent; a small mistake may go unnoticed, and uncorrected, unless a result is checked by a second instrument or an independent set of calculations. Exact agreement should not be expected, but a wide difference between two solutions should alert a navigator to the possibility of a mistake in one or the other of them. Two people working in concert usually make fewer undiscovered mistakes than either working alone.

LOP BISECTORS

3018 When observations of a number of bodies with azimuths *all lying within a horizontal 180° sector of arc* are obtained, a constant error (in both magnitude and sign) may yield misleading results if the fix is assumed to lie *within* the polygon formed by the LOPs; such a fix is often called an "internal" fix. Such constant errors could result from an uncorrected personal error or from unusual terrestrial refraction, which causes the value of the dip, as obtained from the *Nautical Almanac*, to be considerably in error. The correct fix may lie *outside* the polygon, resulting in an "external" fix rather than the usual internal one. Where multiple LOPs well distributed in azimuth are obtained, this problem does not arise, because in this case the error may be assumed to affect all LOPs about equally.

Where three or more observations are made of bodies with azimuths within 180° of each other, it is useful to use *LOP bisectors* to determine the fix. Each angle formed by a pair of position lines is bisected, being drawn in the direction of the *mean of the azimuths* of the two bodies.

For example, assume that because of cloud cover, only three stars could be observed, the respective azimuths being as follows: star No. 1, 224°; No. 2, 000°, and No. 3, 256°. The resulting LOPs are plotted in figure 3018. Note that arrows have been added to each LOP to show the direction of the celestial body; this practice is desirable for any celestial plot. LOPs 1 and 2 will be bisected in the direction 292° – 112°:

$$\frac{(224° + 000°)}{2} = 112°$$

LOPs 1 and 3 will be bisected in the direction 240° – 060°:

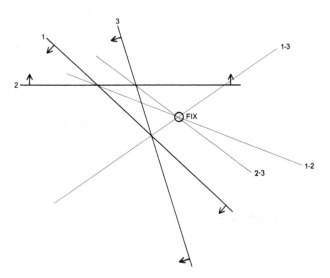

Fig. 3018. The use of bisectors showing the external fix (LOPs in black, bisectors in blue).

$$\frac{(224° + 256°)}{2} = 240°$$

and LOPs 2 and 3 will be bisected in the direction 308° – 128°. In figure 3018 these bisectors are drawn in as blue lines.

The most probable position for the fix lies at the center of any small triangle formed by the three bisectors, rather than in the triangle formed by the three LOPs. Note that this external fix shows an apparent greater "error" (distance from the three LOPs) than is shown by assuming the center of the original triangle, but this disparity is misleading.

It can be seen in figure 3018 that the external fix is a point equidistant from each LOP in the same direction, "away" in this example. Such a point can also be estimated by eye, taking care to always be on the same side of each LOP as indicated by the arrows. This technique is more practical at sea than calculating the bisector directions and cluttering up the plot with several additional lines; it should be sufficiently accurate for practical navigation.

The "external" fix should be found and used *only* when there is good reason to believe that there is an error in each observation of constant magnitude and direction. Barring this condition, the navigator is safer to use the internal fix.

SUMMARY

3019 In this chapter some of the particulars of celestial navigation at sea have been discussed. While typical, they are not all inclusive. On a naval ship, the procedures would likely be more formal than on a yacht, but the basic components of a "day's work at sea" remain valid and should be adhered to as closely as circumstances permit.

Celestial navigation has been largely subordinated by electronic forms of navigation, especially GPS, and celestial itself has been simplified by the use of computer programs (such as the Navy's STELLA program). But the *practice* of celestial navigation provides a reliable backup to such electronic marvels, and an understanding of the *principles* of celestial navigation will prove invaluable in making you a better navigator through a more acute awareness of your position in relation to the Earth and the heavens and an appreciation for what lies behind these cybernetic conveniences.

Chapter 31

The Sailings

Direction and distances for shorter passages are almost always determined graphically, using rhumb lines on a chart or plotting sheet. For longer passages, however, a great-circle path (see articles 203 and 208) can often provide a practical shorter distance with resulting economies of time and fuel; these can be determined graphically as explained in article 305. There are times, however, when a mathematical solution of course and distance is preferred over a chart plot, or when a suitable chart is not available. These calculations are collectively referred to as *sailings*. They were much used in the days before the availability of adequate charts and continue today in the internal computations of microprocessors in the receivers of several advanced electronic systems.

When circumstances dictate the determination of course and distance by calculation or by the use of tables, knowledge of the sailings is essential for a navigator, whether you work with paper and pencil or use a calculator or computer. Great-circle, mid-latitude, and Mercator methods are the only sailings discussed in this chapter as they will provide a suitable solution in almost all situations. Other methods and a more exhaustive treatment of the sailings may be found in *Bowditch*.

PRELIMINARY CONSIDERATIONS

3101 It must be kept constantly in mind that all solutions of sailing problems are made with true directions. Throughout this book, *all directions given are true unless specifically stated otherwise.*

Before proceeding with a discussion of the sailings, the following terms should be familiar to you from your readings in other parts of this book: lati-tude (L) (article 204); longitude (Lo or λ) (article 204); difference of latitude (l) (article 206); difference of longitude (DLo) (article 206); distance (D or Dist) (article 207); great circle (articles 202 and 208); rhumb line (article 209); course (C used for plotting; Cn used for mathematical calculations) (article 109).

The latitude and longitude of the point of departure will be designated L_1 and l_1, respectively, and the coordinates of the destination, L_2 and l_2. The latitude and longitude of the vertex of a great circle (point on circle farthest from the equator) is L_v and l_v.

Departure (symbol p) is the linear measure, in nautical miles, of an arc of a parallel included between two meridians. The term distinguishes it from difference of longitude (DLo), which is the *angular* measure of the same arc. Regardless of the latitude, the difference of longitude between two meridians remains the same, but the departure between those meridians varies with the parallel along which it is measured. Thus, in figure 3101 the difference of longitude between the meridians is constant, whereas the departure becomes less and less as the poles are approached. Departure must be marked east (E) or west (W) according to the direction in which it is measured.

Figure 3101 illustrates the relationship of DLo and departure at various latitudes. At the equator DLo and departure are identical and equal to the difference in longitude in minutes. The distance between the meridians becomes less with increased latitude and varies as the *cosine* of the latitude. At 60°, the departure is one half of that at the equator (cos 60° = 0.5), and the distance around the Earth at the sixtieth parallel is one half the distance around

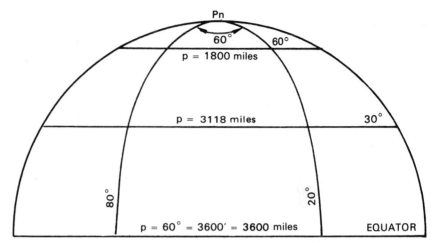

Fig. 3101. Departure and difference of longitude at various latitudes.

the Earth at the equator. The relationship of DLo and p is expressed by the equation

$$p = DLo \cos L$$

or

$$DLo = p \sec L$$

Course angle (symbol C) is the inclination of the course line to the meridian, measured from 0° at the reference direction (*north* or *south*) *clockwise* or *counterclockwise* through 90° or 180°. It is labeled with the reference direction (N or S) as a prefix, and the direction of measurement from the reference direction (E or W) as a suffix. The rules for determining the labels and the numerical limits vary with the method of solution. Course angle (C) is converted to *course* (Cn) by following the instructions of the labels. For example:

$$N40°E = 000° + 40° = 040°$$

$$S50°E = 180° - 50° = 130°$$

$$S30°W = 180° + 30° = 210°$$

$$N15°W = 360° - 15° = 345°$$

Middle latitude or *mid-latitude* (Lm) is the latitude of a point that is normally found by taking the *mean* value of L_1 and L_2 both being on the same side of the equator. (A more exact definition exists, but it is difficult mathematically and the difference is of no practical significance.)

Meridional parts (M). The length of a meridian on a Mercator chart, as expanded between the equator and any given latitude, expressed in units of 1' of arc of the equator, constitutes the number of meridional parts of that latitude. The meridional parts used in the construction of Mercator charts and in Mercator sailing are tabulated in a table in *Bowditch*. In Mercator sailing, M_1 represents the meridional parts of the latitude

of the point of departure, and M_2 the parts of the latitude of the destination.

Meridional difference (m). This represents absolute difference $M_1 \sim M_2$ ($M_1 - M_2$ or $M_2 - M_1$ as determined by which is the larger).

THE VARIOUS SAILINGS

3102   Although several of the more often used "sailings" will be considered in this chapter, the method that gives the most accurate results, and is unlimited in its applications, is *great-circle sailing;* the "cost" of these advantages is a longer mathematical solution of greater complexity. Several other methods involve shorter solutions and give less precise results, although still within acceptable limits for practical navigation; these procedures, which yield rhumb lines, include *mid-latitude* sailing and *Mercator sailing*.

Other sailings of less general usefulness covered in *Bowditch* are *plane* and *traverse sailing*, in which a small area of the Earth's waters is considered to be a flat, or plane, surface with the resultant simplifications in the mathematics of the solution; plane sailing is for a single "leg," and traverse sailing is for two or more legs of a complex set of rhumb lines; these are used by small-craft skippers in navigation contests and predicted log races. *Parallel sailing* is a method involving the interconversion of departure and difference of longitude for a vessel proceeding due east or west; it is now generally obsolete. *Composite sailing* is a modification of great-circle sailing to limit the maximum latitude that otherwise would be reached.

MID-LATITUDE SAILING

3103   The procedures for mid-latitude sailing are based on approximations that simplify the mathematics of the problem and yield somewhat less accurate answers than are obtainable by more rigorous and time-consuming reductions. For ordinary purposes, however, they yield more accurate results than are obtainable in the ordinary navigation of vessels.

Typical mid-latitude sailing problems are: (1) knowing latitude and longitude of points of departure and destination, solving for course and distance; or (2) knowing latitude and longitude of point of departure, and course and distance made good, solving for the latitude and longitude of the point thus reached.

Note carefully that when the course line crosses the equator, the problem *must* be broken down into two separate triangles of north and south latitude and solved separately.

The basic equations for mid-latitude sailing are:

$$p = DLo \text{ (in minutes of arc)} \times \cos Lm \quad (1)$$

$$C = \tan^{-1}(p \div l) \quad (2)$$

$$Dist = l \times \sec C \quad (3)$$

The solution of a problem using the first equation is shown in the following example:

Example: A vessel at Lat. 8° 48.9′ S, λ 89° 53.3′ W is to proceed to Lat. 17° 06.9′ S, λ 104° 51.6′ W.

Required: (1) course, (2) distance.

Solution:

L₁	8° 48.9′ S	λ₁	89° 53.3′ W
L₂	17° 06.9′ S	λ₂	104° 51.6′ W
l	8° 18.0′ S	DLo	14° 58.3′ W
l	498.0′ S	DLo	898.3′ W
½ *l*	4° 09.0′ S		
Lm	12° 57.9′ S		
DLo	898.3′ W	log	2.95342
Lm	12° 57.9′ S	log cos	9.98878 - 10
p	875.4 mi W		2.94220
l	498.0′ S	- log	2.69723
C	S60° 21.9′ W	log tan	0.269723
(2) Dist 1007.1		log	2.69723
(1) Cn 240.4°		log sec	0.30586
			3.00309

The solution above is shown through the use of logarithms. It can be easily and quickly solved with a small electronic calculator or computer having trigonometric function. The basic mid-latitude equations (1) and (2) above would be used as shown, but equation (3) might be changed to

$$Dist = l \div \cos C \quad (3a)$$

to better match normal keyboard functions; angles may have to be converted to degrees and decimal fractions.

When the latitude and longitude of the point of departure and the course and distance steamed are given, the latitude and longitude of the point of arrival may be found by using the following equations:

$$l = Dist \times \cos C \quad (4)$$

$$p = Dist \times \sin C \quad (5)$$

$$DLo = p \times \sec Lm \quad (6)$$

$$\text{or } DLo = p \div \cos Lm \quad (6a)$$

With *l* having been found, ½ *l* is applied to the latitude of the point of departure to find Lm. The latitude and longitude of the point of arrival are found by applying *l* and DLo, in accordance with their names, to the latitude and longitude respectively of the point of departure.

Example: A vessel at Lat. 37° 01.2′ N, Long. 75° 53.7′ W proceeds on a rhumb-line course 072.5° for a distance of 850 miles.

Required: (1) Latitude and (2) longitude of point reached at end of run.

Solution: (by calculator):

l =	Dist × cos C		
=	850 × cos 72.5° = 255.6′ N		
=	4° 15.6′ N		
p =	Dist × sin C		
=	850 × sin 72.5° = 810.7′ E		
l	4° 15.6′ N	½ l	2° 07.8′ N
L₁	37° 01.2′ N		37° 01.2′ N
(1) L₂	41° 16.8′ N		
Lₘ			
DLo =	p ÷ cos Lₘ		
=	810.7′ ÷ cos 39°	09.0′ = 1045.4′
=	17° 25.4′ E		
	75° 53.7 W		
(2)	58° 28.3′ W		

Answer: Lat. 41° 16.8′ N; Long. 58° 28.3′ W.

MERCATOR SAILING

3104 The determination of course and distance on a Mercator chart constitutes a graphic solution of a Mercator sailing problem. This sailing may also be solved by computation.

The equations for Mercator sailing are:

$$C = \tan^{-1} (DLo \div m) \quad (1)$$
$$Dist = l \times \sec C \quad (2)$$
$$\text{or } Dist = l \div \cos C \quad (2a)$$

where m is the absolute difference between M and M₂.

These equations can be conveniently arranged for solution as shown in the following example:

Example: Find the course and distance by Mercator sailing from Cape Flattery Light, Washington, to Diamond Head, Oahu, Hawaiian Islands.

Cape Flattery Light	L_1	48° 23.5′ N		
	λ_1	124° 44.1′ W		
Diamond Head	L_2	21° 15.1′ N		
	λ_2	157° 48.7′ N		
Solution:	L_1	49° 23.5′N	M_1	3309.2
	L_2	21° 15.1′ N	M_2	1296.9
	l	1528.4′ S	m	2012.3
	λ_2	157° 48.7′ W		
	λ	124° 44.1′W		
	DLo	33° 04.6′ W		
	DLo	1984.6′ W		

By calculator:

$$C = \tan^{-1} (DLo \div m)$$
$$= \tan^{-1} (1984.6 \div 2012.3) = \tan^{-1} 0.98623$$
$$= 44.6029° = S\ 44°\ 36.2′\ W$$
$$C_n = 180° + 44°\ 36.2′\ W$$
$$= 224.6°$$
$$Dist = l \div \cos C = 1628.4 \div \cos 44.6029°$$
$$= 2287.0\ mi$$

In Mercator sailing, the limits of C are 0° to 90°, labeled N or S to agree with *l* and E or W to agree with DLo. To convert C to Cn, follow the instructions of the labels. In the above example, start at S (180°). The course is 44° 36.2′ to the west, or 180° + 44° 36.2′ = 224° 36.2′; this is recorded as 224.6°. It is customary to solve for Distance and C to a precision of 0.1′ but to record Cn only to a precision of 0.1°.

These equations can also be used for determining the latitude and longitude of the destination if the course and distance are known, but if the course is near 090° or 280°, an appreciable error in DLo may result.

CHARACTERISTICS OF GREAT CIRCLES

3105 Every great circle of a sphere bisects every other great circle. Therefore every great circle, if extended around the Earth, will lie half in the Northern Hemisphere and half in the Southern Hemisphere, and the midpoint of either half will be farthest from the equator. This point, where a great circle reaches its highest latitude, is called its *vertex.*

A great circle between two places on the same side of the equator is everywhere nearer the pole than the rhumb line between those same points. If the two places are on different sides of the equator, the great circle between them changes its direction of curvature, relative to the rhumb line, at the equator. If the two places are equal distances on opposite sides of the equator, the great circle will bisect the rhumb line between them at the equator.

Since the direction of a great circle is constantly changing, it cannot be drawn on a Mercator chart as a straight line; the course of a vessel attempting to follow such a curved path would have to be continually changed. As this is obviously impractical, the course is changed at intervals, so that the vessel follows a series of rhumb lines. Since for a short distance a rhumb line and a great circle are nearly coincident, the result is a close approximation of the great circle. This is generally accomplished by determining points at regular intervals along the great circle by any one of several methods, plotting them on a Mercator chart or plotting sheet, and steaming the rhumb lines between such points.

It should be apparent that the equator and the meridians are special cases, and that many of the statements regarding great circles do not apply to them. If the course lies along one of these great circles, the solution may be made mentally, since the course is constant (these special great circles being also rhumb lines), and the distance is the number of minutes of DLo in the case of the equator and *l* in the case of a meridian.

COMPARISON OF RHUMB LINES AND GREAT CIRCLES

3106 The difference between the great-circle distance and the rhumb-line distance between two places may amount to several hundred miles. For example, the great-circle distance from Sydney, Australia, to Valparaiso, Chile, is 748 miles shorter than the rhumb-line distance. It is obvious, then, that while the rhumb line is most convenient, it should not be used for all long passages.

Under certain circumstances the great-circle track is *not* materially shorter than the rhumb line between two places. These may be summarized as follows:

1. For a short distance, the rhumb line and great circle are nearly coincident.
2. The rhumb line between places that are near the same meridian is very nearly a great circle.
3. The equator is both a rhumb line and great circle. Parallels near the equator are very nearly great circles. Therefore, at *low latitudes*, a rhumb line is very nearly as short as a great circle.

The decision to use or not to use great-circle sailing depends on whether the distance to be saved is sufficient to justify the trouble involved, as well as on other considerations, such as the latitude of the vertex, and anticipated weather, currents, shoal water, etc., along the different routes.

GREAT-CIRCLE SAILING BY CHART: GNOMONIC PROJECTION

3107   NIMA publishes a number of charts at various scales using the gnomonic projection and covering the usually navigated portions of the Earth. The point of tangency is chosen for each chart to give the least distortion for the area to be covered. Any great circle appears on this type of chart as a straight line and is therefore very useful in great-circle sailing.

However, since the meridians are not shown as parallel lines, no ordinary compass rose can be provided for use in measuring direction over the entire chart, and since angles are distorted, they cannot be measured by protractor or plotter. Latitude and longitude at a particular point on the chart must be determined by reference to the meridians and parallels in the immediate vicinity of the point. Hence, a gnomonic chart is *not* convenient for ordinary navigational purposes. Its practical use in navigation is limited to solving great-circle sailing problems.

To use a gnomonic chart, draw a straight line connecting the point of departure and the destination on the chart (see upper half of fig. 3107). The great circle is then inspected to see that it passes clear of all dangers to navigation. If this requirement is met,

the courses are then transferred to a Mercator chart by selecting a number of points along the great circle, determining their latitude and longitude, and plotting these points on the Mercator chart. These points are then connected by straight lines to represent the rhumb-line courses to be steered. In figure 3107, a line connecting a corresponding point on each chart is shown. Note that points have been chosen at intervals of 5° of longitude to facilitate the picking off of points and plotting them on the Mercator chart. These are convenient and at this interval the error in using rhumb lines to approximate the great circle is small.

It will be noted that the rhumb-line segments determined in the manner just described are chords of the great circle, as plotted on the Mercator chart. The course and distance for steaming each segment can be determined by measurement on the Mercator chart. Courses and distances of tangents to the great-circle can be determined directly from the great-circle charts, but the method is somewhat involved and can best be understood by studying the explanation given on some gnomonic charts. The chord method is easier and is commonly used in practice.

The great-circle distance of a voyage is sometimes determined from a gnomonic chart for comparison with the rhumb-line distance to determine which method will be used.

The great-circle track should be checked on a pilot chart for any potential hazards. If it extends

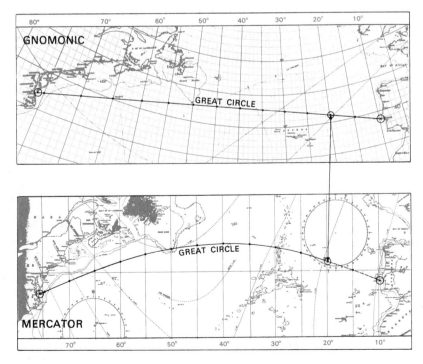

Fig. 3107. Transferring a great-circle track from a gnomonic chart to a Mercator chart.

into high latitudes where weather can be arduous and icebergs a potential hazard, consideration should be given to modifying it to *composite sailing* in which a great-circle track is followed from the point of departure to a *limiting latitude,* thence along that parallel to a point from which another great-circle track will take you to your destination.

GREAT-CIRCLE SAILING BY CHART: LAMBERT CONFORMAL PROJECTION

3108 Although most marine navigators use the combination of gnomonic and Mercator charts for great-circle sailing, the use of the Lambert conformal projection is possible. The advantage of a Lambert conformal chart for this purpose is that both great-circle distance and courses for segments of the great circle may be obtained by direct measurement, saving a transfer of points from the gnomonic to the Mercator projection. Any straight line on a Lambert conformal chart is a close approximation to a great circle, and angles are truly represented on this projection. Although direction can therefore be measured directly on the chart, protractors or plotters must be used, as the meridians are not shown as parallel lines. The course, a rhumb line of each segment of a great circle, is measured at its midpoint.

Since the distance scale of a Lambert conformal chart is so nearly constant that a fixed scale can be used without significant error, distance may be measured either by means of the latitude scale (as on a Mercator chart), by distance scales if printed on the chart, or by use of a special protractor plotter made to the scale of the chart. This latter method permits rapid measurement of both course and distance.

GREAT-CIRCLE SAILING BY CONVERSION ANGLE

3109 If the difference in the direction of the great circle and rhumb line is known, this difference, called the *conversion angle,* can be applied to either one to obtain the other. In any great-circle sailing, the angle the great circle makes with the meridian at the starting point is referred to as the initial great-circle direction. In many texts this is referred to as the initial great-circle course, even though the course by definition must be a rhumb line.

If the distance does not exceed 2,000 miles *and* both points (departure and destination) lie on the same side of the equator, the conversion angle can be found to practical accuracy by the equation:

$$\text{Conversion angle} = \tan^{-1}(\sin Lm \times \tan \tfrac{1}{2}DLo)$$

This equation can be solved graphically by a simple construction as shown in figure 3109. Draw any line *AB*. Draw a second line, *AC*, making an angle with *AB* equal to the mid-latitude between the point of departure and the destination. From the intersection, measure, to any convenient scale, a number of linear units equal to one-half the number of degrees of DLo, thus locating *D*. From *D* drop a perpendicular to the line *AB*. The number of linear units in this perpendicular, to the same scale used for $\tfrac{1}{2}$DLo, is the number of degrees of the conversion angle.

The sign of the conversion angle, in any given case, will be apparent if it is remembered that the great circle is nearer the pole than the rhumb line. For instance, in north latitude if the destination is east of the point of departure, the conversion angle is minus (−); if to the west, it is plus (+).

In practice, the conversion angle is usually modified to provide chord courses. This is done by dividing the conversion angle by the number of legs to be used and *subtracting* this from the conversion angle before it is applied to the Mercator (rhumb line) course. At the end of the first leg, a new solution must be made for the next leg. This is somewhat more trouble than using a great-circle chart, but eliminates the necessity of a lengthy computation if no great-circle chart is available.

Distance is determined by measuring the length of each rhumb-line leg and adding the figures so obtained.

GREAT-CIRCLE SAILING BY COMPUTATION: MATHEMATICAL PRINCIPLES

3110 In figure 3110, "1" is the point of departure (L_1 λ_1) and "2" the destination (L_2, λ_2). "P" is the pole

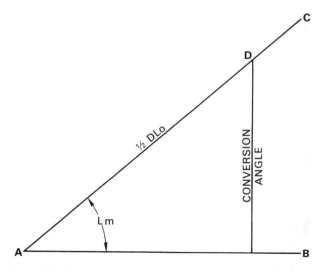

Fig. 3109. Conversion angle determined graphically.

nearest 1, and *EQ* is the equator. The great circles through *P1* and *P2* are meridians. Since latitude is the angular distance of a place north or south of the equator measured along a meridian (P1), the angular distance from the pole to 1 (the point of departure) is 90° − L_1, or the colatitude. Similarly, P2 is the colatitude of the destination. However, the term *colatitude*, as used with respect to the destination, is 90° ± L_2, since P is chosen as the pole nearest the point of departure. That is, if 2 and 1 are on the same side of the equator, or of the same *name*, the latitude of 2 may be considered (+) and the colatitude = 90° − L_2. However, if 2 is of opposite name, or on the opposite side of the equator from 1, it may be considered (−), in which case the colatitude is 90° − (−L_2), or 90° + L_2.

If 1 and 2 are connected by a great circle, a spherical triangle is formed. The length of the arc of the great circle between 1 and 2 is the great-circle distance between these two points. The initial direction from 1 to 2 is the angle P12. The angle 1P2 is the DLo, designated t when used in the special case as part of the navigational triangle illustrated in figure 3110. This is the same triangle used in the solution of celestial observations, 1 then being the assumed position of the observer and 2 the point on the Earth directly under the celestial body observed. Hence, any method of solution devised for one of these problems can be used for the other. However, some methods devised for solution of celestial observations are better adapted to the solution of great-circle sailing problems than others.

The solution of a great-circle sailing problem involves computation for the distance and initial direction, the position of the vertex, and the coordinates of points along the track. Computation is somewhat tedious if not done by calculator or computer, but the results are accurate and this method is sometimes the only means available.

GREAT-CIRCLE SAILING BY COMPUTATION: DISTANCE AND INITIAL DIRECTION

3111   Refer to figure 3111. A perpendicular dropped from the destination, 2, to the meridian P1 will divide the oblique navigational triangle P12 into two right spherical triangles. The length of the perpendicular is designated R, and the foot of the perpendicular y. The latitude of point y is designated K, which is always on the same side of the equator as 2. The arc 1y represents the *difference* of latitude of points 1 and y, regardless of which is greater or whether or not both are on the same side of the equator.

This is designated as K ~ L_1. (Here the symbol ~ is used to mean *algebraic* difference.) Thus, if both K and L_1 have the same name, the smaller is subtracted from the larger, but if they are of opposite name, their numerical values are added. The value K ~ LM_1 has no sign or name, being merely a difference. The side Py is co-K.

If the point of departure and the destination are known, L_1, L_2, and t ($l_2 − l_1$) are the values available for use in the solution. The problem is to find the distance (side D in fig. 3111) and the angle C at 1.

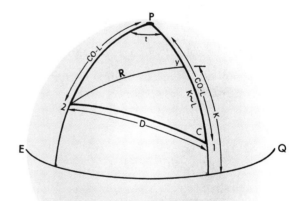

Fig. 3110. The navigational triangle as used in great-circle sailing.

Fig. 3111. The navigational triangle divided into two right spherical triangles by a perpendicular from the point of destination to the meridian of the point of departure.

These can be found by the following equations:

$$\csc R = \csc t \sec L_2 \qquad (1)$$

$$\csc K = \frac{\csc L_2}{\sec R} \qquad (2)$$

$$\sec d = \sec R \sec(K \sim L_1) \qquad (3)$$

$$\csc C = \frac{\csc R}{\csc d} \qquad (4)$$

Any table of log secants and log cosecants can be used for the solution of these equations, but they are most conveniently arranged in the Ageton tables (available on the Naval Institute's web site, www.navalinstitute.org/navtable). Column A contains log cosecants multiplied by 10^5, and column B contains log secants similarly multiplied by 10^5. These values are intended for use without interpolation in most instances, the accuracy being sufficient for practical navigation. In situations, however, where t is near 90°, the results may not be accurate enough; it is advisable to interpolate if it is between 85° and 95°. Numerous rules for naming the triangle parts north or south, and for entering the tables at the top or bottom of the page, must be carefully followed.

GREAT-CIRCLE SAILING BY COMPUTATION: VERIFICATION PROCEDURES

3112   Mathematical errors may occur when a great-circle problem is computed in the foregoing manner. It is advisable to check the answers for gross errors with a small calculator using the following equations. Distances over 1,800 miles and course angles between 0° and 80°, and between 110° and 180°, can be solved with considerable accuracy.

$$D = 60\cos^{-1}\,[(\sin L_1 \times \sin L_2) \qquad (1)$$
$$+ (\cos L_1 \times \cos L_2 \times \cos t)]$$

$$C = \sin^{-1}\,[(\cos L_2 \times \sin t) \div \sin D] \qquad (2)$$

$$L_v = \cos^{-1}\,(\cos L_1 \times \sin C) \qquad (3)$$

$$t_v = \sin^{-1}\,(\cos C \div \sin L_v) \qquad (4)$$

$$D_v = \sin^{-1}\,(\cos L_1 \times \sin t_v) \qquad (5)$$

$$L_x = \sin^{-1}\,(\sin L_v \times \cos D_{v-x}) \qquad (6)$$

$$t_{v-x} = \sin^{-1}\,(\sin D_{v-x} \div \cos L_x) \qquad (7)$$

Note: Equation (1) above assumed that L_1 and L_2 are both of the same name (both north or both south). If they are contrary (the course crossing the equator), insert L_2 as a negative quantity. In equation (2), d is in angular units, $D \div 60$. These are not the only formats used for such equations; other forms may be found in other sources.

GREAT-CIRCLE SAILING BY COMPUTATION: USING PUB. NO. 229

3113   The tables of Pub. No. 229 are readily adaptable to solutions of great-circle sailing problems, because the point of departure and the destination can always be found on the same page.

Pub. No. 229, and the use of its interpolation tables, is described at some length in earlier chapters and will be dealt with only briefly here to describe its use for finding the great-circle distance and initial direction. This is accomplished by entering the tables with latitude of departure as "Latitude," latitude of destination as "declination," and difference of longitude as "LHA." The tabular altitude and azimuth angle may then be extracted and converted to distance and course.

The tabular azimuth angle (or its supplement) becomes the initial great-circle course angle, prefixed N or S for the latitude of departure, and suffixed E or W depending upon the destination being east or west of point of departure.

If all entering arguments are integral degrees, the altitude and azimuth angle are obtained directly from the tables without interpolation. If the latitude of destination is not a whole degree, interpolation for the additional minutes of latitude is done as in correcting altitude for any declination increment; if either the latitude of departure or difference of longitude, or both, are nonintegral, the additional interpolation is done graphically.

Since the latitude of destination becomes the declination entry, and all declinations appear on every page, the great-circle solution can always be extracted from the volume that covers the latitude of the point of departure.

Great-circle solutions fall into one of the four following cases:

Case I: Latitudes of departure and destination of same name and great-circle distance less than 90°.

Case II: Latitudes of departure and destination of contrary name and great-circle distance less than 90°.

Case III: Latitudes of departure and destination of same name and great-circle distance greater than 90°.

Case IV: Latitudes of departure and destination of contrary name and great-circle distance greater than 90°.

The introductory pages of Pub. No. 229 provide instructions for the solution of each of these cases. The solution of a Case I problem is shown below:

Example: Find the initial great-circle course and distance from Land's End, England (50° 04.0′ N, 5° 45.0′ W), to St. John's, Newfoundland (47° 34.0′ N, 52° 40.0′ W). By computation using Pub. No. 229.

Solution: (1) Since the latitude of the point of departure, the latitude of the destination, and the difference of longitude (DLo) between the point of departure and destination are not integral degrees, the solution is done from an adjusted point of departure or assumed position of departure chosen as follows: the latitude of the assumed position (AP) is the integral degree of latitude nearest to the point of departure; the longitude of the AP, which should be within 30′ of the longitude of the point of departure, is at latitude 50° N, longitude 5° 40.0′ W; the DLo is thus 47°.

(2) Enter the tables with 50° as the latitude argument (Same Name), 47° as the LHA argument, and 47° as the declination argument.

(3) From page 96 of Pub. No. 229, Volume 4 (fig. 3113a), extract the tabular altitude, altitude difference, and azimuth angle; interpolate altitude and azimuth angle for the declination increment using figure 3113b. The Dec. inc. is the number of minutes that the actual latitude of the destination exceeds the integral degrees used as the declination argument.

LHA 47°, Lat. 50° (Same), Dec. 47°
Dec. inc. 34.0′, d + 22.9′
   Ht (Tab. Hc)   59° 13.8′
        Tens   11.3′
        Units   *1.7′*
Interpolated for Dec. inc.   59° 26.8′
          Z 77.1°
         C N77.1° W

Initial great-circle course from AP Cn 282.9°
Great-circle distance from AP (90° − 59° 26.8′ = 30° 33.2′) 1833.2 n mi.

(4) Using the Pub. No. 229 graphical method for interpolating altitude for latitude and LHA increments, the course line is drawn from the AP in the direction of the initial great-circle course from the AP (282.9°). As shown in figure 3113c, a line is drawn from the point of departure perpendicular to the initial great-circle course line or its extension.

(5) The required correction, in units of minutes of latitude, for the latitude and DLo increments is the length along the course line between the foot of the perpendicular and the AP. The correction applied to the distance from the AP is −4.3′; the great-circle distance is 1828.9 nautical miles.

(6) The azimuth interpolated for declination, LHA, and latitude increments is N76.3° W; the initial great-circle course from the point of departure is 283.7°.

The accuracy of Pub. No. 229 in calculating great-circle distance and initial direction is indicated by the fact that the actual distance, rigorously computed, is 1,828.98 miles and the initial direction is 283° 43.5′, giving an error of less than 0.1 miles and less than 0.1 degrees.

Points Along a Great-Circle Path by Pub. No. 229

3114 If the latitude of the point of departure and the initial great-circle course angle are integral degrees, points along the great-circle path are found by entering the tables with the latitude of departure as the latitude argument (Same Name), the initial great-circle course angle as the LHA argument, and 90° minus distance to a point on the great circle and the difference of longitude between that point and the point of departure are the tabular altitude and azimuth angle respondents, respectively.

Suppose you wanted to determine a number of points at 300-mile intervals along the great circle from latitude 50° N, longitude 5° W when the initial great-circle course angle is N76° W.

Entering the tables (fig. 3114) with latitude 50° (Same Name), LHA 76°, and with successive declinations of 85°, 80°, 75°, and so on, the latitudes and differences in longitude from 5° W are found as tabular altitudes and azimuth angles, respectively. Note: If the values are taken from across the C-S

Distance n. mi. (arc)	300 (5°)	600 (10°)	900 (15°)	1200 (20°)
Latitude	51.0° N	51.4° N	51.3° N	50.6° N
DLo	7.7°	15.7°	23.7°	31.5°
Longitude	12.7° W	20.7° W	28.7° W	36.5° W

line, the DLo is the supplement of the tabular azimuth angle; the tabular altitudes correspond to latitudes on the side of the equator opposite form the latitude of departure.

COMPARISON OF VARIOUS METHODS

3115 The "sailings" are mathematical procedures involving computations between latitude and longitude of the departure point, course and speed, and latitude and longitude of the destination. In general, two of these three pairs will be known, and the solution will be for the third pair.

The sailings are not often calculated in modern marine navigation, but when needed they provide a

47°, 313° L.H.A. — LATITUDE SAME NAME AS DECLINATION

N. Lat. { L.H.A. greater than 180°......Zn=Z
{ L.H.A. less than 180°..........Zn=360°−Z

Dec.	45° Hc	d	Z	46° Hc	d	Z	47° Hc	d	Z	48° Hc	d	Z	49° Hc	d	Z	50° Hc	d	Z	51° Hc	d	Z	52° Hc	d	Z	Dec.
0	28 49.9	+48.4	123.4	28 16.7	+48.9	123.9	27 43.1	+49.5	124.3	27 09.1	+50.0	124.7	26 34.7	+50.6	125.1	26 00.0	+51.1	125.5	25 25.0	+51.6	125.9	24 49.6	+52.1	126.3	0
1	29 38.3	48.1	122.7	29 05.6	48.7	123.2	28 32.6	49.3	123.7	27 59.1	49.9	124.1	27 25.3	50.4	124.5	26 51.1	50.9	125.0	26 16.6	51.4	125.4	25 41.7	51.9	125.8	1
2	30 26.4	47.9	122.0	29 54.3	48.5	122.5	29 21.9	49.1	123.0	28 49.0	49.7	123.5	28 15.7	50.2	123.9	27 42.0	50.8	124.4	27 08.0	51.3	124.8	26 33.6	51.7	125.2	2
3	31 14.3	47.6	121.3	30 42.8	48.3	121.8	30 11.0	48.9	122.3	29 38.7	49.4	122.8	29 05.9	50.1	123.3	28 32.8	50.6	123.8	27 59.3	51.1	124.2	27 25.3	51.7	124.6	3
4	32 01.9	47.5	120.6	31 31.1	48.1	121.1	30 59.9	48.7	121.7	30 28.1	49.3	122.2	29 56.0	49.9	122.7	29 23.4	50.4	123.1	28 50.4	51.0	123.6	28 17.0	51.5	124.1	4
5	32 49.4	+47.1	119.9	32 19.2	+47.8	120.4	31 48.6	+48.4	121.0	31 17.4	+49.1	121.5	30 45.9	+49.6	122.0	30 13.8	+50.3	122.5	29 41.4	+50.8	123.0	29 08.5	+51.3	123.5	5
6	33 36.5	46.9	119.2	33 07.0	47.6	119.7	32 37.0	48.3	120.3	32 06.5	48.9	120.8	31 35.5	49.5	121.4	31 04.1	50.0	121.9	30 32.2	50.6	122.4	29 59.8	51.3	122.9	6
7	34 23.4	46.8	118.4	33 54.6	47.3	119.0	33 25.3	47.9	119.6	32 55.4	48.6	120.1	32 25.0	49.3	120.7	31 54.1	49.9	121.2	31 22.8	50.4	121.8	30 51.0	51.0	122.3	7
8	35 10.0	46.3	117.6	34 41.9	47.0	118.2	34 13.2	47.7	118.8	33 44.0	48.4	119.4	33 14.3	49.0	120.0	32 44.0	49.6	120.6	32 13.2	50.3	121.1	31 42.0	50.8	121.7	8
9	35 56.3	46.1	116.9	35 28.9	46.8	117.5	35 01.0	47.4	118.1	34 32.4	48.1	118.7	34 03.3	48.8	119.3	33 33.6	49.5	119.9	33 03.5	50.0	120.5	32 32.8	50.6	121.0	9

Dec.	45° Hc	d	Z	46° Hc	d	Z	47° Hc	d	Z	48° Hc	d	Z	49° Hc	d	Z	50° Hc	d	Z	51° Hc	d	Z	52° Hc	d	Z	Dec.
45	57 14.7	+16.9	72.9	57 31.6	+18.7	74.4	57 47.0	+20.4	75.9	58 00.8	+22.2	77.5	58 13.0	+24.0	79.1	58 23.5	+25.9	80.7	58 32.4	+27.7	82.3	58 39.7	+29.4	83.9	45
46	57 31.6	15.4	71.1	57 50.3	17.1	72.6	58 07.4	19.0	74.2	58 23.0	20.8	75.7	58 37.0	22.7	77.3	58 49.4	24.4	78.9	59 00.1	26.2	80.6	59 09.1	28.0	82.2	46
47	57 47.0	13.8	69.3	58 07.4	15.6	70.8	58 26.4	17.4	72.4	58 43.8	19.2	73.9	58 59.6	21.1	75.5	59 13.8	22.9	77.1	59 26.3	24.7	78.8	59 37.1	26.6	80.5	47
48	58 00.8	12.2	67.5	58 23.0	14.0	69.0	58 43.8	15.8	70.5	59 03.0	17.7	72.1	59 20.7	19.5	73.7	59 36.7	21.4	75.3	59 51.0	23.3	77.0	60 03.7	25.1	78.7	48
49	58 13.0	10.5	65.6	58 37.0	12.4	67.1	58 59.6	14.2	68.7	59 20.7	16.0	70.2	59 40.2	17.9	71.8	59 58.1	19.7	73.5	60 14.3	21.7	75.1	60 28.8	23.6	76.9	49

Dec.	45° Hc	d	Z	46° Hc	d	Z	47° Hc	d	Z	48° Hc	d	Z	49° Hc	d	Z	50° Hc	d	Z	51° Hc	d	Z	52° Hc	d	Z	Dec.
80	51 16.2	−34.2	11.7	52 14.9	−33.9	12.0	53 13.6	−33.7	12.2	54 12.2	−33.4	12.5	55 10.7	−33.0	12.8	56 09.2	−32.7	13.2	57 07.6	−32.4	13.5	58 05.9	−32.0	13.9	80
81	50 42.0	35.1	10.4	51 41.0	34.8	10.6	52 39.9	34.5	10.9	53 38.8	34.3	11.1	54 37.7	34.1	11.4	55 36.5	33.8	11.7	56 35.2	33.5	12.0	57 33.9	33.2	12.3	81
82	50 06.9	35.8	9.1	51 06.2	35.7	9.3	52 05.4	35.5	9.5	53 04.5	35.3	9.8	54 03.6	35.0	10.0	55 02.7	34.8	10.2	56 01.7	34.5	10.5	57 00.7	34.3	10.8	82
83	49 31.1	36.7	7.9	50 30.5	36.5	8.1	51 29.9	36.3	8.2	52 29.2	36.1	8.4	53 28.6	36.0	8.6	54 27.9	35.8	8.8	55 27.2	35.6	9.0	56 26.4	35.3	9.3	83
84	48 54.4	37.4	6.7	49 54.0	37.3	6.8	50 53.6	37.2	7.0	51 53.1	37.0	7.1	52 52.6	36.8	7.4	53 52.1	36.6	7.4	54 51.6	36.5	7.6	55 51.1	36.3	7.8	84
85	48 17.0	−38.1	5.5	49 16.7	−38.0	5.6	50 16.4	−37.9	5.7	51 16.1	−37.7	5.8	52 15.8	−37.6	6.0	53 15.5	−37.6	6.1	54 15.1	−37.4	6.3	55 14.8	−37.3	6.4	85
86	47 38.9	38.8	4.3	48 38.7	38.7	4.4	49 38.5	38.6	4.5	50 38.4	38.6	4.6	51 38.2	38.5	4.7	52 37.9	38.3	4.8	53 37.7	38.2	4.9	54 37.5	38.2	5.1	86
87	47 00.1	39.4	3.2	48 00.0	39.4	3.3	49 00.0	39.3	3.3	49 59.8	39.2	3.4	50 59.7	39.2	3.5	51 59.6	39.1	3.6	52 59.5	39.1	3.6	53 59.3	38.9	3.7	87
88	46 20.7	40.1	2.1	47 20.6	40.0	2.2	48 20.6	40.0	2.2	49 20.6	40.0	2.2	50 20.5	39.9	2.3	51 20.5	39.9	2.3	52 20.4	39.8	2.4	53 20.4	39.8	2.5	88
89	45 40.6	40.6	1.0	46 40.6	40.6	1.1	47 40.6	40.6	1.1	48 40.6	40.6	1.1	49 40.6	40.6	1.1	50 40.6	40.6	1.2	51 40.6	40.6	1.2	52 40.6	40.6	1.2	89
90	45 00.0	−41.2	0.0	46 00.0	−41.2	0.0	47 00.0	−41.2	0.0	48 00.0	−41.2	0.0	49 00.0	−41.2	0.0	50 00.0	−41.2	0.0	51 00.0	−41.3	0.0	52 00.0	−41.3	0.0	90

| | 45° | 46° | 47° | 48° | 49° | 50° | 51° | 52° | |

47°, 313° L.H.A. — LATITUDE SAME NAME AS DECLINATION

Fig. 3113a. Pub. No. 229, "same name" page (extract).

Dec. Inc.	Altitude Difference (d)														Double Second Diff. and Corr.
	Tens					Decimals ↓		Units							
	10′	20′	30′	40′	50′		0′	1′	2′	3′	4′	5′	6′	7′ 8′ 9′	
34.0	5.6	11.3	17.0	22.6	28.3	.0	0.0 0.6	1.1 1.7	2.3 2.9	3.4 4.0	4.6 5.2				0.8 ₀₁
34.1	5.7	11.3	17.0	22.7	28.4	.1	0.1 0.6	1.2 1.8	2.4 2.9	3.5 4.1	4.7 5.2				2.5 0.1
34.2	5.7	11.4	17.1	22.8	28.5	.2	0.1 0.7	1.3 1.8	2.4 3.0	3.6 4.1	4.7 5.3				4.1 0.2
34.3	5.7	11.4	17.1	22.9	28.6	.3	0.2 0.7	1.3 1.9	2.5 3.0	3.6 4.2	4.8 5.3				5.8 0.3
34.4	5.7	11.5	17.2	22.9	28.7	.4	0.2 0.8	1.4 2.0	2.5 3.1	3.7 4.3	4.8 5.4				7.4 0.4
34.5	5.8	11.5	17.3	23.0	28.8	.5	0.3 0.9	1.4 2.0	2.6 3.2	3.7 4.3	4.9 5.5				9.1 0.5
34.6	5.8	11.5	17.3	23.1	28.8	.6	0.3 0.9	1.5 2.1	2.6 3.2	3.8 4.4	4.9 5.5				10.7 0.6
34.7	5.8	11.6	17.4	23.2	28.9	.7	0.4 1.0	1.6 2.1	2.7 3.3	3.9 4.4	5.0 5.6				12.3 0.7
34.8	5.8	11.6	17.4	23.2	29.0	.8	0.5 1.0	1.6 2.2	2.8 3.3	3.9 4.5	5.1 5.6				14.0 0.8
34.9	5.9	11.7	17.5	23.3	29.1	.9	0.5 1.1	1.7 2.2	2.8 3.4	4.0 4.5	5.1 5.7				15.6 0.9
35.0	5.8	11.6	17.5	23.3	29.1	.0	0.0 0.6	1.2 1.8	2.4 3.0	3.5 4.1	4.7 5.3				17.3 10
35.1	5.8	11.7	17.5	23.4	29.2	.1	0.1 0.7	1.2 1.8	2.4 3.0	3.6 4.2	4.8 5.4				18.9 11
35.2	5.8	11.7	17.6	23.4	29.3	.2	0.1 0.7	1.3 1.9	2.5 3.1	3.7 4.3	4.9 5.4				20.6 12
35.3	5.9	11.8	17.6	23.5	29.4	.3	0.2 0.8	1.4 2.0	2.5 3.1	3.7 4.3	4.9 5.5				22.2 13
35.4	5.9	11.8	17.7	23.6	29.5	.4	0.2 0.8	1.4 2.0	2.6 3.2	3.8 4.4	5.0 5.6				23.9 14
35.5	5.9	11.8	17.8	23.7	29.6	.5	0.3 0.9	1.5 2.1	2.7 3.3	3.8 4.4	5.0 5.6				25.5 15
35.6	5.9	11.9	17.8	23.7	29.7	.6	0.4 0.9	1.5 2.1	2.7 3.3	3.9 4.5	5.1 5.7				27.2 16
35.7	6.0	11.9	17.9	23.8	29.8	.7	0.4 1.0	1.6 2.2	2.8 3.4	4.0 4.6	5.1 5.7				28.8 17
35.8	6.0	12.0	17.9	23.9	29.9	.8	0.5 1.1	1.7 2.2	2.8 3.4	4.0 4.6	5.2 5.8				30.4 18
35.9	6.0	12.0	18.0	24.0	30.0	.9	0.5 1.1	1.7 2.3	2.9 3.5	4.1 4.7	5.3 5.9				32.1 19 / 33.7 20 / 35.4 21

| | 10′ | 20′ | 30′ | 40′ | 50′ | | 0′ | 1′ | 2′ | 3′ | 4′ | 5′ | 6′ | 7′ 8′ 9′ | |

Fig. 3113b. Pub. No. 229, interpolation table (extract).

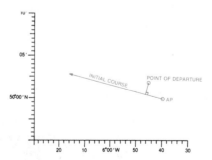

Fig. 3113c. Correction of great-circle distance when using Pub. No. 229.

useful solution of course and distance. Mid-latitude and Mercator sailing provide less accurate solutions than great-circle sailing, but at a considerable savings of effort and time except when a computer or calculator is used with great-circle sailing; the inaccuracies of these easier methods increase proportionately the longer the distance between the point of departure and the destination.

76°, 284° L.H.A.   LATITUDE SAME NAME AS DECLINATION   N. Lat { L.H.A. greater than 180° .... Zn=Z / L.H.A. less than 180° .... Zn=360°−Z

Dec.	45° Hc	d	Z	46° Hc	d	Z	47° Hc	d	Z	48° Hc	d	Z	49° Hc	d	Z	50° Hc	d	Z	51° Hc	d	Z	52° Hc	d	Z	Dec.
0	9 51.0	+43.0	100.0	9 40.5	+43.7	100.2	9 29.8	+44.5	100.3	9 19.0	+45.1	100.5	9 07.9	+45.9	100.7	8 56.8	+46.5	100.8	8 45.4	+47.2	101.0	8 33.9	+47.8	101.1	0
1	10 34.0	42.9	99.3	10 24.2	43.7	99.5	10 14.3	44.3	99.7	10 04.1	45.1	99.8	9 53.8	45.7	100.0	9 43.3	46.4	100.2	9 32.6	47.1	100.3	9 21.7	47.7	100.5	1
2	11 16.9	42.8	98.6	11 07.9	43.5	98.8	10 58.6	44.3	99.0	10 49.2	44.9	99.2	10 39.5	45.7	99.3	10 29.7	46.3	99.5	10 19.7	47.0	99.7	10 09.4	47.7	99.9	2
3	11 59.7	42.7	97.9	11 51.4	43.5	98.1	11 42.9	44.2	98.3	11 34.1	44.9	98.5	11 25.2	45.6	98.7	11 16.0	46.3	98.9	11 06.7	46.9	99.1	10 57.1	47.6	99.3	3
4	12 42.4	42.6	97.1	12 34.9	43.3	97.4	12 27.1	44.0	97.6	12 19.0	44.8	97.8	12 10.8	45.5	98.0	12 02.3	46.2	98.2	11 53.6	46.8	98.4	11 44.7	47.5	98.6	4
70	46 18.0	+6.5	28.7	47 10.5	+7.2	29.2	48 02.7	+8.0	29.8	48 54.7	+8.7	30.3	49 46.3	+9.5	30.9	50 37.6	+10.4	31.5	51 28.6	+11.2	32.2	52 19.2	+12.0	32.9	70
71	46 24.5	5.4	27.3	47 17.7	6.1	27.8	48 10.7	6.8	28.3	49 03.4	7.6	28.8	49 55.8	8.3	29.4	50 48.0	9.0	30.0	51 39.8	9.9	30.6	52 31.2	10.8	31.3	71
72	46 29.9	4.3	25.8	47 23.8	5.0	26.3	48 17.5	5.7	26.8	49 11.0	6.3	27.3	50 04.1	7.1	27.8	50 57.0	7.9	28.4	51 49.7	8.6	29.0	52 42.0	9.4	29.7	72
73	46 34.2	3.3	24.4	47 28.8	3.8	24.8	48 23.2	4.4	25.3	49 17.3	5.1	25.8	50 11.2	5.8	26.3	51 04.9	6.5	26.8	51 58.3	7.3	27.4	52 51.4	8.0	28.0	73
74	46 37.5	2.1	22.9	47 32.6	2.7	23.3	48 27.6	3.3	23.8	49 22.4	4.0	24.3	50 17.0	4.6	24.7	51 11.4	5.3	25.3	52 05.6	5.9	25.8	52 59.4	6.7	26.4	74
75	46 39.6	+1.0	21.5	47 35.3	+1.6	21.9	48 30.9	+2.2	22.3	49 26.4	+2.7	22.7	50 21.6	+3.3	23.2	51 16.7	+3.9	23.7	52 11.5	+4.6	24.2	53 06.1	+5.4	24.7	75
76	46 40.6	-0.1	20.0	47 36.9	+0.4	20.4	48 33.1	+0.9	20.8	49 29.1	1.5	21.2	50 24.9	2.1	21.6	51 20.6	2.7	22.1	52 16.1	3.3	22.6	53 11.5	3.9	23.1	76
77	46 40.5	1.3	18.5	47 37.3	-0.8	18.9	48 34.0	-0.3	19.3	49 30.6	+0.2	19.6	50 27.0	+0.8	20.0	51 23.3	1.3	20.5	52 19.4	1.9	20.9	53 15.4	2.5	21.4	77
78	46 39.2	2.3	17.1	47 36.5	1.9	17.4	48 33.7	1.4	17.7	49 30.8	-0.9	18.1	50 27.8	-0.5	18.5	51 24.6	+0.1	18.9	52 21.3	+0.6	19.3	53 17.9	+1.1	19.7	78
79	46 36.9	3.4	15.6	47 34.6	3.0	15.9	48 32.3	2.6	16.2	49 29.9	2.2	16.6	50 27.3	1.7	16.9	51 24.7	-1.3	17.3	52 21.9	-0.8	17.6	53 19.0	-0.3	18.1	79
80	46 33.5	-4.6	14.2	47 31.6	-4.2	14.4	48 29.7	-3.8	14.7	49 27.7	-3.4	15.0	50 25.6	-3.0	15.3	51 23.4	-2.6	15.7	52 21.1	-2.1	16.0	53 18.7	-1.7	16.4	80
81	46 28.9	5.6	12.7	47 27.4	5.3	13.0	48 25.9	5.0	13.2	49 24.3	4.7	13.5	50 22.6	4.3	13.8	51 20.8	3.9	14.1	52 19.0	3.5	14.4	53 17.0	3.1	14.7	81
82	46 23.3	6.7	11.3	47 22.1	6.4	11.5	48 20.9	6.1	11.7	49 19.6	5.8	12.0	50 18.3	5.5	12.2	51 16.9	5.2	12.5	52 15.5	4.9	12.7	53 13.9	4.4	13.0	82
83	46 16.6	7.8	9.9	47 15.7	7.6	10.0	48 14.8	7.3	10.2	49 13.8	7.1	10.4	50 12.8	6.8	10.6	51 11.7	6.5	10.9	52 10.6	6.2	11.1	53 09.5	5.9	11.4	83
84	46 08.8	8.9	8.4	47 08.1	8.6	8.6	48 07.5	8.5	8.7	49 06.7	8.2	8.9	50 06.0	8.0	9.1	51 05.2	7.7	9.3	52 04.4	7.5	9.5	53 03.6	7.3	9.7	84
85	45 59.9	-9.9	7.0	46 59.5	-9.8	7.1	47 59.0	-9.6	7.3	48 58.5	-9.4	7.4	49 58.0	-9.2	7.6	50 57.5	-9.1	7.7	51 56.9	-8.8	7.9	52 56.3	-8.6	8.1	85
86	45 50.0	11.0	5.6	46 49.7	10.8	5.7	47 49.4	10.7	5.8	48 49.1	10.6	5.9	49 48.8	10.4	6.0	50 48.4	10.2	6.1	51 48.1	10.1	6.3	52 47.7	9.9	6.4	86
87	45 39.0	12.0	4.2	46 38.9	11.9	4.2	47 38.7	11.8	4.3	48 38.5	11.7	4.4	49 38.4	11.7	4.5	50 38.2	11.5	4.6	51 38.0	11.4	4.7	52 37.8	11.3	4.8	87
88	45 27.0	13.0	2.8	46 27.0	13.0	2.8	47 26.9	12.9	2.9	48 26.8	12.8	2.9	49 26.7	12.8	3.0	50 26.7	12.8	3.0	51 26.6	12.7	3.1	52 26.5	12.6	3.2	88
89	45 14.0	14.0	1.4	46 14.0	14.0	1.4	47 14.0	14.0	1.4	48 14.0	14.0	1.5	49 13.9	13.9	1.5	50 13.9	13.9	1.5	51 13.9	13.9	1.5	52 13.9	13.9	1.6	89
90	45 00.0	-15.0	0.0	46 00.0	-15.0	0.0	47 00.0	-15.0	0.0	48 00.0	-15.1	0.0	49 00.0	-15.1	0.0	50 00.0	-15.1	0.0	51 00.0	-15.1	0.0	52 00.0	-15.1	0.0	90
	45°			46°			47°			48°			49°			50°			51°			52°			

76°, 284° L.H.A.   LATITUDE SAME NAME AS DECLINATION

Fig. 3114. Pub. No. 229, "same name" page (extract).

Chapter 32

Bathymetric Navigation

The navigation of a surface vessel or submarine can also be accomplished by bouncing sound waves off the bottom of the sea to measure distances. These distances can be combined to provide a topographical "picture" of the ocean floor. When this data is used to obtain positioning data, it is called *bathymetric navigation* and can be used even in considerable depths of water. Positions are determined relative to the known locations of specific geological features of the ocean bottom.

SIDE ECHOES AND MULTIPLE RETURNS

3201   In theory, echoes are returned from the bottom from all points within the sound cone produced by a transponder; in actual practice, the first echoes tend to mask the later ones, and there may be a significant delay between the return of the first and later echoes. It must be borne in mind that the first return will come from that portion of the bottom that is *nearest* the ship, and that *this portion is not necessarily directly below the ship*. This phenomenon is known as a *side echo*. Subsequent returns will be from other portions of the bottom. In comparatively shallow water, *multiple returns* may occur when the bottom is a good sound reflector. The echo returns from the bottom and is recorded as the depth, but it is also reflected for a second trip downward by the vessel's hull and the water's surface, and then back up for a second reading. Two or more returns can occur in shallower water, particularly when the bottom is of hard material such as sand or rock. Reducing the echo-sounder gain will usually remove indications of multiple return (some models feature automatic gain control).

Another phenomenon that may be puzzling is the appearance at times of a false bottom, suspended in the water. This is caused by echoes returned from the *deep scattering layer*, also sometimes called the *phantom bottom*. In daytime it is encountered at depths of about 200 fathoms (366 m); it usually moves nearer the surface at night. It is caused by echoes reflected from light-shunning plankton and other minute marine life. At times, this layer is sufficiently dense to mask echoes from the actual bottom. Schools of fish, or a single large fish, also can return an echo, making the echo sounder particularly useful to fishermen but a bit more complex for the navigator. Any sharp discontinuity within the water causes sound to be reflected, and an echo sounder often can detect the boundary of a layer of fresh water overlying heavier salt water such as occurs near a river mouth.

A rocky bottom reflects almost all the sound striking its surface, while soft mud tends to absorb it, thus returning a weaker signal. A layer of mud or silt overlying rock frequently yields two echoes.

A navigator must always bear in mind that depths shown on charts may be inaccurate due to changing bottom conditions, such as silting or the formation of sandbars since the survey was made. It is also possible that protruding underwater obstacles may have been missed during the survey that was used to make the chart in use.

Modern surveys are, however, much more accurate than those conducted before the introduction of electronic positioning systems, so that newer charts are more reliable. Electronic systems permit not only an accurate establishment of the survey vessel's position, but extend the range of operations farther from shore. More important, they are able to maintain an automatic plot of positions related to time. By use of a depth sounder in place of the old hand lead a continuous recording of depths can be made and correlated with the position of the survey vessel.

USE OF AN ECHO SOUNDER IN NAVIGATION

3202 Soundings shown on NOS and NIMA charts are obtained by echo sounders using an assumed standard velocity of sound in sea water and are uncorrected for any variation in salinity, density, or temperature. This lack of correction is actually desirable because conditions in any given area remain reasonably constant, and thus the subsequent echo-sounder readings of a ship (also uncorrected) may be directly compared with the charted values.

In bathymetric navigation, the wide-beam characteristics of a typical depth sounder may be advantageous. Often a sea-bottom feature would go undetected by a ship not directly over it were it not for the wide cone of sounding pulses. Because of the cone configuration, the deeper such a feature lies, the greater the horizontal distance at which the ship can locate it. From the bathymetric navigation standpoint, the fact that such an off-track feature is recorded at a depth greater than its true depth is a meaningful clue to its position. The minimum depth recorded by a ship over a seamount will be identical to that shown on the chart only if the ship passes directly over the top, assuming that the charted depth is in fact correct. If the top of the seamount still lies within range of the sound cone, it will be recorded even though the ship is to one side. However, the minimum depth will be recorded as deeper than shown on the navigation chart because of the greater oblique distance from the transducer. Within a reasonable range of values, the difference in minimum depths (between charted and recorded values) will yield distance horizontally from the vessel to the projected point of the seamount top at the surface.

The National Ocean Service produces a series of bathymetric maps of the waters adjacent to portions of the coast of the United States. These maps extend seaward somewhat beyond the 100-fathom curve and show the contour of the bottom in considerable detail. Such maps can be of great assistance in fixing position by means of the depth finder.

Even where a line of soundings cannot be matched to a chart or bathymetric map, echo-sounder data can still be of value to a navigator. While an isolated measurement of depth cannot, of itself, yield a position due to the repetition of the

same depth at many spots, it can provide "negative" information that questions the validity of a fix obtained by other means.

USE OF BOTTOM "LANDMARKS" FOR NAVIGATION

3203 Charted "landmarks" on the ocean floor can often assist the navigator in determining position. Such marks include submarine canyons, trenches, troughs, escarpments, ridges, seamounts, and guyot. These terms, in general, describe submarine topographical features that are similar to their counterparts found on dry land. An *escarpment* is a long, steep face of rock, or long submarine cliff. A *seamount* is an elevation of relatively small horizontal extent rising steeply toward, but not reaching, the surface. *Seaknolls* are smaller versions of seamounts. A *guyot* is a flat-topped seamount, rather similar to the mesas found in the southwestern United States. *Canyons* are found off most continental slopes; they are relatively steep-sided, and their axes descend steadily. A canyon, when crossed approximately at right angles, is easily recognized on a depth sounder or recorder. It will serve to establish a line of position, and the maximum depth noted, when crossing the axis, may further aid in determining position. Trenches, troughs, ridges, and escarpments are often found on the ocean bottom, which may otherwise be featureless; they also can be useful in yielding a line of position. Many guyots occur in the Pacific, and are useful in positioning. A line of position may also be obtained when crossing the line of demarcation between an ocean basin, which is usually very flat, and the surrounding bottom mass.

PRECISE POSITIONING USING SEAMOUNTS

3204 If the apex of an identified isolated seamount is located by means of an echo sounder, a precise position can be determined. If several seamounts are located in the same area, identification must be made by individual shape as well as minimum depth.

It should be noted that this method, while entirely feasible, requires that the vessel be diverted from her track toward her destination in order to make the second pass by the seamount at right angles to the first passing. Such a diversion is not normally welcomed by vessel owners, and for ships on normal ocean passages this method is rather more theoretical than practical. There are conceivable times, however, when a navigator might want to use these techniques.

Echo sounders on many vessels typically generate a 60° cone of sounding pulses. The geometry of such a cone can be considered in terms of isolated features on the sea bed such as a seamount; this is sometimes known as the *side-echo technique,* although the name is something of a misnomer in this case, because the technique actually concerns position to one side of a feature rather than the phenomenon previously discussed under this name. Basically, the technique involves two passes near a seamount at right angles to each other. The point of minimum depth on each track is noted and lines at right angles to the track are drawn at these points; the intersection of these lines locates the seamount with respect to the ship.

The first echo return comes from the portion of the sea bed that is nearest the vessel, and this portion is not necessarily directly below the vessel; in such a case, the depth finder is indicating a side echo. This can be very helpful, because if the seamount apex lies within the sound cone, the depth recorded by the depth finder cannot exceed the depth of the apex multiplied by 1.154. In addition, the horizontal distance from the apex to the ship cannot exceed half the depth indicated by the depth finder (see fig. 3204a). (These factors must be modified if the depth sounder being used has a cone of sound pulses other than 60°.)

Ordinarily, to obtain a fix by means of locating the summit of a seamount, a position some distance away is determined as accurately as possible, and then a course is set for the apex. The distance of the departure position from the apex will depend in part on the existing current, sea, and wind conditions.

Figure 3204b shows the contour lines surrounding the apex of a seamount. Assume that a ship obtained a good running fix due south of the apex, and is approaching on a course of 000°. It is possible that this course will take the ship directly over the summit, in which case the depth finder will give a minimum reading of 1,126 fathoms (the depth at the summit), and provide a fix. Unfortunately, this seldom occurs.

Figure 3204c shows the DR plot as the ship approaches the location of the summit. Soundings are recorded every minute on the plot and also the minimum sounding obtained (times are omitted in this figure for clarity). The shallowest sounding obtained is 1,169 fathoms, and a line is drawn at right angles to the heading line for this sounding. As the soundings begin to increase, it is obvious the ship has passed the area of the summit; a right turn is made to come to a course of 270°, crossing the original track at an angle of 90°. The turn to starboard is adjusted so that the new course will pass as close as possible to the summit's assumed position. Soundings are again noted every minute, as is the minimum sounding, which is 1,149 fathoms. A perpendicular to the ship's course line is again drawn for this minimum sounding.

The intersection of the two perpendicular lines passing through the minimum recorded depths locates the summit of the seamount relative to the ship; the direction and distance separating the intersection of these two lines from the charted position of the seamount is the offset of the ship's track from the seamount. Adjustment of the track may be accomplished by shifting all recorded times and soundings by the direction and distance of the offset.

It is possible that the selected track will pass so far to the side of the seamount that the top lies *outside* the cone of sounding pulses. This is apparent if the navigator observes a minimum depth greater than 1,300 fathoms; this means that the ship was

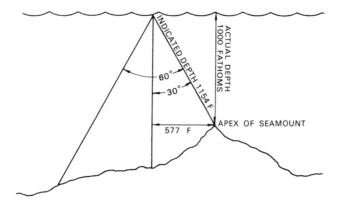

Fig. 3204a. The geometry of a 60° sound cone.

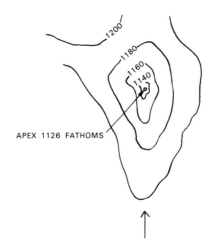

Fig. 3204b. Bottom contour chart.

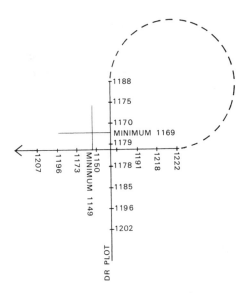

Fig. 3204c. Determining position by means of a seamount.

more than 1,300 yards to the side of the top. For a 60° sound cone, the geometry of the situation leads to this rule of thumb; the deepest value recorded with the seamount top still retained within the cone is twice the distance from ship to seamount top horizontally. Obviously, it is to the advantage of the navigator to choose, if a choice is possible, a seamount with deep minimum depth, other considerations being equal. In the event that the top does not lie within the sound cone, the ship's position can be determined only approximately. It would be desirable to make another pass on a reciprocal course, displaced to one side as indicated by the approximate position, in order to attempt a more precise location of the seamount top.

CONTOUR ADVANCEMENT

3205 If the area has been precisely surveyed and compiled, the contour advancement technique can yield accurate results. No bathymetric anomalies such as seamounts, canyons, or ridges are required; but some variation in depths is necessary. In this case, it is the slopes that are of interest. Ideally, a slope of more than one degree, but no more than four or five degrees, is required. The slope should not be constant, because this method will not work well if the linear distance between contours is equal.

In noting that some slope is required, the presence or absence of contour lines and the scale of the chart used must be kept in mind. Areas that appear devoid of contours and flat on one chart may, upon use of a larger-scale chart, show some relief or slope. After finding that a given area is not

absolutely level, the contour advancement method is facilitated by use of the largest-scale chart available.

Refer to figure 3205a as the base chart. The DR track is depths marked off with observed depths at increments equal to the charted contour interval. These data were obtained while the ship was steaming across the area, using the 700-fathom curve as referencing contour. This is a time-distance plot and is based on ship speed and recorded depths. For example, if the ship had been steaming in the same direction for several miles (over this slope), it would be recording incremental depths differing in time from the recording of the charted depths. The recorded contour crossings are merely extended to the area on this chart and plotted in relative position on the DR track.

By starting with the 700-fathom curve as the first one crossed, the curve is traced onto an overlay and becomes the *reference contour*. The assumed track is also indicated on the overlay. The next step is to shift the overlay in the direction of travel until the reference contour (700 fathoms) matches the plotted (not contoured) position of the next depth for which a contour exists (680 fathoms). Now the 680-fathom curve is traced. It should intersect the reference contour at one or more positions. The overlay is again advanced along the direction of travel to the point where the reference contour intersects the

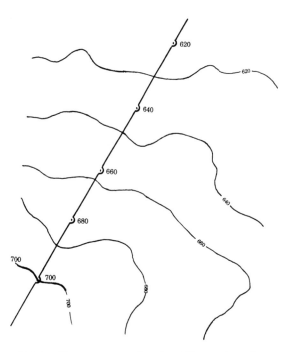

Fig. 3205a. Chart extract showing DR track and successive depth contours.

plotted 660-fathom curve. This contour (660 fathoms) is now traced. The three contours that are now traced should intersect at a point off the assumed track, or some triangle or error will be indicated that can be further defined by continuation of the "advancement." The intersection of lines becomes the position that is used to adjust the ship's track. This adjustment is a linear shift of the DR track and is a fix modified by the time (and therefore positional) lag after determination.

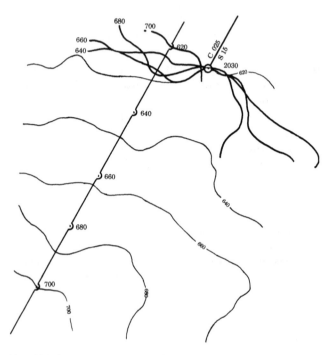

Fig. 3205b. Transparent overlay showing contours successively advanced and position of vessel at common intersection.

This description may appear complex in the absence of an overlay. Actually, the technique is a simple one and easy to master. Figure 3205b depicts the overlay after the contours have been traced by advancement of the 700-fathom curve.

USE OF SONAR IN NAVIGATION

3206   *Sonar* (*so*und *na*vigation *r*anging) operates in the same manner as the echo sounder, except that it radiates its signal in a generally horizontal, rather than a vertical, direction. Excellent ranges on underwater objects may be obtained with sonar, and as the sonar transducer can be rotated horizontally, acceptably precise and accurate bearings may also be obtained.

Sonar can be of great assistance in piloting in thick weather, particularly in rocky areas.

For example, when the harbor in Newport, Rhode Island, is closed due to very heavy fog, a vessel returning to port can come to anchor out of the channel south of Brenton Reef and west of Seal Ledge in a very precisely determined position. Subsequent changes in sonar ranges and bearings would give immediate notice, should she drag her anchor.

In arctic regions, sonar is sometimes helpful in locating ice when steaming at slow speed, since approximately nine-tenths of the ice mass is located below the water surface. Large bergs may sometimes be detected at a range of 6,000 yards or more, but the actual service range is usually less. Growlers may be picked up at ranges of between 1,000 and 2,000 yards, and even smaller pieces may be detected in time to avoid them.

Chapter 33

Doppler Navigation

Doppler navigation makes use of the consequent compression of energy waves caused by the motion of the user—the so-called Doppler effect. While this principle has been used with success with radio waves (such as in the now defunct Navy Satellite [NAVSAT] system) this chapter will focus on the use of Doppler using *acoustic* energy.

ACOUSTIC DOPPLER SYSTEMS

3301   Acoustic Doppler navigation systems are capable of giving a constant readout of speed and distance traveled to a high degree of accuracy. Some models can additionally show speed on the athwartship axis for a measurement of offsetting influences such as current. In shallower waters—depths less than 250 feet (76 m)—some equipments have been developed that can be switched to a "mooring mode," in which speeds on both the fore-and-aft and athwartship axes can be resolved down to 0.01 knot to facilitate docking, anchoring, or mooring to a buoy.

Because acoustic Doppler navigation relies primarily on echoes from the sea bottom, their effectiveness can be limited by water depth. Typically, units can operate from bottom echoes in waters no deeper than 1,500 feet (460 m). In greater depths, "water-mass tracking" must be employed, using reflections from particulate matter in the water with somewhat reduced accuracy of speed and distance measurements.

Doppler systems can also simultaneously be used for depth measurement, often with a preset alarm capability. All information derived from the system—speed, distance traveled, and depth—can be transmitted in digital form to a navigational computer. Here, distance can be combined with heading information from a gyrocompass for an accurate continuing computation of latitude and longitude.

ACOUSTIC DOPPLER PRINCIPLES

3302   The basic principles of acoustic Doppler navigation will be illustrated by an example that considers the sonic energy as being transmitted horizontally through the water, rather than diagonally downward, as is actually the case in marine Doppler navigation. Energy is transmitted as a *continuous wave*, rather than in pulses as for echo sounding. If the sonic projector shown in figure 3302a is considered as being stationary in the water, while transmitting sound on a frequency (f), the transmitted energy in the form of sound waves moves away from the transmitter at the speed of sound (C). This speed is affected by the temperature, salinity, and density of the sea water. The energy travels outward in the form of waves, alternating between pressure crests and troughs. The distance between consecutive crests or troughs is the wavelength (λ) of the acoustic wave.

The wavelength is equal to the speed of sound divided by the frequency, or $\lambda = C \div f$. Therefore, in a period of time each pressure crest travels a distance d equal to C multiplied by t. In the illustration it can be seen that the wavelength in feet (λ) and the distance (d) that a given pressure crest has traveled are one and the same.

Figure 3302b depicts a ship carrying the projector (transducer) moving through the water at a velocity V, and the resulting wave being monitored at a fixed point some distance away from the projector. When transmitted at the same fixed frequency (f, as

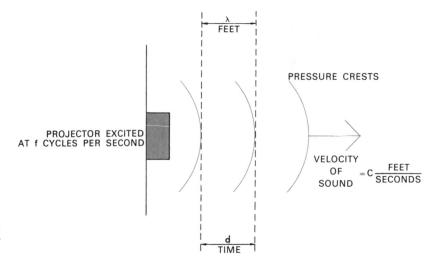

Fig. 3302a. Pattern of acoustic waves transmitted from a stationary underwater projector.

above), the waves, with their pressure crests, are generated at the same time intervals or frequency. The pressure crests are closer together in the water due to the forward velocity of the vessel. The new compressed wavelengths, λ', are equal to the prior undisturbed wavelengths minus the distance traveled at velocity v between pressure crests. Since wavelength and frequency vary inversely in any medium having a fixed speed of sound, the shortened wavelength caused by the ship's velocity results in an increase in frequency received at the monitoring point. Stated somewhat differently, the motion of the source of sound waves toward the stationary observer results in a greater number of pressure crests reaching the observer in a given unit of time; this means a higher frequency of the acoustic waves. The change in frequency is known as the *Doppler shift.*

If the stationary observer in figure 3302b is replaced by a reflector, as shown in figure 3302c,

the transmitted energy will be reflected back to the ship. By adding a hydrophone (another transducer) and receiver, the distance to the object can be determined by measuring the elapsed time between transmission of an outgoing signal and the return of the echo, a sonar distance. In addition, by measuring the Doppler shift of the echo, the ship's speed relative to the reflector can be determined.

Because no reflective surfaces are available in the horizontal plane, the ocean floor is normally used as a reflector in Doppler navigation. A highly directional sound projector and hydrophone are therefore depressed to a predetermined angle below the horizontal. If a second projector and hydrophone, facing in the opposite direction to the first pair and depressed to the same angle, are added, the Doppler shift, as received by the two hydrophones, can be compared. If the Doppler shift, as obtained from the after hydrophone, is subtracted from the shift as obtained from the forward hydrophone, the value of

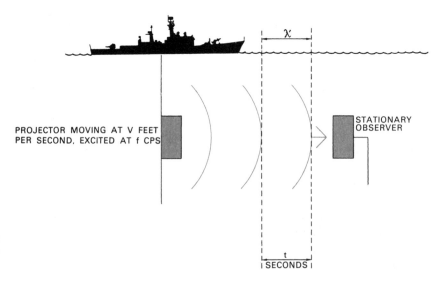

Fig. 3302b. Pattern of acoustic waves transmitted from a moving underwater projector.

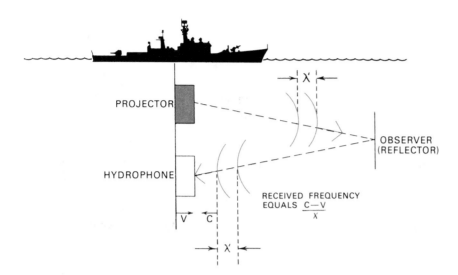

Fig. 3302c. Pattern of acoustic waves reflected back to a moving transmitter receiver.

the shift caused by horizontal motion will be doubled; in addition, any shift due to vertical motion will be canceled. It follows that if four projectors and hydrophones equally distrusted in bearing are employed, relative direction and distance measurements can be very precisely determined. In some systems, only three projector/receiver units are used, with one being common to the two pairs.

SONIC SIGNALS TRANSMITTED THROUGH SEA WATER

3303 So far, only the Doppler shift has been considered, with no thought to the medium—sea water—through which it is transmitted. The existing characteristics of the water can have a significant effect on Doppler navigation, the major considerations being their effect on the *speed of sound*, on *signal attenuation*, and on *volume reverberation*.

Speed of Sound

3304 As stated above, the wavelength, λ, of a transmitted sound wave is equal to the speed of sound, C, divided by the frequency, f, or λ = C ÷ f. The speed of sound in water is affected by such factors as *salinity, temperature,* and *pressure*. It can vary by approximately 3 percent on either side of the standard value, which is generally taken as 4,935 feet per second (1,504 m/s) in sea water near the surface with a temperature of 60° F (15.6° C) and salinity of 34 parts per thousand. Note that this speed differs from the more rounded figure of 4,800 feet per second (1,463 m/s) commonly used in echo-sounding and bathymetric navigation.

An uncompensated variation in the speed of sound as great as 3 percent could cause an unac-ceptable error in a Doppler navigation system. Errors resulting from such a cause can be largely eliminated by transmitting a signal on a constant wavelength rather than on a constant frequency, or by constantly adjusting the depression angle of the transmitter and hydrophone array to compensate for a change in the velocity of sound. Both methods offer certain advantages, but neither is generally considered to be the ultimate answer to the problem. The two methods have been combined with considerable success in some Doppler instrumentation.

Signal Attenuation

3305 The acoustic energy of the sonic signal is dissipated as it passes through the water; this phenomenon is called signal attenuation. As path losses increase with increased frequency due to signal attenuation, tradeoffs between power and frequency must always be taken into consideration in the design of Doppler navigational equipment.

Volume Reverberation

3306 In addition to the reflected echo from the bottom, acoustic energy is returned from debris, bubbles, minute marine life, and thermal boundaries in the water; this is collectively termed volume reverberation. The noise caused by volume reverberation can, at times, drown out the echo reflected from the bottom. This effect is used to advantage with some types of Doppler equipment.

APPLICATION OF DOPPLER PRINCIPLES

3307 The Doppler navigational system as originally developed by Raytheon Company employed four beams of sonic energy, spaced 90° apart. These beams were directed outward and downward at equal angles of inclination from the horizontal. The sonic energy was transmitted from *transducers,* which were activated by an electrical signal from the transmitter. In addition to radiating the outgoing sonic signal, the transducers served as hydrophones, in that they also picked up the echo of the signal, reflected from the ocean floor, and converted the acoustic echo back into electrical energy. This energy passed into the receiver, where it was amplified, and the input from the four transducers was compared to produce the Doppler frequency. It also determined the relative strength of the frequencies, thus providing a sense of motion and its direction.

If the transducer array remained fixed in bearing relative to the ship's centerline, motion would be stated relative to the vessel's coordinate system; that is, the readout would show motion relative to the vessel's heading and would indicate speed over the bottom and cross-track errors (lateral displacement relative to the track). To make it a true navigational system, a transducer array can be constantly oriented to true north by the vessel's gyrocompass, which also serves to stabilize the array and maintain it in a horizontal plane, regardless of any roll or pitch. Motion is thus indicated in the north-south and east-west directions, and readout is both the true direction and distance traveled from a point of departure expressed as distance north or south and east or west. Therefore, the system can present a constant indication of position, expressed as latitude and longitude, and can also continuously plot position on a chart, using an X–Y coordinate plotter. In lieu of continually orienting the transducer array to true north, N–S and E–W components of the vessel's motion can be derived by a microprocessor program.

Accuracy

3308 Geometric arrangement and sonic factors, both of which affect the performance of the system, have been considered briefly. Another limitation on the accuracy of the system is the heading accuracy supplied by the gyrocompass employed. A high-quality gyrocompass under good operational conditions will have a bearing uncertainty of 0.1°, or about six minutes of arc. The Doppler navigational system using a heading reference in which this error remained constant would indicate a position to within about 0.17 percent of the distance traveled from the departure point, and the ship might be to the right or left of the intended track by this

amount. As the errors introduced by the gyro usually tend to be random rather than constant, they average out to a considerable extent. Many runs have been made with this equipment to a considerably higher degree of accuracy than the 0.17 percent error would seem to indicate.

The chief limitation in Doppler navigation using the ocean floor as a reflector is not system accuracy, but rather that it is effective only in depths not exceeding approximately 1,500 feet (460 m) because of signal attenuation; accuracy degrades with increasing depth.

DOPPLER NAVIGATION IN DEEP WATERS

3309 Volume reverberation was mentioned earlier as sometimes having an adverse effect on the Doppler navigational system, as when an echo returning from the ocean floor is masked by an echo from thermal gradients, stratified layers of minute marine life, and so on. Because of this volume reverberation in sonar transmissions, with a continuous-wave transmitter, part of the acoustic energy is reflected back and produces a signal level. Consequently, Doppler navigation is possible *relative to the water mass,* regardless of water depth.

Volume reverberation is thus not an unmixed liability, because it makes possible the use of the Doppler navigational system as an accurate DR system at any sea depth. Motion is sensed relative to the water mass and is read as a change in position. This equipment can be extremely helpful at sea in indicating deviations from the intended heading, such as steering errors.

DOPPLER NAVIGATION EQUIPMENT

3310 Doppler navigational instrumentation has been developed with two very different types of vessels primarily in mind; these are the "super-jumbo" tankers, displacing 300,000 tons or more, and research submarines, often termed deep-submergence vehicles.

These two highly diverse types have one characteristic in common: they are little affected by wave action. At its operating depths, the deep submergence vehicle will be quite unaffected by surface conditions, while the giant tanker, due to its enormous mass, is much less affected than are most other surface ships.

Because of this greatly improved stability, the Doppler systems developed for these vessels do not need to employ a gyro-stabilized pendulous array of transducers. Instead, the four transducers are rigidly affixed to the ship's bottom plating, in such a position that under normal conditions of loading, their axes are directed downward at a specific angle; usually they are located well forward of the midships point. Stabilization is achieved internally by electronic means.

This system of mechanically fixed transducers will perform the same functions and permit the same degree of accuracy as discussed above, and the system should greatly benefit both types of vessels. The deep submergence vehicle, operating in a medium that prohibits almost all conventional navigation, is no longer at the mercy of unknown and variable currents. It can complete an accurate and detailed survey of the ocean floor, and return to the point from which the survey was started.

For the giant tanker, this equipment furnishes a continuous and accurate DR plot at sea; it is of even greater benefit when entering or operating in port. As these ships have large drafts, often well in excess of 80 feet (24 m), they cannot totally rely on the usual aids to navigation to keep in safe waters.

Instead, they often restrict their movements to a limited portion of the normally used channel. The Doppler system is of great assistance in such operations, and can often warn of potential trouble before such could be detected by plotting visual bearings.

USE OF DOPPLER EQUIPMENT IN DOCKING

3311   Pilots and conning officers have frequently experienced difficulty in sensing slight lateral motion in large vessels, such as tankers, during the final stages of coming alongside a berth. Since the momentum involved is tremendous, serious damage can result from even a comparatively slight contact with a pier or camel.

To detect such slight motion, a more sensitive "mooring mode" can be used, or a pair of auxiliary transducers may be installed. These are placed on the athwartship axis, and are intended solely to detect lateral or turning motion when coming alongside a pier and when the engines are stopped.

Chapter 34

Polar Navigation

Navigation in the higher latitudes can be very different from navigation in nonpolar regions. Methods described here are not new or unique; they are, rather, the application of standard procedures to different circumstances.

After first reviewing the geography of polar and subpolar regions, the following broad areas of interest will then be considered: chart projections, environmental factors (as they relate to navigation), determination of direction and distance, fixing position, and determination of the times of celestial phenomena.

THE POLAR REGIONS

3401   No single definition is completely satisfactory in defining the limits of the polar regions. Astronomically, the parallels of latitude at which the Sun becomes circumpolar, at about latitudes 67.5° north and south, are considered the lower limits. Meteorologically, the limits are irregular lines that, in the Arctic, coincide approximately with the tree line. For purposes of this book, the polar regions will be considered to extend from the geographical poles to latitude 70°. The subpolar regions are a transitional area extending for an additional 10° to latitude 60°.

ARCTIC GEOGRAPHY

3402   The Arctic Ocean is a body of water, a little smaller in area than the continental United States—an ocean that is almost completely surrounded by land. Some of this land is high and rugged and covered with permanent ice caps; part of it is low and marshy when thawed. Permanently frozen ground underneath, called *permafrost,* prevents adequate drainage, resulting in large numbers of lakes and ponds and extensive areas of *muskeg,* soft spongy ground with characteristic growths of certain mosses and tufts of grass or sedge. There are also large areas of *tundra,* low treeless plains with vegetation consisting of mosses, lichens, shrubs, willows, and so on, and usually having an underlying layer of permafrost.

The central part of the Arctic Ocean is a basin with an average depth of about 12,000 feet (3,660 m); the bottom is not level, and there are a number of seamounts and deeps. The greatest depth is probably something over 16,000 feet (4,880 m); at the pole the depth is 14,150 feet (4,310 m). Surrounding the polar basin is an extensive continental shelf, broken only in the area between Greenland and Spitsbergen. The many islands of the Canadian archipelago lie on this shelf. The Greenland Sea, east of Greenland; Baffin Bay, west of Greenland; and the Bering Sea, north of the Aleutians, all have their independent basins. Because of ice conditions, surface ships cannot penetrate to the pole, but some have successfully reached quite high latitudes.

ANTARCTIC GEOGRAPHY

3403   The *Antarctic,* or south polar region, is in marked contrast to the Arctic in physiographical features. It is a high mountainous land mass, about twice the area of the United States, surrounded by the Atlantic, Pacific, and Indian Oceans. An extensive polar plateau, covered with snow and ice, is about 10,000 feet (3,050 m) high. The average height of Antarctica is about 6,000 feet (1,830 m), which is higher than that of any other continent, and there are several mountain ranges with peaks rising to more than 13,000 feet (3,960 m). The height at the South Pole is about 9,500 feet (2,900 m).

The barrier presented by land and the tremendous ice shelves in the Ross Sea prevent ships from reaching very high latitudes. Much of the coast of Antarctica is high and rugged, with few good harbors or anchorages.

NAVIGATION CONCEPTS IN POLAR REGIONS

3404 Many of the concepts of measurements used in normal navigation take on new meanings, or lose their meaning entirely, in the polar regions. In temperate latitudes, one speaks of north, south, east, and west when he refers to directions; of latitude and longitude; of time; of sunrise and sunset; and of day and night. Each of these terms is normally associated with specific concepts and relationships. In the polar regions, however, each of these terms has a somewhat different significance, requiring a reappraisal of the concepts and relationships involved.

In lower latitudes, the length of a degree of latitude and a degree of longitude are roughly comparable, and meridians are thought of as parallel lines, as they appear on a Mercator chart, or as nearly parallel lines. Not so in polar regions, where meridians radiate outward from the pole like spokes of a great wheel, and longitude becomes a coordinate of direction. An aircraft circling the pole might cover 360° of longitude in a couple of minutes. Each of two observers might be north (or south) of the other if the north (or south) pole were between them. At the North Pole all directions are south, and at the south pole all directions are north. A visual bearing of a mountain peak can no longer be considered a rhumb line. It is a great circle, and because of the rapid convergence of meridians, must be plotted as such.

Clock time as used in temperate zones has little meaning in polar regions. As the meridians converge, so do the time zones. A mile from the pole the time zones are but a quarter of a mile apart. At the pole the Sun rises and sets once each year, the Moon once a month. The visible stars circle the sky endlessly, essentially at the same altitudes; only half the celestial sphere is visible from either pole. The planets rise and set once each sidereal period (from 225 days for Venus to 29$\frac{1}{2}$ years for Saturn). A day of twenty-four hours at a pole is not marked by the usual periods of daylight and darkness, and "morning" and "afternoon" have no significance. In fact, the day is not marked by any observable phenomenon except that the Sun may make one complete circle around the sky, maintaining essentially the same altitude and always bearing south (or north).

The system of coordinates, direction, and many of the concepts so common to our daily lives are manmade. They have been used because they have proved useful. If they are discarded near the poles, it is because their usefulness does not extend to these regions. They should differ as little as possible from familiar methods, while taking full cognizance of changed conditions.

CHARTS

3405 The familiar Mercator chart projection will normally not be used in higher latitudes, since distortion becomes so great as the poles are approached. Variations of the Mercator projection can be used, thus retaining some advantages without the unacceptable distortion imposed by having the tangency of the cylinder occur at the equator. This is done by rotating the tangent cylinder through 90°. If this is done, the cylinder is tangent to a meridian, which becomes the "fictitious equator." Parallels of latitude become oval curves, with the sinusoidal meridians extending outward from the pole. The meridians change their direction of curvature at the pole (see fig. 3405). Within the polar regions the parallels are very nearly circles, and the meridians diverge but slightly from straight lines. The distortion at L 70° is comparable to that at L 20° on an ordinary Mercator chart. Within this region a straight line can be considered a great circle with but small error. If a cylinder is tangent to a meridian, the projection is called *transverse Mercator*. If it is placed tangent to an oblique great circle, the projection is termed *oblique Mercator*.

Other projections used in polar regions are the stereographic, gnomonic or great circle, azimuthal equidistant, and a modified Lambert conformal. Near the pole, all of these and the transverse Mercator projection are so nearly alike as to be difficult to distinguish by eye. All are suitable. On the gnomonic chart, a great circle is a straight line, and on the others it is very nearly so. Distance and direction are measured in the accustomed manner.

The real problem of polar charts does not involve the projection to be used. The latitude and longitude lines can be drawn to the same accuracy as on any other chart, but the other information shown on polar charts is sometimes far from accurate. Many areas of Arctic regions have not been accurately surveyed. The result is that in less-traveled areas, topography is unreliable, and soundings are sparse.

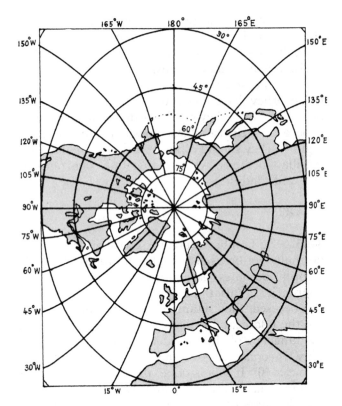

Fig. 3405. A polar transverse Mercator chart with the cylinder tangent at the 90°E – 90° W meridian.

Lines of magnetic variation are located principally by extrapolation. Even the positions of the magnetic poles are only generally stated, and vary irregularly. Consequently, you should take greater than usual precaution to ensure that a safe course is steered. Any advance-warning device is most useful, and should be fully used. Coastal topography or irregular soundings may indicate pinnacles some distance offshore, and if ice conditions permit use of sonar on a forward-looking echo sounder, this should be employed.

The most easily used projection for polar ship operations is often considered to be the Lambert conformal. Plotting is a bit of a problem but land masses are most accurately portrayed, and courses steamed in ice being somewhat erratic, the advantage of a rhumb line course being a straight line is not missed.

ENVIRONMENTAL FACTORS

3406 The effects of polar operations in navigation are many and varied. A thorough study of *Sailing Directions* or *Coast Pilots* is necessary, including those available from foreign nations. For example, the Danish *Pilot* for Greenland contains some excel-

lent land profiles. There are a number of specialized publications available that cover polar areas specifically. A volume of *Sailing Directions for Antarctica*, NIMA Pub. No. 27, contains a large amount of accurate (though incomplete) information. There is also additional information in the ATP and NWP series of naval publications for those to whom such documents are available. In some areas, it may be necessary to work from aerial photographs or preliminary charts, and soundings will be lacking. Occasionally, review of old *Cruise Reports*, or even accounts by early explorers, will yield useful data. Whatever the circumstance, the navigator must plan ahead and obtain all information from whatever source.

Normally cruises will be scheduled during the daylight periods, that is, during the summer months, for the area involved. During these periods the Sun may not set at all, and consequently there may be no navigational twilight. Ice conditions will be more favorable, as will the weather generally, except at the turn of the seasons. Fog at the ice edge is frequently encountered, and good radar navigation is imperative. Warm-water currents also cause fog, not just at the ice edge but near cooler land masses as well. There may be days with below-freezing temperatures, or raw and damp days, but for the most part the weather will be cool and pleasant. Gales are few. Cold-weather precautions should be taken.

Cruising in the off season, though unlikely, is possible and is apt to increase as ship capabilities and the needs of commerce expand. Severe low temperatures, ice conditions, and gales may be expected, especially at the turn of the season. During the dark period, there may be enough light to take good celestial sights, although there may be no actual navigational twilight. The midwinter period will probably be clear and very cold. Bare flesh will stick to metal instruments. Elaborate cold-weather precautions are essential for engineering equipment as well as for personnel.

A phenomenon known as *mirage effect* is caused by abnormal refractions and occurs whenever there is a severe difference between surface and air temperatures. In summer in the north, for example, when the water and ice are much colder than the air above, multiple images may be seen. Landfalls may appear many miles before they are expected.

Unknown tidal and ocean currents, or ice conditions, will make a good DR plot very hard to keep. Close observations for any clues of set and drift are most useful; for example, grounded icebergs may show tidal erosion as well as a wake. If observed for long periods, they serve as a rough tide gauge. Pit logs may not be practical, but timing objects passing alongside can give a rough indication of speed through the water or ice.

Upon entering a harbor or unfamiliar waters it is good practice to send a small boat ahead with a portable echo sounder plus a radio for communications.

One of the principal hazards to marine navigation in polar regions is ice. In some regions icebergs are very numerous. In the upper part of Baffin Bay, for instance, south of Cape York, literally hundreds of icebergs may be visible at one time. During periods of darkness or low visibility, radar is essential in avoiding collision. This method is usually quite adequate, icebergs often being picked up before they are capable of being seen. Smaller icebergs, about the size of a small house, are called *growlers;* these break off from larger icebergs and constitute a major hazard to marine navigation. When the sea is smooth, it is usually possible to detect growlers in time to avoid them without difficulty, but if the sea is rough, they may not be picked up because of excessive sea return near the ship. It must be remembered that about 90 percent of an iceberg is *below* the surface of the water, so that in a rough sea, a growler is practically awash. Sonar has proved useful in detecting the presence of such ice.

DIRECTION

3407 The determination of direction is perhaps the single most difficult problem. Magnetic compasses become largely useless due to the weakness of the horizontal component of the Earth's field and the large and somewhat unpredictable variations, and the presence of magnetic storms adds to the difficulty. Gyrocompasses with proper speed and latitude corrections entered are reasonably accurate, but the directive force weakens as the poles are approached.

Any gyroscopic device will degrade in accuracy in higher latitudes, and will lose all directive effect at the geographic poles. It is therefore necessary to take almost continuous error observations on a celestial body, normally the Sun. One practical method is to mount an *astrocompass* on or parallel to the ship's centerline (see fig. 3407). While a Sun compass can be useful, it needs a shadow from the Sun to give useful data. The astrocompass can be used with the Sun or *any other body.*

Bearings

3408 Bearings may be difficult to plot over long distances, because of the problems encountered

Fig. 3407. An astrocompass.

with chart projections, but considering your bearings as great circles and plotting them as such according to the chart projection employed will help solve the problem. Poor charting means that there are few references upon which to shoot a navigational bearing. In this case, redundancy of observations is important, and an attempt to fix the position of objects while the ship is stopped, to give good visual or radar navigational references for a stretch of steaming, is recommended.

Grid Direction

3409 Some navigators consider that in polar regions it is convenient to discard the conventional directions of true north, east, and so on, except for celestial navigation, and substitute grid north, grid east, and so on. That is, directions can be given in relation to the common direction of all fictitious grid meridians across the chart. The relationship between grid direction and true direction depends on the orientation of the grid. The system generally accepted places grid north in the direction of the North Pole from Greenwich; or 000° on the Greenwich meridian is 000° grid (at both poles). With this orientation, the interconversion of true and grid directions is very simple. If G is grid direction and T is true direction, in the Northern Hemisphere:

$$G = T + \lambda W$$
$$G = T - \lambda E$$

$$T = G - \lambda W$$
$$T = G + \lambda E$$

In the Southern Hemisphere, the signs are reversed. It is not necessary to remember all of these equations, for the last three follow naturally from the first. Grid direction of a straight line remains constant for its entire length, while true direction changes continually, with change in longitude.

In figure 3409, the grid direction from A to B is 057° and from B to A is 237°, the reciprocal. However, at A, longitude 20° W, the true direction is 037° ($T = G - \lambda W = 57° - 20° = 37°$). At B, longitude 100° E, the direction is not 237°, but 237° + 100° = 337°.

It is most convenient to give all directions in relation to grid north. Even azimuths of celestial bodies can be converted to grid directions if desired, both for plotting lines of position and for checking the directional gyro. If wind directions are given in terms of the grid, confusion is minimized, for a wind blowing in a constant grid direction is following widely different true directions over a relatively short distance near the pole. Since drift correction angle relative to a grid course is desired, wind direction should be given on the same basis. A grid direction is indicated by the letter *G* following the direction, as Zn 068°G, or by placing the letter *G* before the nature of the direction, as in GH 144°, for grid heading 144°.

The lines of equal magnetic variation all pass through the magnetic pole and the geographic pole; the former because it is the origin of such lines, and the latter because of the convergence of the meridians at that point. Convergency, however, can be combined with variation to obtain the difference between grid direction and magnetic direction at any point. This difference is called *grid variation* or *grivation*. Lines of equal grid variation can be shown on a polar chart in lieu of lines of ordinary variation. These lines pass through the magnetic pole, but not the geographic pole. Hence, even when a magnetic compass is used, grid navigation is easier than attempting to maintain true directions.

POSITION FIXING

3410   GPS works well in polar regions and inertial navigation can be helpful if available. Overreliance in navigation is never a good idea, so other methods—though difficult—must not be abandoned. A navigator must never miss an opportunity for an LOP; you cannot know when there will be another opportunity. You must obtain all information possible, even though some of it may be incomplete or of questionable accuracy.

Visual methods of position fixing are always good, particularly as charts of polar areas improve, but there will be an almost total absence of such aids to navigation as buoys, lights, and sound signals.

Radar can serve as a warning device as well as for navigation. A good rule is to use only radar ranges.

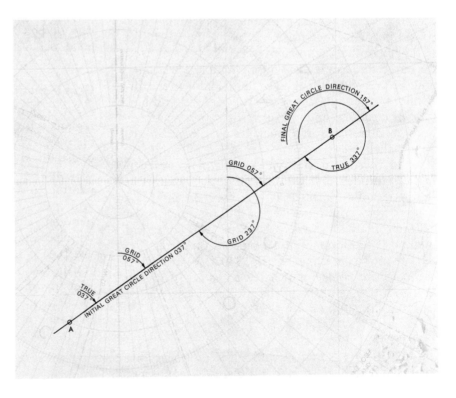

Fig. 3409. Grid navigation.

One helpful technique, particularly in first establishing a position in an unfamiliar area, is to prepare a tracing of the PPI picture, which can then be matched with the chart. Many targets should be plotted on the tracing; target separation should, when possible, be about 5°. This will simplify matching the tracing to the chart, as any error in bearings will not affect the accuracy of determining the ship's position; position is determined by matching the contours on the tracing to those on the chart, rather than by the use of bearings.

One useful wrinkle when using radar in ice is to reduce radiated power, if possible. This reduces range but increases ice definition (resolution), so that leads are more easily perceived. Some radars have an automatic setting for this, others would require reducing magnetron current. Shorter wavelength radars give better resolutions.

CELESTIAL NAVIGATION

3411 Celestial navigation is of prime importance in polar regions, although its practice may be very different from that to which a navigator is accustomed. You must acquire new techniques, familiarize yourself with new tools, accustom yourself to functioning in a very different environment, and never miss the opportunity to obtain a line of position.

Navigation during the summer months involves the problem of positioning the vessel by altitude measurements of the Sun only (except for occasional use of the Moon), as continuous daylight prevents any observations of stars or planets. A navigator, therefore, must depend almost solely on single lines of position of the Sun. In very high latitudes, a particular difficulty may arise twice a year. After the Sun has set below the horizon, (or shortly before it rises for the summer) there may be a period of days or even several weeks when the Sun is not available, yet the sky is too bright for observation of other bodies; at this time, it will not be possible to make any use of celestial navigation.

Tools and techniques that have been found useful will be discussed in the following paragraphs. But we must first consider *time*, on which all celestial navigation is based, as the nature of time itself is somewhat affected in the polar regions.

Time

3412 In previous chapters, the importance of time was stressed, since each four seconds of error of the navigational watch may introduce an error of as much as one minute of longitude. At the equator

this is 1 mile (1.85 km); at latitude 60°, it is 0.5 mile (0.93 km); at latitude 88°, it is only 0.035 miles (65 m). Thus, at this latitude a watch error of 2 minutes would introduce a maximum error of about 1 mile (1.85 km). That is, the maximum change of altitude of a body, at a fixed point of observation, is one minute of arc in two minutes of time, and the average error is not more than half this amount. Thus, for celestial navigational purposes, precise time is of little consequence in polar regions. At the poles, all bodies circle the sky at a constant altitude, except for a very slow change due to the changing declination. Because time zones lose their significance near the poles, it is customary to keep all timepieces set to GMT while in polar regions.

Lower-Altitude Sights

3413 Navigators in temperate climates usually avoid observations of bodies below 15°, and most of them never observe bodies lower than 10°. In polar regions the only available body may not exceed an altitude of 10° for several weeks. At the poles, the maximum altitude of the Sun is 23° 27′; the Moon and planets may exceed this value by only a few degrees. Hence, in polar regions sights must be taken without regard for any lower limit for observations.

The reason for avoiding low altitudes in temperate latitudes is the variable amount of refraction to be expected. In polar regions refraction varies over much wider limits than in lower latitudes. Because of the low temperatures in polar regions, the refraction correction for the sextant altitudes should be adjusted for temperature, or a special refraction table for this area should be used. Refraction is known to vary with temperature and barometric pressure, but there are other factors that are imperfectly known. Refractions of several *degrees* have occasionally been observed, resulting in the Sun appearing several days before it was expected in the spring, or continuing to appear for days after it should have disappeared below the horizon. Since abnormal refraction affects both the refraction and dip corrections, bubble sextant altitudes, if the average of a number of observations is used, are sometimes more reliable in polar regions than marine sextant altitudes on the natural horizon.

Tools and Techniques

3414 A marine sextant is the basic tool for polar navigation, although it is difficult at times to obtain a good horizon. Sun and Moon observations will usually be made at lower altitudes than the navigator is accustomed to using; they must be carefully corrected for refraction. As for all observations made in the polar regions, the "Additional Corrections" for nonstandard temperature and barometric pressure, contained in the *Nautical Almanac*, should be applied. An artificial horizon can be improvised when required. The conventional mercury horizon can rarely be used even aboard a stationary ship; it can, however, be used to advantage on the ice. For ship use, a pan of lubricating oil makes an acceptable horizon. It may be placed on a leveled gyro repeater and should be shielded from the wind.

When the horizon is poorly defined and a star at high altitude is visible, it may be desirable to take both direct and *back* (or *over-the-shoulder*) sights. In this latter technique, the observer faces *away* from the body and measures the *supplement* of the altitude (180° − sextant reading = observed altitude). The arc that appears when "rocking" the sextant is inverted, with the highest point on the arc the position of perpendicularity; practice is required for accuracy in taking back sights. The results of the direct and back sights are compared, and usually averaged.

An aircraft bubble sextant, or a marine sextant with bubble attachment, can be used advantageously in the polar regions. It takes some practice to become accustomed to using it, and a considerable number of sights of each body should always be taken and averaged. Results obtained with the bubble sextant will be improved if there is no ship's motion; it may be desirable to take all way off the ship while sights are being made. Some navigators suspend the bubble sextant from a spring, to help damp out undesired motion.

Celestial Observations

3415   During the long polar day—which at Thule, Greenland, in latitude 76° 32′ N, lasts for four months—the only body regularly available is the Sun, which circles the sky, changing azimuth about 15° each hour. The Moon will, at times, give a second line of position; but when it is near the new or full phase, such a line will be nearly parallel to the Sun line and hence of little value in fixing a position. An average of several observations of the Sun, obtained every two hours, can provide a series of running fixes. An even better practice is to make observations every hour and establish the most probable position for each hour.

The best celestial fixes are usually obtained from star observations made during twilight. With increased latitude, the period of twilight lengthens, permitting additional time for observation. With this increase, the period when the Sun is just below the horizon also lengthens, and it may be difficult to pick up stars or planets unless a sextant with a high-magnification telescope and large mirrors is available.

In the Arctic, with such an instrument, Capella, Deneb, and Vega should be among the first stars visible, particularly when situated approximately at right angles in azimuth to the position of the Sun below the horizon. In the Antarctic, the first stars to look for are Rigel Kentaurus, Acrux, Canopus, Hadar, and Achernar. The brighter planets will be the next bodies to become visible if they are high in declination. A bright aurora may delay the observation of stars and planets after sunset; at times, however, it may assist in defining the horizon. With dark-adapted vision and a good sextant, a navigator can frequently obtain excellent observations throughout the polar night. The Moon should, of course, be observed whenever it is available. Polaris, because of its high altitude and difficult azimuth determination, has very limited use.

Other conditions besides long periods of darkness complicate the problem of locating the horizon in high latitude. Low fog, frost smoke, or blowing snow may obscure the horizon when the Sun is clearly visible. Nearby land, hummocked sea ice, or an extensive ice foot may be troublesome, particularly at low heights of eye. As previously stated, an artificial horizon sextant can be most helpful under such conditions, and can supply good lines of position if the observer is practiced in its use and averages a number of observations.

The plotting of lines of position in polar regions is no more difficult than elsewhere. However, it must be remembered that an azimuth line is in reality a great circle. In moderate latitudes it is approximated on a Mercator chart by a rhumb line. In polar regions, rhumb lines are not suitable because they no longer approximate great circles. This is shown in figure 3415a in which a fix is plotted on a Mercator plotting sheet in the usual way. The solid lines show the actual lines that should be used. In figure 3415b this same fix is shown plotted on a transverse Mercator chart. Note that both the azimuth line and the line of position are plotted as straight lines, as on a Mercator chart near the equator. The assumed position is selected as in any latitude and located by means of the graticule of actual latitude and longitude. The fix is also given in terms of geographic coordinates. In plotting the azimuth line, the direction can be converted to grid azimuth, or plotted directly by means of true azimuth. If the latter method is used, care must be taken to measure the direction from the meridian of the AP. An aircraft plotter or protractor is usually used for this purpose.

Sextant altitudes are corrected in the same manner in polar regions as elsewhere, except that refraction should be corrected for temperature, or a special refraction table used, as indicated above. Coriolis corrections, needed for bubble sextant observations made from a moving craft, reach extreme values near the poles and should not be neglected.

If a body near the zenith is observed, the line of position is plotted as a circle, with the GP as the center, as in any latitude.

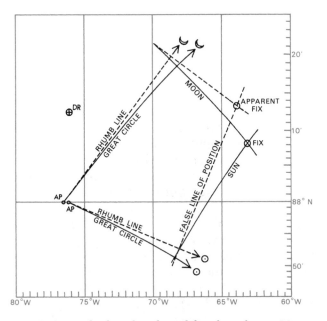

Fig. 3415a. High-altitude celestial fix plotted on a Mercator plotting sheet.

The Geographic Pole as Assumed Position

3416   One special method of plotting lines of position is available above 80° latitude. By this method, the pole is used as the AP. The Hc can then be determined by means of the almanac. The altitude of a body is its angular distance from the horizon; the declination is its angular distance from the celestial equator. At the pole, the horizon and celestial equator coincide, making the altitude equal to the declination. This is why a body with fixed declination circles the sky without change in altitude. At the pole, all directions are south (or north), and hence azimuth has no significance. The lines radiating outward from the pole, similar to azimuth lines in moderate latitudes, are meridians. Hence, in place of azimuth, GHA is used, for it indicates which "direction" the body is from the pole.

To plot a sight by this method, enter the almanac with GMT and determine the body's declination and GHA. Using the declination as Hc, compare it with Ho. If Ho is greater, it is a "Toward" case, as usual. Measure the altitude difference (a) from the pole along the meridian indicated by the GHA, and at the point so found erect a perpendicular to the meridian. If Hc is greater, an "Away" case, measure the intercept (a) along the meridian 180° from that indicated by the GHA, or *away* from the body (see fig. 3416).

In the early days of air exploration in polar regions, this method was quite popular, but with the development of modern tabular methods, it has fallen into disuse, except within 2° of the pole, or above latitude 88°, where it is sometimes used. This, of course, is a very small area. If a ship is near the meridian of the GP of the body (or its reciprocal), the method is entirely accurate at any latitude, even though the altitude difference might

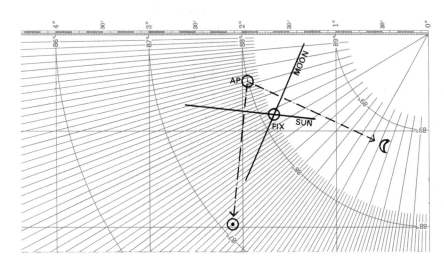

Fig. 3415b. The celestial fix of figure 3415a plotted on a transverse Mercator chart.

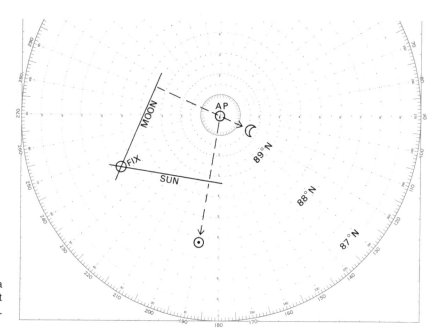

Fig. 3416. The celestial fix of figure 3415a plotted on a Maneuvering Board sheet used as an azimuthal equidistant chart. The pole is used as the assumed position.

be quite large, for this is simply a different way to plot meridian altitudes. However, the straight line used as the line of position is actually the arc of a small circle on the Earth. The radius of the circle depends on the altitude of the body. For bodies near the horizon, the straight line of position, a close approximation of a great circle, can be used for some distance from the meridian of the GP without appreciable error. However, as the altitude increases, the discrepancy becomes larger. Tables have been prepared to show the distance from the straight line to the circle of equal altitude at different altitudes and for several hundred miles from the meridian of the GP, on a polar stereographic projection.

Lines of position are advanced in the same manner as in lower latitudes. If a grid course is being followed, the AP or line of position is advanced along the grid course. The use of the pole as the AP does not complicate this practice.

SUNRISE, SUNSET; MOONRISE, MOONSET

3417 Obviously sunrise, sunset, moonrise, and moonset do not have the same significance in polar regions as in lower latitudes. At the poles, any change in altitude of a body is occasioned only by a change in declination. Since the maximum rate of change of declination of the Sun is about 1′ per hour, and the Sun is about 32′ in diameter, the entire Sun would not be visible for about thirty-two hours after "sunrise," or the moment of first

appearance of the upper limb, if refraction remained constant. In an aircraft high above the pole the Sun might be visible more than a week before it appears to an observer at the surface. Because of large variations in refractions, even the *day* of sunrise is difficult to predict in polar regions.

Ordinary sunrise, sunset, moonrise, and moonset tables are not available above 72° N or 60° S latitudes, nor would they be of much value if they were published. The method usually used is that provided by graphs in the *Air Almanac* as shown in figures 3417a, 3417b, and 3417c; comparable diagrams are not found in the *Nautical Almanac*.

The semiduration of sunlight is found by means of the graph in figure 3417a. The manner of its use is illustrated by the dashed lines.

Example: Find the LMT of sunrise and sunset at L 78° on March 8. Find the GMT if the observer is in λ 93° W.

Solution: From 8 March on the scale at the bottom of the graph draw a line vertically upward to the top of the diagram. To the nearest minute the time indicated by the dots is 1211. This is the LMT of meridian transit, or the center of the period of sunlight. Next, draw a horizontal line from L 78° N at the left (or right) margin to intersect the vertical line. At the point of intersection interpolate by eye between the curves. The semiduration of sunlight so found is 4^h40^m. Hence, the Sun will rise 4^h40^m before meridian transit, or at 0731, and set 4^h40^m after meridian transit, or at 1651. The GMT

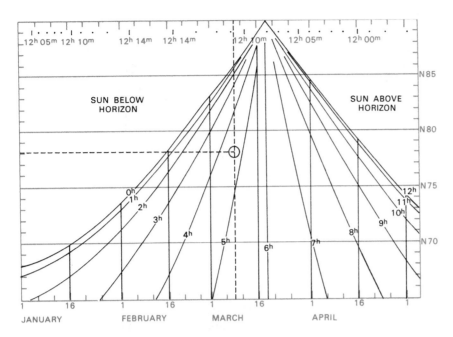

Fig. 3417a. Semi-duration of sunlight graph from the *Air Almanac*.

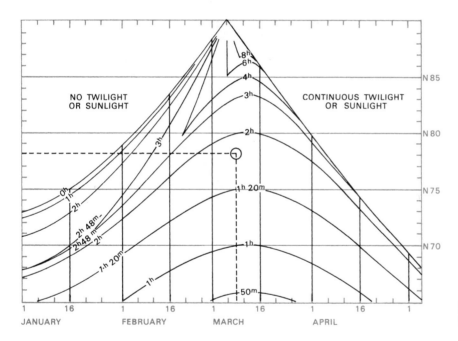

Fig. 3417b. Duration of twilight graph from the *Air Almanac*.

is 6^{h}12^m *later,* so that sunrise occurs at 1343 and sunset 2303. These values are approximations.

Answers: Sunrise, LMT 0731, GMT 1343; sunset, LMT 1651, GMT 2303.

The duration of civil twilight is found in a similar manner by the use of figure 3417b.

Example: Find the LMT and GMT of beginning of morning twilight and ending of evening twilight for the example above.

Solution: Draw a vertical line through 8 March and a horizontal line through L 78° N. At the inter-

section interpolate between the two curves. The value found is about 1^{h}45^m. Hence, morning twilight ends 1^{h}45^m after sunset.

Answers: Morning twilight, LMT 0546, GMT 1158; evening twilight, LMT 1836, GMT 2448 or 0048 the following day.

The time of moonrise and moonset is found from figure 3417c in a manner similar to finding sunrise and sunset. The time of transit of the Moon, of course, is not always near 1200, but may be any time during the day. The phase of the Moon is

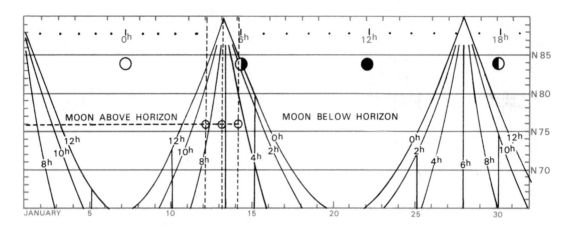

Fig. 3417c. Semi-duration of moonlight graph from the *Air Almanac*.

shown by its symbol, the open symbol being full Moon and the filled symbol new Moon.

SUMMARY

3418 Planning is important in any operation; it is *vital* to the success of polar navigation. Throughout this chapter, emphasis has been placed on the problems and difficulties that will be encountered in polar regions to underscore the need for an understanding of the conditions to be met and for adequate planning and preparation *before* entering the regions. This having been done, the polar regions can be navigated with confidence.

Chapter 35

Despite the best of intentions and efforts, there is always the possibility that a navigator might one day have to take to a lifeboat with severely limited facilities and capabilities. As a survivor of a disaster at sea, you may need to practice your navigation skills under these limitations in order to reach a place of safety. As long as ships ply the sea, ships will go down and a prudent mariner will *plan ahead* for that possibility. You cannot expect that there will be sufficient time to organize your equipment *after* the word is passed to abandon ship. In addition to being thoroughly familiar with the use of available equipment, you must be prepared to improvise.

ADVANCE PREPARATIONS

3501　There are several ways to prepare for the emergency of abandoning ship. The surest way is to make up an emergency navigational kit for *each* lifeboat and life raft, place it in a waterproof container, and lash it securely in place. If that is not practical, have a general kit ready to be taken to the lifeboat when disaster strikes.

The Emergency Navigation Kit

3502　Each emergency navigation kit should ideally contain charts, a portable GPS receiver (with spare batteries), a hand-held compass, a sextant, an almanac, sight reduction tables, a solar-powered calculator, a plotting kit, and notebook. The exact configuration of these components will depend upon the kind of lifeboat available to you, your resources, and the area of operations. Some modern navigators advocate taking a laptop computer with all the navigational software available (electronic charts, sight reduction programs, etc.), along with a

number of charged laptop batteries. While this may be viable in some circumstances, it is not difficult to imagine some inherent problems. Unless there are severe space limitations, this method is certainly worth trying, however.

The best charts for survival craft use are pilot charts for the area to be traveled. Aircraft position charts, published by the National Ocean Service, are also excellent.

If possible, the best sextant available should be taken into a lifeboat. Inexpensive plastic ones should also be in each survival craft if possible; these are sufficiently precise and accurate for lifeboat navigation.

If at all possible, a *Nautical Almanac* should be used, although many navigators prefer the star chart included in the *Air Almanac;* the star chart from a superseded almanac may be saved for emergency use. A *Long-term Almanac* that once appeared in *Bowditch* is available at the Naval Institute's web site, www.navalinstitute.org/navtable. With the instructions for its use and auxiliary tables, it comprises six pages and supplies data on the Sun and thirty of the selected stars. It does not become outdated and is surprisingly accurate; the maximum error in altitude computed by it should not exceed 2.0′ for the Sun, and 1.3′ for the stars. These pages can be photocopied and included as part of your emergency navigation kit. It is necessary to include copies of the refraction and dip tables from the *Nautical Almanac*, as these tables are not a part of the *Long-term Almanac*. Copies of almanacs for recent years can be put in lifeboat navigation kits with instructions on the simple corrections to be applied for use in the current year. These are usable for the Sun, Aries, and stars, with data being sufficiently accurate for emergency situations.

The Ageton tables for sight reduction, formerly published separately as H.O. 211, are also available at the USNI web site, www.navalinstitute.org/navtable. These can be very useful and are discussed in article 2526. An alternative for vessels that operate in limited areas is to photocopy just those pages of Pub. No. 229 or 249 that might be needed.

Fairly heavy plastic bags, such as are used for packaging ice cubes, are of great value for storing books, instruments, radio, and so on, and keeping them dry in a lifeboat. The types that securely seal with a plastic "zipper" are especially valuable.

Information

3503   Current knowledge of certain facts can be of great value in a lifeboat situation. For example, the approximate latitude and longitude of several ports, islands, and so on, in the area in which the ship operates, can prove useful if no chart is available. Obviously, the approximate position of the ship should be known at all times. A general knowledge of the charts, currents, and weather of the region in which the ship operates can be very useful, and the ability to identify stars without a star finder or sky chart will also prove valuable.

ABANDONING SHIP

3504   When the abandon ship order is given, the amount of preparation that can be made for navigation will depend on the time available. There is usually some warning. There are some things that must, of necessity, be left to the last moment, but it is not wise to let this list grow large. All actions in support of lifeboat navigation that will be required in an actual emergency should be a part of every abandon-ship drill. A checklist should be available without a search. The following items should be accomplished if time allows.

Determine the watch error and write it down. Be sure you know what kind of time your watch is keeping (zone, GMT, etc.). Check the date and write it down in the notebook, note the Zone Time being maintained. Write down the position of the ship. If possible, record also the set and drift of the current and the latitude and longitude of the nearest land in several directions. It may be easier to take along the chart or plotting sheet giving this information.

IN THE LIFEBOAT

3505   If you had time to get off distress signals before abandoning your vessel, or if other factors lead you to believe the probability is high that res-

cue efforts will be quickly mounted, it makes sense to remain as near as possible to the last reported position of your vessel.

If, on the other hand, rescue efforts are not anticipated, you should attempt to navigate your lifeboat to land or to heavily trafficked shipping lanes. It may help to remember that long voyages in lifeboats *can* be made, as proved by Captain Bligh, of HMS *Bounty*, who sailed 3,000 miles when cast adrift in an open boat.

Before setting out on any course, it is important to make an estimate of the situation. Do not start out until you know where you are going; determine this carefully and deliberately. This may be the most important decision of the entire journey; make it carefully.

Record the best-known latitude and longitude of the point of departure and the time of day. Let this be the beginning of a carefully kept log.

A number of factors will influence your decision of which direction to head. If a pilot chart is available, study it carefully and be sure you are thoroughly familiar with the average current and prevailing winds to be expected. Consider the motive power available and the probable speed. It may be better to head for land some distance away, if wind and current will help, than for nearby land that will be difficult to reach. Captain Bligh knew that there were islands within about 200 miles upwind, but he knew he could not reach them; his decision to take the long 3,000-mile downwind journey made survival possible. Note the location of the usually traveled shipping routes. These are shown on the pilot chart. If more than one suitable course is available, choose the one that will take you nearest to a well-traveled shipping route.

Consider the size and height of any nearby land, and the navigation equipment available. Remember that the horizon is quite close when the observer is standing in a lifeboat (only about 3 miles when standing in most lifeboats. Consider the probable accuracy with which positions can be determined. A small low island some distance away may be extremely hard to find with crude navigational methods; it may be advantageous to head for a more distant, but higher and more easily seen, landfall.

If the destination is on a continental land mass at a known latitude, it is often wise to direct one's course toward a point somewhat north or south of that place, and then when land is reached, run south or north along the coastline to the objective. This will eliminate the uncertainty as to which way to turn that will exist if land is reached at what is believed to be the correct latitude, but the destination is not sighted.

Will accurate time be available? Remember that the latitude can be determined accurately without time, but the longitude will be no more accurate than the time. If there is any question of the ability to maintain reasonably accurate time (each four seconds error in time results in 1' error in the longitude), do not head straight for the destination, but for a point that is certain to take the boat to the east or west of the destination, and then when the latitude of the destination has been reached, head due west or east and maintain the latitude. This method was successfully used for centuries before the invention of the chronometer.

Having decided upon the course to follow and the probable average speed, including help from current and wind, estimate the time of reaching the destination and set the ration of water and food accordingly.

DEAD RECKONING

3506 Dead Reckoning is always important, but never more so than when in a lifeboat. Determine as accurately as possible the point of departure and keep a record of courses, speeds, estimated ocean currents, and leeway. Do not be too quick to abandon a carefully determined estimated position for an uncertain fix by crude methods. It may be advisable to consider all positions as EPs and carefully evaluate all information available. Your real test as a navigator will be how accurately you can evaluate the information at hand and from it determine your true position.

DIRECTION

3507 At the very start of the voyage, check the accuracy of the compass on the course to be steered. The variation can be determined from the pilot chart, but to find the deviation, if this is not accurately known, locate a bit of wreckage in the water or throw overboard an object that will not drift too much with the wind and take the reciprocal magnetic course to the one desired. After this has been followed for some distance (a half mile to a mile), turn and steer for the object. If there is no deviation, the compass course will be the reciprocal of that first steered. If it is not, the desired compass course is halfway between the reciprocal of the first course and the compass course back to the object.

Under way the compass error should be checked at regular intervals. In the Northern Hemisphere

Polaris can be considered to be due north except in very high latitudes (above L 60° N the error can be greater than 2°). When Polaris is directly above or below the pole, the azimuth is 000° in any latitude. When the Sun, or any body, reaches its highest altitude, it can be considered to be on the celestial meridian, bearing 180° or 000°. If an almanac and a method of computation are available, the true direction of any body can be determined at any time by the usual methods of computing azimuth.

If a compass is not available, an approximation of a straight course can be steered by towing a line secured at the gunwale amidships. If the boat deviates from a straight track, the line will move away from its neutral position approximately parallel to the side of the craft. With a cross sea this method is less accurate, but may be better than nothing at all. Do *not* steer by a cloud on or near the horizon; these move with the wind and a curved, rather than straight, track will result. At night the boat can be kept on a reasonably straight course by steering by Polaris or a body near the prime vertical.

SPEED

3508 Throughout the trip, speed should be determined as accurately as possible. One crude method of measuring speed is to throw a floating object overboard at the bow and note the time required for the boat to pass it. For this purpose a definite distance should be marked off along the gunwale. Make this as long as practicable, but a length that will facilitate calculations—a length that is divisible into 100 a whole number of times, such as 25, 20, 16.7, or 10. In round figures, a boat traveling 100 feet in 1 minute is moving at a speed of 1 knot. If, for example, the length marked off is 25 feet (one-fourth of 100 feet) and an object is thrown overboard at the forward mark, it should be opposite the after mark in 15 seconds (one-fourth of one minute) if the boat is making 1 knot, 7.5 seconds if the speed is 2 knots, 5 seconds if 3 knots, and so on. If the distance were 16.7 feet (one-sixth of 100 feet), the times would be 10 seconds for 1 knot, 5 seconds for 2 knots, and so on. Speed determined in this manner is relative to the *water* and not speed made good over the bottom.

Since objects available for throwing overboard may be scarce, a light line, such as used for fishing, may be attached to the object and the other end secured to the boat so that the object can be secured and used again; this line must be able to run out freely. Alternatively, a small drogue can be improvised from a piece of cloth and a light line; this makes a good log line. Knot the line at intervals similar to those listed above or multiples of these. As the drogue is streamed aft, the time between the passage of two knots through the hand is noted. The drogue should be some distance astern before starting to take time; the knot at which time is started should therefore be 25 feet (7.6 m) or so forward of the drogue.

MEASURING ALTITUDES

3509 If a sextant is available, the altitude of a celestial body can be measured but to assure optimum observations when using a sextant in a lifeboat or in any other small craft, the observer should obtain his altitude at the instant the crest of a wave is directly under his position in the boat. The height of eye used in calculations should be the height in calm water plus one-half of the height of the waves. If no sextant is available, altitudes can be measured in several alternative ways.

A protractor can be used as shown in figure 3509a. A weight is attached to the center of curvature by a string that crosses the outer scale. Some navigational plotters with included protractors already have a hole in the appropriate location where a string can be attached. The observer sights along the straightedge of the protractor (AB) toward the body. Another person reads the point on the scale where it is crossed by the string. This is the zenith distance if the protractor is graduated as shown in figure 3509a; the altitude is 90° minus this reading (62¹/₂° in this example) and hence the observed altitude is 27¹/₂°. Several readings should be taken and all of these averaged for a more accurate value. This method should not be used for the Sun unless the eyes are adequately protected.

In figure 3509b, the weight is attached to a pin at the center of curvature and the protractor held horizontally, as indicated by the string crossing at 90°. The assistant holds the protractor and keeps the string on 90°. The observer moves a pin, pencil point, or other thin object along the scale until this pin and the center one are in line with the body. The body is then in direction AB. When the protractor is used in this way, the altitude is indicated directly. In figure 3509b, an altitude of about 49° is being measured. This method also should not be used for the Sun unless the eyes are protected.

For the Sun, either of the above methods can be used if a pin is mounted perpendicularly at the center of the protractor. In the first method, the reading is made when the shadow of the pin falls on 0°. In the second method, the reading is made at the shadow.

There are several other variations of the use of the protractor. A variation on the second method described above is to omit the weight and the assistant can sight along the straightedge at the horizon. An observation can be made without an assistant if the weight is attached at the scale at 90° and a loop of string placed over the pin at the center of curvature for holding the device. If preferred, a handle can be attached at 90° on the scale and the weight hung from the center of curvature, the protractor being inverted. The first method can be used without an assistant if the string is secured in place by the thumb and forefinger when the observation is made.

If no protractor is available, but you have a pad of maneuvering board paper, one of these sheets

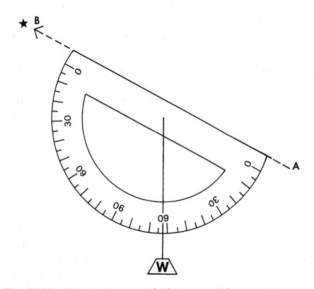

Fig. 3509a. Measuring zenith distance with a protractor.

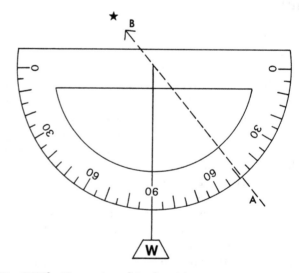

Fig. 3509b. Measuring altitude with a protractor.

may be fastened to any flat surface that can be raised to eye level. The same procedures are used as with a more conventional protractor; pins stuck into the board make sighting easier and more accurate.

Keep in mind that if a weight is used to establish the vertical, there is no correction needed for dip.

HORIZON SIGHTS

3510   A line of position may be obtained without a sextant or other altitude-measuring instruments by noting the time a celestial body makes contact with the visible horizon. The body most suitable for such observations is the Sun, and either the upper or lower limb may be used; the best practice would be to time both when they contact the horizon, and use the mean of the two resulting intercepts. Binoculars, if available, will assist in determining the instant of contact.

Such observations will usually yield surprisingly accurate results; they will certainly be more satisfactory than LOPs obtained from measurements made by improvised altitude-measuring devices.

The uncorrected altitude is noted as 0° 0′, and carefully corrected for dip, refraction, and semidiameter. The correction for dip is made by adding its value numerically to the value of the refraction correction.

Under nonstandard atmospheric conditions, the additional corrections for temperature and barometric pressure should be applied, if a thermometer and barometer are available; in actual lifeboat circumstances, however, this is unlikely.

The sight may be reduced by the tables of Pub. No. 229 or the Ageton tables but it must be remembered that when *both* Ho and Hc are negative, the intercept will be *"toward"* if Ho is numerically less than Hc, and vice versa; this is the *reverse* of the normal procedure.

Any low-altitude observations may yield results that are in error by a few miles under conditions of abnormal terrestrial refraction. However, Captain P. V. H. Weems, USN (Ret.) made ten horizon sights at sea on six different occasions, which gave an average error of 1.95 miles and a maximum error of 4.0 miles.

An azimuth of the Sun should be obtained at the same time the horizon sight is made, as a check on the accuracy of the compass.

The Green Flash

3511   The *green flash* is a common phenomenon in the tropics, and occurs at the moment the Sun's upper limb touches the horizon. It is caused by refraction of the light waves from the Sun as they pass through the Earth's atmosphere; there must be no low clouds on the horizon in the direction of the sunset. These light waves are not refracted, or bent, equally, the longer waves of red light being least refracted, the shorter blue and violet waves being more refracted. The red, orange, and yellow light is cut off by the horizon when the blue and violet light is still momentarily visible. These blue and violet rays cause the green flash.

It is estimated that at sea in the tropics, the green flash may be seen as often as 50 percent of the time and usually lasts for about $^3/_4$ of a second. Using the time of the green flash to obtain a line of position is merely a variation of the horizon sight described above. It is somewhat easier to use the time of the flash than to determine the instant the Sun's upper limb disappears below the horizon when there is no green flash.

NAVIGATION WITHOUT INSTRUMENTS

3512   The ancient Polynesians were able to navigate successfully without mechanical instruments or timepieces by using their knowledge of the heavens and the lore of the sea. Few persons today have acquired this knowledge, hence this chapter has been principally devoted to using, or improvising, instruments and methods familiar to most naval and merchant marine officers and quartermasters and yacht navigators.

The declination of any star is equal to the latitude of the point on Earth directly beneath the star; the GP, and for lifeboat accuracy the declination of the stars, can be assumed to remain fixed. This is the key to no-instrument celestial navigation. In the South Atlantic, for example, Alphard will pass overhead at Ascension Island. Farther north, Alkaid passes directly over Land's End, England; Newfoundland; Vancouver Island, south of the Aleutians; and over the Kuril Islands, north of Japan.

A rough determination of latitude can therefore be made by observing the passing of a star of known declination directly overhead. (The determination of "directly overhead" is not easily done; use the opinions of several persons for an average result.) By comparing the star's declination with the known latitude of land areas, a position east or west of the land areas can be determined. Ancient navigators were able to sail to the proper latitude, then sail directly east or west to a known island by this process.

Directions to land can be determined by observing the flight of birds or by typical cloud formations over islands. A steady course can be steered by maintaining a constant angle with the direction of swells or wave motion. Nearby land can sometimes be detected by sounds or even by a particular smell. A complete dissertation on using the lore of the sea and sky for navigation is beyond the space limitation of this text, but it is mentioned here to illustrate the necessity of using any and all available data or knowledge when routine navigation methods are not available.

Chapter 36

The Practice of Nautical Navigation

The preceding chapters have considered in detail various aspects of navigation: charts, aids to navigation, instruments, dead reckoning, celestial, electronic, and so on. Here in this chapter they will be brought together as a kind of summary of the practice of navigation in order that the interrelationship of each may be understood, and the importance of each to intelligent voyage planning and execution may be recognized.

Well in advance of the time that a vessel will get under way for a specified destination, her navigator assembles various data, charts, and publications for study so that he or she can *plan* the voyage in detail. In the following paragraphs, essentials to the completion of adequate and safe planning are discussed. The order of accomplishing these steps may vary, but an attempt has been made to place the various items in the sequence most frequently encountered in practice.

Once under way, the navigator will carry out many routine functions as well as responding to opportunities for refinement and unexpected circumstances.

Detailed information on these procedures for U.S. naval vessels is included in COMNAVAIRFORINST/COMNAVSURFORINST 3530.4 and should be reviewed in detail by all Navy navigators.

DETERMINING ETD AND ETA

3601 It is customary for the authority directing a vessel's movement to specify only *dates* of departure and arrival, leaving the *times* of departure or arrival to the discretion of the commanding officer or master of the vessel. This permits needed flexibility in determining the most advantageous times for favor-able conditions of tide, current, and weather. Movement orders may specify other limiting factors such as SOA; or perhaps only the time and date of arrival will be prescribed. Where exact ETA and ETD are not given, the navigator must study the various charts and publications as outlined below before these times may be precisely determined.

DETERMINING CHART REQUIREMENTS

3602 You must determine the charts available for use during the voyage. These are located by reference to the appropriate catalog(s) of charts. Most charts for U.S. waters are listed in the four catalogs of the National Ocean Service. Charts of foreign waters, bottom contour charts, and charts restricted to naval usage are listed in the various volumes of *NIMA* catalogs. New editions of nautical chart catalogs are published when accumulated changes warrant such action; only the current edition of any catalog should be used.

Using the appropriate catalogs, examine the *index diagrams* covering the area of interest. Each such diagram shows by colored outlines the area covered by each chart, with its corresponding number. With the chart numbers determined, you can consult a tabular listing for additional information such as chart name, scale, edition and date, datum, and price.

From this information, compile a list of the numbers of all available charts covering any part of the proposed route. If the latest editions of the needed charts are not on board, immediate steps should be taken to obtain them before departure. Charts must be ordered by naval units using the quite complex procedures of the NIMA Automated Distribution

Management System as described in Volume X of the NIMA catalog, which also lists the distribution points serving various geographical areas. Charts of the National Ocean Service may be obtained through NIMA except for a few charts that must be obtained directly from NOS sources. Civilian users will normally obtain charts from local sales agents.

DETERMINING PUBLICATION REQUIREMENTS

3603   The navigator should have available all pertinent *Light Lists, Lists of Lights, Coast Pilots, Sailing Directions*, and other navigational publications for the area to be traversed. On board naval ships, the current allowances established for the type of ship and the fleet to which it is assigned will normally be adequate.

Correction of Charts and Publications

3604   After all necessary charts and publications have been assembled and checked to ensure that they are the latest edition, they must also be checked to verify that all pertinent corrections have been entered, or must be brought up to date if not already corrected.

Charts may be corrected from either the onboard file of *Notices to Mariners* or a NIMA publication, *Summary of Corrections*, a consolidated reprint of all still-valid changes published in *Notices to Mariners*. This semiannual *Summary* is more convenient to use for correcting charts than individual *Notices to Mariners*, but it does not contain chart corrections for the Great Lakes or inland bodies of water and routes that are not normally used by oceangoing vessels.

Besides charts, each publication to be used must be checked to ensure that it has been fully corrected, or action must be taken to bring each volume up to date. The convenient *Summary of Corrections* can be used to correct *Coast Pilots* and *Sailing Directions*, but the file of *Notices* must be used to update *Light Lists, Lists of Lights*, and other navigational publications. These publications are issued in annual editions (in a few cases, at somewhat longer intervals where the number of changes does not warrant annual editions). Between editions, changes are published in *Notices to Mariners*. In most instances, the change is published as an item that can be cut and pasted directly into the basic publication; few pen changes are required except for deletions. Each correction item published in *Notices to Mariners* carries information as to the last prior correction for that chart or publication published so that none will be inadvertently overlooked.

Many publications contain a page where a record can be noted of the entry of each correction.

CONSIDERATION OF TIDES AND CURRENTS

3605   It is usually desirable to get under way or enter port at high-water stand, and as near as possible to the time of slack water, although they seldom coincide. A large ship entering a harbor with comparatively shallow water will be primarily concerned with the time of high water, while a smaller vessel entering a harbor with deep water but variable current will be more interested in times when the current is slack.

Occasionally the draft of the ship will be greater than the charted depth (low water) of a portion of the channel or harbor. This requires the use of Table 3 in the *Tide Tables* to determine how long before and after high water the depth of the water will be sufficient to permit safe passage of the ship. Extreme care must be used in such cases, as the *Tide Tables* are only predictions, and there can be a significant difference between the predicted and actual conditions.

DETERMINING DISTANCE AND SOA

3606   Before making a voyage, it is essential that you first determine the total distance to be traveled. This distance may be obtained by measurement from the charts to be used or by reference to available publications. NIMA Pub. No. 151, *Table of Distances Between Ports*, covering foreign ports throughout the world, or *Distance Between U.S. Ports*, published by the National Ocean Service, should be consulted. Distances between many other combinations of ports will also be found in the pertinent *Coast Pilots* and *Sailing Directions*. If it is your intention to travel the regular route between ports, the distance given in these publications should be used, as it is more accurate than can normally be determined by chart measurement.

Once favorable hours of departure and arrival have been decided upon, the required speed of advance (SOA) can be determined. After SOA has been completed, the speed to be ordered can be determined, taking into account the ship's displacement, condition of bottom, and trim; currents expected to be encountered; and other applicable factors.

PLANNING THE PASSAGE

3607   After completing the preliminary preparations described above, you are now ready to plan the voyage. By commencing the planning phase well in advance you will have sufficient time to study the various publications, to give the proposed track careful consideration, and to obtain any needed charts and/or publications not presently on board.

Chart Selection

3608 Most captains and navigators prefer to have available an overall plot of the entire voyage on one chart. This permits rapid determination of distance made good and distance to go at any desired time during the voyage, and presents clearly the relationship between the route selected and the coastline or adjacent land masses. For this purpose a small-scale (large-area) chart is initially used. Unless the voyage is very short, however, it is not possible to plot the entire track on one chart that is also suitable for piloting. In making this selection, two conflicting factors must be considered and balanced against each other. It is desirable to use a large-scale chart for the greater degree of detail provided. However, the use of the largest scale chart available may often require one or more changes of charts during a run through restricted waters; this is time consuming and could lead to errors at the time of shifting from one chart to the next. Use of a large-scale, small-area chart may also limit the navigator's concept of the "big picture," the area as a whole. It is the practice of some navigators to use the smallest scale chart that contains all essential aids to navigation.

It is quite helpful if any water area that is too shallow for safe navigation has been shaded on the chart in advance. This will allow you to determine at a glance if your vessel is standing into danger.

For piloting during coastwise passages, the most commonly used chart is one from the coast chart series at a scale of 1:80,000. More detailed charts, at scales of 1:50,000 and larger, are desirable for harbor piloting, but are not as useful for offshore waters or approaches.

In selecting a chart to be used for a voyage in pilot waters, consideration should be given to the scale used, ascertaining that it includes all of the landmarks and aids to navigation desired or required in any one area. If the scale is too small, the chart coverage may exclude features best suited for visual observation and fixes.

Once the charts to be used are selected, you should ensure that you are familiar with the details shown on each. The following should be particularly noted:

1. Whether depths are indicated in feet or fathoms.
2. Whether heights are indicated in feet or meters.
3. The distance indicated by the smallest division of the latitude scale.
4. The distance indicated by the alternately shaded divisions of the latitude scale.
5. The distance between adjacent printed meridians and parallels.
6. The significance of the length of the ship and its handling characteristics in relation to the scale of the chart.
7. The geographical limits covered by each chart.
8. Variation of the magnetic compass, correction to variation since printing of the chart due to annual change, and the differences in variation at different points along the track.
9. The patterns of shoal and deep water, and depths, as indicated by the fathom lines; the depth at which water areas change from white to blue.
10. Abnormal patterns of bottom contour lines that may be useful for determining positions by echo sounder.
11. Land contours, marshes, bluffs, prominent mountain peaks, and landmarks that may be useful for radar piloting or identification or which may affect radar interpretation.

Intended Track

3609 Having selected your charts, next plot the route to be followed on both the large- and the small-scale charts. The route is normally plotted first on the small-scale (large-area) chart or charts, and labeled as to track, speed, and distance between points. This allows you to check visually the safety of the track as initially laid down, and to make any adjustments needed.

DR positions for selected times are then plotted along the track, using the speed previously determined. The frequency with which these DR positions are plotted on the large-area chart will depend upon the judgment of the navigator, the proximity of land masses, and the desired course. When making an ocean passage, DR positions every twelve hours are normally sufficient; in coastal piloting, a DR position every hour is common practice.

Naval practice is to lay out PIM (point of intended movement) marks every two hours, facilitating the comparison of intended versus actual movement. The navigation team will normally update the officer of the deck on an hourly basis regarding the ship's position in relation to PIM. PIM marks are normally laid out in Zulu (GMT) time to avoid confusion when changing time zones.

At this time, any special information of interest in the broad planning of the voyage should be noted on the chart. These items may include limits of special danger, restricted areas, and for naval ships, limits of operational control areas and changes in communications responsibility. This information should be noted on the chart in the vicinity of the position at which the event is expected to occur.

You should next translate the general information portrayed on the small-scale chart into detailed graphic representations on the large-scale charts covering the same areas. At this time, careful reference should be made to the instructions and information given in the *Coast Pilots* and *Sailing Directions* for the areas of each chart. If specific routes are recommended or overprinted on the charts, these should be used to the greatest extent possible, for they represent known safe tracks that have been tested over many years. In deciding on details of the final track, you should not only avoid all obvious dangers, but also allow yourself as much sea room as possible in the areas of these dangers.

Points at which the course or speed must be changed are of particular interest to navigators and should always be marked on the chart. For naval vessels operating with other ships, it is often desirable to assign a name or number designation to these points for ease of reference. The ETA at each critical point should be plainly marked on the charts.

Ship Weather Routing

3610 The practice of taking prevailing or expected weather conditions into account when planning your voyage is sometimes called *ship weather routing*. It can be specifically defined as the process of selecting an optimum track for an ocean passage by making long-range predictions of wind, waves, and currents, and their effect on the vessel, which may be large or small. In more general terms, it is taking advantage of all meteorological and hydrographic information to achieve the safest and most economical passage for a ship or yacht. This is essentially routine in aircraft operation, but not as widely used in marine navigation as it might be.

In the U.S. Navy, weather routing is called *Optimum Track Ship Routing* (OTSR) and is done by regional centers of the Naval Meteorology and Oceanography Command. Several commercial meteorological activities provide similar services for merchant ships and yachts.

As shown in earlier chapters, the shortest distance between any two points on the surface of the Earth is the arc of the great circle connecting them. Although this represents the shortest linear distance, it may not represent the most desirable track

for a vessel; another route may produce a least-time track. In the case of passenger vessels, the optimum route is quite often the one that will maximize conditions of passenger safety and comfort. In other operations, minimum fuel consumption may be the determining factor; or, in the case of some cargo vessels, particularly those carrying deck loads, the optimum track may be one that will present the least hazard to the cargo. In general, routes are prepared that combine these considerations. It has always been recognized by seamen that waves, whether breaking seas or swells, have the greatest adverse effect on the movement of a ship through the water. Optimum track routing is therefore normally used to route ships along a track to avoid areas where the waves are expected to be the highest.

The output from a weather routing advisory service is normally in the form of an *initial route recommendation* prepared and made available to the vessel two or three days in advance of the planned sailing date. Subsequently, the advisory service may recommend advancing or delaying the day or hour of the departure. Also available from advisory services are generalized *planning routes* that are developed more from seasonal data than from present and forecast weather patterns. These use information from *Pilot Charts* (and other sources), but are more detailed and specific.

After a vessel sails, its progress along the recommended route is monitored with respect to developing weather patterns. *Diversions* are recommended in terms of change of course or speed to avoid or minimize the effects of adverse weather and sea conditions—conditions that might require a speed reduction by one-third or an increase in transit time of six hours or more. A recommendation of storm *evasion* may be made if conditions become dangerous enough that the planned route should be disregarded and the vessel should take independent action to avoid hazardous conditions.

An essential element of any ship weather-routing system is an efficient two-way communications system. By having the vessel report present conditions, the advisory agency can confirm or modify its forecasts; by receiving changes in routing, the vessel can take advantage of knowledge more recent than that which went into the initial route recommendation.

Hazardous Areas, Danger Bearings, and Limits of Safe Water

3611 Frequently the intended track may, of necessity, place the ship in close proximity to dangers to navigation during the voyage. In addition to such natural dangers as rocks, shoals, and bars, various governmental agencies have reserved certain designated areas for hazardous operations. Gunnery practice and testing ranges, ammunition disposal areas, special anchorages, and spoil grounds are a few examples. Where particularly confined waters or heavy shipping concentrations prevail, special rules may be in effect to limit maximum speed and otherwise restrict vessel movement. At the entrance to many ports, there have been established Vessel Traffic Services (VTS) or Traffic Separation Schemes (TSS) consisting of inbound and outbound lanes with a separation zone between them, special precautionary zones, and special communications arrangements. Each of these special areas, whether natural or manmade, constitutes an additional hazard for the mariner. Each chart should be carefully inspected to determine these dangers, and the *Coast Pilot, Sailing Directions,* and *Notices to Mariners* consulted for detailed information concerning them; appropriate annotations should then be made on each chart in question. In addition, it is a good practice to outline all danger areas and the limits of water considered safe for the draft of the ship, using a colored pencil. Do not use a red pencil if the chart will be used under a red light on the bridge at night, as the red marking will not be visible. For this reason, "nautical purple" (magenta) is frequently used instead.

Where appropriate, danger bearings should be located, plotted, and the information noted on the chart.

Aids to Navigation

3612   Special attention should be given to the aids to navigation expected to be sighted during the voyage. A list recording a complete description of the aids and their light characteristics, the expected times of sighting, and the approximate bearings at sighting is of particular use. A notation should be made on the chart of any aid to navigation that is reported in *Notices to Mariners* as missing, defective, or temporarily replaced with an aid of another type.

While the color and shape of buoys that are a part of the lateral system used in U.S. waters are evident from the printed chart information, it is not always possible to predict the characteristics of special-purpose buoys by chart inspection alone. In like manner, it is not possible to apply the rules pertaining to U.S. buoyage to the various buoyage systems in use in foreign countries; in such cases, careful reference to the *Lists of Lights* and *Sailing Directions*

is necessary to avoid misinterpretation.

Under normal conditions of visibility, a primary seacoast light (a "lighthouse") can be seen in the daytime when within range and can be identified by its color and structural appearance. A complete description of the distinctive features of each is given in the appropriate *Light List* or *List of Lights,* and since this information seldom appears on the chart, notation should be made thereon. Photographs or drawings of many lights appear in the *Coast Pilots* and *Sailing Directions,* while many foreign charts include a sketch of the light near its symbol.

Harbor entrances, bays and rivers, coastal danger areas, and other hazards are normally well marked with lighted aids to navigation that the navigator should personally and positively identify on each initial sighting. Identification can be confirmed by using a stopwatch to time a light through a full cycle of its characteristics. Accurate identification of buoys is particularly important and should not be a matter of delegation, chance, or guesswork. The full characteristics of lighted buoys may not be printed on a chart, particularly small-scale charts, and even when using large-scale charts, information such as the length of each flash and eclipse of major aids does not normally appear. Only by use of the *Light List,* comparing the recorded information with those characteristics actually observed, can you be absolutely certain of the identification of a lighted aid to navigation. Supplementary information appearing *only* in the *Light List* should be added to the chart in a box adjacent to the symbol.

While preparing for the voyage, the computed visibility of all lights expected to be sighted en route should be plotted and labeled on the charts. In computing the geographic range at which the light might be sighted in clear weather, you must allow for the elevation of the light and the height of the lookout's eye.

Tide and Tidal Current Data

3613   Times and heights of the tides, and the times and strengths of currents, for the points of departure and arrival, are computed for the respective dates. This information should be carefully studied before reaching a decision as to the time of departure and arrival. Some ports may have shoals or bars that can be crossed only near the time of high water, while others may have bridges of such vertical clearance that high-masted ships may be required to transit the channel at low water. Ships arriving at or leaving their berths will be assisted by a favorable current, while an unfavorable current may make the maneuver very difficult, especially for a single-screw ship.

Port Information

3614 Information concerning the anchorage or berthing space assigned to the ship may not be received until the ship has reported its ETA to the port authority. If the destination is a port frequently used by naval vessels, an anchorage chart is usually available showing the exact location of all berths, the radius of each, and the range and bearing of its center from a prominent landmark or aid to navigation. Additional information concerning the port—such as pier space, tugs, pilots, communications, harbor facilities, and other pertinent items—is contained in the appropriate *Coast Pilot* (U.S. waters), or *Sailing Directions* (foreign waters), and *Fleet Guide* (for U.S. naval vessels only) which should be carefully read prior to arrival. In addition, the file of *NavArea Warnings, HYDROLANT* or *HYDROPAC* messages, and *Local Notices to Mariners* (U.S. waters only) issued by the Coast Guard District concerned, should be checked to see if any recent changes in aids to navigation have been made, or if any special warnings about dangers to navigation have been issued for the area of interest.

To keep port information as current as possible, every Navy ship must submit a port visit report that is entered into a fluid database that can be searched by fleet users. The information in this database is generally more current than that information found in the *Fleet Guides.*

PREPARING TO GET UNDER WAY

3615 The preceding articles have dealt with the preparations made in the planning stages by the navigator in advance of the day prescribed for getting under way. There remain, however, certain other preparatory steps to be taken that have properly been postponed until the overall plan has been decided upon; the systematic accomplishment of these is no less important to the execution of a safe passage than was careful voyage planning.

Piloting Team

3616 On naval vessels, the piloting team must be assembled for a briefing prior to getting under way (and prior to entering port). Appendix B of COM-NAVAIRFORINST/COMNAVSURFORINST 3530.4 provides a checklist for conducting a proper navigation briefing. During the briefing, the navigator informs the team of everything it is possible to predict, such as all aids to navigation expected to be used (their name, appear-ance, and about where and when they will be sighted), all natural and manmade ranges, any special information concerning soundings, and so on.

It is advantageous that key members of the team be given the material covered in the briefing in written form in order that the detailed plan, the characteristics, and appearances of lights and other important features to be encountered will not be trusted entirely to memory.

Equipment Checks

3617 Forehanded testing will permit time to repair any casualties uncovered. The master gyro should be checked for error, after which the gyro repeaters on the bridge are checked against the master gyro. Such things as the steering system, the depth finder, radios, navigation and signal searchlights, and navigational lighting circuits should all be tested.

With the piloting team on station, a round of bearings should be taken and plotted on the chart, or a gyro observation of a range should be obtained and the amount and direction of gyro error, if any is present, should be determined. If a gyro error is determined, you may offset the parallel motion dial of your drafting machine (if you are using one) by the amount of this error. This procedure permits plotting the reported bearings as they are received from the bearing takers without the necessity of applying gyro error before plotting each line of position.

Because you are generally in a well-fixed position when moored (i.e., you know precisely where you are), prior to getting under way is an excellent time to conduct a comparison of your various navigational assets. In other words, check your position using all means possible (GPS, visual, radar, celestial, etc.) and compare the results. This process will tell you much about your equipment and techniques.

INTEGRATED BRIDGE SYSTEMS

3618 One of the technological advancements that has improved the practice of navigation for mariners is the *integrated bridge system* (IBS). Bridge watch officers must concern themselves with ship management, collision avoidance, and safe navigation. All three make demands on the watch officer's attention and all three are important. An IBS streamlines the watch officer's duties by linking various components that traditionally have been independent. The traditional approach has been for such things as the nautical chart, the radar scope, and the ship's helm to be linked through the watch officer. IBS links these components and many more through an local area network (LAN) and displays them in a centralized console system that makes it easily accessible for a watch officer to access and use in carrying out his or her duties. The attendant automation pays dividends in allowing the watch officer to spend less time inputting/outputting information, moving around the bridge to reach various components, and correlating disparate but vital elements of information.

IBS configurations differ from ship to ship, depending upon the vessel's functions and needs. Not surprisingly, an IBS system for a merchant vessel making cargo runs from port to port will be less complicated and capable than one designed for a flagship in a naval battle group. Components or systems that can be included in an IBS configuration include compasses (both gyro and flux-gate magnetic), GPS, radar, ECDIS, inertial navigation, speed log, meteorological sensors, steering control, depth sensors, and so on. Obviously, an IBS will include one or more computers and the necessary software to integrate the necessary components.

In 1997, USS *Yorktown* (CG 48) was the first major U.S. warship to include IBS technology as part of the Navy's "Smart Ship" concept. Many more have followed, included submarines, aircraft carriers, and patrol craft. Many merchant ships are also equipped with variations of IBS.

UNDER WAY

3619 Once under way, you must constantly strive to take any and all steps that will assure the safety and efficient operation of your vessel. No opportunity for obtaining or verifying your position should ever be squandered. If you are fortunate enough to have a state-of-the-art GPS system, by all means, use it in every way you can, but do not overrely on it—something it will be very tempting to do. Convenience and ease of use are seductive lures but cannot justify the abrogation of your responsibility for the safety of your vessel.

The United States Navy equips its vessels with outstanding navigational equipment that is the envy of navigators with fewer resources, but Navy directives make it clear that the presence of this equipment does not relieve the commanding officer (and his or her navigator) of the responsibility to use celestial navigation whenever possible as a supplement. This philosophy should prevail with all nautical navigators, whether their vessel is an aircraft carrier or a weekend pleasure boat. The tried and true methods of the ancients should be blended with the wonders of modern technology to ensure that your vessel does not needlessly go in harm's way.

Appendix A   Abbreviations

A	ampere; amplitude; augmentation; away (altitude difference)	CH	compass heading
		CIC	Combat Information Center
a	altitude intercept (altitude difference, Hc – Ho); assumed	cm	centimeter
		CMG	course made good
a_o, a_1, a_2	first, second, and third Polaris sight-reduction correction (from *Nautical Almanac*)	Cn	course (as distinguished from course angle)
		CNO	chief of naval operations
AA	*Air Almanac*	co-	the complement of (90° minus)
AC	alternating current	COA	course of advance
ADF	automatic direction finder	COG	course over ground
AF	audio frequency	co-L	colatitude
aL	assumed latitude	comp	compass
aLo	assumed longitude	corr.	correction
AM	amplitude modulation	cos	cosine
Amp	amplitude	cot	cotangent
AP	assumed position	CPA	closest point of approach
app	apparent	cps	cycles per second
Υ_1	longitude of departure	CRT	cathode ray tube
Υ_2	longitude of destination	csc	cosecant
Υv	longitude of vertex	CW	continuous wave
atm	atmosphere	C – W	chronometer time minus watch time
AU	astronomical unit	D	deviation; dip (of horizon); distance; drift (current)
Aug	augmentation		
Az	azimuth angle (Z also used)	d	declination; difference; distance
aλ	assumed longitude (also aLo)	DB	danger bearing
B	bearing; bearing angle; barometric correction (altitude); body (celestial body)	DC	direct current
		Dec.	declination
		Dec. inc.	declination increment
Bn	beacon	deg	degree
C	Celsius (centigrade); chronometer time; compass (direction); correction; course (vessel); course angle	Dep	departure
		Dest	destination
		Dev	deviation
CB	compass bearing	DFGMC	digital flux gate magnetic compass
CC	chronometer correction; compass course	DG	degaussing
		diff	difference
CCZ	Coastal Confluence Zone	dist	distance
CE	chronometer error; compass error		

D. Lat.	difference of latitude
DLo	difference of longitude (arc units) (also dλ)
DME	distance measuring equipment
DoD	Department of Defense
DR	dead reckoning, dead reckoning position
Dr	drift
DRM	direction of relative movement
DRT	dead reckoning tracer
DSD	double-second difference
DST	daylight saving time
dur	duration
DUT1	time signal correction
Dλ	difference of longitude (also DLo)
E	east; error
EHF	extremely high frequency
EM log	electromagnetic log
EP	estimated position
Eq. T	equation of time
est	estimated
ETA	estimated time of arrival
ETD	estimated time of departure
F	Fahrenheit; fast; phase correction (altitude); frequency; latitude factor
fath	fathom, fathoms (also fm)
FM	frequency modulation
fm	fathom, fathoms (also fath)
ft	foot, feet
G	Greenwich, Greenwich meridian (upper branch); grid
g	Greenwich meridian (lower branch); acceleration due to gravity
GB	grid bearing
GE	gyro error
GH	gyro heading
GHA	Greenwich hour angle
GHz	gigahertz
GMT	Greenwich Mean Time
Govt	government
GP	geographical position
GPS	Global Positioning System
Gr	Greenwich (also G)
GST	Greenwich sidereal time
GV	grid variation
GZn	grid azimuth
H	altitude (astronomical); height above sea level
HA	hour angle
ha	apparent altitude
Hc	computed altitude
Hd	head
Hdg	heading
HE	height of eye
HF	high frequency

HHW	higher high water
HLW	higher low water
Ho	observed altitude
Hor	horizontal
HP	horizontal parallax
H_{pgc}	heading per gyro compass
H_{psc}	heading per standard compass
H_{pstgc}	heading per steering compass
hr	hour
hrs	hours
hs	sextant altitude
HT	height
ht	tabulated altitude
Ht. Eye	height of eye
HW	high water
Hz	hertz (cycle per second)
I	instrument correction
IC	index correction
in	inch, inches
INS	integrated navigation system
J	irradiation correction
K	knot, knots; Kelvin (temperature)
kHz	kilohertz
km	kilometer, kilometers
kn	knot, knots (also kt)
kt	knot, knots (also kn)
kW	kilowatt
L	latitude; lower limb correction for Moon (from *Nautical Almanac*)
L_1	latitude of departure
L_2	latitude of destination
l	difference of latitude
LAN	local apparent noon
LAT	local apparent time
Lat.	latitude
LF	low frequency
LHA	local hour angle
LHW	lower high water
LL	lower limb
LLW	lower low water
Lm	mid-latitude; mean latitude
LMT	Local Mean Time
Lo	longitude (also long. or λ)
log	logarithm; logarithmic
log_e	natural logarithm (to base e)
log_{10}	common logarithm (to base 10)
Long.	longitude (also Lo or λ)
LOP	line of position
Lv	latitude of vertex
LW	low water
M	magnetic; maneuvering ship (in relative plot of relative movement problems; meridian (upper branch); meridian parts

mag	magnetic; magnitude
max	maximum
MB	magnetic bearing
mb	millibar
MC	magnetic course
Mer. Pass.	meridian passage
MF	medium frequency
MH	magnetic heading
MHHW	mean higher high water
MHW	mean high water
MHWN	mean high water neaps
MHWS	mean high water springs
MHz	megahertz
mi	mile, miles
mid	middle
min	minute, minutes
MLLW	mean lower low water
MLW	mean low water
MLWN	mean low water neaps
MLWS	mean low water springs
mm	millimeter
mph	miles (statute) per hour
ms	millisecond
N	north
NA	*Nautical Almanac*
Na	nadir
NASA	National Aeronautics and Space Administration
naut	nautical
nm	nautical mile, nautical miles (also n mi)
n mi	nautical mile, nautical miles (also nm)
NIMA	National Imagery and Mapping Agency
NOAA	National Oceanic and Atmospheric Administration
NOS	National Ocean Service (formerly National Ocean Survey)
P	atmospheric pressure; parallax; planet; pole; departure; polar distance
PC	personal correction
PD	polar distance; position doubtful
pgc	per gyro compass
P in A	parallax in altitude
Pit log	pitot-static log
PM	pulse modulation
Pn	North Pole; north celestial pole
Pos	position (also posit)
posit	position (also Pos)
Ps	South Pole; south celestial pole
psc	per standard compass
p stg c	per steering compass
PV	prime vertical
Q	Polaris correction
QQ'	celestial equator; equator
R	refraction

RA	right ascension
RB	relative bearing
R Bn	radiobeacon
RDF	radio direction finder
rel	relative
rev	reversed
RF	radio frequency
R Fix	running fix
RLG	ring laser gyro
RMS	root mean square
RPM	revolutions per minute
S	sea-air temperature difference correction; slow; south; speed
s	second, seconds (also sec)
SD	semidiameter
sec	secant; second, seconds (also s)
SH	ship's head (heading)
SHA	sidereal hour angle
SHF	super high frequency
SI	international system of units (metric)
sin	sine
SINS	Ship's Inertial Navigation System
SMG	speed made good
SOA	speed of advance
SOG	speed over ground
SRM	speed relative movement
st.m.	statute mile
T	air temperature correction; temperature; time; toward (altitude difference); true (direction)
t	meridian angle; elapsed time
Tab	tabulated value
tan	tangent
TB	true bearing; combined temperature-barometric correction
TC	true course
TD	time difference (Loran)
T_G	ground-wave reading (Loran)
T_{GS}	ground-wave-sky-wave reading (Loran)
TH	true heading
TR	track
TZn	true azimuth
U	upper limb correction for Moon (from *Nautical Almanac*)
UHF	ultra high frequency
UL	upper limb
UT	Universal Time
UTC	Coordinated Universal Time
V	variation; vertex
v	excess of GHA change from tabulated value for one hour
Var	variation
VHF	very high frequency
vis	visibility

VLF	very low frequency	Z	azimuth angle (also Az); zenith
W	watch time; west	z	zenith distance; zone meridian (lower branch)
WAC	World Aeronautical Chart		
WE	watch error	ZD	zone description
X	parallactic angle	Zn	azimuth (as distinguished from azimuth angle)
yd	yard		
yr	year	ZT	Zone

Appendix B

Symbols

⌒	dead reckoning	≈	nearly equal to
⊙	fix	>	is greater than
⊡	estimated position	<	is less than
△	symbol used for one set of fixes when simultaneously fixing by two means, e.g., visual and radar; sometimes used for radionavigation fixes	≥	is equal to or greater than
		≤	is equal to or less than
		∞	infinity
		.....	repeating decimal
+	plus (addition)	Δ	a small increment, or the change in one quantity corresponding to a unit change in another variable
-	minus (subtractions)		
±	plus or minus		
~	absolute difference (smaller subtracted from larger)	λ	longitude; wave length (radiant energy)
×	times (multiplication)	μs	microsecond
÷	divided by (division)	♈	Aries
x^2	square of number x	°	degree
x^3	cube of number x	′	minute
x^n	nth power of number x	♀	Venus
$\sqrt{}$	square root	♂	Mars
		⊙	Sun
$\sqrt[n]{}$	nth root	☾, ☽	Moon
=	equals	⊕	Earth
≠	not equal to	π	pi (ratio of circumference of circle to diameter = 3.14159...)

Appendix C   Compass Adjustment

The following discussion will dispense with theory and follow the procedures that experience indicates is satisfactory for adjusting the great majority of compasses. It is recommended that the reader first read and understand chapter 7 before reading this appendix. If the procedures outlined here do not give acceptable results, the services of a professional compass adjustor should be sought. For a more detailed discussion of compass adjustment, see *Handbook of Magnetic Compass Adjustment*, NIMA Pub. No. 226, or the appropriate chapter in *Bowditch* (*The American Practical Navigator* by Nathaniel Bowditch, NIMA Pub. No. 9).

COMPONENTS OF MAGNETISM

Deviation of a magnetic compass is caused by the magnetic properties of metallic objects on a vessel and/or the vessel itself. A complete analysis of the many separate magnetic components that combine to cause deviation is beyond the scope of this book; however, an understanding of the basic concepts and terminology is desirable. The various magnetic components or parameters of the total magnetic field of a vessel are referred to as *coefficients,* and different correcting devices are used to compensate for their effects on the compass.

Since materials of opposite polarity attract each other, the polarity of the magnetic hemisphere and the north-seeking end of a compass magnet are opposite. To identify their polarity, the ends of compensating bar magnets used in binnacles are color-coded; by convention the north end is painted red, and the south is painted blue.

Coefficients of Deviation

The components of the total magnetic forces causing deviation, the coefficients, are arbitrarily defined and designated by letters. As used below, "soft iron" is material in which magnetism is induced by the Earth's magnetic field. This magnetism changes as its orientation with respect to the Earth's magnetic field changes. In contrast, a ship's "hard iron" has the relatively permanent magnetism acquired during construction and fitting-out. Soft and hard iron are further classified as "horizontal" or "vertical" as determined by the orientation of their magnetic axes when induced by components of the Earth's field.

Coefficient A is constant on all headings and may be a combination of other parameters or may be mechanical, as from an incorrectly placed lubber's line.

Coefficient B is maximum on compass headings east or west and zero on compass headings north or south.

Coefficient C is maximum on compass headings north or south and zero on east or west.

Coefficients B and C are caused by permanent magnetism and to some extent by induced magnetism in vertical soft iron. On small craft constructed mainly of wood and/or fiberglass, adjustment is normally made only for these coefficients. Most boat compasses or their mountings will have built-in small correcting magnets for this purpose.

Coefficient D is a form of quadrantal deviation that is maximum on intercardinal headings: 045°, 135°, 225°, 315°, and zero on cardinal compass headings: north, south, east, west.

Coefficient E is quadrantal deviation that is maximum on the cardinal compass headings and zero on the intercardinal headings.

Coefficients D and E are caused by induced magnetism in horizontal soft iron and are compensated for by the use of the soft iron *quadrantal spheres* normally mounted on brackets athwartships on the binnacle. These spheres should be used on all vessels constructed of steel.

Coefficient J is defined as the change of deviation for a heel of 1° while the vessel is on compass heading 000°. It is, in effect, the error caused because the compass, with its gimballing arrangement, remains in a horizontal plane while the vessel, with its magnetic field, rolls and pitches. A slight change in the relative positions of the compass and ship is therefore introduced. This change in deviation caused by the motion of the vessel can cause the compass card to oscillate. Coefficient J is compensated for by a *heeling magnet* placed in a vertical tube directly below the center of the compass.

CORRECTORS IN COMPASS BINNACLE

The compass binnacle is the case and stand in which a magnetic compass is mounted. It consists of a casting of nonmagnetic material about 3½ feet (1.1 m) high, with an opening in the top to receive the compass and with a place for the correctors used for adjusting the compass.

Inside the binnacle, which has access doors, are trays or holders for fore-and-aft magnets and for athwartship magnets. The trays are supported on screws so they can be raised or lowered, with about 12 inches (30 cm) of travel available, and provision is made for as many as eight 4-inch (10-cm) magnets in each set of trays. These are the B and C correcting magnets. In the center of the interior of the binnacle there is a tube to hold the heeling magnets, which can be moved up and down in the tube and secured as desired.

On the magnetic equator there is no vertical component of the Earth's magnetic field and consequently no induced magnetism in vertical soft iron. At other locations, however, notably in higher latitudes, the vertical component can cause the compass to become unreliable over a much larger area than if the force is neutralized. This statement represents an oversimplification of the problem, as the various coefficients are, of course, interrelated. To compensate for or neutralize any induced magnetism in vertical soft iron, a *Flinders bar* (named for its inventor) is used. This is not really a bar but consists of a series of sections of soft iron having no

permanent magnetism; as many sections as are required are installed vertically in a tube on the side of the compass opposite to the effective pole of the ship's field.

The soft-iron quadrantal spheres are mounted on either side of the binnacle in grooved brackets that permit the spheres to be moved in a horizontal plane, toward or away from the binnacle.

The binnacle may also equipped with degaussing compensating coils near the base of the stand. Binnacles for nonnaval vessels are generally of similar design, but without degaussing coils.

PREPARATIONS FOR ADJUSTMENT

The preparatory steps for adjusting the compass can be made before getting under way. The vessel should be on an even keel. All movable magnetic gear in the vicinity of the compass should be secured in the position it will occupy at sea. Small transistor radios, photoelectric light meters, hand calculators, and hand or electric tools can be highly magnetic and should never be permitted in the vicinity of the compass. Degaussing coils should be secured and compass coils given a "dockside" compensation. The binnacle should be exactly on the ship's centerline and should be so solidly secured as to avoid any chance of movement.

The lubber's line of the compass should be exactly in the fore-and-aft plane of the ship. This should be carefully verified. It is best done by sighting with the azimuth circle on straightedges erected on the centerline at some distance forward and abaft the compass; this may be done very accurately when in drydock.

The compass bowl should be in the center of the binnacle. To center a compass bowl in its binnacle, adjust the position by the screws at the ends of the outer gimbal ring knife edges, until no change of heading by compass is observed as the heeling magnet is raised and lowered. Secure the compass bowl in this position by tightening the screws. If the gimbal rings are loose from wear, they should be repaired or new ones obtained. The compass bowl should not move either fore-and-aft or athwartships in the gimbal rings.

INITIAL POSITION OF THE MAGNETS

If the Flinders bar is in place, leave it there. If not, do not attempt to install without expert advice.

The quadrantal spheres should be left in the same position they were in when the compass was last adjusted. If there is uncertainty as to where they should go, place them in the middle of each athwartship arm.

If the heeling magnet is in place, with the correct end up (*red* end *up* if the ship is *north* of the magnetic equator, and *blue* end *up* if the ship is *south* of the magnetic equator), leave it in place. If not, place it in the tube with the appropriate end up.

Remove all other correctors, except the degaussing coils.

UNDERWAY PROCEDURES

Having arrived in a clear area, with plenty of room to maneuver, the vessel must be steadied accurately on selected *magnetic* headings in a definite sequence. Then the proper correctors are applied to eliminate or minimize the deviation as described below. When this is accomplished, the deviation becomes zero or is minimized. Various methods of putting the vessel on the desired magnetic headings are given later in this chapter.

The sequence of magnetic headings is as follows:
1. A cardinal point—E or W (preferably), or N or S.
2. The cardinal point 180° from the first point.
3. A cardinal point 90° from the first.
4. The cardinal point 180° from the third.
5. An intercardinal point—NE, SE, SW, or NW.
6. An intercardinal point 90° from the point used in step 5.
7. Separate runs, steadying for at least one minute on headings 15° apart—000°, 015°, 030°, and so on, through 360°—to find the residual deviations.

Assume that the first heading is *east*. After the vessel has been steadied on 090° *magnetic*, the read the compass and note the deviation. The required correcting magnets will go in the *fore-and-aft* holders below the compass, which should be cranked down to near, but not quite at, the bottom of their travel. The correct direction in which to place the red ends of the magnets may be determined by holding one magnet above the compass parallel to the position it will have in the holder. If the card swings in the proper direction, magnets should be inserted in the holders with that orientation; if the swing is in the wrong direction, the magnet should be turned end for end before it is inserted. The number of magnets to be used is determined by trial and error. *Several magnets near the bottom of travel are preferable to one or two close to the compass;* if more than one magnet is used, all red ends must point in the same direction. When enough magnets have been put in the holder to remove approximately all the deviation on the holder to remove approximately all the deviation on that heading, a fine adjustment is made by cranking the holders up or down until the compass indicates the correct magnetic heading, zero deviation.

Next bring the vessel to the second heading, 180° from the first—in this example, *west*. After she steadies on the desired heading, the deviation, which should be small, should be again noted. Remove *half* of the deviation by cranking the holders containing the fore-and-aft magnets up or down, as necessary.

Proceed next to the third heading—in this example, north or south. All deviation on this heading is removed by using magnets in the *athwartship* holders. Determine the correct direction of the red ends as on the first heading. The holders should again be cranked down almost to the lower end of their travel; insert the magnets as required. Crank the holders up or down to remove all deviation.

Come to the fourth heading, 180° from that of the third. Remove *half* the deviation by cranking the atwartship magnets up or down as required.

On the fifth heading, an intercardinal point, all deviation found on this heading is removed by moving the two quadrantal spheres. *Move both the spheres equally in or equally out,* as required, until the magnetic heading and heading by compass are identical. If the inboard limit of travel is reached without fully removing the deviation, larger spheres are needed; if overcorrection exists at the outward limit of movement of the spheres, smaller ones must be used. It is preferable to use large spheres farther away from the compass rather than smaller ones nearer the compass.

Come next to the sixth heading, an intercardinal point 90° from the one used for the fifth heading, and remove *half* the deviation found by moving the iron spheres. Again, both spheres must be moved in, or out, and by the same amount.

The number and positions of all correctors should be carefully logged.

Finally, swing the vessel through 360°, steadying on each 15° heading *for not less than a minute;* if the compass appears sluggish, steady up for at least two minutes on each heading. Record the *residual deviation* (the deviation remaining after adjustment) for each 15° change of heading. If time is short, or the residuals are only 2° or less, deviations may be taken on only eight headings, or every 45°.

If the vessel is fitted with degaussing gear, energize these circuits and repeat the procedures for determining residual deviations for each 15° heading. Record these as "DG ON" deviations on the deviation table. The deviation caused by these currents is usually larger than that caused by the vessel's magnetism. Some of the deviation caused by the degaussing circuits is offset by the degaussing compensation coils mounted in the binnacle as described earlier. These are not completely effective, however, and deviation must therefore be determined with the degaussing gear activated as well as off.

The proper height for the heeling magnet can be determined after the other steps of the adjustment are completed, by heading north or south when the ship has a steady roll. Observe the oscillations of the compass, and raise the magnet until the compass steadies. This can be easily accomplished on smaller vessels, but is more difficult on larger ones. The position of the heeling magnet may have to be readjusted to keep the compass steady if the ship moves to a substantially different magnetic latitude.

Procedures for Small Craft

Procedures for small craft follow the same basic principles as those for large vessels, but are somewhat simplified. Compensating magnets are normally contained within the mounting for the compass and are adjusted with a *nonmagnetic* screwdriver; these serve the same purpose as the bar magnets placed in binnacle trays.

Occasionally a compass will not have built-in compensating magnets, and in this case a small external bar magnet is placed on either side of the instrument with another just forward or aft of the compass. These must be accurately aligned with the fore-and-aft and athwartship axes of the compass; they are reversed end for end and moved nearer or farther away until the correct amount of compensation is achieved on the E-W and N-S headings. Except in craft with steel hulls, quadrantal spheres are not used. Deviation on intercardinal headings—NE, SE, SW, and NW—is recorded, but no effort is made to adjust the compass for it.

Sailing craft normally carry an angle of heel when under way, and will often require the installation and adjustment of a heeling magnet, which is placed vertically beneath the compass with the correct end up determined by trial and error. The proper up-down placement of this compensator is normally determined at dockside, and will usually require the services of a skilled compass adjustor.

ESTABLISHING A MAGNETIC HEADING

There are several methods for coming to a specified magnetic heading in order to determine deviation. The creative navigator can devise other methods, but four of the more common ones used are discussed below.

Comparison with a Gyrocompass

When a gyrocompass is available, the comparison of the course as shown by gyro and the course as shown by magnetic compass will give the compass error, provided the gyro is running true. If there is a known gyro error, it must be considered. The deviation can then be found by combining the compass error thus determined and the charted variation. This is the method most frequently used by ships with a reliable gyrocompass.

To bring the ship to a desired magnetic heading, apply the variation to the desired magnetic heading to obtain the corresponding true heading, and bring the ship to this heading by gyro.

Comparison with a Compensated Compass

Comparison with a magnetic compass of known deviation (compensated) is a similar method to that of comparison with a gyrocompass, except that it is not necessary to know the variation, as it will be the same for both compasses. This is a method frequently used when there is no gyrocompass installed in the boat or ship.

Bearings on a Distant Object

The bearings of a fixed object at least six miles distant will not change materially as long as a vessel stays within a small area. By observing the bearing of the object by a magnetic compass as the vessel heads in various directions, the deviation can be obtained for each heading for which an observation is taken by comparison with the charted magnetic bearing.

If the distant object is shown on the chart, its magnetic bearing is obtained simply by applying the charted variation to the true bearing by compass rose. If not charted, its magnetic bearing may be taken as the average of a round of compass bearings of the object, observed on equidistant headings of the vessel. The explanation of the last statement is that, theoretically, if a vessel is swung through a circle and deviations are determined on equidistant compass headings, the sum of the easterly deviations found will equal numerically the sum of the westerly deviations, the resulting net deviation for all headings being zero. The error introduced by this assumption is generally very small unless there is a constant error, such as a misaligned lubber's line.

Azimuths of a Celestial Body

This is a derivation of the distant object method, but the navigator must have a working knowledge of celestial navigation to employ this method. The body most frequently used for this purpose is the Sun. A time of day should be selected when the Sun's altitude is below 30° because it is more difficult to measure its azimuth accurately at high altitudes. Azimuths must be computed in advance, usually for every eight minutes of the period that it is anticipated will be required for the adjustment. Having determined the azimuth at eight-minute intervals, the variation for the locality is applied to obtain magnetic azimuths. These are plotted on graph paper, and a smooth curve is drawn through the various points; the coordinates are time and magnetic azimuths.

To put the ship on a desired magnetic heading, pick the magnetic azimuth off the curve for the appropriate time, then find the angle between the desired magnetic heading and the magnetic azimuth. Rotate the azimuth circle on the compass so that the line of sight through the vanes forms this same angle with the lubber's line. Adjust course right or left until the Sun appears in the vanes. Recheck the time and the corresponding magnetic azimuth, and adjust the setting of the azimuth circle, if necessary.

IALA MARITIME BUOYAGE SYSTEM
LATERAL MARKS REGION B

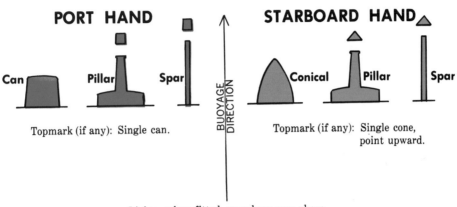

PORT HAND

Can   Pillar   Spar

Topmark (if any): Single can.

STARBOARD HAND

Conical   Pillar   Spar

Topmark (if any): Single cone,
point upward.

BUOYAGE DIRECTION

Lights, when fitted, may have any phase
characteristic other than that used
for preferred channels.

Examples
Quick Flashing
Flashing
Long Flashing
Group Flashing

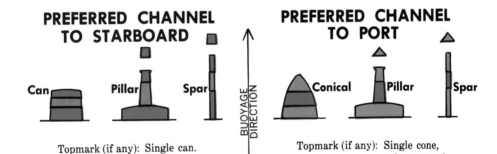

PREFERRED CHANNEL
TO STARBOARD

Can   Pillar   Spar

Topmark (if any): Single can.

PREFERRED CHANNEL
TO PORT

Conical   Pillar   Spar

Topmark (if any): Single cone,
point upward.

BUOYAGE DIRECTION

Lights, when fitted, are composite
group flashing Fl (2+1).

IALA MARITIME BUOYAGE SYSTEM
CARDINAL MARKS REGIONS A AND B

Topmarks are always fitted (when practicable).
Buoy shapes are pillar or spar.

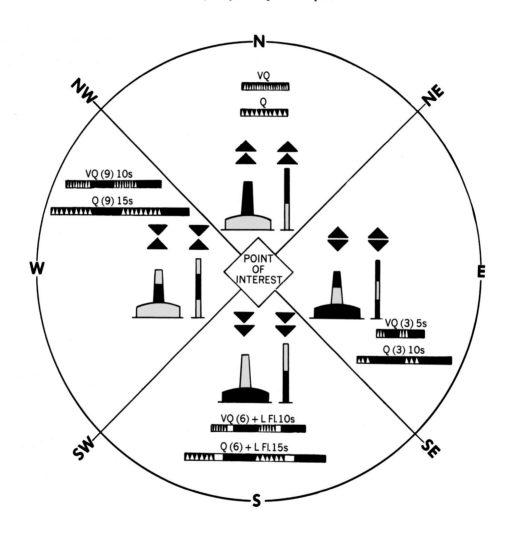

Lights, when fitted, are **white**, Very Quick Flashing
or Quick Flashing; a South mark also has a
Long Flash immediately following the quick flashes.

IALA MARITIME BUOYAGE SYSTEM
REGIONS A AND B
ISOLATED DANGER MARKS

Topmarks are
always fitted
(when practicable).

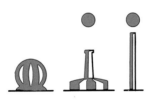

Light, when fitted, is
white
Group Flashing (2)

▭▯▭ ▯▭ Fl (2)

Shape: Optional, but not
conflicting with lateral
marks; pillar or spar
preferred.

SAFE WATER MARKS

Topmark (if any):
Single sphere.

Light, when fitted,
is **white**
Isophase or Occulting,
or one Long Flash
every 10 seconds or
Morse "A".

▭▭ Iso

▭ ▭ Occ

▭▭▭▯▭▭ L Fl.10s

▭▯▭ Morse "A"

Shape: Spherical
or
pillar or spar.

SPECIAL MARKS

Topmark (if any):
Single X shape.

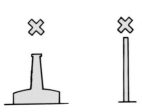

Light (when fitted) is
yellow and may have
any phase characteristic
not used for white lights.

Examples

▭▭▯▭ Fl Y
▯▯▯ ▯▯▯ Fl(4) Y

FICTITIOUS NAUTICAL CHART

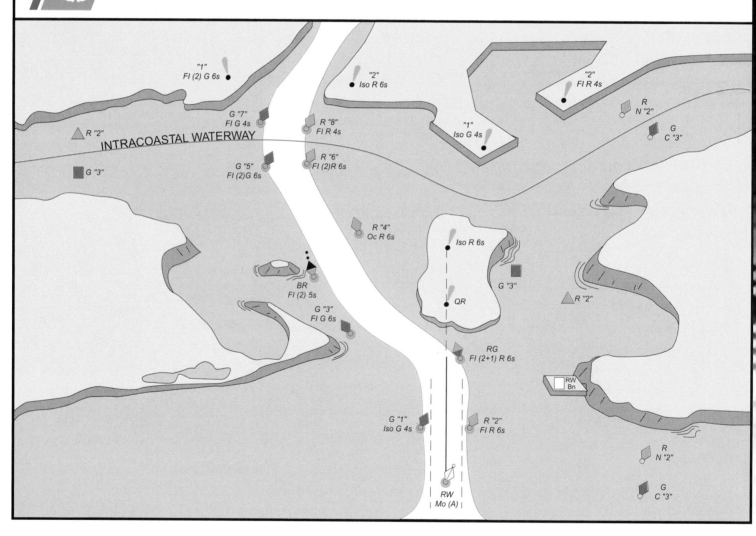

"1"
Fl (2) G 6s

"2"
Iso R 6s

"2"
Fl R 4s

R
N "2"

G "7"
Fl G 4s

R "8"
Fl R 4s

"1"
Iso G 4s

G
C "3"

R "2"

INTRACOASTAL WATERWAY

G "5"
Fl (2)G 6s

R "6"
Fl (2)R 6s

G "3"

R "4"
Oc R 6s

Iso R 6s

R "4"
Oc R 6s

G "3"

BR
Fl (2) 5s

QR

R "2"

G "3"
Fl G 6s

RG
Fl (2+1) R 6s

RW
Bn

G "1"
Iso G 4s

R "2"
Fl R 6s

R
N "2"

RW
Mo (A)

G
C "3"

About the Author

Thomas J. Cutler is a retired lieutenant commander and former gunner's mate second class who served in patrol craft, cruisers, destroyers, and aircraft carriers. His varied assignments included an in-country Vietnam tour, small-craft command, and nine years at the U.S. Naval Academy, where he served as executive assistant to the chairman of the seamanship and navigation department and associate chairman of the history department. While at the academy, he was awarded the William P. Clements Award for Excellence in Education (military teacher of the year). He is the founder and former director of the Walbrook Maritime Academy in Baltimore. He is currently a professor of strategy and policy with the Naval War College and a senior acquisitions editor for Naval Institute Press.

Winner of the Alfred Thayer Mahan Award for Naval Literature, his published works include *Brown Water, Black Berets: Coastal & Riverine Warfare in Vietnam* (Naval Institute Press, 1988) and *The Battle of Leyte Gulf* (HarperCollins, 1994). His books have been published in various forms, including paperback and audio, and have appeared as main and alternate selections of the History Book Club, Military Book Club, and Book of the Month Club. He is the author of the twenty-second and twenty-third (centennial) editions of *The Bluejacket's Manual*, and he is currently working on a *Sailor's History of the United States Navy*. His other works include revisions of Jack Sweetman's *The Illustrated History of the U.S. Naval Academy*.

Along with writing, editing, and teaching, Commander Cutler has served as a panelist, commentator, and keynote speaker on military and writing topics at many events and for various organizations, including the Naval Historical Center, Smithsonian Institution, Navy Memorial, U.S. Naval Academy, MacArthur Memorial Foundation, Johns Hopkins University, U.S. Naval Institute, Armed Forces Electronics Communications and Electronics Association, Naval War College, Civitan, and many veterans' organizations. His television appearances include the History Channel's *Biography* series, A&E's *Our Century*, Fox News Channel's *The O'Reilly Factor*, and CBS's *48 Hours*.